McGraw-Hill Series in Psychology
CLIFFORD T. MORGAN, *Consulting Editor*

DEVELOPMENTAL PSYCHOLOGY

DEVELOPMENTAL PSYCHOLOGY

ELIZABETH B. HURLOCK, Ph.D.

Associate in Psychology, The Graduate School
University of Pennsylvania

NEW YORK   TORONTO   LONDON

McGRAW-HILL BOOK COMPANY, INC.

1953

DEVELOPMENTAL PSYCHOLOGY

To my daughters
DARYL AND GAIL

PREFACE

From conception to death is a long time for the average American of today. During the span of his life, he will change not only in size, proportions, and appearance but also in his attitudes, interests, and behavior. While it is true that all people are different and that the way they change differs according to their innate capacities and environmental influences, there is a fundamental, underlying pattern that is much the same for all.

To understand a person at any stage of his development, it is necessary to know what went before and what is likely to happen in the future. This cause and effect relationship may best be seen by getting a bird's-eye view of the person throughout his entire life span. From a practical point of view, this is important because it will help to dispel any delusion the person may have that this behavior or that attitude "doesn't count." When one takes a look at life from the beginning to the end, it becomes readily apparent that what the person does at one age leaves an impression on his future activities which may never be completely eradicated.

The purpose of this book is to give as complete a picture of the developmental changes of the total life span of the human being as is possible within the two covers of one book. This is a more gigantic task than one may realize because of the tremendous amount of research that has been done at each age level. It would obviously be impossible to report all the important research studies for any one age level. The matter of selection, therefore, became a major problem in planning this book. As many of the latest studies as possible have been reported in addition to the best known of the older studies.

To simplify the use of this book as a teaching aid, the material has been divided into fourteen chapters to meet the standard semester length of the typical American college or university. To break the developmental pattern and to emphasize the change from childhood to maturity as it is recognized in our culture today, a chapter on the meaning of a "mature adult" has been given. As another teaching aid, an attempt has been made to keep the length of the chapters as nearly uniform as possible. For the shorter periods, in the beginning of the life span, this has not been possible nor would it be wise to grant them as much space as the longer periods.

It is hoped that, from a study of the chapters that cover adulthood and old age, the reader will derive a true appreciation of the importance of the earlier years of the life span, the foundation years. It is further hoped that the emphasis placed on cultural influences at every period of the life span will leave the reader with the impression that the human being is truly a product of both his heredity and his environment.

ELIZABETH B. HURLOCK

CONTENTS

CHAPTER 1

Growth and Decline

The human being is never static. He is changing from the moment of conception to the time of death. Growth and development occur in an orderly, patterned way over a span of years. From a microscopically small speck to an individual who measures from 5 feet or less to 6 feet or more, and who tips the scales somewhere between 85 and 250 pounds is the change that will occur in a fifth or less of the entire life span. But growth and development do not stop there. Changes in bodily size and functions are accompanied by changes in mental capacities. For a half or more of the life span, there is a gradual but ever perceptible increase in capacity, thus enabling the individual to adjust himself with greater and greater skill to his environment.

Then, at varying times from the middle to the latter part of the total life span, a period of contraction or of decline starts. As a rule, physical decline precedes mental. The individual starts to go downhill physically before the mental descent begins. If, however, he firmly believes that the two go hand in hand, he is likely to let go mentally when he notices the first signs of physical decline. As a result, his mental decline will be swifter than nature intended it to be and it may even precipitate a more rapid physical decline than would otherwise occur. Thus, growth and decline are the normal changes that are taking place as life proceeds. They are both developmental phenomena. As H. L. Hollingworth has so aptly said, "The ultimate goal of development is death" (1928). Whether the span of life will be terminated abruptly by disease or by accident, or whether it will drag out even beyond the threescore and ten years generally allotted to the individual, will depend upon many factors, both intrinsic and extrinsic, over which he may have little or no control.

Typically, the pattern of human life is that of a bell-shaped curve, rising abruptly at the start, then flattening out to some extent during the middle years, only to decline slowly or abruptly toward the closing years of the life span. At no time can this pattern be represented by a straight line, though plateau periods of short or long duration may be found in the curves for different capacities. As Kahn and Simmons (1940, pp. 352-353) have pointed out,

Man never stands still in his development. All his organs and functions show curves of capacity achievement rather than plateaus. The brain gains and loses

1

weight, basal metabolism reaches a peak and declines, endocrine functions flourish and fade, the powers of taste and the capacity to experience pain and pleasure vary in intensity. There is a rise and fall of physical energy in terms of both force and speed of action: sexual powers wax and wane. Intelligence and related mental functions develop and decline, and there appear to be shifts in interests and attitudes. The skeleton is delicately sensitive to the processes of age and accurately records them. In fact, no organ or function of man has yet been found in which an "age determinant" does not exist.

The processes of growth and of decline are orderly, regular, and predictable. The life career of an individual is a "broad highway along which every individual must travel. Each individual, with his unique heredity and nurture (including prenatal) will travel along the highway at his or her own rate of progress and will attain the size, shape, capacities, and developmental status which are uniquely his or her own at each stage in the life career" (Frank, 1950). While changes of a constructive sort are characteristic of childhood, adolescence, and early maturity just as decline is characteristic of late maturity and old age, one cannot draw a sharp line and say, "Development stops here and decline begins." There is some overlapping of constructive and destructive changes at all ages. In childhood, for example, the thymus gland, or "gland of childhood," gradually shrinks and loses its power of control over the sex organs, thus permitting sex development to take place. Similarly, in late maturity and old age, when the downward movement begins, there is some growth though at a slow rate as compared with the earlier years. Cuts heal themselves, broken bones mend, skin and mucous membranes renew themselves, just as old hair falls out and is replaced by new. Thus, the processes of growth and decline overlap, even though one predominates.

Awareness of Changes. In spite of the fact that changes of a physical or psychological sort are constantly taking place, the individual may not be aware of them. In childhood, puberty, and even early adolescence, when changes occur so rapidly that new adjustments are constantly necessary, the individual is attentive to these changes. Likewise, in senescence, when the downward movement begins to speed up, the individual is aware of the fact that his health is "failing" and that his mind is "slipping." These changes necessitate constant readjustments in the scheduled pattern of his life. He must slow down as the incapacities and infirmities of old age catch up with him.

While the changes of old age are at a much slower pace than the changes of childhood and adolescence, they still require readjustments on the individual's part. Because these readjustments can be made more slowly than developmental changes, they may not be recognized by others or even by the individual himself. Furthermore, because they are unwelcome and suggest to the individual that his life is drawing to a close, he is likely to shut his eyes to them as long as he can or to minimize their severity. Developmental changes, by contrast, are welcome. The child likes to feel that he is growing up and, as a result, he eagerly welcomes each new change which brings him nearer and nearer to the longed-for goal of maturity with its rights, privileges, and independence.

THE LIFE SPAN

The length of the life span varies from individual to individual, from civilization to civilization, and from time to time in the history of the world. At the present time, American men and women, on the average, live longer

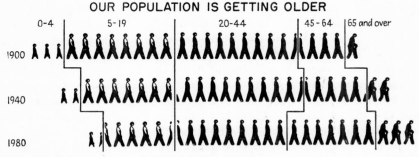

FIG. 1. Changing proportions of the population in different age categories from 1900 to 1980. Those under age twenty constituted about 44 per cent of the population in 1900. They will constitute about 26 per cent in 1980. (*Based on data of L. K. Frank, Human conservation. Washington, D.C.: National Resources Planning Board, 1943. From F. K. Shuttleworth, The adolescent period: a graphic atlas, Monogr. Soc. Res. Child Develpm., 1949, 14, No. 1. Used by permission.*)

than men and women of any other country. And, within our nation, women as a group outlive men. Owing to improved prenatal and postnatal care and feeding, modern medical science, accident-prevention measures, and a host of other factors, the life expectancy of the American man and woman has grown longer with each generation. At the present time, the life expectancy for men is approximately 62 to 65 years; and of women, approximately 68 to 70 years. Figure 1 illustrates the lengthening of the life span in America since the turn of this century.

While it is impossible to predict how long a given individual will live, there is evidence that the length of the life span of the individual is influenced by his hereditary endowment. In certain families, longevity prevails; in others, a shorter life span is more often found. A recent study has indicated that the age of the mother at the time of the individual's birth may play a role of some importance in determining how long that individual will live. In an analysis of the birth and death records of a large number of men and women in Sweden and Finland, it was found that the average life span of a child born when the mother was twenty-four years old or younger was six to seven years longer than that of a child whose mother was forty years old or older (Jalavisto, 1950).

Periods in Life Span. Regardless of how short or how long the total life span may be, it falls into stages or periods which, during the early part of life, are of comparable length. In the latter part, however, the periods may be shortened by devastating illness or premature death. According to Feldman (1941), "Human life proceeds by stages. The life periods of the individual are no less real and significant than the geographical ages of the earth or the evolutionary stages of life." In the early stages, development occurs, while in the latter, there is decline and deterioration. To show how rapid the development is at first, increases in weight may be used as a criterion. From fertilization to birth, weight increase is 11 million times. After birth, increases continue at a progressively slower rate until the late teens or early twenties when growth comes to a standstill. Increase in strength continues from birth to approximately twenty-five years of age, remains at about the same point from twenty-five to forty-five or fifty-five years, after which it decreases slowly or rapidly, owing to retrogression (Bühler, 1935).

Characteristics of Period. Each stage or period in the life span of the individual is "distinguished by a dominant feature, a leading characteristic, which gives the period its coherence, its unity, and its uniqueness" (Feldman, 1941). As Lawton (1943) has pointed out, each period in the life span has "its own problems of adjustment. These age periods are related, not in surface story since the problems change; it is the method of attacking these problems which is likely to remain the same. Throughout the life span, people develop techniques of handling each of their difficulties. Some of these techniques are suitable and efficient, others are inappropriate and wasteful, or a method may be suitable for one age period and not another."

While a number of attempts have been made to subdivide the life span into different stages with the outstanding characteristic or characteristics of each, the "timetable of the life course of man," as outlined by Feldman, seems most complete. According to his "timetable," the stages and leading characteristics of each are as follows:

1. First prenatal, embryonic period: acquisition of human form.
2. Second prenatal, fetal period: beginnings of motility.
3. First period of infancy: head and eye practice.
4. Second period of infancy: reaching.
5. Third period of infancy: dual orientation.
6. First period of childhood: domestication. First period of socialization: central point of reference—adult, parents.
7. Second period of childhood: parting of the generations. Second period of socialization. Activity beyond home: child with own generation. Two zones of child's world—outdoor and domestic.

8. First period of adolescence: quasi adulthood. Third period of socialization. Acts and regards self as grown-up. Own generation as model—others, "old."

9. Second period of adolescence: beginnings of individualization.

10. First period of maturity: self-realization. Sustained application to responsibility.

11. Second period of maturity: self-appraisal. The beginning of retrospection of one's life career.

12. First period of senescence: retirement. Period of contraction. Outside interests and employment given up. A new period of domestication.

13. Second period of senescence: farewell; *l'envoi.* Farewell said in variety of ways; carrying on, calm preparations, hurry, panic, resignation, flight to retrospection, giving up the game with consequent breaking up of habits.

In summarizing these stages, Feldman (1941) has pointed out that in the life cycle, the individual acquires form (1), then is oriented to the world (2 to 5), socialized (*a*) with older generation, (*b*) apart from it, and (*c*) in rivalry to it (6 to 8), and change in time perspective (9) leads to the peak of life (10) while a reverie of temporal perspective marks the descent (11 to 13).

While a detailed breaking up of the human life span into periods of relatively short duration gives a very complete view of the whole span with its outstanding changes and dominant characteristics, it is difficult to subdivide experimental material into such small periods. Therefore, in the analysis presented in the remaining chapters of this book, larger periods will be used and the characteristics of each presented in detail. The periods and the approximate ages of each are:

Prenatal: conception to birth.
Infancy: birth to the end of the second week.
Babyhood: end of the second week to end of second year.
Early childhood: two to six years.
Late childhood: six to ten or twelve years.
Puberty or preadolescence: ten or twelve years to fourteen years.
Early adolescence: fourteen to sixteen or seventeen years.
Late adolescence: sixteen or seventeen to twenty-one years.
Maturity: twenty-one to sixty years.
Senescence: sixty years to death.

Because there are such marked individual variations in the age of puberty or sexual maturity, and because senescence with its decline begins at different ages for different individuals, it is impossible to give any definite age limits for these stages. Roughly, however, they fall at approximately the ages listed above. These rough averages serve a useful purpose as a guide to know when to expect the characteristic changes in attitudes and behavior which normally come at every stage of the human life span. It is for this purpose that they are given.

Developmental Tasks. As the individual passes through one stage of development to another, there are certain things he must learn if he is to be happy and successful. These are *developmental tasks,* or "a task which arises at or about a certain period in the life of the individual, successful achievement of which leads to his happiness and to success with later tasks, while failure leads to unhappiness in the individual, disapproval by the society, and difficulty with later tasks" (Havinghurst, 1950).

Inner and outer forces set for the individual developmental tasks which must be mastered if the individual is to be a successful human being. Some tasks arise mainly from physical maturation, such as learning to walk; others primarily from the cultural pressures of society, such as learning to read; and still others from personal values and aspirations of the individual, such as choosing and preparing for a vocation. In most cases, developmental tasks arise from these three forces working together.

The developmental tasks for each major developmental period may be summarized as follows (Havinghurst, 1950):

Developmental Tasks of Infancy and Early Childhood

Learning to walk.
Learning to take solid foods.
Learning to talk.
Learning to control the elimination of body wastes.
Learning sex differences and sexual modesty.
Achieving physiological stability.
Forming simple concepts of social and physical reality.
Learning to relate oneself emotionally to parents, siblings, and other people.
Learning to distinguish right and wrong and developing a conscience.

Developmental Tasks of Middle Childhood

Learning physical skills necessary for ordinary games.
Building wholesome attitudes toward oneself as a growing organism.
Learning to get along with age-mates.
Learning an appropriate sex role.
Developing fundamental skills in reading, writing, and calculating.
Developing concepts necessary for everyday living.
Developing conscience, morality, and a scale of values.
Developing attitudes toward social groups and institutions.

Developmental Tasks of Adolescence

Accepting one's physique and accepting a masculine or feminine role.
New relations with age-mates of both sexes.
Emotional independence of parents and other adults.
Achieving assurance of economic independence.
Selecting and preparing for an occupation.
Developing intellectual skills and concepts necessary for civic competence.
Desiring and achieving socially responsible behavior.

Preparing for marriage and family life.

Building conscious values in harmony with an adequate scientific world-picture.

Developmental Tasks of Early Adulthood

Selecting a mate.

Learning to live with a marriage partner.

Starting a family.

Rearing children.

Managing a home.

Getting started in an occupation.

Taking on civic responsibility.

Finding a congenial social group.

Developmental Tasks of Middle Age

Achieving adult civic and social responsibility.

Establishing and maintaining an economic standard of living.

Assisting teen-age children to become responsible and happy adults.

Developing adult leisure-time activities.

Relating oneself to one's spouse as a person.

Accepting and adjusting to the physiological changes of middle age.

Adjusting to aging parents.

Developmental Tasks of Later Maturity

Adjusting to decreasing physical strength and health.

Adjusting to retirement and reduced income.

Adjusting to death of spouse.

Establishing an explicit affiliation with one's age group.

Meeting social and civic obligations.

Establishing satisfactory physical living arrangements.

THE FOUNDATION YEARS

Childhood is the foundation period of life. This is the time when attitudes, habits, and patterns of behavior are established and when the personality is molded. What form these take will determine, to a large extent, how successfully or unsuccessfully the individual will be able to adjust to life as he grows older. The poorly adjusted adult, Freud pointed out many years ago, is the product of unfavorable childhood experiences. His neuroticism has not developed overnight nor can it be cured easily because of its deep-rooted origin (Freud, 1920). "Just as the twig is bent the tree's inclined," as Alexander Pope said.

Each stage in the life span has its characteristic forms of behavior, influenced by what has gone before and leaving its impression on what will come afterward. Of all these, the early stages are, unquestionably, the most important. For this reason, more attention in the field of scientific research has been given to them than to the later stages. Because of the plasticity of the human physical and nervous structure, the human being is capable of being molded in a fashion that is impossible in animals where the neuromuscular equipment is nearly ready to function at birth. The human child can develop more varied types of adjustment because he is capable of learning and can make adjustments that, among animals, are impossible. Furthermore, because he can make more adjustments, he can make greater progress and thus rise to a higher level than is possible among animal groups (Punke, 1950).

In spite of the fact that the foundations are laid during the childhood years, changes can and do occur as the life cycle progresses. Sometimes these changes are marked, sometimes they are slight. The extent of the changes depends largely upon environmental factors, though they will not occur unless the individual himself is anxious and willing to do his share. For, in the absence of motivation, changes will come so infrequently and to such a slight degree that they are barely recognizable. Without conscious effort on the individual's part, the changes that occur from one stage of development to another are mainly consolidations and strengthening of traits already established in the early years of life.

GROWTH vs. DEVELOPMENT

Though commonly used interchangeably, "growth" and "development" are not synonymous terms. In the strictest sense of the word, *growth* means an increase in size. The growth period of life extends not from birth nor from the time of conception but from approximately two weeks after conception when the fertilized egg has embedded itself in the wall of the maternal uterus and begins to grow. Growth does not continue throughout life but comes to a standstill at approximately eighteen or twenty years of age among girls and a year or two later among boys.

Development, by contrast, means a progressive series of changes in an orderly, coherent pattern. Each change is dependent upon what has preceded it and affects what will come after. As Gesell (1952) has pointed out, "Development is more than a concept. It can be observed, appraised, and to some extent even 'measured' in three major manifestations: (*a*) anatomic, (*b*) physiologic, (*c*) behavioral. . . . Behavior signs, however, constitute a most comprehensive index of developmental status and developmental potentials." In the early years of life, development consists of changes that lead to maturity not only of body size and function, but also of behavior. After maturity has been attained, development does not end. Changes occur which lead to the period of life known as "senescence," or old age. These changes will continue, sometimes slowly, sometimes rapidly, until death ends the entire life cycle for the individual.

Types of Change. Not all changes which occur in development are the same. There are different types of change taking place, each serving its own function in the pattern of life. These changes are:

CHANGES IN SIZE. Changes in size are especially obvious in physical growth. The individual becomes progressively larger until his mature size has been attained. As old age sets in, the changes occur in the opposite direction and the individual begins to shrink. Paralleling physical growth is mental growth. An increase in intellectual capacity, as shown in vocabulary, reasoning, imagination, perception, and memory ability, continues until the middle or late teens. This is followed by a period of status quo which, in turn, gives way to decrease in mental abilities as age progresses.

CHANGES IN PROPORTIONS. The top-heavy proportions of the newborn infant gradually give way, through the growth years of childhood, to the proportions characteristic of the adult (see Fig. 2). Then, as old age sets in, slight changes in body proportions again appear. With the loss of teeth, the lower jaw shrinks and the chin recedes. The well-developed secondary sex characteristics of the mature man or woman gradually disappear and, as is true in children, the bodies of elderly men and women are more alike than different.

Changes in interests from one age to another illustrate the changes in proportions that come in the area of mental development. In the early years of life, interest is concentrated on self. Gradually, the individual's horizons broaden to include his neighbors, his school, his country, and the world as a whole. As middle age approaches, there is a shrinking of interests. The adult, weighed down by personal, business, and family problems, gradually loses interest in affairs which do not concern him personally. Then, with advancing age, the narrowing down of interests continues until, at old age, physical and mental deterioration combine to limit the interests to self, as was characteristic of the baby.

ACQUISITION OF NEW FEATURES. As development continues, new physical and mental features are acquired. Some of these are learned and some come from maturation or the unfolding of native traits. Acquisition of new physical features ends with the completion of physical and sexual development during the adolescent years. New mental traits, however, develop with every stage in the life span. These, for the most part, are the result of learning. The young child develops a healthy curiosity about everything and explores until he discovers the meanings of these new things. Later, he turns his attention to sex matters and the gratification of the sex urge. Satisfaction from his chosen line of work and pride in his achievements dominate the years of maturity while, in old age, interests in the affairs of his past life and concern about his physical well-being dominate his outlook on life.

DISAPPEARANCE OF OLD FEATURES. As development progresses, certain physical and mental features disappear as their usefulness ends. Baby teeth, which are too small to be useful and too delicate to stand the wear and tear of time, give way to the larger and sturdier second, or permanent, teeth. After the period of reproduction is over, in middle life, the sex glands of the female cease their production of mature ova. Babbling, baby talk, and crying are

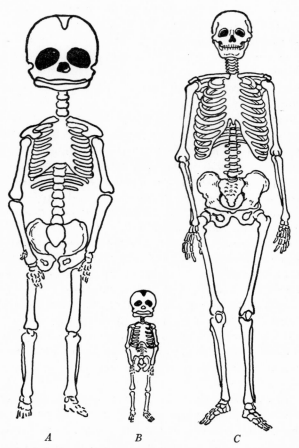

A   B   C

Fig. 2. Changes in skeletal proportions between birth and maturity. Note relative size indicated by B and C and altered proportions indicated by A and C. (*Based on G. Stanley Hall, Adolescence. New York: Appleton-Century-Crofts, 1904, Vol. 1. From F. K. Shuttleworth, The adolescent period: a graphic atlas, Monogr. Soc. Res. Child Develpm., 1949, 14, No. 1. Used by permission.*)

forms of vocalization which outlive their usefulness and gradually disappear as do infantile forms of locomotion, such as creeping, hitching, and crawling. Likewise, falling in love indiscriminately with members of the opposite sex and curiosity about everything that is new and different gradually disappear with the passage of time and are replaced by more mature forms of behavior.

SIGNIFICANT FACTS ABOUT DEVELOPMENT

Studies of development have revealed certain fundamental and predictable facts so important to the understanding of the pattern of development that they are worthy of serious attention. These facts are:

1. *All Individuals Are Different.* This fact has, in recent years, been so definitely proved by measurements with tests of all kinds that now there is no question or doubt about it. According to Gesell (1952), "Every infant has a unique pattern of growth which expresses itself ontogenetically in his behavior characteristics. The entire course of ontogenesis is ballasted by intrinsic maturational determiners." (*Ontogenesis* means development of functions specific to the individual.) How much or how little individuals vary one from another has not as yet been proved as definitely or as conclusively as the fact that they do differ. There are definite indications, however, that the differences in physical structure are less than the differences in intellectual capacity. Personality differences, on the other hand, are far more marked than either physical or intellectual differences, while differences in special aptitudes seem to be the most marked of all.

Individual differences are due partly to differences in hereditary endowment and partly to environmental influences. Even when the environment is similar, individuals react differently to it because of the differences in their individual make-ups. There are many factors in the individual's life which are also responsible for bringing about differences in the individual's physical and mental structure. The most important of these include such environmental factors as food, climate, health conditions, opportunities for learning, motivation to learn, social relationships, codes of behavior set up by the social group to which the individual belongs, and the strength of social approval or disapproval.

From a practical point of view, it is important to know that individuals are different because it means that no two persons can be expected to react in the same manner to the same environmental stimuli. One can never predict with accuracy how an individual will react to any given situation, even when there is ample information about his hereditary abilities. Furthermore, in dealing with individuals, methods that bring success when applied to one may bring failure when applied to another. It is impossible, under such conditions, to lay down rules of behavior that will prove to be successful in handling different individuals, even when they are of the same age level. And finally, individual differences are significant because they are responsible for individuality in personality make-up. This is what makes people interesting and what makes social progress possible.

2. *Development Comes from Maturation and Learning.* The second fundamental fact about human development is that it comes from both maturation

and learning. Learning means development that comes through exercise and effort on the individual's part. Maturation, Gesell (1952) has pointed out, may be defined as

. . . the net sum of the gene effects operating in a self-limited life cycle. Here lies an important key to his constitutional individuality. It is unnecessary to make a rigid distinction between maturational and environmental factors. The physical endowment and the cultural environment interact. . . . There is evidence of a ground plan of development governed by an inherent dynamic morphology, imposed by a combination of racial and familial inheritance. For this reason a child of a given stock in a given culture tends to exhibit at advancing age levels maturity traits which are more or less typical for the group as well as representative of his constitutional self.

Studies of large groups of children of different age levels to see whether, under different environmental conditions, similarities of behavior appear at approximately the same ages, have given us some clues as to whether a trait that was supposed to be a product of maturational influences actually was or whether similarities in teaching methods have brought about these similarities. In the case of walking, for example, much the same pattern of preliminary forms of locomotion is used by all babies, and when they start to walk, they all walk in a similar fashion at first (Shirley, 1931). At puberty, when sexual development brings about growth of the sex organs and of the secondary sex characteristics, similarities in pattern of development of physical traits and of behavioral changes indicate that this development is the result of maturation with little influence from learning (Shuttleworth, 1939).

Attempts to control the environment of the individual, so as to prevent him from having an opportunity to learn, have been few in number but significant in their findings. Elimination of opportunities for practice in reaching, sitting, and standing showed little influence on the development of these abilities. When compared with norms for babies whose environments had offered ample opportunities for practice in these abilities, the baby whose environment had been restricted showed behavior similar to that of babies who had been brought up under normal conditions (Dennis and Dennis, 1938). While maturation in and of itself "seldom produces new developmental items, maturation of structures when accompanied by self-directed activity leads to new infant responses" (Dennis, 1941).

A comparison of identical twins, one of whom was trained while the other served as a control without training, has revealed that in *phylogenetic* functions or functions common to the race, such as crawling, creeping, sitting, and walking, training is of little importance, while in the *ontogenetic* functions, or functions which are specific to the individual, such as roller skating, swimming, or tricycle riding, training is essential to the acquisition of the skill (McGraw, 1935). Using a similar technique with two groups of children matched for ability, the group that receives training in a specific function will advance above the other group provided the training comes after the necessary foundations for the skill have been laid by maturation (Hilgard, 1932). Intensive practice preceding full maturity does not perceptibly affect the maturational processes (Gates and Taylor, 1926).

From studies of the roles played by maturation and learning, it has become apparent that learning must wait upon maturity. Trying to teach a child something before he is physically or psychologically ready will invariably lead to failure. This will be accompanied by a resistant attitude on the child's part to further learning in the same area or even in related areas. As a result, the child will not learn what he is capable of learning when the state of readiness occurs (Blum, 1952).

Delay in learning beyond the time when the individual is ready to learn is equally harmful. Once the state of readiness to learn is present, it should be used before the motivation to learn wanes. A child, for example, who is ready both neurologically and psychologically to dress or to feed himself will lose interest in learning to do these things if he is not given an opportunity to learn when the interest is present. And, in the absence of interest, motivation lags to the point where learning is hindered. The importance of determining the state of readiness of the individual before teaching begins has been stressed by Gesell (1949) thus: "All educability is dependent upon innate capacities for growth. This intrinsic growth is a gift of nature. It can be guided, but it cannot be created; nor can it be transcended by any educational agency."

3. *Development Follows a Definite and Predictable Pattern.* Every species, whether animal or human, has a characteristic pattern of development which is normal for that species. While individual differences exist within a species, these differences are, for the most part, slight and in no appreciable way influence the general trend of development. Studies of the prenatal development of humans have shown that the pattern there is definite and predictable, just as it is throughout the course of postnatal life. From genetic studies of groups of children over a period of years, Gesell (1949a) has concluded: "Although no two individuals are exactly alike, all normal children tend to follow a general sequence of growth characteristic of the species and of a cultural group. Every child has a unique pattern of growth, but that pattern is a variant of a basic ground plan. The species sequences are part of an established order of nature."

The significance of variations in the developmental pattern, Sontag (1946) has pointed out, must not be overlooked. According to him, "Growth and maturational factors progress independently of each other. Any combination of acceleration and retardation in growth in height, weight, intelligence, maturation of emotional processes, or sexual maturation may occur. This irregularity of rates of maturation and growth of various aspects of structure, function, social adaptability and intelligence has many psychosomatic implications." For example, bright children are socially unacceptable to an older group. This, therefore, affects their social adjustments, their sense of personal adequacy, and the development of drives and motivation.

By following a group of individuals over a number of years, it is possible to see the genetic sequences in different areas of development and to note the similarities in the patterns of development from one individual to another. In *physical development,* there are many evidences of the orderly, predictable pattern of growth. During prenatal life, the pattern of development follows the *cephalocaudal sequence,* which means that improvements in structure as well as in control of different areas of the body come first in the head region, then in the trunk, and last, in the leg region. This same sequence is found in postnatal development. Not only do the structures in the head region develop sooner than those in the leg region, but motor control comes first in the upper areas of the body and last in the lower areas.

Studies of the arms and hands of children from birth to eight years have revealed a pattern in their growth and development. From one to four years, children tend to have longer left arms, forearms, hands, and wider left palms than do children five to eight years of age. The five- to eight-year-olds, by contrast, have longer right arms, forearms and hands, and wider right palms than do children from one to four years. With increasing age, the right arm becomes longer than it was earlier (Van Dusen, 1939). Studies of puberty changes show that the pattern of development is regular and predictable for the two sexes. Not only do the sex organs of boys and girls grow and become functionally mature in much the same manner for all individuals of a given sex, but the secondary sex characteristics also appear in a patterned order, and growth in body size proceeds at a predictable rate while these sexual changes are taking place.

At middle age, when the sex life of the individual comes to a close with the menopause in women and the climacteric in men, there is ample evidence that the individuals are following a pattern that is similar for all members of the same sex. There is a slowing down of the sexual functions, accompanied by a lessening in sexual desire, followed by an end of both. Then, as old age approaches, the pattern of deterioration continues the similarity of structural change that was apparent throughout the life span.

The *speed of change* varies for different individuals in prenatal as well as in postnatal life. This, however, does not vary the pattern. All individuals pass through the same fundamental forms, but at different rates. Among the mentally retarded, the pattern is markedly slowed down, while among the gifted, there is an acceleration in the pattern. Even in the case of prematurely born infants, there is no real deviation in the pattern of postnatal development as compared with infants who are born at full term (Gesell, 1930). Within the same individual, there is a consistency in the speed of development. Babies who are slow in creeping, for example, have been found to be slow in climbing and prehension. Even practice does not have any appreciable effect on the speed of behavior or its form. This suggests that such patterns are "determined by internal maturational rather than experiential factors. Children do simpler things first and more complex ones later, but the individual movements, whether of simple or advanced patterns, remain remarkably constant" (Ames, 1940).

In *behavioral development,* there is ample evidence of a common pattern in all individuals. As Ilg and her associates (1949) have pointed out:

Not only does each child appear to have a characteristic constitutionally determined individuality which first expresses itself in infancy and which continues to appear consistently throughout the preschool years (and presumably thereafter) but that in addition, *each age level* has a characteristic pattern of its own which is consistent from child to child. Thus the behavior of any given child at any given age is colored partly by his own basic individuality, and partly by the pattern of his age level. This pattern does not consist so much of what the child can accomplish, as it does of the *way in which he behaves.*

A baby's reaction to his image in a mirror changes in an orderly way as he grows older. At the age of sixteen weeks, the baby's reaction is largely limited to his eyes. Later, the arms, hands, feet, fingers, toes, and tongue are activated by the sight of the image and they participate in his responses. The area of regard likewise expands from a narrow fixation of the face to an inspection of the total body image and the surroundings. By the end of the first year of life, there is increasing perception of depth and distance and a growing social awareness (Gesell and Ames, 1947a). The baby's method of picking up a cube changes in a patterned way with increase in age. There is first a backward sweep, then a circuitous approach, and finally a direct approach (Halverson, 1931). In block building, the young child first carries blocks and manipulates them in irregular masses. At the age of two or three years, he places them in regular rows or piles and builds simple structures. By the time he is five or six years old, he tries to duplicate structures he sees around him (Johnson, 1933). Clearly observable patterns have been noted in the child's position in relation to the blocks he is building with (Ames, 1948).

In writing, both the preferred place of writing and the position of the nonwriting or passive hand change from age to age in a characteristic manner, consistent from child to child (Ames, 1948). Developmental trends in reading behavior show a typical pattern. At fifteen months, the child pats identified pictures in a book. Three months later, he points to identified pictures, and at two years, he names the objects pictured in the book. Between the ages of thirty-six and fifty-two months, he wants to look at the pictures in books while being read to. Reading errors likewise follow a predictable pattern.

The 5½-year-old, for example, makes mostly single-letter substitutions; the 7½-year-old, mostly one-letter substitutions; and the 9-year-old, few one-letter substitutions but mostly errors in long words (Ilg and Ames, 1950).

In the area of emotional development, two distinct emotional responses are differentiated during the first two months of life. A month later, the baby responds to a human face by smiling and, somewhat later, displeasure appears when the baby is left alone. After the sixth month, negative emotions take the lead, with anxiety being differentiated from displeasure. Two months later, possessive emotions toward toys are manifested, and this is followed later by jealousy, disappointment, anger, love, sympathy, friendliness, and enjoyment (Spitz, 1949). Tracing the developmental pattern of the emotions from infancy to senescence, it has become apparent that the pattern remains consistent throughout life (Banham, 1952). This is illustrated in Fig. 3.

√ A characteristic pattern is also seen in the child's identification with and consequent modification of his behavior to resemble that of the individual with whom he identifies himself. The sequence of identifications followed by the average individual in the process of growing up is as follows (Havinghurst, 1950):

(a) Parents.

(b) Teachers and parent-surrogates, such as club leaders and adult neighbors.

(c) Successful age-mates and persons just older than the individual.

(d) Glamorous adults, such as movie stars, soldiers, airplane pilots, athletes, outlaws.

(e) Heroes read about, such as Abraham Lincoln, Florence Nightingale, Louis Pasteur.

(f) Attractive and successful young adults within the adolescent's range of observation.

Through an analysis of the biographies of over 300 people of different ages and professions, it has been found that their experiences follow a fairly definite pattern marked by expansion, stability, and restriction which parallels the biological curve. The typical pattern of activities is as follows: In adolescence and young adulthood, activities are preparatory or provisional in character, and may be considered as nonspecified activities; at the age of thirty years begins a period of "specification and definiteness in work" at which time the life choice of mate and job has already been made and the individual's energies are rather well directed; at forty-five years, the period of testing results and accomplishments begins, during which the individual determines whether he has attained the position, success, and income for which he strove; a period when striving for desired success dominates the life picture follows, and, finally, there is a period of looking back on life as life comes to a close (Bühler, 1935).

Knowing that development proceeds in an orderly, predictable way for all individuals is of great practical value. It is now possible to set up standards

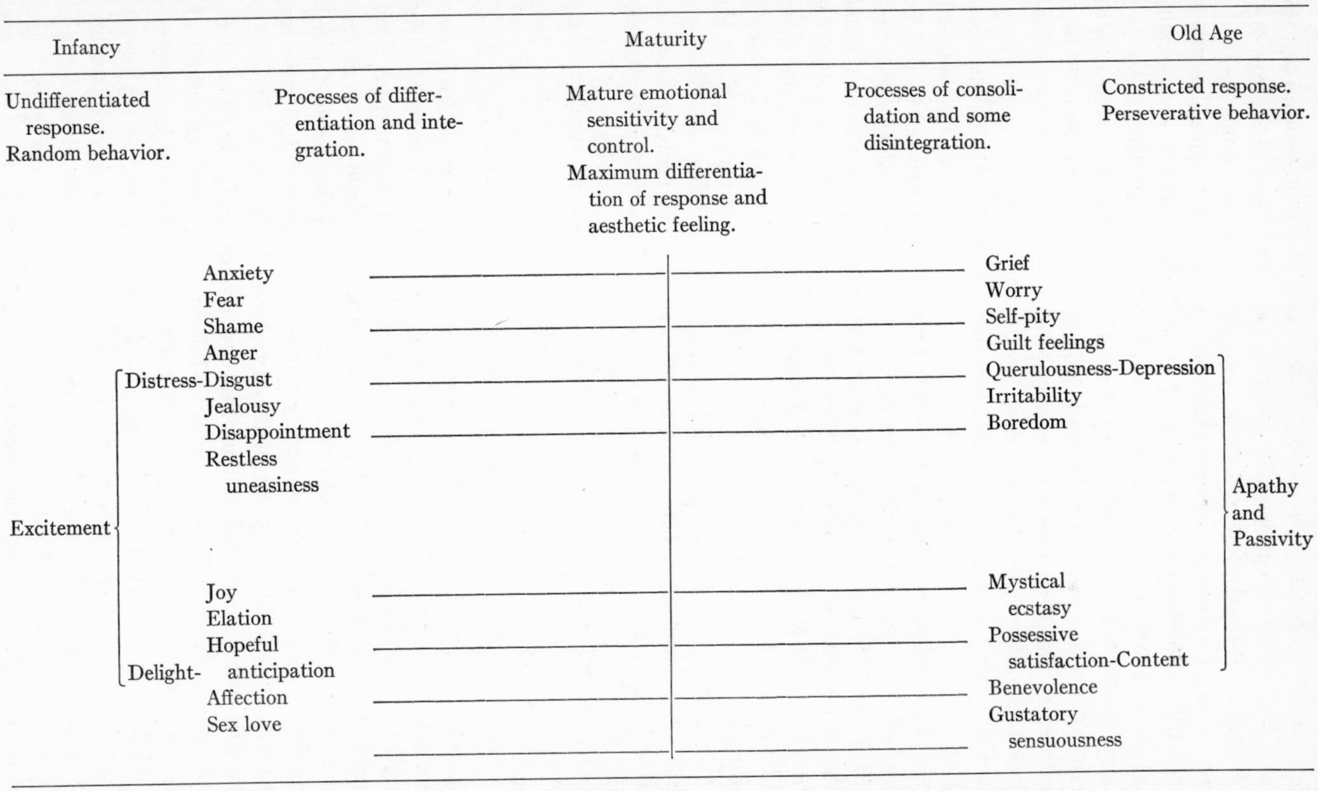

Fig. 3. Schematic presentation of a genetic theory of life-span emotional changes. (*From K. M. Banham, Senescence and the emotions: a genetic theory. J. genet. Psychol., 1951, 78:175–183. Used by permission.*)

Infancy	Processes of differentiation and integration.	Maturity	Processes of consolidation and some disintegration.	Old Age
Undifferentiated response. Random behavior.		Mature emotional sensitivity and control. Maximum differentiation of response and aesthetic feeling.		Constricted response. Perseverative behavior.

Excitement

Distress-Disgust:
- Anxiety
- Fear
- Shame
- Anger
- Jealousy
- Disappointment
- Restless uneasiness

Delight:
- Joy
- Elation
- Hopeful anticipation
- Affection
- Sex love

Grief
Worry
Self-pity
Guilt feelings
Querulousness-Depression
Irritability
Boredom

Mystical ecstasy
Possessive satisfaction-Content
Benevolence
Gustatory sensuousness

Apathy and Passivity

17

in the form of age-height, age-weight, mental-age, or social-development age scales to know what to anticipate in the developmental level of a given individual at any chronological age. And, because all children conform to a greater or lesser extent to a pattern of development, it is also possible to predict with a fair degree of accuracy what one can expect of a given child at a given age. The practical importance of this is great. No longer is it necessary to adopt a "wait-and-see" policy in the training and education of children, as it was in the past. Instead, it is now possible to plan ahead in the training of children. This puts education and child training on a firmer foundation than it ever has been before.

Knowing what to expect and when to expect it avoids the tendency to expect too much or too little of a child at a given age. When too much is expected of a child, he soon develops feelings of inadequacy because he realizes that he is falling below adult expectations. It is equally bad to expect too little of a child. When this happens, it stifles the child's motivation to do what he is capable of doing and, at the same time, builds up feelings of resentment toward the individual or individuals who do things for him when he would like to be independent of adult help. There is another important advantage in knowing what to expect of a child at a given age. This is the correct timing of training and the introduction of incentives to stimulate the child's development. When, for example, the child is ready to learn to read, that is the psychological moment to begin formal instruction in reading. It is also the time to turn the child's attention to pictures, stories, and books, so that he will develop the necessary motivation to learn the skills that are needed to be able to read to himself. In the absence of correct timing, there is a tendency to begin training in reading too soon or too late.

It is equally important to the child to be prepared ahead of time for the development of new physical features, new interests, or new abilities, thus enabling him to prepare himself psychologically for them. Perhaps the best illustration of this is in the case of physical and mental changes which come with sexual maturity. When the child knows ahead of time about menstruation or nocturnal emissions, about uneven growth of facial features which may make the nose seem proportionately too large at first, or about the new urges that come with the maturing of the sex organs, he is able to face these changes without the emotional tensions that are almost inevitable when these changes come suddenly and unexpectedly. While not all tensions of childhood, adolescence, maturity, or even old age will necessarily disappear just because the individual knows about these changes ahead of time, there is every reason to believe that some of the tensions could be minimized and the adjustments made more easily if foreknowledge of what to anticipate were given.

4. *Each Phase of Development Has Characteristic Traits.* Because all traits develop in their own way and at their own rate, it is understandable that, at different ages, certain traits would stand out more conspicuously than

others. In babyhood, for example, the major development consists of gaining control over the muscle patterns of the entire body. In adolescence, on the other hand, social adjustments to members of the opposite sex and adjustments to adult standards of behavior dominate the developmental pattern. From studies of large numbers of children at different ages, Ilg and her associates (1949) have concluded: "Each age level has a characteristic pattern of its own which is consistent from child to child. Thus the behavior of any given child at any given age is colored partly by his own basic individuality and partly by the pattern of his age level. This pattern does not consist so much of what the child can accomplish as it does of the way in which he behaves."

The developmental pattern is marked by periods of equilibrium and of disequilibrium. These alternate in accordance with the principle of reciprocal neuromotor interweaving (Gesell, 1940). During periods of disequilibrium, the child displays behavior patterns which may be judged as "problem" behavior. But these behavior difficulties are not individual aberrations. Rather, they are predictable and are characteristic of the age level. During the preschool years, the periods of disequilibrium come at approximately the ages of fifteen months, twenty-one months, $2\frac{1}{2}$ years, and $3\frac{1}{2}$ years. At these times, tensions, indecisions, insecurities, and similar forms of problem behavior are commonly observed (Ilg et al., 1949). Children may not all show the same behavior at the same ages. More mature children show the characteristic behavior of periods of disequilibrium earlier than do those who mature later.

In a detailed description of the characteristic behavior of $3\frac{1}{2}$-year-old children, Ilg has pointed out the following behavior patterns: physical incoordinations; shifts of handedness; excessive tensional outlets such as nail-biting and rubbing the genitals; stuttering and other speech difficulties; "psychological deafness"; visual difficulties such as holding books close to the eyes; emotional insecurities as shown in easily hurt feelings and night-time fears; deterioration in parent-child relationships; emotional extremes, from excessive shyness to boisterousness; marked expressions of affection, and tendency to be highly imaginative (Ilg et al., 1949).

While it is unquestionably true that some stages of growing up are marked by more difficult behavior than others, there is no stage when the characteristic behavior is not "problem behavior" if judged by adult standards. The two-year-old is into everything and is often very destructive in his attempts to discover what things are and how they work. A year later, the child bothers everyone with his constant questions. At the "gang" stage, boys and girls are ruled more by what their contemporaries think and do than by home standards. In adolescence, the emotional instability, coupled with instability in behavior, might readily be classed as problem behavior if it were not so normal and so universally found at that age level.

Studies of normal growth patterns have revealed that many of these difficult, unsocial, and often hard-to-understand forms of behavior which appear at different times during the years of growing up will gradually wane and disappear, only to be replaced by other forms of behavior as difficult to understand and to live with as the ones that have just been outgrown. Only when a type of behavior that is characteristic of one level of development persists into a later and more mature stage may it rightly be considered problem behavior.

HAPPY AND UNHAPPY AGES IN THE LIFE SPAN

Childhood is traditionally "the happy age of life" because it is a carefree time. Likewise, there is a belief that with the approach of the end of life, the individual is happy not only because age releases him from many of the burdens and responsibilities imposed upon those of younger ages but also because the individual can look back over his life and say, "Well done." Happiness, as experimental studies have revealed, depends not upon the chronological age of the individual, his intellectual level, his socioeconomic status, the religious group he belongs to, or any similar factor. It is dependent upon the adjustment of the individual to the role he plays in life. One very common cause of unhappiness throughout the major part of life is the individual's unrealistic concept of himself. He believes that he has greater capacities than he actually has or than other people recognize in him. Because of this unrealistic self-concept, the individual expects greater success than he is capable of achieving and more acceptance from people than his behavior would warrant. As a result, he feels out of place, misunderstood, and mistreated, a feeling that is certainly not conducive to happiness.

An analysis of the social relationships and life responsibilities of individuals at different ages will give some clue as to which ages should normally be happy and which, by contrast, have far less chance of being happy because of circumstances which normally accompany these ages. It will be noted that the happy ages are not necessarily those which are traditionally believed to be such nor are the unhappy ones the ones usually associated with unhappiness.

Babyhood, which is characterized by a long period of dependency and helplessness, gives rise to a feeling of importance and omnipotence on the baby's part. Naturally this results in a state of satisfaction to the baby and brings him great happiness. Only as he develops to the point where he wants to do many things for himself that he is not given an opportunity to do is he likely to run into many frustrations. Because even homely, sickly babies are appealing, there is little chance that the baby will lack affection from all with whom he comes in contact. The more attractive he is physically or the more handicapped he may be because of some weak physical condition, the more attention and affection he will receive.

Many children, as they grow older, find far less satisfaction in their more mature states than they did when they were helpless babies. Hence they may regress to this infantile state. Many forms of infantilism, such as pretense of helplessness, nail biting, thumb-sucking, and enuresis, are attempts to win back the satisfactions enjoyed during babyhood. When, however, the individual regresses to infantile behavior, he rarely experiences the satisfaction from this state of helplessness that he experienced when he was a baby. The reason for this is obvious. No longer has he the small body of a baby and no longer has he a justifiable claim on the attentions and help of others that he had when he was younger.

In *early childhood*, the individual is no longer omnipotent. Frequently there is a new arrival in the home who now enjoys the position of importance which was formerly his. Furthermore, because he has demonstrated his ability to be independent of adult aid in many areas of his behavior, he is now expected to do things for himself which formerly he relied upon others to do for him. In addition, he meets many environmental conflicts. He is slapped, spanked, or spoken to harshly when he gets into things that arouse his curiosity. He is left to his own devices, to amuse himself as best he can, many more hours of the day than he was when he was younger. And, when he is with adults, his relationship with them often lacks the warmth of love and demonstrations of affection which he formerly experienced.

Even his contacts with other children are more often marked by conflicts than by friendly associations. Other children of his age grab his toys, push him around, fight with him, or ignore him. While some of his social contacts with his contemporaries are satisfying, most are just the opposite. And, if he is sent to a nursery school or kindergarten, there are new individuals to adjust to, most of whom care nothing about him, his feelings, or his wishes. Under such circumstances, early childhood has little chance of being a truly happy age. There are, of course, moments of happiness but, for the average young child, these happy times are overshadowed by the longer and more severe periods of unhappiness. The contrast between what he experiences as he grows older and what he was accustomed to when he was younger intensifies this unhappiness.

With the beginning of *late childhood* comes the beginning of the school age. This brings with it many frustrations and conflicts not only with teachers but also with the child's contemporaries. The school child finds himself constantly in competition with other children in school work, in popularity, and in athletic skills. The more successfully he competes, the greater his chances for happiness. But very few children can stand at the top of the class, few can be liked by all, and few develop such outstanding skills that they are in demand for all games or are sure of a place on every team. The child who is left by the wayside, because his abilities are inadequate to bring him success, is bound to experience unhappiness.

The contrast between what the child experiences when he enters school and what he has been accustomed to at home often proves to be too great for him to adjust to successfully. The unrealistic concept of self and of his abilities, fostered by his early relationships in the home, makes his adjustments even harder than they would otherwise be. As a result, many children seek happiness denied them in their out-of-home relationships by regressing to infantile forms of behavior or by developing compensatory forms of behavior, such as rationalization to explain their lack of social acceptance, projection to try to convince themselves that they are the innocent victims of an unfriendly society, or daydreaming in which they can have the happiness they have not found in real life.

Changes in family relationships do not make matters easier for the older child. No longer is he the cuddly, lovable creature he was when he was a helpless baby. Now he is a gawky, homely, often untidy individual who is asserting his rights and is often contemptuous of the affection his parents spasmodically bestow upon him. Constant criticism of his behavior, nagging because he has not come up to parental expectations, and punishments for misbehavior that he often does not know is wrong are not sources of happiness to any child. How happy or how unhappy the child will be as childhood comes to a close will depend to a large extent upon his social and academic successes. The bright child, the child who through natural endowments or through a long period of professionally directed training gains skills that will win the admiration of others, the child who is appealing in appearance and who from earliest babyhood has learned good manners, and the child who has developed a personality that will make him acceptable in any social group, all have good chances for a happy childhood.

Children, on the other hand, who fall short of the top in different areas of their development, who make poor social adjustments because of poor personality traits fostered during the early years of their lives, and children who have been permitted to develop faulty concepts of their abilities, are doomed to many bitter disappointments as their social horizons broaden. They will be the unhappy children and, unfortunately, they are in the majority. While children usually look forward eagerly to the time when they will be teenagers with all the rights and privileges that *adolescence* brings, they are more often doomed to disappointment than to happy realization of their dreams. For adolescence, in our civilized culture, is a time of great frustrations. The adolescent is neither a child nor an adult. He no longer enjoys the freedom from responsibilities that were his when he was younger nor does he have the rights and privileges of an adult. His status is an uncertain one and thus rarely satisfying to him.

The competitions he experienced in childhood are increased in number and severity as he grows older. Few adolescents meet these new challenges successfully. Most fall by the wayside. The outstanding student, the best athlete, or the most gifted child of a group may discover, as the group grows larger, that his position of superiority is challenged by those who are more able than he. Adolescents, on the other hand, who have held a position of mediocrity during childhood, now find themselves out of the race completely. Each year, as adolescence progresses and as the social group enlarges, the competition becomes stiffer and stiffer.

Adolescence is a period of great idealism. The individual has ideals for himself, for his family, for his community, for his country, and for the world at large. When he compares himself as he is with what he had always hoped and dreamed he would be, the result is usually disillusioning. Nor are matters any better in the family. His family rarely comes up to his expectations and his relationship with them is generally strained to the breaking point by the constant conflicts that arise between their "old-fashioned" ideas and his modern ones. Adolescent idealism usually leads to crusading. Not only does the adolescent try to change the pattern of his home life and reform the members of his family, but he carries his crusade into his school, his community, or to the nation at large. But this is doomed to failure wherever he turns. He discovers that people prefer to go on in the old familiar ruts and that they resent his attempts at change, even to the point of labeling him as a "dreamer" or a "brash and callow youth." The higher the ideals, the more crushing the defeats which the adolescent inevitably experiences.

Then, too, the adolescent meets defeats in his heterosexual relationships. Love affairs which are such happy experiences when all goes well are equally bitter pills to swallow when they do not go well. And they go badly far more than they go well. The young girl who has looked forward for many years to the day when she will be "sweet sixteen and never been kissed" is very unhappy if this dream is fulfilled. She now realizes that not being kissed means that she is not attractive to members of the opposite sex.

With legal *maturity,* the individual feels that the day of release from all the restrictions of childhood will be broken and that, at long last, he can be his own master. But for many young people, such is not the case. The young adult finds himself still tied to parental apron strings whether he likes it or not. Even marriage or economic independence are not always adequate to sever these ties. Then there is the matter of competition. It does not take long for the adult to realize that his childish dreams of setting the world on fire or of getting to the top of the ladder were just figments of his imagination. The competition that bothered him in his school days is now often so keen that he gives up the struggle and tries to resign himself to doing any work that he can get. But he never resigns himself to the disillusionment that this resignation brings.

Far too often, his ideals of marriage are shattered soon after he enters this supposedly blissful state. Financial pressures, personality conflicts, family interferences, and the giving up of freedoms achieved after so many years of bondage are just a few of the many factors that lead to marital unhappiness. Even the arrival of children does not always compensate for these deprivations and tensions. At first, the novelty of parenthood may be adequate compensation. But when the child becomes a troublesome problem, much of the joy that he formerly brought his parents leaves. As the years pass and middle age arrives, the adult finds that pressures at home, in business, or from declining health bring with them the giving up of many of the things he formerly enjoyed. Just when his children outgrow the "problem stages" and are companionable near-adults, they shift their affections elsewhere and leave the parental roof. By this time, the job has become an old story and is boring, or it is a constant source of reproach to him because it has not come up to his expectations.

Then, with *old age* come retirement, loss or decrease of income, readjustments in manner of living, further restrictions of interests and activities because of failing health, and a growing realization that he is now "on the shelf." As his former friends die or retire to the fireside, little is left for him but to wait for death. The helplessness that senility frequently brings with it could be pleasant, as helplessness is in babyhood, but now there is a difference. Members of his family do not have the same feelings about waiting on him as they do when taking care of a baby nor do they gladly deprive themselves of time and money to cater to his wishes. Even if his reasoning powers are failing, he still is mentally alert enough to recognize their resentments. How, under such conditions, can old age be anything but an unhappy age?

Significance of Unhappiness. Cynical as the above may sound, there is more truth than fiction in it. Of course there are times when the individual is happy and these periods may be of greater or lesser length. The happiness that prevails may be very intense while it lasts, or it may be mild in form, clouded by forebodings or memories of past failures. There is no question about the fact, however, that the average individual experiences as many if not more periods of unhappiness than of happiness. Even babyhood, the happiest of all ages, has its moments of sorrow. This is evidenced in the baby's cries when he is frustrated in his attempts to do something or to gain the attention of someone. Periods of physical discomfort or pain likewise bring him momentary unhappiness.

The significant fact about the unhappiness that prevails so generally throughout the life span of the human individual is that it affects the individual's attitudes and, in turn, leaves its mark on his personality. In addition, it reduces his efficiency in whatever work he may undertake. Whether he be a school child, a factory worker, or a business executive, his chances of making the most of his potentialities are greatly reduced by his unhappy mental state.

While unhappiness is inevitable at some time during the life span of every individual, much of the unhappiness that individuals of all ages experience could be reduced if they had more healthy attitudes about themselves, their achievements, their families and society in general. Healthy attitudes depend upon a realistic concept of self. The individual who sees himself as he actually is, not as he would like to be or as his family and friends expect him to be, will be able to face life far more realistically than will the individual whose concept of self has been distorted by wishful thinking on his part.

Retrospective Reports. The best way to find out when people think they have been happy or unhappy is to ask them. This cannot be done with any degree of accuracy while the individual is living through a particular period of his life span. But, in retrospect, he can get a clearer perspective and can see how one stage in his life compares with another. Like all retrospective studies, studies of happiness are subject to error resulting from forgetting accompanied by a tendency to minimize some events that were mildly unhappy when they occurred and to exaggerate the severity of the unhappiness of others.

When a group of college students was asked to rate happiness in childhood and adolescence, 81.6 per cent said they were happy in childhood; 6.6 per cent said they had an unhappy childhood but a happy adolescence; while the rest said they were not happy at either time. In childhood, the home and family relationships are the most important factors in happiness. Games, sports, hobbies, and intellectual interests prove to be a refuge when life is difficult for children (Wall, 1948). When girls from different countries were asked questions about their happiness in childhood and adolescence, childhood was reported to be a happier age than adolescence. Among the English and German girls, wartime incidents were important in causing unhappiness in proportion to family involvement. No pronounced national differences in happiness were reported (Barschak, 1951).

Adult recall of unpleasant experiences has shown that, for the first five years of life, unpleasant memories are mainly of pain and of unpleasant sensory experiences, such as painful injuries, illnesses, corporal punishment, and attacks by animals. From the ages of six to twelve years, unpleasant memories are related to learning to live in a social world, as being teased and ridiculed, forced to do unpleasant things, or feelings of guilt. Adolescents from twelve to eighteen years are made unhappy mainly by feelings of inadequacy and insecurity resulting from death of a relative or friend, school failures, or being refused desired objects (Thompson and Witryol, 1948).

Retrospections covering the whole life span show the earlier years of life in comparison with the latter and indicate how great or how slight the unhappiness is at each age. When a group of sixty-five- to ninety-eight-year-old dependent and nondependent individuals were asked about happiness in different periods of their lives, the single individuals reported that they were happiest when young. Married, divorced, and separated individuals, by contrast, said they were happiest when married and when their children were in the home. Men more frequently expressed a desire to relive their lives than did women. Happiness in old age centers around home and children. When the individual is deprived of both, he is unhappy (Landis, 1942).

CHAPTER 2

How Life Begins

Life begins at the time of conception. The first major developmental period in the human life span is a relatively short one of approximately nine months, which extends from the moment of conception to the time of birth. This period is important for two reasons: first, because what the individual will ultimately be is largely determined at that time and, second, because there is proportionally greater growth and development taking place during this period than at any other time throughout the individual's entire life.

CARRIERS OF HEREDITY

The true carrier of heredity is the *gene,* a minute particle within the human sex cell which is passed on from parent to offspring. The gene is found in combination with other genes in a stringlike formation within each *chromosome.* Each fertilized germ cell, or zygote, contains 24 pairs of chromosomes, one from each pair coming from the father and the other from the mother. This is illustrated in Fig. 4. Each chromosome in turn contains genes from the parent from which it originated. But, because the combination of genes is a matter of chance, it is impossible to predict what the physical and mental characteristics of a child will be, even when the traits of his parents are known. Furthermore, because there are so many possible chromosome and gene combinations, it is understandable that siblings (brothers and sisters) within a family are likely to be very different from one another in physical as well as in mental traits. Only in the case of identical twins is there an identical genetic make-up.

Sex Cells. The maternal and paternal germ cells are developed in the reproductive organs, the *gonads.* The male germ cells, the *spermatozoa* (singular, *spermatozoon*), are produced in the male gonads, the *testes,* while the female germ cells, the *ova* (singular, *ovum*), are produced in the female gonads, the *ovaries.* Ova and spermatozoa differ from each other in the following five ways:

1. The spermatozoon is one of the smallest cells of the body, while the ovum is one of the largest. The ovum is approximately 0.1 millimeter in diameter as

contrasted with a diameter of approximately 0.05 millimeter in the case of the spermatozoon.

2. The ovum contains yolk which can be used to nourish a new individual should the ovum be fertilized. The spermatozoon contains no yolk.

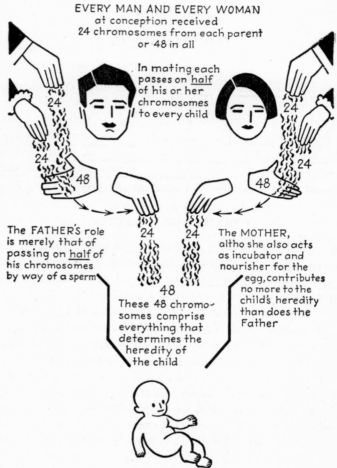

EVERY MAN AND EVERY WOMAN
at conception received
24 chromosomes from each parent
or 48 in all

In mating each passes on _half_ of his or her chromosomes to every child

24

24

24

48

48

24

24

The FATHER'S role is merely that of passing on _half_ of his chromosomes by way of a sperm

24   24

48

These 48 chromosomes comprise everything that determines the heredity of the child

The MOTHER, altho she also acts as incubator and nourisher for the egg, contributes no more to the child's heredity than does the Father

Fig. 4. The hereditary process. (_From A. Scheinfeld, You and heredity. Philadelphia: Lippincott, 1939. Used by permission._)

3. The ovum is round and has no means of locomotion within itself. By contrast, the spermatozoon is elongated with a fine, hairlike tail which can be lashed back and forth to enable the spermatozoon to swim through the semen in which it is found.

4. Normally only one ovum is ripened every menstrual cycle of approximately 28 days as compared with millions of spermatozoa released in one ejection.

5. In the ovum, there are 24 matched chromosomes. In only one half of all spermatozoa are there 24 matched chromosomes. In the other one half of the spermatozoa, there are 23 matched pairs and one unmatched pair of chromosomes. (The significance of this is discussed in the section Sex Determination.)

THE BEGINNING

Before new life can begin, the sex cells from which the new individual will develop go through three preliminary stages of development. These are *maturation, ovulation,* and *fertilization.*

Maturation is chromosome reduction through cell division in which one chromosome from each pair goes to a subdivided cell which, in turn, splits lengthwise and forms two new cells. The mature cell, which contains only 24 chromosomes, is known as a *haploid cell.* Both male and female cells must become mature before they can unite to form a new individual. Maturation of sex cells does not occur until sex maturity has been attained, following the onset of puberty in both boys and girls. In the case of the spermatozoon, there are four new cells, the *spermatids,* each of which is capable of fertilizing an ovum. In the division of the ovum, one chromosome from each pair is pushed outside the cell wall and forms a *polar body.* Three polar bodies are formed in the process of division. Unlike the spermatids, the polar bodies cannot be fertilized, while the fourth cell, the *ovum,* can. If, however, the ovum is not fertilized, it disintegrates and passes from the body with the menstrual flow.

Ovulation is the process of escape of one mature ovum during the menstrual cycle. It has been estimated that in the follicles of the female ovaries there are approximately 30,000 immature ova when the girl reaches sexual maturity. Only about 400 of these ova mature during the female reproductive period, from the onset of puberty, at approximately 13½ years, until the onset of the menopause, in the forties or early fifties. It is believed that the two ovaries alternate in producing a ripe ovum during each menstrual cycle of 28 days. After being released from one of the follicles of the ovary, the ovum finds its way to the open end of the Fallopian tube nearest the ovary from which it has been released. Once it enters the tube, it is propelled along the tube by cilia, or hairlike cells, which line the tube.

When the female menstrual cycle is normal, lasting for approximately 28 days, ovulation occurs between the fourteenth and seventeenth days following the onset of the previous menstruation. Daily observations of 10 women, over a 5-month period, have revealed how irregular and unpredictable ovulation is. When the time of ovulation was determined by the electrical method and by vaginal smears, it was found that this event occurred, on the average, on the 11.8th day of the cycle with a variation from the fifth to the twenty-eighth day. Even for the same individual, there was very rarely a repetition of the spacing of ovulation in consecutive cycles. A variation from the fifth to the sixteenth day was not uncommon. (Altmann *et al.*, 1941). When the ripe ovum reaches the Fallopian tube, it remains there for a period ranging from 3 to 7 days, and then passes into the uterus.

Fertilization, or conception, occurs while the ovum is in the Fallopian tube. It is believed, though not actually proved, that fertilization occurs shortly after the ovum reaches the tube. During coitus, or sexual intercourse, spermatozoa are deposited at the mouth of the uterus. Through strong hormonic attraction, they are drawn into the tubes where they are aided in making their way up into the tubes by rhythmic muscular contractions. Only one spermatozoon can fertilize an ovum. After the spermatozoon has penetrated the ovum, the surface of the ovum changes so that no other spermatozoon can enter. Contrary to popular belief, twins are not formed by two spermatozoa entering the same ovum (see discussion of twins in the section Multiple Births). There are three very important facts about fertilization. The first is that at the time the ovum is fertilized by the spermatozoon, the *heredity* of the new individual is determined. Second, at this time *sex* is determined and, finally, whether the individual will be a *singleton* or will develop into several individuals will depend upon events at the time of fertilization.

HEREDITY. When the spermatozoon penetrates the wall of the ovum, the membrane surrounding the two cells begins to break down and the nuclei from the two cells, which contain 24 chromosomes each, approach each other and merge. As a result of this fusion, the fertilized ovum has 24 pairs of chromosomes, one half of which have come from the male cell and the other half from the female cell. Because the genes from the two parents, and in turn from the grandparents and other ancestors, are assorted by chance during cell division, it is impossible to predict what the newly formed individual will be like. Furthermore, as physical and mental traits of ancestors are carried through the genes of the parent cells, traits may appear in the offspring which are not present in either parent but which may be traced to some near or remote ancestor.

SEX DETERMINATION. There are many traditional beliefs concerning the control of the sex of a child. Because in almost all civilized cultures men have been given places of greater importance than women, it is the wish of practically every man and woman to have a son and heir. There have been many theories as to how this can be done. The most common of the traditional practices are to regulate the time of conception to coincide with the period of the menstrual cycle when it is believed that a male offspring will result, to eat a protein-heavy diet to guarantee a boy and a diet heavy in starches and sweets if a girl is wanted, or to drink certain alkaline potions regularly during pregnancy to produce a boy and acid ones to produce a girl.

In spite of scientific evidence to the contrary, many people still believe that it is within their power to control the sex of their offspring. The seriousness of such a belief is more widespread than most people realize. When parents are convinced that they can produce an offspring of the sex they want, they are generally bitterly disappointed when the child turns out to be of the opposite sex. This disappointment may wane and disappear in time, but it frequently leaves its imprint upon the parents' attitudes toward the child. Furthermore, many men feel that it is the woman who has the power to control the sex of her child and, if she does not produce an offspring of the sex her husband wants, his attitude toward her may be seriously affected.

Since the turn of the century, there has been ample scientific evidence to disprove all the traditional beliefs and practices relating to sex control. It is now reliably proved that neither parent has any control whatsoever over the sex of the child. Whether the child turns out to be a boy or a girl is purely a matter of chance. As for the mother's being to blame if the child is not of the desired sex, that belief has also been disproved. If it were possible for either parent to control the child's sex, that power would be in the hands of the father, not the mother. It is from his germ cells that the types of chromosomes that produce male and female offspring come.

In the human species, there are two kinds of spermatozoon. In the first kind, the spermatozoon contains 23 matched, or X, chromosomes and one unmatched, or Y, chromosome, making 24 chromosomes in all. The second kind of spermatozoon contains 24 matched, or X, chromosomes. The spermatozoon containing the Y chromosome is somewhat smaller in size and differs slightly in shape from the spermatozoon containing all X chromosomes. There are equal numbers of these two types of spermatozoa because they have resulted from the splitting of the spermatids at the time of maturation (see the section Maturation). This difference in chromosome make-up does not occur in ova, all of which have 24 matched chromosomes.

Should an ovum be fertilized by a spermatozoon with all matched, or X, chromosomes, the result is a female offspring. A male offspring is produced by the union of an ovum with a spermatozoon containing 23 X and one Y chromosome (see Fig. 5). Sex determination is entirely a matter of chance. Which type of spermatozoon, the male-producing or the female-producing, will reach the ovum first and penetrate it cannot be controlled. Once the union of the male and female cells has occurred, nothing can be done to change the sex of the newly formed individual. Sex was determined at the moment that fertilization took place. According to statistics, there are 105 male offspring born for every 100 females. This slight discrepancy in the law of chance has been explained in various ways, the most plausible of which is that, because the spermatozoon bearing the Y chromosome (the male-producing) is slightly lighter, it is able to move more swiftly than the heavier 24 X chromosome spermatozoon. As a result, it has a slightly better than a fifty-fifty chance of reaching the ovum first and fertilizing it.

Tradition holds that there are more boys born during wartime than girls. The explanation given for this is that nature is compensating for the disruption of the normal sex ratio brought about by war. A recent study, based

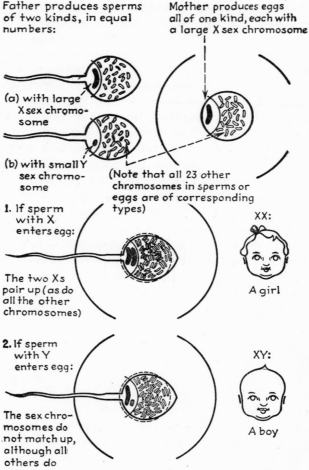

Father produces sperms of two kinds, in equal numbers:

Mother produces eggs all of one kind, each with a large X sex chromosome

(a) with large X sex chromosome

(b) with small Y sex chromosome

(Note that all 23 other chromosomes in sperms or eggs are of corresponding types)

1. If sperm with X enters egg:

The two Xs pair up (as do all the other chromosomes)

XX:

A girl

2. If sperm with Y enters egg:

The sex chromosomes do not match up, although all others do

XY:

A boy

FIG. 5. How sex is determined. (*From A. Scheinfeld, Women and men. New York: Harcourt, Brace, 1943. Used by permission.*)

on data from the United States, Great Britain, Canada, Australia, and New Zealand, showed that the sex ratio did not change appreciably during the years of the Second World War as compared with the years immediately preceding and following the war. There was, therefore, no evidence that war significantly increases the number of boy babies or that the normal ratio of 105 boys born for every 100 girls is changed (Myers, 1949).

It is common, though far from universal, that two-child families will have both children of the same sex. Myers (1949a) has reported that families contain one boy and one girl much more frequently than expected. A more recent study, in which 6,000 two-child families were included, showed that a statistically reliable excess of unisexual sibship existed. This proved to be true also of families in which there were three children. This does not necessarily mean that families can and do have children of only the one sex. Rather, it may be that the sampling of cases was neither large enough nor varied enough to give a reliable result (Bernstein, 1952).

As was pointed out earlier, most parents want a boy who will carry on the family name. How they feel about the sex of the second child has been investigated by asking expectant parents whether they wanted a girl or a boy. Their answers were found to depend almost entirely upon the sex of their older child or children. If all or most were of one sex, then 90 per cent of the expectant parents said they hoped that the new baby would be of the opposite sex (Dahlberg, 1948). Regardless of parental wishes, there is nothing that they can do to make their wishes come true. Predicting sex, like controlling it, at the present time is almost impossible. Studies of the fetal heartbeat have shown that, when the heartbeat is 125 or less per minute, the chances are that the fetus is a boy; when, however, the heartbeat is 144 or more per minute, the fetus is a girl. But, because there are marked individual differences in the rate of heartbeat in fetuses, this test is not infallible. Likewise, differences in the rate of ossification of the bones make it impossible to tell with accuracy whether the fetus is a boy or a girl. In general, however, X-ray studies of fetal bones show that comparable bones ossify earlier in girls than in boys.

At the present time, there is a new technique for predicting the sex of the unborn child which is being tested. This test is based on the presence or absence of a certain chemical substance, believed to be related to the male sex hormone, in the saliva of the expectant mother. When this substance is present in the mother's saliva, the offspring is nearly always a boy. Its absence, on the other hand, is nearly always associated with the birth of a girl. Of 221 boys the prediction was accurate in 98.6 per cent of the cases, and for the 155 girls there was 95 per cent accuracy. While this test is only in its experimental stages, it appears to be more accurate and certainly more practical than previously used tests (Rapp and Richardson, 1952).

NUMBER OF OFFSPRING.. While normally the human female produces one ripe ovum every menstrual cycle, it sometimes happens that two ova are ripened and released simultaneously. When this happens, and when both ova are in the Fallopian tubes at the same time, there is a very good chance that both will be fertilized. This fertilization is not by one spermatozoon but by two. The result will be nonidentical twins (see the section Multiple Births for a complete explanation). If, however, only one ovum is ripened and released, the offspring will be a singleton unless, during the period of the embryo, the zygote splits into two or more distinct parts in the early stages of cell cleavage.

Difficulties in Fertilization. As a result of female glandular deficiencies, especially of the pituitary gland, the normal female menstrual cycle may be interfered with. This usually results in the lengthening of the normal 28-day period. The ripened ovum is, therefore, delayed in its release from the follicle in the ovary or it remains longer than the usual time in its passage down the Fallopian tube to the uterus. Because it must rely upon its own nucleus for nourishment until it becomes embedded in the wall of the uterus, the supply of nourishment may be insufficient to keep it alive. As a result, it dies even though it may have been fertilized.

In the case of old age, malnutrition, chronic alcoholism, wasting diseases like tuberculosis, and other similar conditions which affect the general physical well-being of the man, the spermatozoa are less healthy and vigorous than normal. Consequently, they lack the necessary strength to reach the ovum or, if they do reach it, to penetrate its outer surface and fertilize it. Occasionally, fertilization takes place in the abdominal cavity. This necessitates surgical removal. Sometimes, after fertilization has occurred, the ovum remains in the Fallopian tube instead of moving down into the uterus. This is known as *tubal pregnancy*. Because normal development cannot take place in the tube, the ovum must be removed surgically.

PERIODS OF PRENATAL DEVELOPMENT

The normal prenatal period is 10 lunar months or nine calendar months in length. However, there is great variation in this length. Data from the study of a large number of pregnancies at a maternity hospital in England have shown that the period of pregnancy has a mean of 278 days. The range was found to be wide and there were approximately three times as many premature as postmature births, when the index used for prematurity was $5\frac{1}{2}$ pounds for boys and $5\frac{1}{4}$ pounds for girls (Karn, 1947). The prenatal period is generally divided into three subdivisions, each characterized by its own peculiar type of development. These three periods are: the *period of the ovum,* extending from the moment of conception to the end of the second week: the *period of the embryo,* from the end of the second week to the end of the second month: and the *period of the fetus,* from the end of the second month until birth.

The Period of the Ovum

During the entire two weeks of this period, the zygote, or fertilized ovum, remains practically unchanged in size because it receives little or no nourishment from outside. By the time it reaches the uterus, the size of the zygote, though varying slightly according to how long it has been in the Fallopian tube, is about that of a pinhead. It has been kept alive by the nourishment it received from the nucleus of the ovum. Marked internal changes begin immediately after fertilization, even as the zygote passes down the Fallopian tube into the uterus. The ovum divides and subdivides many times, forming a globular cluster of many cells. Within this cluster, a small cavity forms, causing the cells to separate into outer and inner layers. The *outer layer* later develops into the accessory tissues which protect and nourish the individual during the prenatal period while part of the *inner cluster* develops into the embryo.

During approximately the first half of the period of the ovum, the zygote is free-roving and unattached. During this time, it is nourished by the yolk within the ovum. Should this yolk be used up before the zygote becomes implanted in the wall of the uterus, the zygote will die. However, when the zygote reaches the uterus, it quickly implants itself in the wall of the uterus and disappears from sight. The *placenta,* or sac in which the zygote will develop, begins to form as does the *umbilical cord,* through which nourishment passes from the mother's blood stream and from which waste products are eliminated. *Implantation* occurs approximately 10 days after fertilization. Once this has been accomplished, the zygote becomes a parasite and remains as such throughout the remainder of the prenatal period. At first, the zygote absorbs water and nutritive substance from the wall of the uterus. After the fetal heart begins to beat, food and oxygen pass from the mother's system to that of the fetus through the pure blood from the placenta that flows through the umbilical vein. Through the two umbilical arteries, waste products pass from fetal to maternal blood.

Significance of Period. The period of the ovum is important for three reasons: first, the ovum may die before it becomes lodged in the wall of the uterus; second, implantation may not take place and, finally, the ovum may split off into several individuals. If the ovum has too little yolk to keep it alive until it can lodge itself in the uterine wall and obtain its nourishment as a parasite from the mother, or if it remains so long in the tube that the nourishment in the yolk is used up, the zygote will die. When there is a proper balance between the functioning of the pituitary gland and the ovaries, the walls of the uterus prepare themselves to receive the zygote. This preparation is brought about through the action of progesterone and of *estrogen,* hormones released by the ovaries. The state of readiness for pregnancy consists of a tremendous increase in the glandular and blood-vessel systems of the uterus. If this preparation is too late, because of glandular imbalance, implantation does not occur and the zygote disintegrates and is washed out of the body with the next menstrual flow.

The third significant fact about this period is that, during the early cell cleavage which is taking place, even as the zygote is traveling down the

Fallopian tube, the cleavage may be so complete that two or more individuals are formed. When this happens, identical twins or identical multiple births of larger numbers result (see the section Multiple Births for more complete description of this phenomenon).

THE PERIOD OF THE EMBRYO

The period of the embryo is one of rapid change. From a mass of cells, the embryo develops in the short period of six weeks to a miniature individual. All the essential features of the body, both external and internal, are estab-

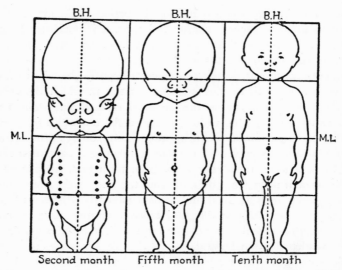

FIG. 6. Body proportions during the prenatal period. *B.H.*, body height; *M.L.*, mid-line. (*From C. Murchison, A handbook of child psychology, 2d ed. rev. Worcester, Mass.: Clark Univ. Press, 1933. Used by permission.*)

lished at this time. After this period, the changes that occur are in actual or relative size and in the functioning of the parts of the body already established, rather than in the appearance of new features. Figure 6 illustrates changes in relative size.

The outer layer of cells, which separated from the inner shortly after implantation, now develops into a placenta, or sac, which protects and nourishes the embryo. After birth, its usefulness has ended and it is discharged as *afterbirth*. Studies of the human placenta have revealed a consistently high correlation between placental area and placental weight. After reaching a certain thickness, the placenta tends to increase in size much more by increase in area than by any further increase in thickness (Dow and Torpin, 1939). The umbilical cord, which in time becomes 10 to 20 inches long and the thickness of a man's finger, develops where the zygote embedded itself in the wall of the uterus, at the time of implantation. There is no direct union of maternal and fetal blood vessels, nor is there a nerve connection between the mother and the fetus.

The inner layer of germ cells divides into the *ectoderm,* the *mesoderm,* and the *endoderm.* The ectoderm produces the epidermis of the skin, hair, nails, parts of the teeth, the skin glands, the sensory cells, and the entire nervous system. At the beginning of the period of the embryo, a neural tube is formed by a groove in the ectoderm. Eventually this develops into the spinal cord and the upper part of the brain. By the fifth week, the principal structures of the brain can be distinguished at the top of the neural tube. From the mesoderm come the dermis, or inner, layer of skin, the muscles, and circulatory and excretory organs. The endoderm produces the lining of the digestive tract, trachea, bronchia, Eustachian tubes, lungs, liver, pancreas, salivary glands, thyroid glands, and thymus.

The rapidity of development taking place during the period of the embryo can be appreciated only when one knows what changes occur at this time. By the end of the period, the embryo has enlarged from the size of a pinhead to an individual 1½ to 2 inches long, and weighing about two-thirds of an ounce. This increase is estimated to be about 2 million per cent. At no other time in the entire life span is growth or development at proportionally so rapid a rate. The form of the embryo is distinctly human though the proportions differ so markedly from those of an adult that one cannot refer to an embryo as a "miniature adult." The head is enormous and the arms and legs are very small. There are *eyes* with *eyelids* in the form of folds of skin above the eyes, *ears* that are low on the side of the head, a broad *nose,* a large bulging *forehead,* a *mouth* that opens, and a very small lower *jaw* which makes the embryo appear chinless.

The rounded, elongated *trunk* contains a *liver,* one-tenth of the entire body volume, from which bile is excreted; *intestines* which are shoved into the umbilical cord; a *diaphragm* which divides the chest from the abdominal cavity; and *sex organs* which are differentiated enough both externally and internally to make it possible to distinguish the sex of an individual when operatively removed. The *arms* have elbows and the *legs,* knees. The *fingers* and *toes* are webbed at this time. There is a *tail* which reaches its maximum development during this period and then regresses. The majority of the body *muscles* are now formed and those of the arms and legs are capable of functioning. There is *cartilage* in the backbone, ribs, and arm and leg bones. Around the cartilage is hard bone which spreads nearer and nearer the surface as time goes on and replaces the cartilage.

In operatively removed fetuses, an examination of the umbilical cord shows regular twists which, it is believed, have come from *turnings* of the embryo in the uterus. It is also believed, though not definitely proved, that *peristaltic movements* begin before the end of this period. *Spontaneous movements* in the form of wormlike contractions of the arms, legs, and thorax can likewise be observed. All of these are of a random, uncoordinated type.

Significance of Period. By the end of this period, the individual is distinctly human. All the important features, organs, and the glands of the body have started to develop and the embryo represents a miniature human. However, this period is not without its hazards. Falls, emotional shocks, malnutrition, glandular disturbances, and other not fully determined causes may dislodge the embryo from its place in the uterine wall, thus resulting in a *miscarriage,* or "spontaneous abortion." There are many popular explanations for miscarriages most of which are now disproved. The majority of these center around the mother's activities, emphasizing the fact that she was too active, she was too excitable, she smoked or drank too much, or that she took too many automobile trips. There is also a popular belief that miscarriage is a "blessing in disguise" because it is nature's way of getting rid of the unfit. This belief has helped to ease the sorrow of many women who otherwise would have suffered from feelings of guilt for the role they played in bringing about the death of their unborn children.

While it is true that a certain percentage of miscarriages come from the elimination of the unfit, most are the result of other causes. Of these, an amount of progesterone insufficient to keep the uterine walls from contracting and thus dislodging the embryo before it is firmly implanted is believed to be the most common and most serious. Other proved causes are insufficiency of the thyroid hormone, insufficiency of vitamin E, pronounced malnutrition or starvation, and serious diseases, such as pneumonia, smallpox, diphtheria, German measles, and diabetes. For reasons as yet unknown, female embryos have a better chance of survival than male. For every 100 females lost through miscarriage, for example, there are 160 males (Ratcliff, 1950).

Furthermore, because this is the time when the different characteristics of the body are being formed, malformations may occur. If these are serious, the individual develops into a *monster* or badly deformed human being. There is a special time in the timetable of prenatal development for the development of each organ. If something interferes to keep the organ from developing at the proper time, "it will never be able to express itself fully since the moment for the rapid growth of some other part will have arrived" (Stockard, 1931). The skull, for example, will be incompletely formed if some disturbance occurs at the time the skull is normally formed. Timing of the disturbance, it appears, is the crucial factor rather than the disturbance itself. The disturbance may be either *internal* (inherent in the ovum from the start) or *external* (acting on the embryo from a very early stage).

Little is known about the internal causes except that heredity plays a part in the occurrence of certain deformities. In lower animals, experiments have shown that changes can be brought about in the very early stages of growth by chemical, thermal, and other agents. In humans, it is known that irradiation therapy by deep X ray or radium, and the occurrence of *rubella* (German measles) in pregnancy affect the developing embryo and cause deformities (Herring, 1947). Glandular deficiencies, as in the case of thyroid deficiency which causes cretinism or deformities of physical structures and mental deficiency, also play an important role in producing monsters.

The Period of the Fetus

The development that takes place in the period of the fetus consists mainly of changes in actual or relative size of the parts of the body already established during the preceding period rather than in the appearance of new parts. This period extends from the end of the second lunar month until birth, which normally occurs at the end of the tenth lunar month. While the actual growth and development are greater than during the preceding period, they occur at a relatively slower rate. From careful measurement of large numbers of fetuses, it has been found that the development that occurs at this time follows the *law of developmental direction,* which holds that development extends from the head to the feet in an orderly pattern (Scammon and Calkins, 1929). In the early part of the period, the body length shows a rapid increase, followed by a steady decline in growth rate toward the end of the period, when increase occurs in the length of the limbs.

The increase in *body length* at this time is slightly over sevenfold. By the end of the third lunar month, the fetus measures approximately $3\frac{1}{2}$ inches in length and weighs $\frac{3}{4}$ ounce; at five months, 10 inches and 9 to 10 ounces; at eight months, 16 to 18 inches and 4 to 5 pounds; and, at ten months, 20 inches and 7 to $7\frac{1}{2}$ pounds. The *head* is almost one-third of the total body length at the beginning of the period, one-fourth at the sixth month, and slightly less than one-fourth at birth. Rapid growth takes place in the *trunk* also. The increase is between seven- and ninefold. Before the third fetal month, the *arms* are longer than the *legs.* Later, the reverse is true. During the entire period of the fetus, both the arm length and the hand length increase eightfold.

At the end of the third lunar month, the *internal organs* are well developed. In some instances, they begin to function at this time. Fetal heartbeat, for example, can be detected through the use of a stethescope by the fourteenth or sixteenth week. By the end of the fifth lunar month, the different internal organs have assumed positions nearly like those in an adult body.

Changes in relative weights of the thymus, thyroid, and adrenal glands occur during this period. At the fourth prenatal month, the adrenals are relatively the largest, the thyroid is immature, and the thymus begins to grow steadily. The greatest decrease in weight in these glands after labor comes in the case of the thymus (Ekholm and Niemineva, 1950). By the third lunar month, short, threadlike prolongations, which later develop into the *axons* and *dendrites* of the *neurons,* appear. Two months later, the complete number of neurons possessed by a mature individual are present, though many are still in an immature state of development. From then on, development consists of extension of the axons and dendrites, acquisition of a covering or myelin sheath, and modification of the synapses. The fetus has reached a state of development, by the end of the seventh lunar month, which makes it possible for him to survive, should he be born at that time. This is known

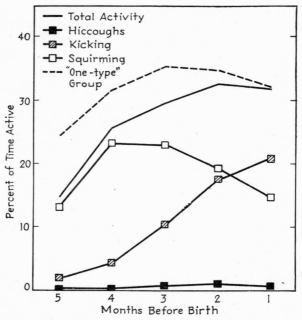

FIG. 7. Types of fetal activity. (*From H. Newberry, The measurement of three types of fetal activity. J. comp. Psychol., 1941, 32:521–530. Used by permission.*)

as the *age of viability*. By the end of the next month, the body is completely formed though smaller in size than the body of a normal full-term infant.

Fetal Activity. The muscles are well developed, and spontaneous movements of the arms and legs appear by the third lunar month. Fetal activity differs markedly in different fetuses, not only in amount but also in type (see Fig. 7). In some instances, the fetus is active as much as 75 per cent of the time; in others, as little as 5 per cent. In some fetuses, constant turning and twisting are noted; in others, the movements are limited to kicks of the legs and thrusts of the arms. There are three types of fetal activity. These are slow squirming, stretching, pushing, and turning movements; quick kicks, jerks, and thrusts of the extremities; and hiccups or rhythmic series of quick convulsive movements. Kicking is the most common of these forms and hiccuping is the least (Newberry, 1941). There is a significant increase in the amount of fetal movement from the sixth to the tenth lunar month, with the greatest increase in the earlier part of this period (Newberry, 1941).

It has been noted that infants who had been most active as fetuses showed certain motor performances at an earlier age than did those who had been less active (Richards and Newberry, 1938). Excessive activity of fetuses may also cause them to be considerably underweight for their body length at birth because energy-producing foods are used up in activity and are not stored as fat (Sontag, 1940). Maternal activity temporarily decreases fetal activity. The reason for this, it is believed, is that after maternal activity, there is an increased supply of oxygen available to the fetus (Schmeidler, 1941). Maternal fatigue does not seem to affect fetal activity which is usually greater at the end of the day than at the beginning. When the mother is severely fatigued, more frequent and more violent fetal activity occurs (Sontag and Wallace, 1936). Fetuses are equally active when the mother is engaged in any activity other than eating which brings about a temporary decline in fetal activity (Richards et al., 1938). Sudden feelings of fear or anger on the mother's part produce immediate and marked increases in the number and violence of fetal movements (Sontag and Wallace, 1934). Fetuses of mothers undergoing severe emotional stress exhibit many times the amount of activity they previously did (Bakwin, 1947).

Sense-organ Development. The condition of the sense organs during the fetal period is difficult to determine except in the case of operatively removed fetuses or in prematurely born infants. There are indications, however, that stimulation of the sense cells in the fetus is impossible because of the constant conditions which exist within the uterus. *Taste* buds, which begin to develop in the third fetal month, are found on the hard palate, the tonsils, and in parts of the esophagus, as well as on the tongue. Because of the constant condition that exists in the uterine environment, there is no adequate stimulation of the taste buds until after birth. *Smell* reactions in prematurely born infants show that the smell mechanism is well developed before birth. But, like taste, olfaction cannot begin until the nasal cavity is filled with air.

Stimulation of the visual cells in the *eye* does not take place until birth, though the eye itself begins to develop in the second or third week after fertilization. The eyes of the fetus move beneath their fused lids as early as the twelfth week after conception. For six or more months before birth, the eyes move with increasing coordination, even though they are in darkness. This is nature's preparation to meet the demands that will be made upon the eyes when subjected to light. Two months before birth, the retina assumes an adult arrangement. Four months before birth, the fovea forms and establishes itself definitively at the final adult distance from the optic nerve head. The eye more than doubles its weight before birth as contrasted with the brain which is three and a half times heavier from birth to maturity, and the body which is 21 times heavier. In spite of the increase in weight, the distance between the fovea and the nerve head remains absolute (Gesell, 1949).

The infant remains partially deaf, even after birth, until the Eustachian tube of the *ear* is opened and the liquid from the middle ear is drained out. However, the fetus can hear strong sounds produced by doorbells, buzzers, and wooden knockers struck against a dish attached to the mother's abdomen. Fetal reaction to such sounds occurs four or five weeks before birth (Sontag and Wallace, 1934). It is impossible to tell whether auditory perception is accomplished by means of the auditory apparatus or whether it represents a vibratory perception sense of other parts of the body (Bernard and Sontag, 1947). *Cutaneous* sensitivity begins in the nose and mouth region, then spreads gradually over the remaining surface of the body. Even in prematurely born infants, little or no response is made to *pain* stimulations, showing that the pain sense is poorly developed during the prenatal period. The *temperature* sense is much the same in premature as in full-term infants. Reactions to stimuli warmer than the body are stronger than to stimuli that are colder.

Significance of Period. The period of the fetus is by far the longest of all the prenatal periods. In spite of this fact, it is relatively less important than the two periods that precede it. By the beginning of this period, all the important features of the body of the new individual have been established and it has begun its life as a parasite, depending on the nourishment and protection it will receive from the mother's body. Only pronounced external factors, such as marked glandular disturbances, will affect the growth and development of the fetus. The effect is usually to retard the development, as in the case of *cretins* whose physical and mental development are deformed as a result of thyroid and pituitary deficiencies. Many fetuses do not have an opportunity to complete the full course of their intrauterine life. Excessive maternal fatigue, malnutrition, glandular deficiencies, falls, emotional shocks, and other causes not fully determined may terminate the fetus' development before it has been completed. Should this occur before the end of the seventh lunar month, the chances of survival are few. Infants born after seven lunar months of prenatal growth have a progressively better chance of survival with each passing day.

MULTIPLE BIRTHS

Normally, in the human species, one individual is conceived at a time. The larger the number of offspring, the less frequent is the occurrence. It has been estimated that *twins* occur once in every 85 births; *triplets,* once in every 7,225 births; *quadruplets,* once in every 614,125 births; and *quintuplets,* once in every 52,200,625 births. Multiple births come from the asymmetrical division of one cell or from several simultaneous fertilizations. Early in the prenatal period, when the zygote divides, it sometimes happens that cells split away from each other. Each group of cells, thus formed, grows independently. While not definitely proved, there was evidence to show that in the case of the Dionne quintuplets, six embryos started to develop independently as a result of the division of cells of the zygote. Only five of them reached maturity, the sixth having aborted (Blatz, 1938).

Twins. For centuries it was believed that all twins (two individuals born at approximately the same time) were alike. Now, scientific research has revealed that there are two distinctly different types of twins, the *identical* or uniovular, which come from a single ovum fertilized by a single spermatozoon, and the nonidentical, fraternal, or biovular, which come from two ova fertilized simultaneously by two spermatozoa. It has been estimated that only approximately one-fourth of all twins are identical. In the case of *identical twins,* when the zygote first divides, two new cells are formed and become separate instead of remaining together. Each part then develops into a complete individual. Because they have both originated from the same zygote, they have exactly the same assortment of genes and chromosomes. As a result, they closely resemble each other in all their hereditary traits. Identical twins are always of the same sex. During their prenatal life, they have one placenta and are enclosed in one chorion coat.

Nonidentical twins, on the other hand, lack similarity in physical and mental make-up because the genes and chromosomes of the two zygotes from which they develop are not the same. Ordinarily, as was pointed out earlier, only one ovum matures in each lunar month in the human female. Occasionally, and for reasons as yet unexplained, two or more ova mature simultaneously. Because of the millions of sperm cells available for fertilization, each of these ova has an equal chance of being fertilized. As they are fertilized by different spermatozoa, nonidentical twins may be of the same or of opposite sexes. Like their heredity, their prenatal environment is different. Each has its own placenta.

Recently, a number of studies have been made to determine not only the physical and mental similarities of twins but also their abilities as compared with ordinary siblings. Even when reared apart, identical twins have been found to show marked similarities. They are much more alike than are fraternal twins in physical measurements, intelligence, and educational achievement (Newman *et al.*, 1937). Only in the case of personality traits is there any indication that the similarity between twins is not greater in the identical than in the nonidentical (Troup and Lester, 1942). In many instances, twin status is detrimental to the personalities of both twins. There are likely to be unusually intense competitive and rivalrous feelings between them, they are torn between feeling and acting as half of a whole and their desire for independence from the dependency that comes with twin status, and there is frequently complementary personality development. Among the more rigid twin personalities, there are divisions of labor attitudes in which one twin expects the personality and behavior of the other to fill the vacuum he leaves. This results primarily from the ambivalent attitudes of the parents, especially of the mother (Kent, 1949).

Triplets. To date, few scientific studies of triplets have been made and most of these, unfortunately, are based on only one or two sets of triplets. Only in the studies of triplets made by Howard have enough sets of triplets been examined to give an adequate picture of their development. Among the pre-school triplets of his group, Howard found retardation in anthropometric measurements and in developmental traits as compared with average single-born children of the same ages. Among the older children, however, there was a tendency for the triplets to approach more nearly the level of single-born children. Personality measurements showed the triplets to be socially and temperamentally like single-born children, with interests and attitudes normal for their sex. When compared with twins, triplets showed a developmental lag. Older triplets, however, more nearly approached the developmental norms than did the younger (Howard, 1946a, 1947).

Quintuplets. The only available study of quintuplets at the present time is the intensive inventory of the Dionne quintuplets, made from the time of their earliest infancy. According to developmental norms for single children, the Dionnes were backward in their development. The age of first walking, for example, was fifteen months as compared with an average of twelve months for single children. In their speech development, they used gesture language at first, as is true of twins, and did not catch up to the norms for single-born children until they were five years old (Blatz, 1938). Intelligence tests, unfortunately, were given only until the quintuplets were three and a half years old, too early for the tests to be of much diagnostic value.

FACTORS INFLUENCING PRENATAL DEVELOPMENT

There are many myths and superstitious beliefs concerning the influence of different prenatal factors on the developing fetus. These "old wives' tales" have not only hampered investigations into the maternal-fetal relationship and how it is influenced by different maternal factors but they also have had a marked influence on the thinking of the mother which, in turn, frequently makes her unwilling to accept advice from her doctor if that advice is in contradiction to advice given her by well-meaning but misinformed relatives and friends.

A famous novel of the late nineteenth century, *Elsie Venner,* written by Oliver Wendell Holmes, placed emphasis on the already-existing "old wives' tales" about prenatal influences. According to this novel, the heroine, Elsie Venner, had a snakelike character which manifested itself throughout the major part of her life. This snakelike character, according to the book, was the result of a snakebite her mother received during her pregnancy. Many similar beliefs prevail today. Red birthmarks are explained by the fact that a mother has had a craving for strawberries which "marked" her child with the characteristic red blotch that comes when blood courses through capillaries that are revealed by especially thin skin in certain areas of the newborn infant's body. Brown birthmarks are attributed to the fact that the mother was frightened by a mole or a mouse and this "marked" the child with a mole that, with a great stretch of the imagination, may be interpreted to resemble either a mole or a mouse, but which probably looks like neither.

When a baby is born with a harelip, the usual explanation is that the mother was either frightened by a hare or that she had a special liking for hares. Then, there are many beliefs about how a mother can produce abilities of her choosing in her unborn child. Reading good literature is supposed to make him a writer or at least to give him an appreciation of the classics. Listening to classical music and frequent attendance at concerts will, tradition says, make the child into a musical prodigy or at least endow him with a taste for music (Fasten, 1950).

The influence that the mother's thoughts, feelings, and emotions were supposed to have on her baby were believed to be brought about through some nervous relationship between the mother and fetus. Present-day knowledge of this relationship indicates that maternal influences are limited and come only through the maternal blood stream. Any abnormality that may develop during the prenatal period may be due to inheritance, to a disturbance or disease of one or more of the endocrine glands, especially of the thyroid or pituitary glands, or to a malfunctioning of the placenta caused by such factors as a deficiency of vitamins or minerals from the mother's blood stream, excessive use of alcohol and drugs, or venereal diseases.

Experimental studies of animals, of miscarriages, and of operatively removed fetuses have shown that the determining influence in producing abnormalities in development is not the agent itself but the period in the developmental pattern in which the agent is introduced (see the discussion of "monster," p. 38). Abnormalities result when the normal course of development is altered by some foreign agent. Because the different parts of the organism are taking form during the early part of the prenatal period, abnormalities of development are more likely to occur during the periods of the ovum and embryo than during the period of the fetus. After the different parts of the organism have appeared, any interference with normal development is less serious.

Fetal environment is very important. This includes many factors, the most important of which are:

Food. According to tradition, a mother must "eat for two." As a result, many women, during their pregnancies, eat much more than they need or want and, as a result, the fetus becomes so large that childbirth is very difficult. Because growth is more rapid during the period of the fetus than during the two preceding periods, the mother's food is most important at that time. Serious malnutrition hinders prenatal growth and development because the fetus does not receive the necessary elements of nourishment from the maternal bloodstream. Weight, body length, vitality, and rate of ossification of the bones are influenced by the amount of protein in the maternal diet (Shock, 1947).

When the prenatal diets of a group of women were carefully evaluated for 3 to 6 months before delivery and graded from "poor" to "excellent," it was found that nearly half of the infants whose mothers' diets had been rated "good" to "excellent" were "superior." Forty-five per cent had only one minor physical deficiency and their pediatric rating was "good." Of the entire group, only one infant had a "poor" pediatric rating. By contrast, 67 per cent of the infants whose mothers' diets were rated as "poor" to "very poor" were stillborn, died within 3 days after birth, had congenital deficiencies, were premature, or functionally immature. Twenty-eight per cent were in "fair" to "poor" condition and only 5 per cent were in "good" or "excellent" condition (Burke et al., 1943).

When the diets of a group of Canadian women of low incomes were improved by supplying additional food during the last 3 to 4 months of pregnancy, their offspring were compared with the offspring of women of the same class who had not had this additional supply of food. The incidence of miscarriages, stillbirths, and premature births was found to be much greater in the latter group than in the former (Eblis et al., 1941). These and similar studies have led to the conclusion that the "ravages of faulty maternal nutrition fall with tragic emphasis on the mothers in poor homes and their children" (People's League of Health Report, 1942).

During the Second World War there were opportunities to study the effects of malnutrition in different European countries. When Leningrad was besieged by the Germans from 1941 to 1943, the severe hunger from which the women suffered affected not only their own health but also that of their babies. The stillbirth rate doubled during the period of particularly severe hunger in the first half of 1942. Generally lowered vitality and frequent congenital softening of the skull bones were reported (Antonov, 1947). The general undernourishment prevalent in Holland was likewise found to affect prenatal development. There was a decrease in birth weight and, to a lesser extent, in birth lengths of infants born during this period. These measurements returned to their previous normal levels when the maternal food supply was increased. There was also a slight increase in malformations of the fetus caused by starvation (Smith, 1947).

Vitamin deficiency is more important than insufficient food because it is likely to cause mental deficiency or some physical abnormality as rickets, nervous instability, scurvy, defective teeth, or general physical weakness.

In an experiment on rats, vitamin-A-deficiency diets of the mothers produced deformities in the eyes of the newborn. Riboflavin-deficiency diets of the mothers resulted in skeletal malformations of the offspring. Vitamin-D-deficiency diets also produced skeletal deformities but of a different nature (Warkany, 1944).

Diseases. When a diseased condition of the mother affects her general metabolism, it influences, to a greater or less degree, the development of the fetus. Diseases which have been found to have the most serious effects are syphilis, gonorrhea, endocrine disorders, wasting diseases such as tuberculosis and diabetes, and toxins or poisons in the mother's blood resulting from lead poisoning or bacteria from certain diseases. The heavy use of quinine by mothers in the malaria season brings about an increase in the number of cases of congenital deafness, because of the effect of quinine on the fetal inner ear (Sontag, 1941). Rubella (German measles), which is a mild disease in children, is a potential danger in developing congenital defects. When mothers suffer from rubella during the first or second month of pregnancy, such congenital defects as cataracts, deafness, and anomalies in the structure of the heart may develop. Mental deficiency is also a common aftermath of rubella. Some mothers, on the other hand, give birth to normal infants even after suffering from severe cases of rubella (Shock, 1947). Recently, the Rh blood factor has been found to be a potential cause of pathological development in the fetus. Incompatibilities in the blood composition of the mother and the developing fetus are likely to result in low-grade intelligence (Shock, 1947).

Because maternal and fetal endocrine glands function in a complementary manner, it is logical to assume that glandular deficiency on the part of the mother will, in some way, affect the developing fetus. To date, there is little scientific evidence to show how great this effect is. A hypothyroid mother, or one suffering from a deficiency of the thyroid hormone, is likely to bear a child who has retarded skeletal development, is inactive, and is retarded in his behavior pattern (Sontag, 1941). Marked cases of thyroid deficiency are known as "cretins," or physically deformed children whose mental development is markedly below that of the average child of the same chronological age. The use of X ray or radium on the maternal pelvis during pregnancy may be detrimental, depending partly on the strength of the X-ray exposure or the radium and partly on the age of the fetus. If used early in pregnancy for therapeutic purposes, they are generally of greater strength. This is likely to have marked effects on the fetus, the most common of which is microcephaly or an abnormally small head and brain, accompanied by mental deficiency. When used at the end of pregnancy for diagnosis or measurements, the exposures are of short duration and have no effect on the fetus (Murphy *et al.*, 1942).

Alcohol. Constant use of alcohol, when it gives rise to such danger signals as irregular heartbeat, nervousness, or insomnia, may affect the fetus detrimentally. While many chronic alcoholics have children who are physically or mentally deficient, it has not yet been determined whether their condition resulted from chronic alcoholism on the part of the mother or whether her weakness for alcohol was caused by some physical or mental weakness which the child inherited. It is maintained that alcohol "acts as a definite but not too drastic selective agent upon both germ cells and developing embryos, eliminating the weak and leaving the strong" (Pearl, 1930). It is also reported that the genes "show a very great resistance to alcohol. Either it [alcohol] does not alter them at all, or it kills them; in either case no modified descendants result" (Jennings, 1930).

Tobacco. When the nicotine in tobacco is inhaled in smoking, it causes disturbances in the mother's blood pressure and heart action. Increase in fetal heartbeat follows, with the maximum effect coming from eight to ten minutes after the mother starts to smoke (Sontag and Richards, 1938). In animals, nicotine has been found to decrease milk secretion though no scientific evidence is available to prove that this holds true for the human mother.

Emotional Experiences of Mother. The mother's emotional experiences, according to tradition, affect the personality of her child. No evidence is available at the present time to substantiate this belief. Knowledge of the existing relationship between the mother and fetus would point to the conclusion that any effect the mother's emotional experiences can have will be through the glandular changes taking place in her body when emotions are severe or prolonged. Infants whose mothers had undergone severe emotional stress late in pregnancy have been found to be unstable and hyperactive for weeks or even months after birth. They sleep poorly and cry a great deal. Most of them gain weight slowly and are difficult to feed (Sontag, 1941, 1946).

Month of Birth. Scientific investigations have shown that the month of the year in which the child is born has some influence on his mental as well as his physical development, but this influence is very slight (Blonsky, 1929). The highest IQ's are found among children born in the spring and summer seasons and the lowest among those born in autumn and winter (Pintner and Forlano, 1933, 1934, 1939, 1943). These differences are, however, too small to be significant. This is illustrated in Fig. 8.

Age of Parents. It is popularly believed that children of young parents are healthier and brighter than children of older parents. It is further believed that parents should have their children when they are young so that they can "grow up with them." These beliefs unquestionably originated in connection with the greater ease with which adolescent girls and young women can bear children as compared with slightly older women. Each successive year is likely to add to the difficulties of childbirth for the mother, especially when the child is her first-born. But there is little or no evidence to show that young parents produce healthier, brighter, or better adjusted children. On the contrary, what evidence there is points in the opposite direction.

Studies of the intelligence of the child in relation to the age of the parents when the child was born show that the older parents have more intelligent children than do younger parents. When fathers are below the ages of thirty

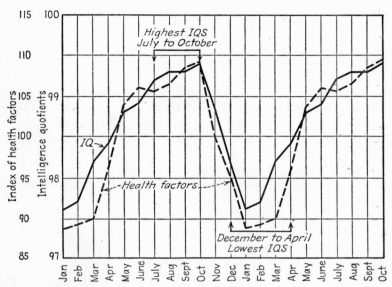

Fig. 8. Average IQ's by month of birth in comparison with monthly indexes of favorable health conditions. Children born in the months July to October have reliably higher average IQ's and these are the most favorable birth months as measured by health indexes. (*Based on an analysis of data of R. Pintner and G. Forlano, The influence of month of birth on intelligence quotients. J. educ. Psychol., 1933, 24:561–584; and of R. Pintner and J. B. Maller, Month of birth and average intelligence among different ethnic groups. J. genet. Psychol., 1937, 50:91–107. From F. K. Shuttleworth, The adolescent period: a graphic atlas, Monogr. Soc. Res. Child Develpm., 1949, 14, No. 1. Used by permission.*)

to thirty-two years and mothers below twenty-six to twenty-eight years, the mean intelligence rating of the children is lower than when the parents are older (Steckel, 1929). The average age of fathers is 33.63 years and of mothers, 29.8 years, at the time of the birth of superior children (Terman, 1926). This difference, however, may be the result of socioeconomic conditions that result in later marriages among the higher and more intellectual groups. This delay is necessitated by the long period of education needed for the higher occupations. Furthermore, there is evidence to show that parents of approximately the same age have more intelligent children than do those who are widely different in age (Steckel, 1929).

CHAPTER 3

Infancy

Infancy, or the period of the neonate (from the Greek *neos,* meaning "new" and the Latin *nascor,* meaning to "be born"), extends from birth to the end of the second week of life when the navel is healed. This is a plateau stage in development because no appreciable change occurs either in physical development or behavior. At this time, the newborn infant must make many adjustments to a completely new environment outside the mother's body. Generally, by the end of the period, the infant has regained the weight lost after birth while these adjustments were being made.

The birth of the infant does not necessarily mean that the prenatal period has been the normal length of 280 days. Some infants are born prematurely, some postmaturely. Under such conditions, it is obvious that the same level of physical and mental development will not be present in all infants. The description of the neonate, given below, will refer to the normal, full-term infant. Additional data will be presented to show what effect prematurity has on the infant's development. Because, to date, there are no scientific data relating to postmaturity, no attempt will be made to describe the development of an infant whose entrance into the world has been delayed beyond the normal time.

PHYSICAL DEVELOPMENT

At birth, the average infant weighs 7½ pounds and measures 19½ inches. Weight in relation to height is less at birth, on the average, in the more active fetuses than in those less active (Sontag and Wallace, 1934). Boys, on the whole, are slightly longer and heavier than girls. There are marked individual differences, however, in infants of both sexes. Ranges in weight are from 3 to 16 pounds, and in length from 17 to 21 or 22 inches. Variability in size is dependent not so much upon sex as upon factors in the prenatal environment, especially prenatal feeding. Infants whose mothers had prenatal diets that were rated as "superior" have been found to weigh 2 to 3 pounds heavier at birth, on the average, than do infants whose mothers had diets that were rated as "very poor." They are likewise approximately 2 inches longer, on the average, at birth than are those whose prenatal environment was not so favorable (Burke *et al.,* 1943).

50

There is a significant relationship between the protein content of the prenatal diet of the mother and the length, height, and general physical condition of the infant at birth. With each additional increment of protein in the prenatal diet, there is an increase in the infant's length, weight, and general condition. Less than 75 grams of protein daily during the latter part of pregnancy results in an infant who will tend to be short, light in weight, and most likely to receive a poor pediatric rating (Burke *et al.*, 1943). During the first few days after birth, losses in weight are usual though not universal. A loss of 6 to 7 per cent of the birth weight is common. By the tenth day after birth, most infants regain part of the weight lost immediately after birth. Light infants, as a rule, show smaller postnatal weight losses than do those who are heavier at birth and they also regain the lost weight more quickly. Infants born in the summer and autumn tend to regain their lost weight slightly sooner than do infants born in the winter and spring (Meredith and Brown, 1939).

The muscles of the newborn infant are soft, small, and uncontrolled. At the time of birth, less development has taken place in the muscles of the neck and legs than in those of the hands and arms. The bones, like the muscles, are soft and flexible because they are composed chiefly of cartilage or gristle. Because of their softness, they can readily be misshapen. The skin is soft, deep pink in color, and often blotchy. The flesh is firm and elastic. Frequently, soft downy hair is found on the head and back, though this soon disappears. Natal teeth occur approximately once in every 2,000 births. They are of the primary, or "baby," type and are usually lower central incisors. Upper incisors appear less often. It is not unusual for the infant to have two teeth instead of just one. Because the presence of natal teeth occurs with significant frequency in families, it suggests that some genetic factor is contributory (Massler and Savara, 1950).

Physical Proportions. A study of the physical proportions of the newborn will reveal that he is not a miniature adult (see Fig. 9). His head is approximately one-fourth of his body length as compared with the adult head which is approximately one-seventh of the total body length. The cranial region, the area over the eyes, is proportionally much larger than the rest of the head while the chin region is proportionally too small (see Fig. 10). The neck is so short that it is barely visible. The eyes are almost mature in size but because of the weakness of the eye muscles they move in an uncontrolled way in their sockets. In the trunk, the shoulders are narrow, while the abdomen is large and bulging. Proportionally, the arms and legs of the infant are much too short. The hands and feet are miniature.

Physiological Functions. Before birth, respiration, nutrition, and elimination are carried on through interchanges in the membranes of the placenta. With the birth cry, the lungs are inflated and respiration begins. Reflex sucking movements occur when the infant is hungry or when the lips are

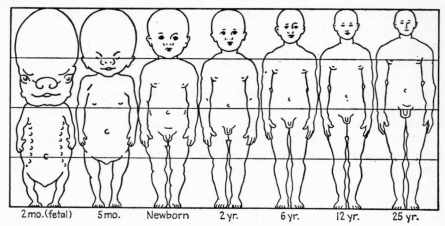

2 mo.(fetal)   5 mo.   Newborn   2 yr.   6 yr.   12 yr.   25 yr.

FIG. 9. Changes in form and proportion of the human body during fetal and postnatal life. Changes in relative proportions of the body are extraordinarily rapid during the fetal period. Changes occurring between birth and the second year are more marked than those between the twelfth and twenty-fifth year. (*Based on W. J. Robbins, S. Brody, A. G. Hogan, C. M. Jackson, and C. W. Greene, Growth. New Haven: Yale Univ. Press, 1928. From F. K. Shuttleworth, The adolescent period: a graphic atlas, Monogr. Soc. Res. Child Develpm., 1949, 14, No. 1. Used by permission.*)

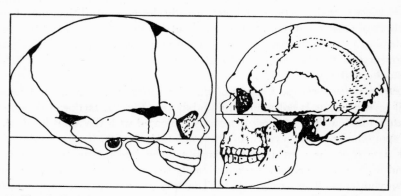

FIG. 10. The skull of the newborn infant as contrasted with that of the adult. This emphasizes the relatively large brain case of the infant and the relatively greater size of jaws and face of the adult. (*Based on material from J. C. Brash, The growth of the jaws, normal and abnormal, in health and disease. London: The Dental Board of the United Kingdom, 1924. From F. K. Shuttleworth, The adolescent period: a graphic atlas, Monogr. Soc. Res. Child Develpm., 1949, 14, No. 1. Used by permission.*)

touched (Norval, 1946). Breast-fed infants develop stronger sucking reflexes than do infants fed by the bottle (Davis *et al.*, 1948). Because nourishment comes in a continuous stream through the cord and placenta before birth, the hunger rhythm does not develop until several weeks after birth. The hunger demands of the newborn are, therefore, irregular not only as to intervals between feedings but also as to amounts. By the age of two or three weeks, a hunger rhythm develops. Then infants can adjust to a feeding schedule (Bakwin, 1947). Elimination of waste products begins a few hours after birth.

There are marked differences between the physiological functions of infants and adults. The infant's blood contains fewer red and more white corpuscles than does that of the adult. Hence, infant resistance to disease is poor. At birth, the pulse rate ranges from 130 to 150 beats a minute but drops to an average of 118 beats a minute several days after birth. This compares with the average adult rate of 70. Respiration rate in the infant ranges from 40 to 45 a minute, as compared with the average rate of 18. Neonatal heart-beat is more rapid than that of the adult because the infant's heart is small as compared with the arteries. Even in the healthy infant, the temperature is higher and more variable than in the adult.

The infant sleeps or dozes for approximately 80 per cent of the time as compared with 49 per cent at the age of one year (C. Bühler, 1930). By the fourth day of life, the amount of time spent in sleep drops to 68 per cent (Pratt *et al.*, 1930). Neonatal sleep is broken by short waking periods which occur every 2 or 3 hours, with fewer and shorter waking periods during the night than during the day. The infant is wakened by internal stimuli, such as discomfort, pain, and hunger. The only environmental stimuli that disturb him are very loud noises and changes in temperature. External stimuli are least effective immediately after feeding and during the latter periods of violent activity, both of the body and stomach, and of hunger (Richards, 1936). The infant falls asleep readily and can be awakened easily because he sleeps lightly. The greatest depth of neonatal sleep comes during the first hour. After that, sleep is lighter and can be broken easily.

The typical sleep curve for newborn infants shows a state of complete waking at feeding time followed by an intermediate stage when there are occasional stirs of the body and irregular movements, then deep sleep for 5 to 20 minutes, followed by an intermediate stage, and then complete waking. Deep sleep is in the middle of the sleep period and, contrary to popular opinion, is very short in duration. Typical sleep curves for infants are shown in Fig. 11. During this time, it is hard to waken the infant. While variations in infant posture during sleep are great, the characteristic position, when prone, is one similar to that of the fetus during intra-uterine life (C. Bühler, 1930). By the end of the first month of life, this position is generally out-grown, owing to the tonus of the baby's musculature (Shirley, 1931).

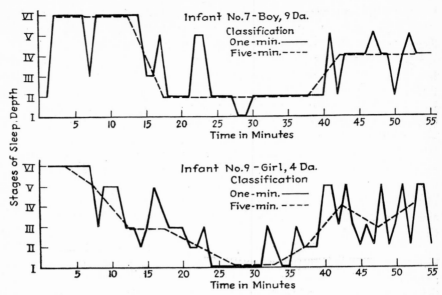

FIG. 11. Typical sleep curves for infants. (*From M. C. Reynard and F. C. Dockeray, The comparison of temporal intervals in judging depth of sleep in newborn infants, J. genet. Psychol., 1939, 55:103–120. Used by permission.*)

Throughout the neonatal period, there is a gradual increase in body movements during sleep, as is true also of the waking periods.

ACTIVITIES OF THE INFANT

It is difficult to record the movements of the newborn infant because they are so rapid, varied, and uncoordinated. In time, these will be coordinated and controlled to form the basis of the skilled movements needed for everyday life. The coordination which gradually takes place comes partly from maturation and partly from learning.

The activities of the infant are generally divided into two categories, *mass activity* and *specific activities* (Irwin, 1930).

Mass activity includes general movements of the whole body. Owing to the neurological immaturity of the infant, mass activity is highly uncoordinated. It may occur independently of specific external stimuli. Movements limited to one area of the body are relatively infrequent because the immature condition of the nervous system results in a diffusion of energy when a stimulus is applied to one area of the body. When a sensory stimulus is applied to any part of the body, activity occurs throughout the entire body. It is most pronounced, however, in the area that has been stimulated. When the left hand is stimulated, for example, the infant moves not only that arm but the other arm as well. In addition, he is likely to kick his legs, twist his trunk, turn his head from side to side and, if the stimulus has been intense, he will cry. Otherwise, he may sneeze or yawn.

Because activity is diffused, the amount of energy expended is great. It has been estimated that the energy expended by an infant is two or three times greater than that expended by an adult when pound to pound comparisons are made. Likewise, because crying is accompanied by mass activity, a great amount of energy is expended and the infant becomes fatigued quickly. The condition of the infant's body has a marked influence on mass activity. Hunger, pain, and bodily discomfort give rise to great activity, while limited activity follows nursing (Davis *et al.*, 1948). Just before nursing, the mean number of movements per minute is 45 as compared with 17 in the period immediately following nursing (Irwin, 1932). Breast-fed babies show slightly greater general body activity than those fed by the bottle (Davis *et al.*, 1948). Caesarean babies are the quietest of all babies (Fries, 1941).

In sleep, infants move about 20 per cent of the time, even in the absence of external stimuli (Pratt *et al.*, 1930). The mean number of movements for sleeping infants is 8.7 and for those who are awake, 51.5 per minute. Changes in light stimulate motility. The greatest amount of activity occurs in moderate light and the least, in dim light. All light is disturbing and becomes increasingly so with added intensity (Weiss, 1934). Sounds also produce an increase in mass activity in infants (Pratt, 1934). When clothing and covers are removed, activity increases. These are most disturbing when the physiological factors are unfavorable (Irwin and Weiss, 1934). The average percentage of movement in the head is 4, in the body, 28, in the arms, 21, and in the legs, 30. Thus, the greatest amount of movement is in the trunk and legs, the least in the head (Irwin, 1930).

Specific activities involve certain limited areas of the body. They include *reflexes* which are definite responses to specific sensory stimuli and which remain unchanged with repetition of the same stimulus, and *general* responses which use larger groups of muscles than are involved in reflexes and which may be aroused by either external or internal stimuli. Most of the important reflexes of the body, as the pupillary, lip, tongue, sucking, flexion, knee jerk, sneezing, and others, are present at birth. The first reflexes to appear have distinct survival value. The others appear within a few hours or days after birth. With practice, the reflexes become stronger. Breast-fed infants, for example, develop stronger sucking reflexes than do bottle-fed infants (Davis *et al.*, 1948).

Several reflexes, as the *Babinski,* the *Moro-embrace,* and the *Darwinian,* which have no survival value, appear shortly after birth but disappear during the early months of life. The Babinski, or fanning of the toes following a gentle stroking of the sole of the infant's foot, is accompanied by movement of the entire leg in the infant. At the age of four months, the speed of the withdrawal has diminished, and fewer segments of the leg are involved. By the age of $2\frac{1}{2}$ years, the response is limited to movements of the ankle and toes (McGraw, 1941). A distinct weakening of the Darwinian, or grasp, reflex occurs by the end of the second month of life. Almost all newborn infants can suspend body weight, but this ability begins to decline rapidly after the first postnatal month (McGraw, 1940).

When the infant is placed flat on his back and the table or mattress on which he is lying is struck hard, he throws out his arms in a movement resembling an embrace. This is the Moro-embrace reflex. At first, there is a marked response of the whole body, accompanied by crying. Gradually, the amount of general bodily activity is reduced. By the eighth month, the Moro reflex consists of a quick, fine body jerk, accompanied by crying (McGraw, 1932).

General responses involve larger portions of the body than the reflexes. Like the reflexes, they are present at birth and are direct responses to external or internal stimuli. Some of the most common of these are visual fixation on light, spontaneous eye movements, shedding of tears, feeding responses such as sucking, swallowing, tongue, cheek, and lip movements, sucking of the fingers, yawning, hiccuping, rhythmic mouthing movements, frowning and wrinkling of the brow, turning and lifting the head, turning of the trunk, body jerk, hand and arm movements, prancing and kicking, leg and foot movements. All of these are uncoordinated, undefined, and aimless. However, they are important because they are the basis from which skilled movements of a highly coordinated type will develop as a result of learning.

VOCALIZATION OF THE NEWBORN

The infant cries at birth or shortly afterward. This is a purely reflex type of activity and results from air being drawn rapidly over the vocal cords, thus causing them to vibrate. The cry of the newborn is uttered with force and loudness and is characterized by regularity of breathing (Irwin and Chen, 1941). The purpose of the birth cry is to inflate the lungs, thus making breathing possible, and to supply the blood with sufficient oxygen. There are marked variations in the birth cry from infant to infant. To a certain extent, the cry is influenced by the physical condition of the infant and by the type of birth. Premature infants or those in poor condition cry in a moaning fashion. Prolonged labor, resulting in exhaustion of the infant, is characteristically accompanied by a short, weak cry. A quick, expulsive form of delivery, on the other hand, is accompanied by a sharp, deep cry.

Shortly after birth, the cry of infants shows variations in pitch, intensity, and continuity. It is then possible to tell, within limits, what is the matter. When the cry is staccatolike, intermittent, and monotonous in pitch, it means general bodily discomfort or hunger. The cry becomes more incessant if the discomfort is not relieved. When discomfort turns into pain, the cry rises in pitch. Should the pain lead to increasing physical weakness, piercing tones then give way to low moans. Rage is expressed through a long, piercing cry during which the breath is held, the infant's face becomes a purplish-red, and there are gulping sounds. Even after rage subsides, there are intermittent sobs.

Cries come from the physiological condition of the infant, generally hunger, pain, discomfort, or fatigue. The cry is in the nature of a reflex and is a response to a definite stimulus (Aldrich *et al.*, 1945). Continuous observations of newborn infants reveal that infants cry more often when hungry and for unknown reasons than for any other causes. Wet diapers are the third most common cause of crying and vomiting the least common (Aldrich *et al.*, 1946). Bodily activity of some sort almost always accompanies the infant's crying. The more vigorous the crying, the more widespread the activity. In pain, hunger, or colic, the bodily activity that accompanies crying is a signal that the infant needs attention. It is thus a form of language (Irwin, 1930).

The amount of crying a newborn infant does is an individual matter. Observations of a group of newborn infants have revealed that the least amount of crying is 48.2 minutes per day and the most, 243 minutes per day. The average for the entire group was 117 minutes per day (Aldrich *et al.*, 1945). Crying was reduced 51.4 per cent when the nursing care of the newborn infant was individualized (Aldrich *et al.*, 1946). Infants delivered by Caesarean section cry less than those born in normal or instrumental births (Fries, 1941). When the amount of crying was correlated with labor time, the correlation was found to be 0.17, little better than chance (Ruja, 1948).

Other Sounds. In addition to crying, the newborn infant makes *explosive sounds* similar to heavy breathing. They are uttered without meaning or intent and occur purely by chance whenever the vocal muscles contract. They are commonly called "coos," "gurgles," or "grunts." These are gradually strengthened and develop into *babbling* which later develops into *speech. Sneezing* is a reflex type of explosive sound which first occurs within a few hours after birth and occasionally before the birth cry itself. Healthy infants sneeze several times a day, thus cleaning the nose of any foreign matter.

Yawning, another type of explosive sound, may be heard as early as 5 minutes after birth. *Whining,* which can be distinguished from crying, occurs during irregular breathing (Irwin and Chen, 1941). *Hiccuping* occurs during the first week of life and ranges in length from 35 seconds to 18 minutes 20 seconds, with a mean of 6 minutes 34 seconds. Hiccuping begins and ends abruptly. It varies from barely audible inspirations to loud sharp sounds. Hiccups usually come in groups of loud sounds interspersed with groups of relatively quiet inspirations (Wagner, 1938).

SENSITIVITIES OF THE NEWBORN INFANT

Because sensation is best studied by the introspective method, and because introspection is impossible at the prespeech level of development, the only criterion that can be used to determine the presence or absence of sensory capacity is the motor response to sensory stimuli that would normally arise when these sense organs are stimulated. However, it is often difficult to tell whether a motor response is made to a stimulus or whether the reaction is a part of general mass activity. Furthermore, absence of response does not necessarily mean absence of sensitivity. It may only mean that the stimulus used was too weak to elicit a response and yet a stronger stimulus might harm the delicate sense organs of the infant. What is known, at the present time, about sensory reactions in the newborn is somewhat limited.

Sight. The retina of the eye, which contains the sense cells for vision, has not reached its mature development at birth. The cones in the fovea are short and poorly defined, though the number of cones per unit area is the same as in the adult eye. This would suggest that the infant at birth is totally or partially color-blind. Within a day or two after birth, the pupillary reflex is well established, as is true of the protective responses of turning the head, closing the eyelids, and crying. The ability to follow moving objects and then move the eye backward, *optic nystagmus,* appears several hours after birth. During the first week of life, most infants respond to light by signs of discomfort (Peterson and Rainey, 1910). Infants seven to nine days old respond in a slightly dissimilar way to colors of the same physical energy (Smith, 1936).

Early ocular fixations, in infants born 8 weeks prematurely, are channelized in the direction of the position of the head. The eyes move saccadically in momentary afterpursuit, though the infant does not give true regard to a dangling object moved slowly across the field of vision. Visual competence at birth exceeds that of the premature. Maturation is more important than experience in this area. On the first day of life, incipient fixation of a near, approaching object can be observed. In the first week, there is sustained fixation of near objects and, by the end of the first month, there is fixation of more distant objects. The infant "takes hold of the physical world ocularly long before he grasps it 'manually' " (Gesell, 1949).

Hearing. At birth, hearing is at the lowest stage of development of all the sensitivities. Many infants are totally deaf at birth and for several days thereafter owing to the stoppage of the middle ear with amniotic fluid. Even loud noises near the ear produce little if any reaction. The average newborn gives no evidence of hearing ordinary sounds during the first 2 days of life, though most make some response to such sounds during the third to seventh day (Bryon, 1930).

Smell. The sense of smell is well developed at birth. This high sensitivity is shown by squirming, crying, and sucking movements, even when the infant is asleep (Pratt *et al.*, 1930). The infant will refuse to take the breast when it has been rubbed with such an odor as petroleum (Preyer, 1888).

Taste. Taste, like smell, is well developed at birth. Reactions to sweet are primarily positive; to salt, sour, and bitter, negative (Shirley, 1931). Wide individual differences in taste thresholds are found, however, among newborn infants (Dockeray, 1934).

Skin Sensitivities. The skin sensitivities of touch, pressure, temperature, and pain are present at birth. Some parts of the body are, however, more sensitive to *touch* than others, especially the lips. The skin on the trunk, thighs, and forearms is, on the other hand, less sensitive. *Cold* stimuli produce prompter and more pronounced reactions than do *heat* stimuli. Sensitivity to *temperature* stimuli is shown by differential sucking reactions to changes of temperature in milk. While marked individual differences exist, the thresholds for the same infants remain constant (Jensen, 1932).

For the first day or two of life, sensitivity to *pain* is weak. Highest sensitivity is found on the lips, eyelashes, soles of the feet, mucous membrane of the nose, and the skin of the forehead. As compared with an adult, the body, legs, underarms, and hands are relatively insensitive. Pain responses appear earlier in the anterior end of the body and develop more rapidly than those in the posterior end. Simple needle pricks, applied to the cheeks, thighs, and calves of the legs produce no reactions before the age of six hours. At forty-seven hours of age, the infant responds to a single prick on the face and, at seventy-six hours, to a single prick on the leg (Sherman and Sherman, 1925). It is impossible to know whether absence of response to pain stimuli in the first hours of life is caused by an undeveloped sensory mechanism or to lack of connections between sensory and somatic centers, or between receptor centers and those mechanisms which govern crying (McGraw, 1941*a*). Sleep increases the threshold of pain sensitivity (Crudden, 1937).

Organic Sensitivities. Hunger contractions are fully developed at birth and appear shortly after birth. They differ from those of an adult only in that they occur at more frequent intervals. They occur every 10 or 15 minutes and end in a complete tetanus or rigid contraction of the muscles. Stomach contractions appear even before the stomach contains food (Carlson and Ginsburg, 1915).

STATE OF CONSCIOUSNESS

Because of the relatively undeveloped state of the most important sense organs, the eyes and the ears, one could not logically expect the newborn infant to be keenly aware of what goes on in the environment surrounding him. His awareness would more likely be "one great, blooming, buzzing confusion" (James, 1890). And, because the mind of the newborn infant is different from that of the older child, and because his experiences are linked to those of intra-uterine life, the newborn infant experiences the world differently, just as "an unmusical person hears a symphony differently from one who is musical" (Koffka, 1925).

EMOTIONS OF THE NEONATE

Studies of the emotions of the neonate date back to the now famous study made by John B. Watson (1925) of Johns Hopkins University. According to him, there are three distinct emotional reactions that occur at birth or shortly afterward and these may be aroused by only a few specific stimuli. *Fear*, for example, is aroused by loud noises and loss of support, especially when the body is not set to compensate for it. The typical fear reaction consists of a jump, a start, a respiratory pause followed by more rapid breathing, sudden closing of the eyes, clutching of the hands, and puckering of the lips.

Rage is a response to the hampering of bodily movements. This is shown by a stiffening of the body, free slashing movements of the hands, arms, and legs, and holding of the breath. No cry is heard at first, though the mouth is open. The *love* response is called forth by stroking the skin, tickling, gentle rocking, and patting. The typical response is smiling, cooing, gurgling, and waving the arms and legs.

While this classification of emotions of the newborn infant was accepted at first, today it is questioned. Are the emotions of the newborn as specific and definite as Watson claimed, or are they general and undefined? In view of the incoordination that characterizes the activities of the newborn, it would be illogical to expect that emotional states at birth be so well defined that they could be readily identified. Subsequent studies have shown this assumption to be valid. Estimations by trained observers of emotional reactions in the absence of a known stimulus were so lacking in agreement as to suggest complete lack of constructive patterning in the responses (Sherman and Sherman, 1929). Increased activity in response to such stimuli as noises is not accompanied by a stirred-up state of the organism and, thus, cannot correctly be labeled "fear" (Pratt, 1934).

Furthermore, crying never accompanies the body startle to loud noises or to being dropped (Irwin, 1930). Instead of specific patterns, the newborn's reactions can be divided into two groups, the "pleasant," or positive, responses, and the "unpleasant," or negative, responses. *Unpleasant responses* can be elicited by changing the infant's position abruptly, by sudden loud noises, by hampering the infant's movements, and by a wet diaper or a cold object applied to the skin. The infant cries in response to these disagreeable stimuli.

Pleasurable responses, on the other hand, can be elicited by patting, rocking, warmth, snug holding, and sucking (Bakwin, 1947). The outstanding characteristic of the infant's emotional make-up is the complete absence of gradations of responses of different degrees of intensity. Whatever the stimulus, the resultant emotion is intense in character and sudden in appearance (Hollingworth, 1928). Observations of prematurely born infants show that emotional reactivity is present several months before birth. It is not known whether the fetus makes any emotional responses. The probability is that they lie dormant until birth as is true of the respiratory mechanism. There is much speculation about this matter but little reliable data. "The ability to respond emotionally is present in the newborn as part of the developmental process and does not have to be learned. Maturing emotions require gratification if optimum health is to be attained" (Bakwin, 1947).

BEGINNING OF PERSONALITY

The foundations of personality, as is true of other physical and mental traits, comes from the maturing of hereditary traits. These traits begin to develop on the delivery table (Zachry, 1940). Even though they are influenced by learning, as a result of direct social contacts, and by conditioning, inheritance plays a major role in the development of personality (Shirley, 1933). There are definite indications of personality at birth (Stagner, 1948). Personality differences are apparent in infants as shown by their responses to food, crying, and motor activities. From these variations, the personality is built (Stagner, 1948; Bayley, 1940; Zachry, 1940). Observations of babies during the first two years of life have revealed a constancy of traits that indicate that the nucleus of personality was present at birth (Shirley, 1933).

Studies of the prenatal environment have suggested that a disturbed prenatal environment, resulting from the mother's emotional or metabolic processes, may cause a modification of the newborn infant's behavior pattern. These are especially important during the latter part of intra-uterine life and may cause a state of hyperactivity and irritability in the newborn infant. Sontag (1946, p. 297) has commented on his findings thus:

As a newborn infant, his muscular activity level is high, as is the level of certain other of his physiological functions. He is the infant who is prone to have an exaggerated bowel activity and a higher fluctuation of heart rate. Such disturbances of somatic function may include cardiospasm. Infants who do not tolerate their feedings, regurgitating them or passing them as undigested curds, often have a history of such disturbing prenatal environment.

Excessive fatigue of the mother, exposure to loud and prolonged noise and vibration, etc., in the fetal environment, cause the possibility of lessening the adaptability of the infant to his new environment at birth, rendering him less able to utilize food successfully. It may also make him nervous, irritable, and given to crying. As a result, the infant will seem less "desirable" in the eyes of his parents, thus affecting their attitude toward him from the very start of his life (Sontag, 1946).

EFFECT OF BIRTH

Contrary to tradition, birth is not the great shock to the infant that one would suppose it to be. The skin sensitivities are not developed well enough before birth to enable the infant to experience the pain which would otherwise result from the pressure of the intense muscular contractions necessary to push the fetus down the birth canal. Because injury to the brain is likely to be the most lasting effect of a prolonged and difficult birth, attempts have been made to see just how much, if any, damage the birth process produces. Electroencephalogram records, taken after feeding and during both sleep and waking periods, have revealed that during waking states, there is a relative absence of rhythmic electrical activity, except in the motor areas where there are several nonpersistent rhythms. During sleep, only about 10 per cent of the cases studied showed a sleep spindle pattern characteristic of older infants and adults. A minimum of disturbance was found, thus suggesting only temporary brain damage (Ellingson and Lindsley, 1949).

How the intelligence of the child has been affected by "natural" or spontaneous birth as compared with instrumental birth has likewise been investigated in children in their early teens. A comparison of the IQ's of those born spontaneously with those who were assisted into the world by instrumental or other operative methods, has led to the conclusion that "instrumental delivery has not had a devastating effect upon the mentality of children who survive." Among the instrumental group, the common forms of problem behavior are hyperactivity (restlessness) and irritability. There is no evidence, therefore, to justify the assumption that behavior difficulties are the result of the shock of birth (Wile and Davis, 1941).

While type of birth per se does not have any appreciable effect on the child's development, indirectly it is of great importance through the effect it has on the parents' attitude toward the child during the years of his childhood. The effect is especially marked on the mother. A difficult birth is likely to make the mother overprotective toward the child. Because it was so difficult for her to give birth to him, she does everything within her power to protect him from any possible harm. This overprotectiveness is often intensified if the mother has been warned by her doctor against having any more children. The mother who gives birth to children easily and with relatively little pain, on the other hand, is far more likely to have a relaxed, unconcerned attitude toward her children than the mother for whom childbirth is difficult. As a result, she will not overprotect her children and will give them an opportunity to develop normally with a minimum of unnecessary restraints. While parental attitude will not influence the level of the child's intelligence, it will have a marked effect on his personality and the development of his native abilities.

PREMATURITY

The prematurely born infant is at a disadvantage from the start because, according to tradition, it is believed that he will never be strong like the full-term infant, and that he is likely to mature into a dullard. Among the ancients, it was customary to take prematurely born infants, along with other defectives, to a mountain where they were allowed to perish. Even in modern civilization, where every possible attempt is made to save the lives of those born ahead of schedule, there is still the belief that, because the development before birth has been incomplete, the infant will never grow up to be like other children. Because of these supposed physical and mental handicaps, parents of prematurely born infants have a tendency to be overprotective of their children throughout the years of their childhood.

In light of these widely accepted beliefs, the following statement by Gesell (1946), based on his research studies of the development of prematurely born infants, is especially interesting and significant. According to Gesell, "The healthy premature infant does not acquire any unnatural precocity from his head start. Neither does he suffer any setback. This should be a great comfort to his anxious mother. She should be assured that the healthy premature infant follows the basic sequence of normal mental growth, making due allowance for his spurious age."

Criteria of Prematurity. An infant is considered premature if the gestation period has been between 28 and 38 weeks long, or when the birth weight is 5 pounds 8 ounces or less. Because the length of the gestation period cannot always be estimated accurately, birth weight is the more commonly used criterion for determining prematurity. Approximately one out of 20 births is premature. The infant mortality rate is high among the prematures, especially in areas where there is no adequate provision for the care of such infants. A prematurely born infant, even with good care, has only one-ninth of the chance for life that the full-term infant has.

The premature infant requires nearly three times as much oxygen as a full-term infant because his breathing is characterized by jerks and gasps. He is often anemic and requires blood transfusions. Because his sucking and swallowing reflexes are underdeveloped, he will require special feeding with a medicine dropper or a tube. As body temperature is not yet properly controlled, the premature infant requires special equipment to duplicate as nearly as possible the constant temperature of intra-uterine life. Furthermore, because he is subject to infection, he requires careful medical supervision. In the modern incubators, the intra-uterine environment is duplicated as nearly as possible.

Prematurely born infants generally develop fast in their early postnatal environment and, when compared with a full-term infant who has just been born, the premature who has had 9 months for developing since the time of conception is more mature. Unfortunately, prematurely born infants are generally judged in terms of age since the time of birth, and this puts them at a decided disadvantage as compared with full-term infants. In fairness to him, "The developmental status of the premature infant must always be appraised in terms of corrected age rather than in those of his spurious chronological age" (Gesell and Amatruda, 1945). A comparison of Negro and white boys and girls showed that, during the first eight months of life, increases in height and weight were greater among boys than among girls. Prematurely born white and Negro infants grow in the same proportions (Glaser *et al.*, 1950).

Characteristics of Premature Infants. Prematurely born infants show the behavior repertory characteristic of full-term infants, though in a less developed form. If the premature's actual age is considered, he shows no appreciable retardation in development (Gesell, 1933). When measured by an infant-development scale, prematurely born infants lag behind those born at full term for a period ranging from 5 months (Melcher, 1937) to 2 years (Benton, 1940). If the birth weight of the premature is taken into consideration, those under 4 pounds are retarded by a month or more through the first 18 months of life: those weighing 4 to 5 pounds at birth, however, overtake the full-term infants by the age of nine months (Shirley, 1938).

In *motor control,* prematurely born infants are somewhat backward. In *postural* and *locomotor* control, not only is their development delayed but they are also frequently awkward, clumsy, and have poor posture (Melcher, 1937). They are either active, or slow and sluggish (Shirley, 1939). Likewise, in control of the *hands,* they are retarded, especially in the use of the index finger for pointing and in the pincer grasp (Shirley, 1939).

Speech also is slower in developing in the prematurely born than in the full-term infant. Baby talk persists longer and more letter substitutions, such as "tix" for "six," are used (Shirley, 1939). Furthermore, more defects, especially stuttering, appear in the speech of the prematures (Hess, Mohr, and Bartelme, 1934). In *sensory behavior* they are more alert than full-term infants. They are especially sensitive to sounds, noises, moving objects, and colors, though they are more easily distracted by voices, traffic noises, and other babies than are those born at full term (Shirley, 1939).

When testing the intelligence of babies, if the amount of prematurity is taken into consideration, there is no significant difference in the IQ scores of prematurely born as compared with full-term infants (Gesell, 1928;

Benton, 1940; Hess, Mohr, and Bartelme, 1934; Knehr and Sobol, 1949). The incidence of mental defect in prematures is no different from estimates for the general population (Knehr and Sobol, 1949), though there is a somewhat higher incidence of serious mental defects among the prematurely born (Benton, 1940). The smallest prematures contribute more than their share to the ranks of the mental defectives. The lowest IQ's are generally found among those who had cerebral hemorrhages postnatally (Beskow, 1949).

In their *relationships with other people,* as they grow older, prematurely born children are generally inferior to other children, though they are more advanced in this area of behavior in the early years of life than in the area of motor development (Jersild, 1947). They are likely to be shy and much attached to their mothers (Shirley, 1939). This is primarily the result of the overprotection given by parents, owing to the physical weakness of the premature at birth (Hess *et al.,* 1934). Prematurely born babies are sometimes "gentle" with moderate affective reactions (Melcher, 1937), but more often they are petulent, shy, irascible, and negativistic (Shirley, 1939). The latter type of *emotional behavior* is likely to result from parental overprotection of the children who were born before term (Hess *et al.,* 1934).

Nervous traits, most investigators agree, are definitely more numerous among children who were born prematurely than among children born at full term. Poor sleep, fatigability, irritability, shyness, temper outbursts, fright, poor concentration, forgetfulness, thumb- and finger-sucking, dogged determination not to comply with directions, hypersensitivity to sounds, and a tendency to burst into tears at the slightest provocation are some of the behavior disorders commonly found among children born ahead of schedule (Benton, 1940; Hess *et al.,* 1934; Shirley, 1939). However, the explanations for the greater incidence of behavior disorders among the prematures have almost unanimously laid the blame on environmental conditions. Because prematurely born children are overprotected at first and then pushed to catch up to other children of their age, they develop nervous traits (Jersild, 1947).

Permanent Effects. Most of the studies of prematurely born children have been limited to the early years of their lives. For that reason, a recent study of a small group of 22 prematurely born infants at ages eight to nineteen years is especially significant. This gives a picture of what one can expect in the way of development of the prematures as they reach maturity. In spite of the fact that the number of cases was too small to be a true picture of what happens to prematurely born individuals as they grow up, it gives clues as to whether the disturbances that have been found to occur in the babyhood or early childhood years persist into adolescence and, if so, how severe the effects will be.

The over-all picture of this small group showed the following characteristics (Howard and Morrell, 1952):

(1) *Physically,* the group showed few defects such as malnutrition, dwarfism, obesity, etc. Eleven were hyperopic. The eyes of prematurely born individuals are frequently defective. Otherwise, prematurity itself does not seem to affect physical growth. (2) *Intellectually,* there is no indication that prematurity per se has either a beneficial or a detrimental effect except that more than the average percentage of prematures suffer intracranial hemorrhages, thus causing brain damage. (3) *Emotionally,* there are indications that with age, the prematurely born children do not make adjustments as well as those who are born at full term. Over half of the group studied had made unsatisfactory adjustments. Contributing factors to their poor adjustment were a poor physical endowment and overprotective parents. Of the group of 22, 12 were of the submissive, passive type, 8 were unusually aggressive, and the others suffered from nail biting, habit spasms, and chronic masturbation. These indications of maladjustment, the authors suggested, may result from deprivation of immediate postnatal maternal tenderness.

CHAPTER 4

Babyhood

(Two Weeks to Two Years)

Babyhood, the stage of development that extends from the end of the period of the newborn infant at approximately two weeks to the end of the second year of life, is characterized by control over the body. With increase in this control comes a gradual ability to be relatively independent of adult aid on the baby's part. The baby who, at birth and for many months thereafter, was totally dependent upon adult care for survival, gradually acquires the ability to do some of the things for himself which formerly he was completely incapable of doing. If given an opportunity to do what he can, the baby will be happy and contented.

Unfortunately, far too often parents cannot or do not adjust their concept of the baby's abilities quickly enough to keep pace with the baby's development. As a result, the baby is frustrated in his attempts to do the things he can and wants to do. Much of the friction between parents and child can be traced to adult lack of understanding of the rapid changes that take place in the capacities and abilities of the human infant during the first two years of life.

PHYSICAL DEVELOPMENT

Babyhood is a period of rapid physical growth. During the first six months of life, growth occurs at a very rapid rate, slowing down gradually during the second half of the first year and proceeding at an increasingly slower rate during the second year (Meredith, 1935). Baby clothes reflect this universal and predictable pattern of growth. Infant sizes, far too large for the newborn unless adjustments are made, are outgrown before the baby is six months old. A second set of clothing is needed for the last six months of the first year while a third set, even larger in size, is adequate to meet his needs from his first to his second birthday.

Weight. The newborn infant weighs, on the average, 7½ pounds, with boys slightly heavier than girls. After the initial loss in weight immediately after birth, weight increases begin. By the end of the second or third week of life, weight loss following birth should have been regained. By the time the baby is four months old, birth weight is normally doubled. This means that the average baby of that age weighs 14 to 15 pounds. At eight months, weight varies from 16 to 19 pounds and, at one year, the birth weight should be trebled, or approximately 21 pounds. By his second birthday, the typical American baby weighs 25 pounds. The slowing down of weight increases during the final quarter of the first year; throughout the second year of life this weight decrease is the result of the great expenditure of energy in learning to eat, crawl, and walk.

Height. Increases in height come at a proportionately slower rate than weight increases. From a birth length of 19 to 20 inches, an increase of $2\frac{1}{2}$ to $3\frac{1}{2}$ inches during the first four months of life makes the baby 22 to 23 inches tall at that age. At eight months, the average height is 25 to 27 inches; at one year, 27 to 29 inches; and, at two years, approximately 32 inches. As is true of weight, variations in height among babies depend upon such factors as sex, parentage, and racial stock. Measurements of weight and height of Negro babies throughout the first year of life showed that those who came from middle-class families were significantly superior to those from the poorer Negro families and that there was no difference between Negro and white babies in these measurements when the groups came from comparable economic levels (Scott *et al.*, 1950). There are also variations in the growth curves for individual babies according to the season of the year. The period from October to December is one of maximum, and from April to June, one of minimum weight gain. Maximum gain in height comes from April to June and minimum, from October to December (Sontag, 1946).

Physical Proportions. Changes in body proportions begin to appear during babyhood. The marked top-heaviness, characteristically present at birth, gradually decreases as the legs and trunk lengthen. The baby appears to be more thickset as a result of greater increase in girth and transverse diameters (Bayley and Davis, 1935) than in length, owing to the proportionally greater increase in weight than in height at this age. The head appears less enormous than at birth owing partly to the development of the lower part of the face, especially the jaw, and the appearance of teeth, and partly to the appearance of a short but actually noticeable neck. Even the nose begins to take on some shape as the cartilage framework develops.

Arms and hands increase in length between 60 and 75 per cent during this period, and legs, approximately 40 per cent. The legs thus are growing at a slower rate than the arms. Babyhood is marked by rapid growth in both hands and feet, not only in size but in muscular development as well. Babies tend to have proportionally longer left arms, forearms and hands, and wider left palms than do children five to six years of age (Van Dusen, 1939).

Bones. As is true of growth in size, babyhood is a period of rapid growth in the bones. The number of bones in the body increases at this age, with bone tissue gradually replacing cartilage or membrane in certain areas. The bones begin to ossify as well as to increase in size and number. The soft spongy tissue of the bones of the newborn gradually hardens, but at different rates in different parts of the body. By the age of eighteen months, for example, the *fontanels,* or soft spots on the skull, are closed in approximately 50 per cent of all babies and, at two years, in approximately all babies. Because the bones are soft during babyhood, the body is pliable. This explains why a baby can get into strange positions, such as sucking his toes when lying on his back. It is at this time also that bones can readily be misshapen if too much pressure is placed on them for too long a time or if the baby is permitted to sleep on a mattress that sags.

Teeth. Of the 20 "baby," or temporary, teeth, approximately 16 have erupted before babyhood is over. The first tooth to make its appearance cuts through the gum generally between the ages of six and eight months, though some babies get their first teeth when they are only two or three months old and some not until their first birthdays have passed. The lower central incisors come in first, followed by the upper incisors. By the age of one year, the average baby has four to six teeth and, by the second year, 16 teeth. The first teeth to cut through, the "biting" teeth, are thin and sharp. As a result, the eruptions are less painful than in the case of the molars, or "chewing" teeth, in the back of the jaw. As these cut through during the second year, teething gives rise to more physical upsets, more discomfort and, in turn, more fretfulness and irritability than during the first year of life when the eruption of teeth is less painful.

Nervous System. Rapid growth in the nervous system characterizes the first three to four years of postnatal life. This growth consists primarily of the development of immature cells present at birth rather than of the formation of new cells. Brain growth is shown in the increase of cranial size, made possible by the loosely connected bones of the skull. It has been estimated that one-fourth of the adult brain weight is attained at birth, one-half by the age of nine months, and three-fourths by the end of the second year.

Sense-organ Development. The sense organs develop rapidly during babyhood and are capable of functioning on a satisfactory level during the early months of life. With the development of coordination of the eye muscles by the third month, the baby is capable of *seeing* things clearly and distinctly. However, because the eye muscles remain weak for many months, eye incoordination is frequent, especially at times when the baby is fatigued, hungry, or has been crying. At about the same age, three months, it is believed, though not conclusively proved, that the cones of the retina are developed well enough to permit him to see all colors. *Hearing* is acute in babies as may be seen in their early response to the sound of the human voice (Gesell and Thompson, 1934; C. Bühler, 1930). At two months of age, babies exhibit a greater acuity to the voice than to such sounds as whistling, knocking, handclapping, and the noise of a spoon (Hetzer and Tudor-Hart, 1927).

Shortly after the baby is two months old, he responds equally well to noises of all kinds.

Smell and *taste,* which are well developed at birth, continue to be acute throughout babyhood. Because of their acuity, foods that are bland in taste to adults are pleasing to the baby, while foods that appeal to an adult are so

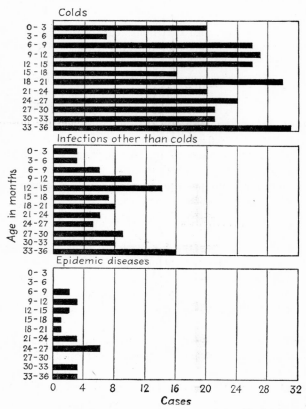

Fig. 12. Common illnesses from birth to three years. (*From N. Bayley, Studies in the development of young children. Berkeley: Univ. California Press, 1940. Used by permission.*)

strong in taste to a baby that he rejects them. Because of the thin texture of babies' skin and the fact that there are as many sense organs for *touch, pressure, pain,* and *temperature* in the skin surface of a baby as there will be when he reaches maturity, a baby is highly responsive to all skin stimuli. He feels heat, cold, and pain acutely and he responds more vigorously to light touch and tickling stimuli than he will when he is older.

Babyhood Illnesses. For the first two to four months of life, nature provides an immunity to disease which safeguards the health of the young baby.

After the first half of the first year of life, this immunity gradually wears off. When pregnant women of low incomes have their diet improved by supplying additional food during the last 3 to 4 months of pregnancy, the incidence of illness in babies up to six months of age and the number of deaths resulting from these illnesses have been found to be many times less than in a control group whose diet was poor and was not supplemented by additional food (Eblis *et al.*, 1941). For the remaining months of babyhood, illnesses are frequent and sometimes fatal. Pneumonia and diphtheria have, in the past, been the most serious illnesses of babyhood. Common illnesses and the frequency of their occurrence in babyhood are shown in Fig. 12.

With modern medical discoveries, however, fewer deaths occur from these illnesses than formerly, especially in cities where better medical attention is available than in small towns and rural districts. In addition to the more serious diseases, minor illnesses such as colds and digestive upsets are common. With prompt diagnosis of these and proper medical care, they can be checked before any serious harm occurs. When, however, they are neglected, as is frequently true in the case of common colds, they can and often do develop with lightning rapidity into more serious disturbances, especially ear infections.

PHYSIOLOGICAL FUNCTIONS

Babyhood is the time when the fundamental physiological habits of eating, sleeping, and elimination should be established. While the habit formation will not be completed when babyhood ends, a good foundation should have been established by that time. Otherwise, the problem of developing good physiological habits will become increasingly difficult as each month passes.

Sleep Habits. From birth to four months, the average amount of sleep is 17 to 20 hours daily. By one year, the amount of sleep declines to an average of 14 to 15 hours and, at two years, to 13 or 14 hours. At first, sleep comes in short intervals of 3 to 4 hours, broken by periods of feeding. As the baby's stomach enlarges, by the end of the first year, the sleep periods become longer. During the second year, the baby sleeps generally from 6 P.M. to 5 or 6 A.M., with a morning nap of 1 hour and an afternoon nap of 2 hours. By the baby's second birthday, the night sleep and afternoon nap remain about the same length as previously but the morning nap is generally discontinued.

For the first three or four months of life, before the baby can move his body from the position in which it has been placed, he becomes tired and fretful if allowed to remain too long in one position. To avoid misshapen bones, the baby's sleep position must be changed from time to time, generally after each feeding. When he can roll, between the ages of four and six months, the baby is able not only to turn his body but also to discover a position that he prefers, often on his stomach. Throughout sleep, the baby's body moves, with the least frequent movements during the early stages of sleep (Boynton and Goodenough, 1930). Motility in sleep decreases with age.

Eating Habits. While sucking and swallowing reflexes are present at birth, even in prematurely born infants, they are far from well developed. The newborn infant frequently sucks in air when he is swallowing, thus causing him to choke or to develop colic pains. From birth until four or five months of age, all eating is in the infantile form of sucking and swallowing. Food, as a result, must be in a liquid form. Chewing generally appears in the developmental pattern a month later than biting. But, like biting, it is in an infantile form and requires much practice before it becomes serviceable. At first, the baby chews in "rabbit style," using only his front teeth and, if the portion he has bitten off is too large for him to cope with successfully, he either holds it in his mouth without chewing or he spits it out. Given a reasonable opportunity for practice, however, and food in a semisolid form to encourage biting and chewing, the baby will have mastered the foundational eating habits by his first birthday.

The use of the bottle and of foods in liquid form during the second half of the first year of life will encourage the continuation of infantile sucking until it becomes such a well-established habit that the baby will have difficulty in progressing to the more mature forms of eating which require biting, chewing, and swallowing of semisolids. To avoid the prolongation of infantile feeding, a cup should be substituted when the baby is six months old so that he will have to drink instead of sucking. In early weaning, thumb-sucking frequently becomes a substitute for sucking the nipple (Levy, 1928). And, as soon as the baby has had some preliminary practice in biting crackers, crisp bacon, or zweibach, his food should be given him in semisolid forms which will offer the necessary motivation to bite and chew.

Food dislikes, which begin to creep into the baby's eating during the second year of life, frequently trace their origin to the prolongation of infantile eating patterns. After becoming accustomed to food in liquid form, it is difficult for the baby to adjust to it in a semisolid form. Furthermore, like all habit breaking, there is emotional resistance to giving up infantile habits after they have become firmly established. This, in turn, adds to the baby's revolt against his food, even though he may like its taste.

Because every baby has his own rhythm of feeding, just as he has his own rhythm of sleep, it is essential that mothers take into consideration the individual baby's hunger rhythm instead of forcing upon the baby an artificial feeding schedule. When an artificial schedule is forced on the baby, it causes a sense of frustration in the baby, it leads to rejection of the food, and it predisposes other emotional upsets on the part of the baby. In the matter of quantity of food as well as in the time of eating, babies should have more liberty in satisfying their wants than they are generally given (Rowan-Legg, 1949).

Habits of Elimination. In establishing habits of bowel and bladder control, timing is far more important than technique. These habits cannot be established until a state of readiness in the development of muscles and nerves is present. Bowel control begins, on the average, at six months and bladder control, between the ages of fifteen and sixteen months. In the case of the former, habits of control are established by the end of babyhood though temporary lapses may be expected when the baby is tired, ill, or emotionally excited. Bladder control, on the other hand, is in a rudimentary state at the close of babyhood. Dryness during the daytime can be expected for a major part of the time except when deviations from the scheduled routine of the day, illness, fatigue, or emotional tension interfere. There are, however, marked individual differences in babies, as there are at all stages of development (Sweet, 1946). Dryness at night cannot be achieved in the average child until several years later.

MUSCLE CONTROL

To be independent, the baby must gain control over his muscles. This is essential if he is to do what he wants to do, when he wants to do it. Muscle control is one of the major areas of development during the babyhood years and, unless environmental obstacles interfere, the baby should emerge from babyhood as a relatively independent individual. Development of control over the muscles follows a definite and predictable pattern governed by the "law of developmental direction." According to this law, muscle control sweeps over the body from head to feet with the muscles in the head region coming under voluntary control first and those in the leg region last. The pattern of motor control is illustrated in Fig. 13.

Maturation and learning work together in the development of muscle control. Through maturation of the muscles, bones, and nerve structures, and through a change in body proportions, the baby is ready to use his body in a coordinated manner. He must, however, be given an opportunity to learn how to do this. Until this state of readiness is present, teaching will be of little or no value. It may even be harmful because it frequently fosters fear or resentment on the baby's part, both of which will militate against his learning the skill. The approximate ages at which muscle control appears in the different areas of the body and the usual pattern of development are as follows:

Head Region. Control of eye movements comes early in life. *Optic nystagmus,* or the response of the eyes to a succession of moving objects, comes within the first 12 hours after birth, and *ocular pursuit movements,* within the third and fourth weeks (McGinnis, 1930). *Horizontal eye movements* develop between the second and third months of life, *vertical eye movements* between the third and fourth months, and *circular eye movements,* several

FIG. 13. Developmental phases in the assumption of an erect posture. (*From M. B. McGraw, Growth: a study of Johnny and Jimmy. New York: Appleton-Century-Crofts, 1935. Used by permission.*)

weeks later. By the end of the fourth month of life, even the most difficult eye movements are normally present (Jones, 1926). While *reflex smiling,* or smiling in response to some tactual stimulus, appears as early as the first week of life, "social smiling," or smiling in response to a smile of another person, does not appear until between the third and fourth months.

The newborn infant, when placed on his stomach, can *hold up his head* during the first 20 minutes of life. When supported in a prone position at the chest and abdomen, the baby can hold his head erect in a horizontal plane at the age of one month and, at two months he can hold his head above the horizontal plane at an angle of 30 degrees. Because holding up the head when lying on the back is more difficult than when in a prone position, this ability does not develop much before the fifth month (Shirley, 1931). By the age of four to six months, most babies can hold up their heads when seated on someone's lap. At this age, the baby's head maintains a mid-position when the body is supine, and he actively rotates his head, turning it freely from side to side. At five months, he turns his head freely when sitting in a chair (Gesell, 1930, 1940).

Trunk Region. The two important developments that take place in the trunk region are the abilities to turn the body by *rolling* and by *sitting up*. At birth, the infant cannot turn his body from the position in which he has been placed, though he can move it slightly by squirming. By the time he is two months old, however, he is generally able to turn from side to back; from back to side at four months; and at six months, from stomach to stomach. The complete turn is generally made at first with several partial turns with rest periods between each turn. When he rolls, the baby turns his head first, then his shoulders, then the pelvis, and last, by pushing-kicking movements of the legs, he makes a turn of his entire body.

A sixteen-week-old baby can pull himself to a sitting position; at twenty weeks, he can sit with erect back when supported; and at twenty-eight weeks, he will sit momentarily without support when placed in a sitting position. The average baby will sit, unsupported, for 10 or more minutes between the ninth and tenth months (Gesell, 1940). Boys achieve this skill slightly later than girls (Peatman and Higgons, 1940). In early sitting, the baby often bends forward with arms outstretched, to maintain his balance. His legs are bowed, with the soles of his feet turned toward each other, thus giving him a wide base for balance. Because early sitting is unstable, the baby frequently topples over when he tries to move.

In pulling himself to a sitting position, the baby first turns from a dorsal to a ventral position, then squats on all fours, and finally pushes himself upright. Not until the second or third year does the baby cease to turn his whole body axis. By the fourth or fifth year, the adult method of rolling up the body symmetrically with the aid of the arms is used (Schaltenbrand, 1928). Sitting down, like sitting up, is difficult for a baby and requires much practice. At first, the baby merely topples over or falls down by giving way in the lower part of the trunk. With practice, aided by demonstration or by trial and error, he gradually learns to bend his knees and slide down instead of keeping his knees stiff. Most babies have learned how to do this by their first birthdays.

Arm and Hand Region. The waving, slashing arm movements and the opening and shutting of the hands of the newborn infant gradually give way to coordinated movements. The first coordinated movement is a *defense reaction* when some stimulus is approaching the face. During the first day or two of life, these movements are poorly coordinated. But, by the end of the period of the newborn, a well-coordinated defensive movement can generally be made in one trial (Sherman and Sherman, 1925). *Thumb opposition,* or the working of the thumb in opposition to the fingers, normally appears in grasping between the third and fourth months, and in picking up objects, between the eighth and tenth months (Gesell and Halverson, 1936). *Eye-hand coordination,* or the direction of the movements of the hands by the eyes, is developed well enough by the sixth or seventh month of life that random reaching no longer exists and the baby can pick up even little objects when he reaches for them (Watson and Watson, 1921).

Leg Region. The earliest form of locomotion comes in the slight shifting of the body as a result of vigorous *kicking* of the legs. This occurs by the end of the second week of life. Then comes *rolling* followed by *hitching,* or locomotion in a sitting position in which the body is pushed backward through the combined pushing of the legs and arms. Rolling and hitching characteristically appear by the sixth month. *Crawling,* in which the body is prone on the floor with the head and shoulders raised by supporting the weight of that area on the elbows, reaches its peak between the seventh and ninth months. In crawling, most of the body movement comes from pulling with the arms and swimminglike movements of the legs.

As greater body strength develops, the baby *creeps* by raising his body from the floor and pushing himself forward on his hands and knees. This generally occurs between the tenth and eleventh months. Sometimes the baby raises his knees from the floor, stiffens his legs, and walks on "all fours" (Ames, 1937). As a general rule, *standing with support* overlaps creeping in the developmental sequence. Gradually the baby will let go, first with one hand and then with the other. The average age for standing alone is one year. The average age for pulling himself to a standing position is 10 to 10½ months with girls slightly ahead of boys in this. The typical standing position is with the feet far apart, the toes turned outward, and the head and shoulders held forward to give the body better balance.

With practice in standing, the baby acquires enough self-confidence to take a step. Gradually, with practice and increased self-confidence, he takes more and more steps, thus *walking with support.* This usually occurs while the baby is acquiring the ability to stand alone. At first, he walks in a stiff-legged manner, with legs far apart, toes turned outward, and arms held outright like a tightrope walker, or close to the body. The head is held erect and slightly forward to maintain balance. Because he cannot watch the floor without throwing his body off balance, because he raises his feet far from the floor, and because of his uneven steps, the baby has many falls when he is first learning to walk. By the age of fifteen months, his walking improves to the point where he can relax his stiff-legged position and walk like an adult.

Later Skills. After body control has been obtained, the baby can use his muscular coordination for new activities. Given an opportunity for practice, an incentive to learn, and a model of behavior to copy, he will acquire many skills that will be useful to him in daily activities. None of these skills will, of course, be perfected in the relatively short span of babyhood years. However, the foundations will be laid at this time, and improvements will follow at a later date.

HAND SKILLS. The ability to grasp and to *hold* two or three objects, such as blocks, bells, cubes, pieces of paper, or rattles, appears at the age of seven months for two objects and at ten months for three objects (Lippman, 1927). By the time he is eighteen months old, the baby can hold his bottle after it has been placed in his mouth and, a month later, he can put it in and take it out without help. During his second year, the baby begins to *feed* himself. At first, he uses a cup held with both hands. Later, with practice, he can hold a cup with one hand. This ability generally appears at the age of eighteen months. At fifteen months, he can grasp a spoon and insert it in a dish. If he carries it to his mouth, he is apt to turn it upside down before it reaches his mouth. Three months later, there is still considerable spilling and a tendency to turn the spoon in his mouth. By the end of the second year, he no longer turns the spoon in his mouth, and there is only a moderate amount of spilling (Gesell, 1940).

By the age of eighteen months, a baby can lift his cup to his mouth and drink well, handing the empty cup to his mother. By the age of two years, he can hold a small glass in one hand and drink from it (Gesell, 1940). By the end of babyhood, most babies can handle a fork. They generally spear the food with the prongs of the fork and spill a major part of the food as they carry it to their mouths. Hand skills in *dressing* develop first in the ability to remove clothing. At the end of the first year, most babies can pull off their socks, shoes, caps, and mittens. By the end of babyhood, they can generally remove all garments unless they are buttoned in the back. From the age of a year and a half, there is an attempt on the baby's part to put on his clothes. Caps and mittens are usually put on first (Key *et al.*, 1936).

During the early months of life, a baby is ambidextrous, with no preference for either hand. At four months, the first contact and manipulation of an object are usually unilateral with the nondominant hand (Ames, 1949). By the age of six months, however, most babies show an unequal use of the two hands and, at nine months, hand preference is definitely marked. No longer are both hands used in grasping or handling objects (Giesecke, 1936). A temporary dominance of the left hand is common during the first year of life (Lederer, 1939). However, there are marked shifts in hand preference at that time and shifts from unilateral to bilateral dominance. By the age of two years, there is a relatively clear-cut use of the right hand (Gesell and Ames, 1947).

LEG SKILLS. After the ability to walk has been achieved, attempts are made to acquire related skills, such as running, skipping, jumping, and climbing. Because the major part of babyhood is devoted to developing the ability to walk these related skills are only in a rudimentary state of development by the close of the period. Running, for example, is little more than fast walking with uneven steps. General clumsiness and many falls are characteristic of the baby's first running. Early jumping is an exaggerated stepping with one foot and then the other. Climbing up and down steps is achieved first by crawling and creeping. Later, when the baby can walk alone, he goes up and down stairs in an upright position, holding on to the railing of the stairs, placing one foot on the step, and then drawing the other foot up to it. By fifty-six weeks of age, about 50 per cent of all babies can climb four steps (Gesell and Thompson, 1938). By the end of the second year, there are definite swimming movements, especially in the lower extremities, and the tendency to remain in a prone position in the water (McGraw, 1939).

Delayed Motor Development. Many babies fall below the norms given above in developing control over their bodies. Because later skills depend upon the development of control of different areas of the body, delayed motor development proves to be serious as a child emerges into childhood and begins to play with other children. The more seriously he lags behind the group in the acquisition of body control, the slower he is likely to be in acquiring the skills other children possess. Furthermore, because the desire to be independent makes its appearance early in the second year, a baby whose motor development lags is frustrated when he tries to do things for himself and fails.

There are many causes of delayed motor development in babyhood, most of which are controllable. The most important of these causes are lack of opportunity to develop muscle control resulting from lack of practice because of a restrictive environment; parental fears of the baby's being harmed by using his muscles too soon; restrictive clothing; lack of incentive to develop muscle control because he is pampered and things are done for him; body size and proportions which make movements of the body difficult; low-grade intelligence which delays motor development in proportion to its deviation from the average; fear engendered by previous accidents or constant parental warnings; and poor health caused by disease and malnutrition.

SPEECH DEVELOPMENT

Because learning to talk is a long and laborious task, many babies try to make known their needs by using substitutes for speech, especially crying and gestures. When these substitutes prove to be effective, the baby's speech development is delayed and he continues to use infantile methods of communication even after he is capable of using words.

Prespeech Forms. There are three prespeech forms which normally appear in the developmental pattern. They are crying, babbling, and gestures. *Crying* is the most frequently used of the three prespeech forms during the

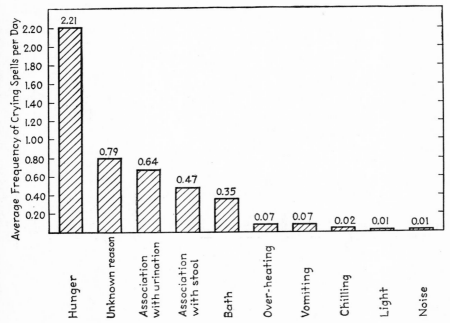

FIG. 14. Causes of crying of an average baby on an average day. (*From C. A. Aldrich, C. Sung, and C. Knop, The crying of newly born babies. VIII. The early home period. J. Pediat., 1945, 27:428–435. Used by permission.*)

early months of life though, from the long-range point of view, babbling is the most important because, from it, real speech eventually develops.

CRYING. The cries of the newborn baby gradually become differentiated so that, by the third or fourth week of life, it is possible to tell from the tone and intensity of the cry and from the bodily movements accompanying it, what it signifies. Pain, for example, is expressed in shrill loud cries, interrupted by groaning and whimpering. Hunger cries are loud and interrupted by sucking movements. Hunger and overheating are the most common causes of crying during the early weeks of life, while noise, light, clothing, and vomiting are the least common causes (Aldrich *et al.*, 1945). The relative importance of the different causes of crying is shown in Fig. 14. As a baby grows older, pain, especially from digestion, strong sensory stimuli, strong disturbances during sleep, failure of an intended reaction such as inability to move because of too-tight covers, loss or removal of a toy, removal of contact with others, and fear of strange places are also common causes of crying (C. Bühler, 1930).

Almost all crying is accompanied by behavior patterns which differ from

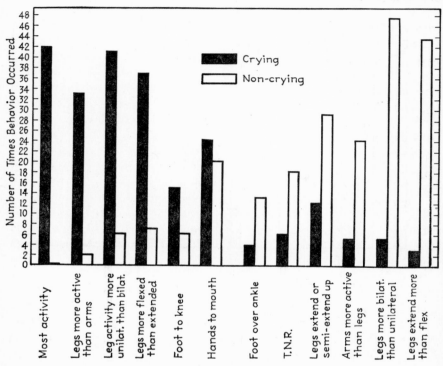

Fig. 15. Differences between bodily activity in crying and in noncrying. (*From L. B. Ames, Motor correlates of infant crying. J. genet. Psychol., 1941, 59:239–247. Used by permission.*)

the patterns in noncrying. In crying, for example, there is vigorous limb activity, strong flexor tendencies, and a disorganization of postures prevailing when crying started. Noncrying behavior patterns, on the other hand, are characterized by greater arm than leg activity, the holding of set postures, and limb extension (Ames, 1941). Behavior patterns in crying and noncrying are shown in Fig. 15.

BABBLING. Babbling develops from the explosive sounds made by the newborn baby. In time, it develops into real speech. The number of·sounds produced in babbling gradually increases and, with practice, the baby can, by the time he is six months old, combine certain vowel and consonant sounds such as "ma-ma," "da-da," or "na-na." Babbling begins during the second or third month of life, reaches its peak by the eighth month, and then gradually gives way to real speech. Because it is not used as a form of communication but as a type of playful activity, its real value from the point of view of speech development is the exercise it gives the vocal mechanism as a preliminary control which will make possible imitation of words spoken by others.

GESTURES. The baby uses gestures as a substitute for speech while adults and older children use them as supplements to speech, to give emphasis to words. Even after he is able to say a few words, the baby will continue to use gestures, combining them with the words he knows, to make his first sentence. Outstretched arms and smiling, for example, readily communicate the idea that the baby wants to be picked up, while pushing away his plate, especially when accompanied by the word "no," quickly tells you that the baby does not want to eat the food placed before him.

Comprehension. At every age, a child comprehends the meanings of what others say more readily than he can put into words his own thoughts and feelings. This is true of babyhood also. The facial expression, tone of voice, and gestures of the speaker help him to understand the meaning of what is being said. This would be impossible if he had to rely entirely upon interpreting the sounds he heard. Pleasure, anger, and fear can be comprehended as early as the third month of life. Until the baby is eighteen months old, words must be reinforced with gestures, such as pointing to an object, if he is to understand the meaning. By the age of two years, according to the Terman-Merrill Scale of Intelligence Tests, the average baby should comprehend well enough to respond correctly to two out of six simple commands, as, "Give me the kitty" or "Put the spoon in the cup," when the objects are placed on the table before him (Terman and Merrill, 1937).

Vocabulary Building. To speak, the baby must learn words associated with objects and activities. His early vocabulary consists primarily of nouns related to persons and objects in his environment, and of verbs which designate action, such as "give" and "hold." Shortly before babyhood is over, a few adjectives and adverbs creep into his vocabulary. Adjectives describing his reactions to people and things, such as "nice" and "naughty," appear first. Prepositions, conjunctions, and pronouns generally are not used until early in childhood. It has been estimated, from studies of large numbers of babies, that at eighteen months of age, the mean number of different words used by babies is 10, and at twenty-four months, 29.1 words. At this age, girls definitely surpass boys in the size of vocabulary used (McCarthy, 1930). However, because the size of the baby's vocabulary depends upon so many factors, especially intelligence, incentive, and opportunity to learn new words, there are marked individual differences. It has been reported that the average vocabulary of a two-year-old contains 272 words (Smith, 1926).

Use of Sentences. The first sentences used by a baby are generally one-word sentences consisting of a noun or verb accompanied by a gesture. "Doll," accompanied by pointing to a doll, expresses the meaning "Give me the doll." One-word sentences appear in a baby's speech between the ages of twelve and eighteen months (Gesell, 1928; Nice, 1933). Gradually, more words creep into the sentences, but the use of gestures is not abandoned until well into childhood. Early word combinations appear between the ages of 17.5 months and two years (Gesell, 1928; Nice, 1933; Shirley, 1933). These early word combinations contain one or more nouns, a verb, and occasionally adjectives and adverbs. Typical early word combinations are "Cup all gone" and "Shut that door" (Gesell, 1940).

Pronunciation. Because speech is learned by imitation, it is essential that a baby have a good model if he is to learn to pronounce his words correctly. But a good model alone is not enough. The model must be presented slowly and distinctly so the baby can hear every sound. He should be encouraged to say the word over and over again, following a repetition of the model, until he learns to say that word correctly. In most cases, mispronunciation of words is the result of crude perceptions rather than of inability to pronounce the elemental sounds (Bean, 1932). "Baby talk," or erroneous speech, generally consists of the omission of one or more syllables, usually in the middle of a word, as "buttfly" for "butterfly"; substitution of letters, syllables, or even words for the word heard, as "tolly" for "dolly" or "choo-choo" for "train"; and interchanges of letters or syllables in the longer and less frequently used words, as "tautmobile" for "automobile." During the first year of life, initial consonants are frequent, while final consonants are infrequent (Irwin, 1951).

Because baby talk is frequently regarded by parents and relatives as "cute," they permit it to continue or they even encourage its use by talking baby talk themselves when they speak to the baby. As a result, an incorrect auditory image is developed. This serves as a model for future pronunciations of that word. Continued mispronunciation of a word results in the formation of a word habit which may be difficult to break and to replace with a habit of correct pronunciation when the baby emerges into childhood and discovers that his playmates cannot understand him or ridicule him because he "talks like a baby."

Delayed Speech. Delayed speech, like delayed motor control, is serious in babyhood because, at this age, the foundations are being laid for the tools of communication which will be needed as the baby's social horizons broaden. In early childhood, with the awakening of interest in people outside the home, the child whose speech lags markedly behind that of other children finds himself in the role of an outsider. If he cannot make himself understood by them, he cannot become one of the group.

There are many causes of delayed speech in babyhood, the most important of which are low-grade intelligence, poor social environment, lack of incentive to talk, an inadequate or defective model, prolonged illness, deafness, and multiple births. The presence of siblings in the family has been found to have a negligible effect on the speech-sound development of young babies (Irwin, 1948a). Mastery of the speech sounds of babies of business, clerical, and professional people has been compared with that of babies of laboring families. No significant difference was found for the first year and a half. After that, however, a significant difference in favor of the former group was noted (Irwin, 1948). Any one or several of these causes can readily delay the baby's speech by several months, not only in the age at which he first begins to talk but also in the size of his vocabulary and his ability to combine words into sentences.

EMOTIONS

From the simple, almost completely undifferentiated forms in which emotions appear at birth, they develop, through maturation and learning, into different emotional states which can be aroused by a wide variety of stimuli. With age, emotional responses become less diffuse, less random, and more differentiated. They likewise become more specialized and directed toward the situation in which they occur. From general emotional excitement, which appears at birth, fear, anger, disgust, distress, delight, elation, and affection gradually develop (Bridges, 1932). Genetic studies of a large number of babies have shown a pattern sequence in emotional development similar in its major aspects for all. In this pattern, different emotional responses appear at particular times and, with increasing age, there is a change in the form the response takes.

Crying and screaming, for example, appear in the first few minutes after birth. By the age of four to eight months, calling is added to crying; between sixteen and twenty months, saying "no" is added, and between twenty and twenty-four months, asking accompanies "no." Similarly, running away when frightened does not appear until the twelve- to sixteen-month period, while hiding the face does not appear until the age of sixteen to twenty months (Blatz et al., 1935; Bayley, 1932). Emotions in babyhood are characterized by behavior responses proportionately great for the stimulus that gave rise to them, especially in the case of anger and fear (Isaacs, 1940). They are brief in duration, though intense while they last. They appear frequently, but are transitory and give way to other emotions when the baby's attention is distracted.

Anger. Anger is the most common emotion in babyhood because there are many anger-provoking stimuli in the baby's environment and because babies quickly learn that anger is an easy way to get attention or to satisfy their desires. In babyhood, anger is often aroused in response to interference with the movements the baby wishes to make, such as putting on his clothes when he wants to play with a toy; thwarting of some wish, such as not being picked up when he cries for attention; and not being able to do what he sets out to do, as getting a box from a shelf that is too high for him to reach. A few of the most common situations that give rise to anger at the close of babyhood are having to sit on the toilet chair, having property taken away, having his face washed, being left alone in the room, or having the adult leave the room (Watson, 1925).

No two babies, of course, experience anger for the same reasons, but the general pattern is the same for all. Thwarting of some wish or interfering with what they are trying to do will invariably lead to an angry outburst. Anger responses in babies show fewer variations than they do in older children. Typically, in an angry outburst the energy is not directed toward any serviceable end. It is expended in screaming, kicking the legs, and waving the arms in a random fashion. Many babies add to this repertoire of actions, holding their breath, jumping up and down, throwing themselves on the floor, and hitting or kicking anything within reach (Goodenough, 1931).

Fear. Unlike anger, fear-provoking stimuli are relatively infrequent in the environment of a baby. The baby is protected as much as possible from the common dangers of life, such as automobiles, falls from high places, loud noises, strange people and places, and animals that come upon them suddenly with a bark or a roar. And, because of their limited intelligence, they are incapable of seeing the threat in such situations as a loss of financial security through the death of the father or the danger to their health when a polio epidemic strikes their community. They do, however, learn to fear certain things in spite of their restricted environment. Through association with the native fear of loud noises or of falling, through imitation of those who are afraid, or through memories of an unpleasant experience, they build up fears of people and things in their environment (Lawton, 1938).

How many or how severe these babyhood fears are will vary greatly from individual to individual. In general, the things most feared at this age are animals; dark rooms; high places; strange persons, objects, and situations; and loud noises. They also fear persons or things associated with loud noises, pain, and tactual-sensory shock, falling, and sudden displacements. Toward the end of babyhood, fears of animals, of dark places, and of being alone begin to appear (Jersild and Holmes, 1935). Even though fears are, for the most part, learned as a result of individual experience and vary from individual to individual, there are two characteristics that are common to all fear stimuli. The first is that the stimulus occurs suddenly and unexpectedly, thus giving the baby little opportunity to adjust himself to it. Fear of strangers, for example, which is so common between the ages of nine and twelve months, comes principally from the fact that a stranger approaches the baby suddenly in place of the familiar person he was prepared to see.

The second characteristic of fear stimuli is that they embody novelty or strangeness. Even a familiar person dressed in an unfamiliar manner, as when the mother wears a hat and coat in place of her usual housedress, may frighten a young baby. As soon as the novelty disappears, so does the fear. The typical fear response in babyhood consists of an attempt to withdraw from the frightening stimulus accompanied by whimpering, crying, temporary holding of the breath, and a checking of the activity in which the individual is engaged. A frightened baby will turn his head and hide his face before he is capable of running away and hiding. His response is thus one of helplessness and his cry is for help.

Joy. Joy which, in its milder forms, is known as pleasure or happiness is bound up at first with physical well-being (C. Bühler, 1930). By the second or third month of life, social situations will likewise give rise to smiling and laughing and, several months later, the baby will respond joyfully to tickling (Leuba, 1941). The most common situations causing laughter in the second year of life are being played with, playing with toys, watching other children at play, and making sounds which are more or less musical (Watson, 1925).

Joy expresses itself in smiling and laughing. Movements of the arms and legs and slight respiratory changes, as may be seen in the pulsations of the abdomen, accompany laughter at this age. When joy is intense, the baby coos, gurgles, or even shouts with glee, and all the bodily movements are intensified. There are definite age trends in the amount and also in the stimuli that elicit smiling and laughing. At eighteen months, the baby smiles mostly at his own activities. The type that amuses him most is his own gross motor activity or his own social approach to a person. At two years, smiles in relation to another person occur less frequently, but now these smiles are accompanied by verbalizations. Smiles in relation to his own activity come next in frequency (Ames, 1949).

Affection. Affectionate responses to people develop in a patterned fashion. Affectionate behavior appears in an outgoing striving and approach. The baby fixes his gaze on a person's face, kicks, holds out and waves his arms, smiles, and tries to raise his body. Because these movements are so uncoordinated at first, he cannot reach the loved one. He can, however, usually reach the loved one by the age of six months. During the second half of the first year, affectionate behavior is directed toward familiar persons, though strangers may win the baby's affection quickly. In the second year, the baby includes himself and his toys in his affection, but it is not until a year later that he responds in an affectionate manner to other children. During babyhood, babies thus develop affectionate responses to persons in their own environments, men and women, adults and children alike. They express their affection in outgoing, expansive ways. Preoccupation with self and withdrawn and withholding behavior are secondary reactions, coming when a baby is rebuffed, smothered with unwanted ministrations, ignored, or neglected. This is often found in two-year-olds who then normally seek other companionship (Banham, 1950).

Curiosity. For the first two or three months of life, until eye coordination is well developed, only strong stimuli directed toward the baby will attract his attention. When, however, the ability to see clearly and distinctly has developed, anything new or unusual will motivate the baby to explore, unless the newness is so pronounced that it gives rise to fear. As fear wanes, curiosity will replace it. Typically, curiosity in young babies is expressed by tensing the facial muscles, opening the mouth and stretching out the tongue, and wrinkling the forehead. By the middle of the first year, the baby leans toward the object that aroused his curiosity and grasps for it. When he reaches it, he handles, pulls, sucks, shakes, and rattles it. This sensorimotor exploration frequently results in damage to the object and harm to the baby.

SOCIAL DEVELOPMENT

The socialization of a human being follows a definite and predictable pattern. Normally, every child passes through the different stages of this pattern. Any obstacle, either from within the child or emanating from his environment, will retard his progress through the different stages of development. This will delay his socialization and, even worse, may result in a fixation at an infantile stage. Geographic isolation, for example, at a time when children normally seek the companionship of other children, may readily result in loneliness which is compensated by excessive reading, by undue interest in a pet, or absorption in a hobby. Later, when this geographic barrier is removed, it is possible and probable that the child will find himself so out of step with the other children of his age that he may withdraw from the group and seek the compensatory satisfaction he formerly derived from the activities he engaged in when he was deprived of the companionship of children.

Early Patterns. At birth, the infant is nongregarious. So long as his physical needs are attended to, it makes no difference to him who ministers to his needs. And, because of the immature state of development of his eye muscles, he cannot see well enough to be able to distinguish one person from another, or to tell what is a person and what is an inanimate object. At this time, he can be soothed as well by caresses from a hot-water bottle or from a soft pillow as by caresses from his mother. He will, however, turn when he hears a human voice at the age of two months (K. Bühler, 1930).

Between the second and third months of life, his ability to see has improved to the point where he can distinguish people. He has now discovered that it is people rather than things who supply his needs. At this age, he shows contentment when with people and is discontented and "fussy" when left alone (Dennis, 1935). This is the beginning of "social behavior." Typically, the first social responses are to *adults*. The baby, by the third month, shows the beginnings of interest in people. This interest is seen in the baby's crying when a person leaves him, by showing displeasure when a person is not looking at him, and by watching their facial expressions. Crying, he soon discovers, brings attention and he then uses crying as a means to an end.

By the fourth or fifth month, the baby makes anticipatory adjustments to being picked up, smiles in response to the person who speaks to him and, a month later, reacts differently to scolding and smiling and to angry and unfriendly voices (C. Bühler and Hetzer, 1928). To attract the attention of other babies or children, he bounces up and down, kicks, and laughs or blows (Kelting, 1934). At this age, the baby differentiates between "friends" and "strangers" by smiling at the former and by sobering or showing fear to the latter (Spitz, 1946).

When the baby is eight or nine months old, he attempts to imitate the speech, simple activities, and gestures of others. At the age of one year, he can refrain from doing things in response to the warning, "NO, no," and he shows, by crying and drawing away, a definite dislike or even fear of strangers. This shy behavior is especially pronounced between the sixty-sixth and eighty-sixth weeks of life (Shirley, 1933). In the middle of the second year, *negativism,* in the form of stubborn resistance to requests and demands of adults, normally appears. Girls, as a rule, show more negativism than do boys (Levy and Tulchin, 1925). Negativism at this age shows itself in physical resistance, in silence, in physical withdrawal, or "tenseness" which is the opposite of "cuddliness" (Plant, 1941). By the end of babyhood, however, the young child can and does cooperate with adults in a number of simple routine activities.

Social reactions to *other babies* or *children* lag behind social reactions to adults in the developmental pattern. The first indication that a baby perceives another comes between the fourth and sixth months of life. A month or two later, the baby smiles at other babies and shows an interest in their crying (Maudry and Nekula, 1939). Between the ninth and thirteenth months, however, interest in other babies increases and is shown in attempts to explore their clothes and hair, to imitate their behavior and vocalization, to cooperate in the use of toys, and in fighting when a toy is taken away by another baby. From the thirteenth to eighteenth month, the baby's interest shifts from play materials to his playmate, resulting in a decrease in fighting for toys and an increase in a cooperative use of them. During the last 6 months of babyhood, the baby is definitely interested in play with others and uses play materials to establish social relationships with them (Bridges, 1931).

Because the first social relationships of a child are in the home, the family group plays an important role in determining what his attitude and behavior in social situations will be. The family group should contribute a readiness to belong and a feeling that he is an accepted part of any subsequent groups that he may enter. When accepted at home, the feeling of belonging will carry over to other groups. The ability to understand and appreciate people will come from contacts with relatives and neighbors (Hattwick, 1940).

PLAY

Play, or any activity that is engaged in for the enjoyment it gives, begins in a simple form in babyhood. It consists primarily of random movements and of stimulation of the sense organs. The free, spontaneous play of babies is characterized by lack of rules and regulations and is more often solitary than social. At first, the baby derives enjoyment from stimulating his sense organs and from playing with his limbs. By the time he is three months old, control of his hands is developed well enough to enable him to play with toys. At this age, he also derives enjoyment from turning from back to side, kicking, bouncing, wiggling, reaching for his toes, and watching his fingers move.

Between the fifth and eighth months, play is less random and consists of play with the toes, bouncing, squirming, head shaking, pulling himself to a standing position, and cooperative motor games, such as "pat-a-cake." In the last quarter of the first year of life, the baby's play consists mainly of kicking, bouncing, leaning over the arm of a chair, rolling, playing with his toes, crawling for a toy, pulling himself to a sitting position, standing, climbing, and moving furniture (Shirley, 1931).

During the baby's second year, play becomes more organized and toys are used for many of the different playful activities. Characteristically, the fifteen-month-old baby's play consists of endless exercise of walking activities, throwing and picking up objects and then throwing them again, and of putting them in and taking them out of receptacles. At eighteen months, the baby pulls toys, carries or hugs a doll or stuffed animal, imitates many adult activities, such as reading a newspaper or sweeping, and actively gets into everything. At this age, his play is solitary and his role when other children are present is that of an onlooker.

In the last half of the second year, the baby feels, pats, and pounds his toys, he is interested in dolls and stuffed animals, he strings wooden beads, he puts them in and takes them out of holes in the top of boxes, transports blocks in wagons rather than building with them, scribbles with crayons, and imitates activities of persons in his environment. When he is with other children, he does not play with them but his play is parallel with theirs. There is little social give-and-take but much grabbing and snatching of another child's toys (Gesell, 1940).

Games and Amusements. Before a baby is a year old, he plays simple little "mother games" with adults or older children. Finger play, peek-a-boo, pat-a-cake, pigs to market, mirror play, and hide-and-seek behind a handkerchief, a piece of cloth, or furniture, are the traditional "mother games" that almost every American baby learns. A baby likes to be amused by being sung to, by listening to music, or by having someone tell him a story. He enjoys having someone point out pictures in a book or even looking at the pictures himself. While he understands little of what he hears, he enjoys the rhythmic sounds of nursery rhymes and lullabies. He also is fascinated by hearing stories about himself, familiar persons, animals, or household objects.

BEGINNINGS OF UNDERSTANDING

Because a baby begins life with no understanding of what he observes in his environment, he must acquire, through maturation and learning, a meaning of what he observes. What meanings he acquires will depend partly on the level of his intelligence and partly on his previous experiences. And, as meanings are acquired, he will interpret new experiences in terms of memories of previous experiences. The association of ideas with objects and situations results in the development of *concepts*.

The baby's *behavior* shows that, at an early age, concepts develop rapidly. For example, his recognition of familiar persons and objects in his environment is shown through his pleasurable responses just as recognition of strange persons and objects is accompanied by fear. Likewise, his responses to his toys, the sight of his outdoor clothes, or the family pet all give indications of his understanding of what they mean. At first, he responds to the total situation rather than to any one part of it. As a result, when objects and situations have elements in common they are responded to as if they were the same.

The baby's earliest perceptions come through the use of sensory exploration. He looks at, listens to, touches, smells, and tastes anything he can get into his hands. Later, as muscle coordination develops, he is able to acquire more meanings through handling whatever is within his reach. He discovers smoothness, roughness, softness, warmth, and other qualities which would not be apparent if he were limited to the use of sense organs alone. Then, as he reaches the end of babyhood, he begins to put together words into sentences. These are generally in the form of questions, beginning with "who," "what," or "why." The baby's limited knowledge and experience result in his inability to distinguish between living and inanimate objects. As a result, he believes that all objects are animate and have the same qualities as human beings. Almost all biographers of baby development refer to instances of animism in the babies they observed (Dennis, 1938).

Space concepts are poor at first. When the baby reaches for an object, he more often reaches in the wrong direction than in the right. Finally, by trial and error, he reaches the object. He rarely reaches for an object more than

20 inches away when he is a year old. This would indicate that he has some estimate of distance. Likewise, *concepts of weight* are very inaccurate at first. The baby perceives a small object as light in weight and a large object as heavy. As a result of this error in perception, he frequently drops the things he is examining because he has not made the necessary muscular adjustment to hold the object that proves to be heavier than he had anticipated.

Concepts of time are also very inaccurate. A baby has no idea of the length of time needed for a specific job, such as feeding himself or putting on his clothes. Furthermore, he has no concept of time duration and, if it were not for a fairly rigid daily schedule, he would not know morning from afternoon. By the time he is two years old, the average baby knows and uses time words, such as "today" (Ames, 1940). *Concepts of self* appear earlier than concepts of other people. Through watching and handling the different parts of his body and by looking into a mirror, the baby discovers meanings about his body. A two-year-old baby can identify at least three parts of the body (Terman and Merrill, 1937). The genitals become a focal point of interest early in life because of their association with the excretory functions. Also, they can be stimulated by touching and patting. Spontaneous erections of the penis appear during the first two years of life (Conn and Kanner, 1940). Genital tension, as indicated by tumescence, occurs under frustrating feeding conditions, as a difficult nipple, a delay in feeding, or withholding the breast (Halverson, 1940).

Social concepts, or the understanding of the thoughts, feelings, and emotional reactions of others, are likewise in the formative stage of development in babyhood. During the first half year of life, the baby can distinguish persons by the tone of their voices and by their facial expressions. He can distinguish angry, frightened, and friendly voices. At one month, he can differentiate the human voice from other sounds; at three months, he smiles when people come near him, though he smiles at an angry person in the same way as he does at one who looks friendly (C. Bühler, 1930). He can distinguish between familiar and unfamiliar persons at five months of age, and he responds to an angry face with crying, though it is not until he is eight months old that he responds to the emotional behavior of others in such a way as to indicate an understanding of their facial expressions (C. Bühler, 1930).

The earliest indication of *aesthetic perception* is to be found in color preferences. While babies at three months of age look at colors twice as long as at gray, there is no significant difference in their response to different colors. But, from the ages of six to twenty-four months, babies respond differently to different colors, with the order of preference as follows: red, yellow, blue, and green (Staples, 1932). A brilliant rose-pink rattle is preferred to a dull blue one by six-month-old babies. At the age of two years, babies can match, with 45 per cent accuracy, colors which differ in hue, brightness, or situation (Cook, 1931).

Music appreciation is shown in the baby's liking for music, especially that with a real tune as one finds in lullabies. A baby perceives as *comic* vocal play or babbling at four months of age and he enjoys tormenting people who dress him or feed him. He also likes to blow bubbles in water given him to drink and he derives enjoyment from dropping things that have been handed to him when he is six months old. At nine months, watching things fall, such as a splash made by milk falling from his mouth onto the floor, is perceived as comic. When he is a year old, he likes to make funny faces and, several months later, hiding from people and laughing when they cannot find him is a source of much amusement. The two-year-old is amused by trying to squeeze through a narrow place or by carrying out different kinds of stunts (Fenton, 1925).

MORAL ATTITUDES AND BEHAVIOR

A baby is neither moral nor unmoral. He must eventually learn to conform to the social codes of the group to which he belongs. This learning will come partly from imitating the behavior of those with whom he comes in contact and partly from the teaching of his parents and others in authority. The whole purpose of discipline during the early years of life is to teach the individual what is right and what is wrong and to see to it that he acts in accordance with this knowledge. Throughout the babyhood years, the baby must learn to make correct specific responses to specific situations in the home and in the neighborhood. It is important at all ages, but especially during the early years of life when moral habits are being established, that discipline be consistent. Acts that are wrong should be wrong at all times, regardless of who is in charge. Otherwise, it will be confusing to the baby and he will not know what is expected of him.

The baby's behavior is guided by impulse. He judges right and wrong in relation to the pleasure or pain of the act rather than in terms of the good or harm to the group. Because of his limited intelligence, he cannot judge behavior in terms of how it affects others but only in terms of its effect on him. An act, therefore, is perceived by him as wrong only when it has some ill effect on him. He has no sense of guilt because he lacks definite standards of right and wrong.

FAMILY RELATIONSHIPS

The individual's attitudes and behavior throughout life are markedly influenced by his early experiences. And, because the baby's early environment is primarily limited to the home, family relationships play a dominant role in determining what sort of individual he will grow up to be. His parents, brothers and sisters, grandparents, and other relatives who come in more or less constant contact with him during these early formative years of life, set the pattern for his attitudes toward people, things, and life in general. While this pattern will unquestionably be changed and modified as he grows older and as his environment broadens, the core of the pattern is likely to remain with little or no modification.

The importance of the parent-child relationship in the early part of life can best be illustrated by cases where babies are separated from their mothers and are institutionalized. When a baby is deprived of emotional interchange with the mother during the third quarter of the first year, a condition may develop which resembles depression in an adult. There is a marked increase in the manifestations of the emotions of displeasure, which may reach the point where anxiety reactions in the nature of panic may be observed. Babies in this condition will scream by the hour, and this screaming is accompanied by heavy salivation, tears, dilation of the pupils, severe perspiration, and convulsive trembling. At the same time, their development is arrested, though a reestablishment of the emotional interchange with the parent will rapidly reestablish the developmental level. This holds true if the separation from the mother has not lasted for longer than 3 months. When the baby has been deprived of emotional interchange with the mother for more than 5 months, the baby's development continues to decline as compared with that of other babies of the same age (Spitz, 1949).

Because early babyhood is a period of extreme helplessness, it is common for parents to develop the habit of caring for and protecting the baby so completely that it stifles the baby's motivation to learn to do things for himself. Or, if the motivation to be independent of parental help is very strong, it expresses itself in a conflict between parent and child. This conflict begins during the latter part of the second year of life and is characterized by frequent and violent temper outbursts.

Furthermore, because parental overprotection retards the normal pattern of development in the acquisition of motor skills, a baby is likely to become angry at himself and at anyone near him if he cannot do what he sets out to do. This results in a changed relationship between parent and child. At first, parental attitudes are wholeheartedly favorable. Only in exceptional cases where there is parental rejection does the young baby experience anything but a warm and loving relationship with his parents and other members of the family. Should he be the first-born, this loving relationship will be accompanied by the constant attention and companionship of his mother during his waking hours and by her help in doing things for him that he needs or wants.

If another child is born in the family before his babyhood is over, it will not disturb him as much as if he were older. While it is true that he will miss the constant attention that he has been accustomed to receive from his parents, his social development has not yet reached the point where he wants constant attention from others. While trying out his newly acquired skills and exploring his environment, he is satisfied to be alone with only an occasional glance of approval or commendation from an adult. His limited intelligence does not enable him to associate the change in his relationship with his parents with the newcomer in the home and, consequently, he is not jealous.

Overdependency may be the result of overprotectiveness on the part of the parent, usually the mother, because she instigates the overdependency. It may also be instigated by the baby and is willingly or unwillingly acceded to by the mother. In babyhood, there are two critical periods when overdependency may begin. The first comes at the end of the first year of life when the baby tests the mother to see if he can depend on her. At this time, the baby is still very helpless and his needs must be met or the effect on his personality of lack of attention will be harmful. But many mothers go beyond the baby's needs and do not encourage independence when it is possible. The second critical period comes at the end of the second year, when there are social demands on the individual to change his old ways of doing things. This causes the baby to cling, if possible, to his status of infantile dependency, instead of trying to develop independence (Stendler, 1952).

The first-born child of the family is more likely to be the victim of maternal overprotection and to develop habits of dependency more often than later-born children except when the later-born child is physically or mentally weak. The oldest child of the family, as a baby, is likely to have experienced more anxiety in nursing and weaning situations, more interference at bedtime, and more cautioning about sickness and danger than the second- or later-born children of the same family. It is because of these attitudes of overprotection on the part of his parents that he develops more often into an overly dependent child than do his siblings who have not been subjected to such treatment (Sears, 1950).

Because the mother is the baby's most frequent companion in his play activities and because the mother takes care of his bodily needs, the beginning of a preference for the mother is generally apparent toward the close of babyhood. A father who spends a reasonable amount of time with his baby, who shares with the mother some of the routine duties connected with baby care, and who gives his undivided attention to playing with the baby when he is with him, will win as much of the baby's affection as does the mother.

A baby needs the continuous care of one person for the first nine to twelve months of his life to give him a feeling of security. The mother is the only person who can be relied upon for this. Professional nurses, relatives, or friends of the family will not give him this continuous care which he needs. When babies are deprived of this, they are found to have, as they grow older, "diffusely impulsive unpatterned behavior that is unorganized and remains unorganized. . . . The behavior remains always infantile" (Bender, 1950).

Even as they grow older, it is difficult to find any educational or psycho-therapeutic method to bring about organized or patterned behavior.

PERSONALITY

While the nucleus of personality exists at birth, maturation and environmental factors begin, from the moment of birth, to influence its development (Shirley, 1933). At first, maturation is more important than environment, causing a radical and gratifying change in personality during the first three months of life. The compulsion and fear characteristic of the newborn stage of development gradually disappear so that by the time a baby is three months old, he "blossoms into a smiling, cooing, pleasantly responsive individual" (Aldrich, 1947).

At this age, the baby's experiences have a basic and continuing effect on his personality (Ribble, 1943). Studies of the effects of the mother's emotional attitudes have shown that exhaustion through overstimulation and inhibition of growth through overtraining are just as harmful as maternal overprotection (Dunbar, 1944). While adults may remember little of what happened during the early years of their lives, these experiences have been of vital importance in the shaping of their personality and have left a lasting impression on it (Hay-Shaw, 1949).

Because the baby's environment is limited almost exclusively to the home environment, and because his parents are his most constant companions, there is no question about the fact that the individual's personality is an "outgrowth of the parent-child relationship in infancy. . . . If the individual possesses a healthy, stable, courageous, and loving father and mother, the chances are that he will be a good student, a good worker, a good husband or wife, a good leader, and a good citizen" (Symonds, 1945).

With the development of muscle coordination, voluntary activity is possible. This opens up new channels for self-expression. An obstructive environment will be opposed by the baby who becomes antagonistic and rebellious as a result of these restraints. Should he be fortunate enough to have an environment which fosters the development of his personality, he will develop into a cooperative and responsive individual (Aldrich, 1947). How greatly environmental obstructions affect the personality development of the baby has been suggested by the study of institutionalized babies. While it is not certain whether the damage is permanent or temporary if the baby remains in an institution for only the first three or four years of life, there is evidence that if he remains longer, the personality distortion will be severe and long lasting.

The common effects of institutional life on the personality pattern of the individual are infantile behavior, as shown in temper tantrums and kicking in response to frustrations; constant seeking of attention; lack of warmth in relationships with others; constant shifting of attention from one person to another; defective language development; impulsive behavior; inability to form normal relationships with others; and lack of normal emotional responsiveness. These are the outstanding personality defects of the emotionally deprived child (Bakwin, 1949).

The effect of the type of contact the baby has with the mother is well illustrated in the case of babies whose mothers show periodic mood swings. From the emotional point of view, these babies showed strange, distorted personalities. In extreme cases, it was possible to observe a suspicious, near-paranoid facial expression and behavior. Babies whose mothers had infantile personalities, as characterized by rapid shifts in their attitudes from hostility to overprotectiveness toward their children literally within minutes, showed a definite and significant retardation in manipulative ability and in social responses. Objectless bodily activity was the baby's outstanding occupation. Follow-up studies of such babies at later stages of development suggested that this may be the forerunner of psychopathy in older children (Spitz, 1949).

A common form of compensatory reaction for deficiency in love, attention, and food is thumb- or finger-sucking. This increases as time after feeding elapses, whether the baby is asleep or awake. It begins soon after birth, increases to the third month, then remains at a plateau until the sixth month, declines to the tenth month, and then rises to the end of the year. The amount of sucking a baby does correlates with the amount of frustration he experiences, especially in connection with weaning. If the conditions that give rise to it are permitted to persist, the thumb-sucking may readily develop into a habit which, as the baby grows older, will be a source of embarrassment to him because such behavior is regarded as "infantile" (Kunst, 1948).

Personality Foundations. Genetic studies of the persistence of personality traits over a period of years have revealed that patterns established early in life remain almost unchanged as the child grows older. While it is true that certain traits of the personality pattern change, the individual's personality retains a "central core," or "center of gravity," which does not change (Breckenridge and Vincent, 1943). The center of gravity is composed of habits and attitudes fixed early in life. Only when radical steps are taken can a change be made in this center of gravity.

While the center of gravity is in the process of becoming consolidated, as is true of babyhood and early childhood, undesirable personality traits can be changed without disturbing the whole personality pattern. As time goes on, the core of habits and attitudes becomes less and less flexible. Then a change in personality traits may upset the personality balance. For that reason, it is vitally important that the habits and attitudes that compose this "center of gravity" be of the sort that will be just as serviceable in adulthood as they are when the child is young. A child who is aggressive at two is likely to be consistently aggressive as he grows older. Following the development of personality in a group of children from the age of six weeks to the middle of childhood has revealed that not only are personality traits persistent but also that it is possible to formulate a prognosis of the child's future personality, at the end of the lying-in period (Fries, 1937; Fries and Lewi, 1938). The prophetic character of the first year's behavior traits is clear-cut evidence of the persistence of personality traits (Gesell *et al.*, 1939). Marked consistency in the personality traits of "Shirley's Babies" was noted during the first years of their lives (Shirley, 1933). Fifteen and a half years later, there was definite evidence that personality similarities had persisted and some of the individuals could readily be identified because of the uniqueness of their personality patterns (Neilon, 1948). Because all experimental evidence to date indicates that personality traits established in babyhood are likely to remain relatively unchanged throughout life, unless remedial measures are used to bring about changes, it is apparent that babyhood is a critical age in establishing the pattern of personality.

CHAPTER 5

Early Childhood
(Two to Six Years)

Early childhood, which extends from the ages of two to six years, is a period when the major development is that of control over the environment. Having acquired a workable control of his own body during the first two years of life, the child is now ready to explore his environment. No longer is he satisfied to be a spectator. He wants to know what his environment is, how it works, how it feels, and how he can be a part of it. This includes people as well as inanimate objects.

Dawn of Problem Behavior. While parents are interested in their children at every age, the home interest in the young child is less sentimental and more practical than it was during babyhood. Most of the problems that parents face with babies center around their physical care. With the dawn of childhood, the child presents many behavior problems for his parents to cope with. He is developing a distinctive personality and is demanding an independence which, in most cases, he is incapable of handling successfully. A young child is often an obstinate, stubborn, disobedient, negativistic, antagonistic individual. He has frequent temper tantrums, he is bothered by nightmares at night and irrational fears during the day, and he suffers from jealousies. All in all, life for the parents and the young child is frequently far from happy. And yet, a "good" child who conforms so completely to adult standards and expectations that he gives his parents little concern is headed for trouble.

PHYSICAL DEVELOPMENT

Growth during early childhood proceeds at a slow rate as compared with the rapid rate of growth during babyhood. The average increase in *height* is 3 inches annually. By the age of six years, the child's height should be approximately 43 to 45 inches. There are, however, marked individual differences among children at this age. No real sex difference occurs, though there is a tendency for girls to be slightly taller than boys between the ages of five and six years. Girls of very superior intelligence are taller and heavier during the preschool years than are girls of superior intelligence, just as those who are superior are slightly taller than are those whose intelligence is average (Katz, 1940). *Weight,* like height, develops at a slow rate during this period with an average increase of 3 to 5 pounds annually. At the age of six years, the child should be approximately six times his birth weight, or 36 to 42 pounds. Boys, as a rule, are slightly heavier than girls, while bright children weigh slightly more than those of average intelligence (Hollingworth, 1926). Gains in weight in general are greater in the fall than at any other season of the year.

During early childhood, *body proportions* change and the "baby look" disappears. The head grows at a slower rate than the other areas of the body. At five years, the surface area of the head is 13 per cent of the total surface area of the body, as contrasted with 21 per cent at birth (Boyd, 1935). The cranial region in relation to the face has a proportion of 1 to 5 at five years as compared with the ratio of 1 to 8 at birth. By the age of six years, the circumference of the head is 90 per cent of its adult size and the weight is 90 per cent of the adult weight. The child's head is broader in relation to length than is the adult's head. There is an appreciable increase in both length and width between the second and fifth years of life, after which the increases taper off. The mean annual increase is greater in length than in width. Among boys, the growth pattern for length and width is similar; among girls it is dissimilar. Increase in size has been found to be more a function of age than of initial size. Short and narrow heads show somewhat greater increase than do long and broad heads (Goldstein, 1939).

Throughout early childhood, the *facial features* remain small. The nose is particularly small and rather flat on the surface of the face. The mouth is likewise proportionately too small because of the small baby teeth. However, there is a more pronounced chin, owing to the development of the lower jaw, and the neck elongates. The soft downy hair of the baby is gradually replaced by hair of a coarser texture which is frequently unmanageable at this age. Up to the age of six years, the *trunk* is twice as long and wide as it was at birth. By the third year, the protruding abdomen of the baby flattens out and the shoulders become broader. The *arms* and *legs* likewise lengthen and the *hands* and *feet* grow bigger. When the child is right-handed, the right arm is proportionally longer than in adults (Van Dusen, 1939). The *bones* gradually harden throughout early childhood so that the chances of their becoming misshapen, as a result of pressure or of poor posture, grows less and less each year. The *muscles* likewise grow larger and stronger, thus making it possible for the young child to do more and to fatigue less quickly than he did when he was younger. By the end of early childhood, there are generally one or two permanent *teeth.*

Physiological Habits. During early childhood, the physiological habits whose foundations were laid in babyhood become well established. The young child eats the same food as the rest of the family and he no longer has to have specially prepared food. At this time, his *appetite* is no longer as ravenous as it was in the early part of babyhood, partly because his growth rate has slowed down and he no longer needs as much food as he formerly did and partly because he has now developed marked food likes and dislikes. This is the age when "eating problems" reach their peak owing to family pressures on the child to eat and to the child's stubborn resistance to parental proddings.

SLEEP HABITS. These habits, well established in babyhood, are often disrupted by the young child's revolt against daytime naps and against going to bed on time at night. In his attempt to stall off the inevitable, the young child is likely to work himself up into a state of emotional tension. This militates against relaxation, which is essential to falling asleep. In spite of daily variations in the amount of sleep, depending on such factors as amount of exercise during the day and type of activity, three-year-olds sleep approximately 12 out of the 24 hours. Each successive year during childhood, the average daily amount of sleep is approximately one-half hour less than in the previous year (Reynolds and Mallay, 1933; Despert, 1949).

Boys generally sleep about 1 hour less than girls of the same age. However, girls go to sleep slightly more quickly than boys and sleep more soundly. Approximately an hour is required for the young child to fall asleep (Reynolds and Mallay, 1933). The sleep posture of the young child changes on the average of once every 25 minutes, with the right side the favored position. During the early part of sleep, movements of the body are less frequent than in the latter part (Boynton and Goodenough, 1930). When a young child has acquired good sleep habits, the presence of other children in the sleep environment does not interfere with the child's sleep (Bott et al., 1928). Going to bed late does not guarantee that the child will sleep late the next morning to compensate for loss of sleep on the preceding day (White, 1931). Parental attitudes concerning sleep are very important. They are often responsible for bringing on sleep problems in the young child (Despert, 1949).

TOILET HABITS. By the time the child is three to four years old, bladder control at night should be achieved. Many young children, however, have occasional night accidents after that age, especially if they are tired or excited during the day. This is true also of daytime accidents. By the time the child is ready to enter school, bladder control should be so complete that even fatigue and emotional tension will not interfere with it. Some young children continue to experience enuresis, or bed-wetting, beyond the time that bladder control is normally achieved. In a few cases, this is the result of low-grade intelligence. In most instances, however, the cause is traceable to nervous tension exaggerated by feelings of inadequacy on the child's part which have been fostered by parental scoldings or punishments for wetting his bed "like a baby."

Diseases. Young children are highly susceptible to disease. Stomach and digestive disturbances, colds, earaches and, in families where there are older children, measles, mumps, chicken pox, and other children's diseases are common. While many childhood diseases are physiological in origin, others are psychosomatic and result from tensions between parent and child. The psychosomatic disorders that are due to parent-child tensions are: anorexia nervosa, ulcerative colitis, enuresis, allergic reactions, asthma, and diabetes. In addition to illness, cuts, bruises, infections, broken bones, strained muscles, and similar minor disturbances are common occurrences. Although most accidents of early childhood are not fatal, many of them leave permanent scars of a physical or psychological sort. They also help to develop in the child a sense of caution which frequently prevents future accidents of a more serious nature.

MOTOR DEVELOPMENT

Early childhood is the ideal age to learn skills which are not only useful at that time but which will serve as the foundation for more highly co-ordinated skills needed at a later age. The young child enjoys repetition and is, therefore, willing to repeat, time after time, an activity until he has acquired the ability to do it well. He is adventuresome and, hence, is not held back by fear of hurting himself or of the ridicule of his associates as so often happens when a child is older. And, because his body is still very pliable, with few conflicting skills to interfere with the acquisition of new ones, he learns quickly and easily. The acquisition of skills is of great personal advantage to a child. The more he can do for himself, the less he will have to depend upon others. At a time when the child craves independence and revolts against adult restraints on his activities, it is very important that he be given an opportunity to learn to do many things for himself.

Hand Skills. *Self-feeding* and *dressing* skills, begun in babyhood, are perfected in early childhood. By the time he is three years old, the child can feed himself with a fork and can spread butter or jam with a knife. Using the knife for cutting is too difficult until the child is a year or two older. Because eating skills at this age are still in the formative stage, the child must concentrate on what he is doing. Should his attention be diverted, he is likely to spill his food or to stop feeding himself until his attention returns to eating. This is true also of dressing. The young child cannot look at or listen to anything else while he is putting on or fastening his clothes. He must give his undivided attention to the job at hand. Because the greatest improvement in dressing skills generally comes between the ages of $1\frac{1}{2}$ and $3\frac{1}{2}$ years, it is important that the young child be given ample opportunity and time to develop the skills necessary for him to assume the responsibility for dressing himself with minimum help from others (Key *et al.*, 1936).

Beginning at the age of two years, most children enjoy manipulating buttons. If these buttons are large and attractive, the child will fumble them and will try to put them in and take them out of the holes. By the time children are three or four years old, they can unfasten and fasten garments, even when the buttons are in such difficult positions as on the shoulders or at the neck, if they look in a mirror. When they are six years old, they can handle all fasteners in any position (Wagoner and Armstrong, 1928). *Brushing the hair* and *bathing* are skills which can be acquired easily in early childhood. At first, the child will need help in getting a straight part in his hair and in reaching the different areas of his body in bathing. But, with practice, he will gradually take over more and more responsibility for these tasks. By the time he reaches the kindergarten age, he should be able to bathe, to dress, to tie his shoes, and to comb his hair with no assistance. Girls, when they wear elaborate party clothes or have hair styles too intricate for them to manage, must depend upon outside help for a longer time.

Because ball games are one of the favorite play activities of children's groups, the sooner a child learns to *throw and catch a ball,* the better will be his chances of becoming a member of the neighborhood group. Between the ages of five and six years most children can become proficient in throwing and catching balls (Gutteridge, 1939). A three-year-old can drive nails into wood with a hammer and a six-year-old can use his carpentry skill to make simple objects like boats and wagons (Strang, 1938). Nursery-school and kindergarten children can use scissors in following the outlines of pictures, and they can mold with clay, make cookies, or sew (Strang, 1938). By using *crayons, pencils, and paints,* young children are able to color outlined pictures, draw or paint pictures of their own, and make a recognizable man. Between the ages of five and six years, children can make recognizable letters, though their writing is slow, laborious, and poor at this age (Hildreth, 1936).

While preference for one hand appears in babyhood, a definite hand preference is not established at that age. Between the ages of $2\frac{1}{2}$ and $3\frac{1}{2}$ years, there is a marked shift to bilaterality. Then, from the ages of 4 to 6 years, unilateral preference predominates (Gesell and Ames, 1947). Because bilaterality does not appear again, except for a brief period around the age of 7 years, it is important that young children who show a tendency to use the left hand more frequently than the right be encouraged to try to use the right hand whenever possible. Since hand skills are being established at this age, it will be easier for the child to acquire these skills with his right hand at the very start, if he is eventually to become right-handed. As Hildreth (1950) has pointed out: "Handedness should be trained, not left to chance, since manual dexterity can affect an individual's educational and vocational success."

Leg Skills. Once the skill of walking has been established, the young child turns his attention to learning other skilled movements requiring the use of his legs. He learns to hop, skip, gallop, and jump by the age of five or six years (Gutteridge, 1939). At this time, not only can he run with very few falls but he can play games at the same time. Climbing skills are likewise well established in early childhood, though many urban children soon exhaust the possibility of climbing in their restricted environments. Should the environment offer opportunities for climbing, the five- or six-year-old is capable of climbing well and of doing stunts such as racing, competing, and climbing in dramatic projects (Gutteridge, 1939). At three years, a child can ascend and descend ladders (McCaskill and Wellman, 1937).

Few children acquire the ability to *swim* before they are four years old. This is due primarily to lack of opportunity to learn or to lack of opportunity for adequate practice to acquire such a complicated skill. Between the ages of three and four years, *tricycling* can be learned. "Stunting," such as riding backward or turning the corner sharply, then enters into the skill (Gutteridge, 1939). Other skills acquired by young children include *jumping rope, balancing* on rails or on the top of a wall, *roller-skating, ice-skating,* if the skates have double runners, and *dancing* (Strang, 1938).

Delayed Motor Development. Early childhood is a critical age for acquiring muscular skills. The child who is hampered by overprotective parents who are afraid he will injure himself, by fear engendered by accidents or warnings to "be careful," by environmental obstacles, or by lack of opportunity to practice until the skills have been formed, becomes awkward as compared to other children of his age. When he tries to do what other children do, he cannot keep up with them. As a result, he is left out of their play. This limits further his opportunity for learning and makes him increasingly more backward in his social contacts. Because early childhood is the beginning of the socialization age, and because play with other children requires the necessary skills to do what other children do, the child who lacks the skills other children of his age possess is limited in his social contacts. This, in turn, makes it difficult for him to become a part of the social group. Each year, as he grows older, play with other children should be an increasingly important part of his daily life. But, unless special training at home or at school is given to him to enable him to catch up to the skills already acquired by other children of his age, he will find himself in the role of a social isolate.

SPEECH DEVELOPMENT

The foundations of speech are laid in babyhood. On these foundations will be built the speech skills which, by the time early childhood is over, will be so well established that the child's future speech will be greatly influenced by them. For that reason, early childhood is a critical period in the developmental pattern of the speech of the individual. The ability to *comprehend meaning* of what others say develops rapidly at this time. The young child can understand most of what is said to him either through comprehension of the words used or of the gestures and facial expressions that accompany these words. A child at the age of $2\frac{1}{2}$ years, when shown a large paper doll and requested to "Show me the dolly's hair" or "Show me the dolly's mouth," is able to do so. A year later, he should be able to comprehend well enough to respond to at least two requests such as, "Give me the kitty," or "Put the thimble on the block." At 4 years, comprehension of the second degree is tested by such questions as "Why do we read books?" and "Why do we have houses?" (Terman and Merrill, 1937).

Building a *vocabulary* of words for general usage proceeds rapidly in the preschool years. The mean number of different words used by 2-year-olds has been found to be only 29.1 as compared with 62.8 at 3 years, 92.6 at 4 years, and 99.5 at $5\frac{1}{2}$ years (McCarthy, 1930). Girls, as a general rule, have larger vocabularies than boys. Throughout the preschool years, the child's vocabulary increases rapidly owing partly to direct teaching of words and partly to his curiosity about word meanings which leads him to ask people what these words mean. Verbs, adjectives, pronouns, conjunctions, and prepositions increase in frequency of use at this age (McCarthy, 1930). Descriptive adjective phrases increase markedly from the ages of $2\frac{1}{2}$ to $4\frac{1}{2}$ years (Carroll, 1939). Pronouns and verbs are more widely used than nouns at this time (Young, 1941). Nouns and interjections decrease in frequency of usage with age, and articles, conjunctions, prepositions, and infinitives increase (Young, 1941).

In addition to building up a vocabulary that will be of general usage, young children learn many *words of a specific kind*. The child learns to use such words as "Thank you," "Please," or "I'm sorry"; he acquires a vocabulary of color words so that, at the age of five years, he can name without error the colors, red, blue, yellow, and green (Terman, 1922). He learns the meanings of numbers so that by the age of five years he can count 3 objects from 12 placed before him and, a year later, he knows how to count out of 12 objects, 3, 9, 5, 10, or 7 of these objects (Terman and Merrill, 1937). All coins are classed as "money" or "pennies" by very young children. However, by the time children are five or six years old, they can distinguish and name pennies, nickels, dimes, and even quarters. The preschool child knows and uses such time words as "morning," "afternoon," "night," "winter," and "summer." Many young children pick up slang or even swear words from their older brothers and sisters, their parents, or their playmates. They use these words in a parrotlike fashion without any comprehension of their true meaning.

Sentence usage follows a fairly definite and predictable pattern in early childhood. Short sentences of three or four words are used as early as two years of age and commonly at three years. These sentences have an excess of nouns but lack verbs, prepositions, and conjunctions. Many of the child's early sentences are incomplete. From the age of three years on, however, complete sentences of six to eight words frequently appear in a young child's speech. All parts of speech are then used. By the time he is six years old, the child should have command of practically every form of sentence structure (Nice, 1925). Young children are apt to use loosely constructed and complex sentences (Davis, 1937).

Up to the age of three or four years, *grammatical errors* are common. The major difficulties are in the correct usage of pronouns, verbs, and verb tenses. It is also very common for young children to be confused about when to use single and plural nouns. Typical errors in verb usage relate to the confusion in the use of "can" and "may," "lay" and "lie." In the case of nouns, it is difficult for them to understand why one does not say "foots" instead of "feet" or "mans" instead of "men." They commonly use the single form of verbs with a plural subject. Because the young child is learning to form sentences, it is most important that grammatical mistakes be corrected when they occur. Otherwise, the child will develop the habit of thinking incorrectly. Through hearing correct speech and through school instruction, many of the grammatical mistakes of early childhood will be corrected.

Some young children pronounce their words clearly and distinctly; some do not. It is not unusual for infantile *pronunciations* to persist until the child is three or even four years old (McCarthy, 1930). The more the child is with other children, however, the more comprehensible his speech becomes. By the fifth or sixth year, most infantile forms of pronunciation are gone. In the early years of childhood, while speech is still in a formative stage, *speech errors* and defects are common. There is still a persistence of such errors as omissions, substitutions, and interchanges characteristic of the baby's first speech. *Lisping,* or letter-sound substitution, as *th* for *z* or *as* and *w* for *r,* is one of the most common speech errors of early childhood. During the transitional stage from first to second teeth, there is likely to be a gap in the front of the jaws where the second teeth will eventually cut through. At this time, there is often a slight lisp which, unless corrected as the new teeth develop, will become established into a habit.

Stuttering, or the repetition of sounds, syllables, or even words, is caused mainly by nervous and emotional tension. Generally, stuttering begins at a very early age, when the child is just learning to talk. Between the ages of two and four years, hesitating, repetitious speech is more or less characteristic of all children (Davis, 1939). At this time, they are mastering the art of self-feeding and self-dressing, they are learning to talk in sentences, and are trying to be independent of adult domination. It also occurs frequently between the fifth and sixth years. These ages represent important breaks in the child's life. At the time of the first, the child is breaking away from babyhood and, at the second, he is breaking away from the home environment and establishing himself in the broader social environment of the school and neighborhood (Blanton, 1929). Stuttering in a minor form is part of the early speech pattern of all children. As children reach the end of early childhood, there is normally a decrease in the amount of stuttering (Davis, 1939). Stuttering is nearly twice as common among boys as among girls.

The common tension-producing factors in the environment of stutterers are:

1. Mothers who are dominating, perfectionistic, or overprotective and overanxious about the health and feeding of their children. Thirty-six out of fifty are of this type (Despert, 1946).

2. Overanxiety about the normal repetitive speech of young children, especially if parents were stutterers as children (Missildine and Glasner, 1947).

Changed parental attitudes and elimination of environmental tensions will generally bring an end to stuttering before the child reaches school age.

Content of Speech. What young children talk about varies from child to child as does their need for speech. At this time, "the pattern of personality is clearly woven into the fabric of speech" (Shirley, 1933). At first, speech generally accompanies motor activity and takes the form of thinking out loud as, for example, when a little boy is playing with his train he will say, "Now I'll put the train on the tracks." Early speech is a monologue in the form of a running commentary on the child's activity rather than a conversation (Smith, 1926). As they grow older, there is an increase in the quantity of their speech. They talk more, though boys, as a rule, talk less than girls. Between the ages of three and five years, experimentation with speech is revealed in the child's enjoyment of rhythmic grouping of sounds, repetitions of sounds and words heard, and in play with rhymes (Rugg *et al.,* 1929). There is also an increase in remarks about people and objects as the child reaches this age, though girls tend to talk more about people than boys do (Fisher, 1934). In their play with other children, children show more tendency to evoke response in their hearers than to verbalize for the sake of doing so (Ganns, 1943). There is a clear tendency for children to talk more to other people and less to themselves as they grow older (Arrington, 1939).

Although only about 2 per cent of the statements of young children are critical, most of them are unfavorable. The purpose of these unfavorable criticisms is to gain the assistance of someone in a situation beyond the child's control and thus the criticism takes the form of *tattling*. Or the criticism is directed at interference with themselves or their possessions and takes the form of a complaint (Smith, 1932). As the size of the group becomes larger, the language of the child becomes more sociable and less egocentric. There is also slightly less criticism, fewer questions, and more commands. Small social groupings are most favorable for the speech of young children (Williams and Mattson, 1942). At the kindergarten age, children talk mostly to other children of their own sex (Arrington, 1939).

The most frequent *topic of conversation* among young children relates to themselves and their activities. When a second person is the subject of a remark, the remark is generally a command for that person to do something (Sprague, 1929). Topics such as likes and dislikes among people, clothes, where one lives, and matters of everyday routine predominate in the young child's conversation (Murphy, 1937). Nearly one-third of their conversations relate to family, mother, father, brothers and sisters, and similar topics (Shirley, 1933). Boasting is common at all ages. The young child boasts about his material possessions such as his toys, his clothes, or the family car.

How the child's environment affects the content of his speech is well illustrated by a comparison of orphanage and nonorphanage children. The orphanage children were found to talk more about the parts of the body, play materials, activities and routines, and buildings and furnishings than the nonorphanage children. The nonorphanage children talked more about other children, adults, clothing, and nature than did the orphanage children, and they mentioned a wider variety of topics (Moore, 1948).

EMOTIONAL DEVELOPMENT

Heightened emotionality, as shown in temper tantrums and intense fears, is common among three- to four-year-olds. This is the third emotional period of childhood and, like the two that preceded it, the predominating emotions are unpleasant. While growth at this age is slow as compared with babyhood, the young child uses up his energy in strenuous and prolonged play. He revolts against naps during the day and stalls at bedtime, hoping to stay up beyond the scheduled hour. As a result, he becomes fatigued as the day advances and this predisposes him to emotional tension. When nursery-school children are given fruit juice at midmorning, they show less negative behavior than children who are given only water. The midmorning fruit juice tends to lessen fatigue which otherwise would predispose the child to irritability and general emotional tension (Keister, 1950).

Most young children feel that they are capable of doing more than their parents will permit them to do and revolt against the restrictions placed upon them. In addition, they become angry when they find they are incapable of doing what they think they can do easily and successfully. When, for example, they cannot make a toy work or a button slip through its hole, they feel frustrated and fly off into a fit of rage. Inexperience and limited knowledge predispose them to be afraid of many things which several years hence they will recognize as harmless. Much the same is true of jealousy. They are unable to understand that the mother's preoccupation with the new baby is necessitated by the baby's helplessness, not by a lessening of her affection for him.

Just before early childhood ends, a fourth emotional period generally develops. This lasts for a year or two and extends into the beginning of the period of late childhood. At this time, there is a slight increase in the rate of growth accompanied by a tendency to fatigue easily as a result of rapid growth and the strenuous play characteristically engaged in at this age. Because the social environment broadens for most children at this time, either in Sunday school, nursery school, or first grade, there is frequently a difficult social adjustment for the child to make. Adjustments at any age are generally accompanied by nervous tension. The younger and less experienced the child, the greater the tension is likely to be. This nervous tension, accompanied by the physical conditions just described, predisposes the child to heightened emotionality.

Common Emotions. Among the emotions experienced at this stage of development are anger, fear, jealousy, affection, curiosity, and joy.

ANGER. Anger is the most common emotion in early childhood partly because there are so many anger-provoking situations in a young child's life and partly because a young child quickly discovers that the use of anger is a quick and easy way to get what he wants, whether it be attention or the fulfillment of some desire. The situations that most frequently give rise to anger in young children consist of conflicts over playthings, conflicts over toilet and dressing, interruptions of interesting activities, and thwarting of wishes (Ricketts, 1934); vigorous attacks from another child, another child's taking a desired object, or another child's calling names (Felder, 1932).

When a young child becomes angry, he expresses his anger in intense outbursts, or "temper tantrums." Tantrums are characterized by crying, screaming, stamping, kicking, jumping up and down, striking, throwing one's self on the floor, holding the breath, stiffening the body, or making it limp. By the age of four years, anger responses are directed more toward a given end than they are when the child is younger. Then there are more attempts to retaliate by hurting the feelings or injuring the body of the offender. Temper tantrums reach their peak of severity between the ages of three and four years. As early childhood draws to a close, temper tantrums become shorter in duration and give way to sulking, brooding, and whining. Up to the age of three years, there are no apparent sex differences in the number and severity of temper tantrums. After that age, boys have more and more intense tantrums than do girls (Goodenough, 1931). Tantrums occur more often indoors than outdoors (Felder, 1932). The violence of the child's tantrums is out of all proportion to what gave rise to them (Isaacs, 1940). Most tantrums last from 1 to 3 minutes (Ricketts, 1934).

FEAR. The young child is afraid of more things than is the baby or the older child. The development of his intelligence makes it possible for him to recognize potential dangers in situations which formerly were not recognized as such. Fear of snakes, for example, does not appear much before the age of $3\frac{1}{2}$ years but, by the age of 4 years, definite fear appears (Jones and Jones, 1928). Among young children, fear at first is general rather than specific. It is more like a state of panic than fear proper. As children become older, fear responses become increasingly more specific. The child shows his fear by running away, by avoiding situations that frighten him, and by such verbal responses as "Take it away" or "I don't want to go" (Bridges, 1931).

Conditioning, or learning by association, imitation, and memories of unpleasant experiences, plays an important role in the development of fear among young children. Fear of certain specific events, such as fright at the sound of applause on the radio and fear of elevators, may lead to fears of similar or associated events, such as fear of all radios and fear of being shut up in a small space (Jersild and Holmes, 1935). Many fears develop from imitating a person who is frightened. It is quite common for preschool children to show fears similar to those of their mothers (Hagman, 1932). And, finally, many fears develop as an aftermath of some unpleasant experience, such as fear of doctors or of dentists (Lawton, 1938).

The number and severity of fears decrease as children grow older. In a follow-up study of a group of children from the time they were three years old until they were six, it was found that the average number of fears at three years was 5.5 and, at six, it had declined to 3.2 fears (Jersild and Holmes, 1935). Decrease in number and severity of fears with age is partly the result of the child's realization that there is nothing to be afraid of in the situation he formerly feared, partly to social pressures which have made him conceal his fear to avoid being ridiculed, partly from social imitation, and partly from adult guidance in acquiring a liking for or a negative attitude toward things he formerly feared (Jones, 1924; Jersild and Holmes, 1935). Fear of unfamiliar persons, environments, and experiences disappears as the child becomes better acquainted with them.

JEALOUSY. Jealousy is an angry resentment directed toward people. It is always called forth by social situations, involving individuals, especially those whom the child loves. Among young children, jealousy is invariably aroused when parents or those who have taken care of the child seemingly shift their interest and attention to someone else, especially a new arrival in the family. Most often jealousy begins between the ages of two and five years, with the birth of a younger sibling. Telling the child ahead of time of the anticipated arrival of the sibling does not necessarily avoid jealousy nor does it determine the attitude of the child toward the sibling (Sewall, 1930). Young children are frequently jealous of their fathers as well as of their siblings. They develop a proprietary attitude toward the mother because of her constant association with them, and they resent her affection for their father. In addition, young children are sometimes jealous of older siblings who are given more privileges than they, or of siblings who are given more attention than they because of poor health or some marked talent they may possess.

In early childhood, jealousy expresses itself in much the same way as anger does except that it is usually directed against another person, the individual whom the child believes has usurped his place in the affections of the loved one. Sometimes jealousy causes the child to revert to such infantile forms of behavior as thumb-sucking, bed-wetting, general naughtiness, or bidding for attention by refusing to eat or by pretending to be ill or afraid. Jealousy is more common among girls than among boys (Foster, 1927). First-born children display jealousy more often and more violently than do their latter-born siblings (Foster, 1927). It is more common in small families of two or three children than in larger ones (Ross, 1930). Over-solicitous mothers or those whose discipline is inconsistent have more trouble with jealousy among their children than do mothers who pay less attention to their children (Sewall, 1930). Jealousy is more frequent among children whose age difference falls between 18 and 42 months than when the difference is less or more (Sewall, 1930). And, finally, the peak of jealousy comes between the ages of two and three years (Foster, 1927).

AFFECTION. Like the baby, the young child learns to love those who give him pleasure and satisfaction. Not only human beings, but animals and inanimate objects, call forth expressions of affection on the part of the young child. Frequently the child expresses affection for a pet or for a favorite toy in much the same way as he expresses affection for the members of his family. Affection for the mother is generally greater than for the father (Simpson, 1935). This is a result of the child's more constant association with the mother than with the father and of the mother's greater understanding of and sympathy for the young child's wants and needs. How great will be the young child's affection for his brothers, sisters, and other relatives will depend primarily upon the pleasantness or unpleasantness of his association with them.

Young children express their affection in much the same uncontrolled manner as they express other emotions. They hug, kiss, and pat the loved person or object. They want to be with the loved one constantly, they cry or whimper when the loved one leaves them, and they want to do what the loved one is doing, even though their assistance may be more of a hindrance than a help. The child feels much the same way about favorite pets and toys as he does about beloved persons. He wants to have the pet or toy with him constantly, even when he goes to bed, and he is frequently merciless in his fondling of it. The most spontaneous and most frequent methods of expression generally occur among children of the lower economic groups (Murphy, 1937).

CURIOSITY. Young children are into everything. Nothing in the house, in a store, or in the homes of others escapes their interest if the object is different from what they have seen before. They even explore other persons' clothing by feeling it. They are intensely curious about their own bodies, the bodies of other children and of adults. They want to know why bodies differ and how they work. Because of the relatively poor muscle coordination of young children and their inexperience in judging the weights of unfamiliar objects, most young children are clumsy, awkward, and destructive in their exploration. Since social pressures in the form of warnings and punishment put an end to some of the sensorimotor exploration the child has previously engaged in, he begins, as soon as he can put words together into meaningful sentences, to ask endless questions, such as, "How does it work?" "Where did it come from?" and "How did it get there?"

The "questioning age" begins between the second and third years and reaches its peak at the sixth year of the child's life. When his questions are answered, the child's curiosity is satisfied because he has been able to obtain information not possible through his own exploration. When, however, he does not receive satisfactory answers or if his questions are unanswered, his curiosity is likely to be dampened and, as a result, his information is limited as compared with that of other children of his age and level of intelligence.

JOY. To young children, there are many sources of joy and many things to laugh about. Physical well-being, incongruous situations, sudden or unexpected noises, slight calamities, or plays on words never fail to bring forth a laugh (Wilson, 1931). Children smile and laugh more in social situations than when they are alone. The children who laugh most frequently play more with children who exhibit the same behavior than with children who are more sober (Gregg, 1928; Brackett, 1933, 1934). Children who laugh most frequently when they play with other children also laugh most when they are engaged in routine activities (Brackett, 1934). Laughter occurs most frequently when the child has completed an act or when there is anticipation of its completion (Blatz et al., 1935).

There is a definite age trend in the amount and also in the stimuli that elicit smiling and laughter. The amount increases from one smile per child every 6 minutes at the age of eighteen months to one smile every $1\frac{1}{3}$ minutes at four years. The ratio of laughs to smiles increases from one laugh to every ten smiles at eighteen months to one laugh to three smiles at four years. The child smiles more in response to the approach of another person than to his own activities, while a baby smiles more at his own activities. While the two-year-old most often smiles in response to an adult, the four-year-old smiles more frequently to other children. Individual differences in the amount and type of smiling and laughing are greater as children grow older (Ames, 1949).

SOCIAL DEVELOPMENT

In the home, the baby first learns to love and to be loved. The success of these early social experiences determines, to a large extent, the success of his later relationships with persons outside the home. As the social world of the young child expands, early parental attachments are gradually outgrown and are replaced by relationships with individuals outside the family circle. How important a role the early parent-child relationships play is shown in the child's adjustments to other children. A comparison of children raised in democratic and nondemocratic home environments has shown the effects of these types of family relationships on the child's reactions to other children. The child who is raised democratically shows behavior of an outgoing type. He may be hostile and dominating as well as friendly. He is not likely to have an inferior status in the group and, on the whole, his bossing is likely to be successful. He engages in activities demanding intellectual curiosity, originality, and constructiveness. He becomes an active participant in nursery-school play.

The child brought up under nondemocratic home conditions, by contrast, is just the opposite. He also shows physical apprehensiveness and lack of skill in muscular activities. While he may be less rebellious and more conforming than the child whose home environment has been more democratic, he does not achieve a degree of social interaction so satisfactory as the child whose home environment has been more democratic (Bakwin, 1948, 1949). Early childhood is the "pregang" stage of social development. At this time the child should acquire the preliminary training and experience needed to become a member of a "gang" in late childhood. Should geographic isolation, parental restrictions, or unfavorable attitude on the part of the child cut him off from contact with other children of his age, the child will be deprived of experiences necessary to make satisfactory social adjustments, not only then but as he grows older.

While babies are content with the companionship of adults, young children are not. Between the ages of two and three years, the child begins to grow restless when his companions are limited to adults. At this time, he shows a decided interest in watching other children and he attempts to make social contacts with them. "Parallel play," in which the child plays independently beside children rather than with them, is the earliest form of social activity with his contemporaries. Following this comes "associative play," in which the child plays with other children in similar, if not identical, activities, and "cooperative play," in which he is a part of a group. Frequently children play the role of an onlooker in which they watch other children at play, talk to other children, but do not actually enter into the play of the group. Types of social participation at this age are shown in Fig. 16.

Social Behavior. Certain forms of social behavior are carry-overs of behavior established during babyhood or are developed as a result of the child's contacts with other children. The most important forms of social behavior necessary for successful social adjustment appear and begin to develop at this time. In the early years of childhood, they are not developed well enough to enable the child to get along successfully with others at all times. However, this is a crucial stage in their development because, at this time, the pattern is set and the foundations are laid. How far this development will progress depends, in large measure, upon the number of opportunities the young child has for social contacts. Children who attend nursery school, for example, make better social adjustments in kindergarten than do those who have never had the nursery-school experience (Jersild and Fite, 1939).

The most important forms of social behavior to appear at this age are negativism, imitation, rivalry, quarreling, cooperation, ascendant behavior, sympathy, and desire for social approval.

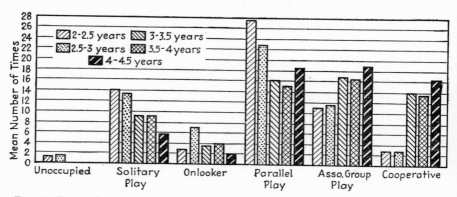

FIG. 16. Types of social participation at the preschool age. (*From M. B. Parten, Social participation among preschool children. J. abnorm. soc. Psychol., 1932, 27:243–269. Used by permission.*)

NEGATIVISM, or resistance to adult authority, begins in babyhood as a result of the aggressive use of discipline in the home or of an intolerant attitude toward childish behavior. At the age of two or three years, negativism is a normal phase of ego development. It is an exaggerated reaction to the need for relinquishing the earlier grandiose concept of self (Ausubel, 1950). The child shows his resistance by verbal response, motor response, or by silence (Rust, 1931). Motor responses decrease with age, and vocal resistance increases (Caille, 1933). Resistance to adult authority reaches its peak around the third year, and thereafter children show negativism to other children and to strange adults in schools or testing situations more frequently than to their parents (Caille, 1933; Rust, 1931).

Perhaps nothing is more distressing to parents than the negativistic behavior of their children. They interpret this as unsocial behavior and try everything within their power to check it. Banham (1952), who has made an intensive study of the obstinate, stubborn, rebellious behavior of children of the two- to three-year-old levels, has interpreted their negativistic behavior thus:

Contra-suggestibility, negativism, and obstinacy in children may be taken as signs of potentiality for good social adjustment. They are forms of behavior that are unsatisfactory in themselves, but that at least show vitality, motivation, and the beginnings of selective sensitivity to complex social situations. They indicate that the child is capable of developing social and emotional attachments and antagonisms. Children become excessively obstinate when demands are made that are impossible for them to execute, when the demands are humiliating, unfair, or exceedingly disagreeable or painful. Obstinate contrariness is a compensatory adaptive reaction, only partially successful, in the interest of self-preservation, growth, and development. It is likely to change to cooperative behavior when the child finds something he can do that will bring satisfaction to him while complying with the wishes of those for whom he cares.

IMITATION. With the beginnings of interest in other children, the child imitates their words, actions, and emotions. The child is, in this way, trying to identify himself with the group.

RIVALRY. The desire to excel or to outdo others is apparent as early as the fourth year of life. When children of two years of age are engaged in the task of inserting pegs in a board, they will look at one another occasionally to see how the other children are getting along. A year later, when working in pairs, rivalry is present but it proves to be more of a distraction than a help. By the age of five years, however, rivalry is a dominant attitude in this situation and it acts as an incentive to increased output (Leuba, 1933). The young child's bragging about his possessions is a subtle form of rivalry. It is commonly displayed in the presence of a third person, generally an adult for whose attention the child is competing (Gottemoller, 1943).

QUARRELING. Much of the quarreling of young children comes from lack of experience in cooperative play. When the child quarrels, he takes away toys that the other child is playing with, he is destructive of the other child's work, and he generally screams, cries, kicks, hits, and bites. These outbursts, though intense, are usually short in duration. After they are over, they are forgotten and the friendly relationship that prevailed before the quarrel is resumed (Dawe, 1934). Quarreling generally starts in a conflict over property, such as toys (Murphy, 1937). It is more frequent in dramatic play, sand play, play with toys, and constructive work than in fine manipulations and bodily activity without apparatus (Green, 1933). The younger the child, the fewer opportunities there are for quarrels because contacts with other children are generally briefer than they are as the child grows older (Muste and Sharpe, 1947), and their quarrels are shorter in durations (Appel, 1942). The age of three years is generally the peak of quarreling. After that, improved social adjustments bring about a decrease in the frequency and intensity of quarrels (Jersild and Fite, 1939). Boys are more quarrelsome than girls, especially when paired with other boys (Muste and Sharpe, 1947).

COOPERATION. Because very young children are self-centered and quarrelsome, there is little cooperation in their play with other children. Even with adults they cooperate little because the adult has a tendency to give in to the child and to allow him to have his own way. By the end of the third year, however, cooperative play and group activities are more frequent and longer in duration. With practice, the child learns to cooperate with other children and to play in an increasingly harmonious manner. The stronger the ties of friendship between young children, the more cooperative is their play (Wright, 1942).

ASCENDANT BEHAVIOR. Almost all young children show a strong tendency to be "bossy." The child attempts to secure materials that he wants from other children and to direct and influence the behavior of his playmates (Mummery, 1947). Girls are significantly more dominating than boys in their play with other children during the preschool years. Among kindergarten children, however, the reverse is true (Anderson, 1937). At home, assertiveness is strongest when there are many restrictions on the child's behavior and when there is little rapport between the child and his parents (Meyer, 1947).

SYMPATHY. Sympathy requires an understanding of the feelings and emotions of others. Children at the age of two or three years do not respond sympathetically to the black-and-blue wounds, swelling, bumps, and minor flesh distortions of others, to stories of a distressing nature, such as Red Riding Hood being eaten up by the wolf, to pictures of accidents, to being crippled, or to funerals. Occasionally a three-year-old will respond sympathetically to persons whose distress is made apparent by the use of bandages colored with iodine and by scars and scratches; to physical dilemmas, such as a fall from a bicycle; and to a child attacked by another child (Murphy, 1937). The child shows his sympathy by attempting to help others, by trying to remove the cause of distress, by protecting those in distress, by warning and telling others about the individual in distress, and by suggesting solutions. Occasionally, however, unsympathetic responses such as laughing at a person in distress occur (Murphy, 1937).

SOCIAL APPROVAL. Like the baby, the young child is anxious to have the approval of others. At first, the approval of adults is more important to him than the approval of other children. But, as interest in being with the group increases, the desire to impress his companions becomes more important than the approval of adults. This desire frequently is so strong, as the child reaches the school age, that the young child is naughty and disturbing in the hope of winning the approval of his playmates. Socially unacceptable behavior is frequently motivated by the child's preference for approval from his companions to that from adults.

Companions. The preschool child's companions are limited in number and variety. For the most part, they consist of the adults in the family, brothers and sisters, and children in the immediate neighborhood. Only if he attends nursery school, Sunday school, or kindergarten does the circle of the child's companions enlarge. Age and home environment are more important factors in the selection of companions than is the level of the child's intelligence (Parten, 1933). By the age of four years, children show a decided preference for companions of their own sex as compared with younger children who show no sex preference (Hagman, 1933; Koch, 1933). Likewise, there is an increase in the child's tendency to choose companions of his own race as he grows older (Koch, 1933).

Imaginary playmates are common among young children, especially when parent-child relationships are unfavorable or when the child has few opportunities for real playmates (Bender and Vogel, 1941). It is a natural developmental phenomenon in many children and is especially characteristic of the age period from $2\frac{1}{2}$ to $4\frac{1}{2}$ years (Ames and Learned, 1946). This is the time when the craving for friendship with other children begins to appear. The child who is unable, for one reason or another, to satisfy this craving frequently compensates with imaginary companions. This, however, is not a satisfactory solution to the lonely-child problem. Having learned to play with an imaginary companion, the child does not get the training in social cooperation essential to satisfactory adjustment to real children. He is likely to acquire the habit of dominating his playmates which is possible with an imaginary playmate but frequently is not possible with a real child. When he discovers that the technique that worked so successfully with his imaginary playmate does not work with real children, the child is likely to become a maladjusted member of the group.

Leadership. In early childhood, the leader is characteristically superior in size, intelligence, and usually in age to the other members of the group. Superior age and intelligence make it possible for him to offer suggestions for play which the other children, because of their habitual reliance upon adult suggestions, are willing to follow. The big child has the advantage over the smaller children because of the child's tendency to respect size as a result of his constant contact with adults and his habits of obedience to their requests. Most leaders in early childhood are tyrannical bosses who show little consideration for the wishes of others, who use brute force and threats to control the behavior of others, and who become sullen and angry when others rebel. When tyranny becomes too great, the leader loses status and is replaced by another. In addition to "bossy" leaders, or the bully type, leaders in early childhood are sometimes "diplomats" who lead others by indirect and artful suggestions or by bargains (Jack, 1934; Parten, 1933). Girls, at this age, frequently assume the role of leadership in groups containing boys. Physical attractiveness, socioeconomic status, religion, and nationality are unimportant qualities of a leader in the early childhood years.

Social Acceptability. When the child begins to play with other children, his acceptance or rejection by them soon becomes apparent. Whether he is popular or not is not necessarily determined by his activity in the group. Sometimes the aggressively bossy child, who pushes himself into everything, is thoroughly disliked by other children. The outstanding trait that makes for popularity among young children is the acceptance of a situation, such as willingness to do what others do, offering no resistance, complying with requests, and accepting gracefully what happens. The popular child is conscientious in his conformity to the group ways. Girls, at this age, are more popular than boys with members of both sexes. Bright children are generally more popular than those who are less bright (Koch, 1933). The unpopular child at the preschool age, on the other hand, is one who attacks vigorously, who strikes frequently, or pushes and pulls. Personal affront and lack of respect for the property rights of others do not win friends for him. Added to the aggressive behavior of unpopular children are frequent attempts to escape responsibility, such as clinging to an adult or running away; dawdling; refusals to comply to the requests of others; and failure to conform to the routine (Koch, 1933).

PLAY

Early childhood is frequently referred to as "the toy age." At this time, toys are essential to the child's enjoyment of his play, even more so than in babyhood, when much of the play takes the form of exploring his toys. The reason that toys are so important to a young child's play is that he imagines his toys have life qualities, that they are capable of talking, acting, and feeling, as he is. Toy play reaches its peak around the seventh or eighth year, after which the child is no longer capable of attributing living qualities to his toys and, as a result, he loses interest in them and turns his attention elsewhere.

Toys. The favorite toys of young children are the "do-with" variety. They can be moved, changed, and manipulated according to the child's wishes. Three-year-olds prefer cylinders to be fitted into holes in a wooden block, blocks, building cubes, and chalk for drawing on a blackboard. Stuffed animals and paints are the least favored toys at this age (Bridges, 1931). The four-year-old shows a definite preference for blocks that can be used for construction, sand, kiddy cars, and seesaws. Dolls, blackboards, and stuffed animals are the least popular play materials for the four-year-old. The favorites of five- and six-year-olds consist of plastic materials, playground apparatus, housekeeping materials, toy animals, transportation toys, and blocks (Vance and McCall, 1934). Less interest is shown in blocks from the age of three years. Mechanical toys occupy the longest play periods on the part of preschool children (Bott, 1928). Boys show a preference for trains, cars, houses, and blocks; girls prefer beads, dolls, and houses (Benjamin, 1932).

Dramatization. Dramatization begins to enter into the child's play between the second and third years. Dolls, soldiers, and stuffed animals become living creatures, and wagons, dollhouses and coaches, all of which are reproductions in miniature of the same equipment used for daily living, make it possible for the child to dramatize scenes from real life in his play. Dramatic play follows a definite pattern in which personification, such as talking to dolls or stuffed animals, predominates before the age of three years. Following this is make-believe use of materials, such as drinking from an empty cup, and then, among those who are four years of age and older, there are make-believe situations involving companions and use of materials, such as playing house (Markey, 1935).

The make-believe play of young children dramatizes events in their everyday lives, the most common forms of which are *domestic patterns,* as cooking and taking care of babies; *selling and buying; transportation activities,* as sailing boats or driving a car; *punishing activities,* as gunplay or policeman; *burning and playing fireman; killing and dying;* and playing *legendary persons,* as Santa Claus or Cinderella (Murphy, 1937). Of these, playing house generally ranks first in popularity (Parten, 1933), with playing school coming to the fore when the child enters school (Lehman and Witty, 1926).

Construction. In addition to dramatization, the young child spends much of his play time in making things. Play with mud, sand, blocks, beads, clay, paint, crayons, scissors and paste, all enable him to construct things in imitation of what he sees in daily life and what is uppermost in his mind at the moment. The drawings of a young child generally follow a developmental pattern. Before the child is three years old, drawings are merely scribbles which even the young child himself cannot identify. By three, however, he names his drawings but it is generally difficult for anyone else to identify them. A year later, there is little scribbling and the drawings take on form and meaning. The five-year-old differentiates parts in his drawings, and they are clearly recognizable for what the child names them to be. The drawings of a six-year-old show improvement in precision and detail over those of the five-year-old. Crayoning and painting follow much the same pattern of development as drawing (Gesell, 1940; Goodenough and Harris, 1950).

It is unusual for children to draw anything bizarre or eccentric (Gesell, 1928). The most popular subjects of their drawings are the human form, with the adult form more common than that of a child. Next in popularity are houses, trees, and furniture. Animals and designs are infrequently drawn (McCarty, 1924). Among young children, objects that are important to a child are likely to be proportionally too large in the drawings, as when a child draws buttons on a man's coat that are almost as large as the man's head (Meier, 1939).

Games. Around the fourth or fifth year, the child becomes interested in playing games with the children in the neighborhood. These "neighborhood games," such as tag, hide-and-seek, cat-and-mouse, cops-and-robbers, advancing statues, and going to Jerusalem, are of the *undefined-group* type in which any number of children can take part. The children copy one another and follow orders from the leader who is generally the child who has organized the game. Games that test skill, such as jumping rope, playing jacks, and bouncing balls, are likewise popular toward the end of early childhood. These are played individually rather than in a group and involve little competition.

Reading. Long before the child can read, he likes to look at pictures in his storybooks and to have someone read to him. Simple fairy and nature stories have great appeal at this age because of the young child's inability to distinguish animate from inanimate objects. The classic fairy tales, such as "Little Red Riding Hood" and "Cinderella," the more modern fanciful stories, such as "Little Black Sambo," the Mother Goose jingles, and stories about animals and everyday people doing everyday things all appeal to young children (Wilson, 1943; Witty *et al.,* 1946). Animals, children, and men are more popular characters in stories for both boys and girls than are women, babies, and fairies (Wilson, 1943*a*).

Radio and Television. In recent years, radio stations have been putting on programs especially suited to the interests of the preschool child. Telling or dramatizing stories for children, clown and animal acts, music, and singing are included in these programs (Wilson, 1941). The characters and types preferred among kindergarten children are Uncle Don, the Lone Ranger, and the Singing Lady (Wilson, 1941). While television is, to date, too new to have offered opportunities for studies of children's interests in different types of programs, there is a general opinion that television appeals more to young children than does the radio because the child can see as well as hear the entertainment it offers.

DEVELOPMENT OF UNDERSTANDING

Concept formation advances rapidly during the years of early childhood. New experiences lead to new meanings which are associated with meanings established in babyhood. The child now begins to notice details which formerly escaped his attention. As a result, he is not so apt to confuse objects, situations, or people that have elements in common, as he formerly did. His concepts become more specific and meaningful to him, though he still perceives wholes rather than parts of the objects (Hurlock and Thompson, 1934). His feelings and emotions influence what he sees (Hildreth, 1941). At first, young children interpret objects in terms of static form and, later, in terms of activity (Amen, 1941).

Animism. Like primitive peoples, young children, because of their limited knowledge and experience, do not distinguish between living and inanimate objects. The young child believes that all objects have the same life qualities as human beings. This tendency to ascribe living qualities to inanimate objects, *animism,* is responsible for many of the faulty concepts of young children. Anything that is in any way active is regarded as conscious (Piaget, 1929). How widespread animism is among young children is hard to determine, primarily because of the young child's difficulty in expressing his thoughts in words. Most baby biographers, however, record instances of animism (Dennis, 1938). Among preschool children, animistic concepts are less frequent than are simple, naïve, physical concepts (Huang, 1943). What few animistic explanations young children give of causality are transmitted to the child by his parents, usually by the mother (McAndrew, 1943).

Techniques of Development. To motor manipulation the young child adds questioning in his quest for meanings. The "questioning age" begins around the third year and reaches its peak when the child enters school. Questioning is used not only to gain new information but to check upon and supplement information gained through experimentation. Boys ask questions at a faster rate than do girls, and they ask more questions involving causal explanations. Girls, on the other hand, ask more questions on social relationships (Davis, 1932). Questions beginning with "What" and "Where" are most common from two to four years, while those beginning with "Why" and "How" and "When" are most frequent after four (Smith, 1933).

Space Perception. The ability to distinguish small distance, established in babyhood, is improved upon at this age. From his play with tricycles, carts, blocks, and other toys, the child becomes familiar with common cues which help him to perceive short distances if they are studied in relation to his body. Longer distances, because they are unrelated to his body, are still very difficult to judge accurately. By the age of four years, perception of short distance is similar to that of an adult (Updegraff, 1930). The child's ability to perceive differences in form increases gradually from two to six years (Wellman, 1937). Perception of relative size also develops at this age. At the age of three years, young children can select the largest and smallest objects from a group of objects of varying sizes. By the age of five years, they can select middle-sized objects. When the difference in size is very small, perception of relative differences becomes increasingly inaccurate (Thrum, 1935). The concept of roundness is well established between the ages of three and six years (Long, 1940).

Weight Perception. Until the child learns that different materials have different weights, he is apt to estimate weight exclusively in terms of size. A ball of cotton, for example, would be judged as heavier than a rubber ball of smaller size. As a result, the young child breaks many objects because he does not make the necessary muscular adjustment to handle them safely.

With experience, he learns that he must judge the material the object is made of as well as its size. By the age of five years, the child is able to tell the difference between 3- and 15-gram weights when they are the same size (Terman, 1922).

Number Concepts. Numbers mean little to young children. While they may use numbers in a parrotlike fashion, their concepts of numbers from 1 to 10 are vague and meaningless in most instances. Children who go to nursery school or kindergarten frequently learn the meanings of numbers from 1 to 5 but have only vague concepts about numbers above that (Douglass, 1925).

Time Concepts. Young children have no idea of the length of time nor do they have means by which to judge it. They cannot tell time by a clock much before they are five or six years old. They have not yet learned how to estimate time in terms of their own activities. Because they do not have a crowded schedule, they are apt to dally over different activities, thus adding to their difficulty in estimating time with any degree of accuracy. Estimating the length of the night is difficult for a young child because he sleeps most of the time and, therefore, has no accomplishments to show how long the time has been. By associating specific activities with different times of the day, with the days of the week, and with the seasons of the year, the child can make more accurate estimates. Morning, afternoon, and night are perceived differently because of the different activities associated with each. Days of the week are known by the different activities that occur on those days. By the time they are four or five years old, most children know what day of the week it is. Only if the month, season, or year is told them at home or in kindergarten are they likely to know them before they are six years old.

Time concepts come into use in a relatively uniform sequence and at about the same time in the life of every child. The use of "today" appears at the age of 2 years, of "tomorrow," at 2½ years, and of "yesterday," at 3 years. At the age of 4 years, children know the difference between morning and afternoon and, a year later, they know the names of the days of the week. At this age, they can tell when they go to bed. The three-year-old can tell his age; the four-year-old, when his next birthday will be; and, the five-year-old, how old he will be on his next birthday (Ames, 1940). When four- to six-year-old boys and girls were asked to draw pictures of a clock, they wrote the numbers of the clock counterclockwise at first. Gradually, as they grew older, accuracy of presentation increased (Springer, 1951).

Concepts of Self. The concept of self, starting in babyhood through exploring the different parts of the body and by looking into a mirror, develops very rapidly during early childhood because of the child's interest in himself. The two-year-old can identify three parts of the body when asked to point to them and, the 2½-year-old, four parts (Terman and Merrill, 1937). By the time he is three years old, he should know whether he is a boy or a girl, what his full name is, and where his nose, eyes, mouth, and hair are (Terman,

1922). At this age, children generally know also the different parts of their bodies, such as their hands, feet, toes, legs, arms, and "tummies," and what articles of clothing belong to the different parts of the body. The six-year-old can distinguish the right from the left side of his body (Terman, 1922). The child's concept of self as a person, as distinguished from anyone else, comes first from comparing his body with the bodies and behavior of others. By the time he is three years old, he can distinguish between a thing belonging to his own person and himself (Lewin, 1935). The negativistic behavior of the two- and three-year-olds is an indication of the growth of self-consciousness. By the time he is four or five years old, the child is aware of himself as an independent person (Allport, 1937).

When the child reaches the school age, he can understand the meaning of competition and can, in some areas of his activity, appreciate how he compares with others. He is capable of a certain amount of self-criticism, is sensitive to ridicule, failure, and also prestige. As a result, he is likely to be self-conscious and shy, especially in such activities as singing, dancing, and drawing (Jersild, 1947). The child's concept of himself as a member of a racial group develops earlier among Negro children than among white children. Negro children in nursery school have a more definite concept of their difference from the group and their similarity to another group than do white children of the same age (Horowitz, 1939). This appears as early as the age of three or four years (Clark and Clark, 1939). The child's awareness of sex differences and of the importance of behaving in a socially approved manner for a member of his own sex appears as early as the second year of life when the child begins to ask questions about physical sex differences, his own body, and the origin of babies (Hattendorf, 1932). The child is aware of differences in urinary posture of girls and of boys, and girls occasionally try to imitate boys (Conn, 1940). They accept these differences without shock and only when there are unfavorable parental attitudes is the child embarrassed (Conn, 1939).

Awareness of sexually appropriate behavior comes early through observation and imitation of adult models (Ferguson, 1941). By the time the child is three years old, he shows by picture choices his awareness of the appropriate role of the father as a man of business and the inappropriateness of boys playing with dolls (Seward, 1946). Boys, in the nursery-school age, have been found to be more clearly aware of appropriate sex behavior than are girls. This is more true of children from the working and executive classes than of children from the middle economic group (Rabban, 1950). As a result of social pressures on the young child to accept the appropriate sex role and to behave in accordance with this role, changes in the behavior of members of the two sexes appear early. At the nursery-school age, boys are more aggressive, extroverted, and difficult to handle than are girls (Hattwick and Sanders, 1938). This awareness of appropriate sex roles is also shown in the excretory behavior of three- to four-year-olds. Cases of excessive modesty, games of rectal thermometer engaged in in secret, and fascinated watching of other children at the toilet all resulted from social pressures in the home to behave in the approved manner (Dillon, 1934). When shown pictures of boys and girls, nursery-school children of both sexes showed a marked preference for pictures of children of their own sex (Springer, 1950).

Social Perception. Social perception, or the ability to understand the thoughts and emotions of others from observing their facial expressions and behavior, is essential to satisfactory social adjustments. Young children, as a result of their constant contact with parents, brothers, sisters, and play-mates, learn to "size up" these individuals with a fair degree of accuracy. Because of their limited contact with strangers, young children frequently size them up incorrectly. Much of the tactlessness of young children can be traced to poor social perception. Awareness of racial differences occurs in the preschool age. When Hawaiian children of different racial backgrounds were shown pictures of children and were asked to identify themselves, their brothers, and sisters, it was found that three- to six-year-olds were aware of differences in the physical characteristics that distinguish different racial groups and could identify their own characteristics in pictures of children of their own race. Non-Orientals emphasized color of hair and eyes as impor-tant determinants; Orientals emphasized the appearance of the hair and the shape of the eyes (Springer, 1950). Among four-year-olds, Negro children have been found to be more often highly sensitized to race than white children. Brighter children of both groups tend to be more alert to racial differences than do the less bright children (Goodman, 1951).

Aesthetic Perception. The young child's perception of beauty depends largely upon the associations he forms. People, things, objects, and places he likes are "beautiful." Those he dislikes are labeled "ugly." When shown pictures of women's faces, many five-year-olds pick out the ugliest. The reason they give for this is that "She looks like my grandmother" or "She looks like my nurse" (Terman, 1922). Children of nursery-school age, when shown pictures of children of different racial backgrounds, tended to prefer children of their own racial background. This was more pronounced for non-Orientals than for Orientals. Children of mixed racial backgrounds tended to choose more non-Oriental than Oriental pictures (Springer, 1950). The young child thinks brightly colored pictures, representing movements of people, animals, or machines, are pretty (Olney and Cushing, 1935). The ability to understand the meaning of a picture plays an important role in the child's appreciation of its beauty. And, because a young child accepts uncritically what an adult says, he is likely to accept this as "pretty" and that as "ugly" because his mother or his teacher labeled it so.

Color preferences of young children are generally for bright hues. Blue, red, violet, green, yellow, and orange are preferred; of the drab colors, black, gray, and brown, with white last, is the order of preference for young children (Garth and Porter, 1934). Girls prefer blue and boys, red. Red-green and red-blue combinations are the favorite ones, with orange-green the least favorite (Dashiell, 1917). Liking for music of certain types is strong among young children. They prefer songs and music with a definite "tune," or rhythm. With repetition of the child's favorite music, the more beautiful he believes it to be. As is true of pictures, the child's ability to understand music plays an important role in his perception of its beauty. By the time the child goes to kindergarten, he can distinguish pitch and intensity, can pitch his voice when a model pitch is given, and can march in time to music.

Comic Perception. Up to the age of three years, the child laughs in response to some pleasurable experience, such as tickling. From then until he is six years old, strange and unusual things, provided they are not so exaggerated as to be frightening, are conceived as funny (Harms, 1943). Among the things most often perceived as funny by nursery-school children are motion and noises made by the child himself or by others; socially unacceptable situations; grimaces made by the child himself or by others; inferiority in others; word play; and imitative laughter (Kenderdine, 1931). The funny antics of domestic animals and the misfortunes of others are likewise sources of humor at this age (Kimmins, 1928). The ability to perceive the comic correlates very highly with intelligence at this age as is true of all other ages.

Errors in Perception. At every age, there is a tendency to perceive things incorrectly. Errors arise partly because of too-hasty observation, partly from misinterpreting what has been observed, partly from misinformation given in answer to questions, and partly from a misunderstanding of the words used in the explanations given. Faulty concepts are very common among young children, especially those from poorer districts (Hall, 1907).

MORAL DEVELOPMENT

Training in conforming to the social codes of the group, begun in the second year of life, must continue throughout childhood. The young child's intellectual development has not yet reached the point where he can learn or apply abstract principles of right and wrong. He must learn moral behavior in specific situations. And, because his retention is still poor, the learning is a slow process. Being told not to do something one day may not readily be remembered the next day or the day after that. This learning is complicated when several different persons, at different times, require that he do different things in the same situation. He cannot understand why an act is wrong today when the same act, yesterday, passed unnoticed.

Moral Concepts. The young child's moral concepts are subjective in nature. He judges acts as right or wrong in terms of the consequences of his own acts. When asked the questions, "What is a good girl (boy)?" and "What is a bad (naughty) girl (boy)?", the answers given show that the authority most often referred to for judgments of good and bad is the mother. Good behavior consists of helping mother do nice, kind things, playing gently with toys, and taking care of his own routine. Behavior called "bad," on the other hand, consists of doing overt acts of violence, such as scratching and biting, not wanting to do what mother asks, crying, saying bad words, and being cross (Radke, 1946). The foundation of moral conduct and the basic moral attitudes of the group to which the child belongs should become well established during early childhood. Because of his mental immaturity, the child cannot understand the whys and wherefores of behavior. He merely learns how to act without knowing why he does so. As early childhood comes to an end, habits of obedience should be established, provided the child has had consistent discipline.

When he is naughty, it is more often from ignorance than from willful disobedience. At this age, the child actually does not know why an act is right or wrong. He conforms to conduct standards set by the home, the school, or his neighborhood to avoid punishment and social disapproval and to gain social approval and reward. He cannot, therefore, be said to be a "moral" individual. He is more rightly called "unmoral." Even though he does not understand why certain acts are good and others bad, the child knows that some acts are labeled "good" and some, "bad." From this information, he lays the foundation for moral concepts that will guide his behavior as he grows older. Even though he may try to evade rules by going to different persons for permission to do something labeled "naughty" by a parent, and even though he may try to test the authority of the person in charge of him, the young child does not question the rules, suggest alternative acts, or bargain with the person in authority as the older child does. Nor does he feel guilty when caught doing something that is wrong. He may, however, become frightened at the prospect of punishment or he may rationalize to explain why he did what he did.

Discipline. The educational aspect of discipline, which consists of training the child to conform to the mores of the group, should be the outstanding part of discipline during early childhood, just as it is in babyhood. As new social horizons open up, when the child first plays with other children or enters nursery school, he must learn how to act in a socially approved manner in these new groups. The child-training methods in use today, as reported by parents, show a swing away from spanking and other forms of corporal punishment and towards reasoning at length with the child, scolding, telling him emphatically what he must do, letting the child choose his own consequences, making him feel ashamed of his behavior, rewards, praise, and promises of extra favors (Long, 1941). Among nursery-school children, isolation, physical punishment, and "natural results of the child's act" are the most frequently used home punishments (Ayer and Bernreuter, 1937).

The effect of discipline on the child's personality is even more important than the effect on his behavior. The more physical punishment is used on children, the less they face reality and the more they depend on adults for attention and affection. "Natural results of the child's acts" foster an attractive personality and an independence of adult affection or attention. Scolding and making the child afraid tend to make him unattractive and dependent

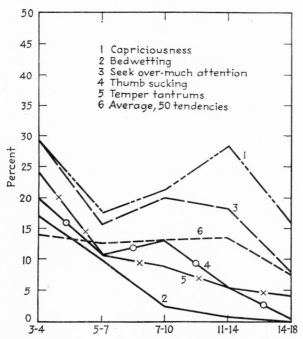

FIG. 17. Most frequent misdemeanors of three- and four-year olds. (*From A. Long, Parents' reports of undesirable behavior in children. Child Develpm., 1941, 12:43–62. Used by permission.*)

(Ayer and Bernreuter, 1937). Very strict discipline during the early years of the child's life may be associated with personality maladjustment, delinquencies, or unhappiness (Stogdill, 1937). It is generally assumed that punishment will prevent the recurrence of undesirable behavior. When preschool children were asked how they felt after their mothers or fathers punished them, the most common answer was that they felt sad, unhappy, or had memories of the pain of the punishment. Very few reported that they felt penitent or resolved to avoid the disapproval of behavior in the future (Radke, 1946). This would suggest that, among young children, punishment does not achieve its goal which is to convince the child that it is to his advantage to try in the future to do what is expected of him.

The types of home punishment most frequently used on young children are verbal appeals, isolating the child, depriving him of privileges, spanking, ignoring, shaming, withdrawing love, and frightening him. Depriving the child of privileges and pleasures is used more frequently by mothers than by fathers (Radke, 1946). Contrary to general opinion, mothers leave punishment to the fathers in only a small percentage of cases (Gardner, 1943). When young children are asked what parents should do when their children are naughty, children are likely to recommend as suitable punishments those which they themselves have received when they misbehaved. In over three out of four of the children consulted, spanking was recommended, while isolating them, scolding, or being cross were only occasionally recommended (Radke, 1946).

Misdemeanors. Young children learn that naughtiness, or willful disobedience of a minor sort, will generally give them more attention than good behavior. If, therefore, they feel that they are being ignored, they are frequently naughty in the hope of getting the attention they crave. Even the temporary discomfort of punishment does not outweigh the satisfaction derived from having adult attention focused on them. The most common misdemeanors of early childhood are capriciousness, bed-wetting, seeking attention, thumb-sucking, temper tantrums, and dawdling. The frequency of different types of misdemeanor in early childhood is shown in Fig. 17. Most of these are associated with immaturity and appear less and less frequently as the child grows older. More girls than boys are hostile and suspicious at this age, and more girls than boys are willful.

EARLY CHILDHOOD INTERESTS

With growth in intelligence comes an awakening of new interests. The young child's interests broaden and intensify as his environment expands and as he comes in contact with more and more people outside the home environment. At this age, his interests center chiefly on himself and all that pertains to his own possessions. This has been brought out clearly in studies of children's wishes (Jersild *et al.*, 1933).

Religion. Religious beliefs are, for the most part, meaningless to a young child. His intelligence has not yet developed to a point where he can understand abstractions nor does he understand many of the words used in his religious training. He may absorb words and phrases so that he can repeat them in a parrotlike fashion but they have little real meaning for him. However, the young child is curious about religion. Many of the questions asked by young children relate to religious matters. Because so many of the mysteries centered around birth, death, growth, and the elements are explained to him in religious terms, his curiosity about religious matters is great. He tries to satisfy this curiosity by asking innumerable questions and he accepts what is told him without questioning or doubting the answers given.

The young child's religious concepts are realistic. He interprets what he hears in terms of what he knows. To him, God is a man who wears clothes different from the clothes of the persons he knows, and who has a flowing beard and hair. Angels are men and women with white wings, while heaven is a place where every human wish is gratified. This is the "fairy-tale stage" of religious beliefs (Harms, 1944). That is why religious stories have such strong appeal to young children. At this age, their preference is for stories relating to the birth and childhood of Jesus and the childhood experiences of such children as David, Moses, or Samuel (Dawson, 1900). The young child's attitude toward religion is a compound of awe and reverence. The pageantry and solemnity of the church service are awe-inspiring. His interest in religion is egocentric. To him, prayer is a way of gaining childish desires. This is in keeping with his personality make-up. He visualizes God as a person who can and will do things for him just as his parents do when he asks them. An analysis of prayers prepared for children by leaders in religious education has revealed that they all relate to specific things that the child seeks through prayer, such as a variety and abundance of good things, direct petitions for specific things, and for help in doing things they cannot achieve by themselves (Fahs, 1932).

The Human Body. The young child is curious about his own body and the bodies of other children. From the age of $3\frac{1}{2}$ years on, there is a greater interest in their own bodies than was shown earlier. This interest takes the form of comments and questions about various parts of the body, of examining them, of calling attention to them, and occasionally, of exhibitionism. The areas that attract a child's attention especially are the navel, the eyes, hair, breasts, and anus. Children are also curious about elimination though their attitude towards it is matter-of-fact and unconcerned (Dillon, 1934). Children under $3\frac{1}{2}$ years of age do not usually differentiate between the two sexes. They accept the differences in the appearance of the genitals as they do differences in hair or eye color and they attach no sex significance to these differences.

From then until the end of childhood, they recognize anatomical differences between boys and girls but only as incidental characteristics. The cues they use to distinguish between the sexes are differences in clothes, hair styles, or names (Dillon, 1934). The youngest age at which hair style is mentioned as a distinguishing characteristic between the two sexes is four years, while clothes, eyes, and hands are noticed at five years (Conn and Kanner, 1947). At this age, there is no sense of impropriety in appearing undressed nor do children make any effort to conceal the manipulation of their genitals in masturbation (Dillon, 1934).

Sex. Young children have strong emotional attachments for anyone whose association with them is pleasant, whether it be a parent, grandparent, servant, pet animal, or child of their own age. The child does not show a preference for members of one sex rather than the other until he reaches the close of early childhood. Then boys begin to show a strong preference for boys, and girls for girls. The young child shows his affection for a loved person, pet, or toy in much the same way that a baby does. He pats, fondles, hugs, or kisses the loved object. In extreme cases, he wants to be with the beloved one constantly and puts up a protest when this is impossible. These protests, however, are generally of brief duration. After the person has left, the child usually turns his attention to something else and becomes absorbed in his new interest. When a loved person leaves the home, dies, or is divorced, the young child soon forgets him and centers his affection elsewhere.

Curiosity about sex matters begins to appear in early childhood. Children at this age are definitely curious about the origin of babies and ask frequent questions about this matter. This curiosity is intensified if there is a new baby in the family or neighborhood, or if a pet animal has offspring. God is frequently referred to as the source of babies, and many children believe they come from a hospital or a store, or that the stork brings them (Conn, 1948). The most common questions asked by young children relating to the origin of babies, physical sex differences, sex organs and their functions, and the coming of another baby are met with parental protests or with misinformation. Questions about intra-uterine growth and about marriage are infrequent at this age (Hattendorf, 1932). Between the ages of four and six years, certain play activities and games are thought of as specifically for boys and others as specifically for girls (Conn, 1951).

Kinsey maintains that the influence of social pressures is beginning to be felt in the child's attitudes toward sex and in his sexual behavior between the ages of three and four years. There is also the beginning of social-level difference in attitudes at this time. The ease or embarrassment with which children at this age discuss the genitals, excretory functions, the origin of babies, and other matters related to sex suggests that the child has already acquired some of the influences of the social attitudes. Social approval and disapproval mean so much to a child at this time that he will avoid doing anything that will expose him to ridicule or criticism. Traditional attitudes toward heterosexual and homosexual relationships are apparent as early as this (Kinsey et al., 1948).

Clothing. The young child discovers that clothing attracts attention to himself. Adults make favorable comments about his clothes, and his playmates not only admire him but often envy him because of them. Children as young as three years of age not only notice one another's clothes, but they refer to the newness, the color, or any feature that is different in the clothing of other children (Murphy, 1937). New clothes have a special appeal for a young child, and he likes others to notice them. If they fail to do so, he calls their attention to his clothes with such comments as, "See my new hat" or

"I have new shoes." The first clothes of a particular type, especially when they are like the clothes of older children, such as the first black shoes or the first long trousers, are worn with intense pride. To the young child, they are insignia of growing up (Macaulay, 1929).

FAMILY RELATIONSHIPS

The young child's environment is limited to the family circle except for short periods of time when he is with neighborhood children or in nursery school. As is true of the baby, the young child's attitudes toward people, things, and life in general are patterned by his home life. This is well illustrated in behavior problems. Eating problems of young children, for example, are characteristically found in young children whose family situation involves domestic discord, an immature mother, or an ineffectual, undependable father (Lurie, 1941). A study of mother-child relationships showed how much effect the mother's influence has on the behavior of the child in his relationships with other children. The mother is anxious to develop in her child certain types of behavior which are compatible with her own standards. This she does by such methods as bribery, punishments, rewards, or other methods. Young children, in their social relationships with others, show much the same patterns of behavior as those they have observed in their family relationships (Bishop, 1951). The child, at this early age, reflects so clearly in his own behavior the behavior of his parent that it is almost possible to know what the personality of the parent is by observing the behavior of the child.

At this age, the child begins to be aware of his status in the family. If he is the first-born, he is likely to feel insecure after the arrival of one or two other children in the family. Not only is more expected of him than before, but he feels that the newcomer is usurping his place in the affections of his parents. To find out how a child reacts when a sibling is born, a case study was made of a child after the arrival of a baby brother. All changes in the child's behavior that were attributable to the baby were noted. It was found that the child tried out a variety of adaptive behavior patterns to adjust to the change in her environment. Vigorous aggression toward the baby was not seen at first, but later, direct and less violent aggressions appeared. The aggressions were directed mostly toward the parents, especially following some frustration induced by the parents. A notable finding was the speed with which the child changed her modes of behavior (Anonymous, 1949).

Should the child be a second- or a later-born child, he may find himself playing the role of the family pet, with attention from older brothers and sisters as well as from his parents. More likely, however, he will discover that his older siblings resent his presence and show it by treating him as if he were a nuisance. Not only will his immediate family play an important role in shaping his personality at this age, but his *relatives*, especially his maternal grandparents, will be influential factors in his life. While he is still young and needs constant attention, relatives will be called upon from time to time to take charge of him while his parents are away from home. Their

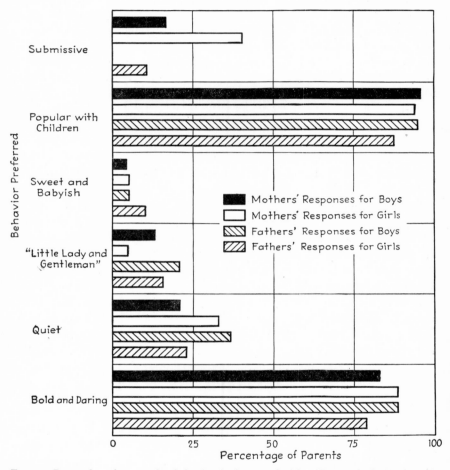

FIG. 18. Parental preferences for behavior in boys and girls. (*From M. J. Radke, The relation of parental authority to children's behavior and attitudes. Minneapolis: Univ. Minnesota Press, 1946. Used by permission.*)

influence, then, will be important in his life. Changes in parental attitudes toward the child come in early childhood. No longer is he the helpless infant who is soft and cuddly as he was when he was a baby. Now he is a rebellious, self-assertive, mischievous individual who is constantly into everything, demanding attention, and refusing to do what he is asked to do unless it strikes his fancy.

The changes that occur in parental attitudes toward the child at this age are reflected in their behavior toward the child. There is less warmth and affection in the parent-child relationship than existed during babyhood. This change is well illustrated in the way the young child responds to parental caresses. While the baby accepts gladly the caresses from his parents, except when held so tightly that he tries to free himself by vigorous kicks and cries, the young child frequently runs away when his parents or other relatives try to caress him. If the caresses are continued after the child attempts to escape, there is an increase in aggressiveness on the part of the child. This he shows by biting, kicking, and hitting. The child will usually accept more caresses when he is sleepy than when he is wide awake and anxious to be active (Wolfle, 1949). While rejection of parental caresses is a normal reaction on the part of young children, it is frequently misunderstood by parents and leads to hurt feelings which, in turn, are reflected in their changed attitude toward the child. Parental expectations of childish behavior are illustrated in Fig. 18.

Preference for Parent. Because the mother spends more time with the young child than the father does and because mothers as a rule have a better understanding of the troublesome behavior of young children than fathers do, young children generally prefer the mother to the father (Nimkoff, 1942). While children of both sexes show a greater preference for their mothers than for their fathers, more girls than boys at this age place their fathers first in their affection (Mott, 1937). The explanation for this may be that fathers are more tolerant of their daughters than of their sons. Both boys and girls show a definite preference for the father when the mother punishes them and vice versa. They prefer the mother for such activities as bathing them or reading to them, and the father for playing with them (Ammons and Ammons, 1949).

PERSONALITY

The pattern of the child's personality, the foundations of which were laid in babyhood, begins to take form and shape in early childhood. The stable, secure, and adaptable child is happy; the unstable one is insecure, lacks adaptability, and is generally troublesome (Rand, Sweeny, and Vincent, 1942). By the time the child enters school, the pattern of his personality can be readily distinguished. Some children are leaders, some are helpers, others are despotic and tyrannize over others, some like to show off, some like to tease and joke, while others are solitary and shun their associates (C. Bühler, 1935). Sex differences appear as early as three years of age, with girls showing stronger reactions to emotional stimuli than boys and making better adjustments to emotional situations than boys do (Klopfer, 1939). Boys, in their play, show more aggressions than girls. When girls do show aggressions, they take the form of producing psychological rather than physical harm (Sears, 1951).

Because young children are anxious to win adult approval and show little concern about the attitude of their contemporaries, they strive to develop personality traits of which adults approve. And, because the adult-approved pattern of personality is characterized by traits that make the child a "perfect little lady" or a "perfect little gentleman," most young children are reasonably polite, agreeable, cooperative, and tractable. This pattern, however, will not prove to be acceptable several years later when the child becomes group-conscious. As a result, he will change and will try to conform to a pattern approved by his contemporaries.

Persistence of Personality Traits. Genetic studies of the same children over a period of time have shown that the pattern of personality remains persistently uniform (Stutsman, 1935). Because of this fact, it is possible to predict with a high degree of accuracy what a child's future personality is likely to be from the pattern established in the early childhood years (Gesell *et al.*, 1939; Fries, 1937; Fries and Lewi, 1938). In spite of the persistence of personality traits, it is possible, at this early age, to eliminate habits and attitudes which predispose a child to act in a socially unacceptable manner. In young children, the core of personality, or the "center of gravity," which is made up of habits and attitudes relating to the child himself and his relationship to other people, can be changed because it is not yet well established. Changing it will not disturb the total personality balance as it is likely to do when the child is older (Breckenridge and Vincent, 1943).

For this reason, it is of crucial importance to see that the environment of a young child is such that undesirable attitudes will not be established. Should any appear, such as the feeling of being unwanted, unloved, or inferior to others, this is the time to nip them in the bud. Parent-child and sibling relationships are of great importance at this age because it is from these relationships that the child builds up the attitudes that eventually form the core of his personality structure. The impact on him of his parents' personality and their attitudes toward him and his training are important in determining what his personality will be (Lerner and Murphy, 1941). It is the mother especially who leaves her imprint on the personality of her child because of her constant association with him (Shirley, 1941).

It is likewise of great importance, as was pointed out earlier in the chapter, that the child's first contacts with other children be of a pleasant sort. Otherwise, he will develop unfavorable attitudes about himself. He is likely also to shun social relationships in the future and to build up compensations of an unsocial sort. Among young children, certain aspects of personality do change, partly as a result of advancing maturity, partly from experience, partly from the social and cultural environment in which he lives, and partly from factors within himself, such as emotional pressures, or identification with people

(Fenton, 1943). A difficult child may become more tractable just as a happy, contented child may develop into a sullen one as he grows older (Bayley, 1940). Attempts have been made to change, under experimental conditions, undesirable personality traits in young children. These changes come about from changes in the child's environment and from direct instruction in the development of desired traits.

To increase self-confidence, for example, nursery-school children were trained in such skills as assembling a mosaic of blocks and learning to know a storybook. Self-confidence acquired from these newly developed skills was then shown in greater interest in directing the activities of other children, in maintaining their own property rights, and in attempting to dominate other children (Jack, 1934). Of even greater significance is the fact that the effects of training are cumulative. Self-confidence increased in one or more skills encourages the child to try to learn other skills and this increases his self-confidence even further (Jack, 1934, p. 1936). Undesirable traits can likewise be weakened or eliminated with training. Children who show immature reactions to failure, such as giving up, asking for help, or rationalizing, can, with training in tasks of graded difficulty which make it possible for them to achieve success most of the time, overcome these immature reactions (Updegraff and Keister, 1937).

CHAPTER 6

Late Childhood
(Six to Twelve Years)

Late childhood extends from the age of six years to the onset of puberty which begins roughly at the age of twelve years in American children of today. This period has been called by various names, each describing one outstanding characteristic of the developmental level present at this time. According to educators, this is the "elementary-school age." Parents regard it as the "smart," or "Big Injun," age, when the child thinks he knows everything and does not hesitate to inform others of his superior knowledge. They also regard it as the "dirty age" because the child glories in being dirty, slovenly, and careless in his appearance.

To the psychologist, this is the "gang age" because, at this time, the major concern of every normal boy or girl is to be accepted by his contemporaries and to be regarded as a member of a "gang." H. L. Hollingworth has suggested that this is the "moron hurdle" over which the individual must pass and make satisfactory adjustments to adult life. The impulsiveness and lack of foresight, so characteristic of the moron, are equally characteristic of the older child. He cannot see beyond his nose and he acts on the impulse of the moment, regardless of the consequences.

PHYSICAL DEVELOPMENT

Late childhood is a period of slow and relatively uniform growth. With the onset of puberty between the tenth and twelfth years, the child's *height* is $2\frac{3}{4}$ times that at birth, or approximately 55 inches. This means a gain of between 2 and 3 inches annually throughout the period of late childhood. During this time, boys are slightly taller than girls. Bright children are taller, on the average, than are those of average or below-average intelligence (Hollingworth, 1926).

Weight increases are likewise slow and fairly uniform at this age. Boys are generally heavier than girls of the same age and bright children are slightly heavier than those who are less intelligent (Hollingworth, 1926). Children of the higher socioeconomic groups are generally taller and heavier than children from the poorer groups (Hopkins, 1947). Children who are heavy at birth maintain this tendency in comparison with other children (Ilg *et al.*, 1949). This is the age at which children who make poor social adjustments frequently turn to overeating as a compensation for lack of social acceptance. As a result, they become obese and lose out in active play, thus lacking the necessary opportunity to acquire the social skills so essential to social success (Bruch, 1943).

Body proportions change during the late childhood years. While the head is still proportionally too large for the rest of the body, the disproportions decrease slightly at this time. At the age of twelve years, for example, the surface area of the head is approximately 10 per cent of the total body surface as compared with 13 per cent at five years (Boyd, 1935). The circumference of the head is 95 per cent of adult size at the age of twelve years. With the gradual eruption of permanent teeth throughout this period, the mouth changes and the lower part of the face increases in size, thus eliminating some of the facial disproportion that existed in the earlier years of life (Allen, 1948). During this time, the nose also enlarges and acquires more shape, owing to the development of the cartilage framework. This helps to eliminate the facial expression of a young child. The trunk elongates and becomes slimmer. There is approximately 50 per cent increase in body length at this time. By the age of eight years, the arms and legs are nearly 50 per cent longer than they were at two years and are very thin with no marked development in the musculature. This is responsible for the spindly, all-arms, all-legs look of the older child. The hands and feet grow very slowly in late childhood.

This is a homely age. Very pretty babies and young children go through this homely stage just as do those who are not so attractive. In the case of the former, however, they generally emerge from this homeliness and blossom into attractive boys and girls. There are a number of reasons for the unattractiveness of the older child's appearance, most important of which are the transition from baby teeth to permanent teeth; stringy, unmanageable hair which results from the transition from the fine-textured hair of the young child to the coarser-textured hair of the adolescent; spindly arms and legs which give the child a young-colt appearance; and poor grooming which comes from the child's lack of interest in his appearance and his revolt against cleanliness, which he associates with "sissies."

Illnesses. During the early part of this period, most children are subjected to different children's *diseases,* as measles, mumps, chicken pox, and whooping cough. Aside from these diseases, late childhood is normally a very healthy age. There may be an occasional stomach upset caused by indiscreet eating, or a cold resulting from the child's refusal to protect himself adequately from rain or snow. These, however, are only transitory and rarely have any serious effect on the child's physical well-being. Accidents are likewise common at this age with boys suffering from more accidents than girls (Hanlon *et al.,* 1949). Poor health conditions, as evidenced in underweight, poor posture, rounded shoulders, bowlegs, and carious teeth, are more common than good health in children of the lower-income classes (Hardy *et al.,* 1941).

The physical defects that have the most pronounced influence on the child's schoolwork are diseased tonsils, serious eye defects, and malnutrition (Woofter, 1940). Defects, showing a decreasing incidence as children grow older, are of the teeth, tonsils, speech, and ears. Those that show an increase with age include defects of vision, nutrition, heart and orthopedic defects (Maxwell and Brown, 1948). Late childhood is the age when *imaginary illness* is not uncommon. The child has learned, from earlier experiences, that when he is ill he is not expected to carry on his usual activities, he receives more attention than usual, and the home discipline is markedly relaxed. When distressing or intolerable conditions exist in the child's life, he may use a trifling illness as a means of gaining outside help. Complaints of illness are thus used to ameliorate these conditions (Preston, 1940).

MOTOR DEVELOPMENT

Because motor skills play such an important role in the child's success in school and in his play with other children, the child whose motor development lags behind that of other children of his age is greatly handicapped. This lag is generally the result of too little opportunity to establish the necessary foundation skills during the earlier years of his life, or to too little opportunity for practice in the skills which his contemporaries consider essential. Given an opportunity, most children take keen delight in motor activity of all sorts. They are healthy, full of energy, and anxious to be on the go constantly. They are willing to practice endlessly to achieve success and they show great pride in their accomplishments, especially if these are recognized favorably by their friends. The only exception to this is when practice requires segregation from the group, as in the case of piano practice. There is then a conflict between the child's desire to be with his friends and his desire to acquire the necessary skill in playing the piano to be able to amuse himself or to win recognition from his friends.

Obesity may be a cause of delayed motor development. In a group of obese children, only 18 per cent of the boys and 22½ per cent of the girls showed the normal degree of activity for their ages, though the younger children tended to be more active than the older. This resulted in a marked delay in ability and willingness to take care of themselves and to take part in active games. Of the group, more than half had difficulties in making social contacts. A majority of the obese sought entertainment in frequenting the movies, persistent listening to the radio, and reading comic strips (Bruch, 1940).

By the age of six years, a child should be able to take complete charge of all the activities needed for *eating, dressing,* and *bathing.* Only occasionally will he need any outside help though the end results may not be up to adult standards. His clothes, for example, may not always be on straight, he may occasionally spill food on the table, and he may not remove all the dirt from the back of his neck or other difficult areas of the body. Gradually, however, these routine skills will become perfected so that the child should be able to perform them with as much speed and excellence as the adult. At school, the older child learns to write, to form numerals, to paint, to draw, to use tools, to sing, and to dance. Day-in and day-out practice of these skills improves their quality and speed. Only when self-consciousness, resulting from a hypercritical attitude toward his achievements, enters into the situation does the child show a tendency to make no improvement in these skills. Unilateral, right-hand preference predominates at the age of six years. The seven-year-old may use his left hand or both hands occasionally in carrying out some activity. From then on, unilateral right-hand preference predominates (Gesell and Ames, 1947).

Problems associated with *change in hand dominance,* from left- to right-handedness, depend on such factors as the completeness of the left-handedness, on the attitude of the child and of others toward his left-handedness, and on attempts at change. Children who lack dominant handedness are more likely to have reading disabilities than are children who are definitely left-handed. Speech defects, defects in writing, reading and spelling difficulties, awkwardness and poor coordination are also common accompaniments of lack of hand dominance. When a child is strongly left-handed, he generally resists conversion successfully and suffers only as he finds himself different from the group. If teased and chided, he may develop feelings of inferiority which are increased by his clumsiness and awkwardness (Bakwin, 1950).

Skills. Throughout late childhood, new forms of skilled performance utilize already present skills in new forms. Old skills are perfected and this results in smoother movements, greater speed and accuracy, and more grace. Because most of the child's play involves skill, such as skating, swimming, and ball play, the child makes rapid strides in the acquisition of all kinds of skills. Children who develop superior skills show superiority also in their schoolwork and social adjustments (Rarick and McKee, 1949). What skills will be acquired in late childhood will depend primarily upon the child's environment, his opportunity for learning, and what is in vogue among his classmates. At this age, marked sex differences exist not only in play skills but also in the level of the perfection of these skills. Boys, for example, are superior to girls in the 35-yard dash, basketball throw, the standing and running broad jump for distance, and soccer kick for distance, while girls surpass boys in the 50-foot hop (Jenkins, 1930). Girls, as a rule, surpass boys in skills involving finer muscles, such as painting, sewing, weaving, and hammering.

SPEECH DEVELOPMENT

Vocabulary. Throughout late childhood, the child's general vocabulary grows by leaps and bounds. From his studies in school, his reading, listening to other people, and his interest in words that leads him to look up in the dictionary words whose meanings are unfamiliar to him, the child builds up a vocabulary which he uses in his speech and writing. Children with reading disabilities tend to be inferior to normal speakers in their vocabulary development (Yedinack, 1949). As is true of every age, his comprehension vocabulary exceeds his use vocabulary. He knows the meaning of many words in a vague way and can understand them when they are used in combination with other words. But he does not know them well enough to hazard using them himself.

Special Vocabularies. Words with special meanings and limited use are also learned at this age. The older child, who has had little opportunity to acquire an adequate vocabulary in early childhood, learns after he goes to school the words which are in common usage in his school environment. By the end of the first grade, if not before, his *etiquette* vocabulary should be as large as that of the adults of his environment. Girls, as a general rule, have larger *color* vocabularies than boys because of the girls' greater interest in colors. Not only the common color words, such as red, blue, and black, but also many of the unusual color names as they are used commercially creep into the older child's vocabulary (Synolds and Pronko, 1949; Pronko *et al.,* 1949). From the study of arithmetic and his out-of-school contacts with money, the older child learns the names and meanings of *numbers* and different denominations of *money.* While the true significance of words relating to large numbers may not be fully appreciated, the child knows in a vague way what they mean. His *time* vocabulary likewise increases and is generally as large as that of the adults with whom he comes in contact.

Slang and *swear words* become important parts of the older child's vocabulary. No longer does he use such words in a parrotlike fashion as the younger child does. Now, such words are used to express thoughts and feelings for which he has no other adequate means of expression. A few adjectives in popular use at the time, such as "lousy," to describe things he does not like, and "swell," for all he likes, takes the place of descriptive words still unknown to him. These words he learns from older brothers and sisters or high-school students in the neighborhood. He thus identifies himself with older children and this gives him a feeling of self-importance. Another source of satisfaction comes from the shocked reaction of his parents and other adults to such language. The more shocked they are, the more triumphant the child. Girls, as a rule, use less slang and less obnoxious forms of slang than do boys. To the typical boy, the rougher the language, the better he likes it and the more he feels that it distinguishes him from girls. Boys take keen delight in using slang and swearing at times when they will attract attention (Melville, 1912; Kasser, 1945). The social environment of the child plays a far less important role in determining the amount and kind of slang he uses at this age than it did during the preschool years. Late childhood is a "slang age," and few children escape using the slang that is in vogue at the time.

A new form of language makes its appearance in late childhood. This is *secret language,* which is used in the child's communication with his intimate friends. He develops this type of language so that others will not learn his secrets. Secret language may take the form of distorting his own speech or he may imitate the secret language used by older children. Like different forms of play, secret language is passed down from one generation of children to another in the same neighborhood. Figure 19 illustrates some typical forms of "secret language." Secret language may be written, verbal, or kinetic. *Written forms* consist of codes formed by symbols or crude drawings to express words or complete thoughts. The common verbal forms are generally known as "pig Latin" or "pidgin English." *Kinetic language* usually consists of the use of gestures and the formation of words by the means of the fingers, as in the language of the deaf and dumb. Girls use secret language more frequently than do boys and they spend more time developing new symbols and word signs than do boys. From ten years of age until early adolescence is the peak of the secret-language age, though most children start to use secret language in some form from the time they enter the third grade.

Sentences. The six-year-old child should have command of nearly every kind of sentence structure. From then until he is nine or ten years old, the length of his sentences will increase (Davis, 1937). These long sentences, so characteristic of children, are generally rambling and loosely knit together. Gradually, after the age of nine years, sentences become shorter and more compact. When conversing with other children, the child uses many phrases instead of complete sentences (Maddock, 1947). Because sentence construction is difficult for a child, *grammatical errors* are very common even at this age. The number and seriousness of these errors will vary, however, according to the correctness or incorrectness of the speech the child hears at home or among his playmates.

Pronunciation. Except in cases where a child has a speech defect of one sort or another, errors in pronunciation are uncommon at this age. A new word may be incorrectly pronounced the first time it is used but, after hearing a correct pronunciation of it once or twice, the child is generally able to pronounce it correctly. The older child does, however, have a tendency to talk at the top of his lungs and to shout as if he thought everyone were deaf. This is not only disagreeable for those who must listen to his shouting, but it also has a tendency to coarsen the tonal quality of his voice. Boys are especially given to shouting because they think a quiet, pleasant, modulated voice is a sign of a "sissy."

Speech disorders are far less likely to begin in late childhood than in early childhood.. However, stuttering, stammering, and slurring, which may have

Fig. 19. Secret language. (*From C. Brownstone, Why children's secret language? Parents' Magazine, May, 1940. Illustrations by Dorothea Warren. Used by permission.*)

started several years earlier, will likely grow worse as time goes on unless remedial measures are taken to correct them. Because these all trace their origins to nervous tension, they are likely to grow worse rather than better after the child enters school, owing to the child's embarrassment when other children laugh at his "funny speech." Except when there is some physical cause, such as a space between the two front upper teeth or malocclusion of the jaws which makes correct pronunciation of the *s, z,* and *r* sounds impossible, few children lisp by the time they reach school age.

Content of Speech. The older child's speech is less egocentric than it was during the preschool years. Favorite topics of conversation, when children are with their contemporaries, consist of talk about their own experiences, home, family and friends, games and sports, animals, trips, and accidents (Zyve, 1927; Dawson, 1937; Maddock, 1947). The younger child of school age is more generally interested and will talk about things of a personal sort than is the older child. The conversations of older children concentrate on a smaller number of topics and they talk less and less about their families and more and more about outside interests. When the older child talks about himself, it is usually in the form of *boasting.* Unlike the younger child, he boasts less about material possessions than about his skill and strength in games. Boasting, as a rule, is very common between the ages of nine and twelve years, especially among boys. The older child also likes to *criticize* and to *make fun* of other people. Sometimes a criticism is to them personally, sometimes behind their backs. When criticizing adults, the child generally puts his criticism in the form of a suggestion of complaint, as "Why don't you do so and so?" or "You won't let me do what my friends do." Criticism of other children frequently takes the form of name calling, teasing, or insults. Questions, answers, commands, and directions are other common categories of the older child's speech (Maddock, 1947).

EMOTIONAL DEVELOPMENT

The older child soon discovers that violent expressions of emotions, especially of the unpleasant emotions, are socially unacceptable to his contemporaries. They regard temper outbursts as "babyish"; withdrawal reactions in fear as indicative of a " 'fraid cat"; and hurting another in jealousy as poor sportsmanship. Hence a child acquires a strong motivation to learn to control the outward expressions of his emotions. While the child may be just as furiously angry or jealous as he was when he was younger, he does not show these emotions by facial expressions or actions except when he knows the group is with him and will not show disapproval of his behavior. Among healthy children, late childhood is characterized by fewer emotional disturbances and less emotionality than any other period (Dingwall, 1949).

At home, however, there is not the same strong motivation to control his emotions. As a result, the child frequently expresses his emotions as forcibly as he did when he was younger. Under such circumstances, it is not surprising that parents regard the child's behavior as "babyish" and criticize or punish him for "not acting his age." Toward the close of late childhood, between the ages of ten and twelve years, there is a period of heightened emotionality. This is caused partly by an excess of energy resulting from slow physical growth, partly from physical well-being, and partly from the social restraints on the child's behavior which cause him to literally, "burst with energy" at times.

Characteristically the emotional expressions are pleasant. The child giggles or laughs uproariously, squirms, twitches, or even rolls on the rug, and in general shows a release of pent-up animal spirits. Not all emotionality at this age, however, is of a pleasant sort. Numerous outbursts of temper and jealousy likewise occur. Girls frequently dissolve into tears when they are angry or they hit, kick, and throw anything within their reach if they are thwarted in what they want to do. Boys, on the other hand, are more likely to express their annoyance by being sullen and sulky. Children who come from homes of low social status have been found to be more unstable emotionally than those who come from good, middle-class homes (Springer, 1938).

Common Emotions. Fear is less common among older children than among the younger. Many objects, situations, animals, and people which terrify young children are accepted calmly by older children. Fears of fire, darkness, illness, disease, doctors, dentists, operations, being hit by a car, and being bitten by a dog are most common at this age (Pratt, 1945; England, 1946). Girls show more fears of different things than do boys (Pratt, 1945). Concrete, rather than imaginary, fears predominate at this age. While fears aroused by concrete and tangible stimuli decrease with age, there is a marked increase in the frequency of fears of imaginary, fanciful, supernatural, or remote dangers; of the dark and imaginary creatures associated with the dark; of matters associated with corpses and death; of boogies and other imaginary creatures; and of characters recalled from stories and pictures (Jersild and Holmes, 1935).

Worries, or fears caused by imaginary stimuli, begin to make their appearance at this age. Family or school problems, problems related to personal and social adjustments, and health, are the most common worries of older children (Pintner and Lev, 1940). School worries, such as failing a test, being late for school, or being left behind in school, are more common than out-of-school worries (Jersild *et al.,* 1941). Girls worry more than boys, especially about school and safety (Zeligs, 1945). Generalized anxiety, however, is more common than any one specific worry (Cummings, 1944).

ANGER. There are more anger-provoking situations in late childhood than in early childhood because the older child has a stronger desire for independence than he had when he was younger and, therefore, is more frequently frustrated in his efforts to achieve this independence than is the more docile younger child. The older child also becomes angry when an activity in progress is interrupted, when he is constantly criticized, when unfavorable comparisons with other children are made, and when he is "lectured." It also annoys him to be blamed for something he did not do, to see someone else cheat or do unfair things, to be punished for something he did not do, or to be accused of lying. And, finally, he becomes angry more often than the young child does from his own ineptitude. He frequently sets levels of aspirations beyond his capacity and, when his achievements fall short of these goals, it makes him angry. Boys are easily irritated by such inconveniences and annoyances as flat tires on their bicycles, doing things they do not want to do, disappointments, and not getting what was promised them. Girls, on the other hand, are most frequently annoyed when they lose or break something, when they are not permitted to play out of doors, when they have their hair pulled, or when they are punched (Zeligs, 1941, 1945).

Instead of flying off the handle in a temper tantrum as a young child does, the older child expresses his anger in sulkiness, negativism, refusal to speak, quarrelsomeness, fussiness, and being generally disagreeable to everyone about everything. The tendency to quarrel, especially with siblings, reaches its peak between the ages of ten and twelve years and then decreases. When an older child expresses his anger in a manner characteristic of younger children, he generally wins the disapproval of other children and finds himself no longer acceptable to the group. Social pressures are thus primarily responsible for changing the form in which anger expresses itself among older children.

JEALOUSY. Sibling jealousy does not die out when the child enters school. Sometimes, however, it is intensified because the child feels that, during his absence from home, the younger child has the whole of his mother's attention while he is among unfriendly strangers. The school child may, if he has experienced jealousy at home, transfer his jealousy to his classmates, especially toward those who are popular or who excel in studies or sports. Instead of the bodily attacks on the child who seems to hold the center of adult attention, as is characteristic of young children, the older child shows his jealousy directly through quarreling, telling tales, ridiculing, teasing, bullying, making disparaging comments, or instigating quarrels. He may express his jealously indirectly by ignoring the child of whom he is jealous, by sarcastic comments, or by engaging in daydreams of the "martyr" type. Identification and sublimation through creative activities are also used as expressions of jealousy at this age (Vollmer, 1946).

JOY. As children grow older, much the same things arouse pleasant emotions as when the child was younger. They never fail to smile or laugh at incongruous situations, violations of conventions, absurdities, slight calamities, sudden or unexpected noises, or anything that seems out of place in the situation in which they are. Their laughter is intensified when they are feeling physically fit. As comprehension of words increases, the child gets more pleasure from play on words and from jokes than he did when he was younger. He is now able to laugh at his own predicament, though he may laugh less at his own achievements than he did when he was younger (Wilson, 1931). On the whole, older children laugh less and smile more than they did when they were younger. Laughing is more frequent when the child is with his contemporaries than when he is alone or with adults (Brackett, 1933, 1934).

Furthermore, it is a highly consistent pattern of behavior. The child who laughs most during play situations, for example, expresses himself in the same manner during routine situations. Children, on the other hand, who laugh little when they are with others, are consistently quiet and sober when they are engaged in routine activities. Expressions of joy are much more controlled in older than in younger children. While the young child may show his pleasure by clapping his hands, jumping up and down in glee, or even by rolling on the floor, the older child rarely behaves in this way because he learns that his contemporaries consider such behavior "infantile." He does, however, show his glee in loud, raucous laughter. Frequently boys slap their companions on the back or head when they are particularly happy, and girls may throw their arms around a friend, hug, and kiss her as expressions of their joy.

AFFECTION. Affection is expressed very slightly by older children. Boys feel that they are "too old" to be kissed or hugged and they are likely to be embarrassed when anyone, even a member of the family, demonstrates any affection for them, especially if the demonstrations are in public. They even resent being called by names of endearment. While girls are not so restrained as boys in this respect, they too dislike being "fussed over" by anyone. And, because both boys and girls dislike people to show affection for them, they are very undemonstrative in their relations with others. They are far more likely to show affection for a pet animal than they are for a person. Their affection for people, however, is shown indirectly by their desire to be constantly with those whom they love, to do things to help them, or to assist them in any way they possibly can. This is especially apparent in the child's reactions to his friends. He wants to be with them constantly. When he is away from them, he tries to keep in close touch with them, by telephone conversations, or by letter writing.

CURIOSITY. Curiosity is not so strong in the older child as in the younger. This may be explained partially by the fact that there is less for the older child to explore because he is already familiar with the commonplace things in his daily life and partly because he has learned from experience that curiosity can get him into trouble and that it is best to check it. The older child is, however, curious about new things that appear in his environment and about those things which, when he was younger, he was not permitted to explore, such as matches, old trunks in the attic, or how the gas stove works. As his environment widens to include areas in the community beyond his immediate neighborhood, his curiosity leads him to explore the new and unfamiliar things in these areas.

The older child uses much the same ways of satisfying his curiosity as he did when he was younger. He examines things that mystify him and he frequently takes them apart to see how they work. Because his motor coordination has improved and his experience has taught him how to handle things with minimum damage, he is far less destructive than he was when he was younger. As a result, there are fewer restraints placed on his exploration than there were earlier. In addition to direct explorations, the older child asks innumerable questions to supplement what he has been able to learn for himself. But, unlike the younger child, he does not have to limit his questions to his parents. He can seek information from teachers, relatives, any adults he comes in contact with, or even from older children.

He soon discovers which ones can and which ones cannot or will not answer his questions and, therefore, limits his questioning to those who give him the greatest satisfaction. And, finally, the older child can draw upon the resources of his school or community library for information. No longer must he rely upon someone to read to him or to furnish him with books. By the time he reaches the third grade, he reads well enough to get meaning out of what he has read. From then on, reading as a source of information becomes increasingly important to him. And, with freedom to select what he wants to read, he can turn his attention to books which contain information that will supplement what he has been able to obtain from direct exploration or from answers to his questions.

SOCIAL DEVELOPMENT

Interest in peer activities, an increasingly strong desire to be an accepted member of the gang, and discontentment away from the gang have given the name "the gang age" * to the closing years of childhood. At this time, social development is taking place rapidly and the child quickly passes from the self-centered, selfish individual, whose social contacts are characterized by constant disagreements and fights, to the point where he is a cooperative, well-adjusted member of a social group composed of his peers. Learning to live in a social world is hard for the child, especially so if he has not had a good preliminary training for it at home during the early years of his life. When a group of adults was asked to recall unpleasant experiences at different times in growing up, it was found that a predominance of these were for the years six to twelve, and were related to unpleasant memories of

* "Gang," as used in the following discussion, refers to a specific type of social grouping characteristic of the late childhood years. The childhood gang is not made up of hoodlums whose primary interest is in mischief-making but rather of boys or girls of the same age whose primary interest is in having a good time together.

learning to live in a social world, as being forced to do unpleasant things, feelings of guilt, being verbally disciplined, being teased and ridiculed, and fighting with friends (Thompson and Witryol, 1948).

No longer is the child satisfied to play at home alone or to do things with members of his family. Even one or two friends are not enough for him. He wants to be with the "gang" because only then will there be a sufficient number of individuals to play the games he now enjoys and to give the excitement to his play which solitary play or play with another child lacks. From the time the child enters school until the physical changes at puberty begin to develop, the desire to be with and to be accepted by the gang becomes increasingly strong. This is just as true of girls as of boys. The greater home restrictions placed upon the girl's behavior and the increasingly heavy burden of home duties frequently keep the girl from taking as active a part in "gang" life as boys of the same age enjoy.

Gangs. Gangs are normal social groupings of the late childhood years. They are not to be confused with lawless groups of adolescents nor should they be regarded as having a bad influence over the child. If, however, they persist beyond childhood when "gangs" generally give way to a new form of social grouping, the "crowd," there is likely to be a trend toward lawlessness on the part of gang members that falls into the category of juvenile delinquency. Typically, the childhood gang is composed of individuals of the same sex. When a boys' gang contains one or more girls, the girls are typical tomboys. A boy who belongs to a girls' gang is a "sissy" who does not fit into a gang of boys. The gang is held together by a common interest in games and sports and there must, therefore, be an adequate number of members to make up the team. In areas where there are few or no facilities for team play, gangs are likely to turn their energies into mischief-making channels.

The gang generally has some central meeting place where each member is sure to find some of his gangmates when they are not in school. This meeting place may be a street corner, a garage, the cellar of a home, a barn, a vacant lot, a deserted house, or the corner drugstore. Boys, as a rule, have their meeting place as far away as possible from parental supervision and interference. Girls, on the other hand, are likely to have their gang headquarters in the home of one of the gang members where there is a minimum of interference from the family, where they can talk without fear of being overheard, and where they have both space and freedom to do as they please. While gang activities vary from community to community, and within the given community, according to the socioeconomic group from which the gang members come, there is a marked similarity in gang activities. Games and sports of all kinds, going to the movies or to athletic contests, picnics, parties, camping, exploring the community, or just sitting around and talking are perennial favorites.

Boys' gangs are, as a rule, more likely to turn their energies into trouble-making than are girls' gangs. They like to torment girls and break up their activities, they enjoy annoying elderly people or fussy neighbors and, in areas of the community which provide few opportunities for wholesome recreation, they frequently spend their time gambling, smoking, drinking, or stealing. Even in good neighborhoods, gangs are likely to become noisy and rowdy. Each individual tries to be heard and noticed, with the result that bedlam generally prevails when the gang gets together. And, frequently, when children get together in a gang, they do things which few individuals would do if alone. The motivating force back of this rowdiness is more often the desire to let off pent-up steam and to have a good time than intentional disobedience or annoyance to others.

INFLUENCE OF GANG. Because it is of vital importance to the child to be an accepted member of a gang, he becomes very susceptible to the suggestions of the members. Insecure in his status and afraid that he will be rejected by the gang unless he conforms wholeheartedly to the standards set by its members, the child bends over backward to be like his gangmates in dress, opinions, and behavior. When a conflict arises between parental standards and those of the group, the child is likely to conform to the latter rather than to the former. Because the influence of the gang is so marked, it should be readily apparent that every possible effort should be made to see to it that the gang to which the child belongs is composed of other children whose background and training are similar in their major aspects to his. This will not only help to reduce the amount of friction that otherwise is inevitable in the home, but it will increase the child's feeling of security and of belonging.

From his contacts with the gang, the child learns to compete with others, to cooperate and work as a member of a team, to accept responsibilities and to see them through, to take the part of others when they are mistreated or neglected, and to be a good sport in adversity as well as in success. This training in socialization, which can be derived through no other medium than day-in, day-out contact with his peers, is of far more value to the child not only in childhood but throughout the remaining years of his life, than the temporary disturbance to parent-child relationships which this training is likely to engender.

Companions. Both boys and girls at this age definitely prefer the companionship of individuals of their own sex. Girls show a more tolerant attitude toward boys than boys show toward girls and, were it not for the hypercritical, "we are superior" attitude on the part of the boys, they would accept them as part of their groups. Boys, however, treat girls with such scorn and contempt for their "weakness" and "silliness" that they put the girls on the defensive. As a result, the battle of the sexes begins to rage. The older child's companions are almost exclusively members of his own sex. With increase in chronological age, there is a trend toward greater stability in friendships (Horrocks and Bulser, 1951).

Studies of large groups of children at different ages from the first through the sixth or seventh grades have shown what factors play the most important roles in the child's selection of friends. Propinquity in the school or neighborhood is important in childhood because, unlike the adolescent or the adult, the child is limited to a relatively small area in the selection of his friends. It has been found that the mean distance between the homes of friends is 0.26 mile as compared with 0.92 mile for children in the same grade who have no real ties of friendship. Furthermore, approximately three-quarters of all friendships are among individuals in the same grade in school (Seagoe, 1933). There is a strong tendency for children to choose as friends those whose chronological and mental ages are similar to their own (Pintner *et al.*, 1937). A wide age difference between two individuals would give them little in common, and hence a basis for a real friendship would be lacking.

Personality traits are likewise very important determining factors in the choice of friends. The personality traits that are most admired by other children at this age have been found to be cheerfulness, friendliness, kindness, cooperativeness, honesty, generosity, and even-temperedness (Austin and Thompson, 1948). Popular children show aggressive, socially overt behavior traits (Bonney, 1943). They are, on the whole, cooperative and adaptable to the group (Hardy, 1937; Lippitt, 1941). The child's reputation and the status he has in the group are based partly on his actual behavior and partly on the picture that people carry in their minds about the social group to which the child belongs (Morgan, 1946). The factors that influence the child's reputation are the level of his father's income, the degree of his success in school, length of residence in the community, place of residence in the community, and religious affiliation (Morgan, 1946).

Social isolates, or children who are socially unacceptable to their peers, are either of the quiet, reserved, withdrawn type or of the aggressive, "problem" type that antagonizes other children (Loeb, 1941). During the "gang age," when social acceptance depends upon the child's ability to adjust satisfactorily to the group, social isolates among boys are those who enjoy fights, try to act older than they are, sneak about, are talkative, or are restless. Girls who are unacceptable to their peers at this age are so because they try to boss others, are talkative, seek attention, enjoy fights, and are restless (Kuhlen and Lee, 1943). The unfortunate thing about unpopularity at this age is that it cuts the child off from social contacts at the very age when such contacts are of vital importance because of the opportunity they offer for the child to learn to make satisfactory adjustments to other children.

Leaders. While an aggressive, dominating child may force himself into the role of leader, these tactics will not work when the child becomes older. The leader of a gang represents the gang's ideal. In the case of boys, the boy must be a good athlete, a good sport, and an all-round superior individual. Because boys and girls of this age begin to hero-worship someone who possesses qualities they admire, the leader who can hold the respect of the gang and thus assure his popularity must be superior in most respects to the rest of the group, especially in intelligence, dependability, appearance, and athletic ability (Partridge, 1934). And this superiority must express itself. The quiet, introverted individual is likely to be overlooked and not selected as the leader, regardless of how many superior qualities he may possess. In all leaders, extroversion is more marked than introversion (Caldwell and Wellman, 1926).

PLAY

Late childhood is frequently called the "play age." This name is likely to be misleading because it suggests that more time than ever before is devoted to play. Consideration of the subject will quickly show that this would be impossible. The school child has far less time available for play than he had before he entered school. The name, "the play age," comes from the fact that there is, during this period, an overlapping of play activities characteristic of the younger years and those of adolescence. The older child clings to some of his favorite toys of the preschool years until he is eight or nine years old while, at the same time, he begins to show an active interest in the organized games and sports of the high-school or college student.

In spite of the decrease in total amount of time available for play with each successive year of childhood, there is an increase in the amount of time spent in the specific play activities. This is accounted for by the fact that the young child's concentration is poor and, hence, he goes from one toy to another or from one play activity to another. With each successive year, his ability to concentrate improves and, as a result, he can enjoy a specific play activity for a longer span of time. Another important change that takes place in the older child's play is the gradual increase in the formality of the play. No longer is the older child satisfied to play whenever it strikes his fancy as he formerly did. Now he must have a regular place in the home, a "game room," or, outside the home, a baseball diamond, a tennis court, or a football field. And these must be of regulation size, with proper equipment and clothing for that sport. And, finally, his play changes from the dramatic, make-believe form, so popular with preschool children, to a highly competitive type. He now regards dramatic play as "baby stuff" and craves the competition that identifies him with older groups.

For the first time in the child's life, socioeconomic differences are beginning to be apparent in the child's play. Children of different social-class backgrounds engage in leisure activities that are both quantitatively and qualitatively different. Among older children, the favored activities of those of the lowest economic group consist of going to the movies, radio, and church. By contrast, in the upper middle-class group, radio, church, movies, and family activities rank in first place. Children of the middle-class group participate more in organized recreational groups, such as the Scouts and YMCA, while those who come from the lower economic groups engage in activities mostly in centers or clubs for "underprivileged children" (McDonald *et al.*, 1949).

Constructive Play. Making things just for the fun of making them and with little forethought of the eventual use that may be made of their products is a popular form of play among older children. *Construction* with wood and tools appeals to boys, while girls prefer finer constructions, such as sewing, drawing, painting, clay modeling, and jewelry making. Arts, crafts, and woodwork are popular activities both in school and in camp.

Drawing, painting, and *clay modeling,* which young children engage in frequently and which they thoroughly enjoy, gradually decrease in popularity as childhood advances. This is not so much because the child loses interest in these activities but rather because of the self-consciousness that comes when he realizes that his production falls below that of other children or when it is criticized by his classmates or teacher. Except when the child is truly gifted, originality disappears very soon (Cappe, 1947). The crudeness and lack of originality in a typical child's drawings are shown in Fig. 20.

Among children in the first three grades, *drawing* takes the form of outlines of commonly experienced objects. At this age, the child tries to reproduce not what he sees but what he knows. Objects that are important to him are likely to be made proportionally too large in his drawings and he draws objects not ordinarily visible, such as the internal organs which may appear in the drawing on the surface of the body (Meier, 1939). After the age of eight years, transparency in the child's drawings is quite rare (Boussion-Leroy, 1950). Drawings of the comic-strip type are popular among children in grades four through six (Witty, 1941, 1941a). Boys are better than girls at reproducing proportions correctly, while girls devote more time than boys to ornamentation. At every age, children of high intelligence are superior in their drawing skills to those of the same age whose intellectual level is average or below average (Goodenough, 1926).

Singing, the most frequently engaged in form of musical expression, is another popular type of creative play. During the early school grades, school songs and folk songs are popular. With increasing age, there is an increased interest in folk, patriotic, holiday, religious, and class songs, as well as in the popular songs and dance music of the day (Boynton and Boynton, 1938). Children like songs of easily perceived tonal values and slow cadence because they are "singable" and can be enjoyed by all, regardless of musical ability. As is true of drawing, the child becomes self-conscious about his voice as he grows older and often abandons singing as a form of play. He sings only when he has to sing at school or when he knows that no one is listening to him.

Collecting. Collecting, which is a popular form of play among young children, increases in popularity as childhood progresses. Girls, as a rule, make more collections than do boys and they keep their collections in a more orderly form. The peak age for making collections generally comes at ten years for boys and a year later for girls, though among bright children the

FIG. 20. Typical drawings of a first-grade child. (*From M. M. Hughes and L. Stockdale, The young child and graphic expression. Childhood Education, 1940, 16:307–314. Used by permission.*)

peak is reached sooner than among those of a lower intellectual level (Durost, 1932). The older child is more selective in his collections than he was when he was younger. No longer does he make collections of anything or everything that attracts his attention. Typical objects collected by children are shown in Fig. 21. He generally limits his collections to a few special types of items and tries to get a wide variety of objects of each item.

These collections are more meaningful to him than were the collections he made when he was younger and, as a result, he generally keeps them in a safe place, such as in a drawer of his desk or bureau, or in his closet. There is marked similarity in what different children of a given age collect. Boys, at the age of seven years, for example, collect marbles, coupons, old magazines, small boxes, and buttons, and girls of that age collect funny papers, samples of schoolwork, paper dolls, small boxes, and rubber bands. The favorite items of collection among eleven-year-old boys are coupons, marbles,

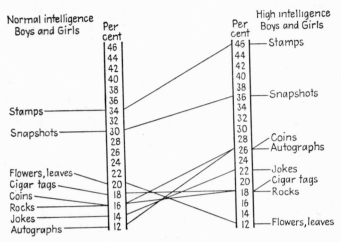

FIG. 21. Objects most frequently collected (as defined by three adult judges on the basis of interview data) by children of normal and high intelligence. A collection is here defined as determined by the nature of the value assigned to the objects or ideas possessed. If the predominant value is representative or relational such as being one of a series, part of a whole, a specimen of a class, then it is the subject of a collection. Note that when this definition is employed, the variety of objects "collected" by children is greatly diminished, and that children of high intelligence make more collections than children of normal intelligence. (*Based on data of W. N. Durost, Children's collecting activity related to social factors. Teach. Coll. Contr. Educ., 1932, No. 537. From F. K. Shuttleworth, The adolescent period: a graphic atlas, Monogr. Soc. Res. Child Develpm., 1949, 14, No. 1. Used by permission.*)

stamps, funny papers, and rubber bands; for girls, the favorites are coupons, letters received, old magazines, beads, and samples of schoolwork (Whitley, 1929).

Games and Sports. Early in the school life of a child, his games are the simple, undifferentiated type characteristic of early childhood. Tag, hide-and-seek, cops-and-robbers, and similar neighborhood games are still played. However, he is now anxious to play the games of older children and he begins to practice basketball, football, baseball, hockey, or whatever sport is in vogue at his school. By the time the child is ten or eleven years old, his games are largely competitive in spirit (Volberding, 1948). No longer is he satisfied with the loosely organized neighborhood games alone. He now wants to spend part of his time playing on a team where each member has his own role.

When the child first becomes a member of a team, he is likely to continue to play an individualistic game, trying to outdo the other team members. This, of course, is a carry-over of the role he played in the neighborhood games. Then each child competed with every other child, pitting his skills against theirs and trying to outplay them. Gradually, he learns to subordinate personal interests, to cooperate with his teammates, to be satisfied with the distinction of being a member of a team, even though he receives no recognition as an individual. Because it takes time for a child to shift from an individual to a cooperative member of a group, the transition is generally not achieved until the closing years of late childhood.

Amusements. The active life of an older child might, at first glance, preclude all amusements. Such, however, is not the case. There are times during the day, and more often in the evening, over week ends, and on holidays, when it is impossible for the child to be with his friends. During these periods of isolation, he spends what time he has free from schoolwork and from home responsibilities in amusing himself, not by playing solitary games but by reading, listening to the radio, watching television, or, whenever he has an opportunity, by going to the movies. In all these activities, he would prefer to have some of his friends with him but, if this is impossible, he can content himself alone for a short period of time.

READING. The older child is too much of a realist to be able to enjoy the make-believe element of a fairy tale. While he continues to be interested in fairy tales for a year or two after entering school, his reading time is devoted mostly to books of adventure. He derives keen satisfaction from imagining himself in the role of the hero of these stories and of doing things which his prosaic life denies him. Books of heroes and heroines, of history, of school life, or of present-day national fame, such as athletic heroes, movie actors and actresses, appeal to his interest in hero-worshiping (Witty *et al.*, 1946). In addition, boys enjoy reading books and stories about popular science, while girls read about nature. The height of the "reading craze" of childhood comes around the twelfth year, when it is not unusual for both boys and girls to read books at the rate of one a week (Terman and Lima, 1927). At this age, marked sex differences in reading interest develop as well as differences resulting from the intellectual level of the child (Thorndike and Henry, 1940).

In addition to reading books, older children show an interest in reading *poetry, magazines,* and *newspapers.* The "better" types of magazines and newspapers are generally favored by children of higher intellectual status (Lazar, 1937). Regardless of intelligence, almost all American children of today enjoy reading the *comics,* especially those of the adventure type. How great this interest is is shown by the fact that in grades 4 through 6, boys and girls read, on the average, 12.94 comic books every week, with boys reading slightly more than girls (Witty, 1941, 1941a). The major interest children of the elementary-school age have in the newspaper is in the comic section (Wilson, 1941).

There are many reasons why comics appeal to children. Not only are they amusing, exciting, easy to read, and cheap, but they may also stimulate the child's fantasy life (Bender and Lourie, 1941). They may present an escape from everyday reality, help the child to forget unpleasant experiences, and give him something to look forward to (Strang, 1943). Boys are attracted to those comics whose contents, action, and stories are predominantly masculine and are written from a masculine standpoint, whose stories feature a good deal of crime and violence, or whose main theme centers around sports and athletics. Girls, on the other hand, show a preference for comic books that feature feminine characters and pursuits, that are typically adolescent, and which contain a certain element of romance and dating (Butterworth and Thompson, 1951). While there is a great deal of criticism of children's reading of the comics, no one has demonstrated conclusively that they are detrimental in any way. On the other hand, normal aggressive reactions in children find release in the fantasies stimulated by comic books (Cavanaugh, 1949).

MOVIES. Movie attendance becomes an increasingly popular form of amusement as the childhood years progress. At last half of the children from grades 1 to 8 prefer going to the movies to reading books or playing games (Seagoe, 1931). Children who are chronologically and mentally older than their friends attend movies more (Heisler, 1948). Up to the age of nine or ten years, comics and cartoons are their favorite movies. After that, they prefer adventure. Boys, on the whole, show more interest in movies of the adventure type than do girls. Because of their deep absorption in what they see, and because of their noncritical attitude that makes them accept in an unquestioning fashion what they see, movies have a marked influence on the child's attitude and behavior (Thurstone, 1931).

RADIO AND TELEVISION. Since the beginning of *radio,* children throughout the nation have devoted proportionally more time to radio listening than to any other form of amusement. One to three hours daily, or an average of 15 hours 39 minutes weekly, was reported by the children studied by Clark (1940). "Problem" children listen more than do nonproblem children; children with lower IQ's more often than those with higher IQ's; and rural children more than urban children. The preferred programs contain detective, adventure, ghost, comedy, and mystery elements (Eisenberg, 1936; Clark, 1940). Girls, as a rule, have a wider variety of program preferences than do boys. The high percentage of children listening to crime and comedy programs suggests that children need tension-releasing experiences. The effects of radio listening differ according to the age and sex of the child. Habitual listening to specific types of programs has been found to be responsible for differences in behavior observed in children (Ricciuti, 1951). *Television,* because of its recent origin as a widespread source of amusement in the American home, has not yet been subjected to scientific analysis. However, reports from teachers and school principals throughout the country indicate that the amount of time spent in television watching exceeds that spent in listening to the radio. This is shown by a drop in school grades whenever a television set is installed in a home or neighborhood.

DAYDREAMING. All children, at some time or other, amuse themselves by daydreaming. The child who has made poor school adjustments and who, as a result, has few opportunities for contact with other children, is likely to spend more time in daydreaming than is the socially well-adjusted child. Girls, as a rule, because home restrictions make it impossible for them to spend as much time with their playmates as boys do, generally daydream more than boys. Typically, the daydream of this age is of the "conquering-hero" type. The dreamer sees himself as he would like to be in real life. While the background and setting of childish daydreams vary from one child to another, the dreamer is invariably the hero or the heroine of the dream (C. Bühler, 1930; Jersild *et al.,* 1933). Daydreaming gives the child an opportunity for self-glorification which may prove to be so pleasant to him that he substitutes daydreaming for real social contacts, thus increasing his poor social adjustments.

DEVELOPMENT OF UNDERSTANDING

As the child's world expands with his entrance into school, so do his interests. And with the broadening of interests comes an understanding of people and things which formerly held little or no meaning for him. Not only is his understanding of his environment increased by the formal teaching he receives in the classroom but it is also broadened by exchanging ideas with his playmates and by his ability to read which reaches the point, during the third or fourth grades in school, where he can comprehend the meaning of what he reads without giving his undivided attention to the mechanics of the reading process. Thus a new avenue of approach is opened up to him. No longer is he dependent upon what others select to read to him for the acquisition of meanings relating to things which formerly aroused his curiosity. Now he is in a position to select reading matter as well as to pursue subjects which have a special interest for him. While he never abandons the methods of exploring formerly used so successfully, those of sensorimotor exploration and of questioning, he nows adds a new and important avenue of approach, reading.

Space no longer is a vague, meaningless thing for an older child. From the use of weights and rulers he comes to learn the meaning of ounces, pounds, inches, feet, yards, and even miles. Schoolwork in arithmetic helps him to formulate more definite ideas of space and distance than he could develop through his own personal experiences. Similarly, *numbers* take on new meanings for him as he begins to use money and as he works with arithmetic problems. The study of history and of geography, with special emphasis on the manners, customs, and modes of living of people in other lands and in different periods of history, broadens his concepts of *time* (Bradley, 1947). Even more important, the rigid schedule of the school day, with the ringing of a bell at the end of a given period of time, enables him to estimate time more accurately in terms of what he can accomplish in a stated period.

A fair appraisal of *self*, as seen through the eyes of his teachers and classmates, free from the prejudices that are likely to color parental concepts, and as viewed through his own eyes as he compares his abilities and disabilities with those of other, children of his age, all help the child to clarify his concept of self. Because the child is egocentric, he is likely to exaggerate his bad qualities, both physical and mental, thus leading to feelings of inadequacy which are reflected in shyness and self-consciousness. By the time the child is seven years old, realistic self-identification with his racial group appears, even when there is an emotional conflict (Clark and Clark, 1950).

Social appraisals, or the ability to size up the personality, abilities, and disabilities of others, likewise develop rapidly at this age as a child spends more and more time with other children. In the absence of adult supervision, children are likely to comment with brutal frankness on qualities of the playmates they dislike. Unpleasant as this may seem, it is a great help to a child who is learning to make his own appraisals of others because he can see, through the eyes of others, characteristics that are socially acceptable and those that are not. The child becomes aware of group differences at an early age. As a result of home and environmental influences, the child recognizes racial, religious, and socioeconomic differences among the children with whom he plays or with whom he is associated in school. And he accepts the adults' attitudes toward these groups, thus giving rise to group consciousness and the beginnings of social prejudice even at this early age (Radke *et al.*, 1949).

Antiminority prejudices are not based on the personal experiences of the children (Radke and Sutherland, 1949) but show a reflection of the set cultural patterns and stereotypes of the child's social environment (Zeligs, 1950). Prejudices have been found to be more common and stronger among children whose intolerance is associated with lack of confidence and security, fearfulness, and suspicion (Gough *et al.*, 1950). Freedom from ethnic prejudice among children, on the other hand, has been found to be associated with attitudes of tolerance and good judgment in child rearing (Harris *et al.*, 1950). When asked for their reasons for intergroup attitudes, children give such reasons as customs, language, physical differences, type of government, and behavior of the people themselves (Zeligs, 1950*a*).

In the same way, the child learns to appraise the *beautiful* and the *comic*. No longer are things beautiful or ugly just because he likes or dislikes them. Beauty and ugliness of color, of nature, or of the human face and form, are conditioned by group standards, rather than by individual reactions (Spiegel, 1950). Similarly, from his group contacts, he discovers that certain things are considered funny while others are not. He learns to laugh when the group laughs and to lift an eyebrow in scorn when others do the same. Seeing others in a predicament; making faces; drawing caricatures of teachers and others in authority; making practical jokes, especially on adults or disliked children; referring to sex and religion; and defying authority, even if this leads to punishment, all make the group laugh, and so each individual child thinks they are funny and laughs too.

In the rapid building of new concepts at this age, and in the absence of an adequate fund of information to act as a critical check on the formation of these concepts, *errors* are frequent. Children, for example, often overestimate or underestimate time, they develop misconceptions about themselves if the group underestimates or overestimates their abilities, they develop a crude and often cruel sense of humor, and they are likely to judge the total personality of others in terms of one or two traits rather than in terms of the personality pattern as a whole. As time goes on and their experiences increase, they become more critical in their estimates, with the result that errors in perception are gradually reduced.

MORAL ATTITUDES AND BEHAVIOR

As the child's horizon broadens and his contacts with other people increase, he discovers that what was considered right or wrong at home is not always viewed thus by those outside the home. As a result, new standards of morality are gradually built up and these frequently conflict with parental standards. The child's moral code is now determined to a large extent by the moral code of the group to which he belongs. Furthermore, his concepts no longer are narrow and specific as they were when he was younger. He gradually generalizes his concepts so that they refer to any situation rather than to a specific situation. For example, he learns that stealing is wrong regardless of whether it means stealing money, material possessions, or the work of others. From the ages of nine to twelve years, children have higher ideals of honesty than they previously had (Beller, 1949). Similarly, the child now regards lying as wrong whether the lie is told to a parent, a teacher, or a classmate, with or without fingers crossed (Macaulay and Watkins, 1926). As a child reaches the end of childhood, his moral code gradually approaches that of adults (Lockhart, 1930).

At this age, there is a marked tendency on the part of children to feel guilty if their conduct falls below the standard of their code. Unlike the younger child who is unconcerned about such matters unless his misbehavior is detected and punished, the older child has a deep personal concern about this matter. Likewise, he no longer accepts in an unquestioning manner punishments meted out by adults for behavior of which they disapprove. Now he has a strong sense of justice and fairness, and he does not hesitate to say so if he feels that he has been falsely accused or unfairly punished. And, unlike the younger child, he is critical of shortcomings on the part of his playmates. He condemns them strongly when their behavior falls below accepted standards and he does not hesitate to ostracize them from the group should their behavior continue to fall below the group standard.

Only when the group as a whole approves and condones behavior that is in direct contradiction to adult standards will the child accept it uncritically. Older children, especially boys, frequently delight in doing things that they know are wrong because of the sense of personal importance they derive. Misbehavior in the school and neighborhood by gangs of older boys or girls is usually motivated by this desire. On the whole, their misbehavior is annoying to adults and is an attempt to throw off the restrictions of adult authority rather than anything else (Wickman, 1929; Stouffer, 1952). In cases of truancy, lying, and stealing, there is generally a background of poor home environment and unfavorable health records (Mullen, 1950). The effects of different types of environment on moral behavior in childhood are illustrated in Fig. 22.

Discipline. Discipline becomes a serious problem with older children. Continuing to use the disciplinary techniques that proved to be effective when the child was younger is likely to lead to strong resentments on the part of the older child. Praise and occasional rewards for good behavior and depriving the child of some pleasure he has anticipated or of some privilege he has been accustomed to and sending him off to his room alone "to think it over" are generally far more effective than corporal punishment which the older child strongly resents. Throughout the closing years of childhood, teaching the child what is right and wrong is just as important as it was during the early years of childhood. But the teaching should take a new form. Emphasis should be placed on explanations of why certain forms of behavior are acceptable while others are not and of helping the child to broaden the specific moral concepts formed when he was younger into more generalized, abstract concepts of right and wrong. Unfortunately, too little emphasis is placed on the educational aspect of discipline at this age, on the faulty assumption that the child should "know by now the difference between right and wrong."

Every child needs discipline. Discipline gives him a feeling of security because he knows where his boundaries, limits, and freedoms are; it helps him to live according to certain standards in order that he will have less feeling of guilt; it gives him an opportunity for praise and love when he does the right thing and an ego-bolstering sense of confidence. Thus, discipline is a developmental need of the child as it is a requirement of society without which the individual's personality will not emerge in its full growth (Geisel, 1951). The child's attitude toward discipline depends upon his age and his environmental influences. When children are young, they like to feel that

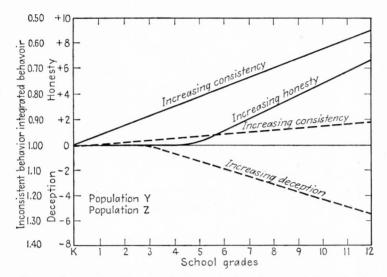

Fig. 22. Contrasting trends of honest behavior and of consistency of that behavior among children in superior (Y) and underprivileged (Z) socioeconomic groups. Children from the superior economic group become more honest and more consistently honest with age, whereas children from the underprivileged group become more deceptive and more consistently deceptive with age. (*Redrawn from Hugh Hartshorne, Mark A. May, and Frank K. Shuttleworth, Studies in the organization of character. New York: Macmillan, 1930. From F. K. Shuttleworth, The adolescent period: a graphic atlas, Monogr. Soc. Res. Child Develpm., 1949, 14, No. 1. Used by permission.*)

parents know best. By late childhood, they rebel against their parents and parental standards when they learn that there are different standards and that different disciplinary methods are used among their friends. The great emphasis on gang standards may lead to open rebellion in the home (Colm, 1951). Children of the lower socioeconomic groups tend to hold an individual child responsible for any violation of rules and to think in terms of punishment more than do children from the better socioeconomic groups. Children from the higher socioeconomic groups consider the environmental basis for misconduct and suggest that misconduct may be the result of circumstances (Dolger and Ginandes, 1946).

SOME CHILDHOOD INTERESTS

What the older child is interested in depends, as it does in the earlier years of childhood, upon what opportunities to develop interests he has. A child brought up in a totally unreligious family may or may not become interested in religion, depending on whether or not he has an opportunity to learn about religion at school or from his discussions with his friends. Similarly, a child whose gang shows a marked contempt for anything but the simplest and plainest clothes will have little or no interest in clothes. Studies of children's interests have revealed certain pertinent facts about them. Older children, in all grades in the elementary school, are preoccupied with people and personal relations. There is a strong element of self-interest and self-reference in children's ideas about life. Among younger children, in the early grades, more emphasis is attached to gifts and material possessions than among older children. The wide variation expressed by children in their interests would suggest that children's interests are, to a large degree, learned (Jersild and Tasch, 1949).

The developmental status of the child, especially the social roles he has acquired, affects the development of his interests. With changes in his concept of self and the role he plays in the social group, certain interests are ruled out as inappropriate while others are strengthened or developed because of their appropriateness. For example, a boy who has become "gang-conscious" may say to himself, "Poetry reading is for sissies, not for me," and substitute for this interest the playing of football because "Real guys are good at football" (Harris, 1950a). There are, however, certain interests which are fairly universally found among the American children of today as a result of the cultural pressures brought on them. These include interests in:

Religion. While the novelty of Sunday-school attendance has worn off, in part at least, by the time the child reaches first grade, he still enjoys going to Sunday school. This offers him an opportunity to be with his friends on a day when otherwise he might not be permitted to play with them or when family plans would limit his companionship to adults. He is, of course, interested in what he learns in Sunday school, but, as each year passes, he is likely to develop an attitude of skepticism toward some of the teaching (Case, 1921). And he does not hesitate to show this skepticism by asking his Sunday-school teacher or his parents to explain certain incomprehensible parts of what he learns, nor does he refrain from arguing and trying to prove that they are not right.

This religious doubt, which generally becomes increasingly pronounced as the child emerges into adolescence, does not disturb him as it so frequently does in adolescence, nor does he feel guilty because he cannot accept, in whole or in part, all that is taught him. Sometimes his arguments about religion are motivated more by the feeling of self-importance that comes when he can put himself in the limelight or put the "teacher on the spot" than by sincere convictions that the teachings are invalid. Religious teaching in the early years of his life has, however, left its imprint on the older child's mind. He has many vague concepts which gradually become clearer and more accurate as he grows older and he can comprehend abstract theories better (Bose, 1929). The clearest concepts generally relate to religious holidays, such as Christmas, while those that are vague and confused relate to spiritual experiences, such as conversion (Bose, 1929).

Most children have a fairly clear concept of God, but it varies from child to child, according to what teaching he has had (Case, 1921; MacLean, 1930). In most of the older child's concepts, there is a marked degree of realism as compared with the fairy-tale element characteristic of the younger child (Harms, 1944). Like the younger child, the older child's attitude toward religion is *egocentric*. To him, for example, Christmas is a day for receiving gifts (Freeman, 1931), while prayer is a means of getting what he wants, whether it be help or material possessions (MacLean, 1930; Fahs, 1932). To teach children the experience of mysticism, children need leisure instead of being overwhelmed with book knowledge (Fahs, 1950).

The Human Body. After having explored the outer areas and orifices of his own body when he was younger, the older child is now anxious to know what goes on inside his body. Being unable to observe bodily functions directly, he tries to satisfy his curiosity by asking innumerable questions and by reading stories or books that describe the body and how it works. School classes in physiology or hygiene have a strong appeal for him because they supply him with the answers to many of his questions. Awareness of physical differences between the sexes begins early in childhood when the young child notices that the hair, clothes, and faces of members of the two sexes are different. Among older children, there is recognition of such differences as in complexion, figure, legs, feet, strength, and gait. Younger children, as a general rule, fail to notice these differences (Conn and Kanner, 1947).

Sex. There is a heightened interest in sex at this age as compared with the casual interest in the subject displayed by younger children. Not only is the older child keenly aware of and interested in genital differences (Conn, 1940), but he also wants to know in more detail about the relations between sexes, the birth process, and how development takes place within the mother's body (Alpert, 1941). After the age of eight years, sexual curiosity is often repressed by the amused or disturbed reactions of adults to the child's sexual manifestations (Hoch and Zubin, 1949). The most common situations to which boys respond erotically before adolescence are seeing females, thinking about females, sex jokes and pictures, and pictures of females.

A child's curiosity has a strong emotional drive but is often cloaked because of his past rebuffs when he asked a question about sex matters. Whispering to his friends, secret talks behind parental backs, smutty stories and jokes, and giggling when sex in any form is mentioned are all indicative of this emotional tone. Given an opportunity at home or in school, older children ask not only more but more varied questions about sex than do younger children (Hattendorf, 1932; Conn, 1940). The age at which children acquire *sex information* and the sources from which it comes vary greatly from child to child. Among boys, approximately 60 per cent gain their information about the origin of babies between the ages of six and eleven years (Terman *et al.*, 1938) and a considerable amount of other sexual knowledge before they reach the age of ten years (Ramsey, 1943).

Most of this information comes from male companions or from their own experiences. When mothers give information about sex matters, the emphasis is generally on sex differences and reproduction. Very few mothers give the child the whole story of reproduction, thus leaving many gaps for the child to fill in as best he can (Hattendorf, 1932). There is a positive correlation between the amount of sex information possessed by parents and child. The children of parents with little factual information about sex tend to have meager knowledge themselves. Some well-informed parents, on the other hand, have been found to have children with little sexual knowledge (Phipps, 1949). One serious obstacle to imparting sex information to children is the child's ignorance of the technical language used to describe the reproductive organs and processes (Conn and Kanner, 1947). If, however, his information is to be, correct and his attitude toward sex healthy, the information must not only be correct but it must also be comprehensive, in words that he knows and understands, and it must come from persons whose own attitudes toward sex are healthy (Conn, 1939).

Sex exploration, either of their own bodies, or mutual exploration of a homosexual or heterosexual sort, such as peeping, matching masculine prowess in the toilet, and masturbation, are found among eight- and nine-year-olds. This is generally accompanied by provocative giggling, obscene language, and secrets (Alpert, 1941). After the age of nine years, there is progressively more provocative heterosexual behavior. When the child's sexual curiosity is satisfied or the matter adequately handled, sexual exploration gradually diminishes. Manual exploration, direct observation of the female reproductive anatomy, exhibitionism, oral contacts, and attempts at intercourse are some of the forms of sexual exploration used by boys (Ramsey, 1943*a*).

Masturbation is a form of sexual exploration that is common among all children, but it is more frequently engaged in by boys than by girls (Levy, 1928; Koch, 1935). Homosexual play is more frequently engaged in than heterosexual sex play. The play companions are usually the child's friends, though the child's initial experience in both homosexual and heterosexual play is usually with an older boy or girl or even with an adult. Most of this sex play ends with the onset of adolescence (Kinsey *et al.*, 1948).

While interest in sex differences and curiosity about all matters relating to sex are far more pronounced at this time than in the earlier years of childhood, the attitude of one sex toward the other becomes progressively less favorable. Toward the end of childhood, marked *antagonisms between the sexes* arise. This generally begins in the first grade at school and becomes stronger each succeeding year. Social distance thus increases from the first grade to high school (Koch, 1944). Not only do members of the two sexes shun each other as much as possible but, in addition, boys derive keen pleasure from bullying and teasing girls. Because there is no evidence of a physiological cause for this antagonism between the sexes, one must conclude that the cause is social in nature and that it comes primarily from early training, especially in play activities and manners which put girls in a disadvantageous position. Only occasionally is a boy of this age interested in a girl and, when he is, he is generally afraid to show it because of the scorn and ridicule he is likely to receive from his playmates.

The Self. The older child begins to think of himself as an individual, distinct and different from other people. He has not, as yet, clear-cut and definite ideas of his abilities and disabilities, nor is he sure of how people will accept him. Because of this feeling of insecurity, he tries to follow the accepted pattern of the group to which he belongs and molds himself into this pattern as closely as he can. Only when he feels secure and accepted at home does he dare to be himself. Because of this, he is frequently troublesome to his parents, a fact which especially worries them when they discover that he causes no trouble in school or when he is with his playmates.

The importance of social pressures in forming the child's concept of himself is shown by the fact that relatively few children, when they first enter school, have any real desire to change themselves, while a large percentage of older children do. This is especially true of girls who, after discovering the more favored position of boys in our culture, say they would like to be boys if they could (Jersild *et al.*, 1933). As childhood draws to a close and the child begins to hero-worship characters in history and in fiction, on the stage or on the screen, or in the world of sports or national affairs, he forms a concept of the *"ideal" self*, the kind of person he would like to be. At first, this ideal is patterned along the lines set by parents, teachers, and others from his immediate environment. Later, as his horizons broaden, people he does not know but has heard or read about form the nucleus of this ideal self (Stoughton and Ray, 1946; Havinghurst *et al.*, 1946).

Vocational Ambitions. As a result of constant questionings, from the time they were very young, as to what they want to be when they grow up, most school children think about their future careers. Their first vocational aims are generally very unrealistic, with little or no consideration of their abilities for the careers they select. As a rule, their first ambitions are to follow in the footsteps of a parent, a relative, or someone outside the family whom they love and admire. Their ambition is to go into a line of work that appeals to them as glamorous or exciting (Jersild *et al.*, 1933; Boynton, 1936; Gray, 1944).

Clothing. Unlike the younger child who regards clothing as a nuisance, except when his clothes give him the limelight because others admire or envy them, the older child is keenly interested in clothes as a badge of conformity to the group. New clothes, clothing of a style usually associated with older children, and clothing in his favorite colors still appeal to the child of school age as they did when he was a preschooler. As a general rule, colors of garments are the only real source of appeal to children up to the age of nine years, and it is because of the garment's color that the child selects it (Macaulay, 1929). Beginning around the eighth or ninth year, slavish conventionality in the style of clothing of the group makes its appearance. At this age, the child is not only becoming self-conscious but he is anxious to be acceptable to the group in appearance as well as in behavior. Both boys and girls at this age want to be noticed as little as possible and, to make themselves inconspicuous, they hide behind a cloak of conventional garments (Hurlock, 1929, 1929a). So long as his clothes are durable, easy to manipulate, admired or approved by the group, comfortable and, above all, conforming in style to the group pattern, that is all that matters to the older child (Hurlock, 1943).

FAMILY RELATIONSHIPS

As the childhood years progress, family relationships generally become worse. The sweet, docile, helplessly dependent younger child grows into a gawky, careless, homely, independent individual who tries hard to throw off the yoke of parental domination. In spite of the broadened environment of the older child, the parents still exert a marked influence on his developing personality. Whether this influence will be good or bad will depend, to a large extent, upon the type of relationship that exists between the child and his parents. Children of *indulgent parents,* especially indulgent mothers, have a difficult time making social adjustments. The child is likely to be selfish, demanding, and tyrannical. He expects constant attention, service, and affection. When he is disciplined or when his wishes are denied, he responds with impatience, outbursts of temper, or assaults. Children of *dominating parents,* by contrast, are likely to be shy, anxious, fearful, and submissive (Bakwin, 1948). The child's behavior toward his own age group is thus influenced by his parents' behavior toward him (Meyer, 1947).

When the child is unable to express his aggressions freely in a home environment, he seeks other outlets when frustrating situations arise. He either projects the blame to the environment or turns it upon himself. As a rule, children are more submissive to their fathers in frustrating situations than they are to their mothers or their contemporaries (Kates, 1951). Absence or presence of parental pressures explains the absence or presence of intolerance and race prejudices (Maloney, 1948). In spite of the older child's desire for independence and his attempts to throw off the parental yoke, he is still more dependent upon his parents for guidance and help than he may realize or may be willing to admit. Prolonged or repeated absence of one parent "creates a poor environmental soil for the growth of the child's character." The maladjustment of the child's personality is usually in proportion to the sum total of physical and emotional absence on the part of the parents (Riemer, 1949).

Family Frictions. From this new independence, friction frequently arises in the home. Parents who are unwilling to give the child the freedom he craves, either for selfish reasons or because they believe he is not old enough to handle this freedom successfully, continue to restrain his actions and treat him as they did when he was little and helpless. Or, if the behavior and attitudes of his gangmates do not come up to parental standards, they criticize the child's friends and try to curb his contacts with them. Added to the friction with his parents, the older child is in more or less constant *conflict with his siblings.* Older brothers and sisters criticize and find fault with his "rowdy" behavior, his crude manners, and his continual shouting. He, in turn, likes to bully and tease, to make fun of, or even to fight with younger brothers and sisters. The result is continuous turmoil in the home which, when parents attempt to put a stop to it, leads to further strain of parent-child relationships.

There are, of course, times of peace and harmony in the home. Older children, if gradually given an opportunity to assume responsibilities, are great helpers in carrying the family burden. And there are times when they show real affection for and interest in their siblings, even to the point of helping in the care of the younger and following the advice and pattern of behavior set by the older siblings. But these favorable relationships are outweighed in number and frequency by the less favorable (McFarland, 1938). Deterioration of relationships within the family spreads to *relatives.* While the younger child frequently shows great affection for grandparents, uncles, aunts, and cousins, the older child is likely to regard them as "too old," "too bossy," or "bores." He resents their authority even more than he resents parental authority and he puts up a protest whenever he is expected to be a part of a family gathering, either in his home or in the home of a relative.

For the first time in the child's life, the *socioeconomic status* of his family becomes important. As he goes to the homes of friends and has an opportunity to compare his home with the homes of his friends, he is satisfied if he has as much as, if not more than, they in the way of material possessions. But he is dissatisfied and unhappy if his home falls below the standard of the homes of his friends. This dissatisfaction becomes increasingly strong with each successive year, reaching its peak during adolescence. And with this dissatisfaction comes increased friction with the members of his family, especially with his parents, whom he blames for not providing him with what his friends have.

Changed Attitudes. In view of the changed attitude and behavior on the part of the child toward his parents, it is not surprising to find a changed attitude on the part of the parents toward the child. When the behavior of parents toward nine-year-olds was compared with their attitudes toward three-year-olds, it was found that parents were less indulgent, less warm and affectionate, more restrictive in their controls, and less intellectually stimulating to the older than to the younger children. While the birth of a younger sibling may be partially responsible for this change, it is also due, in part, to the changed attitude of the child toward his parents and his rebellion against their authority (Baldwin, 1945).

Parental ambitions for the child begin to show their effects on the child's behavior at this age. While many parents form ambitions for their child's future while the child is still in the cradle, these ambitions have little or no effect on the younger child's life. By the time the child reaches school age, on the other hand, parents begin to try to mold him into a pattern they have set for him. In addition, they constantly compare him with their idealized child, or the child they want him to be (Smith, 1931; Anderson, 1949; Radke, 1946). Because few children can or wish to live up to these parental ambitions, they are likely to become troublesome, disobedient, and rebellious. School failures and retreats into the world of fantasy are common effects of overambitious parents (Smith, 1931; Rand *et al.*, 1942; Martin, 1943).

Mothers who have been employed before marriage and who find homemaking boring to the point where they contemplate returning to their former lines of employment often prove to be overly ambitious parents. They show similar demands for conformity and high-standard performance in their children as they had shown in their previous work. Rigid perfectionism on the part of these mothers puts the child in a position where he is constantly subject to criticism and is likely to develop feelings of inadequacy (Berger, 1948).

Parental Preferences. In spite of the child's attempts to break away from parental domination, he is still dependent upon his parents to help him in emergencies or in new situations where he feels inadequate to cope with the situation alone. Because his mother is likely to be ever-present more than his father, he becomes accustomed to turning to her for aid. Furthermore, because mothers, as a rule, have a more tolerant and understanding attitude toward the troublesome behavior of older children than do fathers, a stronger bond grows up between mother and child than between father and child.

As a result, older children, like younger children, generally prefer their mothers to their fathers (Yarnelle, 1932; Mott, 1937; Simpson, 1935). The child's dependence on the mother is well illustrated by the fact that most older children prefer their mothers to stay at home rather than to have out-of-the-home employment (Matthews, 1934).

While younger children accept their parents uncritically, the older child becomes increasingly *critical* of his parents' appearances, attitudes, manners, and behaviors. From contacts with other children and their parents, from reading, and from the stereotypes of parents presented on the screen, the child forms a concept of the *ideal parent*. He then compares his parents with these ideals. If his parents fall short of his ideals in any way, as they invariably do, he becomes critical of their shortcomings and does not hesitate to let them know how he feels.

Younger children are annoyed mostly when parents punish them or interfere with their pleasures (Radke, 1946). Older children, by contrast, resent having their parents, especially their fathers, scold them, lose their tempers, be cross, come home late, use poor English, be careless about their appearance, or have poor manners (Gardner, 1947). They approve, on the other hand, of parents who are companionable, loving, affectionate, understanding, good-natured, and sympathetic (Sowers, 1937), who take an interest in them and their affairs and who do all they can to make the home cheerful and happy (Martin, 1943).

Family Size. It is popularly believed that a child is lucky if he is one of several children in the family but the only child is regarded with pity. Behind this belief is the conviction that a child with siblings learns to conform to other children and to become a social being in a manner which is impossible for the only child. Furthermore, siblings supply ever-ready playmates for the child, an advantage which the only child lacks. Studies of only children have not revealed their inferiority in social adjustments. In social acceptability, only children rate higher than children from a family of several siblings (Bonney, 1942). While it is true that only children are frequently the victims of overprotective parents, they are spared the psychological damage that comes with sibling rivalry and jealousy. The number of misdemeanors of only children is generally smaller than that of children who have siblings (Blatz and Bott, 1927). And, in level of maturity, they generally surpass children from larger families because of the fact that their companions are mainly adults rather than children. As a result, they develop personality traits that make them popular with other children (Bonney, 1942).

PERSONALITY

As the child's social horizons broaden with his entrance into school, new factors of importance begin to influence the development of his personality.

His whole concept of himself must frequently be revised. Having seen himself almost exclusively through the eyes of his parents for the first part of his life, it is not surprising if his concept of himself is biased. Now he sees himself as his teachers, his classmates, and his neighbors see him. Even his parents react differently toward him now and this helps to shatter the foundations upon which his concept of himself was based. With each passing year, the child's personality becomes less and less flexible, and more and more fixed in a set pattern. The shy, retiring, self-effacing individual continues to be such even when he discovers that this does not contribute to his acceptance by the group. The child whose aggressiveness stemmed from parental rejection continues to be aggressive, even though his aggressiveness may take on new and more subtle forms as he grows older.

Admired Traits. As the child spends more and more time with other children, he becomes increasingly aware of the fact that there are certain personality traits other children admire and others they dislike. The pressure of social opinion thus plays an important role in shaping the older child's personality. He tries to mold his personality into the pattern approved by the group in hopes of gaining the social recognition and acceptance he craves. Children who are popular and are accepted by their contemporaries possess the traits admired by their contemporaries. In general, they are more aggressive and overt in their responses than are less popular children and they rate higher in good looks, friendliness, happiness, leadership, and being at ease with adults (Bonney, 1943). Because the two sexes are widely separated at this age, it is not surprising to find that each sex has its own standard of an acceptable personality pattern for its members. Traits that are admired in a girl by both girls and boys would not be admired by either girls or boys if possessed by a boy. Girls, as a group, are expected to be superior to boys in good looks, tidiness, being more grown-up, and possessing more social skills (Bonney, 1944). Children's ideals of acceptable personality traits change, however, with age. In general, the older the child, the more aggressive traits he must possess if he is to be admired and accepted.

Personality Factors. While many of the factors that were in play in the shaping of the personality of the younger child continue to be operative in the latter years of childhood, new factors enter in and play increasingly important roles. While the child's *physique,* especially his size, is important when he first starts to play with children during the preschool years, it becomes one of the dominating personality factors in late childhood.

Being *overweight,* for example, can lead to a "disturbance in the maturation of the total personality" (Bruch, 1941). The *general health* of the child is also an important personality factor. Children who are sickly, who suffer from a series of illnesses, or who have physical defects that cut them off from the play of other children not only feel inferior but are forced to compensate for the lack of companionship of their contemporaries.

Allergic children, for example, develop personality constellations which differ markedly from those of nonallergic children (Riess and deCillis, 1940). Personality changes in allergic children have been found to be strikingly for the better when the allergies were controlled. The explanation given for the improvement was partially the removal of nervous tension caused by asthma and partly the change in parental attitudes (Clarke, 1952). Personality changes frequently follow certain diseases in which there may be a secondary involvement of the central nervous system, as in malaria, pneumonia, pernicious anemia, diabetes, and poliomyelitis (Shock, 1947). Personality changes following polio relate to the extent and severity of the crippling conditions which accompany this disease. When the case is mild, polio has little direct lasting effect on the child's personality or behavior (Harris, 1950).

While the young child accepts in an unquestioning manner the *name* and *nickname* given to him at home, the older child realizes the importance of these. If the name is accepted without ridicule or criticism by his friends, well and good. Should the group, however, comment unfavorably about it, this affects the child unfavorably just as if they commented unfavorably about his appearance. Because most nicknames serve as a form of ridicule of some physical or personality trait that is outstanding in the child, the child is likely to build up resentments against those who use it or to feel inferior if the nickname is widely used (Orgel and Tuckman, 1935). Nicknames such as "Fatty," "Skinny," or "Slumpy" imply physical differences and show how other children feel about these differences (Sontag, 1946).

The *socially approved pattern* of the culture to which the child belongs begins to be felt in the shaping of his personality at this time. Each individual child is gradually molded into this pattern by his parents, his teachers, and by other adults with whom he comes in contact. Any attempt to deviate from this pattern is thus apt to lead to criticism. Because there are pressures and prejudices against those who belong to *minority groups,* the child begins to sense these prejudices soon after he enters school. This gradually builds up a feeling of inferiority which, in time, is expressed in poor social adjustments, antisocial behavior, and in the child's whole outlook on life (Engle, 1945).

In our culture, social prestige is associated with a favorable *socioeconomic status* of the family. The child whose family does not measure up favorably becomes increasingly aware of this as the years pass. He compares his toys, his clothes, his home, his parents' status in the community, and his father's occupation with those of his friends to his personal disadvantage and dissatisfaction (Francis, 1933; Stagner, 1935). Studies of children from rural and urban environments have shown rural children to be superior to those from urban districts in self-reliance, in a sense of personal worth, in a greater sense of belonging, in a greater freedom from withdrawing tendencies, and in absence of nervous symptoms. They showed evidence of greater social skills and are rated superior in school and community relations. They do not, however, show any superiority to the urban children in their sense of personal freedom, in their adjustments in the family, in their adjustments in social standards, or in freedom from antisocial tendencies (Mangus, 1948).

When the child enters school, the *school environment* begins to exert a marked influence on the development of his personality. His teachers influence the molding of his personality. Well-adjusted teachers do much to bring about good adjustment in their pupils; poorly adjusted teachers may have the opposite influence on their pupils. Not all maladjusted teachers cause maladjustments in their pupils, however. A maladjusted teacher can often sympathize better with her pupils who are having difficulties in adjustment than can one who is well-adjusted (Gladstone, 1948).

Intelligence that deviates from the norm of the group invariably exerts a detrimental influence on the child's personality. The child who is duller than the rest of the group quickly senses his intellectual inferiority and the attitude of the group toward him. This builds up a feeling of personal inadequacy which is expressed in every area of his behavior. By contrast, the very bright child not only feels superior to the group and out of step with their interests, but he generally develops an intolerance toward those not so bright as he, a sense of self-sufficiency, a tendency to seek the companionship of children older than he or of adults, a tendency to dominate the situation, and a revolt against authority (Hollingworth, 1940).

While the *home environment* becomes increasingly less important as the child grows older, *family relationships* continue to exert a marked influence. How he feels about his parents, how satisfactory or unsatisfactory his relationship with them is, their attitudes toward him (Symonds, 1938; Grant, 1939), the pattern of home life (Stott, 1939, 1940; Hewitt and Jenkins, 1946), his ordinal position in the family (Adler, 1930; Stagner and Katzoff, 1936), and his relationship with his siblings, all play their role in determining what sort of individual he will develop into. When the environment is made to suit the needs of the child, and when a mutual give and take exists, a healthy, well-balanced personality development results (Graves, 1948). Affectional family relationships influence the development of certain personality traits, especially character development. Sharing in family decisions and attitude toward peer activities are affected by the degree of affectional relationship that exists in the home (Brown *et al.*, 1947).

Children who are brought up in institutions and have not had the benefits of a home environment show personality differences when compared with children who have had the benefits of a home environment and relationships with parents and siblings. Institutionalized children are less mature socially, they have fewer community contacts, they participate less in organized social activities, they have fewer friends, and show less interest in members of the opposite sex than do children whose environment has been that of a home (Bodman *et al.*, 1950).

CHAPTER 7

Puberty

Puberty is a period in the developmental span when rapid physical and psychological changes are taking place. It marks the transition from a childish body, a childish outlook on life, and childish forms of behavior to a mature body with gradual changes in attitudes and in behavior. At this time, the sex organs mature and begin to function. The name for this period comes from the Latin word *pubertas,* meaning "age of manhood." At this age also the secondary sex characteristics, or physical features which distinguish the male from the female body, gradually appear and reach their mature forms.

Bodily changes invariably are accompanied by changes in interests and attitudes. When these changes are rapid, confusion results and the individual feels insecure. This is likely to lead to unfavorable attitudes and equally unfavorable behavior. Charlotte Bühler has labeled this period the "negative phase." "Phase" suggests a period of short duration in the total life span. Fortunately for all concerned, it is short because, at this age, there is a reversal of some of the favorable traits developed during childhood and an exaggeration of those not so favorable. The term "negative" suggests that the child takes an "anti-" attitude toward life or that he is negating some of the good qualities that he has previously developed. Both suggestions are borne out by the typical behavior at this age. Studies reveal that the worst of the negative phase is over with the menarche, or first menstruation in girls (Bühler, 1927; Hetzer, 1927; Leal, 1929).

As far back as the time of Aristotle, it was recognized that when boys are about fourteen years old, they begin to "engender seed." When this occurs, there are changes in their physical structure such as the appearance of hair on the body and a marked change in the tonal quality of their voices. Aristotle also noted that when girls experience their first menstrual flow, their breasts develop and their voices change. Of even greater significance was his emphasis on behavioral changes. He stressed the fact that at this time girls are irritable, passionate, ardent, and in need of constant surveillance because of their developing sexual impulses.

Among primitive peoples, recognition of the changes that accompany puberty are fairly universal. Different rites are observed by different tribes to show their recognition of the fact that the child is emerging from childhood into maturity and is, therefore, reaching the stage when he or she should have the rights, privileges, and responsibilities that accompany maturity. Among some tribes, the rites of puberty are public and are accompanied by singing, dancing, and tests of strength, power, and skill. In other primitive groups, the rites are familial, rather than public. A Mohave girl, for example, begins a 4-day period of seclusion at the onset of the menses. During this period, various restrictions are placed upon her clothing, eating, and general deportment. Her actions at this time are believed to influence her entire future (Wallace, 1947).

AGE OF PUBERTY

Puberty comes at the beginning of adolescence and is, therefore, a part of the adolescent span. It is frequently referred to as the "preadolescent stage." It is difficult or even impossible to give a definite age for puberty because sexual maturity varies so widely in different individuals. Furthermore, different criteria are used to determine just when this stage of development begins and ends.

The widely accepted practice today is to subdivide the puberty age into three stages, as follows:

1. The *prepubescent,* or immature, stage when the secondary sex characteristics are beginning to develop but the reproductive function is not yet developed.
2. The *pubescent,* or mature, stage when the secondary sex characteristics continue to develop but are not yet complete and when sex cells are produced in the sex organs.
3. The *postpubescent,* or mature, stage when the secondary sex characteristics are well developed and when the sex organs are functioning in a mature manner.

The average age for boys to become pubescent is between the ages of 13½ and 14½ years, and for girls, 6 months to a year earlier. Approximately 50 per cent of all boys mature between 14 and 15½ years and approximately 50 per cent of all girls (Crampton, 1908; Baldwin, 1921; Shuttleworth, 1937). When stricter and more reliable criteria are used than are now employed, it may be found that the sex differences that are now believed to exist do not exist at all. The ages at which boys reach different stages of puberty are shown in Fig. 23.

TIME NEEDED FOR MATURING

Children do not turn into men and women overnight. The total time needed for maturing is approximately 3 years for girls and 2 to 4 years for boys. Boys show less uniformity in this process than do girls (Leal, 1929). Approximately 1 to 2 years are required for the preliminary changes from an asexual to a sexual state, the prepubescent stage, and 1 to 2 years for the changes to be completed after the individual's sex organs have become mature. The period of puberty changes lasts from 2 to 4 years. With but few exceptions, this stage has been found to last nearly twice as long as the prepuberty and postpuberty stages in boys (Stolz and Stolz, 1951).

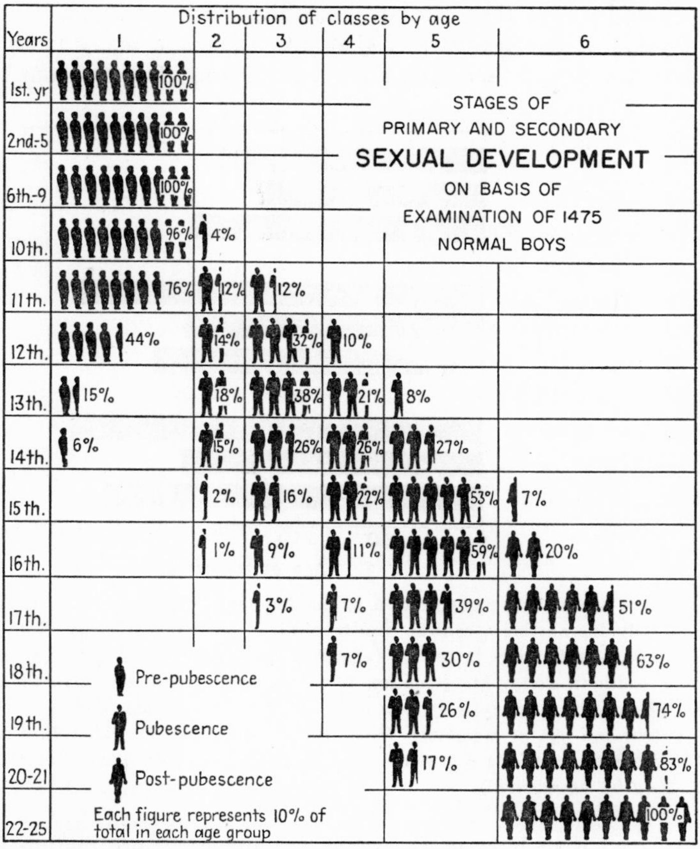

Years	Distribution of classes by age					
	1	2	3	4	5	6
1st. yr	100%					
2nd.-5	100%			STAGES OF		
6th.-9	100%			PRIMARY AND SECONDARY SEXUAL DEVELOPMENT		
10th.	96%	4%		ON BASIS OF EXAMINATION OF 1475 NORMAL BOYS		
11th.	76%	12%	12%			
12th.	44%	14%	32%	10%		
13th.	15%	18%	38%	21%	8%	
14th.	6%	15%	26%	26%	27%	
15th.		2%	16%	22%	53%	7%
16th.		1%	9%	11%	59%	20%
17th.		3%	7%		39%	51%
18th.				7%	30%	63%
19th.					26%	74%
20-21					17%	83%
22-25	Each figure represents 10% of total in each age group					100%

Pre-pubescence
Pubescence
Post-pubescence

FIG. 23. Age distribution of the various stages of primary and secondary sexual development. (*From W. A. Schonfeld, Primary and secondary sexual characteristics. Amer. J. Dis. Child., 1943, 65. Used by permission.*)

Once they start to mature, those who are slow in reaching puberty generally mature more quickly than do those who started sooner. The child who is precocious in his sexual maturing has a shorter childhood with its freedom from responsibilities but he has a longer adolescence, thus giving him more time to make the social and emotional adjustments needed for a successful adult life. By contrast, the child whose sexual maturity is delayed has a longer period of childhood during which he is not expected to assume the responsibilities of maturity. But he is handicapped by a shorter period of adolescence when adjustments to adult life are normally made.

FACTORS INFLUENCING MATURING

Differences between the *sexes* are especially marked between twelve and fourteen years of age because, at that age, there are many more mature girls than boys. At this time, girls are not only larger than boys but they are

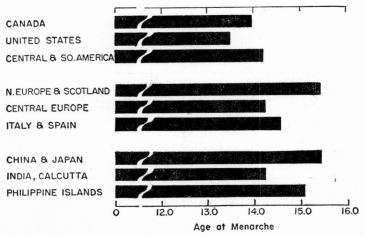

FIG. 24. Average age at first menstruation in the Americas, Europe, and Asia. Data presented separately for northern, central, and tropical or semitropical areas. Note that the menarche is consistently early in central temperate areas and delayed in colder northern and warmer southern areas. Menstruation is earlier in the United States than in any other area. (*Based on an analysis of data of C. A. Mills, Geographic and time variations in body growth and age at menarche. Hum. Biol., 1937, 9:43–56. From F. K. Shuttleworth, The adolescent period: a graphic atlas, Monogr. Soc. Res. Child Develpm., 1949, 14, No. 1. Used by permission.*)

more developed than boys of the same age and are more mature in their attitudes and behavior. Country children, on the average, mature earlier than city children (Baldwin, 1921). In some families, children mature considerably earlier than the average, while in others, maturity comes later (Krogman, 1948). Those, for example, who come from Nordic stock are believed to mature later than those from Mediterranean stock, but, to date, there is little evidence to prove or disprove this belief. Variations in the age of the menarche for girls of different countries are shown in Fig. 24. Comparison of Negro and white boys has revealed little or no difference between the Negro and white groups in the average ages of sexual maturity (Ramsey, 1950).

In *prolonged heat,* girls show not only retarded growth but delayed onset of the menarche or first menstruation. Girls show greater heat susceptibility than boys (Mills, 1950). A comparison of Nigerian school children with control groups in Great Britain revealed that the mean age of the menarche was slightly but significantly later among the Nigerian girls than among the girls of Great Britain. The degree of maturity of Nigerian boys, on the other hand, was essentially similar to that of a control group of boys in Great Britain (Ellis, 1950). Sexual maturity is dependent also, to a certain extent, upon the level of *mental development.* Children of superior intelligence mature earlier, on the average, than do those of average or below-average intelligence (Terman, 1926; Hollingworth, 1926). Children who are feebleminded mature later than those of average intelligence, the degree of retardation depending upon the extent of their mental deficiency. It must be remembered, however, that superior intelligence is generally found among children whose parents are of higher socioeconomic status and, hence, of better health resulting from better prenatal and postnatal care. These factors may play an important role in determining the age at which the children become pubescent.

CRITERIA OF PUBERTY

Because of the practical difficulty in applying a large number of criteria to determine the onset of and the stage of development reached in puberty, attempts have been made to use one criterion. Of those that have been used, some are easy to apply, others are difficult. How accurate this method is, however, is open to speculation. Of the single criteria that have been used to date, the following are the most important.

The *menarche,* or the first menstruation, is a commonly used criterion of sexual maturity among girls. But menstruation means neither the beginning nor the end of the physical changes occurring at puberty. When the menarche occurs, the sex organs and secondary sex characteristics have all started to develop but none are complete when the menarche occurs. All continue to develop for varying lengths of time after the menarche. More correctly, the menarche may be considered a mid-point in puberty. This is borne out by the period of sterility known as the "stage of adolescent sterility" which follows the menarche. This period lasts for 6 months to a year or even longer, during which time menstruation occurs irregularly, with lapses ranging from 2 to 6 months. At this time, ovulation or the ripening and release of a ripe ovum from a follicle in the ovary does not occur and the individual is, therefore, sterile. Even after several menstrual periods, it is questionable whether the sex mechanism is mature enough to make conception possible (Mills and Ogle, 1936; Ashley-Montagu, 1946, 1950; Engle and Shelesnyak, 1934).

Among boys, a popularly used criterion of puberty are *nocturnal emissions.* During sleep, the penis sometimes becomes erect, and semen, or fluid with sperm cells, spurts out. This is a normal way for the male reproductive organ to rid itself of excessive amounts of semen. Several objections can be raised to the use of nocturnal emissions as a single criterion of puberty. Studies of large groups of boys have revealed that not all boys experience this phenomenon or that they do not recognize it as such. Furthermore, nocturnal emissions, like the menarche, occur after some puberty development has taken place and cannot, therefore, be used as an accurate criterion of the onset of puberty.

Enlargement of the neck has been suggested as the most characteristic of all changes in the male reproductive development while *widening of the pubic region* is most characteristic of the female sexual development (Hogben *et al.*, 1948). Whether these criteria could be used alone to determine the onset of puberty is questionable. They could not, until greater refinement is made in the technique, be used to determine the stage of sexual development of the pubescent child.

X rays of the *bone development* of boys and girls show that as growth begins to spurt, at the close of childhood, genital growth always occurs at a certain point in the bone development of the individual. If X rays are taken of the different parts of the body, but especially of the hands and knees, during the preadolescent growth spurt, it will be possible to tell just when puberty begins and at what rate it is progressing (Shuttleworth, 1938; Todd, 1937; Bayley, 1940*a;* Greulich, 1950). From X rays of the hand and wrist, it is possible to predict the age of the menarche in girls. When used in children, predictions of early or late sexual maturing can be made (Greulich, 1950). The practical difficulty in applying this technique is too great to be overlooked, should there be any attempt to make widespread use of it.

Because the second molars, or *"wisdom teeth,"* cut through the gums at puberty, it has been suggested that the appearance of these teeth may be used as a criterion of the onset of puberty (P. Cattell, 1928). Once again, there is the question of practical use of this method, especially among children whose visits to the dentist are infrequent. Furthermore, it does not tell what stage in the total puberty development of the individual has been attained.

Chemical analysis of the first urine passed by boys in the morning to determine whether or not semen is present has proved to be an effective technique, although it is difficult to use (Baldwin, 1928). Urine has also been analyzed to determine the amount of *creatine* and *gonadotropic hormone (androgen)* present. Creatine is normally found in immature boys. If, therefore, the urine is free from creatine, the boy is sexually mature. Androgen is normally not found in the urine of boys under $12\frac{1}{2}$ years of age. After $12\frac{1}{2}$ years, some test positive and after 16, all do, unless there is a marked retardation in their sexual development (Oesting and Webster, 1938; Greulich *et al.*, 1942; Shock, 1945). In all these methods of chemical analysis, the practical difficulty of obtaining specimens of early-morning urine militates against the usefulness of the method as a practical technique.

CAUSES OF PUBERTY

Until recently, the exact cause or causes of puberty changes were a mystery. It was known that puberty changes occur at a fairly regular and predictable time, that the ages differed slightly for boys and girls, and that the changes followed a prescribed pattern similar for all members of the same sex. It was known that, among boys, there was some relationship between the onset of puberty and the development of the testes because, when boys were castrated, pubic hair did not appear nor did their voices change in pitch. Not until studies of the *endocrine glands,* or glands of internal secretion, had advanced to the point where the functions of the different glands were known was there any scientific information on the underlying cause of puberty changes. It has been established that there is a close relationship between the *pituitary gland,* located at the base of the brain, and the *gonads,* or sex glands. In this relationship, it is the pituitary that stimulates the gonads to increased activity. When this occurs, the hormones, or chemical secretions from the gonads, bring about the physical and mental changes characteristic of puberty.

Function of Pituitary Gland. The pituitary gland produces two hormones, both closely related to puberty changes. The first is the *growth hormone* which is influential in determining the size of the individual, and the second is the *gonadotropic,* or gonad-stimulating, hormone which acts on the gonads and stimulates them to increased activity. Just before puberty, it is believed, though not definitely proved, that there is a gradual increase in the amount of gonadotropic hormone from the pituitary gland and an increased sensitivity of the gonads to this hormone. Puberty is thus initiated by these two conditions. After the puberty changes have been completed, the interaction between the gonadotropic hormone and the gonads continues throughout the reproductive life of the individual, gradually decreasing as menopause in women and the climacteric in men occur. When this happens, the reproductive cycle of their lives is terminated.

Function of the Gonads. The gonads are the sex glands of the reproductive system. The male gonads are the *testes* (singular, testis), and the female, the *ovaries*. While the gonads are present at birth, they are in an immature state of development and function until puberty, when their growth and activity are stimulated by the gonadotropic hormone from the pituitary gland. That explains why children are almost neutral as regards sex in their physical development, in attitudes, and in behavior. With the growth and development of the gonads at puberty, marked physical, psychological, and behavioral changes appear. Not only do the sex organs increase in size and become functionally active, but the *secondary sex characteristics,* or physical traits not directly related to reproduction but which distinguish the male from the female body, develop.

The *testes,* which at the age of fourteen years are only approximately 10 per cent of their mature size, grow rapidly for a year or two and then gradually slow down. They have not reached their mature weight when the boy is twenty years old, though they are functionally mature by approximately the middle of puberty, when nocturnal emissions appear. The *ovaries,* likewise, go through a growth spurt at puberty. When girls are twelve years old, their ovaries are approximately 40 per cent of their mature weight. There is an acceleration in growth from then until the age of sixteen or seventeen years when the ovaries are about one-half of their final weight. By the time the girl is twenty years old, her ovaries are their mature size though, like the testes, the ovaries are functionally mature before puberty is ended. Changes in attitudes and behavior appear as these physical changes of puberty take place. It is safe to conclude that their development is due to maturation rather than to learning, and that they are the result of the increased amount of the gonad secretions just as are the physical changes that are taking place.

TESTES. The male gonads or testes have a dual function. They produce *spermatozoa,* or sex cells, needed for reproduction, and they produce one or more hormones that control the physical and psychological adjustments necessary for reproduction. This includes the development of the sex organs, of the secondary sex characteristics, and of the aggressive drives characteristic of the male.

OVARIES. The female gonads, or ovaries, likewise have several functions. Their primary function is to produce *ova* (singular, *ovum*), or germ cells, necessary for reproduction. In addition, they produce *theelin* and *progestin,* regulatory hormones which initiate and bring to a completion the period of pregnancy, the *follicular* hormone, and the *corpus luteum.* The female sex hormones are responsible for bringing about the development in structure and function of the female reproductive organs with their characteristic menstrual cycles and of the secondary sex characteristics of the female body, especially the breasts with their mammary glands, secreting nourishment when reproduction has taken place.

Interaction of Pituitary and Gonads. In both boys and girls, the hormones from the gonads, which have been stimulated by the hormones from the pituitary, act in turn on the pituitary and cause a gradual reduction in the amount of the growth hormone which, as was previously pointed out, is produced by the anterior lobe of the pituitary gland. Eventually, the gonadal hormones stop the activity of the growth hormone completely and thus stop the process of physical growth. If body size is to be normal or near normal, there must be not only reciprocal activity on the part of the gonads and pituitary but also proper timing in this reciprocal activity. When an individual is below average in size at maturity, it means that there has not been enough of the growth hormone in late childhood and early puberty. If, however, the gonadal hormones are not released in adequate amounts soon enough, the individual's growth continues for too long and he becomes larger than the average adult. This is especially true of the limbs.

Abnormal Functioning. Abnormalities in the functioning of the gonads have been studied in both animal and human subjects. When there is an inadequate supply of gonadal hormones because of subnormal development of the gonads an insufficient supply of gonadotropic hormone from the pituitary gland or when there is injury to or destruction of the gonads from a disease such as mumps in boys, removal of the gonads by castration in boys, or the necessity for removing certain areas of the female reproductive apparatus, puberty is delayed and normal development of the sex organs and secondary sex characteristics is prevented. As a result, individuals remain childish in appearance or take on the characteristics of the opposite sex, depending on just when these interruptions occurred in the developmental cycle. Hyperactivity of the gonads or an excessive supply of gonadal hormones, on the other hand, brings about a precocious development of puberty. This condition is known as "puberty precox" and is caused by an imbalance in the functioning of the pituitary gland and the gonads resulting from an excessive amount of gonadatropic hormone at an earlier age than usual. There are medical records of young children who are mature in their sexual development and yet who are as small in stature as other children of their own age.

PHYSICAL CHANGES AT PUBERTY

There are three important physical changes occurring at puberty. These are the development of the *primary sex characteristics,* or the sex organs proper; the development of the *secondary sex characteristics,* or the physical features which distinguish the male from the female; and *rapid physical growth,* accompanied by changes in physical proportions. The first plays a direct role in reproduction, while the second and third are only indirectly related to reproduction.

PRIMARY SEX CHARACTERISTICS

The sex organs during childhood are small and sexually immature. The individual is, as a result, incapable of reproduction. During puberty, the sex organs increase in size and become sexually mature. In boys, shortly after the rapid growth of the testes begins, the growth of the penis is markedly accelerated. The growth at first is in length. This is followed by a gradual increase in circumference. The penis attains its mature length at an earlier age than its mature girth (Greulich *et al.,* 1942). There is a close relationship between the timing of growth of the penis and growth in height. In four-fifths of the cases studied by Stolz and Stolz (1951), the onset of rapid growth in the penis comes within 4 months of the onset of rapid growth in height. There was also an equally close relationship between the endings of these two phases of growth of the testes and the increase in height.

Because the female reproductive apparatus is mostly inside the body, its growth is barely perceptible, except for the enlargement of the abdomen. This is a normal characteristic of early puberty, though a source of great concern to most girls. As the bony framework of the girl's body enlarges, the space within which the reproductive organs are lodged also enlarges, with the result that the abdomen flattens out. The first real indication a girl has that her reproductive mechanism is becoming mature is the *menarche*, or first menstrual flow. This is generally followed by a period of menstrual irregularity during which menstruation comes at irregular and unpredictable times and its duration varies markedly. While the average duration is 4.6 days, this varies from 1 to 7 days, especially in its early appearances (Fluhmann, 1934).

Frequently, headaches, backaches, cramps, and abdominal pain, accompanied by fainting, vomiting, skin irritations, and even swelling of the legs and ankles, occur in the early menstrual periods. As a result, the girl feels tired, depressed, and irritable at the time of her periods. As menstruation establishes itself as a regular function, its irregularity decreases, as do the physical and psychological disturbances which accompany its early appearances.

SECONDARY SEX CHARACTERISTICS

As puberty progresses, boys and girls become increasingly dissimilar in appearance. This change is caused by the gradual development of the secondary sex characteristics. Whether the secondary sex characteristics develop at the same time as the primary sex characteristics, or whether their development precedes that of the primary sex characteristics by a slight margin of time has not yet been definitely proved. The maturation of secondary sex characteristics is shown in Fig. 25. It is believed, however, that the secondary sex characteristics precede the primary in the normal pattern of development and hence are more nearly at their mature state of development when puberty comes to a close than are the primary sex characteristics. In precocious sex development, the pattern of development of the secondary sex characteristics remains the same in both boys and girls, though they appear at an earlier than normal age.

In Boys. Not all secondary sex characteristics begin to develop at the same time in boys, nor do they all reach their mature state of development at the same age. Marked individual differences exist in the ages at which these traits first appear. However, they seem to conform to a fairly regular and predictable pattern of development, varying more in age from individual to individual than in sequential pattern. This pattern is (Greulich *et al.*, 1942):

1. *Pubic Hair.* At first, the hair at the base of the penis is long and downy. This is followed by long, coarse, and rather straight pigmented hairs, which are soon replaced by kinky, deeply pigmented pubic hair.

2. *Axillary Perspiration.* A marked increase in axillary perspiration follows the growth of pubic hairs.

3. *Down.* Down appears on the upper lip, especially at the corners. This becomes longer, coarser, and darker as time goes on.

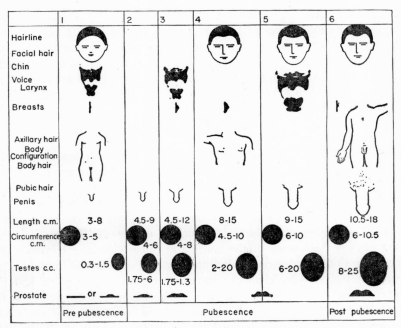

FIG. 25. Stages of sexual development and maturation. (*From W. A. Schonfeld, Primary and secondary sexual characteristics. Amer. J. Dis. Child., 1943, 65. Used by permission.*)

4. *Forearm Hair.* Long, coarse down appears on the forearms.

5. *Leg Hair.* Coarse, pigmented hair appears on the legs and thighs.

6. *Hair on Face.* Long down appears on the sides of the face, in front of the ears.

7. *Pubic Region.* The pubic region is covered with a dense growth of pubic hair.

8. *Armpits.* Short, fine, pigmented hairs appear in the armpits.

9. *Voice.* The voice deepens perceptibly.

10. *Subareolar Masses.* Subareolar masses have attained their maximum size.

11. *Hair on Thighs.* Pubic hair spreads to the adjacent surface of the thighs.

12. *Chin Hairs.* A few hairs have appeared on the sides of the chin and the upper part of the cheek, just in front of the ears.

13. *Body Hairs.* Hair appears around the periphery of the areolae and over the sternum.

14. *Hairline.* The adult type of hairline begins to differentiate on the forehead.

15. *Hair.* Almost all the hair characteristic of a young adult is present on the forearms, arms, legs and thighs.

Of these changes, the ones that have received most attention in scientific investigations, the characteristic form these changes take, and the average ages at which they occur, are as follows:

HAIR. Pubic hair first appears about 1 year after the testes and penis have started to increase in size. Prepubescent or lightly pigmented, straight hair first appears between the thirteenth and fourteenth years, with a median at 13.6 years. At a median age of 14 to 14.5 years, pubescent hair which is more luxuriant in growth and slightly pigmented appears. Six months to a year later, the characteristically kinky twist and greater pigmentation are present. For the average American boy, pubic hair is well developed around the age of 15 years (Greulich *et al.*, 1942). There is a definite tendency for the rate of gain in pubic-hair development to be greater during the first half of the puberty period than during the second half, though marked individual differences occur (Stolz and Stolz, 1951).

Axillary and *facial hair* begin to appear when pubic hair has almost completed its growth. Like pubic hair, axillary and facial hairs are lightly pigmented, fine in texture, and few in numbers at first. Few boys have enough facial hair to necessitate shaving before they are sixteen or seventeen years old. In addition, most boys develop relatively heavy growths of hair on their arms, legs, shoulders, and chests (Greulich *et al.*, 1942). Far less universal among boys is the change of the hairline at puberty from a bowlike curve to a curve with two wedge-shaped indentations over each lateral frontal region.

VOICE CHANGES. Voice changes generally come after some pubic hair has appeared. The median age for the first indication of the deepening of the voice is 13.4 years, though the breaking and conspicuous loss of control do not appear until the body is between 16 and 18 years of age. Following this, there is a year or two before the change is completed and the youth has acquired control of his voice (Ramsey, 1943*a*).

NOCTURNAL EMISSIONS. Nocturnal emissions occur at a median age of 15 years, though the variation from boy to boy is marked. There are marked variations also in the frequency of emissions, varying from 1 to 13 a week (Ramsey, 1943*a*).

BREAST KNOTS. Breast knots, or slight knobs around the male mammary glands, appear between the ages of twelve and fourteen years. They last for only a few weeks, then decrease rapidly in number and size. At about the same time, the male mammary glands enlarge in one or both breasts. Like the breast knots, this is only a temporary condition and disappears within a short time, after which the breasts become flat, as in childhood.

In Girls. The pattern of development of the secondary sex characteristics in girls is regular and predictable, as in boys. The first of the female characteristics to develop are the *breasts,* followed shortly by an increase in the width and roundness of the *hips,* caused partly by the enlargement of the pelvic bone and partly by the development of subcutaneous fat. *Pubic hair* does not appear in any considerable quantity until breast and hip development are well under way, though a few unpigmented hairs appear at the beginning of pubertal changes. This scanty development remains unchanged for a num-

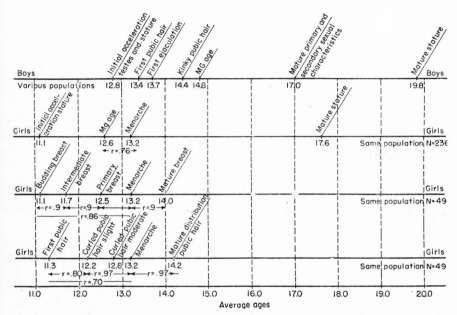

FIG. 26. Schematic picture of the typical sequence and interrelation of events in the process of sexual maturation of boys and girls. (*From F. K. Shuttleworth, The adolescent period: a graphic atlas, Monogr. Soc. Res. Child Develpm., 1949, 14, No. 1. Used by permission.*)

ber of months, when suddenly the hair becomes more pigmented, changes from straight to kinky, and becomes much more luxuriant in quantity.

After the pubic hair is fairly well developed, *axillary hair,* or hair on the armpits, begins to develop and a slight *down* appears on the upper lip. The *menarche* usually, though not always, precedes the appearance of the axillary hair (Pryor, 1936). Just before or just after the menarche, the time of appearance differing from individual to individual, there is a change from the high-pitched, childish *voice* to one of lower pitch with a fuller and more melodious tone. The *shoulders* broaden, the *arms* and *legs* take on a definite shape because of the heavier musculature of the body, and *hair* develops on the limbs. A "timetable" of the sexual maturation of boys and girls is shown in Fig. 26.

RAPID PHYSICAL GROWTH

Puberty is one of the two times during the life span of the individual when rapid physical growth occurs. The first comes during the prenatal period and the first half of the first postnatal year. It then slows down and, from about two years of age until puberty, growth is at a relatively steady and slow rate. The second period of rapid growth is generally referred to as the "adolescent growth spurt." In reality, it is a preadolescent rather than an adolescent spurt because it precedes slightly or comes simultaneously with the physical changes of puberty (Boynton, 1936; Shuttleworth, 1937).

This growth spurt lasts for a year or two before the boy or girl becomes sexually mature and for 6 months to a year afterward. This means that the entire period of rapid growth lasts for about 3 years as contrasted to the 4 or 5 years, as is generally believed. As a rule, this growth spurt starts between the tenth and eleventh years of the child's life, though it may reach its climax as early as ten or as late as seventeen years (Shuttleworth, 1937). Increases in height, weight, and strength come at approximately the same time. Predicting adult stature is difficult until after the prepubescent growth spurt because of marked individual differences in the rate of growth (Simmons, 1944).

Rapid physical growth at puberty is the result of maturation, not of environmental forces such as food or exercise, as is often believed. The pituitary gland which sets into action the gonads, or sex glands, also releases a "growth hormone" from the anterior lobe. This is responsible for the rapid growth taking place at this time. Without adequate amounts of this hormone, *dwarfism* occurs; too much of it produces *giantism*. The timing of the release of the growth hormone is more important than its quantity. The gonadotropic hormone, also released by the pituitary, not only stimulates the development of the gonads but it also acts on the growth hormone and causes a gradual reduction either in its quantity or in its effectiveness. This results in a slowing down of growth.

Individual differences in the pattern of growth depend upon the individual's rate of maturing. Early-maturing individuals have greater spurts of rapid growth with abrupt starts and stops. They attain their adult sizes and proportions quickly. Their growth is regular and symmetrical and there is, therefore, little organic imbalance. Late-maturing individuals, by contrast, have less intense periods of acceleration. As a result, growth is more gradual and even. It continues for a longer time and, therefore, as a rule, late-maturing individuals are larger when growth is completed. But body dimensions and growth of the internal organs may lag behind growth in stature. Hence, growth is irregular and asymmetrical (Reynolds, 1946). Variations in the growth spurt are shown in Fig. 27.

Weight. Girls maturing between twelve and fifteen years of age show an average increase of 14 pounds in the year before puberty. The next greatest increase, 10.1 pounds, occurs two years before puberty and the same occurs in the year of puberty. For boys, the peak of weight increase comes at fourteen years of age, with an average gain of 15 pounds in the year preceding puberty. In the next two years, there is an average gain of 21.3 pounds (Van Dyke, 1930). The pattern of weight increase for boys varies more than in the case of height. During the puberty period, the mean gain in weight is 39.92 pounds,

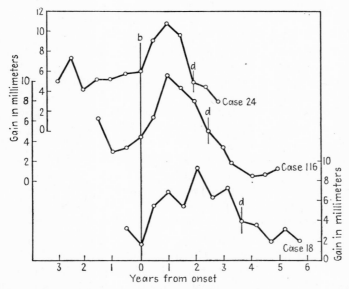

Fig. 27. Growth curve of height for three boys, illustrating variations in the duration of the pubertal growth spurt. (*From H. R. Stolz and L. M. Stolz, Somatic development of adolescent boys. New York: Macmillan, 1951. Used by permission.*)

with a range from 17.2 to 64.81 pounds. Except in cases where there is a marked early adolescent fat period, maximum growth in weight usually comes with or after maximum growth in height (Stolz and Stolz, 1951).

Among boys, when there is a period of fatness at puberty, it generally comes at or near the onset of the period of rapid growth for height and the onset of the spurt in penis growth. During the period of conspicuous fat, boys tend to have marked accumulations of fat around the nipples and over the abdomen, hips, and thighs. In addition, there is usually an increase of fat about the neck, cheeks, and jaw which alters the individual's facial appearance. Generally, the "fat period" lasts for about 2 years, after which the body regains its normal proportions (Stolz and Stolz, 1951). Among girls, the "fat period" comes generally at the onset of puberty but, to date, no scientific investigations of its duration and effect on the female body have been reported. Weight increase comes mostly from growth of the muscles rather than from fat. The muscles are growing rapidly at this time and weigh nearly twice as much at maturity as they do during childhood. The bones are also growing rapidly and they contribute to body weight as do the internal organs. In spite of the increase in weight, pubescent boys and girls often look lanky and scrawny because of the lengthening of their limbs.

Height. The period of most rapid increase in height, as in weight, is in preadolescence and early adolescence. Among girls, the years from ten to fourteen are ones of very rapid growth in height, while for boys, the peak of the increase comes between the ages of twelve and fifteen years. The average annual gain for girls in the year preceding puberty has been found to be 2.9 inches though a 5- to 6-inch gain is not unusual. Two years before puberty, the average increase was found to be 2.6 inches, making a total increase of 5.5 inches in 2 years preceding puberty (Van Dyke, 1930; Boas, 1932; Shuttleworth, 1939). There is a constant relationship between the menarche and maximum annual increment in height, with the greatest increase coming in the year preceding the menarche. The rate of growth decelerates after the menarche (Greulich, 1950).

For boys, the onset of the period of rapid growth in height comes between 10.4 and 15.75 years, with an average of 12.88 years. The age at the end of the period ranges from 13.1 to 17.5, with an average at 15.33 years. The mean age at which boys reach the apex of velocity of their growth in height is 13.99 years. Boys who begin their pubertal growth spurt early complete it early; those who begin late are late in ending. The duration of the period ranges from 1.95 to 4.95 years, with a mean of 2.81 years. There is a slight tendency for early developers to have a longer duration than late developers (Stolz and Stolz, 1951). The greatest increase in height comes in the year following the onset of puberty (Dimock, 1937). The interrelation of height and weight spurts is shown in Fig. 28.

After the age of fourteen years, girls grow at an increasingly slower rate and attain their mature height between the ages of eighteen and twenty years, with barely perceptible gains in height during the last year or two of this period. Among the boys, slight increases in height occur until they are twenty or twenty-one years old. After that, annual increases are barely perceptible. Boys attain their mature height a year or two later than girls, at an average age of twenty-two or twenty-three years. Late-maturing girls continuing to grow after the mature height of early-maturing girls has been completed with the result that they are generally taller at maturity than are the girls who started to mature earlier. The reason for this is that, because growth in height is nearly complete at the time of puberty, late-maturing girls have a longer time in which to grow (Stone and Barker, 1937; Bayley,

1943). In boys, because the advent of puberty accelerates growth in height instead of retarding it, as it does in the case of girls, the early-maturing boys are likely to be taller at all ages than are those who mature later (Bayley, 1943).

Body Proportions. While the body is growing larger at puberty, not all parts increase at the same rate. As a result, the disproportions characteristic of childhood remain, though they change in their emphasis. Certain areas of the body, which in the early years of life were proportionally much too small, now become proportionally too big because they reach their mature size sooner than other areas. This is particularly apparent in the case of the nose, feet, and hands. Until the shoulders broaden, the trunk seems too big in the

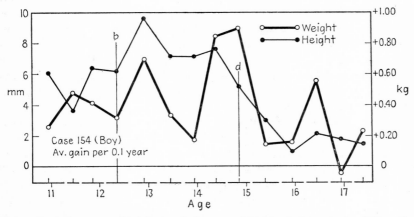

Fig. 28. Typical pattern of height in relation to weight increase at puberty. (*From H. R. Stolz and L. M. Stolz, Somatic development of adolescent boys. New York: Macmillan, 1951. Used by permission.*)

lower region because of the rapid growth taking place in the internal organs. This is especially true of girls whose abdomens protrude to a greater or less extent. Maximum growth in the legs generally precedes maximum growth in the trunk length (Stolz and Stolz, 1951).

Strength. With growth in the muscles comes increase in strength. Strength ratings of boys showed that the average yearly postpubertal gain was greater than the average yearly pubertal gain. There was a close relationship between gains in muscular strength and gains in weight. The apex of strength increase occurred within the pubertal period for height, though in apex growth strength was found to be more closely related to weight than to height gains. It has been suggested that the characteristics of growth of muscular strength have important implications for the classification of adolescent boys into appropriate competitive groups in physical activities (Stolz and Stolz, 1951).

PHYSICAL EFFECTS OF PUBERTY

Rapid growth and bodily changes are likely to be accompanied by fatigue, listlessness, and other unfavorable symptoms. At puberty, this condition is frequently exaggerated by the increase in duties and responsibilities placed upon the individual just at the time when he is least able to shoulder them successfully. Because he is now larger in stature, his parents assume that he can carry more of the burdens of the home than he did when he was younger. In much the same spirit, the school piles work on shoulders not yet broad enough or strong enough to carry them. Is it any wonder, then, that boys and girls who are passing through puberty are tired out and listless much of the time? And, as fatigue invariably predisposes the individual to nervousness, irritability, and general emotionality, is it surprising that the pubescent child is a difficult individual to live with?

Digestive disturbances are frequent and appetite is finicky. Like the woman during pregnancy, the prepubescent child is upset by glandular changes and changes in the size and position of the internal organs. These changes interfere with the normal functions of digestion. Anemia is frequent at this period not because of marked changes in blood chemistry but because of the erratic eating habits of the individual. This, in turn, increases the already present tendency to be tired and listless, thus setting into motion a vicious circle which results in further appetite and digestive disturbances. Headaches, backaches, and a general feeling of wretchedness which accompany the menarche and subsequent menstrual periods are not limited to girls, nor do they occur only at the time of menstruation. Both boys and girls suffer intermittently from them, the frequency and severity depending to a large extent upon how rapidly the pubescent changes are occurring and upon how healthy the individuals were when puberty began.

Children of poor environments, where nutritional diets are poor and good habits of sleep have not usually been formed in childhood, are more likely to be affected unfavorably by pubertal changes than are children whose childhood health has been favorable, provided the rate of maturing is the same for both. Pimples, blackheads, and acne of greater or less severity appear at puberty in almost all boys and girls. As a general rule, brunettes suffer more from skin eruptions than do blondes. Contrary to popular opinion, skin disturbances at this age are not caused by faulty diet alone, though this unquestionably exaggerates them, but rather by changes occurring within the texture of the skin. The disturbances are not limited to the face alone, as many people believe, but often appear on the neck, shoulders, back, and arms.

While puberty may be regarded as a "sickly age" when the individual is not up to par, there are relatively few diseases characteristic of this age. Nor does he suffer from any definite illness which necessitates his being out of school or missing the social life of his companions. If he were actually ill, he would be treated with more sympathy and understanding than he usually is, less would be expected of him, and, of special significance to his social adjustments, much of his unsocial behavior would be understood and tolerated, as it rarely is.

PSYCHOLOGICAL EFFECTS OF PUBERTY

No radical physical change, especially when it occurs rapidly as it does at puberty, can escape having psychological reverberations. How great or how trivial the psychological effects of puberty will be will depend partly upon the speed of maturing with its impact of greater or lesser severity on the general physical well-being of the individual and partly upon the individual's foreknowledge and consequent psychological preparation for the changes. In the absence of preparation, or when the preparation has consisted mainly of inaccurate information which has given rise to unhealthy attitudes, the general effect on behavior is more unfavorable, even when the rate of maturing is slow, than when the preparation has been adequate and wholesome and the speed of development fast.

During this period, both boys and girls are keenly aware of their bodies and the changes that are taking place in them. One of the primary developmental tasks both now and during adolescence is the acceptance of the changing body as a symbol of the changing self. The psychological effects of puberty are also complicated by the social expectancy of parents, teachers, and other adults. A boy or a girl of a given chronological age is expected to act according to standards for that age. The twelve-year-old, for example, is expected to have different interests and to act differently from a fourteen-year-old. When the developmental pattern approximates the group mean, such adjustments will be relatively easy. When, however, there is a marked discrepancy between social expectancy and a child's maturational readiness, there are likely to be problems for him and for society (Stolz and Stolz, 1951). Because the psychological effects of puberty are numerous, they may conveniently be subdivided into two major groups: *sources of concern* and *effects on behavior*. While these two major groups overlap to a certain extent, they are clear-cut and distinct enough to justify such a subdivision.

SOURCES OF CONCERN

Both boys and girls are disturbed by the *changes in their sex organs* and by the *appearance of secondary sex characteristics*. Among boys, there is the fear that the rapidly growing penis will show through their clothing and there is worry because it seems so thin as compared with the penis of adult men. The first straggly *hairs* that develop in the pubic region, under the arms, and on the chest bother the boy, but when they start to appear on his face, his embarrassment becomes real. This is not helped by the joking remarks made by his parents, relatives, or even his friends. Then, when his *voice* begins to crack and he is unsure of its pitch when he is asked to recite in class or when he is expected to talk to friends of the family or adults in authority, his embarrassment reaches its peak and his mental suffering is beyond the realization of adults who have forgotten their own agonizing experiences at the same age.

Because the girl's *genitalia* grow more internally than externally, she has less cause for concern on that score than has the pubescent boy. However, her developing *breasts,* the unexplained protrusion of her abdomen, and the broadening of her hips disturb her in much the same manner as the growing penis disturbs the boy. She is afraid of their telltale signs through her clothing. To avoid embarrassment, especially when she walks or runs, the pubescent girl frequently wears a tight brassière to flatten her breasts and a tight girdle to hold in her hips and abdomen. She often develops a stooping posture to make her hips seem less prominent. And, like the boy, the pubescent girl is concerned about the *hair* that begins to come on her body. Her concern is heightened by the realization that the axillary hair will show when she wears a bathing suit or an evening dress. The appearance of hair on her face frequently alarms her because she is afraid that she may have to shave like a man. Concern about body hair is greater, as a rule, among brunettes than among blondes because the hair of a brunette is more noticeable than that of a blonde. Because her *voice* changes more slowly and less noticeably than the boy's, its change in pitch and tonal quality is of little concern to her.

The *menarche* in girls and first *nocturnal emission* in boys may be traumatic experiences for them, even if they have had some forewarning of what to expect. If the menarche is accompanied by vomiting, pain, headaches, and backaches, all of which are common accompaniments of the menarche, the traumatic effect is heightened. It is not unusual for girls to wonder if they will "bleed to death" or to believe that something serious is the matter with them. What the girl's attitude will be depends largely upon her information and the attitude of her informer. Without wholesome preparation for this experience, the traumatic effect is heightened to a pitch where it is apt to leave an indelible impression on the girl's mind (Conklin, 1933). Subsequent menstrual periods are likely to be disturbing to a girl not only because of the discomforts they bring but also because the girl resents the restrictions this condition imposes upon her activities. Furthermore, she is afraid of any telltale signs that will reveal the fact that she is menstruating. As a general rule, girls become more introverted in their attitudes during the menstrual period, and this tendency is increased with increase in the pain and discomfort experienced (Conklin, 1933).

The boy's first nocturnal emission is much the same traumatic experience for him as the menarche is for the girl. In absence of foreknowledge of this experience, he is likely to believe that something is seriously wrong with him. Furthermore, he is disturbed and embarrassed by the stains left on his pajamas or on the sheets of his bed. Each subsequent nocturnal emission is likely to be a source of embarrassment to him. If, however, he does not experience nocturnal emission, he frequently has tension and discomfort in his penis which may lead to masturbation, to relieve the tension. This, in turn, is likely to lead to shame, embarrassment, or feelings of guilt, depending upon what attitudes toward masturbation were engendered when he was a child.

The sudden *increase in size,* due to the pubertal growth spurt, is likely to disturb girls because they are afraid they will become so large that boys will not want to date them or that they will be wallflowers at a dance. This concern would be markedly lessened if girls realized that rapid growth continues for only a short time. When boys see girls of their own ages literally towering over them, it is not surprising that they are disturbed. Even when they know that girls normally outstrip boys in size for several years, it is hard for them to be objective about the matter and not worry for fear that they will remain small for the rest of their lives.

For both boys and girls, excessive *fat* which frequently comes in the early part of puberty, is a source of great concern. In our culture, fat is considered unattractive and, therefore, it disturbs the individual who does not conform to social expectations. Girls who have a prototype of female beauty based on moving-picture heroines, glamour girls in society, and cover girls on magazines, are very distressed when they look at their own bodies. For a boy, fat is considered sexually inappropriate, especially when there is an accumulation of fat on the thighs, around the waist, and in the mammary region. While this generally disappears as puberty progresses, it may affect personality development unfavorably for many years after the somatic stigma has passed (Stolz and Stolz, 1951).

Body disproportions, which are an inevitable accompaniment of growth, cause concern bordering on alarm for the pubescent child. The too big hands and feet are especially disturbing to a girl because she has been brought up on the tradition that "Ladies have small hands and feet." She shows how great this concern is to her by wearing shoes too small for her feet, by wearing high heels before the arches of her feet are developed enough to wear such heels with comfort, and by holding her hands in her pockets or behind her back so that no one can see them. The temporarily too large nose sends both boys and girls into states of depression every time they look into the mirror. *Skin eruptions,* especially when they appear on the face, disturb both boys and girls. This concern leads them to try out all sorts of beauty aids recommended by friends, parents, or advertisements as "sure cures" for the disfiguring blotches. When the so-called "cures" fail to work, and the blotches appear with increasing frequency and intensity as the months pass, the pubescent boy or girl is sent into the depths of despair and gloom.

Precocious and *delayed maturing* have marked psychological effects on both boys and girls. Those who mature earlier than their classmates feel like misfits among their former friends partly because they are too big and too grown-up in appearance for them and partly because, with the characteristic interests that accompany pubertal development, they have little in common with them. Children, on the other hand, who are slow in maturing, feel embarrassed because of their small, undeveloped bodies; they feel out of things when they cannot bring themselves to be interested in the things which are so absorbing to their more mature classmates; and, if their maturing is markedly delayed, they worry for fear that they will remain little boys or girls for the rest of their lives.

To compensate for slow maturing, many boys and girls withdraw from the groups to which they formerly belonged and develop solitary interests. This, however, is rarely satisfying to them, especially if they have enjoyed an active social life with other children throughout their childhood years and have had a circle of friends to which they belonged. Now they feel lost without their friends and yet, because they have little in common with them, it is not surprising that they find themselves in the role of social misfits. Other children whose sexual maturing is delayed may compensate by trying to dress, act, and feel like their more sexually mature friends. This, likewise, is frequently not a satisfying form of compensation because the individual's behavior often gives his friends the impression that he is "just a kid who is trying to put on airs and pretend that he is older than he is."

A slight deviation from the average age of sexual maturing among members of a group is not a great handicap to any child. But, when the deviations are marked, either above or below the average, the effects on social adjustment are detrimental. Of the two, slow-maturing individuals are more handicapped than those who mature ahead of schedule not only because they lag behind their contemporaries in social development and the acquisition of more mature interests, but primarily because they are likely to develop feelings of inadequacy and inferiority which tend to militate against good social adjustments even after the individuals have become sexually mature. They are likely to continue to be childish and immature in their attitudes (Abernathy, 1925).

The age of sexual maturing affects the two sexes slightly differently. On the whole, early-maturing girls are faced with more serious adjustment problems than are late-maturing girls or than are boys. The reason for this is that the early-maturing girl is not only out of step in her interests and behavior with members of her own sex but also with members of the opposite sex who normally mature a year or two later than girls do. Furthermore, society is more critical of the behavior of girls than of boys. The girl whose sexual development is precocious frequently gets the reputation of being "fast" not only among her contemporaries but also among the parents of her contemporaries. And yet, her behavior is generally normal for her level of development, even though precocious for her chronological age.

An analysis of the personality patterns of a group of men who, as boys, were early maturers showed them to have the following characteristics: alert, energetic, vivacious, spontaneous, physically active, socially extroverted, and aggressive. Fifty-three per cent of the group studied were described thus as compared with 33 per cent of the late maturers. By contrast, 54 per cent of the late maturers were described as slow, quiet, mild in manner, without force, reserved, timid, taciturn, introverted, and socially inept, as contrasted with 31 per cent of the early maturers who were described thus (Kinsey et al., 1948).

EFFECTS ON BEHAVIOR

Marked physiological changes, especially when they come within a relatively short period of time, are likely to be accompanied by psychological changes or changes in attitude toward self, toward other people, and toward life in general. Because growth in stature, growth of the sex organs, and the development of secondary sex characteristics all proceed more rapidly in the early part of puberty than in the latter, the changes in the child's attitudes and behavior are likewise more pronounced in the early part than in the later part of puberty. As might be expected when physical changes bring about a temporary upset in the smooth normal course of growth, the effects on behavior are more unfavorable than favorable.

This expectation is borne out in the case of puberty. Comparisons of different forms of behavior among girls and boys in the prepubescent and pubescent stages with those in the postpubescent stage have shown how marked these changes are. From negative to positive social attitudes occur after the pubescent development is completed or nearly completed just as there is a change from positive to negative social attitudes from the end of childhood to the onset of puberty (Leal, 1929). Among girls, significant and characteristic changes in interests, attitudes, and preferred activities accompany changes in primary and secondary sex characteristics, changes in physical proportions and in physiological functions associated with the attainment of sexual maturity (Stone and Barker, 1937).

When puberty changes occur at a rapid rate, the effects are more marked than when puberty has been slower. Furthermore, good physical and mental health throughout the childhood years are likely to cause less disturbance to behavior and attitudes at puberty than when health conditions are less favorable. Lack of understanding on the part of adults and poor parent-child relationships exaggerate and intensify unfavorable conditions brought about by poor health or unfavorable attitudes fostered in childhood (Hurlock and Sender, 1939). Girls, as a general rule, are more seriously affected by puberty than are boys partly because girls mature, on the average, more rapidly than do boys and partly because there are more social restrictions on their behavior just at the time when they are trying to free themselves from these restrictions. There are, however, such marked individual differences from child to child that it is impossible to predict just how puberty will affect the behavior of any given child, either boy or girl.

Among the many effects of puberty on attitude and behavior, the following have been found to be the most common. All of these, in one way or another, lead to difficult social adjustments for the individual or present problems for his parents and teachers to cope with, thus justifying the name "negative phase" which Charlotte Bühler so aptly applied to it.

Desire for Isolation. As early as babyhood, there is a craving for the companionship of others. This desire reaches its peak in the "gang age" of late childhood. Then, in a relatively short time, sometimes within a week or even over a week end, the child loses interest in his playmates, withdraws from the group, and spends his time alone in his room with his door shut (Furfey, 1926; Vecerka, 1926; C. Bühler, 1927; Hurlock and Sender, 1939). This withdrawal from the group is frequently accompanied by quarreling with former friends and the consequent breaking off of many childhood friendships.

Disinclination to Work. The child who formerly was constantly on the go and never seemed to tire from work or play, now seems constantly tired. As a result, he does as little work as he can. Home responsibilities are allowed to slide and school studies are neglected. As a result, many an "A" student slips into the "just-barely-passing" group while the previously poor student turns into a failure. Unquestionably, this disinclination to work is not willful laziness on the child's part but is a direct outgrowth of rapid physical growth and development which sap his energy. Just at the time when he is least able to assume added burdens and responsibilities, his parents and teachers are likely to expect him to assume them. After all, they reason, he is no longer a child and should, therefore, assume more responsibilities than he did when he was younger. Then, when he shirks these responsibilities, or does them carelessly and slowly, he is blamed for being lazy and slipshod. This, in turn, builds up antagonisms and resentments which result in even less desire on the child's part to do what is expected of him.

Boredom. The pubescent child is bored with the play he formerly enjoyed, with his schoolwork, with social activities and with life in general. And he does not hesitate to show this boredom by refusing to engage in activities he formerly enjoyed or by criticizing them as "stupid" and "babyish." In neither case does he win the sympathy or approval of his friends and playmates. When reproved for this attitude, he sinks into a state of sullen gloom and develops an "I don't care" or a "No one loves me" attitude.

Restlessness. As invariably occurs when a person is bored, the pubescent child is restless. Things which formerly absorbed his interest and held his attention no longer do so. Because his interests are changing, as his body changes, he has not yet discovered new interests that can absorb his attention as his childhood interests did. He, therefore, goes from one thing to another, never completely satisfied with one and always on the search for something that he can enjoy as he previously enjoyed his childhood experiences.

Social Antagonism. The pubescent child is antagonistic in his attitude toward his family, his friends, and society in general. He goes around with a chip on his shoulder and a snarl on his face. Not only does he seem to resent the happiness of others but he seems to go out of his way to dispel

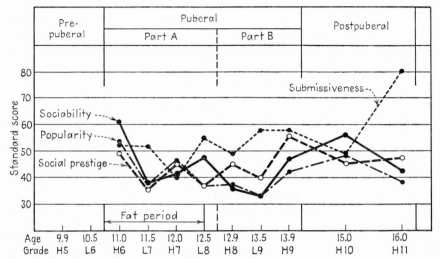

FIG. 29. Ratings on social behavior of a boy during different periods of sexual maturing. (*From H. R. Stolz and L. M. Stolz, Somatic development of adolescent boys. New York: Macmillan, 1951. Used by permission.*)

their happiness by being as disagreeable, as uncooperative, and as antagonistic toward the wishes of others as he can be (Brill, 1921; Hetzer, 1927; Bühler, 1927). Faultfinding frequently leads to family quarrels and the breakup of former friendships (Furfey, 1926). Ratings on social behavior at puberty are shown in Fig. 29.

Sex Antagonism. The antagonism between the sexes which normally develops during the latter part of childhood reaches its peak at puberty. Open hostility between the sexes is common at this age with girls, as a rule, showing a stronger aversion toward boys than boys toward girls. This antagonism is intensified by the girls' resentment of the physical disturbances maturing imposes upon them, especially menstruation, as contrasted with the less severe burden sexual maturing places upon boys. No longer do boys and girls show their antagonism toward one another simply by withdrawing from each other as they did during childhood. Now there is open hostility between the two sexes, expressed in constant criticisms and disparaging comments. Both boys and girls seem to go out of their way to hurt members of the opposite sex by biting comments and bitter sarcasm. These are not limited to their contemporaries but are aimed at any and all members of the opposite sex, regardless of their age, their kinship to the pubescent child, or how pleasant their former relationship has been. Once again, girls are greater offenders in this respect than are boys.

Heightened Emotionality. The tension and confusion resulting from changed attitudes and interests, the disturbances caused by physical and glandular changes, and the general tendency to feel below par physically most of the time result in heightened emotionality at this age. Moodiness, sulkiness, and a tendency to burst into tears at the slightest provocation are characteristic emotional states of the pubescent child. Little pleases them, anything or everything said about them or to them is likely to be taken as a criticism, feelings are constantly being hurt and prides offended (Brill, 1921; Hetzer, 1926; C. Bühler, 1927). There is such a marked and noticeable change from the general good humor that characterized the latter period of childhood that this pubescent moodiness is frequently commented upon by the adults in the child's presence. This only adds to the chip he already carries on his shoulder and increases his belief that no one loves him and the whole world is against him. Semihysterical states of crying are common among girls at this age, while boys are more likely to experience their resentment toward the world in melancholy silence, in sulkiness, or in temper outbursts that are reminiscent of the preschool years.

Lack of Self-confidence. The child who was formerly self-assured to the point where he felt that he could stand his ground in any and every circumstance and who boasted openly about his achievements now passes through a stage where his self-confidence crumbles literally overnight. No longer does he feel that he can succeed in whatever he undertakes as he formerly did. Instead, he doubts his own abilities to such an extent that he hesitates to tackle many of the tasks that he formerly carried out easily and with great success. Lack of self-confidence comes partly from lowered physical resistance which makes every molehill look like a mountain, partly from constant social pressures on the child to do more than he formerly did and to "act his age," and partly from the criticisms of his elders and of his contemporaries of the way he does things or of the fact that he does not do them. Many girls and boys emerge from puberty with so little self-confidence left that regaining it during the adolescent years is one of the major problems they must face. As a general rule, those children who seemed most capable and most confident of their abilities in late childhood are hit hardest in this area by puberty, primarily because more is expected of them than of children who were formerly timid and unsure of themselves.

Preoccupation with Sex. The growth and maturing of the sex organs with the new sensations that accompany these changes and the development of the secondary sex characteristics all focus the pubescent child's attention on sex matters. While children at all ages are, to a greater or lesser extent, interested in matters relating to sex, such as the physical differences between the two sexes, the origin of babies, or the relationships between husband and wife, these interests are objective and impersonal. Now, because of the physical changes taking place in their own bodies, the sex interests of pubescent boys and girls become subjective and personal in nature.

These interests frequently become so strong that they occupy much of the time and thought of the child. Attentive study of the different areas of his body, exploration of the genitals to see what new sensations can be produced by manipulation of different types, careful observation of the forms and shapes of the bodies of other members of his own sex, not only of his contemporaries but of adults as well, to see how they compare with his body, reading books in hopes of gaining information he craves but has not yet found, looking up words in the dictionary in the hope of throwing light on explanations of sex given in medical or technical books, and studying lewd drawings and off-color jokes for clues to further knowledge about this all too-secret subject are some of the many ways in which pubescent girls and boys reveal their preoccupation with sex matters.

Children who have been carefully prepared ahead of time for the changes that will take place in their bodies at puberty and who have been fully informed on all significant points about sex matters are, as a general rule, less preoccupied with sex during puberty than are those who entered this period in complete or partial ignorance of the changes that would take place. Forewarning and preparation alone, however, are not enough to stifle this interest. It is natural and normal that the child should be curious about the changes that are taking place in his body and that he should not only want to understand their significance fully but also to know what effects they have on him personally. The important thing, however, is that when adequate preparation for the changes has been made, the pubescent's attitude toward sex will be of a healthier sort when he enters puberty than when he enters into this phase of his development in complete ignorance or with distorted ideas about what is happening to him.

Excessive Modesty. The pubescent child is very self-conscious about the changes that are taking place in his body, and he makes every possible effort to hide them. Unlike the child who shows little if any modesty even in the presence of strangers, both boys and girls at puberty are likely to be terror-stricken at the thought of having to undress even partially when they have a medical examination. They turn their backs to their classmates when changing clothes in the gymnasium dressing rooms, and they become angry if any member of the family enters the room while they are undressing or bathing. This excessive modesty, which develops quite suddenly at puberty, is a direct outgrowth of the rapid physical changes which are taking place in the child's body. He is self-conscious about these changes and tries to hide them in fear that others will observe them and, perhaps, comment unfavorably upon them. When the child has had little or no forewarning of what changes will take place in his body and when they will come, he is likely to be more concerned about them than if he knew what to expect. Under such conditions, the modesty which normally develops at this age is exaggerated frequently to the point of morbidity.

Daydreaming. Daydreaming is one of the favorite pastimes of the pubescent child. Time which formerly was spent in active play with other children, in schoolwork or home responsibilities, is now spent in reverie. Typically, the pubescent child's daydream is of the "suffering-hero" type in which the dreamer sees himself in his daydream in the role of a martyr, misunderstood and mistreated by parents, teachers, friends, and society in general. Then, when his dream reaches a point where things are almost unbearable, the dreamer suddenly finds the tables turned. No longer is he a martyr but a hero. And, because he has been misunderstood and mistreated, those who were responsible for his martyrdom turn heaven and earth to make amends for their misdeeds.

Needless to say, daydreaming of the suffering-hero type is a source of great emotional satisfaction to the individual who indulges in it. He enjoys his role even when he is suffering great agonies because he knows full well that, in the end, things will turn out in his favor. And, because of his previous suffering, the ending in which he plays the role of a hero who is compensated for all the suffering that has been inflicted upon him is far more satisfying than it would have been had he been a hero from the start. In spite of the satisfaction the pubescent child derives from daydreaming of this sort, the effect on him is harmful because it tends to intensify the already present belief that "No one loves me" and to make him even more antagonistic toward people than he already is. The more frequently the child revels in such daydreams, the more out of step he is with reality and, consequently, the worse his adjustment is to the people he comes in contact with.

Misdemeanors. Misdemeanors, or misbehavior of a minor sort, are frequent at this age. Typically, the pubescent child does nothing so wrong that he can be classed as a "juvenile delinquent." But he is troublesome and frequently he seems to be so intentionally with the hope of irritating people by "getting under their skin." Whispering, inattentiveness, carelessness, tattling, resentfulness, suspiciousness, tardiness, insubordination, rudeness, impatience with restrictions, self-assertiveness, and avoidance of members of the opposite sex are the most frequently reported misdemeanors at this age (Wickman, 1929; Leal, 1932; Hurlock and McDonald, 1934; Long, 1941).

These misdemeanors, which reach their peak of intensity and frequency when boys and girls become pubescent, decline as pubescent development continues and as the individual's sexual development is completed. This would suggest that the general physical stress characteristic of this age, combined with the unsocial attitude of the child, predisposes him to retaliate against those whom he believes do not love him or who are responsible, either directly or indirectly, for the way he feels. For the most part, all these misdemeanors begin to wane as puberty reaches its completion and as the individual becomes mature in his sexual development.

CHAPTER 8

Early Adolescence
(Thirteen to Sixteen Years)

Adolescence is a period of transition. The child is no longer a child nor is he an adult. His status in our modern society is vague and confused. At one time, he is treated as a child by parents and teachers and, at another, as an adult. When he acts like a child, he is reproved and told to "act his age." If, however, he attempts to act like an adult, he finds himself the object of amusement on the part of adults who accuse him of being "too big for his breeches." The term "adolescence" comes from the Latin word *adolescere*, which means "to grow," or "to grow to maturity." As the term is used today, it has a broader meaning than it had in earlier times. Instead of limiting the adolescent period to the time when the individual grows to maturity sexually, it is now extended until the individual is expected to be mentally, socially, and emotionally mature. Legally, in American society, that means when the individual is twenty-one years old.

Among primitive peoples, and in the earlier civilizations, puberty and adolescence coincided. The child was considered mature when his body had completed its development and when he was, therefore, capable of reproduction. With advance in civilization, the transitional period from childhood to maturity has been lengthened as need arose for increased preparation to meet the demands of adult life. As a result, the period of sexual maturing, *puberty,* is now regarded as only part of the adolescent span.

Adolescent Changes. From the beginnings of civilization, it has been recognized that adolescence is a period of change. At first, the changes were thought to be primarily physiological in character, with major emphasis on the sexual development of the child. When these changes were completed and the child's body had been transformed into that characteristic of an adult, his status in society was changed. No longer was he looked upon as a child. Now he was expected to behave like an adult and, to test his capacities for adult behavior, he was subjected to a series of tests at the "puberty rites." Successful passing of these tests guaranteed him the status of an adult, while failure meant that he retained the status of a child, even though he had the body of a man.

As time went on, it became apparent that the changes that took place at this time were not exclusively physical in nature. Changed interests and attitudes led to changed behavior. This, in time, led to the belief that the child would change for the better, and the hope grew that when the child matured sexually, he would leave behind all the undesirable mental and physical traits of childhood. Such, however, does not happen. Changes of a psychological nature do accompany physical changes but these changes are in the direction in which they started. Homely children develop into homely adolescents; tall children into tall adolescents; selfish children into selfish adolescents; and poorly adjusted children into poorly adjusted adolescents. In general, the changes are usually to exaggerate the already existing traits rather than to transform them into socially approved traits.

At the turn of the present century, G. Stanley Hall (1904) reported from observations of large numbers of adolescent boys and girls that adolescence was a period of extremes in behavior, marked by emotional "storm and stress." His emphasis on the heightened emotionality characteristic at this time soon gave rise to the belief that adolescent behavior was abnormal and that it arose from the marked physical changes that were taking place at that time. As scientific interest in studying adolescent behavior grew, it became apparent that many of the forms of behavior Hall had described were normal and were found almost universally among boys and girls at this stage of their development. Furthermore, it became evident that the characteristic behavior attributed to physical causes was, in reality, more the result of environmental factors than physical disturbances.

The culture in which the individual lives is largely responsible for this confused role. It not only determines how long adolescence will be but it affects the behavior and status of the adolescent in that culture. Among primitive groups of people, adolescents rarely show the "storm and stress" characteristic of Americans because of the way they are reared and the highly structured pattern of behavior set for the individual when he reaches adolescence (Mead, 1928). In different socioeconomic groups in the same culture, there are likewise different standards of behavior approved for one group as compared with the standards for another group. This holds true for age roles, family-relationship roles, and standards for sex behavior. Even in the schools, standards differ from school to school (Davis, 1944).

Because physical changes occur more rapidly during early than during late adolescence, the changes in attitudes and behavior are likewise more rapid. The "wants" of a young adolescent (Fig. 30) are indications of such change. In a relatively short period of time, boys and girls change physically from children to adults and their whole concept of themselves as individuals likewise changes. With this comes an awareness on their part that they are "different" and a strong desire to be recognized by the social group as such. Because rapid change always brings with it feelings of insecurity, the young adolescent lacks the poise and feelings of security that are characteristic of individuals in the latter part of adolescence.

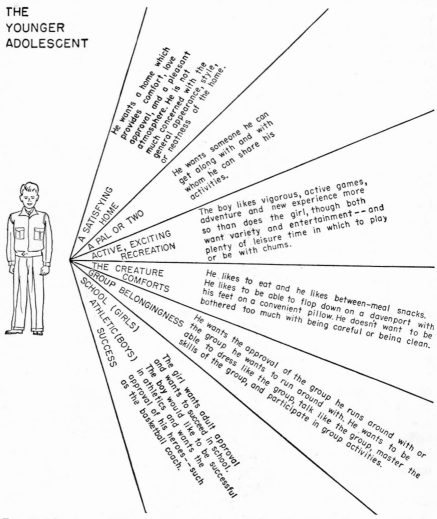

THE YOUNGER ADOLESCENT

He wants a home which provides comfort, love approval, and a pleasant atmosphere. He is not much concerned with the general appearance, style, or neatness of the home.

He wants someone he can get along with and with whom he can share his activities.

The boy likes vigorous, active games, adventure and new experience more so than does the girl, though both want variety and entertainment -- and plenty of leisure time in which to play or be with chums.

He likes to eat and he likes between-meal snacks. He likes to be able to flop down on a davenport with his feet on a convenient pillow. He doesn't want to be bothered too much with being careful or being clean.

He wants the approval of the group he runs around with. He wants to be able to dress like the group, talk like the group, master the skills of the group, and participate in group activities.

The girl wants adult approval and wants to succeed in school. The boy would like to be successful in athletics and wants the approval of his heroes--such as the basketball coach.

A SATISFYING HOME
A PAL OR TWO
ACTIVE, EXCITING RECREATION
THE CREATURE COMFORTS
GROUP BELONGINGNESS
SCHOOL (GIRLS)
ATHLETIC (BOYS) SUCCESS

Fig. 30. The wants of the younger adolescent. (*From M. Malm and O. G. Jamison, Adolescence. New York: McGraw-Hill, 1952. Used by permission.*)

Length of Period. Because of the marked individual differences in age of sexual maturity, it is difficult to give exact ages for early adolescence that will apply to all individuals. It is necessary, therefore, to use only averages as norms and to allow for individual differences not only among members of each sex but also between the two sexes. As a general rule, early adolescence is said to begin when the individual becomes sexually mature. In girls, the criterion of sexual maturity is the menarche, or the first menstruation. This comes, in American girls, at an average of 13 to 13½ years. Therefore, for girls, early adolescence is said to fall between the ages of 13 and 16 years. Because boys mature sexually approximately a year later than girls, early adolescence for them begins at an average age of 14 years and extends to 16½ or 17 years. Roughly, when the two sexes are combined, early adolescence is regarded as the span from 13 to 16 years, or from the junior-high-school to the middle of the senior-high-school years.

CHARACTERISTICS OF EARLY ADOLESCENCE

There are several outstanding characteristics of the early adolescent years that distinguish it from childhood and from the closing years of adolescence. Some of these are unquestionably the result of maturation and accompany the rapid and pronounced physical changes that have taken place. Others, on the other hand, are the result of cultural influences and are more characteristic of American youth than of the youth of other cultures. Of these characteristics, the most outstanding are:

1. *The Young Adolescent Is Unstable.* At this age, instability is extreme. From tears to laughter, from self-confidence to self-depreciation, from selfishness to altruism, and from enthusiasm to indifference are common reactions of young adolescents. One minute the young adolescent is up in the clouds and the next he is in the depths of despair. This instability is largely the result of feelings of insecurity. The physiological and psychological changes which accompany sexual maturity come so quickly that the individual is unsure of himself, of his capacities, and of his interests. The greater demands placed on him by home and school add to his feelings of insecurity and intensify his instability. Added to this is the fact that he is often treated in an ambiguous manner by both parents and teachers. One minute he is told he is too young to drive a car and the next he is given a responsibility usually assumed by an adult. He thus finds himself in a new and overlapping situation where his role is not structured (Bair, 1950).

2. *The Young Adolescent Is Unhappy.* Instead of being one of the happiest and most constructive periods in life, adolescence is too frequently spoiled by adults who make the period more full of conflict than necessary. They fear the adolescent will not grow up to be sufficiently obedient, cooperative, or grateful, or that he will go astray sexually (English, 1947). While there are times of happiness, these are often overshadowed by periods of extreme unhappiness and discontent. The young adolescent is concerned about his appearance, especially when it does not come up to his expectations. He is greatly concerned about the awkwardness and clumsiness that develop at this age. Not understandng the normal pattern of growth, he is likely to feel

that his growth is complete and that there is no further hope for improvement. The social and economic status of his family are likely to make the young adolescent unhappy. Unless his family measures up to the families of his friends in social status or income, and unless he finds himself in a position of acceptance on the part of his contemporaries, he will be unhappy, often to the point where he develops an antagonistic attitude toward his family and threatens to leave home.

The discontent that the adolescent feels about his appearance is often accentuated by disappointment when his mental capacities or personality does not come up to his expectations. He would like to be at the top of his class in school, he would like to have abilities that would win recognition for him and, above all, he would like to be popular. Feelings of inadequacy and insecurity are the outstanding unpleasant memories of adolescence as reported by adults. School failures, loss of friends, quarrels with parents and friends, breakup of friendships with members of the opposite sex, death of relatives or friends, feelings of inferiority, and lack of popularity are recalled as the outstanding sources of concern to the adolescent. Because they are remembered over a period of time, it is unquestionably true that they were sources of great unhappiness when they occurred (Thompson and Witryol, 1948).

3. *The Young Adolescent Has Many Problems.* Every age has its problems. But, for the young adolescent, problems seem more numerous and more insurmountable than at other ages. In childhood, his problems were usually met with the help of his parents or teachers. Now he feels that his problems are his own and that his parents and teachers are "too old" to understand and to help him. Since many of the problems that confront a young adolescent relate to areas of life, such as heterosexual relationships in which he has had no previous experience, he often feels at a loss to know how to tackle them.

An interesting insight into the personal problems of the young adolescent boy or girl comes from a study based on essays written by high-school boys and girls in which they described the problems that were of greatest concern to them. Over 7,000 problems were listed and these were divided into six major categories, as follows:

1. Study-learning relationships.
2. Occupational adjustment.
3. Personal adjustment.
4. Home-life relationships.
5. Social adjustment.
6. Health problems.

The largest percentage, 46 per cent, mentioned problems in category 1, study-learning relationships. The greatest source of concern related to relationships with teachers, amount of home study, teachers' unfairness and stern attitudes. Girls showed more concern than boys about school progress, marks, and tests. Less than one-fourth of all the students were concerned about their futures, category 2, but this concern increased from grades 9 to 12. The major sources of concern to both boys and girls related to need for vocational guidance, inability to choose a vocation, and choice of subjects to prepare for their life work. Eleven per cent of the boys and girls expressed concern about personal adjustment, category 3. Their major concern centered around problems related to feelings of inferiority and superiority. Ten per cent had problems related to home-life relationships, category 4.

Financial problems proved to be more serious to boys than to girls but girls were more concerned than boys about parent-child relationships. Social adjustment problems, category 5, bothered 8 per cent of the students. The problem of making friends proved to be especially serious for girls, but it grew less as they became older. Girls expressed concern about the need for social guidance, especially in boy-girl relationships. The problem of least concern centered around health, category 6. Among the older girls, the concern related especially to the need for sex guidance. The conclusion drawn from this study was that "high school pupils have many problems and they are extremely sensitive to them" (Pope, 1943).

Girls have been found to have more problems than boys at this age. When a group of high-school students was asked to check their problems on the Mooney Problem Check List, the average number of problems checked by boys was 30.6 as contrasted to an average of 36.3 for girls. With increase in age from fourteen to sixteen years, the number of problems for boys decreased while the number for girls increased. Boys were more concerned with school problems while girls reported more problems related to getting along with people than school problems. When asked why the school caused problems for them, typical answers were: "Teachers don't practice what they preach," "Dull classes," "Trouble with teachers," and "Teachers don't like me" (Garrison and Cunningham, 1952).

In addition to the problems the adolescent himself faces, adults whose responsibility it is to guide and supervise the lives of these young people find early adolescence a "problem age" for them. While every age is, in its own way, a "problem age," early adolescence seems to be more troublesome than the periods that preceded it. One of the most troublesome aspects of this age is the obstinacy of the young adolescent. He will not listen to reason, he does just the opposite of what he is asked to do, or he just "moons" around. This troublesome age comes at a time in the life span of the individual when there are strong conflicts between his desires and those of the social group. He wants to be acceptable to his growing circle of friends and acquaintances but he discovers that the same behavior will not please everyone. There is an increase in the number of social interests he has, there are new responsibilities and obligations for him to assume, and there are conflicts between his desire for independence and his need for parental support. These lead to conflicts which make him resistant and obstinate when he finds that he cannot do what the group expects him to do and, at the same time, do what he wants to do (Banham, 1952).

PHYSICAL DEVELOPMENT

The rapid physical growth, characteristic of puberty, begins to slow down when the individual reaches early adolescence. However, growth is far from complete when puberty ends and it is not entirely complete at the end of early adolescence. However, there is a slackening of the pace of growth and there is more marked internal than external development. This cannot be so readily observed or identified as growth in height and weight or the development of the secondary sex characteristics.

Height and Weight. When sexual maturing is delayed, increases in height and weight may precede growth in body dimensions and growth in the internal organs. Thus, growth becomes irregular and asymmetrical which is in direct contrast to early sexual maturing which is accompanied by more regular growth. In the case of the calf of the leg, for example, early-maturing children were found to have larger calves than were late-maturing children (Reynolds, 1946). Furthermore, early-maturing children have greater spurts of rapid growth and their periods of acceleration and of stopping come more abruptly than is true of slow-maturing children. By contrast, the slow-maturing child has less intense periods of acceleration, his growth is more even and regular, and it continues for a longer time, often into late adolescence (Leal, 1932; Richey, 1937).

Because girls, as a whole, mature sooner than boys and because growth in height and weight generally spurt at that time and then slow down as puberty comes to a close, the girl reaches her mature height at the close of early adolescence if she has matured at the average age. Slow-maturing girls, on the other hand, do not reach their mature size until early in the late adolescent period. The fifteen-year-old girls is 64 to 65 inches tall, the average height of a mature American woman of today. The average sixteen-year-old boy is 65 inches tall and still has 2 more inches to grow to attain the height of the average American man. Much the same pattern holds true for weight increases. Because there are such marked individual differences in weight not only between the sexes but also within each sex, it is difficult to say just what an adolescent will weigh at a given age.

Body Proportions. The body proportions of a young adolescent are not those of an adult. Gradually, disproportions, so characteristic of the growth years, right themselves and reach one by one their mature level of development (see Fig. 31). In both length and width, but especially in width, the *head* dimensions are larger among girls who mature early than among those who mature late. The mature size of the head is attained about a year earlier in early- than in late-maturing girls (Goldstein, 1939). When the adolescent is thirteen or fourteen years old, only about 5 or 6 per cent of growth in cir-

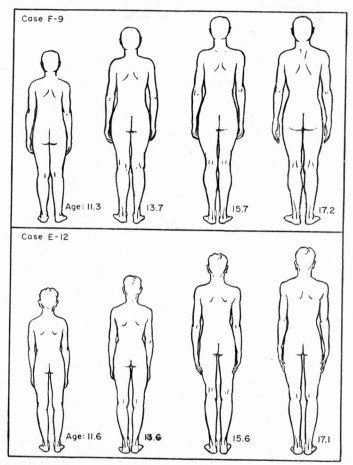

FIG. 31. Contrasting the growth of an early-maturing boy (above) and a late-maturing boy (below). (*Based on Nancy Bayley and R. D. Tuddenham, Adolescent changes in body build. Yearb. nat. Soc. Stud. Educ., Part 1, Adolescence, 1944, 43. From F. K. Shuttleworth, The adolescent period: a graphic atlas, Monogr. Soc. Res. Child Develpm., 1949, 14, No. 1. Used by permission.*)

cumference remains uncompleted. *Facial* disproportions are even more marked in early adolescence than are head proportions. At this time, growth in length of the face is rapid, while growth in width occurs at a slower rate. The upper part of the face develops faster than the lower. The forehead becomes higher and wider, the nose becomes longer and wider, and the slight depression above the nose is filled out with cartilage. The lips become fuller and the mouth begins to widen.

The *trunk*, which grew slowly during childhood, lengthens in early adolescence and, instead of being square in shape as was true of the childhood years, a waistline appears. At first, this is higher in the trunk than it will be in late adolescence when the trunk completes its growth. Rapid growth in the girth of the chest comes at this time. The hips broaden as do the shoulders. The *legs*, which just before puberty took a spurt in length, grow more slowly in length than in girth at this time. The pattern of growth for the *arms* is much the same as for the legs. In early adolescence, the growth in length slows down and growth in girth gives shape to the long spindly arms of the pubescent boy or girl. The *hands* and *feet* reach their mature size before the arms and legs, and this is a matter of great concern to most adolescents.

Bones and Muscles. Marked changes occur in the size and structure of the bones at this period of growth. The bones lengthen, thus adding to the height of the individual. The pelvic arch, especially in girls, broadens, and this gives shape to the hips. The bones change internally also. The cartilage and fibrous tissue of children's bones begin to harden at puberty and continue through adolescence. As a result, the bones are harder, denser, and more brittle than they were during the childhood years. At fourteen years of age, the girl's bones are almost mature in this respect, but for boys the development is not complete for a year or two later. The four second molars begin to erupt at puberty and should have completed their development by the time sexual maturity is attained. The third molars, or "wisdom teeth," start to erupt in early adolescence, though all four of these usually do not come in until the late adolescent period. Because the second and third molars are large teeth and cut through the gums where there were no teeth before, their eruption is generally accompanied by pain, physical upsets, and emotional disturbances.

Rapid growth in the muscles accompanies growth of the bones in early adolescence. This adds to the body weight of the boy or girl. How marked the increase is may be seen by the fact that, at the age of eight years, the weight of the muscles makes up 27 per cent of the gross body weight; at fifteen years, 32 per cent; and at sixteen years, 44 per cent. Because the musculature of boys is greater than that of girls after puberty development has been completed, the boy's body looks and is heavier than the girl's body. For girls, the greatest increase in muscle tissue in relation to total body weight comes between the ages of twelve and fifteen years, and for boys, between fifteen and sixteen years. Because muscle growth and bone growth usually do not develop at the same rate, incoordination and clumsiness frequently appear in early adolescence. This occurs when muscle growth forges ahead of bone growth. When, however, the bones grow faster than the muscles, cramps and "growing pains" are common experiences. Both of these experiences are difficult for the young adolescent to understand and to adjust to successfully.

Skin. Changes in the *skin* are marked during early adolescence. The *apocrine* sweat glands, which are limited to the armpits, mammary, genital, and anal regions, begin to enlarge shortly before puberty but do not reach their full development until puberty is well advanced. Even before the axillary hair develops, there is an increased activity in the glands in the armpits and this becomes very pronounced during the early years of adolescence. In girls, the activity is marked during the premenstrual and menstrual portions of the menstrual cycle. The *sebaceous,* or oil-producing glands of the skin, which are closely associated with the hair follicles, become large and especially active at puberty. At first, they are associated with disproportionally small hairs which cause a temporary maladjustment in their functioning. This causes a skin disturbance, or "acne," which affects the skin on the face, neck, and sides of the nose especially.

The matter from these glands cannot drain properly because the ducts are temporarily too small, and hard plugs or "blackheads" form at the openings of the ducts. When the plugged pores are overfilled, they often become inflamed and "pimples" appear on the surface of the skin. Not only do the glands of the skin change at puberty but the texture of the skin itself changes. The soft, thin, transparent skin of the child gradually becomes thicker and coarser as sexual maturity is attained. The pink-and-white coloring of the child, which accompanies the transparent skin, becomes sallow and colorless. This is especially true of boys, whose skin is coarser than that of girls. In both boys and girls, there is more hair on the face than in childhood. This hair is coarse and pigmented, especially in the case of boys.

Hair. The hair on the face develops in a characteristic manner during early adolescence. In boys, the downy hairs at the corners of the mouth become conspicuous because of their size and pigmentation. Gradually these spread to the middle of the upper lip and become a "juvenile mustache." Then the down of the upper part of the cheek becomes longer and more pigmented. Following this comes the growth of hair on the sides and the lower border of the chin. Finally, hairs on the side of the face, just in front of the ears, and on the throat, develop into a "beard." A similar pattern occurs in girls, though the hairs are less coarse and less pigmented.

Pubic hair and *axillary* hair, as was pointed out in the chapter on Puberty, develop during the puberty period and reach their mature form in texture and pigmentation during the early adolescent years. There is also growth of hair on the arms and legs, on the chests of boys, and frequently on their shoulders. While the pubic and axillary hair of boys and girls are similar in texture and pigmentation, there is a marked sex difference in the amount of hair on the rest of the body. Girls have far less hair on their arms and legs than do boys and rarely ever have hair on their chests, shoulders, or backs, except when there is a glandular disturbance.

Internal Organs. Internal growth, though not readily apparent, is marked during early adolescence. There is a change in the relative size of the organs of the *digestive* system. The stomach becomes longer and less tubular than it was in childhood, thus increasing its capacity. The intestines grow in length and circumference, and the muscles in the stomach and intestinal walls become stronger and thicker, resulting in stronger peristaltic motions. The liver increases in weight and the esophagus becomes larger. The rapid growth of the body which started at puberty necessitates an increase in food intake at this time. In caloric content, the young adolescent's daily food intake equals that of an adult who does hard manual labor (Shuttleworth, 1937). Not only are large amounts of food consumed at every meal but the young adolescent is likely to eat more or less continuously between meals (Hicks and Hayes, 1938). Heavy emphasis is placed on sweets and starches in the young adolescent's diet.

The changes in the *circulatory* system are marked in the increase in the size of the heart and in the length and thickness of the walls of the blood vessels. Growth in the size of the heart is relatively greater, however, than growth in the diameter of the veins or arteries. As a result, a large heart must pump blood through small arteries. Until this condition is corrected, during late adolescence, too-strenuous exercise may cause an enlargement of the heart or valvular disease. Tension in the arteries, resulting from disproportions in the size of the heart and of the arteries, causes much of the restlessness that is characteristic of the young adolescent.

The greatest increase in weight and volume of the lungs comes at puberty. Lung increase keeps pace with the increase in width and depth of the chest which is taking place at that time. After puberty has been completed, there is little increase in lung size. In adolescence, as a result of the increased size of the lungs, breathing is slower than it was in childhood though the volume of inhaled and exhaled air is greater. Up to the age of fourteen years, there is not much difference between the two sexes in lung capacity. After that, boys surpass girls to a marked degree.

Because of the increased activity of the gonads at puberty, there is a temporary imbalance of the whole endocrine system during early adolescence. The glands, which during childhood were dominant, now take a less prominent position in the endocrine system, and those which were formerly less prominent now become dominant. The thymus gland, located in the chest, was one of the dominant glands during the early years of life. Now it is practically inactive. The adrenal glands, attached to the kidneys, lose weight during the first year of life and do not regain their birth size until the middle of adolescence. Among girls, the thyroid glands, located in the throat, enlarge at the time of the menarche and this produces irregularities in the basal metabolic rate of girls. In both boys and girls, there is a temporary rise in the basal metabolic rate early in adolescence and then this sinks again (Bruen, 1933; Molilch and Cousins, 1934). The sex glands develop rapidly at that time and become functionally active. They do not, however, reach their mature size until late in adolescence or early in adulthood.

Health Conditions. After the puberty changes are, for the most part, complete, the adolescent's health begins to improve. The ailments he experienced at puberty, none of which was severe enough to invalid him, gradually clear up and the young adolescent feels better with each successive month. True, he frequently experiences digestive upsets, caused by indiscreet eating, and colds, caused by carelessness or lack of proper precautions. But, for the most part, these are mild and of short duration. Few adolescents, however, are free from minor ailments. Defective teeth, eye troubles, stomach upsets, headaches, earaches, and asthma are a few of the common disorders the young adolescent experiences occasionally or chronically. Many of these disorders are carry-overs of conditions that existed in childhood and have become progressively worse with time. Carious teeth, for example, frequently become worse in adolescence because of neglect or crowding the diet with starches and sweets. Eyestrain becomes a more serious problem for the young adolescent than it was for the child because of the heavier burden of schoolwork. There is no evidence to show, however, that changes in vision are marked at adolescence or that they are by any means universal, as is popularly believed (Sloane and Gallagher, 1950).

Psychological Significance. Physical development and changes in body proportions or functions have a marked effect on the adolescent's attitudes and behavior. The more insecure and the more anxious he is to be accepted by his contemporaries, the more pronounced the physical effects are on the individual's whole attitude. This holds true for boys and girls alike, with a slight tendency for girls to be more concerned about some areas of their physical development while boys are more concerned about others. The young adolescent is especially likely to be concerned about one physical characteristic which he considers homely or sexually inappropriate. In many cases, the adolescent's attitude does not reflect that of the social group but is a matter of personal dislike.

When young adolescent boys were questioned about what physical characteristic or characteristics were of especial concern to them, the majority of the group reported lack of size, particularly height, fatness, poor physique, lack of muscular strength, unusual facial features, acne, and skin blemishes. Very large or very small genitalia and lack of shoulder breadth, which from an adult point of view might seem to be of greater concern, proved to be of little concern. To girls, the sources of greatest concern proved to be tallness, fatness, facial features, general physical appearance, tallness and heaviness, smallness and heaviness, and eyeglasses. Of least concern to them were a scar on the face, one short arm, and big legs. To our present-day American girls, fatness is one of the chief sources of concern regarding their physical appearance (Stolz and Stolz, 1944). A study of nicknames has revealed that those most disliked by adolescents are the ones that refer to anomalies of physical development, especially those that refer to unfortunate physiognomic characteristics (Habbe, 1937).

Because young adolescents must adjust to dramatic physical changes that have occurred during puberty, and because they must accept their size and shape as the physique they will have for the rest of their lives, their attention is naturally focused on their physical development. When a large group of tenth graders was asked how they saw themselves physically, the girls reported that they thought of themselves as heavy and they were concerned about it. The boys thought they were about right in weight, but they were concerned about thinness in their upper arms and chests. Girls were concerned about being too tall, boys about being too short. Slow-maturing boys and girls expressed high concern about this. They also showed great concern about blackheads and pimples. Two-thirds of the group expressed a desire for some change in themselves physically, especially in proportions, weight, height, and complexion. Among girls, the greatest concern centered around blackheads and pimples, irregular teeth, oily skin, gaps in their teeth, and wearing of glasses. Least concern was expressed about heavy eyebrows and lack of beard.

Much the same things concerned boys. They listed first blackheads, pimples, oily skin, large nose, irregular teeth, dry skin, homeliness, and wearing glasses. They were least disturbed about foreheads that were too low or too high. When asked to rank what they would like to change most for self-improvement, the boys listed in first place, proportions, height, weight, strength, complexion, and features. To girls, the strongest desires for self-improvement centered around their proportions, complexions, weight, hair, height, and features (Frazier and Lisonbee, 1950). From a study of a group of boys who presented personality difficulties, it was found that the most serious problems concerned apparent or actual delays in the onset of sexual maturation, the failure of the growth spurt to materialize at adolescence, and inadequacies of masculine development. Deviations from the group pattern proved to be important (Schonfeld, 1950).

MOTOR CAPACITIES

Development of muscular power follows growth in muscle size. This, however, will not alone guarantee muscular skills. The individual needs training, opportunities for practice, absence of environmental obstacles, and a strong motivation to develop skills. At no time is motor development below the level of his contemporaries more serious than it is to a young adolescent. Unless his muscular skills are on a par with those of his friends, at the time when the desire for muscular activity which normally accompanies the growth of the muscles sets in, the young adolescent finds himself so out of step in this area of his development with his contemporaries that he cannot take part in the games and sports they enjoy. This has serious impact on his social adjustments and on his concept of himself.

Adolescent Awkwardness. Not all young adolescents are awkward but few escape awkwardness in some degree. Adolescents whose sexual maturation has proceeded at a slow rate or those who have attained a high level of proficiency during the childhood years are likely to experience less awkwardness than are those who have matured rapidly or whose motor proficiency has lagged behind the level attained by their contemporaries. Some young adolescents are awkward in all of their movements; some are awkward in movements of the legs primarily; some are awkward mostly in the use of their hands. General awkwardness in early adolescence is less universally found than specific awkwardness in limited areas of the body.

Adolescent awkwardness comes from the pattern of muscle growth that characteristically occurs at puberty and early adolescence. During childhood, the muscles grow slowly and relatively uniformly. This enables the child to develop control of his body as changes occur in the muscular development. As a result, he should have good muscular coordination. The situation is changed in early adolescence. Not only do the muscles and bones grow rapidly but they bear a new ratio to one another. The muscles are elongated and pulled into new patterns. As a result, the motor achievements acquired in childhood are upset and this brings about a state of awkwardness and clumsiness. This condition will persist until new controls and new achievements are achieved.

Boys and girls are subject to adolescent awkwardness though in boys awkwardness is likely to be more pronounced than in girls. Unless the girls' growth spurt has been unusually rapid, girls are less awkward than boys because the boys' framework is typically larger than that of the girls. Furthermore, because boys have less fat than girls, they look more gawky and awkward than girls at this age, a fact that contributes to their feelings of inadequacy. This, in turn, contributes to the awkwardness of their movements. Using a battery of motor-coordination tests, it was found that the most pronounced awkwardness in boys occurs with the sudden beginnings of growth at puberty and becomes less and less pronounced as puberty progresses (Dimock, 1935).

It may take several years for the young adolescent to acquire muscular coordination. Until this occurs, he is likely to be embarrassed and self-conscious, not only because of the clumsy things he does but also because he thinks of himself as an adult or a near-adult and it hurts his pride to have people laugh at him or criticize him for his clumsiness. In spite of the nervous tension that tends to exaggerate the clumsiness that is almost inevitable at puberty and immediately afterward, the adolescent gradually builds up new habit patterns to replace the old ones and his awkwardness then diminishes. This process would be hastened if the element of embarrassment could be eliminated.

Muscular Strength. Increase in muscular strength accompanies the growth of the muscles. Because the greatest growth of the muscles comes at puberty and immediately afterward, that likewise is the time when muscular strength increases most rapidly and noticeably. Among boys, physical strength, as measured by a battery of strength tests, was found to double between the ages of twelve and sixteen years (Dimock, 1935). The most rapid development of strength comes in the year following the attainment of postpubescence (Jones, 1944).

There is a definite relationship between strength and skeletal maturing in boys. At the age of 11 years, early-maturing boys have been found to be significantly stronger than late-maturing boys. The beginning of pubertal growth in strength occurs at the skeletal age of 14 years. It comes slightly after the first signs of postpubescence and about half a year before the maximum growth in height. The superiority in strength of early-maturing boys over late-maturing boys continues until at least 17½ years of age, and may even continue after that, though there are no records of genetic studies of the same group of boys to show whether or not this is true (Jones, 1946a). The relationship of strength to age of sexual maturing is shown in Fig. 32.

Among girls, the pattern of development of muscular strength differs markedly from that of boys. Early-maturing girls show a rapid increase in strength up to the age of twelve years, after which there is a slow rate of increase. Late-maturing girls are relatively retarded in strength development, though in time, their level of strength reaches that of girls who mature earlier. In both early- and late-maturing girls, the greatest increase in strength comes near the time of the menarche (Jones, 1944).

At all ages after puberty, boys surpass girls in strength-of-grip tests. This superiority increases with increase in age. The reason for this difference is that the muscles of girls do not develop as much as do those of boys during adolescence. This sex difference is evident in the fact that, at 11 years of age, there is a difference of approximately 4 kilograms of pressure between the sexes while at the age of 17½ years, the difference has increased to 20 kilograms. Furthermore, girls generally attain their maximum strength at about 17 years of age, while boys do not attain their maximum until they are 21 or 22 years of age.

Skills. To determine the degree of skill attained, tests of speed and accuracy have been applied to adolescent boys and girls. Speed of *voluntary movement,* as measured by tests of tapping, increases continually from the onset of early adolescence until sixteen or eighteen years of age, but at a slower rate of increase after thirteen or fourteen years. An eight-year-old, for example, has two-thirds as much speed as a seventeen-year-old, while a thirteen-year-old has six-sevenths as much as a seventeen-year-old. The amount of gain in accuracy, as measured by tests of tracing and aiming, is small after fourteen years of age.

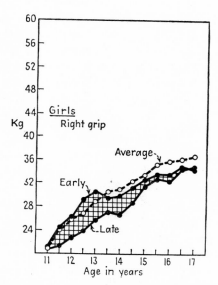

FIG. 32. Age changes in strength of right grip for early, average, and late-maturing groups of girls classified by age at menarche. The difference between early- and late-maturing groups is significant at ages 12½, 13, and 13½. (*Based on Harold E. Jones, The sexual maturing of girls as related to growth in strength. Res. Quart., 1947, 18:135–143. From F. K. Shuttleworth, The adolescent period: a graphic atlas, Monogr. Soc. Res. Child Develpm., 1949, 14, No. 1. Used by permission.*)

A study of a group of boys and girls over a 4-year period revealed that growth in ability to perform motor acts reaches its maximum at the age of fourteen years for girls and at seventeen for boys, though sex differences were found to be greater among the older than among the younger children (Espenschade, 1940). Tests to measure agility, control, strength, and static balance showed the greatest increase in ability for boys after fourteen years of age. In tests involving dynamic balance, on the other hand, boys showed an adolescent lag, because of rapid changes in body proportions and center of gravity (Espenschade, 1947).

Girls improve in tests of agility up to fourteen years and then lag, it is believed, because of changes in interests rather than because of lack of capacity. After then, there is a marked sex difference in favor of boys (Espenschade, 1947). Tests of involuntary movement in boys show an increase in motor coordination throughout the adolescent years. This increase is more rapid after puberty than before. The period when improvement in motor coordination was most substantial coincided with the period when growth in height and weight was most rapid (Dimock, 1935).

Muscular Fatigue. Typically, the pubescent child experiences muscular fatigue. Because of this, he is likely to be listless, lazy, and avoid all exercise whenever possible. When tests of fatigue were given to adolescents to measure the amount of work done in a given period of time in relation to loss of efficiency, it was found that fatigue decreased as adolescence proceeded. In tests of tapping, for example, there is little decrease in output resulting from fatigue. Sex differences are slight, though boys show fatigue slightly less than girls do. Tall adolescents, owing to their tendency to stoop in hopes of making themselves look less tall and conspicuous, generally suffer from fatigue more than do adolescents who feel that their height is about right. This is especially true of girls.

ADOLESCENT EMOTIONS

Traditionally, adolescence is a period of storm and stress, of heightened emotional tension. And, traditionally, this heightened emotional tension comes from the physical and glandular changes taking place at this time. Studies of the normal growth pattern of the adolescent have revealed that this traditional explanation is invalid. While it is true that growth does continue through the early years of adolescence, it is at a progressively slower rate with each successive year. What growth is taking place is primarily a completion of the pattern already set at puberty.

It is necessary, therefore, to look for other explanations of the emotional tension so characteristic of this age. And the explanations are to be found in social conditions that surround the adolescent of today. The pressures and expectations of the social group on individuals who, throughout the years of childhood, have had little if any preparation to meet the changed conditions that will face them at adolescence, are chiefly to blame for adolescent emotionality. This becomes evident when comparisons are made with adolescents in primitive societies. There, adolescence is a happy age, free from the storm and stress so characteristic of adolescents in highly civilized societies (Mead, 1928).

Not all adolescents, by any means, are subject to storm and stress of an exaggerated sort. True, most of them do experience emotional instability from time to time. This is logical because the adolescent is making adjustments to new patterns of behavior and to new social expectations. And, as is true of adjustments to new experiences at any age, there is bound to be some emotional tension connected with these adjustments. Prolonged and continuous emotional tension, on the other hand, is symptomatic of poor adjustments. It indicates that either the adolescent is too immature socially and emotionally to play the new role adolescence brings or that his environment has not been adjusted to meet his new needs. In either case, poor adjustments will result and they will give rise to emotional tension of an intense and prolonged sort. This may be shown directly in temper outbursts, reminiscent of the early childhood years, or it may be revealed indirectly in "show-off," rebellious, immature, and emotionally unstable behavior (Anderson, 1940).

Characteristics. Studies of adolescent emotions, using the questionnaire technique (Wheeler, 1931), the diary analysis method (C. Bühler, 1927), and the controlled diary, in which adolescents record the frequency, intensity, and causes of emotional experiences (Gates, 1926; Stratton, 1927; Meltzer, 1933; Anastasia, 1948) have all shown that in many respects, adolescent emotions differ from those of children. Of these differences, the following are most characteristic:

1. ADOLESCENT EMOTIONS ARE INTENSE. While it is true that temper tantrums of children are intense (Goodenough, 1931), as are their fears (Jersild, 1947), and that they lack degrees of intensity, the emotions of the adolescent are not only intense but intensity is characteristic of all of their emotions. When they fall in love, for example, there is an intensity to this emotion which is rarely found among children. While physical and glandular changes, in part, may be responsible for this (see Fig. 33), social causes are more likely to be at the root of the trouble. The frustrations which the adolescent experiences from all sides added to the problems of adjustment to new conditions of life throw him off his even keel and lead to emotional outbursts of greater or less severity. This is a source of embarrassment to the adolescent who likes to think of himself as an adult. Falling below his ideal of what he would like to be adds to his concern and thus heightens still further the already present intense emotions.

2. ADOLESCENT EMOTIONS LACK CONTROL OF EXPRESSION. Like the child, the adolescent lets go when he is emotionally aroused and seems unable, for the time being, to control his behavior. He differs from the child in this respect, however, in that many more of his emotional expressions are verbal than are those of the child. The angry adolescent, for example, is more likely to express his anger by name calling and swearing than he is by kicking, screaming, or hitting, so characteristic of children. Furthermore, the expressions of emotions on the part of adolescents differ conspicuously from those of children in that in the case of the former, they have little or no relationship with the emotion with which they are associated, while in the latter there is a close relationship. Giggling is the common expression of all happy emotions, and weeping is the common emotional response to all unpleasant emotions on the part of adolescent girls. The adolescent boy's typical emo-

tional responses to all pleasant experiences consist of nervous mannerisms, such as standing on one foot and then on the other, pulling at the tie, or looking "sheepish," and unpleasant emotions of all sorts are expressed by looking sullen and gloomy, refusing to speak or do what they are asked to do, and swearing, either audibly or under the breath. These masculine and feminine stereotypes of emotional expressions generally reach their peak in early adolescence.

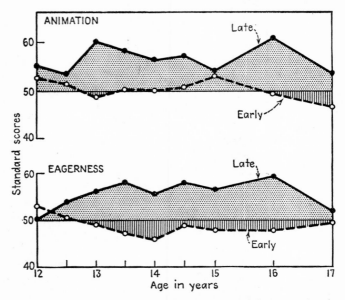

FIG. 33. Scores for two expressive traits among early- and late-maturing boys. (*From M. C. Jones and N. Bayley, Physical maturing among boys as related to behavior. J. educ. Psychol., 1950, 41:129–148. Used by permission.*)

3. ADOLESCENT EMOTIONS LACK CONSISTENCY. Emotional shifts from joy to sadness, from anger to love, often occur within a short period of time among adolescents. While a child may have his emotional ups and downs, these are dependent more upon his physical condition than upon environmental causes. In adolescence, however, these swings do not come from physical causes but from environmental conditions and from the adolescent's self-appraisals. When, for example, there are no restricting influences in the young adolescent's environment and when things are going well for him, he is happy. Let some obstacle cross his path, or let him fall short of the goal he set for himself, and his emotional state will quickly swing to states of depression as intense as the happiness he just experienced.

4. ADOLESCENT EMOTIONS FREQUENTLY TAKE THE FORM OF "MOODS," OR DRAWN-OUT EMOTIONS. Instead of expressing themselves and clearing the

system of the pent-up energy aroused with every emotion, the adolescent's moods are often bottled up emotional states which may last for hours or even days. Because adolescent emotions are characteristically intense, the moods are likewise intense. Since the emotions most likely to be subjected to control are the unpleasant ones, such as fear, anger, or jealousy, adolescent moods are characteristically morbid and gloomy.

5. SENTIMENTS BECOME STRONGER IN ADOLESCENCE. At the close of child-hood, "sentiments," or emotions with an intellectual association or ideal, begin to develop. Group loyalty and patriotism are the most common senti-ments at that age. In adolescence, sentiments are not only more frequent but they are also stronger. Personal pride, family pride, loyalty, patriotism, reverence, love for the beautiful, and kindliness are some of the most com-monly experienced sentiments at this time.

Common Emotional Patterns. The emotional patterns of the adolescent years are much the same as those of childhood. They differ from childish emotions, however, in the type of stimuli that give rise to these emotions and in the form of expression they take. The following are the most impor-tant emotional patterns of the early adolescent years:

ANGER. Adolescent anger differs from that of childhood not in the number of anger experiences at the two age levels but rather in the stimuli that give rise to anger, in the duration of anger, and in the type of response made. Anger situations in adolescence are, for the most part, social. This is in marked contrast to those of childhood. Then the child becomes angry when some activity he is engaging in is interrupted or when he is kept from doing something that he wants to do. The adolescent, by contrast, is made angry when he is teased, when people are unfair to him, lie to him, impose upon him, are sarcastic or bossy. He also becomes angry when things do not go right or when he is unable to accomplish what he sets out to do (Hicks and Hayes, 1938). While many young adolescents do fly off the handle in a temper tantrum, not unlike that of a child in its intensity, the more common form of angry response is sulkiness or being generally disagreeable. The sulky individual refuses to talk or to do what he is expected to do. Any overt response he may make is generally in the form of talking. He calls people names, he makes extravagant statements about "hating" them, himself, and life in general, and he often swears at or tongue-lashes the person who has made him angry.

Instead of trying to get his revenge by hitting and kicking, as a child does, the adolescent frequently substitutes belittling or ridiculing the person he would like to fight with. A persistence in infantile behavior during anger is not unusual in early adolescence. Frequently young adolescents throw things, stamp their feet, hit, kick, and, in the case of girls, cry when they are angry. Gradually, however, the adolescent comes to realize that such overt expres-sions are regarded as signs of immaturity and he learns to control them.

In their place, then, he substitutes verbal forms of fighting which are often deferred until a time when the fighting will be most effective.

ANNOYANCES. Annoyances are a form of anger, though not so severe as anger. They fall in the general category of "irritations," or unpleasant feelings. After childhood is over, annoyances are usually more frequent than anger situations (Cason, 1930). They are built up from unpleasant experiences through conditioning. They are most frequently associated with human behavior, nonhuman things and activities, and clothing and manner of dress (Cason, 1930). There is a tendency for the individual not to do the things which he finds annoying in other people (Cason and Chalk, 1933).

FEAR. By the time the child has reached adolescence, he has learned from experience that many of the things he formerly feared are not dangerous or harmful. As a result, his former fears vanish. However, in place of fears of real people, objects, or situations, the adolescent is more likely to fear things and situations which are primarily a product of his imagination. He works himself up into a state of fear about things that *might* happen, though he may have little reason for believing that their occurrence is possible or even probable. Because fears at all ages are learned either through conditioning or imitation, there are marked individual differences in what adolescents fear. In general, however, adolescent fears may be divided into three major categories: *fears of material objects,* such as fire, airplanes, or animals; *fears of social relationships,* as meeting people, being at parties with members of the opposite sex, or having to speak to a group; and *fears of a general kind,* as fear of death, of lack of popularity, or personal inadequacy, especially in sex relationships.

Fears of the second type, those related to social situations, are by far the most common in adolescence. This is natural since the adolescent is very anxious to be socially acceptable and he is, therefore, afraid that he will not measure up favorably or win the esteem of other people, particularly his contemporaries. General fears are likewise common in adolescence, especially those that relate to people or to social situations. Unlike the child, the adolescent has relatively few fears related to material objects.

A large number of the fears of high-school students center around their school activities. Fears of school tests, school grades, speeches or oral reports, class recitations, teachers, report cards, athletic contests, unpopularity, homework, tardiness, and specific school requirements are some of the most commonly reported fears during high-school days. Most of these fears are determined and caused in school. If the student is to do good work in school, the emotional tension brought on by constant fear of one school requirement or another should be lessened if the students are to enjoy their studies and have a feeling of security in the school life (Noble and Lund, 1951).

Like the young child who is afraid of people and new or strange social situations, the young adolescent is very shy in the presence of all but his most intimate friends. He wants to make a good impression on strangers, on adults, and on members of the opposite sex but he lacks confidence in his ability to do so. The resulting fear makes him shy and ill-at-ease, an almost universal characteristic of young adolescents. This differs markedly from the fears of situations which older children have and which make them cautious.

The typical fear response in adolescence is rigidity of the body, accompanied by paling, trembling, and perspiring. Unlike the child who runs away and hides when he is frightened, the adolescent infrequently responds in this way because he knows it would be a socially unacceptable form of behavior which would label him as a " 'fraid cat" and would win for him the scorn of his contemporaries. However, the adolescent does run away before the situation that might give rise to fear occurs. In other words, he *avoids* such situations. He then finds some justifiable excuse for his behavior and thus rationalizes his avoidance of a situation that he is afraid to face directly.

WORRY. Worry is a form of fear that comes primarily from imaginary rather than from real causes. Worries about examinations, about making a speech before a group, or about taking part in some athletic contest come from the adolescent's imagined fears that he will not make a good impression or that he will not measure up to his own or other people's anticipations. These worries are generally as intense if not more so than fears which come from real situations. And they can have an effect on the physical and psychological well-being of the individual as devastating as real fear does. Among young adolescents, schoolwork is the most common source of worry. Those whose schoolwork is not satisfactory worry more about it than do those whose work is satisfactory. Tests and examinations in school are the chief source of worry connected with schoolwork (Hicks and Hayes, 1938). Young adolescent girls worry also about their appearance (Stone and Barker, 1937), about lack of understanding between themselves and their parents, boy-and-girl relationships, difficulties in making friends, suitable places for recreation, vocational choice, religion, health problems, clothes, money, and such personal problems as personality weakness and lack of emotional control (Hertzler, 1940). Boys worry more than girls about ability and money (Pressey and Robinson, 1944).

JEALOUSY. While jealousy is commonly thought of as an infantile emotion, it appears in an intense and well-camouflaged form during early adolescence. As is true of the jealous child, the jealous adolescent feels insecure in his relationship with loved individuals. The young adolescent is interested in members of the opposite sex en masse and craves popularity with them. Those who attain this desired goal arouse jealous reactions in those who are overlooked or scorned by members of the opposite sex. When interest in one member of the opposite sex appears, as it frequently does at the close of early adolescence, the individual who loses the loved one to another is as intensely jealous as the child whose position as center of attention in the family is suddenly usurped by the new arrival in the family.

When children are jealous, they either attack the individual whom they believe has usurped their place in the parent's affection or they revert to infantile behavior in order to win the attention they feel they have lost. The adolescent, instead of making bodily attacks upon those of whom he is jealous, makes verbal attacks. These attacks are generally in such a subtle form that it is often difficult to recognize them as such. The most common forms of verbal attack consist of sarcastic comments, ridiculing the individual, preferably in the presence of his parents or friends, and making derogatory comments about the person behind his back when he cannot defend himself. Regression to infantile forms of behavior is far less common among adolescents than among children. Girls sometimes, however, do whine and cry when their feelings are hurt or when they feel that they have been neglected. Emotionally immature boys rarely engage in this infantile type of behavior though they may make bodily attacks upon the individual who has aroused their jealousy, just as they did when they were children.

ENVY. Envy, like jealousy, is directed against an individual. It differs from jealousy in that the emotion is not stimulated by the individual of whom the adolescent is jealous but rather by the material possessions of this individual. It is a form of covetousness which is rarely found in any marked degree among children because children lack the ability to appreciate the true value of material objects. So long as a child has material possessions similar in outward appearance to those of his friends, any inferiority there may be in their quality does not disturb him. To an adolescent, however, quality as well as quantity is important. He not only wants as many things as his friends have but he also wants his possessions to be as good as theirs. Differences in size of the home, in the make of the family car, in the quality of his clothes, and in the number and type of vacation trips his family can afford are important to him.

As is true of jealousy, the typical envy reaction is verbal in form. The envious adolescent may criticize and make fun of possessions superior to his in an unconscious attempt to convince himself—as the fox did in the fable about the grapes he could not reach and therefore called "sour"—that they are not worth having. More likely, however, envy will express itself in complaining about the inferiority of the quality of his possessions, in exaggerating to his parents the number and superior quality of the possessions of others, and in saying that he is going to "get a job and have the things his friends have." These verbal expressions, which are more common in girls than in boys, are a bid for sympathy and attention on their part.

AFFECTION. While children may have as strong affectional associations for pets and favorite toys as they do for people, this does not occur in adolescence. The adolescent's affections are concentrated on people with whom he has a pleasurable relationship and who have made him feel secure and loved. As a general rule, the affectional relationship with members of the family is less strong among adolescents than it is in childhood, owing to the strained family relationships that typically exist at this time. On the other hand, affectional relationships with people outside the home, generally with a few members of their own sex, with an adult whom they hero-worship, and with a few members of the opposite sex are common. Only when a pleasant and understanding relationship exists with his parents or his siblings is the affectional relationship with members of his immediate family as strong as it is with individuals outside the home. The number of people for whom the adolescent has a strong affection is small, as compared with that of the child. As a result, his emotional reaction toward these few individuals is typically stronger than it is for the large group the child is fond of. Furthermore, as all emotions have a tendency to be stronger in adolescence than in childhood, it is logical that his affections for the few people he is truly fond of would be very intense.

Adolescent affection is an absorbing type of emotion that drives the adolescent to seek constantly the companionship of the individual or individuals for whom his affection is strongest. When he is away from them, he tries to keep in constant touch by telephone calls and letters. In addition, the adolescent tries to do everything he can to make the loved one happy, whether it be helping him with his schoolwork, planning forms of entertainment he will enjoy, or giving him presents. As early adolescence is a self-conscious, shy age, there is little demonstration of affection in kissing, hugging, and hand-holding, as is true of the early childhood years. He does, however, reveal his affection by watching and listening to the loved one with rapt attention and by smiling constantly when in the presence of the loved one.

JOY. Joy, which in its milder forms is known as "happiness" or "delight," is a general, rather than a specific, emotional state. While it is influenced markedly by the physical condition of the individual, it does not occur in adolescence only when a favorable physical condition is present, as is true of the early years of childhood. Joy, on the contrary, comes from good adjustments to his work and the social situations with which he is identified, from his ability to perceive the comic in a situation, from a release of pent-up emotional energy following worry, fear, anger, or jealousy, and from feelings of superiority which result from successful achievements on the adolescent's part.

The characteristic joy response is stereotyped in form and differs little from one individual to another. The entire body, as well as the face, is relaxed. There is a tendency to smile and, if the situation warrants it, smiling is followed by laughter. Each individual has his own characteristic form of laugh, though boys in general have laughs that are lower in tonal quality than girls have. Giggling frequently accompanies the joy emotion in girls, while boys are more likely to laugh so uproariously that their whole bodies shake. Uproarious laughter among girls is considered "unladylike" and, for that reason, girls seek more socially acceptable forms of expression.

CURIOSITY. By the time the individual has reached adolescence, his natural curiosity has been suppressed by environmental restraints. Not only is he reproved or punished for getting into things that arouse his curiosity but his questions are often unanswered or he is made to feel that he is being a nuisance by asking so many questions. Furthermore, by the time he reaches adolescence, there is not much that he has not already explored if his environment remains unchanged throughout the childhood years. As a result, there are fewer things to stimulate his curiosity than there were when he was younger. There are, however, new things entering the young adolescent's life and these are a source of curiosity to him. Members of the opposite sex present new experiences and the whole matter of sex and the relationships between the two sexes stimulate his curiosity. New areas of knowledge are opened up through his studies in junior and senior high school and the broader social relationships in the community likewise arouse his desire to learn more about them.

Then, too, there is the ever-present interest in the constant changes that are taking place in their own bodies. Naturally these arouse the young adolescents' curiosity, especially if their preparation information about these changes has been lacking or is only slight. The new physical sensations that accompany the maturation of the sex organs are sources of curiosity to the young adolescent, especially in the case of boys. While direct exploration of the things that arouse his curiosity occurs in adolescence as it does in childhood, the major response in curiosity consists of talking with anyone and everyone, asking questions, and making comments. From this, the adolescent not only learns new facts but he also acquires points of view which he might not otherwise have if his exploration were limited to questioning.

SOCIAL BEHAVIOR

While the social development of the adolescent started in babyhood and continues throughout the years of childhood, with a temporary setback during the period of puberty, the most difficult of all social adjustments for the individual to make come during adolescence. These adjustments are related to members of the opposite sex, in a relationship that never existed before in the individual's life, and to adults outside the family and school environments. A good foundation of social adjustments, established during the early years of life, will go a long way toward helping the young adolescent to adjust successfully to the new social demands placed upon him. A poor foundation of social adjustments, on the other hand, will add seriously to the difficulties every adolescent normally experiences at this time. Many young adolescents are so incapable of meeting these new demands successfully that they abandon the attempt and regress to earlier forms of social relationships or they develop compensatory forms of behavior to replace the normal social behavior of their contemporaries.

Influence of the Social Group. The individual at every age is a product of his social environment. As a baby, his environment is limited to members of the family and their influence is paramount in shaping his personality. As childhood advances and the child's social horizons broaden, the social group outside the home plays an increasingly important role in determining what sort of individual he will be. In early adolescence, this influence is intensified by the adolescent's desire to be socially acceptable and the consequent effect of striving on his part to conform in every way to patterns approved by the group.

A new factor enters into the young adolescent's social life which never before existed. Now he is no longer identified with just one group outside the home, the "gang," as he was in childhood. The broadening of his interests and experiences means that he is identified with several groups, often of distinctly different types of individuals with different interests and different points of view. His teammates, for example, may not be the same group that he associates with for social affairs, while that group, in turn, may be composed of entirely different individuals than the group that makes up the high-school dramatic society in which he is an active member.

How much or how little influence these different groups will have on the adolescent will depend to a large extent upon his degree of intimacy with each group. That, in turn, will be dependent upon the degree of success he achieves in his social adjustments with each group and his acceptance by the members of the different groups. In addition, within each group there are degrees of intimacy in his relationship with the different members of that group. These have been subdivided into three categories, according to the degree of intimacy that exists between the individual and other members of the group. In the *primary interactions* there is the closest intimacy. The number of persons with whom the individual has such relationships is small and these are regarded as his intimate friends. *Secondary interactions* are less intimate relationships, while the *tertiary interactions* are purely casual relationships. In the case of the primary and, to a lesser degree, the secondary relationships, the influence of members of the group on the adolescent is pronounced. Tertiary relationships have little influence on the adolescent's behavior (Brown, 1939).

Changes in social attitudes and behavior are not entirely the product of group influences. With sexual maturing come changes which are so universally found among boys and girls of different environmental backgrounds that they cannot be attributed to environmental factors but rather to maturational factors. After pubescence has been completed, the young adolescent boy characteristically shows positive social attitudes as contrasted to the negative attitudes normally found at the time of puberty. These positive social attitudes include impatience with restrictions, sympathy for the weak, gregariousness, interest in social causes, desire to reform others, and loyalty to a person but not to a school. Much the same changes occur in girls except that loyalty to a person is replaced by loyalty to a clique (Leal, 1931).

The most pronounced shifts in social interests and activities come between the ages of twelve and fourteen years (Dimock, 1935a). Of these shifts, the most significant are from variety and instability of interests to fewer and deeper interests; from talkative, noisy, and daring to more dignified, controlled behavior; from an identification with the herd to identification with a small select group; from family status being an unimportant factor in influencing relationships with contemporaries to an increasing influence of the family socioeconomic status in the selection of friends of both sexes; from informal to formal social activities; and from occasional dating to dates and "steadies" (Meek, 1940).

Social Groupings. The "gangs" of childhood days gradually break up at puberty and in early adolescence as the individual's interests shift from the strenuous play activities of childhood to the less strenuous and more formal social activities of adolescence. In their place come new social groupings. Like the child, the adolescent feels the need for companionship with his contemporaries and from this he derives feelings of security which he lacks when his companionship is limited to adults.

Degrees of intimacy, or "social distance," between friends appear for the first time during the early years of adolescence. No longer does the individual feel much the same way about all of his friends as he did when he was younger. Some he prefers to others and some are so congenial that he prefers their companionship to that of other friends. Social distance depends partly upon the degree of intimacy that exists between two individuals and partly upon the degree of emotional warmth. Frequency of contact is responsible, in part, for the degree of intimacy that exists (Runner, 1937). The most common social groupings in early adolescence are *chums, cliques,* and *crowds.*

CHUMS. The adolescent's closest friends and best friends are his "chums," or, as boys prefer to call them, his "pals." How many chums the adolescent will have varies from one individual to another, and from one time to another in the same individual. As a rule, shortly after puberty, a girl will select one other girl as her confidante (Hetzer, 1926; Vecerka, 1926). Much the same pattern is followed by boys (Furfey, 1926; Kupky, 1927). As time goes on, the number of chums may and frequently does increase but it never is as large as the number of less intimate friends. And because of the satisfaction the adolescent derives from such social relationships more time is spent with chums than with other friends. Chums are generally of the same sex and have interests and abilities of a similar sort (Bogardus and Otto, 1936). Their relationship is so close and so satisfying that it is natural that chums would have a marked influence on each other. While they may disagree at times and may even quarrel bitterly, the bond of friendship between them is so strong that the quarrels are soon patched up and forgotten.

CLIQUES. Cliques are small exclusive social groupings. They are made up of three or four intimate friends who have much in common in both interests and abilities (Runner, 1937). Frequently, they are made up of several pairs of chums, though this is not necessarily true in all cases. As the adolescent years advance and boy-girl friendships become more frequent, cliques are often made up of a girl and her chum and a boy and his pal. Early cliques, however, are made up of individuals of the same sex. Cliques, like chums, are far more lasting social groupings than are the friendships of childhood days. They are held together by strong ties of affection and common interests which are frequently lacking in the friendships of childhood.

CROWDS. The largest of the social groupings of adolescence is the *crowd*. Unlike the "gangs" of childhood, the adolescent crowd is composed of individuals with common interests and common abilities. And, because the crowd is larger than other social groupings of adolescence, there is social distance among its members. Typically, it starts with a clique as its foundation. Then new members are added, either single individuals, chums, or other cliques. Naturally, under such conditions, not all members are equally congenial and, as a result, social distance or degrees of intimacy are bound to be found. As is true of cliques, crowds at first are made up of members of one sex. Later, with the development of interest in members of the opposite sex, the crowd becomes heterogeneous in its membership, with an equal number of members of both sexes.

Crowd activities are predominantly social in character. In this respect, also, they differ from the childhood "gangs" whose major activities center around adventure, excitement, and mischief-making. Unlike the "gang," the crowd has no recognized leader, no carefully planned activities, and no regular meeting place. The major interests of its members center around talking, playing games or dancing, and eating. While these may seem unexciting and even meaningless, as judged by adult standards, they fulfill the strong need every adolescent has for companionship with his contemporaries.

Unfortunately, not all adolescent boys and girls belong to crowds. Certain adolescents are excluded from crowd membership because of the poor socio-economic status of their parents; their national background (Additon, 1930); geographic isolation from a group of their contemporaries; difference in interests, abilities, or privileges which their contemporaries enjoy; or, most important of all, personality traits which other adolescents dislike. Whatever the cause, the adolescent who is not accepted as a member of a crowd is unhappy and feels that he is missing out on the fun that is rightly his.

There are *advantages and disadvantages* in crowd life. On the positive side, being a member of a crowd gives the adolescent a feeling of security, it offers him invaluable experience in getting along successfully with people, it offers pleasant leisure-time activities, it offers an opportunity to develop social skills, such as talking and dancing which will prove to be useful not only throughout the adolescent years but also for the years of maturity, and it gives him an opportunity to meet and know members of the opposite sex in socially approved situations. On the minus side, crowd life may prove to be so absorbing to an adolescent that he neglects his duties and responsibilities at home, at school, and in the community; it is likely to encourage an intolerant, snobbish attitude toward contemporaries who do not belong to that crowd or any other crowd; and it makes a difficult if not intolerable situation for adolescents who do not belong to a crowd and who, as a result, miss the fun that crowd members enjoy.

As is true of the childhood gang, the adolescent crowd has a powerful influence on the thoughts, attitudes, behavior, and personality patterns of its members. When a conflict between family patterns and those of the crowd arises, the adolescent is far more likely to accept those of the crowd than those of his parents. He feels that his parents are out of date and old fashioned in their ideas while his contemporaries know what is being done today. Furthermore, it gives him a feeling of security in this new area of his life if he conforms in a slavish way to the codes and roles of his crowd.

Adolescent Friendships. The young adolescent soon learns that friendships are not established just because individuals happen to be in the same class in school. Now there is a strong element of selection not apparent in the earlier years. To be accepted as a friend, he must conform to the socially approved pattern of his contemporaries and he must have personality traits that they like. The problem of friendship selection is complicated in the latter part of early adolescence by the newly awakened interest in members of the opposite sex (Hildreth, 1933). Figure 34 shows this new interest. So long as his friends were limited to members of his own sex, he knew what was acceptable to them and what was not. Now, however, a new element enters into the problem. He must be acceptable to members of the opposite sex if he is to establish friendships with them and, because of inexperience in this area of his behavior, he is unfamiliar with what they consider acceptable.

In the selection of friends, the adolescent is not guided by adult advice as he was when he was younger. He wants to select his own friends and resents adult interference in this matter. As a result of his inexperience, especially in the choice of friends of the opposite sex, he frequently chooses individuals who, at first, seem congenial but who, as time goes on, do not measure up to his standards. As a result, a quarrel ensues and the friendship is broken, often permanently. There is a tendency, as adolescence progresses, for friendships to become more stable than they were in the earlier years (Horrocks and Bulser, 1951). This would suggest that the adolescent, through experience, is learning to evaluate his contemporaries better and to be more selective in his choice of friends than he was when he was younger.

While degrees of intimacy exist between friends in adolescence, the young adolescent likes to have a large number of friends of different degrees of

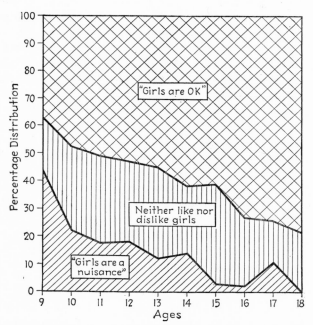

FIG. 34. Anonymous reactions of 700 boys nine to eighteen years old to a question concerning their attitude toward girls. At age nine 43 per cent said "Girls are a nuisance." (*Based on unpublished data of R. T. Sollenberger. From F. K. Shuttleworth, The adolescent period: a graphic atlas, Monogr. Soc. Res. Child Develpm., 1949, 14, No. 1. Used by permission.*)

intimacy (Hicks and Hayes, 1938). This, he feels, is an indication of his popularity. As he grows older, however, he narrows down the number and regards the "right" kind of friends as more important than a large number. What is looked upon as the "right" kind differs from one year to another and within different groups. Childhood friends, selected because they were good play companions, are not necessarily the "right" kind of friends for the young adolescent. Now play of the childhood type has given way to other interests and, as a result, new types of friends are frequently selected to replace the friends of childhood days. The adolescent now wants friends who have interests in common with his, who understand him, and who make him feel secure.

To make him feel secure, the young adolescent chooses as his friends those whose interests, abilities, and socioeconomic status are similar to his (Hicks and Hayes, 1938; Dimock, 1937). Similarity is also seen by the fact that young adolescents choose friends who, for the most part, come from their own neighborhoods and are in their classes at school (Furfey, 1927). These similarities ensure congeniality, they guarantee a degree of understanding and sympathy between friends, and they make it possible for friends to discuss their problems and come to some solution of these problems.

Since interest in members of the opposite sex is just beginning to appear as early adolescence draws to a close, the young adolescent has not yet set up criteria of a definite type for these friends. Because boys are slower in maturing than girls, the young adolescent boy shows far less interest in friendships with girls than girls show in boys. This means that a young adolescent girl has little selection if she wants to have friends among members of the opposite sex. She must take any boy or boys who are enough interested in girls to want to be friends with them, regardless of whether they come up to her standards or not.

Social Isolates. There are many young adolescents who are social isolates in the sense that they do not have any close friends nor do they belong to any cliques or crowds. This makes them unhappy and resentful, often producing lasting effects on their personalities. They may develop substitute satisfactions, such as friendships with older or younger individuals, an absorbing type of hobby, daydreaming, or similar compensations. None of these, however, is as satisfying to them as friendships with their contemporaries, and, as a result, they are likely to develop personality traits which will detrimentally affect their future social adjustments.

Traits that make young adolescents unpopular include showing off; bullying and antagonizing others; feeling misunderstood or "picked on," carrying grudges; being resentful; using escape mechanisms such as alibis; domineering and bossing others; and being highly nervous, timid and withdrawing, or stubborn, sullen, and sulky (Dimock, 1937). Manners also begin to be important at this age. An adolescent whose manners fall below the norms of his contemporaries is likely to be regarded as a "boor" by them (Strang, 1931).

Geographic isolation, when it means living so far away from other individuals of the same age as to necessitate using different forms of transportation to be with their friends, usually results in social isolation for the individuals who are far removed from the group. A comparison of a group of high-school students from rural districts, who were transported to school in school buses, with town students showed that the town students as a group were rated higher in popularity than were the rural students. Girls from rural districts are at a greater disadvantage than are boys. Both boys and girls, but especially girls, participate less than town students in school functions because of their isolated social position in the student body. Bus students were likewise found to have fewer mutual friends than town students. In general, bus students are not accepted by their peers on an equal basis with town students (Bonney, 1951).

Popularity. The popular adolescent is one who has one or more intimate friends or chums, belongs to a clique, and is generally a member of a crowd. Because he is accepted, he feels secure and happy and this, in turn, gives him the necessary self-confidence to try to develop the characteristics that will add still further to his popularity. Having been popular in childhood, however, does not guarantee popularity in adolescence. The young adolescent expects his friends to possess certain traits that are not important to a child, while, on the other hand, traits which may have made him popular in childhood, such as being noisy, daring, and even rude to his elders, will have just the opposite effect in adolescence.

The socially acceptable adolescent is active, socially aggressive, and extroverted (Kuhlen and Lee, 1943). When he is with others, he cooperates and helps willingly, he is courteous and considerate of others, he assumes leadership in a group, he is truthful and "aboveboard" in his conduct, he controls his temper in annoying situations, he is unselfish with his belongings, he displays resourcefulness and initiative, he is willing and carries out accepted responsibilities, he observes rules and regulations, and he contributes well-considered suggestions to the thinking of the group (Dimock, 1937). High-school students who stand high in prestige among their classmates are those who have many friends, are friendly, well-mannered, cooperative with a group, enjoy hearing or telling a joke, and who are loyal to their friends (Anastasia and Miller, 1949).

Sex differences regarding preferred traits in friends of their own sex have been noted. Boys prefer boys who enjoy practical jokes, who enjoy working at their own hobbies, who are neat in appearance, and who are grown-up in their behavior. Girls, on the other hand, hold high in prestige girls who are cooperative with a group, who are assured with an adult, and who are serious-minded. These sex differences are in line with the traditional concept of a masculine boy and a feminine girl (Anastasia and Miller, 1949). Girls from small families have been found to be superior to girls from large families in social acceptability as measured by a sociometric test. The sex and age of the siblings had no effect on the girls' social acceptability (Damrin, 1949). Studies of only children have likewise revealed that absence of siblings does not create personality traits that make the individual unpopular but rather encourages a higher level of maturity which is admired and respected by individuals of the adolescent years just as it is during childhood.

Leaders. Popularity alone will not guarantee leadership though it is unusual to have a leader who is disliked by a majority of the group. To be a leader an adolescent must have qualities which are superior to and admired by the members of the group of which he is a leader. And, because the interests and activities of adolescents are more varied than they are during childhood, the qualities that make for leadership in one group may not make for leadership in others. In general, however, leaders are more active than nonleaders in social activities. They participate more and their participation is of a more aggressive sort. A comparison of extracurricular activities participated in by leaders and nonleaders among high-school students revealed that each leader averaged 6.8 activities as compared with 1.75 for the nonleader. Leaders spend more of their time in games of all sorts and at parties; nonleaders prefer solitary activities, such as reading, that offer little chance for leadership (Smith and Nystrom, 1937).

There are certain qualities that adolescents expect their leaders to possess. While larger-than-average *height* is an advantage, it is not as important as personality (Bowden, 1926). Most young-adolescent leaders are, however, slightly above average in height (Bellingrath, 1930; Partridge, 1938; Reynolds, 1944). Making a good *appearance,* with the aid of good grooming, good clothes, and a generally attractive, though not necessarily, beautiful face and body build, is more important than height.

Slightly above average *intelligence, academic achievement* above average, and above-average *level of maturity,* due either to age or to early maturing, are characteristics generally found among leaders during the early years of adolescence (Reynolds, 1944). Leaders, as a rule, come from families of higher *socioeconomic status* than do nonleaders. *Personality,* however, seems to be the outstanding quality that determines whether the adolescent will or will not be a leader. Dependability, loyalty, extroversion, wide range of interests, self-confidence, speed of decision, liveliness, good sportsmanship, sociability, sense of humor, poise, originality, and tact are a few of the qualities an adolescent leader possesses (Stray, 1933; Sward, 1931; Partridge, 1938).

The level of *sexual maturity* in early adolescence is a factor of importance in determining the leadership ability of the individual. The more mature the boy or girl, other factors being equal, the greater will be his chances for leadership. This, to a certain extent, depends upon the activity in which the individual is a leader or a follower. In athletics, the more mature boy has a better chance of being a leader than has the immature boy of the same chronological age. The explanation for this is that strength develops with sexual maturing and, as a result, the early-maturing individual is stronger at a given age than is the individual who was slower in developing (Latham, 1951).

INTERESTS

New interests develop during the adolescent years as a result of the changes that have taken place in the physical and emotional development of the individual at the time of sexual maturity and as a result of the new status the adolescent has in the social group. He is no longer a child and, therefore, new areas of activity and new experiences are opened up to him. Furthermore, he thinks of himself as no longer a child but as a near-adult and he is anxious to "put away childish things" just as society expects him to do (Stone and Barker, 1937, 1939).

What interests the individual will have at any age will depend upon so many different factors, such as his sex, his intelligence, opportunities for learning, the environment in which he lives, what his contemporaries are interested in, his own innate abilities, and the interests of his family, that it would be impossible to list all that are characteristically found in the early years of adolescence. Adolescent interests may, however, be roughly divided into three categories: *social* interests, *personal* interests, and *recreational* interests. All young adolescents possess these interests to a greater or less extent, and they all have certain specific interests that fall within these categories.

Social Interests. Social interests are those that relate to social situations and people, such as parties and conversations. After a period of little interest in any form of social activity, during puberty, the young adolescent becomes markedly interested in all forms of group activities, as well as activities with one or more intimate friends. These interests do not, however, develop overnight. Rather, they grow gradually, the rate depending to a large extent upon the satisfaction the adolescent derives from such activities and the opportunities he has to engage in them.

Interest in *parties,* which was strong during the early years of childhood and then lagged as childhood progressed, is revived in early adolescence with the awakening of interest in members of the opposite sex. During the junior high-school age, interest in parties with members of the opposite sex first begins to manifest itself because young adolescents like to be with members of the opposite sex and to play games or dance with them (Hicks and Hayes, 1938). At this age, girls are more interested in parties than are boys. They even go so far as to try to train the boys to dance and to be their party escorts. Left to their own devices, boys would not become interested in parties until a year or two later than girls because of their later sexual maturing (Stolz *et al.,* 1937). Even in the high-school groups, more girls than boys attend the school parties (Sullenger, 1938).

While most young adolescents are tongue-tied when they are with adults, they talk endlessly when they are with their friends. In fact, *conversations* are one of their favorite forms of social activities. Just getting together in a group and talking about the things that interest them or disturb them gives them a feeling of security that goes a long way toward helping them to puzzle out problems that have been a source of concern. Even after seeing his friends at school, the adolescent is hardly in the house before he calls up one of his intimate friends on the telephone and continues his conversation with that friend until his family puts a stop to it.

The favorite topics of conversation among young adolescents differ for the two sexes. Girls talk mostly about parties, dates, jokes, books, movies, movie stars, ball games, and teachers, while the favorite topics of conversation among boys include ball games, jokes, dates, movies, and politics (Jones, 1943). A shift of interest in conversational topics has been observed among high-school boys as they progress from freshman to senior year. The younger boys talk mostly about sports, girls, school, teachers, and studies, in this order, while the older boys concentrate mostly on conversation about girls, sports, social activities, dates, and sex, in this order (Fleege, 1945).

The young adolescent is sincerely interested in *other people,* especially those whom he feels have been misunderstood, mistreated, or oppressed. This interest is shown in active participation in school and community affairs which are planned to help others less fortunate than they and in championing their causes by arguments and discussions (Leal, 1929). He begins to show an interest in *government* and in *politics,* and even in *world affairs* but, for the most part, this interest is expressed mainly by reading and discussions.

Interest in others becomes so strong among many adolescent boys and girls that they bend their efforts to *reforming* their families, their friends, and even their schools and communities. The young adolescent is very free in offering suggestions, whether solicited or not, and in attempting to force his ideas and suggestions on others, regardless of their attitudes and feelings about the matter. Criticisms of parents and attempts to reform them are characteristic of almost all young adolescents, but especially of girls (Sowers, 1937; Stott, 1940). The junior and senior high schools likewise come in for a large share of the adolescent's criticisms and attempts at reform (Jones, 1943). Most of the criticisms are of a destructive rather than of a constructive sort, and suggestions offered for reforms are more often impractical than practical.

Personal Interests. Interest in themselves is the strongest interest young adolescents have. This comes partly from the rapid bodily changes which took place during puberty and which continue, at a decreasing rate, throughout early adolescence, and partly from the realization that social acceptance is markedly influenced by the general appearance of the individual. The girl, for example, "feels a necessity to prove to herself and to the world that she is essentially feminine; the boy needs to demonstrate that he has those masculine qualities which will require others to recognize him as a man" (Stolz *et al.,* 1937).

With the awakening of interest in members of the opposite sex, interest in *appearance, in dress,* and in *personal adornment* increases. This is true especially of girls because they realize how important appearance is to popularity with members of the opposite sex (Stone and Barker, 1939). Interest in appearance covers not only clothes and personal adornment but every aspect of appearance. Hair, body size, facial features, skin, and nails are all focal points of interest to the young adolescent. Any feature that does not come up to standard is likely to be the source of great concern to the young adolescent.

Both boys and girls discover, even before childhood is over, that *clothes* go a long way toward covering up undesirable physical features and toward enhancing good features. They make use of this knowledge during early adolescence when personal appearance becomes important to them. Young adolescent girls, owing to modesty resulting from bodily changes, denounce ostentation in dress while, at the same time, they stress the physical attributes they wish to set off by their clothes, such as their eyes and their hair. They feel that clothes, whether for work or for play, should be as bright and cheerful as possible. They also show interest in fashion (Macaulay, 1929).

High-school girls regard right clothes as necessary to happiness. Wrong clothes can lead to uneasiness in social situations and a good appearance can be an aid in building self-confidence. They select clothes that appeal to boys rather than to girls when their interest in boys appears (Silverman, 1945). Becomingness of color and style is more important to girls than is usefulness. Because the adolescent's happiness and self-confidence depend upon his contemporaries' attitudes toward his clothes, he is anxious to conform to what the group approves of in the matter of dress (Hurlock, 1929). Young adolescents like to express their thoughts, feelings, and emotions on paper. The *diary* is an outlet for their present interests and concerns (Hollingworth, 1928). They also like to write *compositions* about topics of interest to them (Coleman, 1931) and to express their opinions about their classmates in the *social columns* of their school papers. These are often expressed in exaggerated, daring, and exciting terms which are frequently cruel and humiliating to the individuals referred to (Cameron, 1938).

A strong desire for *independence*, which made its appearance in a milder form in the closing years of childhood, develops in early adolescence. It is as if an overwhelming urge were released among these young adolescents to assert their independence, to explore new and thrilling kinds of relationships with one another, and to proclaim their rights of self-expression as individuals (Cameron, 1938). Resistance to adult authority is most pronounced in early adolescence when the individual is in the throes of trying to establish himself socially (Stolz *et al.,* 1937). This leads to many clashes with parents and other adults in authority with the result that there is more or less constant friction in the home.

The common causes of friction at home, during the early years of adolescence, are coming home late, quarreling with and teasing siblings, and disobedience (Hicks and Hayes, 1938). There is also friction regarding personal appearance, habits, and manners; differences in thinking between the adolescent and his parents regarding vocational, social, recreational, and educational choices; and in the activities used to attain these goals. Friction often comes not so much from the situations themselves as from the way the parent

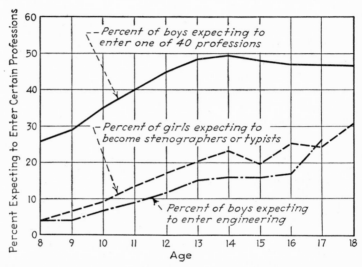

Fig. 35. Vocational aspirations of boys and girls at different ages in adolescence. (*From F. K. Shuttleworth, The adolescent period, Monogr. Soc. Res. Child Develpm., 1938, 3, No. 3. Used by permission.*)

handles them (Block, 1937). The most serious frictions come from social situations and activities (Lynd and Lynd, 1929).

As boys and girls reach the end of their high-school days, they begin to think seriously about their *careers*. The unrealistic vocational aspirations of childhood give way to a more realistic concept of what certain lines of work require in the way of ability and education, and of the assessment of the individual's capacities. This change is shown in Fig. 35. Early in his high-school career, the young adolescent's attention is focused upon his choice of future work because of the necessity of training for this brought on by our present-day trend toward specialization. The young adolescent's attitude toward working shows a strong need for vocational guidance (Jahoda, 1949).

The young adolescent boy frequently is more seriously concerned about this problem of vocational choice than is the girl because, to him, it will be a life career while, to her, it will be, in most cases, just a stopgap until she marries. In the case of boys, therefore, making a mistake in choice is far more serious than it is for girls. Girls, as a rule, show a preference for occupations of a more sedentary type, while boys prefer occupations which enable them to move around and to travel (Lehman and Witty, 1936). Parents and teachers are generally the most important factors in the determination of a high-school student's choice of career (Beeson and Tope, 1928; Austin, 1931).

As young adolescents have a relatively unrealistic idea of what their abilities are (Hurlock and Jansing, 1934), they are likely to be influenced by the waves of occupational interest that sweep over the group to which they belong (Clark and Withers, 1931). Nor do they take into consideration job opportunities (Kroger and Louttit, 1936). What they want is a job that has glamour and excitement, regardless of their real ability for it or the chances that such jobs will be available for them. They also want jobs with high prestige, even if these jobs pay less than those with less prestige (Hildreth, 1933; Hicks and Hayes, 1938).

Because of the unrealistic attitude most young adolescents have toward careers, it would be logical to assume that they would be very changeable in their vocational selections. This is true in a large majority of cases. The adolescent decides upon one job, then changes to another as he hears about those that appeal to him more. An investigation of the stability of vocational interests of high-school students, using the Kuder Preference Record for ninth- and twelfth-grade students, showed that the greatest area of interest remained highest for 52 per cent of the group, second for 34 per cent, and third for 28 per cent. The lowest remained lowest for 43 per cent, and the next lowest for 35 per cent (Mallinson and Crumrine, 1952).

Recreational Interests. While both boys and girls show a change in the recreations they enjoy in adolescence as compared with childhood, the change is more marked for girls than for boys. In general, there is a breaking away from recreations that require much expenditure of energy and a liking for recreations of the amusement type, where the player is a passive spectator. This may be explained partially by differences in physical strength between the two sexes but it is more likely to be the result of the greater home responsibilities carried by the girls and of the sapping of their strength which might otherwise be used for strenuous play. In early adolescence, just as is true of the early part of late childhood, there is a carry-over of some of the play activities of the early years and the introduction of new and more mature forms of recreation. Gradually, the childish forms of play drop out so that, when early adolescence comes to a close, the individual's recreational pattern is much the same as it will be during the latter part of adolescence and into the early years of maturity (Lehman and Witty, 1930; Furfey, 1929; Partridge, 1938; Abt *et al.*, 1940).

Because of the pressures of schoolwork, home duties, extracurricular activities at school, and afterschool or week-end jobs, most young adolescents have far less time for recreation than they had when they were younger. As a result, they select the types of activities that they enjoy most or in which they excel. This limits the number of activities (Witty, 1931; Hicks and Hayes, 1938). There is also a tendency to prefer sedentary to more active forms of play (Lehman and Witty, 1927; Stone and Barker, 1939).

Interest in *games* and *sports* which require great physical energy reaches its peak in early adolescence (Rothney, 1937). Of all games, swimming is most popular with both boys and girls at this age. Ice-skating, basketball, football, and tennis rank below swimming in popularity (Hicks and Hayes, 1938). A larger percentage of girls than of boys enjoy sports as spectators (Sullenger, 1938). The junior-high-school girl's interest in games and sports depends somewhat upon her physical strength. Girls with high strength and physical-fitness indexes, as measured by tests, exceed girls in corresponding low groups both in total number of play activities engaged in and in total time devoted to play activities. Girls in the low group were found to exceed girls in the high group in playing musical instruments, bicycling, and playing with pet animals. By contrast, girls in the high group engaged in a preponderance of physical activities involving competition and subordination of individualistic activities (Van Dalen, 1949). Boys, on the other hand, prefer to be active participants in such sports as football, basketball, and swimming (Dimock, 1937). They prefer organized sports to the neighborhood games of childhood (Reaney, 1916). Games of intellect and gambling come into popularity at this age, especially among boys.

Hobbies of a constructive sort occupy much of the leisure time of young adolescents (Sullenger, 1938; Dimock, 1937). Boys like shopwork, and girls show an interest in sewing clothes, knitting sweaters and socks, and trying out different cooking recipes. Both girls and boys like to draw, but they are self-conscious about their artistic productions (Dimock, 1937; Oakley, 1940; Hurlock, 1943a). Caricatures, drawing human forms, and printing words in a decorative fashion are the favorite subjects of adolescent drawings (Hurlock, 1943a).

Exploring the community, overnight or week-end trips to the country, and bicycle trips are popular at this time. The young adolescent likes to make *collections* but his collections are more selective than those of a child and they are kept in a more orderly fashion. As a rule, their collections have a sentimental value for them, such as programs of athletic contests, souvenirs of a pleasant date, and school papers with high grades (Sullenger, 1938; Whitley, 1929; Lehman and Witty, 1930). *Social dancing* begins to be popular during the junior-high-school days and becomes increasingly popular as time goes on (Hicks and Hayes, 1938; Sullenger, 1938; Stolz *et al.*, 1937). Boys are slower in developing this interest than are girls, primarily because of their retarded sexual development (Punke, 1936). When girls do not have boys as partners, they frequently dance together (Stolz *et al.*, 1937).

Reading, just for fun, becomes less popular in early adolescence than it was at the close of childhood. The young adolescent has less time than the child to read for the fun of it because of school and home pressures. Boys, at this age, prefer science and invention, and girls show a preference for romantic stories (Terman and Lima, 1927). They also specialize in the type of subject matter that appeals to them, and they read magazine stories more often than books (Dimock, 1937; Hicks and Hayes, 1938). Like the child, the young adolescent enjoys reading the comics, either in newspapers or in comic books (Witty and Coomer, 1942). Tabloids have an especially strong appeal to the slow reader at this age (Center and Persons, 1936).

Movies that appeal to young adolescents, as is true of reading, must have a romantic as well as an adventure theme. They also like comedies. Educational pictures, as is true of sex and society themes, have little appeal. Girls, on the whole, prefer pictures with a love theme; the preference of boys is for pictures with an adventure, mystery, or comedy theme (Sullenger, 1930; Hicks and Hayes, 1938; Witty *et al.,* 1941). What the adolescent sees, however, depends largely upon what is available in the local theaters. In small communities, where there are only one or two movie houses, the young adolescent's selection is limited to what is being shown when he wants to go to the movies. In selecting a movie, the most potent factor influencing the choice is the featured actor or actress. The sophisticated type of actor or actress or those who play romantic roles have greater appeal than do those whose acting ability may be greater but whose type of roles appeals less to the adolescent (Edman, 1940). Girls prefer actresses, while boys prefer actors and their choices of movies are motivated by these preferences (Sullenger, 1930).

Throughout the years of early adolescence, going to the movies is one of the favorite recreations of both boys and girls. The popularity of moving pictures comes from the fact that they provide "vicarious satisfaction for those fundamental desires which life most often inhibits and suppresses" (Lehman and Witty, 1927a). Movies are a form of escape mechanism which serve a useful purpose when life becomes too complicated for the young adolescent to meet successfully. Whether the adolescent goes to the movies alone or with his favorite friends, the experience is enjoyable. Unlike the child, he does not want to accompany his parents or go in a family group (Dale, 1935).

Because of the great interest in movies, it is not surprising that they have a profound influence on both boys and girls at this age. Girls, especially, are influenced by the feminine stereotypes they see on the screen, and they try to imitate their clothing, their hair styles, their speech, and their actions. Reading about their favorite actresses in the different movie magazines is one favorite source of reading pleasure. Much of the criticism and faultfinding with their parents and homes can be traced to the fact that the adolescents do not feel that their parents and homes come up to the standards set by the screen (Blumer, 1933; Forman, 1935).

Listening to the *radio* and watching *television* have, in recent years, become universal favorites among adolescents in America. As most American homes, even those of mediocre or even poor economic status, have either radio or television sets or both, the adolescent can get his amusement at home without the cost of going to the movies. One to 3 hours a day, or even more, is spent by the majority of adolescents on this form of amusement (Hicks and Hayes, 1938). Many young adolescents listen to the radio while they study, claiming that it helps them to concentrate better. There is an increase in preference for programs of dance and popular music as adolescence progresses. Humorous sketches and plays also have great appeal. Among boys especially, mystery, crime, and detective programs are popular. Both boys and girls like programs of the quiz type and those which feature amateurs (Hicks and Hayes, 1938; Jersild, 1939; Clark, 1940). Because television is such a recent innovation, to date there have been no studies of program preferences among adolescents.

Much of the adolescent's time that might be spent more profitably on his homework or other duties is spent in *daydreaming*. As is true of the pubescent child, daydreaming is a source of great satisfaction to the individual because, in his daydream, he can be the sort of person he would like to be in real life. But, unlike the suffering-hero daydream of puberty, the characteristic daydream of early adolescence is that of the conquering-hero in which the dreamer sees himself as the hero he would like to be in the type of setting that appeals most to him, whether it be on the football field, in the classroom, or on the dance floor (Hollingworth, 1928; Symonds, 1945). The theme and the setting of the adolescent daydream are often influenced by the movies that the adolescent has seen (Blumer, 1933).

While daydreaming is, unquestionably, a waste of time that might be spent more profitably in other activities and while it often leads to an unrealistic concept of self on the part of the dreamer, it also serves as an outlet for pressures that might not otherwise be met satisfactorily by the adolescent. In this respect, daydreaming serves much the same purpose as movies do in the lives of young adolescents (Zachry, 1940). Too much and too frequent daydreaming may and often does lead to a form of escapism from situations that are difficult. If the habit of retreat from reality into the daydream world becomes firmly established, it will lead to poor social and personality adjustments as time goes on (Hollingworth, 1928).

RELIGIOUS ATTITUDES

Human beings normally turn to religion during times of stress and strain, when they feel insecure and at a loss to know how to cope with their problems. This is true of early adolescence. But, if religion is to meet the needs of the young adolescent, it must be such that he can understand its true meaning, it must be personal in that it relates in some way to his own life, and it must be free from dogma. Far too often, the religious beliefs of childhood do not meet the needs of the adolescent. As a result, he tries to revise his religious beliefs to fit into his more mature level of understanding and to meet the more mature needs he faces.

Typically, adolescence is a period of *religious awakening*, when childish religious beliefs are examined critically and evaluated, then are revised to meet the new needs of the individual. Because all of this takes time, the major part of adolescence is devoted to the problem of religious revision. At first, the young adolescent faces his childish beliefs in a critical way, often dogmatically rejecting all or most of them. This, as a rule, begins when the average child is 12 years old or when the bright child's mental age is 12 years, regardless of what his chronological age is (Hollingworth, 1933). The median age for rebellion against parental teaching is 14½ years for girls and 15½ years for boys (Allport *et al.*, 1948).

Environmental influences are also important in bringing about religious awakening. The adolescent who has grown up in a family where religion plays a dominant role in the family life is likely to be more concerned about religion than is one whose family paid little attention to religion. Blows of fate, such as the death of a relative or near friend, and severe personal hardships also help to focus the adolescent's attention on religion. Religious discussions with his friends or teachers bring religion to the foreground and motivate a critical examination of it on the part of the adolescent. He is often confused by different opinions and this leads him to question his own beliefs (Remmers *et al.*, 1951).

Whether or not the religious awakening will be slow and gradual or catastrophic will depend partly upon the temperament of the individual and partly upon the pressures from his environment, especially from the home and from his friends. Most adolescents, however, are not urged to make, but rather are discouraged from making, hasty decisions about their religious faith. As a result, they meet the problem in a calm, critical manner, thus bringing about a better solution to the problem than if it were clouded by strong emotional factors. Among a group of college students, 27 per cent of the boys and 35 per cent of the girls had experienced the emotional type of conversion. For the rest, it was a gradual conversion (Allport *et al.*, 1948).

Most young adolescents meet religious beliefs of childhood with a hypercritical attitude. They have a tendency to reject all or at least a majority of their former beliefs because they have found a few of them difficult to accept now. They question those beliefs which do not stand the test of scientific scrutiny, and they refuse to accept on faith any teachings as they did when they were children. The more dogmatically religion was taught to them when they were children, the more skeptical they are likely to be when they are adolescent.

Pattern of Religious Doubt. Typically, religious doubt follows a predictable pattern. The adolescent first becomes skeptical of religious *forms,* such as prayer and duties toward God. Later, doubts are more likely to center around religious *contents,* such as knowledge and belief, and the nature of God and of man (Hollingworth, 1933). Sin, what becomes of people after they die, failure to go to church, and disliking church, are a few of the problems concerning religion that trouble young adolescents (Kuhlen and Arnold, 1944). As adolescence progresses, these problems give rise to new ones with their accompanying doubts. Girls, as a rule, are less subject to religious doubt than are boys (MacLean, 1930). Doubting is invariably accompanied by emotional tension. The more pronounced the doubting and the more closely it is related to subjects where doubt is frowned upon, the stronger will be the emotional accompaniment. In general, the more dogmatic the religious teaching of childhood has been, the greater will be the emotional accompaniment of doubting.

Religious doubt may be met by rationalization, consisting of quoting the Bible or the teachings of famous ministers to justify a religious concept the adolescent doubts; rejection of all childish religious concepts; or adjustment of childish concepts to meet the more mature needs of the individual. Of these three methods, only the last proves to be satisfactory to the individual either at the time of doubting or as he grows older (Brown, 1939). Absence of religious doubt is a bad sign. It means either that the individual has an intellectual level too low to question beliefs that proved to be satisfactory to him when his intellectual development was on a lower level or it means that his religious teaching has been so dogmatic and so threatening that he is afraid to doubt for fear of possible evil consequences. As a result, he continues to accept the beliefs of his childhood with a logic-tight mind and a tendency to inhibit any questions that might arise in regard to them. This eliminates any possibility of revision of his beliefs which is essential if they are to prove to be satisfactory to him as he reaches maturity.

Church attendance and other *religious observances* play a far more important role in the life of the young adolescent than most adults believe. The typical high-school student of today has a favorable attitude toward church (Remmers *et al.,* 1951). While the adolescent may revolt against going to Sunday school unless the teaching is of a liberal sort that fits his more mature needs, and while he may object to accompanying the family to church, this does not mean that he has rejected religion. Rather, it suggests that the matter of selection should be left to him so that he can find the Sunday school or the church that will meet his needs best. Girls, as a rule, attend both Sunday school and church more than boys do (Hicks and Hayes, 1938; Punke, 1936). Youth organizations within the church have a strong appeal to the young adolescent. While these organizations are usually more social than religious in function, they do serve to act as a tie between the young person and the church at a time when the tie could easily be broken as a result of the doubts experienced by the adolescent (Bell, 1938). Church attendance may fall off at this time as may active participation in church activities, but, generally, this is due to lack of activity on the part of the group, to lack of friendliness within the group, or to the fact that the meetings are "dead" (Weaver, 1944).

While *prayer* to a child is an egocentric experience in which he asks God for something he wants, whether it be a material object or some desired skill, the typical prayer of an adolescent is a means of confession of wrongdoing or sin, an opportunity to express thanks or to talk to God, to ask for guidance in meeting some especially troublesome problem, or merely to comply with a habit established in childhood days. Relatively few adolescents use prayer to ask for personal benefits (Pixley and Beekman, 1949). A nationwide poll of high-school students revealed that the typical student says prayers once or twice a day (Remmers *et al.*, 1951).

MORAL ATTITUDES AND BEHAVIOR

Adolescence puts a strong strain on the moral standards and behavior of the individual. When firm foundations of morality have been established during the years of childhood, they will stand up under the strain. At adolescence, the individual must make decisions for himself and must learn to guide his own behavior according to standards he has learned when he was a child. No longer can he expect the guidance of adults nor can he rely upon them to tell him what to do or what not to do. It is assumed that he knows what is right and what is wrong. Only in new areas of behavior, as in his relationships with members of the opposite sex, do adults feel that there is any real need for further moral training. Between the ages of twelve and sixteen years, there is a steady increase in moral discrimination which, given the right attitude on the individual's part, should lead to a gain in quality of moral behavior (Dimock, 1937).

Moral Concepts. No longer is the individual willing to accept in an unquestioning manner the concepts of right and wrong of either his parents or of his contemporaries, as he did when he was a child. He now builds up a moral code of his own, based upon the moral concepts established during childhood days but changed and modified to meet his more mature level of development. Inconsistencies in moral concepts, which he soon discovers from his discussions with other people and from his observations of their behavior, prove to be confusing to the young adolescent. In spite of this confusion, most young adolescents are able to work out a code of moral standards which differs from that of their childhood days and which will serve them well not only now but after they reach maturity. Things which, during childhood, they thought of as "wrong," they now learn to accept, such as smoking, playing cards, divorce, pawning jewelry, and playing hooky (Stone and Barker, 1939).

Changes in attitudes toward lying from childhood to adolescence show the influence of individual thinking on the part of the adolescent. While older children almost unanimously condemn lying on moral grounds, adolescents admit that "social lies," or lies to avoid hurting other people's feelings, are justified. As social sensitivity increases with age, so does a more tolerant attitude toward lies of this sort (Tudor-Hart, 1926). Much the same sort of confusion is apparent in the attitude of junior-high-school students toward stealing. Their judgments of whether an act is or is not "stealing" were found to depend somewhat on whether the property was private or corporate. Stealing private property was considered worse than taking corporate property. This shows that their concepts are not clearly formed. Only about 12 per cent of the students questioned had absolute standards for stealing in all situations (Stendler, 1949).

As a result of his taking moral matters into his own hands, the young adolescent frequently sets higher moral standards for himself and for others than can be attained at all times. When his behavior falls short of his standards, the young adolescent feels guilty and suffers from a troubled conscience. This leads to disillusionment and anger, directed partly toward himself because of his shortcomings and partly toward others whom he blames for his shortcomings. If feelings of guilt occur too frequently or are too severe, they may lead to attempts at suicide, to retreat into a daydream world, or to the "I don't care" attitude which results in his doing just the opposite to what he would like to do. Perfectionism is not limited to his own behavior. The young adolescent's standards of morals by which he judges others are just as high as those by which he judges his own behavior. This leads to friction, quarreling, and the straining of relationships which, previously, were strongly cemented by admiration and affection. Much of the friction in the home can be traced to the intolerant attitude the adolescent has toward the behavior of the members of his family, especially of his siblings.

Moral Behavior. Adolescents are, for the most part, consistent in following their moral beliefs with actions of an equally high sort. The tendency to do things behind others' backs, to lie, or to take things if there is a good chance they will not be caught is far less frequent at this age than when the individual was younger. Frequently, the child does things he knows are wrong because of the thrill he gets when he can "get away with it." Not so with the young adolescent. To him, such behavior is "wrong" and, because it is wrong, there is no thrill in it for him. It becomes a matter of honor to try to live up to what he believes is right. There are, of course, exceptions to this general rule. Some young adolescents who are socially and emotionally immature continue to do things they know are wrong, just for the thrill of it. Others act according to their moral codes but these codes fall short of social standards. Still others are engaging in the sowing of wild oats as a revolt against strict parental domination and discipline throughout their childhood years.

Often a young adolescent does the wrong thing because he does not know how to deal with the situation in a better way. He needs guidance in acquiring techniques in dealing with new and difficult situations. This is well illustrated in the frequent coming home late that parents complain about. The young adolescent means to obey the family rule and return home on time but, when he is with a group, he does not know how to break away without being conspicuous, without running the risk of having his friends call him a "baby" because he must be at home earlier than they, or because he does not want to spoil the fun of the person he is escorting. Adolescent girls run into the same problem and are at as great a loss to cope with it as boys are (Strang, 1951).

Common *misdemeanors* at this age include whispering in school, truancy, going out without telling parents, staying later than permitted, willful disobedience, bullying other children, destruction of property belonging to others, and rudeness (Blatz and Bott, 1927; Ackerson, 1931; Hurlock and McDonald, 1934; Strang, 1951). The peak of misdemeanors generally comes around the age of fourteen years, after which they are less frequent and less serious. Girls, as a general rule, display fewer misdemeanors than do boys. The number and frequency of misdemeanors also vary with age and the kind of environment the adolescent lives in (Strang, 1951). This is illustrated in the case of truancy. Many more school truants come from broken homes, homes on relief, and homes where there is delinquency than from better homes. Classroom-disorder cases are frequently found among those who are retarded in their grade placement, who have reading disabilities, who have poor work habits, show aggressive, antisocial behavior, are subject to temper tantrums, and lack self-confidence. They, too, frequently come from poor home environments (Mullen, 1950).

Punishments. The young adolescent needs punishment when he willfully disobeys, just as the child does. But the punishment used should suit his level of development and not be embarrassing to him. Because the adolescent is sensitive to the opinions of his contemporaries, he resents being embarrassed before the group in school and he resents any punishment that seems unfair to him or which he associates with children. The commonly used punishments in the home at this age are spankings and corporal punishments of all sorts, deprivations of different kinds, scoldings, being talked to, and having privileges taken away (Strang, 1951).

SEX INTERESTS

Early sex interests are centered mostly on physical differences. With the development of the sexual capacities of the individual at the time of puberty comes a change in the form of interest that adolescents take in members of the opposite sex. No longer are boys and girls primarily interested in physical differences, although this interest never completely vanishes. The new interest that develops during the early part of adolescence is romantic in nature. This is accompanied by a strong desire to win the approval of members of the opposite sex. *Heterosexuality,* or interest in members of the opposite sex, depends not alone on sexual maturity. Opportunities for contacts with members of the opposite sex, especially when these contacts prove to be satisfying to the individuals involved, also play an important role in determining when this interest will develop and how strong it will be.

The adolescent who is cut off from such contacts, either by geographic isolation, family interference, or personal factors that make the individual unattractive to members of the opposite sex, will be unhappy and insecure. Unsatisfactory adjustments to members of the opposite sex during the early years of adolescence do not limit themselves to that age. Instead, their influence may be permanent and interfere with opportunities for marriage or poor marital adjustments. Furthermore, at an age when interest in members of the opposite sex is beginning to dawn, rejection by such individuals will have a very detrimental effect on the individual's concept of self.

Heterosexual Interests. While it is true that heterosexual interests develop with the attainment of sexual maturity, these interests are intensified and take new forms as a result of environmental influences. Boys, it has been found, first become sex conscious between 9 and 16 years, with an average age of 12½ years. When asked what first brought sex to their consciousness, the boys reported that it was due to "boys' talk," "girls," and "parents." Three-fourths of them felt that their introduction to sex had been bad (Hughes, 1926). Erotic responses in young adolescent boys are produced by such stimuli from their environments as female nudity, daydreaming, obscene pictures, motion pictures, sex conversations, burlesque or stage shows, and dancing (Ramsey, 1943). While there is no similar evidence regarding the stimuli that give rise to similar experiences in girls, it is reasonable to assume that they would be much the same as in the case of boys.

After the first ejaculation, 99 per cent or more of the male population become regular in their sexual activity. This involves monthly, weekly, or daily ejaculations which occur at fairly regular intervals after the first experience. In this respect, males differ from females. As time goes on the male may change the sources of his sexual outlet and his frequency may vary, but almost never is there a complete cessation of his sexual activity until old age stops all response (Kinsey *et al.*, 1948).

The boy's first ejaculation generally comes from masturbation or nocturnal emission. For boys of all social levels in early adolescence, masturbation is the chief source of sexual outlet. After this age, masturbation is never as frequent for boys or men again, though it is still engaged in. Other sources of sexual outlet gradually replace it. Nocturnal emissions of high-school boys are most frequent among those who became pubescent early, up until the age of about fifteen years. After that, these early-maturing boys depend upon other sources of outlet, such as masturbation and heterosexual coitus (Kinsey *et al.*, 1948).

How soon or how late heterosexual interests will develop will depend, to a large extent, upon the level of sexual maturity attained by the boy or girl. Some boys are completely disinterested in sex at the age of fourteen years, while others are so preoccupied with sex that everything else seems insignificant to them. Much the same is true of girls. While the intensity of the interest is dependent, to a marked degree, upon the stage of sexual development attained at a given age, environmental influences must also be taken into consideration. Being with a group whose major interest is centered in members of the opposite sex will have a marked influence on the attitude of a boy or of a girl who otherwise would have little interest.

Hero-worshiping. In the transition from aversion toward members of the opposite sex characteristic of puberty and falling in love with members of the opposite sex, it is quite usual for both boys and girls to center their affections first on a member of their own sex, older than they, who has qualities they admire, and then, later, on a member of the opposite sex who is distinctly older than they. When the attachment is for a member of the same sex, this is usually referred to as a "crush." When, however, the attachment is for a member of the opposite sex, it is known as "hero-worshiping." *Crushes* usually develop at puberty, when there is a strong aversion toward members of the opposite sex. The typical crush behavior is that of adoration for an individual, a strong desire to do all that is possible to please and to win the favor of that individual, and to be constantly in the presence of the loved one. There is little, if any, physical contact in this relationship (Hollingworth, 1928; Bühler, 1933; Hurlock and Klein, 1934; Landis *et al.*, 1940).

Hero-worshiping is far more common than crushes and it comes later. Typically, fourteen- and fifteen-year-olds fall in love with an older person of the opposite sex, a person they know, a hero or heroine on the screen, or a person who is prominent in public life. They have the same absorbing interest in that person that a person in love has. But there is rarely any physical contact. Affection is shown by constant thinking and talking about the loved one, by trying to imitate the individual, and by attempting to know as much as possible about that person.

"Boy-crazy," "Girl-crazy" Stage. Just before early adolescence draws to a close, interest in members of the opposite sex of approximately the same chronological age replaces interest in older individuals. At first, girls like any boy who will pay any attention to them. They do not discriminate. Much the same is true of boys. Girls in general rather than any girl in particular have a strong appeal for them. By the time a girl is sixteen years old, she normally shows a definite interest in boys of her own age. Boys of sixteen, by contrast, are still shy and hesitant in the presence of girls, though they secretly have a stronger interest in them than they show by their behavior. This difference is due primarily to differences in age of sexual maturing. Boys, at this time, retain much of their surface antagonism toward girls (Furfey, 1926; Lehman and Witty, 1927; Sullivan, 1934; Kuhlen and Lee, 1943; Goodenough, 1945).

Early love between the sexes is often referred to as "puppy love" by amused adults. Because of the newness of the love situation, and because of the feelings of insecurity that invariably accompany a new and difficult situation, young adolescents frequently try to cover up their embarrassment by pretending to be at ease and sophisticated. Wisecracking, or mental fencing, teasing, roughhousing, and pulling each other around are backhanded ways of showing mutual interest and are most frequently resorted to when other people are present. It is a bold, aggressive form of behavior as contrasted with the shy, tongue-tied behavior that accompanies crushes or hero-worshiping (Goodenough, 1945). Because interest in the opposite sex is always accompanied by a desire to attract the attention of individuals of the opposite sex, the shy, retiring, and self-effacing behavior of the young adolescent gradually gives way to showing off, especially in the presence of members of the opposite sex.

In spite of the desire to be noticed by members of the opposite sex, young adolescent boys and girls are extremely shy and self-conscious when this desire is realized. This shyness is heightened when they are with a group of other boys and girls though it is present when they are alone with just one member of the opposite sex. Shyness and self-consciousness may show itself in quiet, tongue-tied behavior but, among most adolescents, an attempt is made to cover up their shyness and this leads to noisy, boisterous laughing, aggressive reactions toward the opposite sex, and a tendency to talk too much about nothing (Campbell, 1939). As early adolescence draws to a close, there is a beginning of pairing off, especially among the more mature members of the group. Instead of going around in crowds, or in small groups, they begin to go around in pairs. This is more characteristic of young adolescent girls, however, than it is of boys. The more mature girls date boys a year or more older than they, while their less mature contemporaries continue to associate with boys only in groups.

Curiosity about Sex. Curiosity about sex matters, which became very pronounced at puberty with the development of physical changes characteristic of that age, begins to wane during early adolescence, provided the individual has been able to get the information he wishes to satisfy his curiosity. There is still, however, a lively interest in sex though this is not likely to preoccupy the time and interest of young adolescents as much as it did earlier, during the puberty period. When girls or boys get together with members of their

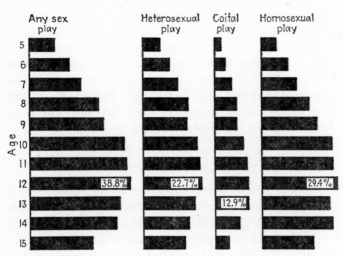

Fig. 36. Per cent of males involved in sex play at each preadolescent age. (*From H. C. Kinsey, W. B. Pomeroy, and C. E. Martin, Sexual behavior in the human male. Philadelphia: Saunders, 1948. Used by permission.*)

own sex, they are likely to talk about sex. The more intimate the group, the more intimate the subject of sex becomes. No longer do they seek information about the fundamental facts of sex. This knowledge they already have. Instead, they discuss such matters as what is real love, how can one tell if love is real or not, what is the sex relationship in marriage, problems related to menstruation, and sexual feelings and attractions (Davenport, 1923).

Like the child, the young adolescent obtains most of his sex information from contemporaries of his own sex, from books, and from courses of study at school. What information he obtains from his parents is likely to be so superficial that it fails to satisfy his curiosity. There is a positive but low correlation between what parents and teen agers know about sex (Phipps, 1949). He, therefore, turns to whatever source is available and, because he finds his intimate friends are always anxious to discuss sex matters, he discovers that this is one of the most fruitful sources of information (Burgess, 1934; Ramsey, 1943).

Experimentation with sex, to satisfy curiosity, begins during early adolescence or even during the puberty period. Manual manipulation, accompanied by a direct observation of the female reproductive anatomy, exhibitionistic sex play, attempts at intercourse, and oral contacts are common at this age. Petting, in the form of kissing, manual exploration, and manipulation by the boy of the girl's breasts and reproductive organs, has been reported by boys of the early adolescent years (Ramsey, 1943). *Masturbation,* as a form of sexual experimentation, is common among both boys and girls during the early years of adolescence. While masturbation is often engaged in by children, it comes to a peak in frequency and in degree of satisfaction obtained during this period. From an occasional indulgence to indulgence several times a day have been reported (Ramsey, 1943). Because of the social taboos associated with masturbation, most boys and girls have strong feelings of guilt during and after indulgence. These feelings, however, are generally not strong enough to prevent the indulgence. The frequencies of different forms of sexual experimentation are shown in Fig. 36.

FAMILY RELATIONSHIPS

The relationships of the young adolescent to the members of his family deteriorate as adolescence progresses. The fault lies on both sides. Parents far too often refuse to modify their concept of their child's abilities as he grows older, and, as a result, they treat him in much the same manner as they did when he was younger. In spite of this, they expect him to "act his age," especially when it comes to assuming responsibilities. Another source of conflict comes from the use of standards of behavior that were in vogue when they were adolescents. It is very common for both mothers and fathers to reply to an adolescent's request to do something his friends are doing with the preface to their refusal, "When I was your age." This annoys the adolescent, especially if a majority of his friends are permitted to do the thing his parents refuse to allow him to do. The adolescents who are most seriously affected by this parental attitude are those whose parents grew up in another country or in another part of this country where mores differed from those of the community in which the adolescent is growing up.

The blame for the friction between parents and adolescent children is not all on the parents' side. No one is more irresponsible, more difficult to live with, more unpredictable, or more exasperating than a young adolescent, with the possible exception of a preadolescent. Parents' patience is sorely tried during this transitional period of their children's lives and they cannot be blamed if they sometimes lose patience completely with their children. This, unfortunately, makes matters worse and the relationship between parents and adolescent suffers.

While the sources of friction between the adolescent and his parents are myriad, two very common sources of friction are almost universally found. The first stems from the methods of discipline used by parents and the adolescents' resentments against what they consider to be "childish" forms of punishment and unreasonable restraints on their behavior. The second common source of friction arises from the hypercritical attitude of the adolescent toward his parents, his siblings, and his home life. Parents who have made great sacrifices of time, energy, and money to give the adolescent the best home they can and as many advantages as they can afford, naturally resent this seeming lack of appreciation on the part of their children.

Deterioration in family relationships during the early years af adolescence is not limited to the parent-child relationship. Relationships with their siblings suffer just as seriously as do those of parents and adolescents. The young adolescent treats his younger brothers and sisters with scorn and constantly finds fault with whatever they say or do. He is jealous of his older brothers and sisters because they enjoy privileges denied him and he resents the criticisms of these older brothers and sisters aimed at his immature behavior. Relatives, especially those of the older generation, no longer are in favor with the young adolescent. He finds family gatherings "boring" and he does not hesitate to show how he feels. He deeply resents any criticism on the part of his relatives concerning his behavior and he objects to their giving him advice of any sort.

PERSONALITY

The pattern of personality becomes well set by the time adolescence is reached. While it is not as inflexible as it will be later, there is evidence of rigidity at this time. A study of a group of extremely prejudiced as compared with a group of unprejudiced eleven- to sixteen-year-old boys and girls revealed that the prejudiced showed up as illiberal, rigid, and punitive in their attitudes toward people. The ratings these young people received were positively related to the ratings obtained by their parents which suggested that the attitudes had been established early as a result of the dependent status of these individuals when they were children (Frankel-Brunswik, 1948).

New factors enter into the individual's life at this time. These will leave their mark on his personality. What effect they will have, however, will be determined to a large extent by the foundation already established. An adolescent who finds himself in the role of a social outcast will be affected differently by this experience depending on what concept of himself he established when he was younger. If he had a fairly well established inferiority complex when adolescence began, his status in the adolescent group will intensify his feelings of inferiority. If, however, his concept of himself was that of an important person, his present role may modify this concept or it may leave it unaffected while he builds up rationalizations to explain to himself and others why he is not socially acceptable to his peers.

Personality Changes. The questions of how much and in what areas personality changes occur during adolescence have received attention in experimental investigations. During early adolescence, boys become more interested in the opposite sex, they enjoy jokes on themselves, they are more enthusiastic and willing to take a chance, and they are more anxious to be popular. Girls show the most marked changes in interest in the opposite sex and less interest in active games. They also act older than their ages. As the adolescent grows older, sex differences in personality patterns become more apparent (Kuhlen and Lee, 1943). Changes in attitudes among boys between the ages of twelve and sixteen years are most pronounced in self-criticism, in criticism of others, in social insight, and in feeling different from the group (Dimock, 1937).

The changes that take place in personality patterns are due, partially at least, to the influence of social pressures. There are certain socially approved and socially disapproved personality traits for both boys and girls. In his desire to be socially accepted and to win the approval not only of his contemporaries but of the social group as a whole, the young adolescent strives to develop personality traits that will win for him approval and acceptance. The young adolescent boy who is admired by his contemporaries must be a leader in games, daring, fearless, and personally acceptable. The approved pattern for girls includes such personality traits as good sportsmanship, activity, ability to organize games and parties, and being glamorous and fascinating (Tryon, 1939). Broad-mindedness, cooperativeness, and reliability are personality traits both boys and girls expect their contemporaries to have (Pressey and Robinson, 1944).

Personality Factors. Much the same factors influence the adolescent's personality as is true of the childhood years. The difference, however, is in emphasis. Some factors which were of relatively little importance during childhood now prove to be of great importance, while those of dominance in childhood may lose some of their strength in adolescence.

The adolescent becomes increasingly aware of likenesses and differences in *personal appearance*. Being different in appearance makes the adolescent feel inferior, even if this difference adds to his physical attractiveness (Stolz and Stolz, 1944). Being different is likely to make an adolescent critical of others and of himself and to make him develop a feeling of superiority as a form of compensation (Dimock, 1937). Any physical defect the adolescent may have now becomes a source of embarrassment to him, even though as a child this defect was of little significance (Stolz and Stolz, 1944). To the high-school student, *clothes* are important more because they improve appearance than because of their attention value. Clothes are selected to bring out their good qualities and to cover up their defects (Hurlock, 1929a). This is so important to a young adolescent that he is willing to make sacrifices in order to have such clothes (Silverman, 1945). When girls make a poor appearance, they withdraw from activities of other young people, they dislike prominence and leadership activities, and they develop a negativistic attitude. Girls who make a good appearance, by contrast, enjoy being with both girls and boys and in participating in social activities (Silverman, 1945).

Poor health, throughout childhood and adolescence, may or may not leave its mark on the adolescent's personality. Individuals who have suffered from allergies throughout the major portion of their lives develop into ascendant, extroverted, emotionally unstable individuals (Riess and deCillis, 1940). If illnesses are limited to the childhood years, the individual usually makes reasonably good adjustments in adolescence because of the development of "wholesome attitudes toward the realities of environment" (Hardy, 1937a). How successfully or how unsuccessfully the adolescent will adjust to illness depends to a large extent upon parental attitudes. The adolescent's *name* now becomes a source of concern to him. Names that are a handicap to an adolescent are those which are associated with stereotypes that are frowned on by society; that are displeasing when combined with certain surnames; that have been made unpleasant by certain associations, either personal or social; and those which lend themselves to nicknames that carry unpleasant connotations (Allen *et al.,* 1941). The adolescent will dislike any name that makes him shy, embarrassed, or sensitive (Eagleson, 1946). Nicknames that make the individual feel inferior are also disliked (Orgel and Tuckman, 1935).

In spite of the fact that adolescents spend less time with their parents than they did when they were younger and in spite of the strained relationship that frequently exists at this time, the *family* leaves its mark on the adolescent's personality. An unhappy family life produces marked emotional instability in the young adolescent (Stagner, 1948). Parents who always welcome the children's friends to the home, who share joys and sorrows with their children, and who have enjoyable times with them are more likely to have well-adjusted sons and daughters than are parents whose relationship with their children is less favorable (Stott, 1939). Adolescents from broken homes, on the other hand, show many personality maladjustments (Torrance, 1945).

Family resemblances in personality are frequently noted. This is especially true of neurotic traits. The older the individual, the less his personality is influenced unfavorably by that of his parents (Hoffeditz, 1934). Studies of juvenile delinquency have shown that a large percentage of juvenile delinquents come from homes where the parental personality model is poor and where the influence of the parents is bad (Healy, 1915). During the time when the young adolescent has a crush on a member of his sex or hero-worships an individual of the opposite sex, the adolescent's *ideal* plays a role of importance in shaping his personality. While ideals may come from the adolescent's remote or immediate environment, they are equally effective in setting a standard which the adolescent tries to imitate (Hill, 1930). *High-school teachers,* because of their close contact with the young adolescent, are frequently factors of great importance in molding the individual's personality (Hart, 1934).

Personality Maladjustments. The problem child is likely to turn into a maladjusted individual during adolescence unless remedial steps are taken to overcome the problem behavior. Clinical studies have revealed that relatively few forms of maladjustment appear for the first time during adolescence unless there has been some marked physical or glandular change in the individual, or unless he has experienced some sort of severe trauma. More maladjusted adolescents have a case history of problem behavior dating back to the early years of childhood (Yellowlees, 1940).

Adolescence, but especially the early part of the period, is inevitably a time of stress and maladjustment. This contrasts with the relative stability and tranquillity of the latter part of childhood. At this time, the individual is trying, by trial and error, to adjust himself to the new and strange role of the adult and to an environment suited more to adults than to children. Whether he will learn the adult roles and thus pass through this period successfully or fall a victim to mental disease and maladjustment in the form of regressive behavior will depend primarily upon the foundations laid in childhood and upon the degree of patience, understanding, and kindly guidance he receives from his parents (Jones, 1951). Among institutionalized adolescents, most had suffered from family troubles and had shown symptoms of emotional disturbance in early childhood (Warren, 1949).

Personality maladjustments may be roughly divided into two categories: those which are individually satisfying but socially unacceptable and those which are socially approved but a source of excessive, disturbing, and long-continued conflict to the individual (Strang, 1938). The former generally lead to delinquency in one form or another. Personality maladjustments reveal themselves through "danger signals" of greater or lesser severity during the early years of adolescence. The most common danger signals that are symptomatic of underlying trouble are irresponsibility which leads the adolescent to neglect his work or other duties in a desire to win social approval and to have a good time; aggressiveness of an exaggerated form which shows itself in a cocksureness in everything the adolescent says or does; feelings of insecurity at home or outside the home which cause the individual to conform to the group in a slavishly conventional manner; homesickness when away from the familiar surroundings of the family; feelings of martyrdom, not only at home but also when the adolescent is with his contemporaries; excessive daydreaming to compensate for lack of satisfaction from daily life;

regression to earlier levels of behavior in an attempt to win favor and recognition; and rationalization, usually in the form of projection of the blame on others, to explain his shortcomings.

The poorly adjusted adolescent is an unhappy individual. He finds himself playing the role of a social isolate, he misses out on the good times his contemporaries are enjoying, and he finds little compensation for these losses in his relationships with the members of his family. While most young adolescents experience unhappiness in some degree, the poorly adjusted individuals not only experience unhappiness in more pronounced forms but they experience it more often. As a result of their unhappiness, they try to develop compensations which will take the place of the normal pleasures they miss and which they see their contemporaries enjoying. This results in more severe maladjustments and eliminates what hope they might otherwise have of becoming acceptable members of a group of their contemporaries. The personality defects which, throughout childhood, seemed too trivial to parents and teachers to be of concern and were thus neglected, now exert their influence on the lives of the adolescents in such a manner as to exaggerate the unhappiness which otherwise might have been mild and transitory.

CHAPTER 9

Late Adolescence
(Seventeen to Twenty-one Years)

Late adolescence, like early adolescence, is a transitional period in the individual's life. The adjustments to a mature status and to mature levels of behavior, begun during early adolescence, are gradually completed as the individual reaches the status of legal maturity. Many of the problems that arose in the early years of adolescence and which were not satisfactorily solved at that time are solved now. Other problems which arise as new areas of interest and new responsibilities and privileges develop must likewise be solved before the individual can be socially and emotionally mature.

Problems of Late Adolescence. New problems, often more difficult to meet than the ones formerly met, present themselves. As a result, the older adolescent often finds himself so weighted down by his problems—and their solution seems hopeless to him—that he does nothing but fold his hands and bemoan his fate. Others, who are more aggressive in their approach toward life, may contemplate or even attempt suicide as a way out of their difficulties. Still others meet their problems by trying to run away from them. Most adolescents, however, solve the majority of their problems with greater or less satisfaction before adolescence is over or during the early years of adulthood.

When a group of college men was asked to give an account of their problems, they listed the following (Heath and Gregory, 1946):

1. Problems of social adjustment, as shyness, feelings of inferiority, social sensitivity, making friends, meeting and getting along with girls, and immaturity per se.
2. Problems of adjustment to family, as parental discord, divorce, separation, or remarriage, antagonism toward parents, or death of a parent.
3. Problems related to career and life work.
4. Problems of finances in college.
5. Problems related to the need for discussions centering around the individual.
6. Academic problems.
7. Sex problems.

As may be seen from the problems listed above, even when an adolescent remains in an academic environment in the latter years of adolescence, his problems relating to his academic work are far less numerous and less serious

256

than are the problems reported by younger adolescents who are still in high school. When Symonds asked boys and girls of senior-high-school and college ages to rank in order of seriousness their problems, he found that the prob-

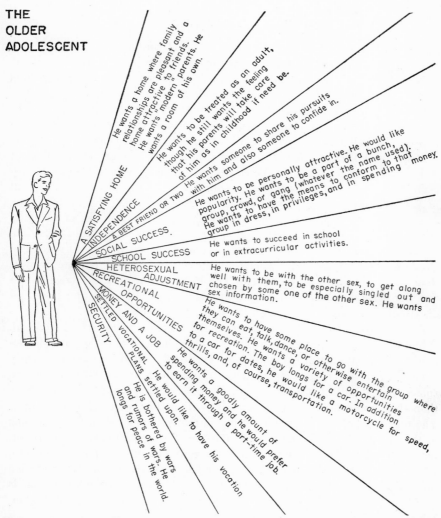

THE OLDER ADOLESCENT

FIG. 37. The wants of the older adolescent. (*From M. Malm and O. G. Jamison, Adolescence. New York: McGraw-Hill, 1952. Used by permission.*)

lems of boys and girls were closely similar. The most serious problems related to money, health, study habits, and personal attractiveness. Boys were more concerned over matters relating to money and sex, while for girls, the greatest concern centered around the problem of personal attractiveness (Symonds, 1935). Sex problems of greatest concern at this time relate to conduct, behavior, and experience (Kirkendall, 1948). The typical wants of an older adolescent, as illustrated in Fig. 37, show the intensity of their problems.

PHYSICAL GROWTH

The growth spurt that started at puberty and continued at a diminishing rate during early adolescence gradually halts during late adolescence. What increase there is in height and weight at this age is barely perceptible. This enables the older adolescent to integrate the functions of the different muscular patterns and, as a result, the awkwardness that was characteristic of the preceding period gradually rights itself. Each year, as adolescence progresses, the individual displays better coordination of the body.

Height and Weight. How tall or short, how heavy or light the adolescent will be when his growth is completed depends upon such factors as hereditary endowment, prenatal and postnatal feeding and health, racial stock, general environmental conditions, opportunities for exercise during the growth years, and climatic conditions. A study of American college freshmen of today as compared with those of 30 years ago has revealed that the girls of today are about an inch taller and 3 to 4 pounds heavier than the girls of 30 years ago. Freshmen boys of today are 2 inches taller and weigh 9 to 14 pounds more than the freshmen of 30 years ago. The explanation for this increased size was the general reduction in illness during the growth years and improved distribution of fruits and vegetables to all areas (Mills, 1950).

Age of maturing has an influence on the ultimate size of the individual. While early maturing results in bigger bodies during the early part of adolescence, the late-maturing individuals eventually catch up and frequently outstrip their earlier-maturing contemporaries. The result is that when growth comes to a standstill, the later-maturing individuals generally end up taller than their contemporaries who, several years earlier, were taller than they. The reason for this is that puberty marks the end rather than the beginning of the period of accelerated growth. Early-maturing individuals, as a result, have not had as long a time to grow as those who mature later (Shuttleworth, 1939; Bayley, 1943). The average mature heights of early- and late-maturing individuals is not significantly different, though there is a difference that is slight in favor of those who mature late (Richey, 1937; Stone and Barker, 1934).

Individual differences in weight are far greater both between the sexes and within the two sex groups than are differences in height. As is true of height, the times when the greatest increases in weight occur are when growth in height is most rapid, just before and just after the individual becomes sexually mature. When puberty has been completed, increases in weight slow down. At corresponding ages during early adolescence, the early-maturing individuals are heavier than those who mature later but there is no evidence to show that this difference will continue after the period of the growth spurt has come to an end. The scrawny look of the young adolescent gradually gives way to the rounded curves of the older adolescent. What increases there are in fat during late adolescence are generally distributed in areas of the body where previously there was little or no fat. The arms and legs develop curves, the hips and breasts of the girl round out, and the long, thin face of the young adolescent loses its angular look.

Predicting adult size in late adolescence is not difficult. While it is true that boys do not attain their full stature until they are twenty-two or twenty-three years old and girls when they are approximately twenty years old, the increase in height and weight in late adolescence is so slight that, by the close of early adolescence, the individual knows, within several inches and pounds, what his size will be for the rest of his life. Several methods have been used to predict adult height. Using skeletal age as a basis (Simmons, 1944), age of maturing in relation to height and weight at the age of maturing (Shuttleworth, 1939), and X rays of the bones (Bayley, 1946) all give some indication of what the adolescent can anticipate in the way of a mature stature.

Body Proportions. The disproportions of the young adolescent, which were the cause of such great concern to him, gradually right themselves in late adolescence as the individual's body takes on the form of the adult. Gradually the features which lagged behind in their growth catch up with the more rapidly developing features and, as a result, they now are in correct proportion as measured by adult standards. The too-large nose, for example, now seems to be in correct proportion as the lower jaw, the last part of the face to attain its mature size, grows larger and as the lips become fuller. As the *chest* broadens and the *trunk* elongates, the waistline drops and the scrawny look of the young adolescent's body disappears. By late adolescence, the *breasts* and *hips* of a girl are fully developed so that her body now has the pleasing curves of the mature woman. When boys are late in maturing, they characteristically have slender hips and long legs, and those who mature early are typically broad-hipped (Bayley, 1943). Late-maturing girls, by contrast, have slightly broader hips than those who mature early. In the case of both boys and girls, late-maturing individuals tend to have slightly broader *shoulders* than those who mature early.

The effect of age of maturing is shown in the relative length of the *legs* of both boys and girls as they approach maturity. The legs, which at puberty were relatively longer than the trunk, are arrested in their growth with the onset of puberty and, as a result, the individual is short-legged. In late-maturing individuals, the leg growth continues for a longer time and, consequently, the individual is long-legged when he has attained his mature proportions. The legs of early-maturing boys and girls have a tendency to be stocky; those of late-maturing individuals tend to be more slender. Much the same pattern is found in the proportions of the *arms*. Early-maturing individuals have a tendency to have short arms, and those who mature late are long-armed in proportion to the length of the trunk. The shape of the upper arm follows the growth of the muscles which reach their mature size shortly after late adolescence begins.

Skin and Hair. Changes in skin texture and coloring, which proved to be a source of great concern to young adolescents, are nearly complete when late adolescence begins. *Acne* and other *skin disturbances* gradually disappear and the skin now is free from blemishes except in cases of indiscreet eating or at the time of the menstrual period in girls. The excessive oiliness of the young adolescent's skin, resulting from the temporarily increased activity of the sebaceous, or oil-producing glands, subsides and the skin and hair of the older adolescent are less oily than they were several years before. By late adolescence, the *hair* on the face, the body, and the head has reached mature growth. The older adolescent boy must now shave daily if he wants to have a neat appearance. The girl finds that she, too, must remove the hair from her armpits frequently if she wants to wear evening clothes or bathing suits without embarrassment. The hair on the arms, legs, chest, and shoulders of boys and on the arms and legs of girls will be as luxuriant in late adolescence as it will be during the years of maturity.

The changes in the structure and functioning of the *internal organs,* begun during early adolescence, continue through late adolescence until a mature level of development has been reached. The *heart,* which at the age of twelve years is 7 times as heavy as it was at birth, grows rapidly so that, at the age of seventeen or eighteen years, it is 12 times as heavy as it was at birth. This means that the heart nearly doubles during the adolescent years. By contrast, the increase in the *veins* and *arteries* is only 15 per cent. At the end of adolescence, the ratio of the size of the heart to the arteries is 290 to 61, as compared with a ratio of 25 to 20 at birth. Throughout childhood, there is little difference between the sexes in *blood pressure*. With puberty, there is an increase in blood pressure for both boys and girls, with boys having a higher blood pressure than girls (Burlage, 1923). From $11\frac{1}{2}$ to $17\frac{1}{2}$ years of age, there is a decrease of 8 to 9 beats per minute for both boys and girls (Shock, 1944). There is a rise in blood pressure for boys from 80 to 85 millimeters at the age of 6 years to 115 at the age of $18\frac{1}{2}$ years, and for girls, from 80 to 85 at 6 years to 105 at 19 years.

At the age of seventeen years, the lung capacity of girls has almost reached its mature level; for boys, the mature level is not reached for several years after that. Because of this, the difference in *lung capacity* for the two sexes becomes increasingly greater from the beginning of adolescence to the time when the mature level of development has been reached. In boys, the greater increase in the size, capacity, and power of the lungs is made possible by the broadening and elongating of the bones of the chest. The rapid growth in the *digestive system* that took place during early adolescence slows down during late adolescence. With this slowing down and the slowing down of growth in height and weight comes a decrease in appetite. No longer is the adolescent's stomach a bottomless pit as it was during the early years of adolescence.

Added to the decrease in appetite is a strong motivation on the part of the older adolescent to curtail his food intake so as to keep his figure from becoming too fat. This motivation is especially strong among older adolescent girls in America today. They want to have figures that will approximate the ideals they see on the screen and, as a result, they are willing to forgo the pleasures of eating they enjoyed several years earlier. This motivation to have a slender figure is strengthened by the desire to improve the complexion which, they know, can be ruined by indiscreet eating. As a result, the preponderance of sweets and starches that made up the diet of the young adolescent is now replaced by a better balanced diet with fewer starches and sweets. There is also less between-meal eating than there was earlier due, largely, to the fact that the hunger pangs are not so frequent nor so intense as they were during the period of rapid physical growth.

Good health and *resistance to disease* are the rule rather than the exception to the rule during late adolescence. Adolescents who have had a healthy childhood are more likely to be healthy in late adolescence than are those whose childhood was marked by a series of illnesses. Similarly, good health habits established in childhood will go a long way toward guaranteeing a healthy adolescence. Like the younger adolescent, the older adolescent frequently uses illness as a form of escape from unpleasant duties or responsibilities. Because he worries about different situations he feels inadequate to meet successfully, he often makes himself sick by bringing on headaches, digestive disturbances, or sleeplessness. His real upsets are frequently exaggerated out of all proportions and lead the adolescent to believe that he is too sick to face the situation that confronts him. *Imaginary* illness is more frequent among girls than among boys and is more often brought on by social situations in which members of the opposite sex are involved rather than by school or college work.

MOTOR SKILLS

The awkwardness which is so common during the early years of adolescence is generally a thing of the past when late adolescence begins. The older adolescent has gained control of his enlarged body and has learned how to use it as successfully as he did when he was younger. Furthermore, the increase in physical strength that accompanies the growth of the muscular system motivates him to make use of his newly acquired strength. In boys, where muscular strength surpasses that of girls, pride in achievement motivates them to acquire skills of a complicated sort which they were incapable of acquiring when they were younger.

Marked sex differences in physical strength appear in late adolescence. This is the result not of exercise but of the maturation of boys' muscles to a degree that far surpasses that of girls. Boys, as a rule, do not realize that their muscular superiority comes from natural development and are likely to feel above girls because of their excellence in this area of their development. Girls, on the other hand, withdraw from situations where their muscular inferiority would be obvious, such as athletic contests or games where speed is an essential factor.

For boys, on the other hand, "competitive athletic skills are among the chief sources of social esteem in the period preceding maturity" (Jones, 1944). This accounts for the strong interest most older adolescent boys have in competitive sports, either as active participants or passive spectators, and for the fact that girls, during the later adolescent period, show a declining interest in sports as participants but an increasing interest as spectators. Because of the social esteem associated with muscular strength, physical strength plays an important role in the social adjustments of boys in the late years of adolescence. Observations of the social adjustments of a group of physically strong boys as compared with a group of physically weak boys over a period of 6 to 8 years revealed that popularity increased with time for the strong boys but the change was in the opposite direction for the weak boys. Social-adjustment scores followed much the same pattern.

Commenting on the results obtained, Jones (1946) observed:

> The boy who is slightly deficient in physical traits may experience, in relation to his own aspirations, a slight handicap in social relations in his age group. Often this is readily compensated by other personal characteristics. But evidence has been presented that a more conspicuous deficiency may lead to cumulative and interactive handicapping effects in reputation and in the individual's reaction to his position in the group. An opposite and more advantageous spiral of consequences may occur in cases of outstanding physical superiority.

Because physical strength is not so important as a factor of prestige among girls as it is among boys, girls concentrate their efforts on developing skills where strength is not important. They take delight in dancing in the most intricate manner or in diving and other sports where muscular coordination is far more important than strength. When they do compete in athletics, it is with girls whose abilities are more on a par with theirs than are the abilities of boys. Boys, likewise, take pride in skills, such as driving cars at high speed and dancing in the most intricate manner in vogue at the time.

EMOTIONS IN LATE ADOLESCENCE

The heightened emotionality, so characteristic of the early years of adolescence, gradually subsides, provided environmental adjustments are made to meet the new capacities and demands of an older adolescent. There is, however, likely to be a period of emotional tension toward the end of adolescence, generally between the ages of eighteen and twenty years, which comes from new problems that normally present themselves at that age and to the rebellion against adult restrictions, especially on the part of girls. At this time, problems related to their romances are very real. So long as the romance is moving along smoothly, the adolescent is happy. But when things begin to go wrong, the adolescent sinks into states of despondency as intense as the happiness he previously experienced. Then, too, there are worries about his future which become very serious when he faces the end of his schooling.

For the adolescent who spends the major part of the latter years of adolescence preparing himself for his future career, the restraints that come from financial dependency upon his family are a source of great concern to him. He resents being told what to do; he may have fallen in love and want to marry, which is impossible so long as he is dependent; and he resents the fact that adults outside the home do not treat him as an adult any more than his parents do. In our modern culture, with the necessity for periods of preparation for a life work that are longer than ever before in the history of civilization, with the trend toward later marriage, and with the freedom in selection of a life mate which was never so great as it is at the present, it is inevitable that heightened emotionality should occur at this time in the individual's life.

Emotional Patterns. The older adolescent experiences much the same emotions as the child and the young adolescent, but there is a difference in the frequency with which different emotions are aroused, in the intensity of these emotions, in the typical responses made, and in the types of stimuli that give rise to them.

ANGER. Of all the emotions, anger is more often aroused in late adolescence than any other emotion. *Thwarting of self-assertion,* or restraints on the adolescent's desire to do something he wants to do which *interrupt habitual activities,* are the two most common causes of anger at this age. Illustrations of situations that thwart self-assertion are unjust accusations, insulting or sarcastic comments, and unwelcome advice. When such habitual activities as studying or sleeping are interrupted, they give rise to anger (Gates, 1926). People more often cause anger among adolescents than do things. Failure to accomplish what one sets out to do, to come up to one's own expectations, likewise gives rise to anger. Girls respond more often and more violently to social situations than do boys, while boys are more often angered by things than are girls. Typical of the response-to-person situation is expressed in the comment, "The girl made slighting comments about a friend of mine," and of reaction-to-things comment, "Broke a shoestring in a hurry to get to breakfast" (Meltzer, 1933).

In a detailed analysis of anger-arousing situations, where 52 per cent of the anger responses came from thwarted plans, it was noted that of the 311 situations that made up this percentage, the interfering agent consisted of people in 135 instances, institutional factors in 65, accidents, chance factors, and the malfunctioning of inanimate objects in 89, and organic needs or conditions, such as illness or sleep in 22 instances. The second most common category, found in only 20.9 per cent of the angers, consisted of inferiority and loss of prestige, including personal inadequacies as the most frequent cause with "criticism or belittling" and "opinion crossed" the next most frequent. Angers arising from schoolwork (12.7 per cent), family relationships (9.9 per cent) and from abstract problems, such as incidence of intolerance or seeing a classmate cheat (4.5 per cent), were far less frequent than angers coming from the first two causes. For the college women who reported these angers and their causes over a period of one week, there was a mean of 15.7 instances of anger during the week, or slightly more than two anger experiences a day per student. The reports varied from 0 to 42 anger responses indicating a wide range of individual differences (Anastasia et al., 1948).

The older adolescent has generally learned to keep his angry responses under control to the point where he no longer kicks, hits, and throws things. He does, however, try to get his revenge in other ways, the most common of which is tongue-lashing. Name calling, sarcastic comments, swearing, and ridiculing others are his way of hitting back. In addition, he may substitute for the violent reactions of the earlier years such activities as pacing the floor, going for a walk, throwing things within his reach, becoming sulky and refusing to speak, or by mannerisms which he knows irritate people, such as whistling under his breath or tapping on the table (Gates, 1926; Meltzer, 1933). How marked the social inhibitions on angry responses are may be seen by the fact that college students report what they would like to do when they are angry in comparison with what they actually do. Impulses to scream, cry, tell others what they think, or do physical injury to the offender are generally inhibited and, in their place, are substituted verbal responses of a far milder form. Unfavorable reactions on the part of the individual, in the form of general irritability, tiredness, and feeling ashamed of themselves, followed inhibitions of angry responses (Meltzer, 1933).

Furthermore, the duration of an angry outburst on the part of an older adolescent is longer than that of a child because of the restraints placed by the individual on his angry outbursts. The angrier the individual, the longer his anger lasts (Gates, 1926; Meltzer, 1933). The same type of thing that annoyed a young adolescent arouses anger when he is older. People, things that don't work as they are supposed to work, and his own physical or mental characteristics that fall below his expectations continue to annoy an older adolescent as they did several years before. Now, however, he has learned to shut his eyes to some of the things he formerly responded to or to accept a more philosophical attitude toward things he cannot control. As a result, he will be less disturbed by things than he formerly was, if he develops emotional maturity as the adolescent years progress.

FEAR AND WORRY. The older adolescent fears fewer things but worries more than he did when he was younger. Among college students, there is a decline in the number of fears experienced as the students go from freshman to sophomore year. The greater number of fears of the younger students is an indication of their immaturity. The fears of the older students, such as fear of mismating, of performing in public, of losing confidence in self, and of automobile accidents, are much the same type as adults experience. Nearly three-quarters of these fears were acquired from personal experiences (Means, 1936). By the time adolescence comes to a close, the individual should be relatively free of fears that come from the external environment. There should also be a waning of fears of people and of social situations as the individual's social experiences increase and his opportunities to meet all types of people develop. Fears of his own ineptitudes, or fears arising from imaginary situations may, on the other hand, remain or may even increase as adolescence progresses.

An analysis of the fears recorded by a group of college girls over a period of one week revealed that the largest number was for *anticipated* situations, as compared with anger which arises mainly from situations already present. The largest number of fears centered around schoolwork (40.2 per cent) and the next largest number (30.8 per cent) centered around feelings of inferiority and loss of prestige. More than half of this latter group arose from social situations or personal appearance. Fears regarding illness and physical danger were about equally divided between fears about themselves and about their families. There were relatively few fears about family relationships, financial difficulties, and abstract problems. The individual reports ranged from 2 to 36 fears reported as having been experienced during the preceding week, with a mean of 12.2 (Anastasia *et al.*, 1948).

Like the younger adolescent, the older adolescent does not run away from a frightening situation, no matter how great his fear may be. He stands his ground, even though he may become tongue-tied and shake so that all can see him. If he anticipates an unpleasant situation or one that may prove to be frightening to him, such as having to speak before a group or meet members of the opposite sex who are strangers to him, he is likely to shun the situation, offering some plausible excuse for his absence. He becomes quite adept at this as he grows older and plans his activities in such a way that he can truthfully say, (I have another engagement") when something comes up that he does not want to do or that he is hesitant about facing.)

Worries, or imaginary fears, are far more common and more intense than are fears of real situations at this age. Few adolescents escape worrying at some time or other, especially when they hear their friends say they are worried about this or that. The chief sources of worry are not being as successful in their work as they would like to be, concern about the impression they will make on others, hurting other people's feelings, and not working hard enough. Their least causes of worry consist of going insane, growing old, dying, and being ashamed of the shabbiness of their homes when their friends come to see them. The more remote the possibility of an unpleasant experience, the less they worry about it (Bonner, 1936; Lunger and Page, 1939; Marsh, 1942). Marked sex differences in the cause of worrying have been found. Among boys of the older adolescent years, the chief causes of worrying are future financial security, the possibility that they will have to support their parents in old age, not being able to support those who might become dependent upon them, being disinterested in their work, and becoming ill. Girls, on the other hand, worry more than boys about not being socially popular and the possibility that no one cares for them. In the case of both boys and girls, the more they worry, the poorer social adjustments they make (Marsh, 1942).

JEALOUSY. Toward the middle or end of adolescence, interest in members of the opposite sex in general changes to an interest in one individual of the opposite sex. With this shift of interest comes a proprietary interest in that individual accompanied by a feeling of uncertainty about that individual's feelings. Under such conditions, jealousy is inevitable. Like the child who is unsure of his mother's love after the arrival of a new member of the family, the adolescent is never sure of what the loved one is doing when out of sight. Both boys and girls experience intense jealousy in their heterosexual relationships at this age. In the case of girls, however, the jealousy is likely to be more intense than in the case of boys because it is they who must play the passive role and not take aggressive steps to hold onto what they want as boys do.

Any suspicion of a waning of interest on the part of the loved one or an unexplained lateness for a date or a last-minute canceling of a date will give rise of suspicions on the girl's part that invariably include the possibility of another girl for whom the boy has developed a romantic attachment. When jealousy is aroused, it usually expresses itself in verbal fighting rather than in bodily attack as is true of children. The use of sarcasm when speaking to the person who has aroused the jealousy, of the "sticking a knife in the back" by talking against that person when he is not there to defend himself, or the use of veiled suggestions about his character or moral standards are typically adolescent forms of hitting back at those against whom the individual's jealousy has been directed.

ENVY. The older adolescent is fully aware of the prestige value of expensive clothes, a car, and a large home. He realizes that those who are popular are in a favored socioeconomic position where they can have material possessions which many of their friends do not have. Furthermore, those who hold leadership positions are more likely to be from the favored than from the less favored socioeconomic groups. And, finally, in heterosexual relationships, boys and girls who have plenty of this world's goods have an obvious advantage over those who are less favored. It is not surprising, then, that material possessions have strong appeal for the older adolescent. His envy may become so strong that it is a dominating factor in producing unhappiness at this age. When an adolescent is envious of the possessions of others, he rarely keeps this fact to himself. Instead, he complains about his own bad fortune, he labels those who have what he would like to have as "lucky," and he makes others uncomfortable by his self-pity. Other adolescents take jobs to earn the necessary money to get these things or they find an easy approach to the problem through stealing. Back of much juvenile delinquency is envy of others more fortunate than the delinquent.

HAPPINESS. There are, in general, four types of situations that give rise to pleasant emotional reactions at this age. The first consists of good adjustments to the situation in which the individual finds himself. When the adolescent "fits," he is happy. When, on the other hand, he feels that he is a misfit, he is unhappy and discontented. The ability to perceive the comic element in a situation is the second cause of happiness in adolescence. What an adolescent perceives as comic, however, varies according to his intellectual level, how he feels at the moment, what his previous experiences have been, and many other factors. The one thing that older adolescents rarely perceive as comic is a situation in which they are personally involved and in which the source of ridicule concerns them. While he thoroughly enjoys laughing at others, it is quite a different story when the joke is on him. His inability to enjoy subjective humor stems from the fact that he is insecure in his feelings and is sensitive to the opinions of others.

Situations in which college students find humor have been classified in six categories, as follows (Kambouropoulon, 1926, 1930):

1. Laughter when there is no objective cause, no humorous event or situation to arouse it, as laughter occurring when others are laughing without knowing why this laughter takes place.

2. Laughter which has no objective cause, as when people fall down or are awkward in their behavior.

3. The mental inferiority of another person as seen in the stupidity, mistakes, absent-mindedness, social blunders, or naïve remarks of children.

4. The inferiority of another person as it is brought out by witty remarks or satirical comments.

5. Incongruity of the situation, especially when a person in authority is in a predicament.

6. Humor caused by incongruity of ideas, as is apparent in puns or clever remarks not directed at only one person.

Like the younger adolescent, the older adolescent may experience joy in situations in which he feels superior, and in situations which offer an outlet for pent-up emotional energy, especially that of an unpleasant nature such as anger, fear, or jealousy. There is far less of the uncontrolled giggling and crying among older adolescents than among younger and, as good social adjustments are gradually being made, the older adolescent derives less intense satisfaction from feeling superior to his contemporaries than he did when he was younger.

AFFECTION. Because the older adolescent concentrates his affection on one individual at a time, it is more intense than at any previous time in his life. There is a marked trend toward concentration of affection on one individual of the opposite sex, together with an idealization of that individual, which adds to the intensity of the emotional reaction. Not all older adolescents, however, concentrate their affection on one individual or on members of the opposite sex. Many have deep affection for a small circle of friends of the same sex, some concentrate their affection on a member of the same sex whom they hero-worship, while still others have a deeper affection for a parent than for anyone else. If, however, the adolescent is well adjusted, he generally falls in love with a member of the opposite sex before the adolescent years come to a close.

SOCIAL BEHAVIOR

In late adolescence, there is a narrowing down of the circle of intimate friends or chums and a broadening of the group. This means that the older adolescent has fewer intimate friends than he had when he was younger, more friends of a less intimate type, and more acquaintances. Another outstanding difference that becomes apparent at this age is the shifting of interest in friends of the same sex to friends of the opposite sex. While the older adolescent still maintains his friendships with members of his own sex, there is a growing preference for friends of the opposite sex. This change occurs slightly earlier in girls than in boys because of the more precocious sexual development of the girl. Improvements in different forms of social behavior are shown in the ratings given in Fig. 38.

Forms of Social Behavior. The slavish conventionality of the younger adolescent, which came from feelings of insecurity in the broader social situations he met for the first time, gradually gives way to *self-assertiveness*. Instead of trying to submerge his individuality so that he is just one of a group cut from the same pattern, there is now a desire to be recognized as an individual and to win the approval of the group. To achieve this end, the adolescent will wear brightly colored, conspicuously cut garments, regardless of whether they are becoming, in good taste, or appropriate for the occasion. So long as they attract attention, they fulfill their purpose as he sees it. He develops

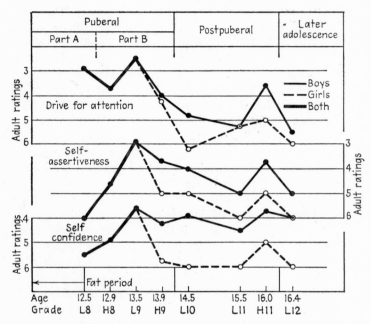

FIG. 38. Ratings on different types of social behavior for a boy at different stages of sexual development while in social situations with boys, girls, and both. (*From H. R. Stolz and L. M. Stolz, Somatic development of adolescent boys. New York: Macmillan, 1951. Used by permission.*)

an ex-cathedra manner of talking, posing as an authority on any and every subject. He tells off-color jokes which he knows will hold his listeners spellbound and he laughs uproariously at the jokes of others, not because the jokes are funny but because he likes others to think he has a keen sense of humor.

While most of the showing off at this age is crude and rude, it gives the adolescent satisfaction of a sort he never had when he was afraid of the group. Now he feels secure enough in social situations that he dare take a chance of expressing himself, and the release from fear of social situations alone is a source of satisfaction for him even if the attention he attracts to himself is more often unfavorable than favorable. As time goes on, he discovers that the reactions of the group are not always favorable. He then learns to modify his self-assertiveness and to emphasize only those forms of showing off where he has discovered that the social reactions are favorable. This is especially apparent in the change from loud, conspicuous clothes to clothes of more subdued shades with major emphasis on line rather than on color, and from the "Big-Injun" type of boasting to boasting of a more subtle type.

Social discrimination, or what is popularly known as "snobbishness," generally reaches its peak during the years of late adolescence. There is a strong tendency on the part of both boys and girls to discriminate against those whom they consider their social inferiors, either because of race, color, religion, or socioeconomic status. An interesting study of social discrimination among college students was made by asking students what type or types of individuals they would exclude from their fraternities or rooming houses. The greatest prejudice was found to be against Negroes, anarchists, loafers, students below average in intelligence, members of national groups not widely represented in the United States, such as Turks and Hindus, and people of unconventional morals. There was also a prejudice against students whose families had the stigma of a member who had served a term in jail, and students from families of low social standing (Katz and Allport, 1931).

The adolescent is intentionally rude to people whom he considers his inferiors. He makes a point of talking against such individuals, behind their backs, and takes delight in seeing to it that they are excluded from parties and other social gatherings. This intolerance normally begins to wane as adolescence comes to a close. He is strongly *resistant to adult authority.* The belief that he should have the rights and privileges of adulthood, which became strong during the early years of adolescence, now reaches an intensity that frequently leads to open rebellion against adult authority both at home and outside the home. When opposed in what he wants to do, the older adolescent threatens to leave home or actually does so, he storms against his parents and teachers, he tells those in authority, especially his parents, that he "hates" them, and he makes a scene when outsiders are present, hoping that they will champion his cause. Because girls in our culture are surrounded on every side by more restrictions than are boys, the adolescent girl of today does not accept placidly these restraints as did girls of several generations ago. Instead, she rebels as openly as boys do and may seek any way out of an environment that frustrates her.

Quarreling is a natural outcome of resistance to adult authority. The older adolescent is constantly at swords' points at home, either with his parents or his siblings, and he carries a grudge around for supposed injustices he receives outside the home. In his relationships with friends of his own sex, there is some quarreling but this is less frequent and less violent than with friends of the opposite sex. Unlike the child, the adolescent does not forgive and forget easily. When his pride is hurt, it is difficult for him to forget.

As a result, many friendships are broken and many hurt feelings established. Because the adolescent has a tendency to idealize the loved one, there is a bitterness when the loved one falls short of the ideal. This leads to words which often would be better left unsaid. Then, of course, the older adolescent has a tendency to try to reform those whom he loves and this is a source of friction.

Social Groupings. The older adolescent, like the younger, has friends of different social levels. His most intimate friends, or *"chums,"* are limited in number and are the ones with whom he spends most of his time. There is a degree of intimacy between chums that gives great satisfaction to the individuals involved. This intimacy comes from similarities in abilities and interests. Chums are very much alike in their fundamental standards and ideals, in determination, and in neatness of dress, though they may differ in personal interests, activities, and hobbies. Thus they complement each other in ways in which each is lacking (Bogardus and Otto, 1936). The average amount of time chums spend together is more than 2 hours daily, though girls spend more time with their chums than boys do. An investigation of how long individuals had been chumming showed that the average length was over 4 years. These intimate friends are of the same sex, and the degree of intimacy among girl chums is greater than among boys.

Cliques formed during the early part of adolescence persist into the latter part as dating takes a place of major importance in the lives of individuals of both sexes. These cliques are made up of intimate friends among the girls who bring into the group boys in whom they are interested. Sometimes the boys have been chums before they joined the clique and they are brought into the group for girls who have no special friend among the boys. Regardless of how the formation takes place, the individuals who are primarily responsible for its formation are the girls, and the degree of intimacy between them is usually greater than between the boys.

The clique of late adolescence becomes a unit of the larger social grouping, the *crowd.* Crowds are, for the most part, composed of two or more cliques which band together for parties and larger social functions where a fairly large number is needed to have a good time. Like the clique, the crowd is bound together by similarities of interest and standards of behavior. These guarantee a congeniality that would not be present if there were few interests in common or if the standards of conduct were widely different. Girls, on the whole, are more likely to band together in cliques than are boys who prefer the larger gathering of a crowd and whose social relationships are not so rigidly structured (Campbell, 1940).

Friends. In late adolescence, number of friends is less important than having the right kind of friends. The older adolescent thus limits the number of his friends but increases the circle of his acquaintances. He spends less and less time with members of his own sex and increasingly more time with members of the opposite sex. As a result of this new trend, the social distance between members of the same sex broadens while that between members of the two sexes narrows. By the end of adolescence, both boys and girls are spending more time with, and they have a greater interest in, friends of the opposite sex than in friends of their own sex.

In the selection of friends, the older adolescent is strongly motivated by the desire to have as friends individuals who can help him to make satisfactory adjustments to members of the opposite sex and who are themselves popular. A girl, for example, does not want to be seen with another girl whom the boys have labeled a "drip." If, however, the girl is popular, that will increase her own prestige in the boys' eyes. Similarly, a boy who is insecure in heterosexual relationships prefers boys who have the "know-how" he lacks. Older adolescents do not select friends alone for the reason that these friends will help them in their social adjustments. Other factors enter in too. Important factors from the environment consist of propinquity, socioeconomic status, community of interests, and tradition. Personal factors of importance in the selection of friends, whether they be of the same or of the opposite sex, include age, race, physique, "looks," intelligence, and personality (Partridge, 1934).

FRIENDS OF THE SAME SEX. Because of the strong interest boys and girls have in members of the opposite sex and in social activities with members of the opposite sex, the selection of friends of his own sex is influenced by these new interests. Now, friends of the same sex must not only be congenial but they must also be acceptable to the other members of the crowd to which the individual belongs. In the selection of friends of the same sex, there is a greater tendency for "birds of a feather to flock together" than for "opposites to attract," as is commonly believed (Fleming, 1932). Studies of similarities and differences between close friends have revealed that they are alike in such traits as intelligence, chronological age, sociability, dominance, emotional stability, self-sufficiency, introversion or extroversion, pleasingness of personality, social adjustments, social intelligence, and similarity of opinion on important moral, religious, social, and political problems (Vreeland and Cory, 1935; Winslow, 1937; Van Dyne, 1940).

A greater similarity exists between close friends among girls than among boys. Boys, on the other hand, tend to select as their friends other boys who have more pleasing personalities than theirs, who have more social intelligence, and who are better adjusted (Fleming, 1932).

The older adolescent generally has friends who live in different parts of the community than he or even in different communities. His most intimate friends, however, are those who live close enough to him that he can see them often and can do things with them without too much effort. There is no such thing as a *general* prejudice against individuals. Prejudice is a *specific* attitude toward certain specific relationships (Lundberg and Dickson, 1952).

An adolescent might have a friendly relationship with another adolescent of different religious, racial, or social status at school or at college, and yet not include that individual in the circle of his most intimate friends or even try to bring him into the crowd to which he belongs.

Church groups show a tendency to prefer as friends their own members. This is especially strong among members of the Baptist and Presbyterian groups. Nonchurch members show the greatest preference for each other. It is a case of "hanging together." No one denomination, on the other hand, has a reliable advantage over others in developing the kind of individual who wins friends (Bonney, 1949). The socioeconomic status of the adolescent's family is more important to girls than to boys in the selection of their friends. A girl expects her friend's family to be equal to or superior to hers in socioeconomic status.

FRIENDS OF THE OPPOSITE SEX. By late adolescence, both boys and girls have definite standards of what they expect friends of the opposite sex to be. While it is true that they revise these standards as time goes on and as they learn from experience that certain qualities they believed very important at first, such as good looks, are less important than qualities they attached only minor importance to, such as ambition and ability, there is at all times a standard approved by the group which the adolescent accepts and uses in the selection of his friends.

How definite and rigid these standards are is well illustrated by the anonymous answers given to the question, "What do you like and dislike about members of the opposite sex?" Girls reported that they do not like an unkempt appearance, such as unpressed trousers or shirttails out. They do not like a boy's hair to be greasy or to be cut so short that it is bristly. They like boys to have good manners; to be complimented by boys; to have a boy speak to them on the street, even when they are with another boy; to dance well but not to brag or talk incessantly about themselves or spend too much time talking to their parents. Boys dislike the use of too much make-up and too short skirts; they like girls to have good manners and social skills such as talking and dancing well; to be natural, not show-offs and gigglers; to plan something to do when they are out on a date but not to make undue demands on their pocketbooks; to be introduced to their parents; and not to be too forward (Pressey and Robinson, 1944).

The characteristics boys most dislike in girls include being a "gold digger," always having to be taken somewhere, being self-centered, being fickle, wearing too much make-up and looking cheap, talking baby talk, using vulgar language, telling shady stories, swearing, talking about other dates, making-up in public, and sulking or pouting. Girls dislike most boys who are vulgar-minded, who drink, who are conceited and brag, who swear in front of girls, who sponge off other boys, and who wait until the last minute to ask for a date (Wood, 1946).

It is interesting to note how standards for friends of the opposite sex change from the high-school to the college age. While, at both ages, boys have a great admiration for girls who have a sense of humor, they admire quietness when they are younger but dislike it greatly when they are older. At first, they are indifferent to a girl's looks, so long as she has other compensatory qualities, but later in adolescence, they dislike girls who are not good-looking. Much the same is true for daring. The older the adolescent, the more he admires a daring girl. The young adolescent girl admires a boy who is quiet and inactive but, later on, she shows a dislike for such traits. At all ages, she likes boys to be masculine, tidy, and to have a sense of humor (Chaffey, 1944).

APPRAISAL OF FRIENDS. The adolescent is hypercritical of his friends of both sexes and is intolerant of their weaknesses. They talk freely about the good and bad qualities of their friends behind their backs and they do not hesitate to tell them to their faces what they think of them. Few boys and girls consider their friends perfect in every way. While a few are afraid to tell their best friends secrets for fear that these secrets will be revealed, most have implicit faith in the secrecy of their friends. Boys rely on their best friends to back them up more than girls do, but boys more often than girls envy their best friends (Lucina, 1940). While most adolescents take teasing and criticism in a good-natured way, some resent it and a quarrel ensues. This is often the beginning of the straining of friendship ties which, as time goes on, may result in a breakup of the friendship.

Leaders. The older adolescent, like the younger, looks upon his leader as the individual who represents him in the eyes of society. Because of this, he wants his leader to be such that others will admire and respect him. For that reason, appearance is an important quality of leadership, regardless of what social grouping the individual leads. Furthermore, he must have ability above that of the rest of the group so that the members of the group can look up to and respect him. Because there are so many different kinds of groups in late adolescence—athletic, social, intellectual, religious, and class or community groups—the leader of one group will not necessarily have the ability to be a leader of another group. Leadership is now a function of the situation, as it is in adult life. Leadership is not a general quality but a specific one (Spaulding, 1933; Janney, 1938).

Among older adolescents, leaders may be subdivided into three general types, each with specific functions to perform which require specific abilities and personal qualifications. They are the *intellectual* leader who has higher scores on mental tests, who has better scholastic standing, and who has more interests of an intellectual nature than the other members of the group; the *social* leader distinguished by superior dress, manner, appearance, and bearing; and the *religious* leader who has a marked interest in religious activities. Only when an individual possesses the qualities that a leader in a particular group must have will he achieve leadership in that group, even though he may be a leader in another group (Dunkerley, 1940).

PERSISTANCE OF LEADERSHIP. While leaders come and go in childhood, this is not true of adolescence. The individual who is a leader in his freshman year of high school is more likely to be a leader throughout his entire high-school career than is the individual who has not held a leadership position. The training and experience derived from being a leader, plus the prestige which puts him in a focal point of attention when leaders are to be selected, give the individual an advantage over those whose experience in leadership has been limited or who have never held such a position. High-school students who go to college are four times as likely to be leaders in college if they have been leaders in high school than they are if they have not been leaders during their high-school days. Furthermore, those who are leaders in high school are far more likely to continue their education in college than are those who have not been leaders (Courtenay, 1938).

LEADERSHIP TRAITS. Leaders in late adolescence, as is true in the earlier years of the individual's life, are somewhat larger and make a better appearance than do nonleaders. While *physique* in and of itself is not responsible for leadership, it gives prestige to the individual and, at the same time, contributes favorably to his concept of himself (Moore, 1935; Cabot, 1938; Partridge, 1938). On the average, the leader has superior *health*. Because of this, he has more energy and is more eager to do things, both of which contribute to the quality of initiative (Fleming, 1935). There are no physical *monstrosities* among leaders, though marked individual differences in body build exist (Bowden, 1926). Now, more than ever before, a leader must be well dressed and well-groomed. Even though he is physically attractive, this is not enough. A good appearance depends as much on *clothes* and on *grooming* as on good physical characteristics. When a group is made up of members of both sexes, a pleasing appearance, aided by stylish, becoming clothes, is an essential characteristic of a leader.

The *family background* and the *socioeconomic status* of the individual are important in determining leadership. Among the fathers of college leaders, more are in the professional, managerial, and clerical groups than is true of fathers of nonleaders (Cobb, 1952). The leaders come from the higher-income brackets where their parents are better educated than are the parents of nonleaders (Hunter and Jordon, 1939; Reynolds, 1944). Among girls who are leaders, more of their siblings are boys than girls (Cobb, 1952). As measured by a masculinity-femininity test, girls who are leaders have a tendency to be more masculine than feminine (Cobb, 1952). Superiority of leaders over nonleaders is apparent in intelligence (McCuen, 1929; Reynolds, 1944; Cobb, 1952), in academic achievements (Sward, 1933; Reynolds, 1944), in chronological age (Moore, 1935), and in level of maturity as expressed in breadth of interests (Cobb, 1952).

A pleasing personality, including such traits as extroversion, self-confidence, individuality, originality, and good sportsmanship, is an essential quality of a leader in late adolescence (Terman, 1926; Sward, 1931; Cowley, 1931; Fleming, 1935). A leader at this age must be of the ascendant type, with good insight and judgment (Bowden, 1926). The leader is an individual who is most familiar with the standards and interests of the group and can judge the attitudes of the members regarding group interests. The leader's thinking is in terms of the group, rather than of himself as is true of non-leaders and he holds the position of leadership because of his "sensitivity" to the opinions of other members of the group (Chowdhry and Newcomb, 1952). Good emotional control and absence of neurotic tendencies are also qualities of leaders (Remmlein, 1938; Cobb, 1952).

Social Acceptability. The older adolescent, like the younger, is happy and well adjusted only if he achieves a reasonable degree of social acceptance. Being unpopular with either sex or with both cuts him off from the social life of his contemporaries and leaves him with no opportunities for the type of recreation that his contemporaries engage in. While social acceptability is affected very little by the size of the family from which the adolescent comes, there are indications that the larger the family, the less acceptable is the individual to his contemporaries (Bonney, 1949).

Among boys, the popular older adolescent is cheerful, natural, sociable, quick of apprehension, original, conscientious, energetic, tactful, kind, well-controlled emotionally, and very low in perseveration. The unpopular individual, by contrast, is unreliable, changeable, inert, tactless, subject to emotional instability, moody, casual, not so kind, and stands very high in perseveration (Cattell, 1934). Popular girls at this age come from unbroken homes, participate in sports and other outside activities, and are in the upper quartile of the group in intelligence-test scores (Washburne, 1941). Among both boys and girls, the qualities most admired for members of both sexes are character, kindly disposition, congeniality, sincerity, and a sense of humor. The qualities that are less important to popularity are thoughtfulness, enthusiasm, good manners, and common sense (Bogardus and Otto, 1936).

INTERESTS IN LATE ADOLESCENCE

Environment and sex are the two major factors that determine what the older adolescent's interests will be. Boys and girls from small towns or rural districts have interests which are in keeping with their environment; those from large cities develop interests as a result of the different opportunities the city environment offers. City adolescents are more interested in sex, ambitions and ideals, personal attractiveness, and getting along with others than are adolescents from small-town and rural environments. Because of the greater opportunities for earning money in the cities, the city adolescent is less interested in and concerned about money than is the rural adolescent (Symonds, 1936).

Late adolescence is the age when the full impact of socially approved patterns of behavior for the two sexes are felt. Girls are supposed to behave in keeping with their sex and boys with theirs. As a result of the socially approved standards, it is not surprising that, at this age, girls have interests that are very different from those of boys. A comparison of interests of boys and girls revealed that boys show a reliably greater interest than do girls in health, safety, money, study, recreation, and civic affairs. Girls show, on the other hand, more interest than do boys in etiquette, personal attractiveness, and getting along with people. Even in areas where both sexes show marked interest, the interest is of a different sort for the two sexes. In the case of health interest, the emphasis placed on health by boys related to strength, endurance, and general physical fitness. The girl's interest in health, by contrast, emphasized personal attractiveness; dieting, for example, was to improve her figure, not her physical fitness (Symonds, 1936).

Types of Interests. To cover the range of interests of older adolescents, they may be subdivided, arbitrarily, into the three major categories used in the description of interests among younger adolescents, as presented in the preceding chapter. These subdivisions include *social, personal,* and *recreational* interests.

SOCIAL INTERESTS. *Parties* of all types, especially those that include members of the opposite sex, rank first among the social interests at this age. The boys who, during early adolescence, showed little interest in parties and dances and who had to be persuaded by the girls to attend now show as keen an interest in parties as girls do. But, if the party is to be to the liking of the boy, it must be informal. *Talking* to anyone and everyone is a favorite activity of an older adolescent. No longer does he limit his talking to his intimate friends as he did several years earlier. Now he talks to anyone who will listen and frequently he does not care whether they are paying attention to him or not. Talking is a form of thinking out loud for him, and he derives keen satisfaction from verbalizing his thoughts, thus clarifying them.

Studies of what older adolescents talk about when they get together with members of their own sex have revealed that the favorite topics of conversation are dates, sports, clothes, and drinking for boys; for girls they are dates, clothes, food, and dancing. Nothing of great seriousness is discussed when older adolescents meet with their contemporaries. Rather, their conversations are a form of indoor sport (Stoke and West, 1930, 1931). Sex and smutty stories likewise are popular topics when adolescents are with intimate friends (Stoke and West, 1931). The relative importance of different conversational interests is shown in Fig. 39.

The older adolescent, especially when the major part of his time is spent in college or in some other educational institution, becomes keenly interested in *government* and *national and world affairs*. He reads and talks about these matters far more than he did when he was younger and he forms definite opinions which are often radical and unrealistic (Bell, 1938). Because of his

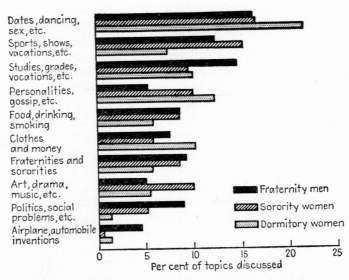

FIG. 39. Relative importance of conversational interests as revealed by the type of topics discussed by fraternity men, sorority women, and dormitory women. Note that the differences between men and women are not much greater than those between women in sororities and in dormitories. Studies, grades, vocations, art, music, drama, politics, social problems, etc., together constitute less than one-fourth of the total topics discussed. (*Based on a regrouping of data of Stuart M. Stoke and Elmer D. West, Sex differences in conversational interests. J. soc. Psychol., 1931, 2:120–126. From F. K. Shuttleworth, The adolescent period: a graphic atlas, Monogr. Soc. Res. Child Develpm., 1949, 14, No. 1. Used by permission.*)

relative ignorance in this area, he feels unsure of himself and, as a result, is often swayed by persuasive speakers and writers who are likely to hold a radical point of view. The radicalism of youth is generally found in countries where freedom of discussion is permitted or where there are attempts to mold the thinking of youth along these lines.

PERSONAL INTERESTS. The older adolescent has three major personal interests: *appearance, independence,* and his *life career.* These are so dominant that they absorb much of his time and thought. When their personal problems are solved or partially solved, and when they make a place for themselves in the social group, older adolescents become more stable and predictable.

As a result, they settle down and make better adjustments to life (Stolz *et al.*, 1937).

The older adolescent's interest in *appearance* is heightened by the realization that appearance plays a role of great importance in social adjustments. Popularity with members of his own sex as well as with members of the opposite sex is determined by whether the individual fits into the group ideal in appearance as well as in behavior. To girls, this is even more important

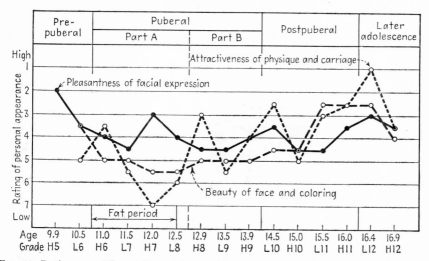

FIG. 40. Ratings on different items of personal appearance at different stages of sexual development. Note the low ratings on face and physique during the early adolescent-fat period and the higher ratings as the boy became more mature. (*From H. R. Stolz and L. M. Stolz, Somatic development of adolescent boys. New York: Macmillan, 1951. Used by permission.*)

than to boys because of the nonaggressive role they are expected to play. To make a good appearance, an adolescent girl is willing to sacrifice many of the luxuries and even necessities of life in order to have the clothes and beauty aids that will make her as attractive as possible (Hurlock, 1929, 1929a; Barr, 1934; Silverman, 1945). Improvement in appearance is illustrated in the ratings in Fig. 40.

With the realization that growth is completed or so nearly completed that any change that will take place in the future will be too slight to be noticeable, the older adolescent swings from the characteristic negative attitude he formerly had about his appearance to a positive one. While he is still concerned about his height, his weight, or any physical feature that he regards as homely, his attitude is not one of despair as it was when he was younger (Stolz and Stolz, 1944). Instead, he is concerned with how he can improve his looks and he accepts with greater or less resignation his body build and features. Knowing that clothes, hair styling, and beauty aids of all sorts can do wonders to improve appearance, both boys and girls spend proportionally more time than they can afford to spend before the mirror, reading helpful hints in newspapers and magazines, and discussing the matter with their friends.

The areas of interest are so widespread that they cover almost the entire body. The hair, nails, facial features—especially the mouth—eyebrows and eyelashes, the hands and feet, all receive attention from the adolescent who tries different methods of improving them. Rigid diets are strictly adhered to in an attempt to produce the desired figure, and exercises are strenuously engaged in to reduce some areas and enlarge other areas of the body. The characteristic body odors that come with the functioning of the sweat glands, especially at the time of the menstrual period in girls, is so disturbing to the adolescent that cleanliness becomes an obsession and all types of deodorants are used to kill any possibility of an offending odor (Silverman, 1945).

Because of their great value as aids in improving the individual's appearance, and because of their help in camouflaging physical traits that fall below accepted standards, the adolescent is more interested in *clothes* than in any other aspect of his appearance. While conspicuous clothing that draws favorable attention to the individual is more often worn by the older adolescent than by the younger, there is a gradual trend toward the use of extremes in style and cut rather than in colors, as is true when the adolescent first uses clothes for their attention value. Too much jewelry, too bright colors, and too extreme styles, the adolescent learns, are regarded as in bad taste and win for him attention of an unfavorable sort.

Both boys and girls, but especially the latter, are willing to submit to discomfort if they are compensated by increased personal attractiveness (Silverman, 1945). Because older girls are more self-confident and self-assured than are those in the preadolescent or early-adolescent years, modesty is not as strong a motivating force as it was when they were younger. They are willing to wear clothing that emphasizes their curves, and they are not so embarrassed about the display of their figures as younger adolescents are. Boys, too, like to emphasize their masculinity by having broad shoulders and narrow hips, which are often achieved by tailoring skills.

The desire for *independence*, which has been growing gradually throughout the years of childhood, reaches its peak of intensity in late adolescence (Cameron, 1938). If adult authority is relaxed gradually so that the adolescent can see himself reaching his goal, there is far less friction between the adolescent and his parents or others in authority than when he sees no improvement in his status. Adolescents who are in the throes of establishing themselves and are meeting obstacles at every turn are the most antagonistic to adult authority, especially to their parents (Stolz et al., 1937).

Because independence in all areas of his life is a new experience, even for an older adolescent, he needs help in meeting his new responsibilities successfully. Even when students go away from home to college or to work, they are rarely prepared for the degree of independence their new status brings them. They need help and advice in meeting problems related to their studies, their choice of vocation, personality defects, sex information, religion, a philosophy of life, and adjustments to people of all types, especially members of the opposite sex (Katz and Allport, 1931). When a resistant attitude toward his parents exists, the older adolescent generally turns to outsiders for this help.

The common sources of friction between the older adolescent and his parents consist of too many instructions, nagging, being asked too many questions about what they have done or where they have been, and criticisms of their behavior (Arlitt, 1942). When the older adolescent's family is on a lower social level than that of his friends, or when they come from a foreign country with different mores and different ideas about what adolescents should and should not do, there is invariably friction between the adolescent and his parents. Any unduly exaggerated home condition, such as divorce, death of one parent, or prejudice in favor of one child, will cause friction (Pressey, 1929).

Typically, the older adolescent expects too much independence too quickly. This desire is often exaggerated when the adolescent discovers that his friends have more independence than he or when he sees movies in which the main characters are more independent than he is permitted to be (Blumer, 1933). If his parents are unwilling to give him the independence he wants, the adolescent is rebellious and unhappy. This often leads to his running away from home, giving up his schooling, or even marrying to establish the independence his parents have denied him. Too strict home training during this period builds up a dislike for parents, a combative attitude on the adolescent's part, social maladjustments, and a tendency to do things behind parental backs (Watson, 1934).

The interest in a *life career* that began to be dominant in early adolescence often becomes a source of great concern to an older adolescent when he is confused about what he would like to do or what he is capable of doing. The more he hears or talks about different lines of work, the less sure he is of what he would like to do. Then, too, there is interest in and concern about how he can get a job of the type he would like. This problem rarely disturbs a younger adolescent who thinks that all he has to do is make his choice and the job will then be waiting for him. With the realization of how much it costs to live and the earnings a young person can expect, the older adolescent approaches the choice of his career with a practical and realistic attitude which he did not have formerly.

Older adolescents are less influenced by family preferences in the choice of their careers than they were when they were younger. Except in the case of business, boys are more likely to make independent choices than to follow in their fathers' footsteps (Cunliffe, 1927; Anderson, 1932). Mothers of today are more willing to consent to the choice of vocation made by their daughters than was true a generation or two ago, even if the mothers have had little influence in making the vocational decision (Leonard, 1932). Interest in a particular line of work, which is usually closely correlated with ability, is the dominant motive in the older adolescent's choice of his life work (Thorndike, 1921; Austin, 1931; Cunliffe, 1929).

While the older adolescent is more realistic in his concept of his abilities and disabilities than he was when he was younger, there is still a tendency to ignore the role played by individual abilities and job opportunities in the selection of a life career. Many adolescents believe that *wanting* to do a certain kind of work is all that is necessary in order to get and hold a job. They ignore the role played by intelligence, special training, and natural aptitude for a particular job.To show how unrealistic they are about job opportunities, 70 per cent of a group of boys said that they wanted to enter a line of work in which only 35 per cent of the population is employed. From 30 to 40 per cent of the boys showed a preference for professional careers, while only 8 to 10 per cent of the population goes into such work. By contrast, 1 per cent said that they wanted to go into laboring jobs, and yet 30 per cent of the population finds itself in such work (Rainey *et al.*, 1937).

Desire for glamorous jobs, which is so strong in early adolescence, gives way to an interest in more prosaic occupations, such as law, engineering, and business as the adolescent years progress (Jones, 1943). Desire for prestige is also a strong motivating force in the older adolescent's selection of his life career. In general, there is a popular belief that each generation should surpass the preceding one and this leads adolescents to want to enter a line of work with greater social prestige and greater financial rewards than their fathers and grandfathers enjoyed.

The difficulties in selecting a life career that a younger adolescent faces begin to disappear as adolescence progresses. The boys and girls who mature earlier and who, therefore, are more mature in their interests than are the slower maturing adolescents, generally decide upon a life career before they reach the end of adolescence. Students who make a vocational choice while still in high school are younger, brighter, more mature, and more studious than are those who are undecided about this matter (Jones, 1938). The vocational choices made during the latter part of adolescence prove to be more stable and permanent than those made during early adolescence while the individual is still in high school (Canning *et al.*, 1941; Taylor and Carter, 1942).

In an analysis of changes of interests over a period of 22 years, Strong found that these changes occurred most frequently and most rapidly from the ages of 15 to 25 years, and then more slowly and less frequently until 55 years of age. In a breakdown of the changes during adolescence, it was found that one-third of the changes occurred between $15\frac{1}{2}$ and $16\frac{1}{2}$ years, one-third between $16\frac{1}{2}$ and $18\frac{1}{2}$, and the last third between $18\frac{1}{2}$ and 25 years. It is apparent, thus, that interests are becoming more stabilized as the adolescent grows older (Strong, 1951).

RECREATIONAL INTERESTS. As adolescence progresses, the range of interests in different forms of recreation diminishes, more time is spent on the few forms of recreation the adolescent derives enjoyment from, and less time in all is spent on recreation than at earlier periods of the individual's life. With the pressures from studies, work, home responsibilities, and occasional community obligations, the older adolescent's leisure time to spend as he pleases is limited. As a result, he selects those forms of recreation that give him greatest pleasure, either because he excels in them and this adds to his social prestige or because they offer opportunities for social contacts, especially with members of the opposite sex. The narrowing down of recreational interests comes gradually, as adolescence progresses, and is usually more pronounced in girls than in boys. The narrowing down of recreational interests is illustrated in Fig. 41.

There is a gradual decline of interest in strenuous physical exercise and in *organized games.* Unless the adolescent has enough ability to excel, and to play on a team, he prefers to be a spectator rather than an active participant. Whenever possible, the older adolescent thinks up excuses to avoid strenuous activities and prefers to devote his time to recreations that require less effort on his part. This is particularly true of girls. Parties, picnics, going to the movies, listening to the radio or just sitting around and talking are preferred to the active games enjoyed at an earlier age. Only when games permit playing with members of the opposite sex, such as tennis, bowling, or skating, does the average older adolescent engage in them voluntarily. College men are "prone to spend too much time in sedentary forms of avocations which are apt to be more amusing than recreative" (Stoke and Cline, 1929).

Games of intellect, especially when they offer a chance for gambling, assume a position of importance in the recreational life of the older adolescent never before occupied to such a marked degree. Crossword puzzles, anagrams, and all sorts of guessing games of an intellectual sort are popular at parties of adolescents. Boys as well as girls like to play cards though, to boys, the interest is heightened if a small stake is involved. Playing cards is a popular amusement for parties of members of one sex or when both sexes are involved.

When time permits, the older adolescent has a *hobby*. This is likely to be useful rather than merely a means of filling in idle time, as is true of younger children. Many girls make clothes as a hobby, and boys keep collections of sports events or of some other interest that is absorbing to them at the time.

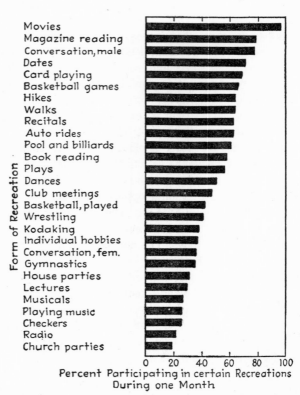

FIG. 41. Per cent of male college freshmen participating in certain recreations during one month. Ninety-six per cent went to movies, 79 per cent read magazines, etc. Data obtained by personal interviews. (*Based on data of S. M. Stoke and W. F. Clive, The avocations of one hundred college freshmen, J. appl. Psychol., 1929, 13:257–263. From F. K. Shuttleworth, The adolescent period: a graphic atlas, Monogr. Soc. Res. Child Develpm., 1949, 14, No. 1. Used by permission.*)

The hobby may take the form of drawing (see Fig. 42) which is generally of the caricature type at this age (Hurlock, 1943) or of playing the piano or singing, just for their own amusement or the entertainment of their friends.

Dancing is a form of recreation that few older adolescents can afford to shun if they want to be popular or to be invited to join in the activities of their contemporaries. While many older boys and girls, especially the former, have no real interest in dancing, an increasingly large number learn to dance and attend dances as the adolescent years progress. From early to late adolescence, there is a gradual decrease in the number of individuals who do not dance (Punke, 1936). Among college students or among older adolescents who do not go to college, about 92 per cent of the girls know how to dance. When a girl does not dance, she finds general social adjustment difficult.

FIG. 42. Typical drawing by an adolescent.

Her inability to dance makes her retreat from social contacts in which she might be a failure (Leonard, 1932).

While the young adolescent is more interested in dancing as an activity than in the dance partner, the reverse is true in the latter part of adolescence. Not only do older adolescents derive keen satisfaction from being with a member of the opposite sex who is socially acceptable to them but it gives them a feeling of satisfaction to be popular, as evidenced by the number of "cut-ins" from other individuals. "Dancing is thus an exciting and pleasurable recreation, as it affords a partial satisfaction to the sex impulses which cannot as yet achieve full and specific expression" (Hollingworth, 1928).

The older adolescent reads for pleasure, if his work or social life permit. At this age, when his leisure time is limited, he would rather spend it with his contemporaries than spend it alone, *reading*. When he does read, it is more likely to be fiction than nonfiction, and short stories rather than books. Romance, adventure, strong characterization, fantasy, and social awareness are prominent in books and stories popular with the older adolescent. When they read newspapers, they now read the serious parts as well as the comics and sport sections. The magazines they prefer are the popular ones of light fiction, rather than the serious type (Lehman and Witty, 1927*a;* Terman and Lima, 1927; Jordon, 1930; Wall, 1948*a;* Abraham, 1952).

There are relatively few nonreaders among older adolescents. Even those who are no longer students seem to retain the reading habits established in school for a time after they leave school. However, how much they read and what they read depends upon the level of their intelligence, the amount of time available for reading, their cultural and socioeconomic background, and many other factors (Wall, 1948*a*). In residential, middle-class communities, for example, reading is more widespread and of a much higher quality than it is in poorer sections. Reading material is also more readily available in the better parts of the community (Miller, 1936). What older adolescents read is a "product of their culture. Look into their homes, study the schools they attended, talk to their parents . . . and you will then have a picture of how they think, react, and also how and what they read" (Abraham, 1952).

The older adolescent, like the younger, enjoys listening to the *radio* for the major part of the time he is at home. As a matter of fact, he actually does not listen to it but it seems to give him pleasure to have it turned on while he is dressing, reading, or studying. In that way, it acts as a form of companionship in the absence of human companionship. Girls, as a whole, prefer romantic stories, popular and classical music, and quiz programs; boys prefer adventure, mystery, popular music, and quiz programs (Clark, 1940). The effect of radio listening on the older adolescent is more intellectual than emotional. His point of view and his attitudes toward important problems are markedly influenced by what he hears over the air.

As a general rule, the older adolescent attends *movies* less than the younger adolescent. This does not necessarily mean a waning of interest in movies but rather a greater interest in other forms of recreation. As interest in members of the opposite sex grows, there is a stronger desire to engage in recreational activities in which members of the opposite sex can take part and which give opportunities for conversation. The type of pictures the older adolescent prefers are those that follow the pattern of his reading and radio-listening interests. Romance stands in first place of preference for girls, and adventure and mystery are more popular with boys. But, as movie attendance during late adolescence is more often with members of the opposite sex than with friends of the same sex or members of the family, it is the girl who usually decides what movie will be seen. The leading character of the movie is responsible for its selection more often than any other factor (Bell, 1938; Edman, 1940).

RELIGIOUS ATTITUDE AND BEHAVIOR

The intensity of religious doubt, with its accompanying feelings of guilt, gradually subsides as adolescence draws to a close. The older adolescent either rejects all religious beliefs and becomes an agnostic or an atheist, or he revises his religious beliefs to fit into his more mature intellectual status. In either case, the problem has been solved and the emotional tension that normally accompanies any problem that is yet unsolved gradually disappears.

The older adolescent, like the younger, still has plenty of problems to solve before he arrives at a satisfactory religious belief. He is concerned about not liking church and not going to church, about sin, heaven and hell, wondering about what becomes of people when they die, conflicts of science and of religion, and wanting communion with God (Kuhlen and Arnold, 1944). He has conflicting ideas about death ranging from a brutal destruction to a liberation (Bernarda, 1949).

Adolescents who go to college and come in contact with different religious beliefs are more likely to be seriously concerned about their own religious problems and doubts than are those who remain at home and limit their social contacts to individuals whose religious beliefs are much the same as theirs. Many of the half-thought-out religious beliefs of a younger adolescent are clarified when he goes away from home and discusses his problems freely with his contemporaries (Griffen, 1929). When science or other courses present facts that contradict many of his earlier beliefs, it is not surprising that the adolescent shows a trend toward unorthodox beliefs after being in college (Katz and Allport, 1931). Those who accept religious beliefs unquestioningly at this age are usually more suggestible than those who reject beliefs (Howells, 1928).

As a result of doubt and rejection of some of his earlier beliefs, the older adolescent emerges from his serious doubts with new religious beliefs and a greater tolerance for the religious beliefs and practices of others than he formerly had. Significant changes occur regarding such beliefs as "Every word in the Bible is true," "God is someone who watches you to see that you behave yourself," and that "it is sinful to doubt the Bible." Beliefs about sin, heaven and hell, and prayer are also changed. In general, the beliefs that undergo the greatest change are the specific beliefs that are taught to or picked up from other children. Many doubts are not entirely cleared up, even though they may become less serious to the individual as he grows older (Kuhlen and Arnold, 1944).

In answer to a questionnaire, 8 out of 10 college women and 6.8 out of 10 college men said they needed religion in their own lives. The degree of this need was found to be influenced by the upbringing the students had had and the amount of religious training they had during their childhood years. The direct relationship between childhood religious training and the individual's need shows that "early training is likely to be the principal psychological influence upon an individual's later religious life." Of the principal types of influence in the childhood experiences, the most important are parental influence, fear and insecurity, personal influence of others, and conformity with tradition (Allport *et al.*, 1948).

While college education influences the religious beliefs of adolescents and brings about changes in these beliefs, the changes are not so marked as is popularly believed. Seniors in college have been found to have only slightly more liberal religious beliefs than freshmen, indicating that a change in their religious beliefs took place even before they entered college (Katz and Allport, 1931). Many of the changes in beliefs that occur during college years started during high-school days and are completed during college. The more abstract the religious attitude, the less likely it is to be changed by college experiences (Griffen, 1929). However, the religious thinking of college seniors is of a higher order than that of freshmen. During their college years, adolescents tend to improve the quality of their thinking regarding religious matters (Mull, 1947).

Contrary to popular belief, very few college students are atheistic. If they are not firm believers in some form of religion, they are neutral or somewhat favorable to the idea of God. There is far less change in the students' attitudes toward God and the church during the four years of their college life than one might expect. They come to college with a more or less definite idea about God and the church, fostered by their home training, and they leave college with much the same idea (Gilliland, 1940). While college experiences lessen some of their beliefs, they do not appreciably change beliefs that are already firmly established (Dudycha, 1933).

Effects of Religious Changes. The older adolescent is far less disturbed emotionally by his religious doubts and the changes in his religious beliefs than the younger adolescent is. In fact, changes bring about a new and satisfying conviction for them (Katz and Allport, 1931). Many older adolescents develop an attitude of indifference toward religion and thus experience no emotional tension (Leonard, 1932). In spite of the younger adolescent's doubts and revolts against religion, more often than not the older adolescent clings to the religious faith of his family. If both parents have different religious faiths, there is a strong tendency for the adolescent to accept the faith of the mother rather than of the father. Very few adopt a faith that is different from the faith of their parents. Church membership in the denomination of their parents is highest among Catholic youth and lowest among those whose parents have no church affiliation (Bell, 1938).

Religious Observances. Changes in religious beliefs are accompanied by a decline in church attendance and in different church activities. The reason given for this is not lack of interest in religion but rather the belief that going to church is not essential to leading a good life. Only about 10 per cent of older adolescents say they never attend church, though a fairly large number attend only occasionally (Katz and Allport, 1931; Brown, 1939). The largest number who attend regularly belong to the Catholic denomination and the smallest number, to no denomination at all (Bell, 1938). As a result of changes in religious beliefs and attitudes which so often occur during the closing years of adolescence, it would be logical to expect a certain number of older adolescents to shift their church affiliation to one that meets their needs more than the church of their parents. Among college students, Allport investigated the problem of whether the group he studied stayed with the church of their upbringing. He found that orthodox Catholics did so more than Protestant Christians or Jews. When shifts did occur, they were principally to more "liberal" faiths or out of religion completely (Allport *et al.*, 1948).

Participation in church recreations is far less popular among older adolescents than it is among younger. The same holds true for activities within the church, such as singing in the choir (Orr and Brown, 1932; Bell, 1938). The older adolescent prays less than he did when he was younger, and he regards prayer as a source of help in times of trouble rather than as a means of making up for some wrong done, as he was inclined to believe when he was younger (Kuhlen and Arnold, 1944).

MORAL BEHAVIOR

The most pronounced changes in attitudes toward right and wrong come between early and late adolescence. The change is marked by a tolerance toward certain acts that were formerly condemned, such as smoking and divorce, and an intolerance toward other acts, such as bribery. Thus, the change is more in the form of shift of emphasis than in the establishment of new codes of behavior. The older adolescent believes the same acts are wrong now as he did when he was younger but some seem more seriously wrong and some less serious than before (Pressey and Robinson, 1944).

At this age, the influence of "double standards," or codes of behavior for each sex, is important for the first time. Formerly, the behavior of both boys and girls was regulated by standards that were approximately the same. True, boys were given more freedom than girls and fewer questions were asked about their whereabouts or their activities. Now, especially in the area of sex behavior, the girl discovers that certain acts are classed as "wrong" when the girl is involved while, in the case of the boy, the same acts are condoned. Because modern girls have been brought up in the same schools as boys, have equaled or even excelled them in academic grades and in extracurricular activities, they rebel against the double standards and maintain that what is right for them is right for boys also, just as behavior classed as wrong, when carried out by a boy, is wrong too. There is a tendency, however, to judge girls more harshly for wrong acts than boys are judged for the same acts (Katz and Allport, 1931).

Moral Concepts. The moral concepts of an older adolescent closely approximate those of an adult. He has definite knowledge of what society judges as right and wrong and the degree of severity attached to a wrong act. Little change will take place in the moral concepts he holds now and those he holds when he is a mature individual (Jones, 1946). There is, however, a lessening of the intolerance he had several years earlier. No longer does the older adolescent condemn himself or others as severely as he did when behavior falls below accepted standards. The older adolescent realizes from experience that a discrepancy invariably exists between moral beliefs and moral behavior, with the former higher than the latter. However, there is a close correlation between moral beliefs and moral behavior with those having the higher beliefs acting in a more socially approved manner than those whose moral standards fall short of society's standards (Bartlett and Harris, 1936).

Discipline. Parents and teachers of today regard the older adolescent as old enough to know what to do and how to do it. Therefore, if the individual's behavior falls short of expected standards, some disciplinary methods must be used. In place of the corporal punishment that was administered to older adolescents who violated rules several generations ago, the new trend is to substitute other punishments for corporal punishment. In the rural and small-town areas, however, corporal punishment is more widely used than in urban areas, and in the lower socioeconomic groups it is used more than in the higher. Urban boys and girls are punished more than are those from rural or small-town areas, and boys receive more punishments than girls.

Disobedience, getting home late, being impudent, and neglecting work are the most common offenses for which parents punish their older sons and daughters. The commonly used methods of punishment consist of being made to stay at home, scoldings, and being slapped (Stott, 1940*b*). Overstrict discipline makes adolescents dislike their parents, it makes them irritable and ashamed of their parents, and it tends to make them rude to their parents. In addition, it leads to worrying and poor social adjustments on the part of those who have been subjected to too strict punishments and home discipline (Watson, 1934).

Juvenile Delinquency. A juvenile delinquent is one whose "accepted pattern of adjustment is at variance with the accepted codes of conduct which society is attempting to enforce" (Partridge, 1938). In many instances, the juvenile delinquent is an individual who has been troublesome and naughty at home, in school, and in his neighborhood. As he grows older, his troublesomeness increases instead of decreases and his acts are more offensive to society than they were when he was younger. In a smaller number of cases, the individual who has conformed to social dictates during childhood and has been regarded as a "good" child, kicks over the traces in adolescence and seems to be trying to compensate for all the years of being a strict conformist to society's rules. Overstrict discipline and too great parental expectancy can be regarded as the causes of the trouble.

During a war period, juvenile delinquency generally increases. Then, when the war is over, there is a decrease in the number and severity of juvenile-delinquency cases. At the present time, the trend is reversed and juvenile delinquency is on the uptrend again. In the year 1951, increases throughout the nation were 10 per cent above 1950, in New York City and New York State, 20 per cent. This alarming increase is accompanied by more serious types of crime than previously reported, with the increase in sex offenses and narcotics addiction (Freeman, 1952).

Juvenile delinquency is serious not only because of the harm it does the social group as a whole but also because it is symptomatic of maladjustment on the part of the delinquent. The adolescent who is unable or unwilling to get satisfaction from conforming to social dictates derives satisfaction from hurting the social group as a revenge for real or imagined wrongs inflicted by the group. Unless the cause of the maladjustment is detected and corrected, the individual will become more and more seriously maladjusted with the result that he will contribute to our roll of adult criminals. The majority of adult criminals in this country are those who "lose their way socially while they are still in adolescence" (Hollingworth, 1928). The peak of juvenile delinquency comes between the ages of nineteen and twenty years.

FORMS OF DELINQUENCY. Juvenile delinquency takes many forms, just as childish misdemeanors do. For the most part, however, those which are regarded as most serious are the forms in which damage to property of others occurs or bodily harm is inflicted upon those who are not responsible for the act or only indirectly so. Sexual delinquencies and the use of narcotics obtained illegally are the outstanding forms of juvenile delinquency brought to the courts in the larger city areas. In addition, other forms of delinquency include stealing, cheating, vagrancy, intoxication, disorderly conduct, destruction of property belonging to others, and attempts at homicide or suicide. Among girls, sex delinquencies rank high (Johnson, 1941) followed by running away, stealing, and ungovernability (Maller, 1937) (see Fig. 43).

For the most part, delinquencies of boys are more frequent and more serious than in the case of girls, though since the turn of the present century the number of cases ôf delinquency brought to the courts has shown a steady increase in the percentage of female offenders. The most common charges brought against boys are for stealing, burglary, and disorderly conduct with

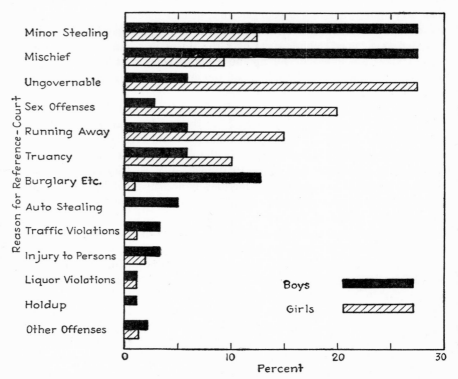

FIG. 43. Relative importance of reference of boys and girls to juvenile courts. (*From F. K. Shuttleworth, The adolescent period, Monogr. Soc. Res. Child Develpm., 1938, 3, No. 3. Used by permission.*)

an increase in number of charges for reckless driving and the sale and use of narcotics in the urban areas. More boys than girls are committed to institutions and more boys than girls are repeaters (Maller, 1937). Up to the middle of adolescence, most cases of juvenile delinquency involve offenses against property; after that, the most common offenses are against persons, in the form of sexual irregularities, attempts at homicide and suicide, and disorderly conduct.

CAUSES OF JUVENILE DELINQUENCY. The largest number of juvenile delinquents come from the poorer areas of a community. This would lead to the conclusion that poor environmental factors, in the form of poor home conditions, parental neglect, poverty, lack of opportunities for wholesome forms of recreation, undesirable companions, and lack of moral training and guidance on the part of parents are all responsible to some degree for the low moral conduct of the young people. Furthermore, the level of intelligence of the average juvenile delinquent is below that of the average for the population and there is a tendency for cases of emotional instability and maladjustment to be common in this group (Rogers and Austin, 1934; Sullenger, 1934; Durea, 1935; Bartlett and Harris, 1936; Healy and Bronner, 1935; Maller, 1937; Zucker, 1943; Shulman, 1949; Wattenberg, 1950; Henriques, 1949; Glueck and Glueck, 1950). For the most part, the motives of juvenile delinquents are those of normal but immature people rather than of criminals (Kelchner, 1941).

SEX INTERESTS AND BEHAVIOR

Romantic attachments normally follow the infatuations of the hero-worshiping and boy-crazy, girl-crazy stages of early adolescence. There is a marked difference between early infatuations for members of the opposite sex and the love attachments that may lead to marriage. Infatuations come at an earlier chronological age and are an indication of emotional immaturity. When one infatuation ends, the adolescent quickly becomes reinfatuated, and this falling in and out of love progresses with as many as eight to ten infatuations a year. It is not uncommon for both boys and girls to have several infatuations simultaneously, a condition which never exists in the case of a love attachment. Infatuations are briefer, lighter, and more promiscuous than love and, for the most part, are not found in late adolescence except in the case of emotionally immature adolescents (Ellis, 1949).

When romantic attachments are formed, they are so intense and so absorbing that the individuals involved have little time or thought for anything else. Their work suffers, their responsibilities are neglected, and they find happiness only when they are together. As a result of this all-absorbing interest in one individual, the older adolescent loses interest in group activities and prefers to be alone with the loved one. This is the period of "dating" when boys select from the girls they know one girl whom they prefer to be with and whom they find congenial for all their activities. Any activity in which the girl cannot participate, such as a team sport with a group of boys, loses its appeal for them when dating becomes their favorite form of recreation. For girls especially, during the period of late adolescence, dating is the favorite recreational activity (Lehman and Witty, 1927).

Dating. "Dating" is to the modern generation what "escorting" was in the past. It is not the same as courtship, though it may and frequently does lead to courtship and marriage. It is a "process of paired association between members of opposite sexes before marriage" (Lowrie, 1951). It involves freedom and lack of commitment or public obligation for any sort of future action. This is what distinguishes dating from courtship where the objective is marriage.

There have been arguments advanced for and against dating. On the negative side is the criticism that dating is a competitive form of association between the sexes in a "period of dalliance" between puberty and marriage which is largely dominated by a quest for thrill, in which each individual tries to deceive the other by pretense of love and devotion. Under such conditions, it is not a preparation for marriage. The reasons advanced for this belief are that dating gives prestige to the participants, it determines the individual's status in his own age group, it provides thrills and is fun, its exploitive element is very harmful, and the capacity to love is permanently injured as a result of too much dating (Wallin, 1937; Mead, 1949).

On the good side are arguments in favor of its educational value. These are that dating offers opportunities for contacts with the opposite sex, for an increase in the range of contacts, opportunities for social engagements and for the selection of companions without parental interference, and an opportunity to determine mutual interests before becoming emotionally involved. Furthermore, in a society in which parental controls over marriage are relaxed, as they are in present-day America, dating offers opportunities to make a right selection which is essential to successful marriage. It also helps the adolescent to learn to adjust to others, especially members of the opposite sex, and to judge the opposite sex objectively and sensibly, which will result in a sounder choice of mate (Burgess and Locke, 1940; Lowrie, 1951). Dating ends when a pairing is repeated continuously and courtship then begins.

When a group of older adolescents was asked to check their most serious reasons for dating, the reasons associated with marriage, affection, and the selection of a mate were the most commonly given. Next in importance were educational reasons, such as gaining poise and ease, and learning to adjust. The least frequently given reasons included competition, prestige, fun, getting to social affairs, and necking. Girls put more stress on the educational aspect of dating and boys emphasize the fun aspect (Lowrie, 1951).

Going Steady. In the typical American courtship pattern, "going steady," or continuous dating of one individual instead of many, generally starts after a year or two of dating. Because there is always "safety in numbers," parents are rarely concerned about dating except when the adolescent dates individuals of whom his parents do not approve or goes to places of entertainment considered too sophisticated for his age level. But it is a different story when the adolescent begins to go steady, especially if this starts when the adolescent is still in high school or college and has had only a limited experience in dating individuals of the opposite sex. There is always the possibility that when two young people start to go steady, they will want to get married.

Furthermore, it is serious because the individuals involved have not had enough dating experience to establish ideals of what they want in a life mate. Many boys and girls, especially the latter, are not satisfied with the individuals they are going steady with but, having started to go steady, they are out of circulation and would miss out on the fun their contemporaries are having unless they continue to hold onto the date they already have (Mather, 1934). The older the adolescent, the more critical he is likely to be of the individual he is going steady with, suggesting that he is forming a more clear-cut concept of what he wants in a member of the opposite sex than he had when he was younger.

As is true of dating, there are advantages and disadvantages in going steady. The advantages include a feeling of security and assurance of dates for all social occasions; more likelihood of "nice" dates; it makes the girl feel popular; it costs the boy less money than when he is dating a number of girls; and it gives the young people an opportunity to know each other, thus knowing whether they want to consider marriage. The disadvantages suggested by young people seem to outweigh the advantages. They have stressed the facts that it is harder to stop than to get started; it leaves the girl without an escort if the boy has to work or goes away from home; it is likely to shut young people off from their friends; it often causes arguments in the family, especially if parents disapprove or feel the young people are too young to consider marriage; and it is hard to get back into circulation after going steady, especially for girls (Wood, 1946).

Early dating usually consists of going out to places of amusement with one or two other couples. The inexperienced adolescent finds it easier to meet this new social situation successfully in a group than when alone with one individual. As time goes on and the adolescent learns from experience how to act and what to talk about on a date, the trend is away from a group and toward single dates. How soon or how late this will come in adolescence depends largely upon the opportunities for practice in dating the individual has had. While girls prefer dancing, going to the movies, or riding in a car as dating activities, boys generally prefer some athletic activity, such as tennis or swimming, rather than dancing (Punke, 1944).

Selection of "Dates." In a social group where the male is the aggressor, the selection of the individual he will go with is almost exclusively his choice. The girl in American society must wait to be selected, and this puts a burden of responsibility on her shoulders to make herself attractive to members of the opposite sex so that she will be assured of selection. While no two adolescent boys find the same characteristics in girls equally attractive, there are certain characteristics that are almost universally admired by boys and others that are admired by girls in the boys they go with. Of the bases of attraction, the following play the most important roles:

PHYSICAL ATTRACTIVENESS. Most adolescent boys are so looks-conscious that they will not consider dating a girl unless she appeals to them as attractive, not only of face but of body build (Baber, 1936).

MANNER OF DRESSING. Clothes must be up to date and stylish as well as becoming. Both boys and girls expect the individual they associate with to be attractively dressed to the point where others will notice and be impressed. For that reason, both boys and girls become clothes-conscious and clothes-preoccupied to the point where they often spend far more money on clothes than they can afford in order to make a good appearance (Hurlock, 1929; Silverman, 1945).

AGE. While girls, owing to their precocious sexual development, generally prefer to date a boy a year or two older than they, an age differential of more than that is regarded as too high. Boys likewise prefer a girl a year or so younger than they, because they feel more at ease with her than with a girl of their own age, but an age differential that is too great leads to the accusation of "robbing the cradle."

INTELLIGENCE AND EDUCATION. Greater compatability exists between boys and girls when they are about equal in intelligence and educational background than when the difference is too great. Many adolescent boys do, however, date girls less intelligent and less well-educated than they but, in the long run, they find less congeniality in such girls than in girls more nearly their equal in these qualities.

PERSONALITY. A pleasing personality, or one that is patterned according to the boy's concept of a good all-round sport, frequently compensates for lack of physical attractiveness. No longer are socially and emotionally immature individuals considered attractive. Therefore, a boy or girl who seems young for his or her age is not likely to be attractive to members of the opposite sex.

SIMILARITY OF INTERESTS. Congeniality in any human relationship, whether it be within the same sex group or not, demands interests in common. While two individuals who are markedly different in interests may attract each other, there is little basis for a lasting friendship or for a romance. Similarity in interests, on the other hand, is one of the major factors in holding two persons together.

RELIGIOUS AND ETHNIC BACKGROUNDS. In spite of protests on the part of many parents, young people of today date and marry individuals of religious and ethnic groups different from their family background. Boys are likely to make more out-group choices than girls, though boys of the higher socioeconomic groups make fewer out-group choices than do boys from the lower socioeconomic groups (Lundberg and Dickson, 1952).

RESIDENTIAL PROPINQUITY. Most adolescents date individuals from their own school classes or from the neighborhood in which they live. Only when adolescents go away to college, travel extensively, or leave home to work in another community, do they have many opportunities to meet and get to know members of the opposite sex from other communities. Within a given community, there are social barriers between groups. As a result of these barriers, adolescents do not have an opportunity to meet members of the opposite sex who live within a short distance of them and who might be congenial if they had an opportunity to become acquainted.

While all the factors listed above are important in attracting members of the opposite sex (Bossard, 1932; Dreikurs, 1935; Baber, 1936; Rockwood and Ford, 1945), some are more important than others. When high-school and college students were asked, "What sort of girl does a boy like to go with, and what sort of boy does a girl like to go with?" the girls' ratings of boys put the following traits in this order of importance: real brains, cleanliness, good health, dependability, and cheerfulness. Contrary to what one might expect, the girls rated "good looks" in eleventh place. The boys' ratings of girls put real brains in first place, followed by good health, good looks, cleanliness, and cheerfulness (Mather, 1934).

Expressions of Love. Unlike the younger adolescent who hero-worships an adored member of the opposite sex from afar, or who engages in a form of horseplay while in the "boy-crazy, girl-crazy stage," the older adolescent is no longer satisfied with such mild forms of contact. Because the sex drive is accompanied by an emotional state of great intensity, it must seek an outlet in some form that is socially approved or, if not socially approved, in a form that will give the individuals enough satisfaction to outweigh the possible social disapproval which would follow, should the matter be known.

While the desire for *physical contact* is strong at all ages when the love emotion is aroused, it becomes more powerful than ever before when the individual's affections are concentrated on one individual, as happens when the adolescent starts to go steady. This strong desire for physical contact is expressed by "necking," a form of physical intimacy characterized by casual kissing and fondling; by "petting," a form of direct sexual stimulation that is intended to produce or actually does produce erotic responses (Rockwood and Ford, 1945); or by intercourse with the loved one.

There is no question about the fact that adolescents of today, because of the greater freedom they are allowed, knowledge of contraceptive methods, the modern trend of entertaining members of the opposite sex away from the parental roof, and the belief that everyone expects to pet if she is to be popular, engage in petting and necking far more promiscuously than was done in the past. It is quite usual for a boy to expect at least a kiss after his first date with a girl, and for those who are going steady to engage in petting of an extreme form or in sexual intercourse (Kinsey *et al.*, 1948).

Most girls start to pet between the ages of sixteen and seventeen years. At first, they pet openly, when with other members of their crowd, but later, as they grow older and petting becomes more intimate, they generally pet in private (Lynd and Lynd, 1929; Rockwood and Ford, 1945). Most girls are willing to engage in petting because they are infatuated with the boy, because they are curious, because others do it and they haven't the courage to resist, or because they do not know how to get out of it (Smith, 1924; Wood, 1946). When girls do not permit petting, they soon discover that they have fewer dates than girls who do permit it (Lynd and Lynd, 1929).

Between the ages of sixteen and twenty years, there is more petting, some of which is indiscriminate, than at the time of sexual maturing or in adulthood. Most boys and girls of today regard petting as a normal form of sexual expression and, for the adolescent boy in the last years of high school or college, it takes the place of masturbation and other forms of sexual outlet engaged in earlier. The frequency of petting varies from individual to individual, just as is true of other forms of sexual outlet. There is evidence to show, however, that in all social groups, it is more frequent than it was even a generation ago (Kinsey *et al.*, 1948).

The older adolescent begins to think seriously of marriage and family when his interest is centered on one person. When college students were asked questions to discover their attitudes toward marriage and family, they revealed that they were not so socially radical as college students are often accused of being. Men students, however, were found to be more liberal and less resistant to change than women students. Neither sex was in favor of any violent alterations in marriage and the family institution. They show a thoughtfulness about marriage problems that was not found a generation ago (Bernard, 1938).

How many romances an individual will have before he finds a life mate will depend largely upon the individuals involved and the opportunities their environment offers for romances. An urban youth, for example, has much more chance of falling in love again when a former romance ends than has a youth in a rural community where members of the opposite sex are limited in numbers and are likely to be going steady with someone else. When 100 men and 100 women were asked to tell how many love affairs they had before finding their life mates, the average proved to be 6.8 love affairs for each (Hamilton, 1929). Each new love affair is an exciting adventure but, when it ends, the adolescent will take it with less intense feeling than he previously did because he now knows from experience that he will fall in love again just as he did before.

What causes adolescent romances to end varies widely from one individual to another. An interesting study of the causes reported by a group of adolescents showed that in 20 per cent of the cases, geographic or social separation brought about the end of the romance; 15 per cent ended in marriage; 13 per cent in dissatisfaction with the other person; 12 per cent in drifting apart; 10 per cent were terminated by another person; 9 per cent resulted in transfer of affection to another person; and the rest were ended by scattered causes (Folsom *et al.*, 1938). It is interesting to note what a small percentage ended in marriage.

When an adolescent is in love, he is unhappy when away from the loved one. This leads to a strong desire for *constant association,* either by being together, or by keeping in constant contact with the loved one by telephone calls or letters. As is true of chums, the older adolescent makes a *confidante* out of the loved one. To her, he confides his hopes, ambitions, joys, and sorrows. Girls, more often than boys, treasure *keepsakes* that remind them of the loved one. These range from letters to pieces of jewelry, such as class pins or rings.

Curiosity about Sex. By late adolescence, the typical American boy and girl of today are familiar with the important facts relating to sex. How accurate their information is and how wholesome their attitudes are will be determined largely by the type of sex instruction they had when they were younger. A satisfactory romance at this age often compensates for an unhealthy attitude toward sex built up during the earlier part of the individual's life. There are a number of topics related to sex which are familiar to the older adolescent but which he does not understand completely. In many instances, there are medical or technical terms that confuse him and about which he has no way of getting information to clarify his confusion. Such topics are soul kissing, why some women cannot have babies, the cause of venereal diseases, the effect of saltpeter, and the effect of birth control on future fertility (Parker, 1938).

The older adolescent is not satisfied with talking or reading about sex. To satisfy his curiosity, he must have firsthand experience and see for himself what sex means. That is what motivates the necking and petting that adolescents engage in when they have dates with members of the opposite sex. While there is affection or even infatuation for the individual with whom they neck or pet, the primary motivation is not expression of affection but rather satisfaction of curiosity. The older adolescent engages in more frequent petting and in a greater variety of petting techniques than are used by the younger adolescent (Ramsey, 1943).

Curiosity is one of the dominant motives in premarital intercourse. While there is a growing tendency for older adolescents to engage in premarital intercourse, there are still strong feelings against it on the part of many girls. Even among engaged persons, the same feeling exists. Very often, after satisfying their curiosity about this matter, girls refuse to indulge before marriage, even though the boy they are dating insists upon it or threatens to break up the friendship unless the girl grants his wish. Many girls who disapprove of premarital intercourse engage in it not so much because of curiosity but to win popularity (Butterfield, 1939; Bernard, 1938; Rockwood and Ford, 1945).

FAMILY RELATIONSHIPS

As the adolescent years progress, parents generally come to the realization that their sons and daughters are no longer children. As a result, they give them more privileges while, at the same time, they expect more in the way of work and assumption of responsibilities on the part of the adolescent. When this parental adjustment to the changed status of the son or daughter is made, the tension that marked the parent-child relationship in early adolescence generally relaxes and the home becomes a pleasanter place in which to live. The more parents are willing to treat their older adolescent children as peers, the better the relationship between them. There are, however, many families in which this change does not occur. As a result, the resentment on the part of the adolescent grows stronger and stronger as time passes.

At every age, parent-child relationships leave their mark on the individual's personality. The older adolescent, after experiencing throughout his life poor or good relationships with his parents and siblings, emerges from these home situations with a personality pattern that helps or hinders him in his social adjustments outside the home. As Stott (1939) has pointed out: "In the family situation are provided the setting, the stimulation and guidance which determine, very largely, whether the child shall develop into a personally well adjusted and socially useful individual."

When the family relationships are good not only during adolescence but also during the earlier formative years of his life, the adolescent is a well-adjusted individual. Such an individual has grown up in a home where opportunities for responsibilities and freedom to meet them were offered, where parents showed an understanding of the needs of their children, and used the guidance type of discipline rather than no discipline at all or the domination type. Such parents are companions to their children and this helps to foster a wholesome relationship in the home. Poorly adjusted adolescents, by contrast, generally come from home settings where the family relationship is poor and where the adolescent has had inadequate or the wrong type of training and guidance through the formative years of his life (McKinney, 1939).

Siblings, who, during early adolescence are frequently a thorn in the side of the adolescent, are now taken in a calmer and more philosophical manner by the older adolescent. He is capable of understanding the behavior of younger siblings better than he could when he was younger, and after developing a certain degree of poise and self-confidence which he formerly lacked, the older adolescent is not so easily embarrassed or upset by the behavior of his younger siblings. In many instances, the older adolescent develops a parental attitude toward his younger siblings, and this eliminates much of the friction that previously existed in the home. Older siblings are treated more casually, and less envy is shown toward them than was true earlier. Even grandparents and older relatives are accepted by the older adolescent more graciously than they were several years earlier. All in all, family relationships in late adolescence are on a better and sounder basis than at any previous time in the individual's life.

PERSONALITY

The personality pattern established during childhood years and changed to a greater or lesser extent in early adolescence as a result of the radical physical and emotional changes that occurred at that time, now stabilizes itself and takes the form it will maintain with few modifications throughout the remaining years of the individual's life. A measurement of personality traits of college students which was then compared with the traits they remembered from their childhood days revealed a continuation of these traits in the same or related forms in adolescence. Students who remembered having an unhappy childhood were found to be very emotional in adolescence. Similarly, the adolescent who was found to be lacking in self-confidence remembered having been that way from the time he was a child (Stagner, 1948). Ascendant behavior among college students traced its origin to conditions in the childhood experiences of these individuals just as those who were submissive had childhood experiences that fostered submissive behavior (McLaughlin, 1930).

"Pleasing Personality." The older adolescent is well aware not only of the advantages of a pleasing personality as an asset in popularity but he is aware also of what constitutes a pleasing personality. The traits admired by his contemporaries in members of his own sex as well as in members of the opposite sex are discussed in conversations and are stressed as reasons for the success of the individual. It is logical, therefore, that the older adolescent would use as a standard for the shaping of his own personality the pattern he knows is admired by his contemporaries. While younger adolescents may admire an individual who is aggressive, daring, and restless, the older adolescent knows that such traits are indicative of immaturity. Likewise, he discovers that certain traits not considered important in early adolescence, such as broad-mindedness, cooperativeness, and reliability now hold a place of dominance in the personality pattern that is regarded as "pleasing" (Pressey and Robinson, 1944).

There is a marked relationship between emotional stability and what is considered a pleasing personality. While children may not notice emotional ups and downs unless they are very pronounced, and while they may look with amusement upon a child who flies off the handle in a temper tantrum or who bursts into tears when he cannot have his way, the adolescent notices and scorns such displays of emotions. He even scorns the individual who laughs too uproariously or who does not hide his jealousy and envy from others. To the older adolescent, a pleasing personality requires that "The general tendency of the emotional response can be depended upon" (Fleming, 1932*a*).

The well-adjusted adolescent who gets along with all types of people in all types of social situations has the personality traits that go to make up a pleasing personality. Because the correlation between personality and popularity is so high, every adolescent who wants to be popular—and there are few who do not—will strive to develop those traits which he has discovered contribute to his popularity. With this strong motivation, many adolescents who begin the adolescent period with personality traits that have made them socially unacceptable throughout their childhood years emerge into maturity with well-adjusted personality patterns that contribute to their social acceptability and success in work as well as in social situations.

Personality Maladjustments. In spite of the individual's attempts to improve his personality during adolescence and in spite of help given him in school and in college, many older adolescents are so poorly adjusted that they fail to do the quality of work they are capable of, they have few friends of either sex, they are at swords' points with the members of their families, and they are extremely unhappy individuals. Sometimes their unhappiness motivates them to threaten or to carry out their threat to commit suicide, sometimes they retreat into a daydream world as compensation for what they have not had in life, and sometimes they are so badly adjusted that they become institutional cases.

The adolescent *nervous breakdown* is generally a signal of serious maladjustment. The usual time for this to occur is shortly after the period of late adolescence starts, during the senior year of high school or the freshman year of college. This is the time when there is a strong awakening of the sex life of the individual, when new and difficult adjustments to members of the opposite sex must be made, and when the adolescent must orient himself to the new environment of being away from home in college, or of adjustment to a job. More often than not, the adolescent who experiences a breakdown at this age is accelerated educationally and, because he is younger than his classmates, his problems of social adjustment are exceptionally difficult because of his more immature state.

The causes of breakdowns at this age have been divided roughly into three categories: *overwork,* due to fear of flunking, to having too many outside activities or home responsibilities, to being "pushed ahead" by overambitious parents, or to trying to earn money while continuing their schoolwork. As a result of overwork, the adolescent gets insufficient sleep and exercise, and he has too few opportunities for wholesome recreation; *mental factors* such as anxiety, overexcitement, worry, nervous shocks, and general discontent with everything; *diseases,* such as measles, neuralgia, or heart trouble (Gardner, 1929).

Personality maladjustments during late adolescence are far more numerous than is generally realized. Many individuals who are regarded as "difficult to live with" or generally "troublesome" are incipient cases of maladjustment which sooner or later must have recourse to clinical help if they are to be saved from more serious mental disorders (McLaughlin, 1930). In addition, there are large numbers of adolescents who are receiving psychiatric help. The extent to which personality maladjustments are found among older adolescents was not popularly recognized until after the Second World War when governmental reports indicated that more young men had been rejected for service in the armed forces because of psychiatric reasons than because of physical reasons.

Among students in both high school and college, maladjustments are common. This does not mean that education per se is responsible for maladjustments but rather that the high academic standards, the pressures to maintain a satisfactory standing in their classes, and the high competition in the extracurricular activities put a strain on individuals just at the time when they are trying to make adjustments to the new and difficult area of heterosexual relationships. Girls, on the whole, are more disturbed than boys primarily because girls find it more difficult to attain status in an educational system planned for and dominated by men and boys (Bridges, 1927; Bell, 1934; Remmers *et al.,* 1938).

The *effects* of personality maladjustment are apparent in the behavior of the individual. The most outstanding effects include *immaturity,* or childishness, which is shown in inability to make decisions or in dependency on parents; *overcomplacency,* which shows itself in lack of motivation and a tendency to follow the crowd; *social inadequacy,* as shown in inability to get along with others; *nonconformity,* as shown in unconcern about the censure of others; *lack of interest in studies or work; habitual worry and anxiety;* and *temporary perturbation,* in which the individual is thrown temporarily out of adjustment by particular emotional upsets (Woods and Chase, 1937).

Happiness vs. Unhappiness. While late adolescence as well as early adolescence is typically an unhappy age, the relative degree of unhappiness is an indication of the success or of the failure the adolescent is making in his adjustments to life. When adjustments are progressing successfully, the adolescent will be less unhappy than when the adjustments are proving to be unsuccessful. The longer the unhappiness lasts and the more intense it is, the stronger the indication of maladjustment on the part of the adolescent.

A well-adjusted individual has goals which are within his capacities and he uses sustained and definitely directed efforts to attain these goals. The maladjusted individual, by contrast, has neither clearly defined goals within his capacities nor plans to attain these goals. In addition, he is unhappy because he cannot attain his goals due to the fact that they are beyond his capacities (Washburne, 1941). A comparison of the problems of happy and unhappy adolescents indicated that the problems of these two groups are similar. Those who are unhappy do not have problems that are peculiar to them but rather their unhappiness stems from the fact that they make poorer adjustments to their problems than do happy individuals (Symonds, 1937a).

The happy adolescent is concerned with facing reality and with affairs outside himself. By contrast, the unhappy adolescent's concern is centered around his own personal problems, his intimate relationships with others, and his personal unhappiness. Because they have not been able to solve the new and difficult problems that adolescence brings into their lives, the unhappy adolescents remain unhappy longer than those who make more successful adjustments and, in many instances, they will carry their unhappiness into the adult years.

CHAPTER 10

The "Mature" Adult

Of all mammals, modern man alone is unequipped to assume an independent role after attaining his "major physiological maturity" (Sherif and Cantril, 1947). The human individual is sexually mature at some time between the ages of twelve and sixteen years; he is intellectually mature between the ages of fourteen and sixteen years; and his education is complete or nearly complete a year later. He is not, however, given the legal status of an adult until he is twenty-one years old. By that time, it is assumed that he will attain maturity in all aspects of his development.

An "adult," in the strictest sense of the word, is an individual who has grown to mature size. It is assumed that this will be accompanied by maturity of behavior. An adult is not necessarily a paragon who never slips back into immaturity, but rather one who makes mature responses most of the time (Cole, 1944). Few adults in our culture are mature in every respect. Most of them revert to childish or adolescent behavior from time to time. As a result, their behavior is characterized by a combination of mature and immature responses.

As the body grows and develops, it matures functionally. The acquisition of functions is correlated in sequence and tempo with fairly definite life stages. Each successive age period in the developmental pattern is accompanied by striking changes in emotional attitudes, social adjustments, occupational interests, and life ambitions (Doll, 1938). Since the individual can function only as a total personality, the attainment of adult status must be postponed until *all* the major lines of growth have been completed. Complete sexual gratification, for example, demands more than physiological maturity. The emotional development and the social and economic independence that go with a total adult personality are also required (Ausubel, 1950).

Effective operation of earlier-maturing functions is impeded by delay in the maturation of related functions, and the rate of the earlier-maturing functions may even be retarded because of the slower development of other functions. This brings about a delay in the attainment of adult status which is found in few cultures except that of present-day America. The individual, from the time he was a child, expected that he would be treated as an adult when he attained sexual and physical maturity. It is a rude awakening for

305

him when he discovers that adult status will be withheld for a number of years. This causes many frustrations and leads to much of the unhappiness and discontent characteristic of adolescents in our culture (Ausubel, 1950).

DETERMINING MATURITY

Primitive Cultures. Among primitive peoples, there are definite standards of what constitutes a mature person. While these standards may vary from group to group, each group formulates its own standards and then subjects its members to tests to determine their fitness to be accorded the status of adulthood. These tests are part of the *puberty rites,* or initiation ceremonies, that are part of the ritual for most primitive tribes. In these puberty rites, the qualities considered most important in an adult are put to test by the elders of the tribe. Until the tests are successfully passed, the status of adulthood is withheld.

While the purpose of puberty rites is much the same for all tribes, namely, to test the individual's readiness and fitness to assume the rights and responsibilities of an adult in that group, the forms the tests take differ from tribe to tribe. Because strength, endurance, and courage are considered by most tribes to be the essential qualities of a male adult, boys are given tests to determine whether, when they reach the age of puberty and are sexually mature, they have attained psychological maturity as well. In these tests, the qualities of a man are tested by such measures as knocking out of teeth; cutting off parts of the hair or shaving the head; circumcision; tattooing; laceration; fasting; and torture with heat, thirst, hunger, or exposure. Frequently the youth are sent out to hunt wild animals alone or are sent on dangerous expeditions without adult aid.

To make the break with childhood significant to the youth, these rites usually take the form of elaborate ceremonials witnessed by all the adult men of the tribe as well as by other initiates. Their solemn, awe-inspiring form adds to their purpose of making the young members of the tribe realize that adult status will not automatically be theirs. They must prove that they are worthy of this status. Passing of the traditional tests gives the youth the privileges of adopting the hair styles, bodily ornamentations, clothing, and of carrying weapons like the other adults of the tribe. With this change in appearance comes a change in the tribe's attitude toward him. Now he is an adult and, as such, he is expected to act as an adult and not revert to childish ways.

Because the position of girls in primitive cultures is less important than that of boys, not all tribes have puberty rites for girls. The mature woman's role in primitive cultures is usually limited to that of wife and mother. For this role, girls receive preparation throughout childhood by helping their mothers. Then, at the time of her menarche, or first menstruation, it is customary for the pubescent girl to be segregated from her family and from the rest of the tribe. Upon her return, she is presented to the tribe in ceremonials in which the family makes it known that she is now ready for marriage. In these ceremonials, some tribes give the girl tests of womanly skills. If she passes the tests, she is permitted to signify her mature status by styles of hairdress and body ornamentation similar to those of the women of the tribe. Like the boy, she is then accepted by the tribe as a mature woman and is expected to behave in accordance with her new status.

Failure to pass the puberty tests on the part of either boy or girl brings disgrace both to the individual and to the entire family. This disgrace takes the form of sending the young person back to the family where he is treated as a child. He is denied the privilege of wearing the insignia of an adult and of taking part in any of the tribal affairs reserved for adults. Because every child knows what disgrace would befall him if he should fail to pass his puberty tests and because every family feels that failure would reflect seriously upon the family social status and prestige, there is strong motivation on the part of families to prepare their children adequately for these tests. When passing tests is a prerequisite to adult status, there is no tendency on the part of parents to encourage their children to remain dependent upon them.

Civilized Cultures. By contrast with the elaborate preparation for maturity among primitive peoples, *civilized peoples* of today neglect this aspect of child training. This is especially true in present-day America where only in the higher socioeconomic groups is there anything comparable to the puberty ceremonies of primitive tribes. The "coming-out" party of the debutante is a method of indicating to the community that a girl is no longer a child but is now ready for matrimony (Bossard and Boll, 1948). The modern coming out, however, differs markedly from the puberty ceremonies of primitive tribes. While there is preparation for this important event in the girl's life, the preparation is limited to teaching her how to behave in social situations. No attempt is made to prepare her for assuming the role of wife and mother. Furthermore, lack of social success does not bring disgrace to the girl or loss of family prestige, as it does when a member of a primitive tribe fails a puberty test. It is not a test of maturity, but rather a measure of her ability to make successful adjustments in a limited type of social situation.

In the case of boys, there is no experience comparable to that of the puberty rites of the primitive youth. While the boy is expected to grow up and "act his age," there is little preparation for manhood other than for his chosen vocation. When he reaches the age at which our culture says he is legally mature, he automatically receives all the rights and privileges of an adult, without any form of assessment of his readiness to assume these responsibilities. To complicate matters even further, during the growth years there are no standard criteria of what behavior one could normally expect of him. There is no social stigma attached to failure to come up to these standards. Hence, he has no real motivation to prepare himself for maturity and, in the absence of tests to see whether or not he comes up to social expectations, he frequently is unaware of the fact that he is immature (Benedict, 1938; Ausubel, 1948).

MALADJUSTED vs. WELL-ADJUSTED ADULTS

Studies of *maladjusted individuals* have shown that at every age they are immature as compared with their better adjusted contemporaries. Their immature behavior comes not from intellectual inferiority but from over-dependence on adult guidance and help. They are "young for their ages" as compared with their more mature and, hence, better adjusted contemporaries. The unemancipated adult, for example, has been found to be timid, disinclined to go out socially, rebellious, uncooperative, prone to homesickness, and selfish in his motives (Conklin, 1936). He asks special consideration from his employer, he drifts from occupation to occupation, he has tantrums, he refuses to leave the parental roof and, if he marries, he is likely to marry a person old enough to be his parent (Hollingworth, 1928). Some maladjusted adults are helplessly dependent upon others; others make dramatic over-compensations to cover up social and emotional attachments to home and parents (Cole, 1944).

From studies of the maladjusted adults, it has become apparent that they differ radically from well-adjusted adults in certain areas of their behavior. It is possible, therefore, to build up standards from such comparisons and indicate what traits a mature person must have if he is to make good social adjustments and the relative importance of the different criteria that are used to indicate maturity. A *well-adjusted adult* is a mature adult. He gets along well in all types of situations and with all types of people. This is in contrast to the immature adult who is so poorly adjusted that he has difficulties in getting along wherever he is or with whomever he is because his behavior is on a lower level of development than theirs. To describe fully a well-adjusted adult in our present-day culture, Lawton (1951) has given 20 characteristic forms of behavior normally found in well-adjusted adults. They are as follows:

1. The well-adjusted person is both able and willing to assume responsibilities appropriate to his age.

2. The well-adjusted person participates with pleasure in experiences belonging to each successive age level. He neither holds on to those of an earlier period nor anticipates those of a later period.

3. The well-adjusted person willingly accepts the experiences and responsibilities pertaining to his role or position in life, even though he may object to the role or position.

4. The well-adjusted person attacks problems that require solution. He does not find means to evade them.

5. The well-adjusted person enjoys attacking and eliminating obstacles to his development and happiness, after he has convinced himself that they are real, not imaginary obstacles.

6. The well-adjusted person can make decisions with a minimum of worry, conflict, advice-seeking, and other forms of running-away behavior.

7. The well-adjusted person abides by a choice he has made until new factors of crucial importance enter the picture.

8. The well-adjusted person finds his major satisfactions in accomplishments and experiences in real life, not in the realm of daydreams.

9. The well-adjusted person's thinking is a blueprint for action, not a device for delaying or escaping action.

10. The well-adjusted person learns from his defeats instead of finding excuses for them.

11. The well-adjusted person does not magnify his successes nor extend their applications from the areas in which they originally occurred.

12. The well-adjusted person knows how to work when working and how to play when playing.

13. The well-adjusted person can say "No" to situations which, over a period of time, run counter to his best interests even though they may provide temporary satisfactions.

14. The well-adjusted person can say "Yes" to situations that will ultimately aid him even though they may be momentarily unpleasant.

15. The well-adjusted person can show his anger directly when injured and act in defense of his rights with indignation and action that are appropriate in kind and amount to the injury.

16. The well-adjusted person shows his affection directly and gives evidence of it in acts that are fitting in amount and kind.

17. The well-adjusted person can endure pain and emotional frustration whenever it is not in his power to alter the cause.

18. The well-adjusted person has his habits and mental attitudes so well organized that he can quickly make necessary compromises called for by difficulties he meets.

19. The well-adjusted person can bring his energies together and concentrate them on a single goal he is determined to achieve.

20. The well-adjusted person does not try to change the fact that life is an endless struggle. Instead, he knows that the person who fights himself least will have the most strength and the best judgment left for the outside battle. (Abbreviated from pp. 213–214.)

WHY PSYCHOLOGICAL MATURITY IS ESSENTIAL

There was a time in the history of civilization when youthful vigor and strength were more important than the wisdom and experience that come from maturity. But such is no longer the case. In a peaceful civilization, where the main life pursuits are centered around production and distribution of what has been produced, strength and vigor are far less important than judgment and initiative. The successful individual in modern civilized life

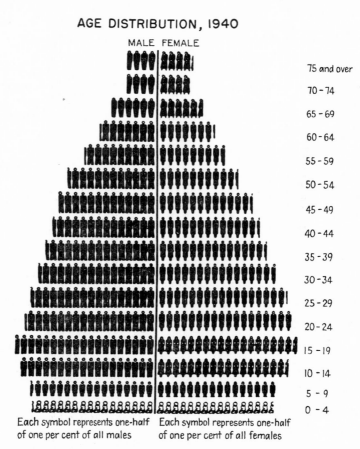

AGE DISTRIBUTION, 1940

FIG. 44. Age and sex distribution of the population in 1940. The small proportions at ages 0–14 reflect declining birth rates, low mortality rates, and the great decline in marriages during the depression years. (*Based on data of L. K. Frank, Human conservation. Washington, D.C.: National Resources Planning Board, 1943. From F. K. Shuttleworth, The adolescent period: a graphic atlas, Monogr. Soc. Res. Child Develpm., 1949, 14, No. 1. Used by permission.*)

must not only have superior mental capacities; he must also harness what abilities he has so that he can use them to the greatest possible advantage.

Furthermore, with the advancement of science, human life has been prolonged. Today the entire life span is longer than it ever was in the history of the world and each developmental age is likewise longer. The period of adulthood, when taken alone or in combination with old age, is far longer than the period of preparation for life and of the periods of childhood and adolescence combined (see Fig. 44). And because there are more mature people than there are children or adolescents, the pattern of modern life is set for the mature, not for the immature. Hence, if an individual is to succeed in a culture where the pattern stresses maturity, he must be mature not only in body but also in his characteristic behavior patterns.

In spite of the demands for maturity of behavior, there is a tendency for the modern generations to be less mature for their years than their parents or grandparents were at comparable ages. They have knowledge superior to that of their parents or grandparents because of superior educational and cultural advantages but, in the areas of initiative, self-reliance, and independence, modern youth is behind the youth of past generations. This is not so much the fault of modern youth as it is a product of their home environments and the culture of modern American society. The demands of the cultural environment in which the individual lives play an important role in determining how mature he will be. This is well illustrated in the case of sex differences in degree of maturity. In our culture, the demands on men for maturity of behavior are greater than on women. As a result, men as a group display a higher level of maturity than do women (Bernreuter, 1933).

OBSTACLES TO MATURITY

In spite of the demands for maturity and the recognition of the need for maturity if the individual is to be well-adjusted to life and hence successful, there are many obstacles to the attainment of this desired goal. Of the many obstacles, the following are the most important:

Tendency on the Part of Parents to Encourage Dependency. In days when life was more difficult than it is today, every member of the family was expected to shoulder his share of the burden as soon as he was capable of doing so. There was too much to be done to expect the parents to do it all. As a result of carrying burdens of a mature sort, children grew up into capable, responsible adults. By contrast, modern youth is growing up in a nation where nearly everything is done with push buttons and can openers. With modern knowledge of contraceptives and the high cost of living, American families of today are voluntarily kept small. Hence the work involved in homemaking is even further reduced. As families grow smaller, more time and attention can be devoted to each child. The mother of today has time to do things for her children which mothers in the past could not do.

Stress on the Importance of Happiness in Childhood Has Led to Indulgence. Most parents are anxious for their children to have a happy, carefree childhood, especially if their own childhoods were unhappy or if they had to assume responsibilities of a heavy, confining nature. Under such conditions, they bend over backward to give their children what they did not have and they often overdo it. Then, too, educators and scientists have stressed the fact that a child is a child and you cannot expect adult behavior from him. Far too often, this has been so misinterpreted that parents expect less than the child is actually capable of. Instead of looking upon childhood as a period of preparation for adult life, overzealous parents have regarded it as an end in itself and have lost sight of the importance of laying a sound foundation for adult life at this time.

Lack of Motivation on the Individual's Part. Many young people have little or no motivation to become mature. True, they want the rights and privileges that accompany maturity but they do not want to accept the responsibilities that maturity brings. Having seen the sacrifices and hard work of their parents, they are anxious to avoid similar experiences. The youth is often disillusioned by the marital discord he sees in his own home or in the homes of friends, and he discovers from afterschool jobs or from what he hears that life in the business world is often nothing but a hard and unrewarded grind. Is it any wonder, then, that he is disillusioned and would like to avoid putting himself in a position where he too would face such realities? (Frank, 1944.)

TIME WHEN MATURITY IS ESTABLISHED

While an individual may receive the rights and privileges of maturity on his twenty-first birthday, that alone does not make him mature. Whether or not he will measure up to the status of a mature person will depend to a large extent upon the training and preparation he has had. A comparison of a group of well-adjusted individuals with a similar group of poorly adjusted individuals revealed marked differences in their home lives and in parent-child relationships during childhood years. The outstanding characteristics of the well-adjusted individuals' home lives, such as happy homes and recreations shared by the whole family, were not to be found in the home lives of poorly adjusted individuals (Stout and Langdon, 1951). Studies of orphan children or children without a stable home environment have shown how important it is for a child to have a source of "good identification" in order to achieve maturity. When the child has no stable or permanent individuals to serve as adult models, as is true of institutional cases, he will copy "chance" individuals. This has been shown to lead to forms of behavior, such as extremes of regressive behavior, which make the attainment of maturity impossible (Holmes, 1951).

The individual who grows up in a large family has experiences and training that fit him to become more mature than the individual has who comes from a small family. Some of the advantages of coming from a large family are (Bossard and Sanger, 1952):

1. The *ability to adjust* to changes in role, in status, and in responsibilities.

2. *Cooperation.* All members must work together, must learn to organize and submit to authority.

3. *Specialization* so that one becomes proficient and confident of his particular ability.

4. *Discipline* in a large family is frequently in the hands of older siblings who, for the most part, are less tolerant than parents. The child soon learns to toe the mark and to conform to rules and regulations.

5. There is no opportunity for *overprotection* in a family where there are many children. Each child must learn to do things for himself as soon as he can.

Adjustment problems of freshmen college girls have been found to be directly related to parental patterns. The most common problems the girls experienced and their relationship to home influences cited by the girls were *homesickness* resulting from lack of parental affection, overprotection, and catering to personal whims and caprices; *oversolicitousness,* excessive caution, and constant vigilance on the part of mothers which make adjustments difficult for girls when they are away from home; *parental domination by remote control* which often brings about maladjustments when girls use their new freedom unwisely; and *incompatibility with parental views* which may cause mental stress on the part of the girl or the use of subterfuges to enable her to do what she wants without her parents' knowledge (Jameson, 1940).

While other factors in the individual's life experiences may contribute to the degree of maturity he shows when he reaches adulthood, there is little question about the fact that the major causes of immaturity are the type of training he received at home, parental attitudes toward him and his interests, and the degree of motivation he is encouraged to have. No matter how strongly a school may encourage independence on the part of its students, and no matter how many rights, privileges, and responsibilities the students may have, a student whose home environment encourages dependency will measure unfavorably with students whose home environments carry through the same kind of training the child is receiving at school.

CRITERIA OF MATURITY

To be a truly mature individual, the adult must be mature in all areas of his behavior. Until recently, there have been no definite and specific standards of what constitutes maturity in different areas. Now, however, attempts are being made to determine just what maturity in a given area of behavior means. This has been done by observing and measuring individuals who are rated as "mature" and then comparing their characteristic behavior with that of individuals who are rated as "immature." From these studies, we now have standards of a fairly definite and predictable sort.

PHYSICAL MATURITY

Different parts of the body reach their mature levels of development at different times. This holds true for size and proportions as well as for functioning. The brain is nearly as large as it will be before puberty sets in. But there is still a considerable amount of internal development to take place and, because of this, the functional level of the brain does not reach maturity

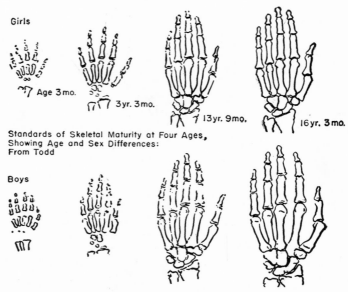

Standards of Skeletal Maturity at Four Ages,
Showing Age and Sex Differences:
From Todd

FIG. 45. Ages and sex differences in ossification of the hand and wrist. (*Unpublished material of Nancy Bayley traced from illustrations in T. W. Todd, Atlas of skeletal maturation. St. Louis: Mosby, 1937. From F. K. Shuttleworth, The adolescent period: a graphic atlas, Monogr. Soc. Res. Child Develpm., 1949, 14, No. 1. Used by permission.*)

until the middle or late teens. Measurements of different bones indicate that the skeleton stops growing at an average age of eighteen years. Final weight for the mature body, on the other hand, is not attained until the early twenties. Tissues other than bones continue to develop after the bones have reached their mature size. The third molars, or "wisdom teeth," for example, frequently do not erupt until the late teens or early twenties. While the secondary sex characteristics are normally mature in size and functioning in the late teens, the sex organs proper may not be mature in size for a year or two later. Physical maturity, as shown in the ossification of the bones of the hand and wrist, is illustrated in Fig. 45.

Effects on Behavior. It is assumed that when the individual becomes mature in size and functioning, especially of the sexual apparatus, he will automatically become mature in his outlook on life and in the quality of his be-havior. This popular concept is frequently expressed in the admonition to children and adolescents, "Act your age." Observations of behavior of pre-pubescent and postpubescent boys and girls have revealed that there is un-questionably a marked change in their interests and behavior after sexual maturity has been completed or nearly completed. This change is shown not in their behavior toward members of the opposite sex alone but in the general quality of their behavior in all social situations (Leal, 1929, 1931; Stone and Barker, 1939).

These changes occur not only because of physical and glandular changes that accompany sexual maturing but also because of the individual's changed concept of self. The boy or girl who has reached mature or nearly mature stature and who looks like an adult thinks of himself as an adult. He, there-fore, begins to regard his former patterns of behavior as "childish" and to feel that he must now show the world that he is no longer a child but an adult. The keen sensitivity of adolescents to public opinion and their strong desire to win social approval act as powerful sources of motivation to changed patterns of behavior on the part of the individual.

The glandular changes that accompany sexual maturity likewise influence the quality of the individual's behavior. When a comparison of sexual ma-turity with maturity of behavior in boys was made, it was found that there was a significant relationship between the developmental age of the boys and their physical measurements. This is actually due to the presence of the sex hormone in the blood stream. Furthermore, it is possible that physical growth inspires greater maturity of conduct, as may be seen by the fact that boys feel they must act in accordance with their size and general physical develop-ment (Rauth and Furfey, 1932).

An interesting comparison of two groups of boys, one of whom was early maturing and the other late maturing showed that the early-maturing group, because of their mature bodies, was accepted and treated by adults as more mature than their contemporaries who were slower in maturing. As a result, they acted in accordance with social expectancy and behaved in a more mature manner. The late-maturing group, by contrast, behaved in an im-mature manner because they were treated as such and they were not expected to act in a more mature manner. Furthermore, because they felt the need to compensate for their physical disadvantage, they often strove for attention and this added to their immature forms of behavior (Jones and Bayley, 1950).

INTELLECTUAL MATURITY

From genetic studies of large groups of individuals, it has been fairly definitely established that for the child of average intelligence, the mental development reaches its mature level between the ages of thirteen and fifteen years; for the child of superior intelligence, the mental development does not reach its mature level until some time between the ages of sixteen and twenty-five years. The criteria used to determine intellectual maturity are:

Maturity of Interests. An important area in which intellectual maturity reveals itself is in the interests of the individual. As has been shown in the preceding chapters of this book, the interests of the individual change from year to year. This change comes partly from physical changes, especially at the time of puberty, partly from the growth of intelligence and the accompanying development of understanding, and partly from the broadening of experiences that comes with growing up. An individual who, at maturity, retains interests characteristic of an earlier stage of development may be regarded as "immature" in that area of his development.

"Interest maturity," according to Strong (1933), "refers to the quantitative measurement of change of interests with age." It is a measure of the intellectual maturity of the individual. In the case of men, interests remain essentially the same from the ages of twenty-five to fifty-five years. While some interests grow stronger and some weaker with advancing years, the interests themselves are similar throughout this period. Before maturity, between the ages of fifteen and twenty-five years, there is a noticable change in interests. *Stability of interest* is thus a characteristic of intellectual maturity.

The intellectually mature individual shows a keen interest in current problems. This interest is displayed not only in discussing such problems with others but also in informing himself about the correct facts relating to these problems. The intellectually immature individual, by contrast, is primarily interested in problems that are directly related to himself and his personal needs. This transfer from subjective to objective interests comes with intellectual maturity. Frequently even before adolescence is over, the individual has an awareness of and an interest in problems of international, national, or community importance. Definite opinions about such problems as child labor, employment of married women, and wages show an interest and thoughtful consideration which is not seen in cases when individuals claim they have "no opinion" or say they are "not interested" (Bell, 1938).

Maturity of Attitudes. An intellectually mature individual can and will change and modify his attitudes should he realize that his attitudes are narrow, biased, or even incorrect. The intellectually immature individual, by contrast, will cling to an attitude developed earlier in life, even though there is evidence to indicate that this attitude is not in accordance with his more mature level of intellectual development. The intellectually mature individual is not swayed by propaganda. In spite of convincing and persuasive speakers, he will cling to a given attitude if he is convinced that it is right. The individual who can be swayed by propaganda, by contrast, displays an intellectual immaturity generally characteristic of children or adolescents who, because of feelings of insecurity regarding their knowledge and points of view, are easily swayed by those whose prestige is high or who speak or write in a convincing fashion.

An intellectually immature individual is likely to have opinions similar to those of his parents, teachers, or intimate friends. The intellectually mature individual, on the other hand, will frequently have opinions that differ radically from those with whom he comes in close contact, such as his family or friends, if he believes their opinions are narrow and biased. Personal opinions are, on the whole, more likely to be immature than are opinions about social and economic conditions where there is more likelihood that they will be discussed and a broader, more mature point of view obtained (Rosander, 1939; Remmers and Weltman, 1947). As a result of higher education, combined with opportunities for frank and free discussions relating to problems about which the individual may have fairly definite attitudes and opinions, there is likely to be a liberalizing of these opinions (Jones, 1936).

Freedom from Superstitious Beliefs. Superstitions are unfounded beliefs, passed down from generation to generation and accepted uncritically by each subsequent generation. The more superstitions the individual clings to, in spite of educational advantages, the more intellectually immature he is. While the individual is still young and gullible, it is logical that he should accept the superstitious beliefs of his parents or contemporaries in an uncritical fashion. But, as he grows older and learns from courses in science and in history that such beliefs are totally without sound foundation, he should be willing to discard these beliefs. The intellectually mature individual is free, or almost completely free, from superstitious beliefs. Clinging to such beliefs and acting in accordance with them is an indication of intellectual immaturity.

Education alone is not enough to decrease the number of superstitious beliefs the individual holds. While education may give the individual information that is in direct contradiction to such beliefs, there is still a tendency to cling to them. Girls, of the whole, are more superstitious than boys at all ages (Lundeen and Caldwell, 1930; Caldwell and Lundeen, 1934; TerKeurst, 1939). College education does, it has been found, help the individual to free himself from superstitious beliefs, especially those relating to good and ill fortune and to foretelling of the future. Seniors are, however, more open-minded about all superstitions than are freshmen (Dudycha, 1933a, 1934). College education is too broad and general to break down superstitious beliefs completely, though it tends to develop a skepticism which the individual may apply to beliefs that seem illogical and unfounded when his scientific knowl-edge is in direct contradiction to these beliefs (Valentine, 1936). The intellectually mature individual will have such a pronounced degree of skepticism that he will either discard all beliefs that are unfounded or in direct contradiction to scientific knowledge or he will withhold all opinions until he has positive proof to prove or disprove such beliefs. He will not accept them in an uncritical manner.

Self-appraisal. The intellectually mature individual will be able to see himself as others see him and to appraise his abilities and disabilities with reasonable accuracy. Regardless of how much he may wish to be different, he will not engage in wishful thinking but will face facts realistically. Unlike the child who sees himself as he would like to be and is then hurt and angry when he discovers that others do not see him as he sees himself, the mature adult will look at himself fairly and squarely, even if what he sees is not to his liking. From competition with others, in school, on the athletic field, and in social activities, the individual gradually builds up a realistic concept of himself, with his abilities and disabilities seen in their true proportions.

An intellectually immature adult, by contrast, will refuse to face reality because it is painful for him to do so. He may, like the child, continue to see himself as he would like to be and literally shut his eyes to any weaknesses he may have. As a result of this, he can continue to be happy so long as he does not compete on equal terms with others. And he avoids this whenever possible to maintain his delusion of grandeur. Other immature individuals see their faults but exaggerate them out of all proportions, thus giving themselves an excuse to complain and bid for the sympathy and attention of others whom they regard as more fortunate than they.

An analysis of vocational aspirations over a period of 7 years, from the sixth through the twelfth grades, showed that both boys and girls were able to appraise their abilities with a fairly mature outlook even during their junior high school years. More than three-quarters of the boys and girls, realizing their limitations, maintained that they would be satisfied to be "happy, ordinary persons with a good job," while only a small percentage said they wanted to be "very great" persons or "one of the leaders" in their home town. Girls, even more than boys, had a realistic concept of themselves to the point where they realized that being a great personage was a remote possibility for them and, therefore, they were content with the idea that they could be happy even though average in ability (Jones, 1943).

While studies of self-appraisals in different areas are limited, there is evidence from the behavior of individuals at different age levels that the individual gradually becomes more realistic in his self-appraisals as he grows older. It is easier to be realistic about some areas of abilities than about others and, as result, self-appraisals in such areas will reach a mature level sooner than in more personal areas. This is true of vocational aspirations as contrasted with the more personal and self-gratifying aspiration to be popular not only with members of one's own sex but also with members of the opposite sex. An individual may have a very mature self-appraisal about his vocational abilities but an equally immature one regarding his popularity, especially with members of the opposite sex. A truly mature individual must be realistic in his self-appraisals in all areas of his abilities, personal as well as those that are less personal.

EMOTIONAL MATURITY

An emotionally mature individual is one whose emotional behavior is comparable to that of a normal adult. More specifically, emotional maturity is "freedom from narcissism and from ambivalence; in other terminology, it is release from egocentrism, the achievement of socialized impulses, of insight; emotional acceptance of the reality principle and an 'analyzed' condition are also approximate synonyms" (Willoughby, 1932).

Criteria. Because it is difficult to know just what constitutes a "normal adult," so far as his emotional behavior is concerned, a number of attempts have been made to give specific criteria of emotional maturity. Three are especially significant and worthy of serious consideration. According to Hollingworth (1933), the mature person is capable of *partial response,* whereas an emotionally immature person reacts in an all-or-none manner; he can *delay* an overt emotional response, while the immature individual "cannot wait"; and he gives an *integrated response* in which his emotional reaction has reference to total character, as contrasted to the child who reacts in a fragmentary manner, without control from character.

Cole (1944) has suggested three criteria of emotional maturity. They are:

1. *The Ability to Bear Emotional Tension.* The emotionally mature individual selects a convenient time and place for letting off emotional steam and a socially acceptable outlet. This enables him to inhibit emotional reactions. The child or the emotionally immature individual, by contrast, "blows up" when he is angry, jealous, or frightened, letting go at the time the emotional stimulus is present. While every individual must have an outlet for a strong emotion sooner or later, whether the outlet be direct or indirect, the emotionally mature individual selects the appropriate time and place for this.

2. *Indifference toward the Kinds of Emotional Stimuli That Give Rise to Childish or Adolescent Emotionality.* The emotionally mature individual learns to ignore many of the stimuli that formerly aroused his emotions and responds mainly to stimuli that are serious in nature. By contrast, the immature individual becomes angry about superficial matters, has his feelings easily hurt, and takes things personally when he is criticized.

3. *Outgrowth of Adolescent Moodiness and Sentimentality.* The emotionally mature individual is stable in his emotional responses. This contrasts with the emotionally immature individual who has a tendency to swing from one mood to another, to have marked "ups and downs" for relatively no reason, and to have strong sentiments that literally sweep him off his feet.

Solomon (1948) has given the following basic features of emotional maturity together with ages at which such maturity can be expected to be achieved:

1. *Independence* (emotional independence from parents) which normally comes at the age of eighteen years but which may come prematurely in rejected children or in those with overbearing parents. It comes later, if ever, in cases of abnormal parent fixation, oversolicitude of parents, or "smother love."

2. *Realism* which lies in the middle of the road between overoptimism and overpessimism. The age when this type of emotional maturity is achieved has not yet been determined.

3. *Self-control* which gradually increases up to the ages of twenty to forty years.

The different criteria of emotional maturity, as given above, all stress emotional control in the form of control over emotional responses and in learning not to respond emotionally to stimuli where no emotional reaction is justified or necessary to physical or mental well-being. Because learning in any area is a slow and difficult process, the individual must have adequate time to achieve success along these lines. Furthermore, there must be adequate motivation. So long as parents will tolerate childish emotional outbursts, the young child has little motivation to develop any control over his emotions. This motivation is generally present when he enters school or when he starts to play with other children who, he soon discovers, will not tolerate his emotional outbursts as his parents do.

Aids to Emotional Maturity. There are a number of aids which have proved to be beneficial in the attainment of emotional maturity, the most important of which are:

CONTROL OF ENVIRONMENT. Controlling the environment so as to eliminate as many frustrating experiences as possible does wonders to keep childish and adolescent emotional reactions to a minimum. As was pointed out above, the matter of control of environment becomes an individual responsibility when the adult years are reached. When an adult finds the environment in which he lives or works is proving to be a source of constant irritation and frustration, he can generally change his environment or change the elements of the environment which are proving to be most annoying to him. A worker, for example, need not stay in a job where the working conditions are not to his liking. The training and ability that enabled him to get that job will likewise enable him to get another job. And, when the pressures of emotional tension are removed, his chances of success will be greatly increased.

IMPROVEMENT OF HEALTH. Any unfavorable physical condition, no matter how trivial it may prove to be, is likely to be a predisposing cause of emotional tension. Until this cause is corrected, it will be difficult for the individual to maintain emotional calm and to keep on an even emotional keel. Headaches, digestive upsets, or actual illness are all controllable now with the aid of medical science. The individual who wants to attain emotional maturity owes it to himself to seek medical aid for any physical disturbance he may have and to make it his business to keep in the best of health at all times.

ELIMINATION OF FATIGUE. Fatigue, like physical disturbances, predisposes the individual to emotional tension and thus militates against the attainment of emotional maturity. But, as is true of poor health conditions, fatigue is and should be controllable. Regulation of amount of exercise according to one's age and occupation, adequate amount of sleep, elimination of eyestrain, and elimination of any physical condition which is normally accompanied by more or less constant fatigue, such as diseased tonsils and adenoids or anemia, will all help the individual to be in a state of readiness to meet emotion-provoking situations in a more mature fashion than would be possible if the fatigue remained unchecked.

ELIMINATION OF PRESSURE. A person who works under pressure is not only fatigued from his experience but he is also predisposed to emotional outbursts of an immature type. While emergencies can and do arise at different times in the life of an individual, when working under pressure becomes essential, these times are relatively few and far between. For the most part, the individual who works under pressure is inefficient. He does not plan his time and work systematically nor does he get started on the job in time to be able to work at a congenial pace. The introduction of efficient methods of work and a better time concept would eliminate the unnecessary pressures from his daily life and thus free him from the emotional tension these pressures invariably give rise to.

REALISTIC LEVELS OF ASPIRATION. Many individuals, both children and adults, have an unrealistic concept of their abilities and disabilities. Their aims or goals are thus often far beyond their reach, no matter how hard they may try to attain them. The result is constant frustrations with the accompanying disappointments and disillusionments. Like the child, nothing makes an adult angry so quickly and so violently as not to be able to do what he wants to do and is striving to do. If, however, the adult whose immature emotional state stems from reaching for the moon would revise his concept of his abilities and formulate levels of aspiration within his reach, he would be able to eliminate many of the anger-provoking situations from his life.

SOCIAL INSIGHT AND UNDERSTANDING. Much of the unnecessary emotionality of childhood can be traced to lack of social insight. Owing to his limited ability to reason and his even more limited experiences, the child will often misinterpret social situations and respond to them emotionally when no emotion is justified. This is well illustrated in the jealous reactions of an older child to the care and attention a younger sibling receives. As a child grows older and understands *why* the younger sibling must have more time and attention from his parents than he has, the jealousy he formerly experienced usually disappears. Likewise, many remarks made by others are misinterpreted by children and even by adolescents. A mature adult, on the other hand, should have enough insight to realize that such remarks were probably not meant as they sounded and, hence, there is no cause for offense or hurt feelings.

HARMLESS OUTLETS FOR "EMOTIONAL STEAM." As has been pointed out before, children usually react emotionally to a situation, regardless of whether the time and place are appropriate or not. The mature adult, on the other hand, realizes that untimely emotional outbursts are regarded as "childish" and, as a result, he learns to defer his emotional outbursts until an appropriate time and a suitable place. Because this means deferring an emotional expression, often beyond the time when the individual can successfully keep his emotions under control, the mature adult will learn to use ways of working off "emotional steam" that will be harmless to him and to others while, at the same time, giving him the relief from emotional tension that otherwise would come from a direct emotional outburst. Some of the most widely used and most successful safety valves for emotional tension are strenuous physical exercise, a hearty laugh or cry in socially approved situations, such as at a movie, diverting his attention to some absorbing interest or hobby, or doing manual work in the home, the garden, or in the office.

DEVELOPMENT OF SENSE OF HUMOR. As is true of social insight, a sense of humor or the ability to perceive an element of the comic in a situation regardless of how serious it may be, is lacking in children. Because of this, things often upset them unnecessarily. While adolescents may have a sense of humor when it comes to a situation in which they are not personally involved, few adolescents can laugh at themselves. Until the adolescent gains enough self-confidence and assurance to be able to see humor in any situation, regardless of whether or not he is personally involved, he will continue to react to emotion-provoking situations in a childish manner. The cultivation of a sense of humor, when combined with the development of social insight, will go a long way toward helping a mature adult to reduce his emotional reactions to a minimum and to limit them to situations where such emotional reactions are justified.

SOCIAL MATURITY

Social maturity has been defined as "the growth and development of the individual, conditioned by both internal and external factors, which enables him to adapt himself successfully to his fellow men and to adapt his fellow men to himself." The pattern of social maturity includes the following forms of behavior: group compatibility, kindness and sympathy, efficiency, fair play, emotional adjustability, courtesy and politeness, dependability, neatness and orderliness, self-confidence, cooperation, originality, curiosity, leadership, and cheerfulness (Pechstein and Munn, 1939).

To achieve social maturity, the individual must be mature in different areas of social behavior. Of these areas, the most important are:

Emancipation from Home. Emancipation from home means the ability to stand on one's own feet, make one's own decisions, support one's self and family without assistance and, most important of all, be happy when away from the familiar scenes of childhood. This does not mean rejection of the family by constant criticism of different members of the family or by constant revolt against parents. Nor does it mean indifference to the family. An individual who behaves in this manner to his family is emotionally immature and shows social immaturity as well. A socially mature adult, by contrast, treats the members of his family, whether they be parents, grandparents, siblings, or other relatives, as friends. In the role of a friend, he has understanding, affection, feelings of loyalty and responsibility, respect, and consideration for the different members of his family.

Emancipation from the home is popularly known as "cutting the parental apron strings." Scientifically, it is known as "psychological weaning." A "psychologically weaned" individual is able to get away from family supervision and become an independent individual. In the process of becoming independent, as is true of the physical weaning of a baby, there are often states of depression and emotional outbursts accompanying this new adjustment (Hollingworth, 1928). The longer the individual has depended upon his parents, either physically or psychologically, the harder and longer the adjustment period will be. This is especially true when the individual has grown up in a large family or has been an only child. In the former case, there is likely to be much supervision and bossing not only by parents but also by older siblings. The only child, on the other hand, has not been subjected to sibling bossing but he is likely to have developed feelings of dependence which make it just as hard for him to let go as it is for his parents. Like the child who has grown up in a large family where he has been accustomed to depending upon others, the only child is likewise a victim of too much supervision and finds it hard, therefore, to stand on his own feet. In his attempts to become independent, he will meet many difficulties which will undermine his self-confidence, often to the point where he gives up any further attempt to be independent. Most adolescents, however, before adolescence has passed, have "left home" in their feelings (Hollingworth, 1928).

DIFFICULTIES IN EMANCIPATION. Many years ago, G. Stanley Hall (1904) wrote: "Parents still think of their offspring as mere children, and tighten the rein when they should loosen it." Even today, when parents who are more liberal than were parents at the turn of the century, there is a tendency to hold adolescent boys and girls down when they should be given more freedom, more responsibilities, and more opportunity to learn to be independent. Most parents hate to see their children grow up and go away from them and few are willing to allow them to have their independence when they are old enough or mature enough for this independence. As a result, there is likely to be a deep-rooted objection to parental authority and hatred toward the parents on the part of their children (Wheeler, 1931).

There are many complications of emancipation, the most important of which are (Meyers, 1946):

1. Emancipation requires much sacrifice by parents not only in relinquishing authority but also in self-control and restraints to allow the child to develop and in adjusting to the changed relationship of parent and child.

2. Emancipation is more than a mere letting go by parents. It is the product of positive steps to cultivate responsibility.

3. Emancipation is complicated by small family size.

4. Emancipation should be consummated in a manner that leaves good feelings all around.

5. Emancipation is complicated by the necessary prolongation of economic dependence.

6. There are many factors operating against parental relaxation of controls.

7. Emancipation is made more difficult by a rapidly changing system of values on the adolescent's part.

8. Emancipation is complicated by the intelligent nature of the adolescent.

EMANCIPATION AND PERSONALITY. Emancipation or lack of it leaves a pronounced mark on the individual's personality. Whether or not this mark will be permanent depends to a large extent upon how complete the emancipation is. Comparisons of the personalities of emancipated and unemancipated individuals have revealed differences worthy of serious consideration. Among adolescent boys, those who are most emancipated are superior to those who are least emancipated in possessing a greater sense of personal adequacy and are better integrated in their attitude toward other boys. Emancipation is affected more by such physical characteristics as being taller, heavier, and stronger than the norms for an individual's age than by chronological age (Dimock, 1937).

A comparison of emancipated and unemancipated college men and women revealed that the greatest difference was dependent upon sex. Seventy-two per cent of the emancipated group were men as compared with 28 per cent of women. In intelligence, the emancipated group was somewhat superior, as was true also of age. They had also been away from home in college for a longer time (Sherman, 1948). In a comparison of emancipated and unemancipated college women, the emancipated were found to be more stable emotionally, to be more dominant, less sociable and gregarious, slightly older and more intelligent than the unemancipated women. Little difference between the parents of the emancipated and unemancipated women was found (Sherman, 1948).

Lack of emancipation does not always result in rebellion and hostility toward parents and all adults in authority. During childhood, the unemancipated individual is frequently overactive, talkative, overalert, engages in attention-getting behavior, shows a hunger for affection, and has crushes. Toward puberty, however, he frequently becomes listless and apathetic

(Martin, 1943). The adolescent who is unemancipated may be docile, polite, and easily managed. But, his lack of emancipation affects his social adjustments. He lacks independence and has little self-confidence and few friends. At maturity, the unemancipated individual is frequently unmarried or, if married, has an unsuccessful marriage or is divorced. There is often a strong mother attachment or an open hostility toward the mother along with the attachment (Meyers, 1946).

AGE OF SOCIAL WEANING. While it is generally assumed that psychological weaning takes place between the approximate ages of twelve and twenty years, there is evidence to show that the foundations for this weaning are laid earlier in childhood. The foundations are in the form of short and experimental departures from home, "like the short flights of fledglings away from the nest." One of the ways in which the psychological weaning begins comes from the child's experience in visiting in the homes of other people. From these visits the child is provided with a series of experiences which are beneficial not only in social weaning but also in social learning.

When children and adolescents are prevented by their parents from visiting, even when parents try to compensate for this by inviting friends of the child to their own home, the young people show definite resentment against their elders for denying them this privilege. Those who do visit away from home start early in their lives by going to the homes of relatives for visits ranging in time from a few hours to a few weeks or months. As a result of such experiences, children feel a sense of personal achievement and an opportunity to experiment with freedom. From their visiting experiences, children get an insight into life as it is lived by others and a broadening of their views from experiencing the customs as practiced in other homes. In this way, childhood visiting experiences may be regarded as a step in growing up, in becoming a person, and in being weaned from the parents (Bossard, 1951).

Visiting away from home is not the only way in which psychological weaning can be achieved. Throughout the childhood years, the individual who remains at home or with his parents for the major part of the time can be given freedoms, responsibilities, and out-of-the-home activities that will encourage him to stand on his own feet when he is psychologically capable of doing so. However, knowing that parents are readily available to meet any emergency that may arise, psychological weaning does not take place as quickly or as completely as when the individual is away from the sheltering protection of the home. That is why camps, boarding schools, and colleges prove to be such valuable experiences in growing up.

Duties of Citizenship. A mature individual is a citizen of a community, of a state, and of a country. As such, he has certain obligations to perform. In a democracy, the duties of citizenship are heavier than in a monarchy or any other form of government where citizens have few rights. In childhood, the contributions the individual can make as a citizen are more negative than positive. He is giving his community or country nothing but devotion and loyalty, but he is preparing himself to assume the duties of citizenship when he is legally mature and is granted these rights and privileges. Throughout adolescence, there is generally a livelier interest in community and national affairs than there was when the individual was younger. Now he can make positive contributions in the form of aiding in all sorts of community drives or even in serving his country in time of emergency. At this time, his interest in such affairs leads him to many discussions and arguments which frequently make him see many weaknesses which, in his youthful zeal, he tries to reform.

On the individual's twenty-first birthday, he automatically becomes a citizen, with all the rights and privileges of citizenship. If he is socially mature, he will use these rights and privileges in a positive manner. No longer will he limit himself to obeying the laws or to helping in some of the community activities. He will vote, he will serve on the jury when called, he will defend his country when emergencies arise, and may even act as an elected or appointed public servant (Zachry, 1940). When he sees a need for reform, he will not limit himself to grumblings and criticisms but will take positive steps to bring about the reform. By contrast, the socially immature individual will neglect the duties of citizenship even to the point of not bothering to vote.

The individual who is socially responsible or who has a high level of social maturity so far as his fellow men are concerned has a "deep concern over broader ethical and moral problems, with a strong sense of justice, with a rather high but somewhat rigid set of self-demands and standards, of rejection of privilege or favoritism, an inability to enjoy unearned rewards, an almost excessive emphasis on carrying one's share of burdens and duties, a strong and unflagging sense of confidence in self and in the basic rightfulness of the larger social worlds, and a rejection of the light, trivial, and dangerous" (Gough *et al.*, 1952).

Absence of Prejudice. It is not necessary to like people or to have them as friends to be able to get along with them in business, social, or community life. The socially mature individual makes good social adjustments with all types of people. He accepts an individual for what, not who, he is. Prejudice against an individual because of his race, color, religion, or socioeconomic status is an indication of social immaturity. Many children develop prejudices against certain individuals or groups through imitation of prejudiced attitudes on the part of their parents. Racial prejudice generally undergoes development and reconstruction as the individual passes from childhood to adolescence. When opportunities to learn about people of other racial groups through study or personal contact are given, the individual's racial attitude becomes more desirable. This is especially true of the higher intellectual levels (Minard, 1931). In many instances, racial attitudes are affected unfavorably by racial stereotypes. "Racial prejudice is thus a generalized set of stereotypes of a high degree of consistency which includes emotional responses to race names, a belief in typical characteristics associated with race names, and an evaluation of such typical traits" (Katz and Braly, 1935).

Changes in attitudes where prejudice formerly existed come from such experiences as developments during a war period or familiarity resulting from closer personal contacts with individuals. Whether the change will be away from prejudice or toward greater prejudice will depend largely upon the character of the association or the favorable or unfavorable aspect of the development (Kuhlen, 1941; Zeligs, 1950a). As a general rule, however, individuals become less prejudiced and more liberal in their social attitudes as they leave school and college and come in contact with all types of people in daily life. This is more true for urban individuals than for those living in rural districts (Zeligs, 1950).

Self-reliance. The ability to rely upon one's self should normally replace childish dependency as the individual grows up. The unemancipated individual is, as a result, less self-reliant than is the emancipated one. How self-reliant an individual is will depend largely upon the individual's experiences at home, in school, and with his contemporaries. Self-reliance does not develop overnight. It comes only after a long period of training in learning to be independent. For that reason, if an individual is to be socially mature when he reaches maturity, it is essential that he have an opportunity to develop the ability to stand on his own feet before he acquires the habit of depending upon others for help in meeting the different problems of everyday life.

On the whole, parents are less likely to see the importance of giving children an opportunity to develop self-reliance when they are young than are specialists in child training. Furthermore, their attitudes toward self-reliance are less favorable and, hence, they are less likely to provide the experiences that will encourage the acquisition of this personality trait (Oj'emann, 1934). There is a relationship between the educational status of parents and the degree of favorable attitude they express toward children's freedom (Koch *et al.*, 1934). Older parents favor control over their children more than do younger parents. City parents favor granting most freedom to their children during the adolescent years. Contrary to what one might anticipate, fathers prove to be no stricter than mothers in respect to the amount of freedom they are willing to grant their children (Stott, 1940a).

When an analysis was made of parental attitudes toward the amount of freedom they were willing to grant their adolescent children and the personalities of their children, it was found that a home situation, in which both parents were agreed that adolescents should have considerable freedom from parental domination, was favorable to the development of self-reliance. Adolescents who came from city homes, where parents had a more favorable attitude toward developing independence than had farm parents, proved to be more independent and more self-reliant (Stott, 1940a).

Self-sufficiency. A mature individual can amuse himself and be happy when alone. It is not essential that he be with one of his contemporaries or with a crowd to be happy. As a mature adult, he should be able to amuse himself with reading, radio listening, television, or any hobby he has cultivated and enjoy different forms of recreation alone, such as playing the piano, going to the movies, or engaging in some solitary sport. True, the presence of a friend would add to his enjoyment, but this should not be essential. As a mature individual, he can make adjustments to solitude when solitude is essential. The immature adult, like the child or the adolescent, cannot make such adjustments and is therefore unhappy when circumstances force him into solitude. Instead of using his solitude in a pleasurable manner, he frets and does all that he can to end the solitude as quickly as possible.

Attitude toward Friends. The attitude the individual has toward his friends is an indication of the degree of social maturity that he has achieved. It is objective and far less personal than it was when he was younger. This does not mean that he lacks affection for his friends. On the contrary, what affection he has is of a far deeper, more stable, and more lasting type than one normally finds in the friendships of children or of adolescents. Instead of selecting friends primarily because their relationships with him are emotionally pleasant, or because he hero-worships them on account of some outstanding achievement, as he did when he was younger, the mature adult evaluates people critically and objectively before he establishes a friendship relationship. He accepts their faults openly instead of trying to shut his eyes to them. And he does not criticize his friends for their faults or try to change them as he did when he was an adolescent. He accepts his friends as they are, and likes them in spite of their faults.

Like the adolescent, the mature adult is loyal to his friends. But mature loyalty is not of the blind sort that characterizes friendships among more immature individuals. He is no longer willing to condone behavior that falls far below his standards just because his friends engage in it. Now he is loyal when he feels his friends are misunderstood or mistreated, or when he feels they need his help to meet their difficulties. He is able to differ from his friends in his manner of dress, in his interests, and even in his opinions and still remain friends. He can afford to be an individual, as they can, and still be a devoted friend. And, finally, a mature adult feels that a small circle of intimate friends who are congenial and loyal is worth far more than a large circle of casual acquaintances. He measures "popularity" by the depth and length of friendships, not by the number of friendships.

Socially immature individuals have an attitude toward friends that is characteristic of that of children or of adolescents. They want to be "popular" at any price and, as a result, they try to conform to an accepted pattern they hope will bring them the desired goal. They are willing to go out of their way to "live up to the Joneses" and to court the favor of others by lavish entertaining and expenditure of money. They try to win the favor of those whom they admire because of financial success or social achievement, just as the hero-worshiping adolescent does, and they are willing to accept blindly the qualities in individuals they dislike or distrust if these individuals are "popular" or in the "right crowd."

Group Conformity. Slavish conformity to dress, manners, and actions of the group to which the individual belongs is a sign of social immaturity. So is revolt against the accepted customs and traditions of the group. Going to extremes in what he says, wears, or does comes with revolt against accepted practices of the group. The unconventional extremist, like the strict conformist, is behaving in an immature fashion. A mature individual, on the other hand, conforms not so much because he approves of existing patterns of behavior or because he is afraid not to conform but rather because he realizes that each individual must be willing to fit his individual wishes into the pattern approved by the group as a whole.

SOCIAL IMMATURITY

The socially immature individual can be spotted not only by the poor adjustments he is making to work and social situations but also by certain forms of behavior which, in themselves, are indicative of social immaturity. Of these forms of behavior, the following are the most characteristic of a socially immature individual:

Homesickness. It is to be expected that when a young child goes away from home for the first time, to camp or to visit friends and relatives, he will be homesick. Even older children are frequently homesick when they make their first major break from home to camp or boarding school. But they will quickly adjust to the new situation and be happy if they are socially mature. This is not true of the socially immature individual. He not only does not adjust but his unhappiness increases as time goes on. Back of this unhappiness is a feeling of insecurity accompanied by strong emotional reactions. It does not necessarily mean a strong parent-child relationship nor an abnormally strong love for the parents. In fact, some individuals who suffer from homesickness have looked forward eagerly to leaving home and to having the freedom their parents denied them. But, when they achieve this goal, it does not bring them the happiness they had anticipated. Homesickness is thus an indication of lack of psychological weaning (Jameson, 1940).

Among adolescent girls, homesickness is far more common than among boys. In college girls, it is predisposed by such factors as extreme fondness for the home, people, and social functions; a strong feeling of belonging to and sharing in one's home; the habit of confiding in members of the family and depending on their advice and guidance; and missing the attentions of the local boy friend (Jameson, 1940; McCann, 1941, 1943). College girls who are homesick only once after arriving at college are, on the whole, as socially well adjusted as girls who never experience homesickness. They do, however, show some anxiety and lack of emotional stability. Girls who repeatedly experience homesickness in college show signs of lack of adjustment all around. They come from homes where there is much friction. The home thus "plays a major role as a predisposing factor for homesickness" (Rose, 1947).

Regression. When an individual finds it difficult to adjust satisfactorily to a more mature level of social behavior, he may regress or return to a lower level of social behavior in which he formerly found satisfaction. While regression may occur at any stage in the individual's life, it is most likely to occur during adolescence when adjustments to members of the opposite sex are normally made. Many adolescent boys and girls find these adjustments so difficult and the results so unsatisfactory that they return to the "gang stage" in their social behavior and try to find satisfaction from the companionship of members of their own sex. An immature adult is likely to have the major part of his social contacts with parents, members of his family, or contemporaries of his own sex.

Snobbishness. Normally, an adult develops a tolerant attitude toward all individuals, regardless of their sex, race, creed, color, or socioeconomic status. The prejudices of childhood and adolescence should be overcome and should not affect the quality of his behavior. In the case of the immature adult, on the other hand, prejudice is still strong in adulthood. The immature adult, like the adolescent, will not only try to shun the individual whom he regards as his inferior but he will even go out of his way to show, by word or action, the contempt he holds for this individual, not necessarily as an individual but rather as a member of a group against which he is prejudiced.

Poor Mixer. The socially immature individual is a "poor mixer." He has not learned to get along with reasonable success with all types of people and, like the child or the adolescent, he feels ill-at-ease when he is with any but his intimate friends. Sometimes this comes from lack of opportunity for practice in making social adjustments of all sorts, especially with members of the opposite sex; sometimes it comes from snobbishness or a feeling of superiority on the part of the individual which causes him to shun all except those whom he considers "good enough" for him; and sometimes it comes from marked feelings of personal inadequacy resulting from unsuccessful social contacts during the earlier years of the individual's life.

Lack of Social Skills. An individual normally learns to do what his associates are doing, whether this means playing baseball, dancing, or engaging in social conversations with his friends. The mature adult has developed enough social skills so that he can fit into any group situation and feel confident that he can adjust with reasonable success to this situation. The socially immature individual, on the other hand, lacks the necessary social skills to make good social adjustments. As a result, he feels ill-at-ease in social situations and frequently shuns them. Whether this lack of necessary skills comes from lack of opportunity for learning or from a resistant attitude on the individual's part, the result is much the same. The individual feels out of place in a group and, consequently, makes poor adjustments to the group.

PSYCHOSEXUAL MATURITY

The psychosexually mature individual not only makes good adjustments to members of the opposite sex but he has a healthy attitude toward sex. The individual who is immature in this area of his development shuns members of the opposite sex whenever possible, is ill-at-ease and unhappy when thrown with members of the opposite sex in work or social life, and has an unhealthy attitude toward all aspects of sex behavior and sex relationships. On the whole, in our culture, men achieve psychosexual maturity at an earlier age and in larger numbers than do women.

Pattern of Development. From a detailed study of a large group of women who were mature and those who were immature in their sex attitudes and behavior, it has been possible not only to determine the pattern of normal development and the expected level of development at different ages but also to find out what is responsible for psychosexual immaturity. There are certain practices, attitudes, and experiences which are common among American adolescent girls and women at given ages. Those who come up to these norms may be regarded as "mature" for their age level. Those, on the other hand, who fall below the expected pattern may be regarded as "immature." Variations in the pattern have been found to be *temporal*. They take the form of precocity or immaturity, depending on whether the individual's development is ahead of or behind the expected level of development for that chronological age.

The pattern consists of three major subdivisions, each falling within a range of several years. They are as follows (Landis *et al.*, 1940):

1. *Fifteen- to Seventeen-year-olds.* Psychosexually mature girls for this age have gone out frequently with boys but have not yet had complete sex experience. Their sex experience has been limited to petting. Their sex information is fairly complete but the girl is constrained in discussing such matters with her parents. While still interested in doing things with other girls, she is definitely interested in boys, more in dates than in a serious manner. The psychosexually immature girl, on the other hand, shows no interest in boys and restricts her interests and activities to girl friends or members of the family. She has a definitely unfavorable attitude toward sex which may show itself in complete lack of interest or in disgust toward sexual matters.

2. *Eighteen- to Twenty-one-year-olds.* While the psychosexually mature girl of this age is not yet independent of her family, her activities and associations are mainly outside of the home. She has a fairly complete fund of sex knowledge, has gone out with a number of boys, and feels she is attracted to one of them but is not yet thinking specifically in terms of marriage. Her attitude toward sex is one

of healthy interest. As yet, she is not preoccupied with boys but spends more and more of her time in planning and daydreaming about particular individuals.

The girl of this age who is psychosexually immature has little interest in boys and has had few dates. Her physical contacts with them have been limited to kissing and even this has not been particularly enjoyable to her. She usually has a negative attitude toward all sexual matters. Her sex information was not complete until she was 18 years old nor did she have any strong curiosity about sex. She usually masturbates occasionally and is primarily interested in herself. An extremely immature individual has never had any dates or love affairs. Her sex information is still incomplete and she masturbates frequently or excessively. She is still very closely attached emotionally to her family and is extremely narcissistic. Her attitude toward sex is either one of disgust or apathy.

3. *Twenty-two- to Twenty-five-year-olds.* A psychosexually mature woman has by now completely resolved her family ties and is free from any pronounced signs of narcissism. Her heterosexual intimacies have included some sex play and petting. She is free from any unfavorable sex attitudes. This shows a marked contrast with the psychosexually immature woman of the same age. She has had her first date at 19 years and has gone out with few men since. Physical intimacies with men have rarely gone beyond a kiss. Her sex information is not complete until after she is 18 years old. She may masturbate occasionally and show evidence of narcissism or a poorly resolved family situation. The extremely immature woman has had no dates or attachments to men and has not yet acquired complete sex information. She masturbates frequently or excessively, shows extreme narcissism and a close attachment to her parents.

Causes of Psychosexual Immaturity. Immaturity in this area of life can be more serious for a woman than immaturity in other areas of her development. It will militate against a marriage or, if she does marry, she will not experience the same satisfaction from her sex life as a more mature woman would nor is she likely to make the same success of her marriage as she would if she were more mature in her attitudes and behavior. Furthermore, if she does not marry but devotes her life to a job or career, she will find adjustments to her working conditions and associates difficult if not actually unsuccessful unless her work limits her exclusively to associations with members of her own sex.

In an attempt to discover the underlying causes of psychosexual immaturity, Landis and his associates (1940) made an intensive investigation into the physical and psychological characteristics of a group of extremely immature women. Their investigation revealed three characteristics associated with psychosexual immaturity: *physical underdevelopment, frequent illness during childhood,* and *little curiosity about sex.* The physically underdeveloped women frequently had a tendency toward male characteristics. This suggests that the psychological character of psychosexual immaturity has a "substratum" in the physical make-up of the individual. "Those individuals whose attitudes, experiences, and contacts with other people were of a childish or immature nature showed a tendency toward a childish underdeveloped physique." There was a tendency for those women who had experienced frequent illness during childhood to miss out on the activities of their contemporaries and this led to emotional dependence upon their parents. Lack of curiosity about sex was unquestionably related to lack of normal physical development of a sexual sort.

A study of the love attitudes and behavior of a group of college girls has led to the hypothesis that a girl's adult love attitudes and behavior are influenced by the amount of love she experienced in her early family environment, by the head start or delay of her first heterosexual love experiences, and by the number of friendly social contacts she has with males. Adult heterosexual love relations are importantly conditioned by early family love relationships, especially with the parent of the opposite sex, and also by biological factors and favorable socioeconomic factors (Ellis, 1949). In the case of men, when the father is missing from the home, because of death or divorce, there is a tendency to show a lower level of courtship behavior than is characteristic of men of the same age who come from unbroken homes (Winch, 1949). This may be explained by the fact that the young man in such a position feels an obligation to remain with his mother and, for that reason, there is less advancement in his heterosexual adjustments than there would have been had the family not been broken.

Appropriate Sex Role. The psychosexually mature individual will accept his or her sex role and will try to fulfill this role successfully with minimum resentment toward being a member of that sex. The psychosexually immature individual, on the other hand, will resent being a member of the sex to which he belongs and will either try to assume the role of the other sex or will show bitter resentment against the sex to which he belongs. In our culture, where men unquestionably have many advantages which women of their own intellectual, cultural, or socioeconomic status lack, there is far less resentment and protest on the part of boys and men than on the part of girls and women.

The "masculine protest," or the woman's dissatisfaction with her sex and her striving to achieve the masculine role in society or to revenge herself on society for having been born a woman, makes women aggressive or masculine. Now that business and professional opportunities are opening up for women as was unheard of even a few generations ago, women are able to express their masculine protest in action instead of feeling sorry for themselves or complaining about their lot in life as women of previous generations did.

The masculine protest does not first develop when girls reach sexual maturity or when they achieve the status of a mature woman. It generally traces its origin back to early childhood when cultural mores prescribe the behavior of the little girl and deprive her of many of the privileges that boys of her age and even her family enjoy. The situation is not improved as time goes on. With the onset of puberty, the girl experiences menstruation with all its discomforts, inconveniences, and deprivations. She soon discovers that this is a typically feminine characteristic and that boys have no experience comparable to it.

Furthermore, the mores of the group prescribe more rigidly the girl's behavior after she is sexually mature than do those of boys. A girl discovers that there are many things she cannot do without winning social disapproval and that the very same things, if done by a boy, pass unnoticed or are condoned. A modern woman does not accept without protest the necessity of giving up a career she has worked hard to attain, should she marry, and devoting her time to housework which does not equal her career work in interest and personal satisfaction. Women find men combining marriage and a career while they must choose between the two. Is it any wonder, then, that the masculine protest waxes instead of wanes as time goes on?

When a group of women was asked if, at any time in their lives, they had wanted to be a boy or a man, 61 per cent said that they had wanted to be a boy at some time or other during the early years of their lives. Of this group, 28 per cent had the desire to be a boy before they were twelve years old and the remaining 43 per cent, after they were twelve years old. The reasons they gave for this desire were the social restrictions and customs imposed upon girls and, second, the physical handicap that accompanies being a woman (Landis *et al.,* 1940).

An analysis of the behavior characteristic of women who experience the masculine protest has shown that the most typical reactions consist of masculine forms of behavior, aggressiveness, pleasure derived from putting men at a disadvantage, and a desire to dominate men, either in the home or outside the home. Such women have a competitive attitude toward men, they prefer a career to home activities, and they take pleasure in feeling dominant in the love relationship. They belittle men's importance, they have little real affection for men, even if they marry, nor do they form strong attachments for men.

There is no physical correlate for the masculine protest. Therefore, it is socially conditioned. It is a product of our present culture which gives women equal educational advantages with men and then denies them the rights and privileges in other areas of their lives. As a result, the girl develops into an aggressive, energetic woman who is not satisfied with the typical female role and to whom achievement and social status are very important. Because she is unable to achieve a status in society equal to that of men, she is constantly irritated by being frustrated in the feminine role (Landis *et al.,* 1940).

There is no counterpart to the masculine protest on the part of the typical man. From earliest childhood, he has accepted his sex role willingly and has enjoyed the prestige of being a member of the "stronger sex." He has also enjoyed rights and privileges at all ages that were superior to those of girls of the same ages and, as a result, he had no reason to feel that society was mistreating him. While men occasionally feel that they have the harder lot in life because they must be the breadwinners of the family, there is no desire on their part to be a woman as women so often wish they were men. In this area of psychosexual maturity, men achieve a mature status not only at an earlier age but also in greater numbers than do women.

Religious Maturity

While maturity in the area of religious beliefs and observances is not essential to successful adjustment to life and has not, as a result, been subjected to inquiry as is true of the other areas of maturity described above, it is nevertheless important because it contributes to the individual's happiness. No adult with a childish form of religion can be contented with his beliefs, no matter how satisfactory these beliefs were to him when he was a child. Unless he can revise his religion to meet his more mature needs, that area of his life will be unsatisfactory, sometimes to the point where he rejects all religious beliefs and observances completely.

The brighter the individual, the more essential it is that he attain a satisfactory form of religion as he passes through adolescence and into adulthood. During the time when adolescents normally begin to doubt the religious teachings of their childhood days and are attempting to revise their religious beliefs to be more in keeping with their more mature intellectual status, the individual needs not only encouragement and help to make this revision satisfactorily but, of even greater importance, he must not be made to feel guilty because he has doubted what was taught him when he was younger. When feelings of guilt are strong, the individual will not seek help in this task nor will he allow himself to face the fact squarely that he does not find his childish religion satisfactory to him any more. He may continue to show outward signs of religious acceptance, such as attending church and engaging in prayer, but this is not enough to achieve maturity in this important area of his life.

During the process of religious reconstruction, which normally begins late in adolescence after the intense skepticism and doubt of early adolescence have subsided, it is not unusual for the individual to accept parts of a number of religious beliefs and to reject those parts which seem unsatisfactory to him. By the time he has finished this process of reconstruction, it may be that his religious faith does not actually fit into any of the orthodox faiths from which he has drawn parts of his own faith. As a result, he has a *philosophy of life* which means more to him as the years go on than any particular faith could.

The mature adult attends religious services, not necessarily regularly but often enough to feel that he is a part of the church organization. His attendance is voluntary, not forced by fear, habit, or any other motive of the sort that might prompt the attendance of a more immature individual. He does not necessarily worship in the church of his parents' faith but selects a denomination that meets his own needs, or a church where he feels that the minister gives him something worth while to think about in his sermon. Frequently mature adults select a church more because of the minister than because of the denomination. He engages in prayer if he feels that it is personally beneficial to him, not because of habit or fear of evil consequences if he does not pray. In the reconstructed religion of many mature adults, prayer does not play a role; if it does, the role is of very minor importance. And, finally, the mature adult takes part in different organizations that have a religious or semireligious background.

The *immature* adult, by contrast, may accept the religious faith of his father in much the same form that he accepted it during his childhood. He neither doubts nor questions the doctrines he learned as a child, nor does he attempt to see the good in religions other than his. He develops a logic-tight mind toward religion even though his education and experience might justify his reconstruction of his childhood beliefs. This narrow-minded, bigoted individual refuses to discuss religion with others and, if forced into a religious discussion, he generally approaches every criticism and argument with the flat denial of any good in any religion other than his and the statements that his religion is the "only true religion." This immature individual turns to prayer when emergencies arise, just as he did when he was a child, hoping that God can do things for him instead of his putting forth efforts to do things for himself. He prays regularly, not so much because he derives any real benefit from it but rather because he is afraid of the evils that will befall him if he does not pray. In much the same spirit, he goes to church regularly and contributes money and efforts to the church and its different organizations. In each case, he is motivated not by a sense of responsibility or a true desire to help a worthy cause but by subjective, personal motives.

Perhaps the most outstanding characteristic of an immature individual in this area of his development is his unwillingness to see any good and any value in a religion that is not his own. He refuses to admit that other religious faiths can meet the needs of other people as well as, if not better than, his faith can and, as a result, he becomes hypercritical of all individuals of other faiths. This is the basis of the snobbishness and social discrimination that so often arises against those of different religious faiths. The more remote a religion is from his own, the more severely he condemns it and the more superior he feels to those who have accepted this faith. An immature adult may and frequently does become atheistic or agnostic in his religious attitudes. He may take the passive attitude of disbelief, which is characteristic of *agnosticism,* and merely ignore religion, or he may take an active, vindictive attitude toward all forms of religion, condemning them as "worthless" or "accepted only by morons." The latter type of rejection of religion is *atheism.*

The atheist is far more vocal and more vindictive in his attitudes and speech than is the agnostic.

A significant study of religious attitudes was made recently in Utah, where there was an opportunity to contrast the Mormon faith with that of other denominations. One of the important findings of this study was that the greatest antagonism to religion on the part of college students came from those whose parents were most orthodox. This was especially marked among the Mormons as compared with the Protestants. The most favorable attitudes toward religion were found among those students in whose family relationships there had been a minimum of conflict about religion. The greatest aversion to the church comes between the ages of twenty-one and twenty-two years, resulting from early childhood and adolescent dependence on parents and the uncritical acceptance of institutionalized patterns. Later, in a mature adult, there is a more favorable attitude toward the church resulting from the assumption of family and community responsibilities, with the accompanying appreciation of the social values of certain religious mores (Telford, 1950).

Moral Maturity

Unlike the child who is guided in the determination of right and wrong by narrow moral concepts related to specific acts, and unlike the adolescent who has such lofty, idealistic moral concepts that neither he nor anyone else could hope to live up to them completely, the mature adult has a moral code that is realistic and workable. He does not limit his moral concepts to what one person has told him they should be but forms them rather from his broader experience with society as a whole. He knows what society expects and, even though he may disagree with some of the moral concepts, he follows them because he realizes that no one can be a law unto himself. In this adult moral code, there is *stability*. Things that are right are right in all environments, not right in one and wrong in another. Nor does right vary according to the person or persons with whom the mature individual happens to be. If it is right to do something now, with one group, it will be just as right to do it with another group, even if that other group has different standards of morality. A code of honesty or truthfulness will not change with the environment. It will hold good in all environments.

The adult moral code is formulated not by the opinions of a small group, as is true of childhood morality, but by the mores of the group as a whole combined with the individual's own ideals and consciously thought out standards of morality. As a result the morally mature individual acts in accordance with his code not because he is afraid of being caught and punished but rather because he believes it is the right thing to do. In this manner, he shows a sense of responsibility and dependability that contrasts markedly to the irresponsibility and undependability of the morally immature individual.

The mature individual may not approve of existing rules, regulations, and laws but he makes reasonable adjustments to them. He may criticize them from time to time and may even take action to change them. Unlike the adolescent who criticizes any rule or regulation that he finds interfering with his personal interests, the mature adult limits his criticisms to those rules and regulations which he feels are unworkable, unjust, or out of step with present times. Furthermore, the mature individual realizes that it takes time and effort to bring about changes. He therefore does not become discouraged if his attempts at reform meet defeat or seem slow in their progress as the immature individual does.

And, finally, the mature individual is tolerant of lawbreakers. Unlike the immature individual who brands all transgressors as "criminals" and accuses them of "wickedness" when their conduct falls below society's standards, the mature individual tries to understand and to sympathize with such individuals. When punishment is necessary, the mature individual gives it reluctantly; the immature individual not only metes out punishments eagerly but he gloats over those who he feels "deserve" such punishments. This intolerant attitude toward those whose conduct falls below standard is commonly found in adolescents but, like many other aspects of adolescent behavior, should have been left behind at the adolescent level. A brief and concise picture of the morally mature individual has been given by Cole (1944) in the following statement: "Perhaps it is not too much to say that childish morals are based mainly on habit, adolescent morals on lofty but nebulous ideals, and adult morals mainly on pragmatism, the adult being good because goodness works better than badness."

CHAPTER 11

Adulthood
(Twenty-one to Sixty Years)

Maturity, which is legally achieved in our culture at the age of twenty-one years, extends to approximately the age of sixty years, at which time decline begins to set in. At first, this decline is barely perceptible and is generally limited to physical changes. Because maturity is by far the longest of all the periods of human life, it is not surprising to find that, within this period of approximately 40 years, marked physical and psychological changes take place. In early maturity, the young man or woman looks more like an adolescent than like a grown man or woman. Likewise, his intellectual development has been completed and his schooling is, in a majority of cases, likewise complete. He is thus ready to take his place in the world, working side by side with other mature individuals.

Up to the age of thirty years, it is quite common for both men and women to be immature in certain areas of their behavior, at the same time showing marked degrees of maturity in other areas. Gradually with new achievements and new expectations from the social group, much of the immaturity that characterized the behavior in the early part of this period disappears. This results in a more even development on a more mature level thon one normally finds in adolescence or in the early years of maturity. There are, however, many individuals who remain immature throughout the major part of their adulthood and who, as a result, can make successful adjustments to life only so long as their environments remain simple and in keeping with their immature level of development. This is well illustrated in the case of the overprotected wife and mother who is taken care of by a doting husband as long as he lives and whose care is later assumed by doting sons and daughters who try to protect their mother from the world just as their father did. Should they not, however, assume the protective role, their mother would quickly find herself incapable of adjusting to an environment that has been planned for adults who have been accustomed to stand on their own feet.

Social Expectancy. The period of maturity is not designated by any marked biological boundaries, such as puberty and the climacteric, as is true of primitive peoples who use these biological landmarks to mark off the years of maturity. With advance in civilization, there has been a growing tendency to push up the recognized age of maturity until now, in our culture, it comes 7 or 8 years after the individual has become sexually mature. Similarly, the climacteric no longer means old age. As a result, maturity today is a long and poorly differentiated period of the life span. Awareness of the biological and psychological changes that occur at this time has been reduced to a minimum since modern medical aids and clothing help to keep men and women of different ages looking, feeling, and acting much as if they were of the same age.

The mature individual of today is expected to find a life occupation in which he can achieve a reasonable degree of success. Because of this success, he is expected to be financially independent and in a position to take care of his family adequately. He is expected to change his interests and activities as he grows older and to act in accordance with his age. And he is expected to assume the responsibilities of an adult, which means not only to regulate his own life but also to rear a family and contribute to the welfare of society (Kahn and Simmons, 1940). High-level social expectancy may lead to feelings of frustration which, if too severe, will lead to a breakdown. When his own levels of aspiration and social expectancy are beyond his abilities, he breaks under the strain of trying to achieve the impossible.

PHYSICAL DEVELOPMENT

Before adolescence has come to a close, the physical growth of the individual is complete, or so nearly complete that what few changes occur thereafter will be barely noticeable. The differences in physical appearance between the two sexes, which began to be so marked in adolescence, continue as time goes on. Men become increasingly masculine in appearance as they grow older and women become increasingly feminine. This tendency to be different reaches its peak around the middle part of maturity and then wanes as middle age sets in.

The average American man of today is 67 to 69 inches tall and weighs from 160 to 170 pounds. He is broad-shouldered; narrow-hipped; has heavy musculature in his shoulders, arms, and legs; and has a heavy growth of hair on his face, chest, arms, and legs, as well as of the axillary and pubic hair. While he probably will take on weight as time goes on, and while he probably will develop a bulge over his abdomen when he is nearing the forties, the average man of today is weight-conscious to the point where he does not permit his weight to get out of hand as was true of middle-aged men a generation or two ago. The average American woman measures from 62 to 64 inches, depending upon the racial stock from which she comes, the socio-economic status of her family, and her general health condition during the growth years. Her weight ranges from 125 to 140 pounds, though there are even more pronounced individual differences in feminine than in masculine weight. While the young woman who is contemplating marriage or has just married may be very weight-conscious, there is a tendency for her to grow careless of her figure during the thirties and forties, only to become weight-conscious in the mid-forties as her figure tells her age or as her doctor warns her of the dangers of excess weight.

Sex Differences. At maturity, there are marked physical differences between the two sexes. Men have larger chests, longer arms and legs in comparison with the trunk, broader shoulders, narrower hips, and bigger heart and lungs in proportion to other internal organs. Typically the female has larger hips; proportionally larger abdominal organs, such as the intestines and stomach; and a more delicate skin with less hair on it. Males have less adipose tissue and more muscles and bones than have females. This difference tends to increase rather than decrease with age. In 90 per cent of the cases, the fat/bone index differentiates the sexes accurately (Reynolds, 1949).

Sex differences in the endocrine systems of men and women account for marked differences in body processes, as evidenced in biochemical changes. Men have higher blood pressure than women up to about the age of forty years, after which both are about the same. The greater production of energy by men demands greater food intake (Sutliff and Holt, 1925). Women sleep more than men and hence conserve their energy more (Thompson, 1936). Furthermore, women can adjust better than men to external changes in temperature by a reduced metabolism on being exposed to heat and with a speeded-up metabolism when exposed to cold (Hardy *et al.*, 1941). Male ability to respond to situations that demand sudden and extreme physical energy is superior to that of women because of the relatively constant level of blood sugar in men as compared with the marked fluctuations in women during the menstrual and childbearing period (Johnson and Terman, 1940).

Menstruation. Among women, there are variations in physical and psychological states accompanying menstruation which are not duplicated in men. Just before and during the early part of the menstrual period, the woman frequently experiences cramps, headaches, backaches, general nervous tension, and a tendency to be easily upset. As a general rule, these physical accompaniments are far less severe than they are during the menstrual periods of young adolescent girls. Among many women, there are no serious physical disturbances at all, though there may be a tendency to greater irritability and nervousness than is experienced at other times during the menstrual cycle. The common physical accompaniments of menstruation are illustrated in Fig. 46.

In a survey of reported effects of the menstrual cycle on women workers, menstruation was found to have little effect. What effects there were were found to be largely subjective and to reflect the influence of tradition (Seward, 1944). A psychological observation of 10 women daily over a period of 5 months revealed that the most universal and conspicuous reaction was an outburst of physical and mental activity before the onset of menstruation coupled with high tension and irritability and preceded or accompanied by depressions. Another high in activity was found to dominate the ovulative

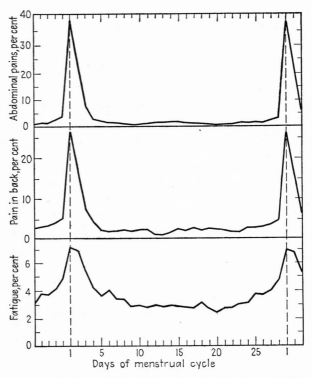

FIG. 46. Percentage distribution of abdominal pain, pain in back, and fatigue in relationship to the menstrual cycle as observed by 167 women who kept daily records over a period of 6 months. Cycles ranging from 21 to 37 days were adjusted to a 28-day base. Note that subjective feelings of pain and fatigue are most often observed on the first day of menstrual flow. (*Redrawn from R. A. McCanico, M. C. Luff, and E. E. Widdowson, Physical and emotional periodicity in women. J. Hyg., 1937, 37:571–611. From F. K. Shuttleworth, The adolescent period: a graphic atlas, Monogr. Soc. Res. Child Develpm., 1949, 14, No. 1. Used by permission.*)

phase of the cycle, but this type of activity was free from nervous tension and generally bore the character of elation (Altmann *et al.*, 1941).

There is a growing belief among doctors and psychologists that the so-called effects of menstruation are partly mental, resulting from social tradition, rather than purely physical in origin. These social traditions trace their origin to primitive man who showed an abhorrence for uncleanliness and an awe and fear of blood. As a result of these beliefs, many rites and taboos grew up. A menstruating woman, among primitive peoples, was not permitted to prepare food because it was believed that by doing so she would poison those who ate it. She could not look at or touch weapons of war or of the chase because it might bring bad luck to those who used these weapons. Among some primitive peoples, the menstruating woman was believed to be mentally unstable and to have certain supernatural powers.

The effects of these primitive superstitions still persist. When asked specifically how menstruation affects them, a group of women listed their physical and emotional symptoms. Among the physical symptoms, 14 per cent said they experienced headaches; 40 per cent, backaches; 63 per cent, increased fatigue; and 60 per cent, cramps. Of the mental and emotional symptoms, 59 per cent reported increased irritability; 49 per cent, let-down feelings or depression; 25 per cent, emotional or crying spells; and 21 per cent, feelings of anxiety. Only 15 per cent reported feelings of well-being and 34 per cent said they experienced a desire for extra activity combined with a desire to change things (Brush, 1938). The general reaction of women to menstruation is introvertive in nature. The frequency and intensity of introvertive reactions increases rapidly with increase in pain and discomfort (Conklin et al., 1927). Many women report that their sex desire is intensified by menstruation. This accompanies the heightened general emotional tension present at that time, and frequently occurs just before menstruation as well as during the menstrual period (Davis, 1926).

Physical Decline. As men and women reach middle age, in the mid-forties, certain physical and physiological changes occur that are almost universal. They are so characteristic of the period that few fail to recognize them. In the case of women, this change is often referred to as "fair, fat, and forty." There is the typical "middle-age spread" which results in a thickening of the body in the area of the waistline. It has been said that middle-aged people stop growing at the ends and begin growing in the middle. The hairline begins to recede, especially in men, and the hair becomes thinner. In men, baldness at the crown or on the top of the head is very common from forty on. If the first gray hairs have not already made their appearance by the time the man or woman reaches forty, they do so shortly afterward. Before the age of fifty, most men and women have a predominance of gray hair and some are even snowy white. Among men, there is a gradual growth of stiff hair in the nose, ears, and eyelashes during middle age and, among women, there is increased growth of hair on the upper lip.

The skin on the face, neck, arms, and hands becomes coarser and begins to show wrinkles. Men find with each successive year after forty that they need to shave less than previously because of the slower and less luxuriant growth of hair on their faces. It is not uncommon for the eyes to look less bright than they did when the individual was younger. If the man or woman has done hard manual work for the major part of his early life, his muscles will still be strong in middle age, though they will have less resiliency than previously. The average American, however, has not continued to be as active physically during the early years of maturity as he was when he was younger and, as a result, he looks and acts as if his muscles were soft and flabby. This is especially apparent in the areas of the chin, the upper arms, and the abdomen. This adds to the general appearance of flabby fatness and results in a slowing down of the individual's walk and other bodily movements. The bones become gradually more brittle with a consequent greater tendency to break easily and to require a longer time to heal after they are broken. Some middle-aged people develop difficulties with their joints and limbs, thus causing them to walk with difficulty and with a degree of awkwardness rarely found in younger people.

There is a beginning of a gradual deterioration of sensory abilities as the individual reaches middle age. The most marked and most troublesome changes come in the eyes and ears. *Presbyopia,* or farsightedness, comes from the gradual loss of accommodative power of the eyes resulting from a decrease in the elasticity of the lens. Between the ages of forty and fifty years, the accommodative power of the lens is usually insufficient for ordinary close work with the result that the individual who never before wore glasses must now have reading glasses or even bifocals. Hearing is likewise apt to be slightly impaired with the result that the individual must listen more attentively than formerly when people speak or he must ask them to repeat what they said. Sensitivity to high pitches is lost first, followed by progressive losses down the pitch scale.

While declines begin to be apparent as early as twenty years, they are not readily apparent in everyday experiences until the individual nears fifty. Because of the loss in ability to hear, most middle-aged people start to talk very loudly. When reminded by members of their family and friends that they can "hear without being shouted at," the middle-aged person often goes to the opposite extreme and talks so softly that it is difficult to hear him. With further losses in hearing ability, the individual frequently talks in a monotone (Anderson, 1949). The sense of smell grows weaker in men, as a result of the increase in the hairy network of the nose, and this affects the sense of taste. As a result, at the time when the individual should be using less salt than formerly to avoid increased blood pressure, he is likely to use more salt and other forms of seasoning than ever before, hoping to make his food more tasty.

Changes in the exterior of the body do not occur without a parallel change in the internal organs and their functioning. These changes are, for the most part, the direct or indirect result of changes in the body tissues. Like rubber bands, the walls of the arteries become brittle as middle age progresses and this leads to circulatory difficulties. Increase in blood pressure, especially among these who are overweight, may lead to heart complications unless radical changes are made in the individual's diet and mode of life. There is increasing sluggishness in the functioning of most of the glands of the body. The pores and skin glands are slower than they formerly were in ridding the skin of waste materials with the result that there is an increased tendency to body odors. The different glands connected with the digestive process likewise function more slowly with a consequent increase in number and severity of digestive disorders. To add to this problem, many middle-aged men and women must have dental plates which increase the difficulty of chewing. In addition, few individuals revise their eating habits to keep pace with the slowing down of their activities and this likewise adds a burden to the functoning of the digestive system.

Most middle-aged men and women become aware of the external and internal changes that come with advancing age and try to put a stop to these changes or to hide them from others. Touching up or dyeing gray hair is very common among American men and women today. When they become aware of the increase in weight and flabbiness of the muscles which proclaim their age so visibly, many men and women go on strict reducing diets or have massages to harden their muscles and break up the fat deposits in areas of their bodies where fat tells their age. Furthermore, they select clothing which is especially designed to cover up telltale marks of middle age and they use more cosmetics than the younger person needs or uses. Because of these forms of camouflage, many Americans of today appear to be younger than they actually are.

As a general rule, men in our culture show signs of aging sooner than women. This may be explained by the fact that women who know that their attractiveness to members of the opposite sex depends so much upon their physical appearance see to it that signs of middle age are quickly covered up. There is also a tendency for the rate of aging to differ in different socioeconomic groups. In general, men and women of the higher socioeconomic groups appear younger than their years while those of the lowest socioeconomic groups look older than they actually are. This may be explained partially by the fact that those of the more favored groups work less, expend less energy, and are better nourished than those who must earn their living by hard manual work. Furthermore, those who come from the less well-to-do groups are unable to afford the beauty aids and clothing that cover up telltale signs of growing old.

Menopause. The menopause in women is the period when her menstruation ceases and when her ability to bear children comes to an end. This comes from glandular changes which affect the functioning of the sex glands. The average age for the menopause in American women of today is between the ages of forty-five and fifty years though there are marked individual differences in these ages. The menopause is a period of several years' duration, and the changes which occur generally take place in a fairly predictable pattern. The Graafian follicles cease to open and the mucous membrane of the uterus is no longer replaced at periodic intervals as it formerly was. The ovaries become mere masses of connective tissue, and menstruation becomes less and less until it finally ceases. Then the entire genital apparatus becomes inactive.

These changes in the reproductive apparatus are accompanied by a disturbance in the delicate balance of the entire endocrine system which results in a number of physical symptoms, such as hot-and-cold flashes, dull, constant oppression above and left of the sternum, a sense of uneasiness throughout the chest, attacks of anginalike pain, breathlessness unrelated to effort, long sighing respiration, paresthesia of various parts of the body, palpitation (or a sense of it) with no change in heartbeat, vague lower abdominal distress, decrease in sexual desire with decrease in ovarian function and lessening of the menstrual flow, varying degrees of impotence, prostatic involvement, unstable vasomotor reactions, lowered metabolic rate, nocturnal sweating, headaches, dizziness, nausea, increase in weight, easy tiring after ordinary exertion, and constipation.

The physiological and glandular changes that take place with the menopause result in changes in the physical appearance of the woman. As the ovarian hormone becomes less dominant, the male hormone secretions which have been present since birth but which have been dominated by the female hormone secretions now come to the fore. As a result, the woman is less feminine in appearance than she was during the period from puberty to the menopause. Three characteristic changes occur, though they differ markedly from woman to woman in their intensity. Hair develops on the upper lip and at the corners of the mouth. This is coarser than the fine down which is usually found on women's faces and is often pigmented. The high-pitched voice, characteristic of women, deepens, though it rarely becomes as low in pitch as that of the typical man. And, finally, the curves of the female body flatten out as a result of the dwindling of adipose tissue. This is especially apparent in the breasts, which become flabby as the milk glands atrophy.

The psychological manifestations of the menopause include malaise; lack of interest; depressive states; indecision; hyperirritability; feelings of self-pity; fear of decreasing feminine attractiveness; nervousness; morbid worry; suspicion of husband, family, and friends; feelings of inferiority; changes in mood; decreased memory; lessened power of concentration; weeping spells; ideas of self-destruction; a tendency to be easily worried and upset by trifles; faultfinding; lack of plasticity; exaggerated sense of responsibility; apprehensiveness; and inattention to dress (Kuhlen, 1948).

As is true of menstruation, there are many *traditional* beliefs regarding the effect of the menopause. In general, the woman is believed to lose her charm, vigor, and womanliness. Being conscious of these traditional beliefs, women are affected unfavorably. There is little evidence, however, that these beliefs are true. When a woman has had an adequate and satisfactory sex life, has borne children, and has had a happy marriage, she generally passes through the menopause period with few discomforts and with a minimum of emotional upsets. When, however, she has not been married, if she is childless, or if her sex life has been unsatisfactory, the changes that accompany the menopause are likely to be more difficult and disturbing, with the result that she experiences more emotional upsets. For the most part, the evidences we have regarding menopausal upsets comes chiefly from women who have sought medical attention at this time and, therefore, this evidence is not representative of the general population. While there may be some psychological disturbance, it is certainly not as severe in most women of today as tradition holds it to be. In a study of 100 patients passing through the menopause, 80 per cent had shown prior disturbances that were purely psychogenic (Fessler, 1950). In many instances, the emotional disturbances that accompany the menopause are merely intensifications of states which formerly existed.

To test the assumption that depression of ovarian function at menopause is associated with emotional instability, thinking difficulties, hot flushes, fatigue, despondency, and insomnia, Seward and Seward studied a group of women with the menopause syndrome who were injected with estrogenic hormone for several weeks and then with normal saline solution as a control. A number of psychomotor tests were given to the group and subjective ratings were made. In both cases, the results were found to be almost entirely negative. This suggests that therapeutic effects can be achieved by adjusting the woman's attitude and by increasing her confidence through the use of hormone treatment (Seward and Seward, 1937). Expectancy of difficulties at this age may bring them about but generally neuroticism and emotionality do not increase at this time. Women between the ages of forty-five and fifty years have been found to be especially calm. When anxiety and stress are present, they more often come from psychological than from physical causes (Willoughby, 1935, 1937).

The extreme nervousness and emotional instability that traditionally accompany the menopause have not been found to exist as a universal symptom among all women. The forties have been described as the "calmest period of adult life" (Willoughby, 1935). While there are some nervous women in the forties, there are also nervous men of this age and there are nervous women in the fifties. Nervousness seldom appears first at the menopause (Hamilton, 1929). Within the American culture, there are variations in the types and intensity of disturbances that accompany the menopause. Upper- and middle-class women have more psychological disturbances at this time than do women from the working classes, though there is no difference in the amount or intensity of the physical difficulties experienced by women of different socioeconomic classes (Havinghurst, 1950).

The effect of the menopause on the sexual desires of women varies greatly. Whether this variation is physical or psychological in origin is yet unknown. The chances are that both play a role in bringing about changes in sexual desires. Among some women, there is a premenopausal "thrust of activity" in which the women seem to be making up for lost time. This may take different forms, such as having another child before the childbearing time is over forever, or it may result in an increased interest in social activities, many of which had been abandoned during the child-raising years of early maturity. Some women go through a "dangerous age" when there is increased sexual excitability, accompanied by flirtations and love affairs. A woman in the "dangerous age" dresses and acts like a woman many years younger than she, in hopes of having a last fling before it is too late (Havinghurst, 1950).

Many women, believing that the menopause marks the end of her sexual life just as it marks the end of her childbearing function, become morbid and neurotic. Other women show increased sexual desire after the menopause is completed, and this is frequently increased by her release from fear of pregnancy. Because, traditionally, women who have passed through the menopause are no longer interested in sexual matters and are supposed to have lost their sexual appeal for men, many women whose sexual desires are increased at this time find their lives frustrating, and this may result in unhappiness or even neuroticism (Harsh and Schrickel, 1950).

Male Climacteric. In men, the climacteric is not comparable to the menopause in women. It comes at a later age, generally in the sixties or seventies, and occurs at a very slow rate. With the general aging of his entire body comes a very gradual weakening of the male sexual and reproductive powers. This decline in sexual power and desire does not affect seriously his reproductive functions. In fact, it is possible for men to produce offspring through the fifties and sixties, and even into the seventies in some instances. This contrasts markedly to women, who lose their reproductive function much earlier and at a time when their sexual desires may be increased, rather than decreased, depending partially upon the general state of their health.

The psychological effect of anticipating decline in sexual powers among men is well illustrated in a study of men in the fifth and sixth decades of life who complained of disturbed sexual desire, depressed feelings, flushes, impotence, fatigue, and minor aches and pains, in absence of demonstrable organic changes. While these are frequently diagnosed as evidences of the male climacteric, there was little evidence of testicle androgen deficiency. Furthermore, testosterone therapy was not uniformly favorable, suggesting that it was a case of psychiatric illness, rather than the male climacteric (Landau, 1951).

During the fifties, as the gradual decline in the sexual powers of the man occurs, there is a decline in the male hormone secretion which allows the female hormone secretion to come to the fore. As is true of women at the menopause, the man loses some of his typically masculine characteristics and takes on some of the characteristics of the female. The voice becomes somewhat higher in pitch, there is less hair on the face and body than formerly, and frequently the body becomes slightly more rounded due to deposits of adipose tissue. Accompanying this tendency toward a more feminine appearance is a gradual increase in feminine interests and forms of behavior. Because there is a popular tradition that hair on the face, body, arms and legs, is a sign of virility, the lessening of the hair during middle age is likely to be a source of great concern to men. Even the beginning of baldness disturbs them because they believe that it is indicative of a decline in their sexual powers. Anxiety about virility is one of the chief causes of its loss. As a result, the middle-aged man who worried about his increasing baldness or the fact that he does not have to shave as often as he did when he was younger, merely accelerates the pace of decline in his sexual powers (Harsh and Schrickel, 1950).

Health Conditions. The peak of physical efficiency is generally reached in the mid-twenties. After that, there is a slow and gradual decline in general physical fitness up to the age of forty to forty-five years, after which the rate of decline is accelerated. Among men, the rate of decline is generally more pronounced than among women, especially among those of the upper socioeconomic groups. The reason for this sex differential may be traced to the fact that the men of the upper socioeconomic groups have the constant emotional tension that accompanies work of the higher levels while their wives have lives of comparative ease. Among the members of the lower socioeconomic groups, on the other hand, the women work as hard, if not harder, than the men. Many of them carry jobs outside the home to help support the families, at the same time rearing children and taking care of their homes.

Increase in blood pressure, digestive disturbances, and an increase in all varieties of disease except those that are epidemic in nature come with the approach of middle age. As a result, many men and women are advised by their doctors to revise their living habits and to select simpler and less strenuous forms of exercise. From the age of forty-five years on, the increase in number and severity of diseases and chronic disturbances becomes more pronounced. Adjustment to declining health with middle age is more difficult for the average man than for the average woman. To men, having to slow down is interpreted as meaning that life is coming to a close and they resist making the change as long as possible. Some even go so far as to try to prove to themselves and others that their doctors were wrong and, as a result, they do irreparable damage to their bodies. Others, welcoming a chance to take life easy, go to the opposite extreme, give up all exercise, and thus accelerate the rate of physical decline. Women, by contrast, generally accept the slowing down that comes with middle age in a philosophical way.

MOTOR ABILITIES

Because of the physical strength and good health that are normally present in early maturity, the individual is generally at the peak of his physical efficiency. At this time, he can acquire skills even better than in adolescence when his body is still developing. And he can count on his ability in a given situation which is generally impossible during adolescence when uneven and rapid growth throw the muscular patterns temporarily out of balance. In *strength* the individual is at his peak between the ages of twenty and thirty years. After that, a slow but steady decline becomes apparent. When, however, the individual has been trained to use his strength at the right time and in the right manner in athletics or in jobs that require strength, there is far less indication of decline than in the case of those who do not know how to use their strength to its best advantage. Tests of reaction time show that the maximum *speed* of response comes between twenty and twenty-five years, with relatively slight declines coming progressively up to fifty years of age. The rate of decline is greater for complex reactions, such as pursuit reactions, than for the simpler reactions, such as digital and foot reactions (Miles, 1931).

In *learning new motor skills,* the learning is quicker on the part of young adults than on the part of those who are approaching middle age. When a group of university students was given the task of learning to write with the nonpreferred hand, those between the ages of twenty and twenty-five gained in speed more than those who were thirty-five or older. For the younger group, the average was 35 letters per minute as contrasted to an average of 18 letters per minute for the older group. For the older group, the largest gain was 25 letters per minute as contrasted to the smallest gain of 16 letters per minute in the younger group. These results indicated that the ability to improve one's motor speed in learning a new task drops off very rapidly with age while the ability to improve in quality shows little relationship to age (Thorndike, 1928). Maximum efficiency in learning a finger maze is attained between the ages of eighteen and twenty-nine years, after which there is a slow but steady decline in the speed of learning (Miles, 1933).

While ability to learn new skills declines with age, motor skills acquired at an earlier age and not used over a period of time can generally be restored with relatively little practice under appropriate conditions. However, many of the declines in old skills as well as in new ones can be traced primarily to declines in reaction time, steadiness, strength, and sensory control through vision and hearing. This puts the older individual at a great disadvantage in sports as well as in many kinds of work in the business and industrial world where speed is of prime importance (Anderson, 1949). Not all skills decline at the same time or at the same rate. Those that have fallen into disuse earlier show more marked declines than do those that have been used for a longer time.

There is no specific chronological age at which different motor skills begin to decline. As a general rule, however, the decline sets in at a slow and gradual rate in the early forties and is accelerated in the fifties. Some of this acceleration is unqeustionably due to the less active life led by the middle-aged individual. Then, too, the matter of motivation should not be over-looked. The older individual feels that it is not worth his effort to acquire new skills unless they are essential to his work on the grounds that he is "too old a dog to learn new tricks." His attitude toward improving already existing skills is "What's the use?" As a result, he does not put forth as much effort to learn as he did when he was younger.

Learning of new skills is greatly hampered by habits, skills, and attitudes learned at an earlier age. Each year, as the individual grows older, these previously learned patterns prove to be an increasingly serious handicap to the acquisition of new skills. Old patterns of motor coordination interfere with ones the individual is now trying to establish and attitudes established at an earlier age make him more resistant to the change which new skills would bring. Because this phenomenon is so universal with advancing age, older workers in factories and offices find it difficult to establish themselves in new jobs because of the resistance on the part of employers to taking on older workers who are likely to be slow in learning the methods of their organization because of work habits established in their former jobs and their mental resistance to making the change to a new system of work.

MENTAL ABILITIES AND LEARNING

It is popularly assumed that the individual in his early maturity is at the peak of his ability to learn and that, as time goes on, this ability will decline. The age at which tradition holds the decline starts is at the time of the menopause in women and at approximately the same age in men, the mid-forties and early fifties. It is also popularly believed that early maturity marks the peak of the intellectual capacities of the individual and, like learn-ing, there is the beginning of a decline in intellectual capacity with the onset of the changes in the physical and sexual functions.

There is, unfortunately, no way at present to determine how great the actual decline in a given individual's mental abilities is because his abilities were not measured and the records were not kept for comparison with measurements taken when he grew older. There have been no genetic studies, with the exception of Terman's follow-up study of children of very high IQ's, of the same groups over a long enough period of time to determine whether or not there is an actual deterioration of mental abilities in the same individuals as they grow older. Comparisons of averages of different groups of different age levels may not be 'valid unless they were equal at the same ages in early maturity or even during the adolescent years. And such evidence is not available.

General Intelligence. In tests of general intelligence, the peak of ability comes around the age of eighteen years after which there is a slow and very gradual decline in mental ability as time goes on. In late maturity, about 10 to 25 per cent of the subjects do as well as the most efficient group (Miles, 1933; Miles and Miles, 1932). While there is some loss in score with age, individuals who are given a time-limit or speed test show a more marked decline than when the individual is given a power test in which accuracy, not speed, determines the score (Lorge, 1936, 1940). Because most tests of intelligence for adult subjects make use of verbal tasks, subjects who have never attended high school and whose occupation is that of a manual laborer, show a greater decline with age than do the subjects who continued their education into high school or college and who continued to get practice in verbal abilities in their occupations (Goodenough, 1945).

An analysis of the different mental abilities tested by a test of general intelligence has shown that different mental abilities decline at different rates. In the Alpha Tests, as used by Jones and Conrad (1933), six out of the eight tests showed a decline in average scores from twenty to sixty years of age. In the other two tests, there was no appreciable change. The greatest decline came in tests involving problem solving and seeing new relationships, while no decline was found in the word-opposites test which measure vocabulary and the range-of-information test, both of which are benefited by the experience that comes with age.

Vocabulary scores show a constant rise to about thirty years with little decline up to sixty (Foulds and Raven, 1948; Foulds, 1949). The ability to form comparisons and reason by analogy reach their maximum level by approximately fourteen years, remain constant to twenty-six, and then decline to sixty at a slow but consistent rate. The ability to recall information increases to the age of twenty-five years and then remains constant until the mid-fifties, after which it declines (Foulds and Raven, 1948). Creative imagination is independent of age (Miles, 1933). The capacity to form comparisons and reason by analogy shows a slow but remarkably uniform decline after the mid-twenties (Raven, 1948). Speed of reading, which shows a decline with age that is very marked after the age of fifty years, may be partially responsible for the differential rate of decline of different mental abilities as measured by standard tests of intelligence (Anderson, 1949).

As in all other areas of ability, decline varies from one individual to another. Some people remain intellectually "young" into middle age or even later. Some, on the other hand, begin to age mentally during the late twenties or early thirties. While attempts have been made to discover if there is any relationship between the age and rate of mental decline and the intellectual

level of the individual, so far there is no conclusive evidence of a real relationship. Those whose mental growth in childhood was rapid are neither
more nor less likely to show rapid decline in maturity and middle age than
those whose early mental growth was at a slower rate. There is some evidence,
on the other hand, that rapid mental growth in the early years is accompanied
by slow decline as time goes on, while slow mental development is followed by
more rapid decline (Goodenough, 1945).

Learning Capacity. The learning capacity of the human being is greater for
a longer period of time than is popularly believed, contrary to the old saying,
"You can't teach an old dog new tricks." Then, too, with maturity come new
interests and responsibilities that preoccupy the time and attention of the
individual. This leaves him less time for learning than when he was younger.
Many adults develop feelings of self-consciousness and inadequacy concerning
learning. They regard it as a childhood occupation and feel that, like toys,
it should be put away with childish things. Furthermore, there is a strong
belief that when one reaches maturity, he should have learned all that is
necessary for him to learn and that further learning indicates a deficiency
on his part. The longer adults resist learning new things, the more out of
practice they become and, hence, the more slowly they learn. This merely
accentuates the already present belief that they are "too old" to learn.

Studies of learning have indicated that the young adult is capable of learning as well as a child or an adolescent, provided he is not hampered by
self-consciousness, a defeatist attitude, or the belief that age makes him
incapable of learning. Many adults fail to learn as much as they are capable
of learning or for as long a time as they might, partly because they underestimate their powers of learning and partly because learning is not important
enough to them to motivate them to make the necessary effort. As Thorndike
has pointed out, "Nobody under forty-five should restrain himself from trying
to learn anything because of a belief or fear that he is too old to be able to
learn it" (Thorndike, 1928). As the individual grows older, there is no
question about the fact that it takes him longer to learn than it did when
he was younger. The end result, however, or the quality of his learning, comes
up to the same standard as that of a younger person. When individuals of
forty-five were compared with children and adolescents, it was found that the
older group had to take 15 to 20 per cent more time to learn than the eighteen-
to nineteen-year-old group required for the same tasks. When the older individual is willing to take a little more time and if he is persistent in his efforts,
he will be able to accomplish as much as the younger individual (Thorndike,
1928).

As is true of learning motor skills, learning in the mental area is influenced
differently by age according to the material to be learned. Some types of
learning are affected detrimentally by advancing age, some are helped by it.
In learning Esperanto, an artificial language, individuals up to the mid-forties

were found to learn as well as school children, but in tests of learning in which they were required to respond to directions given orally, their performance was inferior (Thorndike, 1928). In any area where past knowledge or experience can be used, such as in vocabulary materials, the older subjects are generally at an advantage as compared with younger subjects. There is less decline in learning meaningful material than for learning of nonsense material (Miles, 1933).

The ability to retain what has been learned depends not only upon the degree of learning but also upon the type of material learned. Adults have a good retention for meaningful material until middle age, after which there is a slow but observable decline in their retention. Meaningless material, on the other hand, is retained less well. There is, unquestionably, less motivation on the part of the adult to learn meaningless material, such as nonsense material, than there is to learn meaningful material. Hence, as the material has been less well learned, it is forgotten more quickly. Not until the individual approaches sixty is there a marked decline in ability to remember material recently learned and to reminisce or recall material learned at an earlier period in the individual's life.

Conservatism. It is taken for granted that, with advancing age, people become increasingly less adventuresome and more conservative. The radicalism of youth, not only in opinions, in dress, and in behavior, but also in their willingness to try out anything that is new and different, is well known to all who come in contact with youth. That is why change so often originates among young people and why, when older people are in control, change comes about so slowly. To find out when conservatism begins to appear in the thinking of adults, a group of individuals of different ages was given a questionnaire relating to the acceptance or rejection of new products, of new packaging of products, of desire or lack of desire for change in social, political, or economic organizations and for changes in the internal or foreign policy of the government. In the groups over forty to forty-five years of age, the majority of the individuals questioned were conservative. In the groups under forty, there were also many conservative people, though the proportion was not so great as in the older groups. Thus, there was no real evidence that conservatism is a function of age. Rather, it seems to be a product of the personality make-up of the individual and to be associated with the degree of self-confidence and security the individual has (Pollak, 1943).

Inflexibility. As age advances, unwillingness to adjust to new situations is very commonly found. Adults tend to maintain their earlier established beliefs. When groups of students and their parents were compared in their willingness to accept change, it was found that the parents over forty years of age were less willing to change than were parents under forty. Parents of the entire group were more resistant to change than were their sons and daughters (Bean, 1933). In a *Fortune Magazine* (1946) poll regarding the third-term political issue, it was found that older adults were less willing to break from political tradition than were younger adults. Older adults prefer the status quo. The mental inelasticity which comes with age has been explained in different ways. According to Lorge (1936), "Older persons have habits, ideas, or other tendencies that are more invariant than in the young and which may interfere with acquisition of new points of view." The more schooling an individual has, the more willing he is to adopt a new point of view, regardless of his age, though in all levels of education, the younger the individual, the more ready he is to accept new ideas and new practices. Among middle-aged persons, traditional views and time-worn modes of behavior are adhered to with little or no reason for doing so (Bean, 1933). Acheson (1933) has likewise found that education, reading, and discussion lead to taking beliefs "out of cold storage" and to examining them critically. As a result, the inflexibility usually associated with age gives way to a greater flexibility of attitude.

EMOTIONAL STABILITY

Maturity is a period of emotional calm. In the early part of maturity, during the twenties, there is frequently more emotional tension than there is later, owing to problems of adjustment to a vocation, to courtship and marriage, and even to adjustments to living away from the parental roof. These problems are generally solved with a fair degree of success by the end of the twenties, and this permits the adult to establish a pattern of life for himself that will remain relatively unchanged until he approaches old age. Furthermore, as the general health condition of the adult is good, this predisposes the individual to emotional calm in a manner not characteristic of children and young adolescents whose health condition is far less stable.

Habits of emotional control are generally well learned by adulthood. The individual has learned from experience through childhood and adolescence that emotional outbursts are regarded with scorn by his friends and, as a result, he has acquired the ability to control these outbursts. Furthermore, he has learned not to respond emotionally to many situations which formerly stimulated an emotional outburst. Fears, angers, and jealousies are far less common during the adult years than they were earlier because the individual has learned that most situations do not justify such emotions.

Whenever a set pattern of behavior is upset, there is likely to be emotional tension. The child, for example, frequently experiences emotional tension when he makes his first break from home and enters school. At middle age, there is generally an upset in the individual's life pattern. Not only must strenuous activities, such as sports and dancing, be revised but the pattern of daily living is often upset. The woman who for the major part of her adult life has been preoccupied with running a home and rearing children finds that her life work is coming to an end as her children reach maturity and leave home for school, college, jobs, or marriage. With middle age, the man's occupation likewise changes. His status is less secure each year as he grows older, and there is always the possibility that poor health will force him into premature retirement. Then, too, his home life may prove to be less stimulating than it previously was. His wife is aging, just as he is, and his children are leaving home. As a result, boredom frequently sets in for him as it does for the woman.

All in all, there are many reasons why a middle-aged person would be predisposed to emotional tension not experienced during the earlier years of adulthood. Only when adequate provision has been made for these changes which are inevitable with advancing age is there any possibility that the period of middle-age stress and strain could be eliminated or reduced to a minimum. In most men and women, it comes upon them suddenly and, like any sudden upset in a set pattern of behavior, it is disturbing. Most men and women make reasonable adjustments to the physical and psychological changes of middle age within a period of time. As a result, the emotional tension subsides and emotional calm once again appears. By the mid-fifties, most individuals are fairly well adjusted to middle age and are no longer upset by it. They have adjusted their pattern of life, their interests, and their activities to fit into the changes which have taken place in their organisms. Life then moves along smoothly for them until the onset of old age.

Sex Differences. Traditional beliefs regarding sex differences in emotionality among adults are so widespread that they have produced a social expectancy which, in turn, has influenced what sex differences do exist. While it is true that there is a cycle in the sex life of the woman not found in the sex life of the man, this in and of itself would not produce sex differences in emotional behavior. Social expectancy unquestionably has played a role of great importance in the type of training for emotional control the two sexes receive from the time they are young children. Because it is so firmly believed that girls are naturally more emotional than boys, they receive less training to control their emotions than do boys. Furthermore, until recently, adult women were thought to be more feminine and, hence, more charming if they displayed their emotions than if they had the control that men are expected to have.

Experimental evidence has borne out the popular belief that women are, on the whole, more emotional than men. To test emotionality at different ages, Willoughby (1935) gave the Thurstone Personality Schedule and Root's Introversion Items to women and men from fifteen to seventy-five years of age. At all ages, he found sex differences, with women significantly more emotional than men. The curve of emotionality rises to the mid-twenties, declines to the climacteric in middle age, then rises to the early sixties, followed by a slight decline or remains stationary into old age. The first rise in the curve may be attributed to the problems of adjustment to life and to sex in particular and the second to changes occurring with advancing age. The low level of emotionality in the period from the late twenties to the climacteric reflects the lessening of sexual tensions, the relative remoteness of incapacitating age, and maximum earning power (Willoughby, 1937).

Married women, it has been found, are more emotional than spinsters; little difference in emotionality exists between married and unmarried men. There is a rise among both men and women in introvertive interests such as quiet amusements, avoidance of crowds, and reading, which is not indicative of worry, anxiety, emotional disturbance, or neuroticism but rather indicates a reorientation of interests with advancing age (Willoughby, 1935). It accompanies the period of emotional calm that normally comes in the middle of the adult years.

A comparison of the emotional reactions of men and women has shown in what emotions women and men differ most. Women are more actively sympathetic than men and are more concerned with their nearer relationships than men are. Women express fears more strongly than men and more than the fearsomeness of the object justifies. Women are more disgusted than men by coarse and impolite language and about sexual immorality. They show more sympathy for the meek and those who are helpless or visibly in distress, and they express more pity for female distress than men do (Terman and Miles, 1936).

Annoyances. While fear, anger, and jealousy decline with age, there is an increase in the number and type of situations that will annoy an adult. Annoyances increase up to middle age and then decrease as the individual reaches old age. Some annoyances, acquired in the earlier years of life, drop out and others are acquired. Among middle-aged and elderly people, the most frequent annoyances come from seeing suggestive dancing at a social dance, from walking on ice-covered, slippery sidewalks, from hearing persons refer to a sex subject, from seeing a woman smoke in public, from very noticeable powder on a woman's face, or liquor on a person's breath. Less frequent sources of annoyance consist of a person with a gushing manner, hearing people make bad grammatical mistakes, having to get up in the morning, hearing a person scratch his fingernail on a blackboard, seeing a person wearing clothing not appropriate to the occasion, and seeing a woman wear high heels. Borderline moral wrongs are more annoying to middle-aged than to younger people but the former are more tolerant of ordinary annoyances than are those in the latter group (Cason, 1930).

Neuroticism. Poor emotional adjustments, as shown in neuroticism, are more frequent among younger adults than among those who are approaching middle age. There is no question about the fact that adulthood brings with it many problems of great seriousness which the individual must solve to his own satisfaction if he is to be well-adjusted. Some individuals make these adjustments with relative speed and success. Others, whose earlier lives have not been well-adjusted, find the adjustments of adult years far more difficult and their success in adjustment is, as a result, more meager.

Willoughby (1935), in a measurement of neuroticism in husbands and wives, came to the conclusion that wives were consistently more neurotic than husbands. This suggests that the marriage situation bears more heavily on the wife than on the husband. A comparison of married and unmarried women showed that among the unmarried group, which was composed of teachers, the peak of neuroticism came at thirty years, after which there was a decline, showing that a fairly good adjustment was being made by these individuals. Among the married women, there was also a steady decline in neuroticism with advancing age showing, likewise, improved adjustments (Phillips and Greene, 1939).

ADULT INTERESTS

Interests at every age depend upon a number of factors, most important of which are opportunities for acquiring them, the life activities of the individual, the people with whom he is associated, the level of his intelligence and education, and his general health condition. As is true of childhood and adolescence, there is a wide variety of interests among individuals of any age level. In any given culture, however, there are certain interests which are more or less uniformly found. This holds true of the adult years just as it does of the earlier years of life.

In the early years of adulthood, many of the interests are similar to those of the closing years of adolescence. They center around personal attractiveness, especially of members of the opposite sex, courtship, marriage, raising a family, and making satisfactory vocational adjustments. Because the life pattern for married adults differs markedly from that for unmarried adults of the same age levels, it is logical to suppose that there will be marked differences in the interests of individuals depending on their marital status. Likewise, because the life pattern for women is so different from that of men, sex differences in interests are inevitable.

Methods of Study. Studies of adult interests have made use of vocational-interest blanks to discover the characteristic patterns of vocational and avocational interests for the purpose of vocational guidance. Interviews and observations of activities, as well as analyses of conversations in different situations, also throw light on the matter of interests in the adult years. These studies have, unfortunately, been made on cross sections of individuals of different age levels at the time the studies were made. They tell us merely what people of different ages are interested in today but they do not prove conclusively that there is a decline in interest in certain areas, as is often claimed, because there is no indication that certain interests ever existed in the groups studied (Thorndike, 1949).

For example, when middle-aged people of today show little interest in attending movies or listening to the radio, it may mean merely that they never acquired such interests when they were younger, because of lack of opportunities to develop such interests, and therefore there has been no decline after all. Older people, who grew up in a culture devoid of many of our amusements and at a time when many of the present-day recreational activities were disapproved of, established different habits and these persisted to influence the activities of those individuals during maturity (Kuhlen, 1940). The only valid way to study changes of interest from one age to another is through genetic studies of the same group over a period of years, from childhood into old age. The only study of this sort to date is that made by Terman who has followed a group of individuals of very superior intelligence from kindergarten into middle age (Terman and Oden, 1947).

Changes with Age. It is popularly believed that there are marked changes in interest with age. This is not borne out by evidence from experimental studies (Reid, 1951). The tendency is not to change interests with age so much as to narrow down slightly the range of interests as age advances with the result that, as middle age approaches, there are fewer interests than there were during the years of early maturity. As changes in duties and responsibilities occur in early maturity and as changes in health come in middle age, there is normally a shift of emphasis on already existing interests rather than on the establishment of new interests. New interests may be established as the individual grows older but, unless there are changes in his environment, opportunities to develop new interests, and a strong motivation to do so, the chances are that new interests will develop only infrequently as time goes by.

Changes in interests do not all come at the same time. Approximately one-half of all changes come between the ages of twenty-five and thirty-five years; 20 per cent between the ages of thirty-five and forty-five years; and the remaining 30 per cent, between forty-five and fifty-five years. There is little or no change in interests between the ages of fifty-five and sixty-five years. These shifts in interest are probably more cultural and environmental rather than actual age changes. The period of most rapid shift in interests comes in adolescence, when there is the most marked change in the physical and psychological make-up of the individual (Strong, 1951). As Strong (1931) has pointed out, at "twenty-five years the adult is largely what he is going to be and even at twenty years he has acquired pretty much the interests he will have throughout life."

Shifts in Interests. Though the number of interests changes little as age advances, the shifts in emphasis on different interests are marked. Interest in active recreations, such as sports and dancing, declines with age and in its place comes an interest in more cultural and sedentary use of leisure time, such as reading and card games. Interest in sex changes differently for the two sexes. For men, this interest increases up to the ages of thirty-five or forty years and then decreases at a slow rate. For women, by contrast, the interest begins to decline in the thirties but at a much more rapid rate than for men. This interest, as is true of almost all interests that have developed

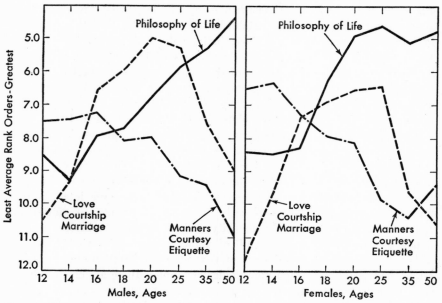

Fig. 47. Changing interest in three life areas. (*Based on unpublished data of Percival M. Symonds. From F. K. Shuttleworth, The adolescent period, Monogr. Soc. Res. Child Develpm., 1938, 3, No. 3. Used by permission.*)

from childhood, never declines to the zero point, though it waxes and wanes at different ages in the individual's life. Interest in personal adornment increases for women up to middle age and then declines. For men, this interest which has been less pronounced increases rather than decreases in middle age.

Interest in manners and courtesy, which ranks high in adolescence, decreases as time goes on. Likewise, interest in money, which to the adolescent and young adult is not only a strong interest but also a serious problem, loses its hold on the individual's attention as he reaches middle age and is in a financial position to supply most of his needs and wants. By contrast, interest in a philosophy of life, which during the adolescent years was not too strong, increases in importance as the individual grows older (see Fig. 47). This is true also of interest in civic affairs and in mental health. Social problems, such as popularity, recede into the background as age advances and in their place come the more personal problems. From these examples, it may be seen how interests change as the individual grows older and as his activities change (Symonds, 1936a).

Sex differences in interests are apparent from earliest childhood when cultural influences determine what the activities of the two sexes shall be. The

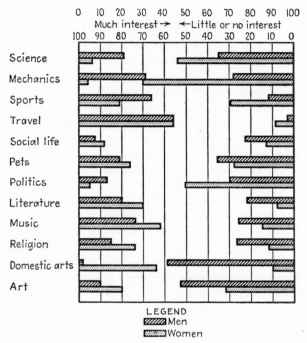

FIG. 48. Interests of men and women. (*From L. M. Terman and C. C. Miles, Sex and personality. New York: McGraw-Hill, 1936. Used by permission.*)

most marked differences in interests between the sexes come in late adolescence and early maturity. For men, the strongest interests are in success, sexual adjustments, and personal adjustment in society while, for women, the dominant interests are in a personal philosophy, planning a daily schedule, and problems of mental health and personal attractiveness. As they grow older, both men and women become more interested in feminine lines of interest, though differences do exist between the two sexes, in lesser degrees, as time goes on. Perhaps the most marked sex differences are to be found in the area of recreations where men prefer activities with men more than with women and activities of an informal sort to those of the more formal type which women prefer (Symonds, 1936a). Sex differences in interests are shown in Fig. 48.

Sex differences in interests are due partly to differences in education from earliest childhood, partly to different objectives and roles, partly to innate differences, but mainly to social expectancy. Women are expected to assume a typically feminine role and men a typically masculine role (Strong, 1936). When women are in professions similar to those of men, such as medicine and life insurance, there is little sex difference in men and women engaged in the same occupation (Seder, 1940). Because interests change less in adult years than is generally supposed, the importance of developing a wide range of interests during the years of childhood and adolescence is emphasized. If the young person is given an opportunity to acquire many interests while he is young, the chances are that he will hold a major part of them throughout his life.

Types of Interests. Of the almost universally found interests among American adults of today, the following are the most important:

PHYSICAL APPEARANCE. By adulthood, most men and women have learned to accept their physiques and to make the most of them. While their height, weight, facial features, and coloring may not be to their liking, they have learned that little can be done to alter them but much can be done to cover them up or to improve them. As a result, the adult's major concern with his appearance is to improve it. This leads to interest in all sorts of beauty aids, to diets, and to exercises which will improve the figure. The adult's interest in looks begins to wane during the late twenties. But, with the first signs of aging, this interest is again revived. As signs of aging appear with greater frequency and severity, the interest becomes stronger and stronger.

Many adults, after a few years of trying to cover up physical signs of aging, accept the fact that they are growing older and show less and less concern about it. When this happens, their interest in appearance once again begins to wane. Other adults, especially those to whom remaining young in appearance is of importance in the business, professional, or social world, do not resign themselves to increasing signs of aging and lose interest in their looks. Instead, their interest becomes stronger and stronger until it becomes one of the dominant interests of their lives. As a result, they engage in many activities that make themselves and others believe that they are younger than they actually are.

CLOTHING. Clothing and personal adornment, one of the major interests of the adolescent years, remains strong during the early years of maturity. This is especially true of unmarried men and women. Frequently, more time and money are spent on clothing than the individual can afford, because he knows it plays a role of major importance in achieving success in whatever area of activity he is interested. Even as early as the childhood years, the individual comes to regard clothes as a part of himself. They are used largely to "make real the role that is to be played in life" (Murphy, 1947). Among men, clothing is important as an indication of social status and economic success.

The man knows that he cannot "afford" to be poorly dressed. He is aware of the fact that his clothes tell the world not only what sort of person he is but also how successful he is.

It is not alone important for women to establish socioeconomic status by the clothes they wear but also to attract members of the opposite sex, to win the approval of members of their own sex, and to maintain a favorable status in the business or professional world, if they work outside the home. Because women's clothing is more individualized than men's, a woman may express her personality through the type of clothes she selects. For this reason, many women seek individuality through clothes to compensate for lack of individuality in their personality make-ups. As Ross (1917) has pointed out: "The ultimate *raison d'être* of fashion is the passion for self-individualization." In addition, through imitation, he asserts, "The individual asserts his equality with the superior by copying him in externals."

When a group of men and women was asked "Why are 'success' and clothes related?" the following reasons were given: "A well-dressed person more easily gains the confidence of people in the business world; consciousness of good personal appearance frees the individual from the fear of adverse criticism; the personality of the individual is judged by his external appearance; and social advantages are frequently obtained as a result of a pleasing personal appearance (Dearborn, 1919).

When a group was asked questions relating to their interest in clothing, their replies brought out the following facts: More adults dress for their own sex and for both sexes than for the opposite sex alone; usefulness and cost are dominating factors in the selection of clothing by both men and women; becomingness of color of a garment is one of the chief motives in its selection by women while, for men, color is less important than arbitrary preference and utility.

When effects on the individual's behavior were examined, it was found that the following influences of clothing were very important: nearly two-thirds of the men and only one-half of the women said they would be willing to deprive themselves of certain pleasures in order to be in style; even fewer said they would be willing to deprive themselves of the necessities of life; few men and slightly more women admitted that they would be willing to adopt a prevailing style, even though they disapproved of it; professional advancement and a desire to put up a "good front" were the most powerful motives in determining whether men and women should spend a disproportionate amount of money on their clothes; most men and women were conservative to the point where they wanted a style to be well established before they adopted it; most men and women selected clothing to make themselves inconspicuous; and estimates of others were, in almost every instance, affected by the person's appearance (Hurlock, 1929a).

MONEY AND MATERIAL POSSESSIONS. Interest in money and material possessions generally reaches its peak during the early years of maturity. The young adult who, as an adolescent, envied those whose economic status was superior to his, is motivated by a strong desire to earn enough money to have the possessions he formerly wanted but was unable to have. Many young women, even after marriage, continue to hold down jobs not because they enjoy the work but rather because they want the money that will enable them to have the things they crave. Because success in the business world is generally judged by the economic and social status of the individual, as shown by his clothes, his home, his cars, and his other possessions, the typical young man of today is eager to rise as fast as possible in the business world in hopes of getting the things he and his family want.

Much of the unhappiness and discontent of young adults stems from the fact that they do not have the material possessions they want or that their friends and neighbors have. Many divorces stem, likewise, from the fact that young people cannot adjust successfully to deprivations, especially when they have anticipated the attainment of certain possessions when they married. Among adult criminals, one of the most common causes of crime is the desire for easy money and the attainment of possessions the individual would not be able to get through his own abilities.

As the individual approaches middle age, his desire for money and material possessions usually begins to wane. As was pointed out earlier in this chapter, interest in money decreases in middle age, either because the individual now has an adequate amount to satisfy his desires or because of the strengthening of other interests which now replace the money interest. The families of middle-aged persons are generally grown-up and in homes of their own. Furthermore, interest in material possessions also begins to wane. Most individuals discover that material possessions can be a great care and responsibility. As a result of their general desire to eliminate some of the burden of responsibilities they have been carrying for many years, the middle-aged man or woman begins to think of disposing of some of his possessions, now that his family is grown and the need for many possessions decreases. Only when there is a sentimental attachment to certain possessions is there as great an interest in them as there was when the individual was younger.

RELIGION. By the time the individual reaches adulthood, he has either resolved his religious doubts and formulated a philosophy of life, based on religion, that will be satisfactory to him, with minor changes, for the rest of his life, or he has rejected religion as having little or nothing to offer him. In both cases, religion has less interest for the individual than it had when he was younger. The early twenties have been called the "least religious period of life" (Allport et al., 1948). The young adult who has given up his faith has a sense of insecurity, displays various neurotic signs, and has an awareness of conflicting ideas and impulses not found among those who are conspicuously more solid and secure in their religious beliefs (Murray, 1938).

When the responsibilities of parenthood are assumed, there is generally a return to religion. Parents of young children feel that it is their duty and responsibility as parents not only to teach their children the fundamentals of their own faith and to see that they receive proper religious instruction in Sunday school, but also to set a good example for them (Allport *et al.*, 1948). Consequently, religious practices which prevailed in their own homes are now revived in the home where there are children, even if these religious practices are somewhat modified to fit into the pattern of life today (Bossard and Boll, 1950). Regular attendance at church is now a part of the parents' life and they begin to take an active part in some of the church organizations and activities.

Interest in religion, as a rule, becomes stronger rather than weaker as age advances. The middle-aged man or woman is more interested in the church and its activities than he was when he was younger and he attends church services more often (Hall and Robinson, 1942). And because many of the interests that preoccupied him when he was younger have been abandoned or have grown weaker with age, interest in religion fills a need in his life to replace old interests that are no longer dominant. Many middle-aged individuals find in religion a source of comfort and happiness they never experienced in the religion of their younger years.

TALKING. The self-consciousness that holds back many adolescents in social situations has generally been overcome by the time the individual reaches adulthood. As a result, most adults are interested in talking, especially with those whose interests are similar to theirs. Women, perhaps more than men, enjoy talking to people and getting a new point of view from these conversations. During the adult years, the environment in which the individual finds himself has a marked influence on his conversational topics. Unlike the child who talks about what is of interest to him at the moment, regardless of the situation in which he finds himself, the adult tries to adapt his conversation to fit into the situation (Carlson *et al.*, 1936). He also tries to adapt it to the people with whom he is. Women, as a rule, are more expert in this than are men.

Adults generally talk about personal, day-to-day matters relating to themselves and very little about public affairs. Only when public affairs reach into the individual's daily routine are they discussed by the average adult (Watson *et al.*, 1948). Young adults talk more about themselves than do older adults. Their interests are closely bound up with their families and their own personal affairs. The conversations of older adults center more around jobs, prices, and more practical matters while those of younger adults are related more to frivolous matters, such as social affairs, clothing, looks, and dancing (Watson *et al.*, 1948).

Sex differences in interests have been revealed in all the studies made of adult conversations. When talking to men, men discuss money, business, and sports mainly. Women, on the other hand, when talking to women, discuss persons of the opposite sex, clothing, building, interior decoration, and children (Landis, 1927). Men tend to pursue a given topic longer than women (Stoke and West, 1931). When women talk with men, their conversations show not so much a mixture of the interests of both sexes as a tendency for women to adapt themselves to subjects of chief interest to men (Moore, 1922). When public affairs are discussed, they are a more popular topic of conversation with men than with women (Watson et al., 1948).

A common characteristic of advancing age is the intensification of traits that are already present. The adult who does not enjoy talking with people generally becomes more and more taciturn as middle age and old age arrive. The individual who, on the other hand, has always had a lively interest in talking to other people develops an even stronger interest in talking as he grows older. The telephone and over-the-fence talks with friends become more frequent and longer as women grow older and the man who, as a young man, enjoyed talking to anyone who would listen to him now talks so endlessly that people try to avoid him if possible. In his work, he is likewise long-winded. Among older and otherwise capable workers, there is often a tendency to talk too much and work too little. As a result, they frequently lose their jobs because their output falls below that of younger men. The older person who talks too much not only tells things that should not be told but he frequently bores others because he talks in a disorganized fashion, with frequent references to things that happened in his youth, none of which are of much interest to his listeners (Anderson, 1949).

RECREATIONS. By the time the individual reaches adult years, his recreational interests are fairly well formed. With the responsibilities he must assume in adulthood, the typical adult has even less time for recreation than he had in adolescence. As a result, he must narrow down the recreations to those that not only give him the greatest enjoyment but also to those that are most practical for him from the point of view of both time and money. Young unmarried people of both sexes not only have more time and money for different recreations than do those who are married but more of their recreational interests are outside the home than are those of the married group. With age, there is a marked decrease in the number of recreations outside the home. This holds true for the married as well as for the unmarried (National Recreation Association, 1935).

The narrowing down of recreational interests generally begins late in the thirties and continues for the rest of the individual's life. A survey of the leisure-hour activities of 5,000 people showed that those between the ages of forty-six and sixty years checked fewer activities than those between twenty-one and twenty-six years. Only musical and educational activities increased with age. All others were found to decrease in frequency of participation. The "desire" to participate was found to be influenced by age in much the same way as actual participation (National Recreation Association, 1935). Of all forms of recreation, reading has been found to be the least stable, and playing a musical instrument the most stable activity during the adult years (Thorndike, 1935).

An analysis of the different forms of recreation commonly engaged in by American adults of today will show how interest in different recreations waxes and wanes with age. *Dancing* is popular into early adulthood and then decreases in popularity with increasing age and the assumption of home and business responsibilities (Hall and Robinson, 1942; Thorndike, 1935). In a group of Missouri adults, 51 per cent said they never danced in the twenties, 74 per cent in the thirties, and 97 per cent in the fifties and over (Briggs, 1938). Active participation in *sports* and *athletic events* of all sorts likewise wanes in adult years. While the man or woman may still enjoy reading about sports, attending different athletic contests, or listening to them over the air, participation reaches a very low point as the individual advances into middle age (Briggs, 1938; Hall and Robinson, 1942; Thorndike, 1935). With advancing age there is a steady falling off of interest in *card playing* and *entertaining*. While 84 per cent of a group of young adults, under twenty-four years of age, said they entertained occasionally, only 47 per cent of the older group did so (Briggs, 1938).

Belonging to a club or lodge is the ambition of the majority of adolescents. By adult years, this interest wanes. Among the members of a group of Missouri adults studied by Briggs (1938), only 67 per cent belonged to such organizations and of those who did, only 20 per cent attended the meetings frequently. Business and professional men say they join such organizations and attend their meetings for professional reasons (Lynd and Lynd, 1929). Attending concerts, lectures, or church, on the other hand, is not greatly affected by advancing age (Briggs, 1938).

There are many adults who do not have *hobbies* and others who do not form them until financial success gives them greater leisure as they grow older. The adult who does not have a hobby is generally one who finds his work so absorbing that he feels no need for the additional outlet provided by a hobby (Young, 1940). Most adults, however, do not find their work so absorbing that they do not feel the need for some form of recreation that will engage their interest and attention. And there are many who find their work so boring or frustrating that they form a hobby as a type of compensation (Harsh and Schrickel, 1950). Individuals with hobbies increase in number steadily up to the age of sixty-five years, after which there is a decline. At different ages, different types of hobbies attract both men and women. Men, as a rule, prefer their work to their hobbies and derive more satisfaction from the former than from the latter (Super, 1941). The hobbies of men, on the whole, increase in number and in degree of interest less with age than do those of women. This may explain in part, the poorer adjustments made in old age by men than by women (Landis, 1942).

Among the men and women of Terman's group of "geniuses" whose development he had studied from early years, interest in hobbies was marked. Nearly two-thirds of the group reported an active interest in two or more avocational pursuits and more than a third in three or more. The women of the group showed a greater variability in their interests than did the men. Men who were most successful vocationally had greater avocational interests than did those who were least successful (Terman and Oden, 1947).

Adult hobbies are, for the most part, of a constructional nature. They include such activities as preparing and cooking food, painting, watching sports events, furniture making and repairing, taking moving pictures and developing films, music, gardening, cultural reading, and dressmaking (Hall and Robinson, 1942; Briggs, 1938). The adult may make a hobby of *collections*. These are not made up of things of momentary interest but things that have some intrinsic value. Stamps, postal cards from all over the world, books, *objets d'art,* fine needlework, buttons, and dolls of different countries and different eras are just a few of the types of things adults collect as a hobby.

The young adult, because of his many responsibilities, generally has less time for *reading* than he had when he was an adolescent. As a result, he must be more selective in what he reads. While reading remains one of the favorite forms of recreation throughout the adult years, there are marked shifts with age in the interest value of different topics. Interest in romance, for example, decreases with age while interest in governmental and religious activities increases. There is also an increase in the quality of the material read as the individual grows older (Hall and Robinson, 1942). The proportion of people reading books and the time spent on them decreases with age. On the other hand, there is more magazine and newspaper reading as people grow older. Among young adults, fiction has more appeal than nonfiction; among the middle-aged and older adults, the reverse is true. While readers of all ages like short stories, humor, and continued stories, with age there is an increased interest in news, in political articles, and in editorials (Gray and Monroe, 1929).

Among both men and women, newspaper reading ranks in first place, with men spending more of their reading time on newspapers than women, though single women have been found to read the newspapers more than married women (Johnson, 1932). Most adults read the headlines of newspapers, even if they do not read the whole paper (Wall, 1948). Papers that are classed as "superior" are read less than the illustrated dailies by adults under thirty years of age (Wall, 1948). With advance in age, however, the better type of newspaper is read and the shift is also seen in the quality of material read within the newspaper (Briggs, 1938). Analyses of what men and women read in the newspapers have revealed that the range of reading interests for adults is narrower than it is for adolescents (Wall, 1948). The items of greatest interest include sports, cartoons, photographs, personal violence, disaster, finance, and trade. The items of least interest relate to state news, education and schools, church, home, gardens, and radio (Gerberich and Thalheimer, 1936). Comics are read by more than three-quarters of all newspaper readers at all ages and of both sexes (Johnson, 1932).

The adult, far more than the child or the adolescent, likes to listen to *music*. A liking for both cultural and modern music shows an inverse relationship with age. The young adult prefers modern to classical music while the middle-aged adult prefers classical to modern music. The older individual becomes indifferent to modern music or he actually dislikes it (Rubin and Rabson, 1940). Going to the *movies* proves to be a less interesting recreation as the individual grows older. Adults, as a whole, attend movies rated as "good" or "excellent" in much greater proportions than do school children. Adults also like comedies, farces, and romantic productions. While children and adolescents are generally guided in their choice of movies by the actor or actress performing in them, adults generally are not. Adults are, likewise, less influenced in their choice by the previews and advertising than are adolescents (Edman, 1940).

People under forty listen to the *radio* more than do those over forty. Older adults show a greater preference for radio than reading as a recreational activity. Except as a source of news, they prefer the radio to the newspaper. Younger men show a preference for sports and orchestra dance programs while older men prefer the programs of old song favorites and news events. With age, women are less interested in dance orchestra and jazz song programs and more interested in old song favorites and orchestra programs. Older people are indifferent to both classical and modern music programs (Lazarsfeld, 1940, 1941; Rubin and Rabson, 1940). *Television* has, in recent years, become a popular form of amusement for adults as well as for children. A comparison of families with and without television sets revealed that television affects the pattern of leisure-time activities of all members of the family. TV families show a considerably lower level of participation in other types of activity outside the home, such as going to the movies, as well as in the home. The effect on the time spent in reading and nighttime radio listening was especially marked. A comparison of the effects of television on families of different socioeconomic status revealed that those of the lower groups were more influenced by television watching than were those of the higher socioeconomic groups (Coffin, 1948).

MORAL STANDARDS

Throughout late adolescence and into the twenties, the individual is engaged in revaluing his moral principles and establishing those which will be satisfactory to him throughout the remaining years of his life. As new interests open up and new responsibilities are assumed, a broader and more flexible code of morals is needed. Frequently, the revision of moral codes is difficult for the individual, especially when his early moral training has been inadequate or inconsistent. Several interesting research studies have been made to determine the moral attitudes of individuals of different ages. When a group of college students, their parents, and grandparents, were given a list of questions to determine what standards were used as a basis for their conduct, it was found that the parents and grandparents used mostly right and wrong standards. The college students, by contrast, preferred to make their moral decisions according to prudence or intellectual judgment rather than according to absolute standards of right and wrong. Parents, it was found, stood between the students and their grandparents in this matter while the greatest difference was between the students and their grandparents. Public opinion was found to be the least frequent basis used for determining moral standards for the three age groups. For the most part, the standards of behavior varied mostly with age, with the older groups showing far less tolerance than the younger groups (Anderson and Dvorak, 1928).

When a group of women college graduate students was asked their opinions regarding such matters as womens' smoking, discussing sex questions with men, reading popular sex literature, drinking, petting, and free love, the group which ranged in age from thirty to thirty-four years had changed most in their attitudes toward these matters since their college days. The older women had changed less, and the group from twenty-five to twenty-nine years of age were not only the most liberal in their views about these matters but they had changed least of all since their college days (Acheson, 1933). Judgments of "correct," "excusable," and "wrong" for certain moral problems were found to be far more rigid among older women than among younger. The older group judged most of the acts as "correct" or "wrong," with few that they considered "excusable" (Jones, 1946). A *Fortune Magazine* (1946) survey of moral attitudes revealed that those over forty years of age are more rigid than those under forty. In such matters as whether a husband or wife should have had sexual intercourse prior to marriage, the older group tended to be more rigid than the younger. Likewise, the older group tended to be less liberal than the younger in their attitude toward relaxing the divorce laws. Variations in age and socioeconomic status in sex morality worries are shown in Fig. 49.

While age is the primary cause of rigidity in moral attitudes, there have been found to be sex differences in rigidity at different ages. When men and women were given a list of acts of various degrees of "wickedness" and asked to grade the badness of each, it was found that the women showed a greater tendency to excessive censure than did the men. Women were harsher in judging petty offenses than men and less harsh than the men in the case of more serious offenses. In offenses characteristic of the opposite sex, women

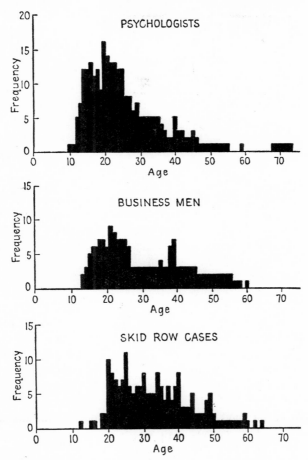

FIG. 49. Sex morality worries of adult men. (*From R. A. Dykman, E. K. Heiman, and W. A. Kerr, Lifetime worry patterns of three diverse adult cultural groups, J. soc. Psychol., 1952, 35:91–100. Used by permission.*)

were more severe than men in judging male offenses and more lenient toward female offenses. This led to the conclusion that the male has, on the whole, a more "objective" moral judgment than the female, who tends to exaggerate minor offenses (Terman and Miles, 1936).

Many of our adult criminals are individuals who began their criminal careers long before they reached maturity. Not all adult criminals, however, have a record of juvenile delinquency behind them. And like the juvenile delinquent, the adult criminal is frequently a repeater. Penalties imposed by the courts and terms of imprisonment are not adequate to reform him into a law-abiding citizen. With age, there is some decrease in criminality among ex-prisoners. Of the 63 factors investigated by Glueck and Glueck (1950), "aging" was found to be the most significant. Those who have not gained stability by the age of thirty-six are not likely to do so afterward.

ACHIEVEMENTS

Adulthood is the period of achievements. The individual who during the years of preparation lays the groundwork for his future occupation with a minimum of shifting from one vocational aim to another and who receives the necessary training to develop his innate abilities is more likely to achieve success in mature years than is the individual who shifts from one type of work to another. Adults who achieve distinction in adult life have had a preparation for these achievements in many years of relevant activity, combined with a noticeable continuity of purpose and interests. Thus, their accomplishments in adult life are dependent upon earlier sustained training and interests (Harsh and Schrickel, 1950).

Studies of achievement have revealed that the peak of achievement in adult years depends largely on the area in which the individual attains distinction (Lehman, 1949). In athletics, for example, the peak of achievement comes earlier than in science or in literature. Furthermore, when the individual reaches his peak will be dependent partially upon the criteria used to determine the level of his achievement. If success is measured in terms of financial reward, the peak will come at a different age than if it is masured in terms of quality or quantity of output. In *athletic abilities,* the peak of performance comes in the mid-twenties, though it varies somewhat for the different types of activity. Over half of the world's records in different sports, made during the past 50 years, have been made by persons around the age of twenty-four years (Lehman, 1938; Anderson, 1949).

In *literature* the peak of achievement comes at different ages, depending upon the type of writing. For lyric poetry, the peak comes near the age of 25 years, for short stories, at 35 years, for religious and philosophical writing, between the ages of 45 and 55 years, and for scientific prose, at $52\frac{1}{2}$ years (Heidler and Lehman, 1937; Lehman, 1943). *Scientific achievements* reach their peak at an average age of 47 years, while the productions of men of affairs do not reach a peak until slightly later (Thorndike, 1928.) For invention, the peak comes at an average age of 35 years; for mathematicians, at 35 with a secondary peak at 45; for astronomers, at 45 to 55; for chemical discovery, at 35; and for composers, earlier than the other types, with ages varying from the mid-twenties to the early thirties (Lehman, 1941, 1943).

The age of greatest *earning power* varies according to the type of work the individual does. The day laborer who requires little training for his work and whose success depends primarily upon physical strength, speed, and endurance, reaches his peak much earlier than the professional or executive for whom a long period of training and of experience is needed before he can hope to earn more than a bare livelihood. A study of Methodist ministers showed that there was a steady increase in their salaries up to the age of forty, following which was a plateau in their earning capacity until fifty-six, after which there was a decline in earning capacity. High- and low-salaried men showed approximately the same-shaped curve except for the high-salaried group where the age changes were most pronounced (Thorndike, 1928).

Studies of early and late productivity have revealed that individuals who are high producers in comparison with their contemporaries at an early age continue to be superior in this area as they grow older. Furthermore, they are individuals who work intensively in their chosen areas instead of shifting about from one line of work to another, and they either create a stimulating environment of their own or they move into an environment that will produce this stimulation. A young man with musical talent, for example, has little opportunity to achieve success or fame if he remains in the country town in which he was born. He must move to a city where there is an opportunity for him to develop his musical talent and to get the stimulation that comes from association with others whose interests and abilities are on a par with his.

SOCIAL BEHAVIOR

During maturity, the craving for popularity and the desire to have a large number of friends wane. This is especially true of married men and women. In place of a large number of friends, their interests are generally centered on the members of their families. This includes not only the immediate family but relatives on both sides. With them the adult spends most of his free time and with them he engages in social activities for which he selected outsiders when he was a child or an adolescent. The adult is far less dependent on outsiders for companionship if he is married than if he is single.

The unmarried adult, by contrast, is often lonely during his free time. This is even more true of unmarried women than of unmarried men. The friends of their youth and the people with whom they work are, for the most part, married, engaged, or preoccupied with dates and other activities with members of the opposite sex or with members of their own families. As a result, the unmarried woman frequently finds herself without companionship, not because she is socially unacceptable as is true during childhood and adolescence, but because her friends are tied up with their families and have made their social lives around the family circle.

The early years of adulthood are frequently lonely years for men as well as for women. When young men, because of economic reasons or because they have not yet found anyone with whom they would like to spend the rest of their lives, are living at home or are away from home, they often find themselves at loose ends during their leisure time. Their friends of earlier years and their business associates, as is true of the unmarried woman, are occupied with family activities or are preoccupied with courtship. As a result, the type of social life they enjoyed during adolescence, when there was always a congenial group to talk to or to do things with, is no longer there and they find themselves alone many times when they would like to have companionship with their contemporaries.

Havinghurst (1950) has described the loneliness of early adulthood and has given the reasons for it thus:

Early adulthood is the most individualistic period of life and the loneliest one, in the sense that the individual, or, at the most, two individuals, must proceed with a minimum of social attention and assistance to tackle the most important tasks of life. . . . Early adulthood seems, then, to be a period of storm and stress in America, and especially in the middle-class part of American society. The basic reason for this, when expressed in sociological terms, is that this is a relatively unorganized period in life which marks a transition from an age-graded to a social-status-graded society. During childhood and adolescence one climbs the age-ladder, getting new privileges and taking on new responsibilities with each step up the ladder. . . . This simple age-grading stops in our culture somewhere around 16 to 20. It is like reaching the end of the ladder and stepping off on to a new, strange cloud-land with giants and witches to be circumvented and the goose that lays the golden eggs to be captured if only one can discover the know-how. In the adult society prestige and power depend not so much on age as on skill and strength and wisdom, and family connections. Achieving the goals of life is not nearly so much a matter of waiting until one grows up to them, as it was in the earlier years. There must be a strategy, based on an understanding of the new terrain, which can only be got by scouting around and getting the lay of the land for a few years. This is what young people do, and it often takes several years to learn how to get about efficiently and to go where one wants to go in the adult society in America (abbreviated from pp. 64–65).

In the process of adjustments to adult life, the individual goes through many changes in his social interests and activities. There are shifts in friendships, changes in forms of recreation, changes in attitudes toward the opinions of the group, and changes in dependency upon group approval. The adult generally establishes a satisfactory and relatively stable social life for himself as he reaches the thirties. Middle life very often brings with it a renewed interest in social life and the establishment of a wider circle of friends and acquaintances than the individual had during the earlier years of adulthood. In many cases, the social life and interests of middle-aged men and women resemble those of older adolescents. There is a craving for the excitement of parties and a desire to be on the go all the time. Popularity, as expressed in a large number of friends and constant calls from these friends, comes to be important to the middle-aged individual as it was to the adolescent. There is a tendency to engage in flirtations with members of the opposite sex and a preoccupation with dress and grooming, in hopes of appearing younger and more attractive. This is often called the "dangerous age" because, at this time, the individual frequently breaks up the established pattern of family life, seeks excitement and adventure outside the home, and neglects the family.

When a group of older men and women in a rural area in North Carolina was studied from the point of view of their interest and participation in community affairs, it was found that the period from fifty-five to fifty-nine years was the peak for social participation, after which there was a sharp drop in social activities of all types (Mayo, 1951). As the individual reaches the sixties, however, his declining energy generally puts a stop to this too active social life. He finds he cannot take it any more and, as a result, his interest in social activities rapidly wanes. Popularity, generally bought by entertaining and expenditures of money he feels are wasted on things that do not count, loses its appeal for him. As a result, he settles down to the home circle and spends most of his time with his family, his children's newly established families, and friends of years' standing.

Friends. As is true of every age, friends in adulthood are selected on the basis of congeniality of interests. The adult, who in his work or social life comes in contact with those whose interests are similar to his, finds them more congenial than individuals whose interests are different. As a result, a friendship is established. It is popularly believed that friendships established during childhood will persist throughout life and that the friends of one's youth, because they are "old" friends, will be one's best friends. There is no evidence to prove that such is the case.

In early adulthood, much the same sort of social grouping exists as existed during the adolescent period. The social distance that marked off degrees of friendship then is operative in adulthood. There is a small group of intimate friends or confidants which frequently is made up of old friends unless the life interests of the individual have changed so that old friends are no longer congenial. Then there are less intimate friends belonging to the "crowd" whom the individual sees infrequently, for parties or other social gatherings. And, on the outer rim of the friendship circle is the large list of acquaintances whom the individual knows but slightly and with whom he comes in contact infrequently.

Degrees of social distance within this friendship circle change from time to time during adult years. Intimate friends may drift apart as their interests change or their places of residence change. This ebb and flow within the friendship circle results in an instability of friendships which, to an adolescent, would be very disturbing. To the adult, however, it is of little consequence. His major interest is in the family circle and, therefore, friendships are of less importance than they were in either childhood or adolescence. Forming of new friendships becomes increasingly difficult as age advances. By the late thirties or mid-forties, most men and women have a circle of friends as large as they want and, because their interests are stabilized by this time, their friends are not so likely to change as they did when the individual was younger and when there was a greater shift in his interests.

Leadership. Studies of persistence of leadership have revealed that "once a leader, always a leader," holds true in a large percentage of adolescent leaders. Not only do these individuals attain positions of leadership in business or community affairs during their adult years but their chance of making a success in whatever line of work they enter is greater than for those who were followers during their school days. The experience gained from their leadership status in school, the prestige associated with leadership, and the self-confidence being a leader engenders in the individual all contribute to his success in adult life.

When a group of men and women who had graduated from a small-city high school was analyzed and rated for leadership and success in their adult occupations, it was found that those who had been leaders in extracurricular activities during their school days rated higher in "success" as measured by further educational achievements, occupational level attained, ownership of property or business, positions of honor or of trust, and confidence and esteem of fellow workers, associates, or employers. Sixty-five per cent of the school leaders were rated as successful in adult life, while only 15 per cent of the nonleaders in school became successful in adult life. This would suggest that leadership is the "best prognosticator of success in later life" (Crowley, 1940).

As Shannon (1929) has pointed out, "Whatever is required to excel in the extracurricular life of the high school seems to be the same thing that contributes most to success later." Terman found much the same to be true of the group of boys and girls of very high intelligence he studied into their adult years. While they were in college, they participated to a greater extent in extracurricular activities than college students as a whole. Among the graduates and nongraduates of colleges in adult years, there were more in positions of responsibility and leadership than is true of college graduates as a group (Terman and Oden, 1947).

CHAPTER 12

Adulthood

(Continued)

The adult years present many new problems, different in major aspects from the problems experienced during the earlier years of life. Consequently, the individual must use a new and different strategy, based on an understanding of the new terrain, if he is to make a success of his adjustments. This will necessitate scouting around and trying out different adjustments for a few years while he gets the lay of the land (Havinghurst, 1950). The more scouting around he does at this time, the more likely he is to be happy as the years pass. Adjustments to the problems of maturity made too hastily on the other hand, are rarely as satisfactory in the long run as slower and more carefully considered adjustments.

Adjustments are always difficult and are invariably accompanied by emotional tension. While the individual is trying to get the lay of the new land in which he finds himself, he is likely to be upset emotionally and, like the adolescent who finds himself in a new and different land, the young adult goes through a period of emotional storm and stress. In an attempt to decide what his life career will be, where he wants to live for the remaining years of his life, or with whom he wishes to share his life, the young adult is in a state of indecision during which he tries out first one solution to his problem and then another until he finds a satisfactory one.

Complications to adjustments at this time come partly from parental pressures and partly from the individual's own unrealistic concepts of what he wants and what he is capable of. Few parents are willing to allow the young adult to make his own choices. This complicates his decisions and presents barriers to clear thinking on his part. In an attempt to satisfy his parents' wishes and his own desires, he frequently makes a compromise which is satisfactory neither to him nor to them. Then, too, his own unrealistic concepts, based on childhood dreams for his future, add other complications to the attainment of a satisfactory adjustment. The young adult who always wanted to be a successful doctor, for example, finds it difficult to adjust to a career as a hospital orderly or an ambulance driver.

From the beginning of adulthood until the early or mid-thirties, the average American of today is preoccupied with problems related to adjustments in the different major areas of his life. These adjustments will not all be made at the same time, nor will their final form be accepted simultaneously. While adjustment is being made to one area, there is a marked preoccupation with that interest. Then, when the adjustment is satisfactorily made, the individual's attention shifts to another form of adjustment. It is difficult, if not actually impossible, for a young adult to solve two such major problems as the choice of a life career and a life mate simultaneously. He therefore solves one problem and then turns his attention to the other.

By the mid-thirties, the average adult has established a life pattern that will remain, with only minor changes, for the rest of his life. Many adults do not need this long to establish themselves in their life patterns. Shortly after they reach maturity, they have married, established themselves in the type of work they will do for the remaining years of their lives, and have settled in a community where they intend to live permanently. This early solution to their life problems may prove to be satisfactory in the long run and it may not. If the decision has been based on strong drives, interests, and abilities, well and good. If, however, the decision has been made hastily to satisfy parental urgings or their own desires, the chances are that a time will come when they regret their hasty decisions.

While adulthood brings with it many adjustments for every individual, there are certain adjustments that are almost universal in our culture. These are vocational adjustment, marital adjustment, adjustment to parenthood, adjustment to singleness, and sex-role adjustment.

VOCATIONAL ADJUSTMENT

Vocational adjustment becomes increasingly difficult for each successive generation of young adults. This is due partly to the ever-increasing number of different types of work available from which the individual must make his choice, partly to the long and often costly preparation needed for the type of work the individual selects, and partly to the individual's ignorance of his capacities. The choice is further complicated by the unrealistic vocational aims that children and adolescents often have. When an individual has had vocational aspirations far beyond his capacities for a number of years, it is difficult, if not impossible, to make a satisfactory adjustment to the type of work his abilities and training force him into.

And yet, to the average man, adult happiness is largely dependent upon a satisfactory vocational adjustment. If he is unhappy in his work, if he feels that he is capable of a higher paying and more responsible job than he has, and if he dislikes his work associates, he will be unhappy in his home life, his social life, and every other area of his life. The well-adjusted individual must be successfully adjusted to his work as well as to other important areas of his life. Much unhappiness in adult life today stems from vocational maladjustments. Men alone do not experience vocational maladjustments. With the increasing number of women in the vocational field, women of today are subject to the effects of vocational adjustment, just as men are. Among young women, misfits in the business world are not serious because the average young woman looks upon her job as a stopgap before marriage.

If, however, she is planning to have a career, with or without marriage, the right choice of career is as important to her as it is to a man. And, because she finds many of the lines of work in which she is interested either shut to women or dominated by men, she feels blocked and unhappy when forced into a line of work in which she has little interest or in which she sees little opportunity for advancement because of her sex.

Vocational Selection. The gigantic task of finding the right niche becomes apparent when one realizes that, at the time of the Second World War, there were 25,000 major civilian occupations from which the soldiers came. It has been estimated that, in our country, there are at least 100,000 distinct occupations from which the individual must make the choice of his life career (Anderson, 1949). Each year, as new discoveries and inventions appear, new types of work are created. Only after the individual leaves school and tries to fit himself into our complex modern society does he realize how serious the task of vocational selection actually is. For that reason, many young adults who have had little specific training for a particular line of work in high school or college go through a period of trial and error in which they try out one job after another.

Vocational Preparation. Once a decision is reached, the next step is preparation for the vocation selected. This is often so long and costly that it necessitates great sacrifices on the individual's part, the most serious of which is the postponement of marriage. When a vocation has been selected in a haphazard manner, mainly on the basis of a temporary interest or the advice of well-meaning relatives and friends whose assessment of the individual's abilities may be as unrealistic as his, and when this decision has been followed by a period of preparation, it is common for the individual to feel that it is too late to make a change, even when he realizes that neither his interest nor his ability fits him for a successful pursuit of his chosen work. As a result, he remains in this work and becomes increasingly dissatisfied with it as each year passes.

Occupational Status. The importance of a satisfactory choice of career becomes apparent when one realizes that the status of the individual in adult society is determined largely by his occupation. Both in and out of work, he associates mainly with individuals in lines of work similar to his. They not only have interests in common but their earnings determine where they will live and with what social groups they will associate. If, for example, the individual's abilities are above the level of his occupation, he will not only derive little satisfaction from the work itself but, in addition, he will derive little satisfaction from association with his work companions and even less from the social group with which he lives. By contrast, the individual whose work is well suited to his abilities finds satisfaction both in his work and in his associations with the people with whom he works and lives (Roethlisberger and Dickson, 1943).

The occupational role of the man in our culture determines the social status of the family, especially in the upper and middle socioeconomic groups. The woman is expected to assume the role of a housewife and, as a result, her status is unimportant in establishing the family social status. Among the members of the lower economic groups and, to a lesser extent, the middle-class groups where the wife may work for a short time after her marriage until her first baby arrives, the occupational status of the woman is of minor importance in the determination of the family social status. Only when her earnings, added to those of her husband, make it possible for the family to live in a better neighborhood than would be possible with his earnings alone does her occupation play any role in establishing the family social status.

The occupational status of women is far less satisfactory than that of men. Among unmarried women and even among the married women who continue to work after marriage, the attainment of an occupational status that fits their abilities is frequently denied them. In many of the professions, as well as in the skilled laboring work of the factory, the woman is often forced into a position below her capacities while the position she is equipped by ability and training to hold is given to a man not because his ability is greater than hers but because of his sex. This naturally militates against job satisfaction among women and results in a poorer adjustment to work and out-of-work activities than would occur if there were opportunities for free competition among workers of both sexes.

Age of Vocational Drive. The urge to success is, for the average boy or girl, strongest during the years of late adolescence (Symonds, 1937). At that time, young people think in terms of setting the world on fire by their accomplishments. Like their vocational aims, this desire for success is very unrealistic in that it does not take into account the individual's abilities or, in most cases, not even his chosen line of work. Much of the enthusiasm of youth carries over into the early years of adulthood. It takes the form of preoccupation with the chosen work and the expenditure of tremendous energy in hopes of winning success and advancement. This results in the peak of vocational accomplishment or productivity between the age of thirty and the mid-forties. At this time, productivity is the result of ambition and of initiative (Lehman, 1943).

The individual who has not made a satisfactory adjustment to his work by this time and who has not shown at least reasonable success in it, is not likely to do so as he grows older. From the mid-forties on, the vocational drive of the individual begins to wane. While many men and women reach their peak of vocational achievement at this age or even slightly later, their drive decreases as time goes on. At middle age, the vocational drive is replaced by a desire for security. Having a job with security back of it now means more to the individual than climbing higher in the vocational ladder.

Job Satisfaction. An analysis of men's attitudes toward their jobs showed age cycles in job satisfaction. In the early twenties, there is a period of satisfaction. At this time, young men are just getting started in their work and are glad to have any job at all, regardless of whether or not it comes up to their aspirations. Furthermore, with the confidence of youth, they believe that they have the necessary ability to get ahead. With this confidence to spur them along, they are willing to expend more energy than the job demands and frequently take extra courses of study to prepare themselves for advancement. Then, around the age of twenty-five years, dissatisfaction begins to appear. This comes from the fact that they do not feel they are getting ahead as rapidly as they should or they begin to realize that they are job misfits and that they will not be satisfied in this line of work for the rest of their lives.

This period of unrest and dissatisfaction lasts until the mid-thirties, after which there is generally a period of satisfaction because of greater achievements and better financial rewards. By the mid-forties, another period of dissatisfaction sets in. This comes partly from change in emphasis of interests which results in the worker's finding more satisfaction outside his work than in it and partly from the fact that his work has lost some of its former attractiveness for him and he has not yet developed other sources of satisfaction. After a period of adjustment, ranging from one to five or more years, the individual develops new nonvocational interests which help to improve his general adjustment to his work (Super, 1939).

The basis on which the individual selects his vocation will have a marked influence on the degree of satisfaction he derives from it. If the selection was made because of a strong interest in activities related to the type of work he does, there is a far greater chance for job satisfaction than when the work was selected for economic reasons. Under such conditions, the individual gets more satisfaction from his avocations than from his chosen line of work. When avocation and vocation are similar, the individual will get greater satisfaction from his vocation than when they are dissimilar. And, because an avocation is the manifestation of a dominant interest, the avocation becomes the major source of satisfaction if it competes with the vocation (Super, 1941).

Employment and Morale. Employment with a regular source of income is essential to the happiness of a large percentage of the population. During the adult years when men or women have families dependent upon them for support, being employed, even if the work is not entirely to their liking, is better than being unemployed. In an attempt to discover just how seriously unemployment affects the individual's morale at different ages, two studies have been reported which throw considerable light on this problem. Among unemployed men over forty-five years of age, the morale scores were found to be slightly higher than for younger men. The explanation given for this was that older men maintain their traditional faith in American opportunities for ability to bring advancement.

When two groups of professional engineers, one of which was made up of employed and the other of unemployed men, were questioned to determine their attitudes toward their employers, religion, and their occupational morale, it was found that 68 per cent of the unemployed were more bitter toward employers than were the employed, 75 per cent had poorer "occupational morale," and 58 per cent were more critical of religion than was the median employed man. The work attitude of the youngest men in the group was the least affected by unemployment. Unemployed men in the thirties were, on the average, the most bitter toward employers and had the lowest occupational morale (Hall, 1934).

Sex Preferences in Work. There are certain occupations which are considered appropriate for women in our culture and others that are not. Among those that are considered inappropriate for women are occupations which require heavy lifting, which involve working in all kinds of weather or in dangerous places, or which require long shifts of duty (Women's Bureau, 1941). It is also popularly believed that women do not belong in certain professions that are traditionally masculine, such as engineering, medicine, law, and the ministry. In spite of these beliefs, some women have been able to enter work that was closed to them a generation or two ago and have proved themselves equal to men in this work. Likewise, during war periods, women are given work in some factories which in peacetime are considered inappropriate for them, and they have proved their worth in such work.

When given a choice of occupations, women as a whole prefer indoor occupations. Only in the case of social work and journalism, both of which are partly outdoor occupations, are there any lines of work preferred by women which require their working out of doors. Artistic and decorative occupations are more favored by women than by men. Women also show a preference for lines of work involving direct ministration to the comfort, convenience, and welfare of others, such as social work, nurse, cook, private secretary, and dressmaker. Men, by contrast, prefer occupations associated with adventure, bodily risk, muscular strength, and bodily exercise. In addition, they prefer occupations pursued exclusively or predominantly by men. This contrasts to women who prefer occupations that are pursued by both men and women, or in which there is a female monopoly, such as nursing and home economics (Terman and Miles, 1936).

Attitudes at Middle Age. The vocational readjustment of the middle-aged individual has been complicated in recent years by two major factors. First,

the increasing life span of both men and women with the consequent prolongation of their years of usefulness; and second, the relatively new policy
in business and industry to hire only younger people partly to minimize the
expense the organization must carry for retirement pensions and partly
because of the widespread belief that maximum productivity can be achieved
best by hiring and training young workers.

With the high cost of living and the heavy taxation that face all workers
today, men become increasingly aware of the fact that their days of earning
good salaries draw to a close as they reach the mid-forties or early fifties.
Hence, if they have not been able to make adequate provisions for old age
up to then, they realize that their future chances of doing so will be limited.
Furthermore, they know that their chances for advancement after middle age
will be slight and that, in place of advancement, there is a likelihood that
they will have to take a position in their organization with less responsibility
and, consequently, a lower salary. The realization that they are being pushed
aside by younger workers does not add to the vocational satisfaction of the
middle-aged worker.

So long as a man in middle age retains his job, no matter how discontented
he may be with it, he is reasonably certain of employment until he reaches
the compulsory retirement age. The unions see to that. But, should a period
of depression come at this time, the unions cannot keep him on the job and,
because middle-aged workers are regarded as less efficient and, hence, less
valuable to their employers, they are usually the first to be laid off. The
possibility of unemployment in middle age, combined with the realization
that reemployment at that age will be almost impossible, is a constant threat
hanging over the head of a middle-aged worker. This causes job dissatisfaction and is a constant threat to the happiness of the middle-aged man.

Changing jobs in middle age, even when the change is to a closely related
line of work, is almost impossible. The employment practice, mentioned above,
which is designed to take new and young workers on the grounds that their
days of usefulness will be greater to their employers than is true of older
workers and that even though an older worker may have greater skill, he is
less adjustable to new work situations, makes it almost impossible for a
middle-aged worker to change jobs, no matter how unsatisfactory his present
work conditions may be.

The middle-aged woman who, after bringing up her family, may want to
work to supplement the family income or to fill in idle hours, finds the
situation even more difficult than men do. Because she has not been working
during the earlier years of adulthood, she is unfamiliar with the new methods,
even though she may have had training and experience in similar lines of
work when she was younger. She finds competition with younger women
far stiffer than men do and, as a result, she discovers that getting any job
at all, with the exception of work in the domestic or related fields, is almost

impossible. This intensifies the adjustment problems for middle-aged women, especially those of the lower-income brackets. Like men, they face the problems of old age with deep concern, especially when their husbands are older than they and in poor health which, they know, may leave them in a precarious economic position when they reach old age.

MARITAL ADJUSTMENT

To the average young adult, marriage is the most important and, at the same time, most serious adjustment that must be made. While the adolescent thinks almost exclusively in terms of love, ignoring such important factors in marriage happiness as congeniality of interests and family backgrounds, the adult approaches marriage in a more realistic manner, facing the many problems that marriage entails before embarking upon this all-important lifetime adventure.

Age of Marriage. In the past, not only in our culture but in most cultures in Europe and in other civilized parts of the world, marriages in the teens were common. Today, the usual age for marriage is during the twenties. This varies somewhat according to the socioeconomic status of the group to which the individual belongs, with those of the lower socioeconomic groups marrying, on the average, 1 to 5 years earlier than those of the higher socioeconomic groups (Glick and Landau, 1950). The reason for this age differential is primarily economic. Men and women of the lower socioeconomic groups have completed their education and are already established in work when they reach the age of legal maturity. For the most part, their earning capacity is close to its peak at that time. The age of marriage varies according to peace and war, prosperity and depression (Glick and Landau, 1950). Ages at first marriage for different socioeconomic groups are shown in Fig. 50.

Men and women of the higher socioeconomic groups, by contrast, have just barely finished their education when they reach legal maturity, and, in many cases, specialized training for a profession or executive business career must be continued into the early years of maturity. As a result, many individuals in this group must defer marriage until their education has been completed and until they have had an opportunity to establish themselves in their chosen careers. By contrast with occupations in the lower economic levels, these careers are frequently poorly paid at first, and this adds another obstacle to early marriage.

The peak ages for love affairs and marriage come in the early and again in the late twenties. Following this, there is a decreasing frequency of love affairs until the forties, when there is another peak, especially for women. This is the time when divorce and remarriage occur most frequently and when individuals who in their earlier years were prevented from marriage by economic or family responsibilities find themselves now free to marry. After the mid-forties, there is a steady decline in love affairs and marriage (Hamilton and MacGowan, 1929). Analysis of census data has shown that the average age for first marriage for men was 26.1 years in 1890 as compared with 22.7 years in 1949. The average age for women was 22.0 years in

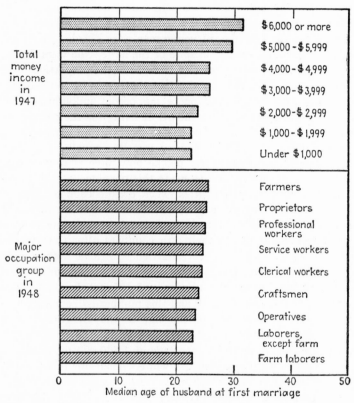

FIG. 50. Age at first marriage for husbands married less than 5 years, by income in 1947 and occupation in 1948, in the United States. (*From P. C. Glick and E. Landau, Age as a factor in marriage. Amer. sociol. Rev., 1950, 16:517–529. Used by permission.*)

1890 as compared with 20.3 years in 1949. In 1949, only 9 per cent of American men married for the first time before they were 20 years old and only 7 per cent after they were 35. The age of first marriage for women was more restricted. One-half of the American women in that year married between 19 and 24 years, 15 per cent before 18, and 7 per cent after 30 (Glick and Landau, 1950).

Sex Ratio. Recent statistics have shown that the proportion of married men and women in America is increasing rather than decreasing. In the early days of American history, marriage was essential to both men and women for economic reasons. The maintenance of a home and all means of livelihood depended upon the joint efforts of men and women. In those days, the population was approximately evenly distributed between the two sexes, another factor that contributed to the high proportion of married individuals. With geographic expansion and with increase in industrialization, the proportions of the married began to decline. This decline was intensified during war periods, because a large number of young men were killed.

Since the turn of this century, in spite of the large-scale wars that America has been involved in, there has been an increase in the proportions of married adults. This may be explained by the fact that areas of the country which in pioneer days had a disproportionate number of individuals of one sex are now equalized, by the higher standard of living for the whole population which makes it possible for more people to marry at an early age than was possible when the wealth of the country was less equally distributed, and by the increasing number of elderly people now alive who were married in their youth or later when conditions made this possible.

Until the depression of the thirties, when drastic changes were made in our immigration laws, there were more men than women in America. For the most part, the immigrants who came to America to seek their fortune were men who intended to return to their own countries after their fortunes had been made. Many of them, however, married American women and settled down in America. In 1930, males twenty-one years of age and over exceeded females twenty-one years of age and over by 1,125,000. In 1944, by contrast, females exceeded males by 331,000, and this number is increasing as a result of the Second World War and of the war in the Far East. For women between the ages of eighteen and forty-five years, the most marriageable years of a woman's life, there is a shortage of 1,500,000 men. The situation is even more serious for Negro than for white women, for there is a shortage of approximately 25 per cent of potential husbands for them. Among Europeans, this situation has existed for many generations, but it is a new trend in American society (Anderson, 1949). Because of the disproportionately large number of women, courtship behavior and the attitudes of young women in our culture are undergoing changes which are proving to be disturbing to members of the older generation.

Problems in Marital Adjustment. Marital adjustment is a far more difficult adjustment than most people realize. It is more than a case of falling in love and living happily ever after, as our fairy tales of childhood days intimate. And it is far more than just adjusting to one person, the marriage partner. While it is true that a person does not "marry the family" of the marriage partner, he or she automatically becomes a unit in a new family group after marriage. This involves adjustments to a whole new social group, one in which the individual may not be a welcome member. Then, too, there are marked adjustments in the pattern of living that must be made when one changes status from an unmarried to a married individual. To many people, especially as they grow older, changes in patterns of living are very difficult adjustments to make and, like all adjustments, they are likely to be emotionally disturbing.

Choice of Mate. Success or failure in marriage depends more upon the right choice of mate than upon any other one factor in the marriage pattern. For that reason, it is most important that the choice be made wisely and with a complete understanding of the entire situation. In earlier generations in our culture, the decision was largely in the hands of the parents of both young people. Because they were not emotionally involved and because of their broader experience, it was believed that a wiser choice could be made than would be possible by the young people themselves. Since the turn of the present century, there has been a gradual swing in the opposite direction. Today, the choice rests almost entirely with the young people with minimum advice or help of any sort from parents, relatives, or any outsider. Because of inexperience and inability to foresee the many problems and adjustments that marriage invariably brings, the choice is often far from wise.

While the primary responsibility for the choice of a mate lies in the hands of the persons involved, rather than of their parents, it is a choice made today by both men and women, rather than by the man alone. Now the woman plays a far more aggressive role than would have been considered sexually appropriate a few generations ago. This change in the courtship pattern has been brought about partly by the trend toward equality between the sexes in education, privileges, and modes of behavior, and partly by the change in sex ratio. At a time when the male sex is proportionally greater than the female, there will be keen competition among eligible males for the eligible females. When, however, the ratio shifts in the opposite direction, the tables are turned and the competition of women for the eligible men grows increasingly keener as the ratio becomes more and more unfavorable to the women.

Not all members of the opposite sex are attractive to all individuals. What one woman may find attractive in a man, another may find unattractive. Likewise, not all men find the same woman attractive to them. There are marked individual differences in this as in all other forms of human behavior. For the most part, the selection of a mate is greatly influenced by past experiences in the individual's life, the attitudes he has formed, and the ideals he has established. This point of view has been expressed by Dreikurs (1935) as follows:

The choice of a mate represents not the outcome of a biologically operating animal urge, but that it is an action depending mainly on *psychic aims* which correspond to the psychic structure of the individual. . . . Personal motives always determine the choice of a mate. . . . There is no question but that in the matter of a love-partner each individual has a certain "taste," a predilection for certain kinds of people and that he is attracted by certain qualities. But · his "taste," his predilection and that which attracts him are not fixed by fate. In any given case they can be adapted to the conditions of real life. One's predilection and the choice of one's mate are stages on the road to the right or faulty solution of the problem of love.

In attracting members of the opposite sex, some factors are more important than others. Those that rank high during the adolescent years will not necessarily be the most important ones during adult years. And as people reach middle life, their choice of a life mate will be on a basis different from that of the earlier years of adulthood. Likewise, members of the two sexes want different qualities in their mates. Men, for example, rank looks higher than women do; to women, the intellectual and educational background of a man is of great importance because they determine how successful he will be vocationally and, hence, how good a provider he will be.

Of the many factors that play a role of importance in the selection of a mate in adult years, the following are the most important:

1. APPEARANCE. There is no question about the fact that adult men and women like the individuals they associate with to make a good appearance. The first attraction to a member of the opposite sex is frequently on the basis of looks. Men, on the whole, are more "looks-conscious" than women as is shown by the fact that while 68 per cent of a group of young men questioned said that they would not marry a young woman who was not good looking, 79 per cent of a group of young women said that they would be willing to marry a young man who was not good looking (Baber, 1936). Small appearance differentials between husbands and wives contribute to good adjustment in marriage, especially when the wives are rated as better looking than their husbands (Kirkpatrick and Cotton, 1951).

The adult has discovered that clothes are important not only to enhance the natural beauty of the individual but also to cover up or to divert attention from physical characteristics that are unattractive. Women, even more than men, use clothing as a camouflage. For that reason, women and men, during the days of early maturity when selection of a mate is a problem of primary importance to them, are far more preoccupied with clothing than they are later, after the selection has been made. How important clothing is to a young adult may be seen by the fact that a large percentage of both men and women say that they would be willing to deprive themselves of certain pleasures and even of some of the necessities of life in order to be in style (Hurlock, 1929).

As individuals approach middle age, appearance is a less important factor in the selection of a mate than it is earlier. While it is true that both men and women of middle age are looks-conscious when they are anxious to marry, they are realistic enough to realize that their youthful charm is a thing of the past and that they must rely more upon clothing to enhance their attractiveness than was necessary when they were younger. After death or divorce, middle-aged men and women frequently show a renewed interest in their appearance when they are hoping to remarry.

2. SIMILARITY OF ABILITIES. While some men prefer their wives to be "beautiful but dumb," this is far from a universal desire. When a group of college students was asked, "Would you prefer the person you marry to be less intelligent, more intelligent, or equal to you in intelligence?" 95 per cent of the men and women said they preferred their future mates to be equal to or more intelligent than they. Only 0.9 per cent of the men and no women preferred a mate of less intelligence (Rockwood and Ford, 1945). Men of high intellectual level select as wives women whose intelligence is equal to that of the average college graduate (Terman and Oden, 1947).

3. SIMILARITY OF AGE. The general tendency in our culture is for women to marry men approximately 2 years older than they. Marked differences in ages between husbands and wives are the exception to the rule. The slight differential in age between husbands and wives can be explained by the earlier age of sexual maturing on the part of girls with the consequent superiority in social and emotional maturity. Because boys and girls of approximately the same chronological age grow up together, attend school together, and belong to the same crowds during adolescence, the girl has little opportunity to meet young men older than she. As a result, her selection of a mate is limited to the young men whom she has known throughout her school years. Furthermore, there is greater congeniality and understanding among those of approximately the same ages than when the age difference is greater. This has been shown repeatedly in studies of friendships of individuals of all age levels.

An age differential of 3 to 5 years, in favor of the man, is the preferred age difference for the majority of young men and women (Baber, 1936; Rockwood and Ford, 1945). While there are some romances with older men or women, there are very few with persons recognized as younger than themselves (Hamilton, 1929). An analysis of census data for the year 1949 has shown that, in the case of first marriages, the average wife is 2.8 years younger than her husband. One-half of all American women are from 1 to 5 years younger than their husbands. Only 10 per cent of American women are the same ages as their husbands in their first marriages, while 78 per cent are younger and 12 per cent are older (Glick and Landau, 1950).

4. SIMILARITY IN BACKGROUNDS. When it comes to the selection of a marriage partner, the socioeconomic status of the individual is taken into consideration. While there are some instances of "Cinderella marriages," in which a wealthy man marries a very poor girl from humble parentage and equally humble background, most marriages are between individuals whose backgrounds are similar in religion, interests, economic status, and cultural advantages. The "cultural likeness" of marriage partners may be explained by the fact that young people are segregated in religious and social classes and in

nationality groups in their social lives and great pressure is brought to bear on them by parents and friends to "marry within their groups." Any attempt to select a marriage partner outside the approved group is likely to be met with stern disapproval by the family and social group to which the young person belongs (Burgess and Wallin, 1943).

How marked an influence similarity of background has on marriage selection may be seen in the fact that 91 per cent of marriages are between men and women of the same religion. Among Jews, 97.1 of all marriages are with individuals of the same faith, as compared with 93.8 per cent of Catholics and 74.4 per cent of Protestants. Social class, as determined by residential area, likewise has a marked influence on marriage selection. More than half, 58.2 per cent, of marriages are between individuals from the same class of residential area. Men select wives from lower-class areas more often than women select men from lower-class areas. In conclusion, it is evident that "the person one marries is very similar culturally to one's self." This supports the theory of homogamy rather than heterogamy in marriage (Hollingshead, 1950).

5. PERSONALITY. A pleasing personality is an asset in mate selection as it is in the selection of friends. Frequently a pleasing personality outweighs other factors and compensates for physical, cultural, and educational deficiencies. By adulthood, most men and women have learned from past experience that social adjustments to individuals whose dispositions are unpleasant are difficult and, as a result, they take this matter into consideration when selecting a life mate (Baber, 1936). There is a strong tendency for both men and women to be attracted to a member of the opposite sex whose personality is the opposite of his, as in the case of introversion and extroversion (Gray, 1949).

6. RESIDENTIAL PROPINQUITY. Because place of residence is determined largely by the socioeconomic status of the family to which the individual belongs, and because friendships are established between people who live within the same residential areas, residential propinquity plays a role of great importance in the selection of a mate. This also means social, economic, religious and ethnic propinquity which, as was pointed out above, are important factors in marriage selection. Most men marry women who live within a few blocks of them (Clarke, 1952). Less than 20 per cent of marriages are between people who live in different communities (Bossard, 1932). Young people marry closer to home than older ones (Harris, 1935).

7. OCCUPATIONAL SELECTION. The type of work young people do plays a role of great importance in the selection of a life mate. Many young people meet their future mates in their jobs or in work closely related to their jobs. To a girl, the selection of an occupation is important because it determines whether or not she will have opportunities to meet young men or whether she will be isolated from masculine contacts because of her work. The business

field offers women the best opportunities for marriage, while the professions are most likely to bar women from marriage (Popenoe, 1932). The more educated a woman is, the more likely she is to go into a line of work and, hence, into a social environment, where women predominate. Furthermore, the woman's selection of work determines from what occupational level she will select her future husband (Marvin, 1938).

Sexual Adjustments to Marriage. Of all adjustments in marriage, this is not only the most difficult to achieve but the one which, if not satisfactorily achieved by both husband and wife, is most likely to lead to unhappiness and marital discord. Unlike other adjustments the adult must make, there has been little or no opportunity for either men or women to have preliminary experience related closely enough to this adjustment to enable them to make it easily or with a minimum of emotional tension. Strong social taboos against premarital intercourse and even against petting have kept many young men and women from the preliminary practice in sexual behavior which will aid them in adjustments to the marriage relationship. Furthermore, the belief that sexual relations produce states of ecstasy not paralleled by any other experience has led many young adults to be so disillusioned at the beginning of their married lives that the attainment of later sexual satisfaction is impossible.

Among men, the peak of the *sexual drive* comes in the late teens and begins to decline in the early twenties, when the man is old enough to consider marriage. Among women, by contrast, the peak does not come until the late twenties, several years after they are normally married. This discrepancy in ages of maximum sexual desire in favor of the male sex is especially important when one realizes that women, as a rule, marry men a year or two their seniors. Consequently, the peak of the woman's sexual desire does not come until the male sexual desire has started to wane significantly (Kinsey *et al.*, 1948).

Added to this is another matter of great significance, the periodicity of the female sexual desire. Among women, there is a bimodal monthly curve of sex desire (Tinklepaugh, 1933). While the times of greatest sexual desire may vary slightly for different individuals, all investigations have reported such periodicity. This does not occur in men. The strength of the male sexual desire does fluctuate from time to time, but the fluctuations are due primarily to physiological causes, such as fatigue and general good health, to psychological causes, such as states of depression and elation, or to the stimuli in the individual's immediate environment, such as an unusually attractive member of the opposite sex or the presence of a member of the opposite sex whose behavior revolts him.

Evidences of the strength of the male sex desire are seen in the number and frequency of outlets for this desire. While this varies markedly according to the educational and social level of the individuals, there is evidence that marital intercourse occurs frequently in the early years of maturity and then begins to wane as individuals reach the thirties. It is interesting to note that early-maturing boys have higher rates of sexual outlets than late-maturing boys. They not only have a head start but they continue to be more active later. This difference is explained as being due partly to physical factors and partly to lack of social restraints which come later and affect the late-maturing boys more than those who mature earlier (Kinsey *et al.*, 1948).

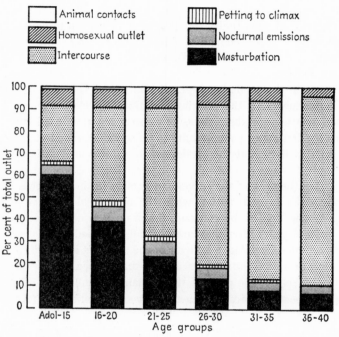

FIG. 51. Sources of orgasm for total U.S. male population. (*From H. C. Kinsey, W. B. Pomeroy, and C. E. Martin, Sexual behavior in the human male. Philadelphia: Saunders, 1948. Used by permission.*)

During the years of early adulthood, men and women, both married and unmarried, engage in autoerotic practices more frequently than is ordinarily believed. The strong sex drive of early maturity must have some outlet and, if social taboos and other cultural restrictions make it impossible for this drive to express itself through normal channels, the expression comes through channels that are socially tabooed. Masturbation is the most common form of autoeroticism in adulthood, though other forms are used (Davis, 1929; Landis *et al.*, 1940; Hamilton, 1942; Kinsey *et al.*, 1948). Sexual outlets for men of different ages are shown in Fig. 51.

A study of the effects of first pregnancies upon the sexual adjustments of young couples has revealed that when there was good adjustment before pregnancy, there was good adjustment during pregnancy and following the birth of the child (see Fig. 52). In only a minority of the cases did those with poor adjustment before pregnancy improve later. The level of sex desire was found to be somewhat lower for both husbands and wives after pregnancy

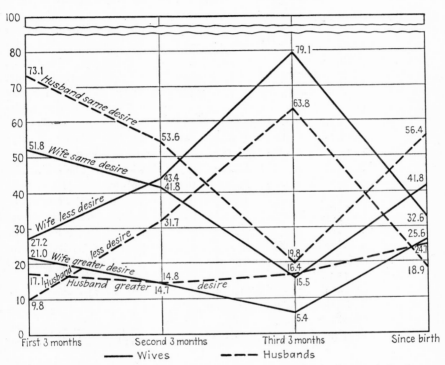

FIG. 52. Percentages of husbands and wives rating sexual desire in three periods of pregnancy and following the birth of the child, as compared with desire before pregnancy. (*From J. T. Landis, T. Poffenberger, and S. Poffenberger, The effects of first pregnancy upon sexual adjustment of 212 couples. Amer. sociol. Rev., 1950, 15:766–772. Used by permission.*)

than before. Wives who had confidence in the contraceptives they used experienced better sex adjustment after the birth of the child, while fear of another pregnancy and childbirth hindered good sex adjustment on the part of other wives. Wives whose health was better than usual during pregnancy had better sex adjustments after giving birth to their children than did those whose health was poor during pregnancy (Landis *et al.*, 1950).

The frequency of marital intercourse drops steadily with age. This decline comes partly from decline in general physical and psychological capacity, but it is affected also by psychological fatigue, loss of interest in repeating the same experience with the same individual, and preoccupation with business and social affairs. It is interesting to note that when individuals in middle age remarry, they develop new techniques, their interest is aroused by a new partner, and their sexual activity is increased. The attainment of orgasm every time intercourse is attempted by persons of middle age is not as usual as during the earlier years, and this detracts from the enjoyment formerly experienced (Clark, 1949).

Because sexual relationships are new and difficult, many adults do not make these adjustments satisfactorily. Many more marriages go on the rocks because of failure in this area of adjustment than in any other. Recently, several important investigations have been made to determine the attitudes of women and of men toward intercourse and other forms of sexual behavior and to interpret the findings in terms of the causes of unfavorable attitudes of members of both sexes. Among the women questioned by Landis, only 38 per cent reported that this adjustment was adequate, 23 per cent reported it inadequate, and 7 per cent said they had never experienced orgasm and were actively repulsed by some phase of the sex relationship. Their attitudes toward sex varied from very favorable to very unfavorable. Those who reported lack of sex feeling or interest were, for the most part, women who had poorly resolved ties to their families. Digust toward all sex matters was associated with limited heterosexual experiences and sex information. More women with good sexual adjustments in marriage reported premarital hetero-sexual intimacies than was true of those who reported poor adjustments (Landis *et al.*, 1940).

From a study of 6,000 marital histories and 3,000 divorce histories, Kinsey has come to the conclusion that, when these adjustments are poor, only with idealism and determination can a marriage be kept together. In upper-level marriages, where divorce is proportionally more frequent than in lower-level marriages, the sexual factors that most often cause difficulty are the failure of the man to show skill in sexual approach and technique and the failure of the woman to participate with the abandon that is necessary for the successful consummation of any sexual relation. Both of these difficulties, Kinsey maintains, stem from the same source, the restraints developed in premarital years and the impossibility of freely releasing these restraints after marriage. For the man, the main problems center around the lack of facility, of ease, or of suavity in establishing rapport in a sexual situation. This is not due to lack of information regarding techniques but rather to subconsciously operating ideas of right and wrong, cleanliness, and what is abnormal or perverted. These unfavorable influences are felt more frequently in the adjustments of upper-level men than in those of men of the lower level.

On the part of women of the upper levels, Kinsey reported, inhibitions are more extreme than those of the average man. Some of these women object to intercourse with their husbands, while a larger number of them remain uninterested in intercourse throughout the years of their marriage, they object to each new technique their husbands attempt, and they charge their husbands with being lewd, lascivious, lacking in consideration, and guilty of sex perversion in general. The woman who has no concept of the fact that sexual contacts may involve a great deal more than genital union will find it difficult to give up her preconceived ideas regarding the right and wrong of such matters and to accept sexual relations with any degree of abandon after marriage.

Premarital petting, Kinsey maintains, is valuable to both men and women in that it helps to free them from the inhibitions that would otherwise plague them throughout marriage and thus interfere with good sexual adjustments. From petting, the girl has learned something about tactual stimulation and, as a result, has less of a problem in resolving her inhibitions after marriage than has the woman who, as a girl, had few contacts with boys and who engaged in little or no petting. There is considerable evidence, Kinsey maintains, that premarital petting experiences contribute definitely to the effectiveness of the sexual relations after marriage. In conclusion, he states, "Whether premarital petting is right or wrong is, of course, a moral issue which a scientist has no capacity to decide. What the relations of premarital petting may be to a subsequent marital adjustment is a matter the scientist can measure" (Kinsey *et al.*, 1948).

Extramarital intercourse, which occurs most frequently in the upper and lower socioeconomic groups, may lead to a breakup of the marriage when it is discovered. If, however, it is undiscovered, it may give the satisfaction denied in marriage and thus prevent a breakup of the marriage. Such relationships, however, most often cause difficulties when they involve emotional and affectional relations with the new partner who takes precedence over the old. When a marriage is helped by extramarital relationships, it is because the individual has learned new techniques or has acquired new attitudes which have released some of the inhibitions that previously existed. After an "affair," both husbands and wives may make better sexual adjustments to their marriage partner than they did before they had the affair (Kinsey *et al.*, 1948).

Burgess and Cottrell (1939), in an analysis of the factors responsible for poor sexual adjustments in marriage, have come to the conclusion that there are three major factors. These are (1) *organic difficulties,* owing to the structure and functioning of the organs, which are infrequent; (2) *unfortunate attitudes,* which are the most common source of trouble, and which include general lack of sexual desire on the part of one of the partners but not on the part of the other; no general lack of sex desire but a specific lack of sex desire for a particular person; and unfavorable attitudes caused by a shifting of attitudes between aversion and desire; (3) *lack of information,* which causes the individual to feel insecure and awkward in early sex relationships.

Social Adjustments in Marriage. With marriage, the adult acquires a whole new social group. This is made up of individuals of different ages, of different cultural backgrounds, and of different interests. He must adjust to people who are not of his choosing and, as an in-law, they are likely to be far more critical of him than they would be of others who have no blood relationship. Furthermore, because they are members of the "family," they frequently assume the privilege of trying to ·direct his life as they would hesitate to do if he were not a member of the family. While the social adjustments of marriage are difficult for all young adults, they are likely to be more difficult for women than for men. The woman is in the home more than the man and, hence, is more accessible to the members of the family. Middle-aged men and women who marry for the first time, or who remarry after a death or divorce in the family, are faced with even more serious social adjustments than are young people. Not only do people become more critical and set in their ways as they grow older but there is frequently the complication that comes with resentments from members of the family, especially the children, when it is a second marriage.

With marriage, every adult must reorganize his life. He must learn to live with a person whose background is different from his and whose interests, attitudes, and emotional states are far less familiar to him than he realizes during the days of courtship. He must learn to share what he has—material possessions, wealth, time, interests, and activities—with the marriage partner, and he must realize that he is not free to do as he pleases as he was before he married. This reorganization of the pattern of living is always difficult and requires time. Even young people, whose life patterns are not fully established, find adjustments to marriage hard to make, and these adjustments are often accompanied by emotional storm and stress.

With each passing year, as the individual's life pattern becomes more set, adjustments to living with another person whose own life pattern may be markedly different are increasingly difficult. The adult's personality and his concept of self are important factors in the social adjustments to marriage. The quiet, introverted, shy individual will have a more difficult adjustment to make than will the friendly extrovert. The tendency to have an exaggerated idea of his own importance and an unrealistic concept of his abilities likewise militates against an easy adjustment to marriage.

The husband's occupation plays an important role in determining the pattern of his life. Since most men are established in a line of work before they assume the responsibilities of marriage, the man has generally made a fairly satisfactory adjustment to his occupation before he marries. For the woman, however, marriage may prove to be very difficult, especially if she has been accustomed to having a career of her own which she must now give up or must combine with her new responsibilities of running a home. Adjustments are further complicated if her husband's occupation requires much traveling or working at hours difficult to fit into a home schedule.

If the social adjustments of marriage were limited to the marriage partners, there should be a fairly good adjustment made within a reasonable amount of time. This, however, is not the case. Adjustments must also be made to the family circle of the spouse. Family backgrounds that differ markedly because of educational, social, cultural, or financial factors intensify the difficulties of adjustment. Two very important areas in the cultural backgrounds of marriage partners that have a pronounced influence on marital adjustment are religion and family customs. In the case of religion, more trouble can be caused by different religious backgrounds than by almost any other cultural difference. Sources of trouble stem not so much from the marriage partners themselves but from the attitudes of the families of both husband and wife.

Every family has its own mores or customs of doing things. Many of these family customs are survivals of customs brought over to America from the country from which the family originated. When racial backgrounds are different, family customs are often so different that they present a major adjustment problem in marriage between two individuals whose childhoods were spent in homes where certain customs came to be important to them. How to resolve the differences in these customs presents a problem of adjustment of pronounced importance in marriage (Bossard and Boll, 1950).

At middle age, a new adjustment problem in the social area arises in the majority of American families, that of caring for aging parents. In many cases these parents need physical care, financial help, or both. Sometimes it means bringing the parents into the home, while, at other times, it means financial sacrifices to enable the parents to live in their own homes. In the former case, the social-adjustment problems are usually very great because, when there are children in the home, three distinct generations, each with its own interests and attitudes, find it difficult to live harmoniously. Another problem of adjustment at middle age comes when the children of the family grow up and leave for homes of their own. The husband and wife, who for years have been accustomed to the companionship, the interests, and the activities of their children, now are alone and must adjust to a life together with few outside contacts. This is often a difficult adjustment to make, especially if the love which formerly helped them to make satisfactory adjustments in their early years of marriage has begun to wane or if one of the marriage partners has found a new love interest away from home.

TIME NEEDED FOR ADJUSTMENT. Adjustment to marriage will not take place quickly. The more individuals are involved, the longer and the more difficult the adjustment will be. For the young adult, adjustments of all sorts, especially to people, are easier than when the individual grows older and his habit patterns are well established. The first year or two of marriage is when the major adjustments to one another, to members of the families, and to friends of both husband and wife normally take place. This can be a very stormy period in the marriage career and it often is. Marriages in the thirties or in middle age frequently require a longer time for adjustment and the end result is usually not as satisfactory as in earlier marriages.

An excellent preliminary to this adjustment is the courtship period. In past generations, the period of courtship was considerably longer than it is today. During this period, the young people were not only able to become thoroughly acquainted with the likes and dislikes, emotional habits, personal characteristics, and temperamental patterns of their prospective mates but they also had an opportunity to become acquainted with the families and relatives of each. By the time of marriage, the major social adjustments had been partially made. Today, the problem is greatly complicated by the shorter courtship and engagement periods. Many courtships are so short and the marriage follows so soon after the engagement has been announced that there is little time for social adjustments. As a result, what should have been done as a preliminary before marriage must be done after marriage. Certain adjustments which cannot be made before marriage, such as the sexual adjustment and adjustment to managing a home without the aid of parents, are difficult enough without adding to them the burden of other adjustments which could be made, in part at least, before marriage.

Happiness in Marriage. How happy or unhappy a marriage will be depends upon the degree of adjustment both marriage partners make. And, because there are many areas in which adjustments must be made, the problem of marital adjustment is a very major one. Successful adjustment in one area alone will not guarantee happiness. In the past, happiness in marriage was taken for granted. Women and men had been trained from the time they were children for their roles in adult life and they were prepared to accept the bad with the good as part of the whole marriage pattern. Moral and religious prejudices against divorce were so great that a marriage was maintained at all cost.

Today, with the new freedom for women, with the relaxed mores regarding divorce, and the opportunities women have to maintain themselves and their children after divorce, there are many more evidences of unhappy marriages than there were in the past. This does not mean that there are proportionally more unhappy marriages today than there were in past generations. Rather, it means that society is more aware of these unhappy marriages because of the legal separations and divorces. When conditions become intolerable today, the marriage is broken up; in the past, the marriage was held together, regardless of the personal sacrifices and unhappiness of all members of the family.

Men, as a whole, make better adjustments to marriage than do women. They grow discontented with marriage sooner than women do, however, though women find more causes for dissatisfaction with marriage than men do. The most common causes of dissatisfaction women find with marriage include temperamental difficulties, sexual difficulties, and lack of personal freedom. Economic problems in marriage prove to be more disturbing to women than to men (Hamilton and MacGowan, 1929).

In summarizing the matter of marital happiness, Terman (1938, p. 111) has pointed out: "What comes out of a marriage depends upon what goes into it and that among the most important things going into it are the attitudes, preferences, aversions, habit-patterns, and emotional-response patterns which give or deny to one the aptitude for compatibility. In other words, we believe that a large proportion of incompatible marriages are so because of a pre-disposition to unhappiness in one or both of the spouses."

Factors in Marital Happiness. There have been a number of studies of happily and unhappily married couples and an analysis of the factors which, in each case, contributed to the success or failure of the marriages. The important factors that aid or handicap adjustment will be summarized briefly, and the relationship of each to the happiness of the marriage indicated. Of the many factors, the following are the most important:

AGE. Age at the time of marriage has been found to be a small factor in marital happiness, as is the age difference between husband and wife (Terman and Buttenwieser, 1935). The happiest wives are those who are 4 to 10 years older than their husbands; the happiest husbands are 12 or more years older than their wives (Terman *et al.*, 1938). Marriage late in life is happier than early marriage. It is happiest when the wife is 1 to 3 years older than the husband. The next happiest is when their ages are equal, and next, when the husband is much older than the wife (Hamilton and MacGowan, 1929).

LENGTH OF COURTSHIP. Well-adjusted mates have a longer courtship and period of engagement than have the poorly adjusted (Locke and Karlsson, 1952).

INTELLIGENCE. Happily married couples are similar in general intelligence. Among adults of very high intelligence, there is a slightly higher level of marital happiness and sexual adjustment than among less gifted adults (Terman and Oden, 1947).

CULTURAL BACKGROUND. The educational background of husbands and wives affects their adjustment in marriage. Those whose educational background is equal are happier than those whose educational background is unequal. Men and women who have never attended college are happier in marriage than college graduates (Hamilton and MacGowan, 1929). Adults who as children attended Sunday school and church, who were married in church, and who as adults had church membership make happier marriages than do those with little religious background (Burgess and Cottrell, 1939).

Similarity in family background also contributes to good adjustment in marriage (Burgess and Cottrell, 1939). Being of the same social class is favorable to good adjustment in marriage while being of a different social class is unfavorable. The reasons given for this are that many individuals are unwilling to learn a new pattern of living after marriage and that the pattern set by marriage will not be satisfactory to both individuals if they come from different backgrounds. In general, cross-class marriages are poorer risks than are same-class marriages (Roth and Peck, 1951).

FAMILY RELATIONSHIPS. The pattern of family relationships the adult has seen in his own home throughout his childhood years leaves an indelible impression on his mind and influences his reactions to members of his own family. If he has been accustomed to happy, harmonious family relationships, the chances are that his own marriage will be far happier and his relationships to the members of his own family far better than if his childhood home had been an unhappy one. Happy marriages of parents usually set the pattern for happy marriages of their children (Terman and Buttenwieser, 1935).

Coming from a large family is more favorable to marital adjustment than being a member of a small family. The youngest child of the family is a poorer marriage risk than the older children, while the only child is a particularly poor risk. Absence of conflict with parents, especially on the husband's side, is important to good marital adjustment (Burgess and Cottrell, 1939). Too little regard for or too strong attachment to one or both parents means a poor marital adjustment (Hamilton and MacGowan, 1929; Terman, 1938). The adult who, as a child, was too strictly disciplined at home makes a poor adjustment to marriage (Hamilton and MacGowan, 1929). Men who get on reasonably well with their mothers are most happily married, especially if their wives resemble the mother physically and temperamentally (Hamilton and MacGowan, 1929). The attitude of the parents toward the mate before marriage is very important in determining the happiness or unhappiness of the marriage (Locke and Karlsson, 1952).

Factors in the family relationships of the individuals who are married that play roles of little or no importance are frequency of seeing the parents or in-laws after marriage, or residence with relatives (Burgess and Cottrell, 1939). The number of siblings of the opposite sex either marriage partner had likewise is a factor of little or no importance to marital happiness (Terman, 1938).

ECONOMIC STATUS. It is popularly believed that one of the most common causes of marital unhappiness is poverty and that having a stable income, adequate to provide the needs and wants of the family, will guarantee happiness. The correlation of income with happiness in marriage scores has been found to be zero (Terman, 1938). The size of the family income is, however, more important to the happiness of the wife than to the husband (Hamilton and MacGowan, 1929). Having a regular income and saving some money prior to marriage facilitate the adjustments to marriage (Burgess and Cottrell, 1939). Economic factors are important in marital stability, not only for the comforts they offer but also for the symbolic character of income and its social meaning. There is a close relationship between the position of the husband, security of the family, income size, and marital stability (Goode, 1951).

OCCUPATION. While Terman (1938) has reported that the husband's occupation has little influence on the happiness of marriage, Burgess and Cottrell (1939) maintain that it does. The relationship between occupation and marital adjustment is not dependent upon the financial returns of the occupation but rather upon the nature of the occupation itself. Some occupations are less satisfactory than others from this angle. Those that are the least likely to lead to good marital adjustment include occupations which require a high degree of mobility for one of the marriage partners, such as traveling salesman, and occupations which are farthest removed from social controls which demand reasonable adjustment in marriage, such as acting.

CHILDREN. It is popularly believed that no family can be happy unless there are children. Presence or absence of children has been found to have little influence on marital adjustments (Terman, 1938; Landis *et al.*, 1940). There is evidence, however, that one of the most common causes of disagreements between husbands and wives relates to the care of the children (Landis *et al.*, 1940). Presence of children has no effect on marital happiness, but it may make divorce less likely (Terman and Buttenwieser, 1935).

SOCIAL INTERESTS. Men and women who are sociable and enjoy social activities make better adjustments to marriage than do those who are lacking in social interests (Locke and Karlsson, 1952). Outside interests in common contribute to a successful adjustment to marriage (Terman and Buttenwieser, 1935). There is a definite relationship between the number of organizations to which a husband and wife belong and their chances for happiness in marriage. There is also a relationship between the number of friends of their own sex both men and women have and their success in marriage (Burgess and Cottrell, 1939).

PERSONALITY. The individual's personality, as is true of adjustments in every area of life, plays a role of great importance in adjustment to marriage. A well-adjusted, happy person has a far greater chance of making a good adjustment to marriage than has a person whose emotional instability, feelings of inadequacy, or feelings of inferiority lead to neuroticism. Happy people make happy marriages; unhappy ones make unhappy marriages (Terman, 1938). When a woman has charm and social poise, they aid her in working out a good adjustment to marriage (Landis *et al.*, 1940).

The personality characteristics of an unhappy spouse have been found to be as follows: touchy; loses temper easily; critical of others; shows dislike;

easily affected by praise or blame; unconventional in attitudes toward drinking, religion, and sexual ethics; lack of self-confidence; and dominating in relations with members of the opposite sex (Terman, 1938). Husbands and wives are more likely to be happy if they are similar in their attitudes toward avoiding an argument and are more likely to be unhappy if they resemble each other in admitted ability to accept just criticism without "being sore" (Terman and Buttenwieser, 1935).

Attempts at domination on the part of husband or wife are likely to lead to poor marital adjustments. When equality in taking the lead in family activities prevails, there is likely to be a happy adjustment in marriage (Locke and Karlsson, 1952). When, however, the wife is definitely dominant, there will be trouble in the form of social and sexual maladjustment. If, however, the husband is very markedly dominant over the wife, there is usually a divorce. Personality measurements of divorced women showed that they lacked "sweet femininity" but commanded respect for their rugged strength and self-sufficiency. A high degree of marriage compatability is accompanied by a willingness on the part of both husband and wife to admit the superiority of the spouse, especially when this admission comes from the wife, and by the tendency of both husband and wife to rate themselves above average on most personality traits (Kelly, 1936).

Terman's analysis of the personality patterns of happily and unhappily married men and women and of divorced men and women has led him to the conclusion that each group is characterized by a typical personality pattern. The happily married are emotionally stable, socially adaptable, are conservative, have uplifting interests, and show both sympathy and tolerance, though men stand higher in these traits than do women. The unhappily married are introverted, show neurotic traits, volitional inadequacies, and intolerant attitudes. The divorced show much the same traits as the unhappily married, though they are more pronounced. In addition, they have more intellectual interests than have the married groups (Terman, 1938).

CHILDHOOD EXPERIENCES. Childhood experiences leave an indelible impression on the individual's mind and affect his future attitudes. In the case of marital adjustments, an unhappy childhood and adolescence will predispose the individual to an unhappy marriage while a happy childhood will lead to good marital adjustment (Terman, 1938; Locke and Karlsson, 1952).

ATTITUDES TOWARD SEX. As was pointed out in the section on sexual adjustments in marriage, the individual's attitude toward sex plays a role of great importance in determining how well he will adjust to marriage. Socially attractive women, as a rule, have more favorable attitudes toward sex than do socially unattractive ones because the former are likely to have been more popular with members of the opposite sex during adolescence (Landis et al., 1940). Likewise, dissatisfaction with one's own sex and premarital attitudes of disgust toward sex topics predispose the woman to make an unfavorable marital adjustment. When virginity is the ideal, the virgin is the most likely to be happy in marriage (Landis *et al.*, 1940). The wife's adequacy to achieve orgasm and similarity of the two partners in degree of sex drive are essential to a healthy attitude toward sex (Terman, 1938; Kinsey *et al.*, 1948).

Frigidity on the part of women and impotence on the part of men may be the result of unfavorable attitudes toward sex. These militate against good adjustment to marriage because the unfavorable attitudes affect every area of the marriage relationship (Landis *et al.*, 1940). Frequently these unfavorable attitudes stem from the wrong type of sex education or from adult attitudes toward sexual play during the childhood years. How healthy or unhealthy the attitudes are is largely a matter of adult attitudes toward the normal curiosity the child shows toward sex matters.

Divorce. Divorce is an indication of poor marital adjustment. It comes only after a period of great emotional tension between husband and wife, when all possible solutions to their problems have proved futile. Marital incompatibility is marked by friction and disagreement. The greatest disagreements relate to the care and rearing of the children, friends, ways of dealing with the in-laws, matters of recreation, matters of conventionality, and religious matters. Least disagreement centers around such matters as attitude toward drinking and smoking, demonstrations of affection, intimate relations, social graces, table manners, handling of family finance, and tastes in food (Landis *et al.*, 1940).

There has been a steady and alarming rise in the divorce rate in America since the turn of the present century (see Fig. 53). In 1890, for example, there were 0.5 divorces for every 1,000 marriages as compared with 3.3 for a similar number in 1947. In 1890, there was 1 divorce for every 16 marriages as compared with 1 for every 4 marriages in 1947. Of the divorces granted, two-fifths represent marriages that have lasted 5 years or less and two-thirds occur within the first 10 years of marriage. During a period of economic depression, the divorce rate decreases; during a period of prosperity, it increases. The explanation for this is not that good or bad times make marital adjustments easier for the individuals involved but rather that people can get along financially better after a divorce if economic conditions are such that both partners can work (Anderson, 1949; Jacobson, 1950).

There are also more divorces among childless couples than among families with children not because children aid the marital adjustments of their parents but because childless couples can manage better after divorce than can those who have children to support and care for. The largest proportion of divorces comes during the first few years of marriage, the critical time when the adjustments to marriage must be made. While satisfactory adjustments may not be made at this time, if there are children born during the early years of marriage, the chances are that a potential divorce is checked for the sake of the children. The frequency of divorce has been found to vary inversely with the number of children in the family (see Fig. 54). For childless couples, there are 15.3 divorces out of every 1,000 marriages as compared with 11.6 divorces out of every 1,000 marriages where there is one

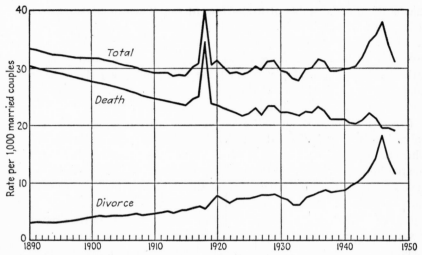

FIG. 53. Marital dissolutions by death and divorce in the United States, 1890–1948. The figures for divorce include annulments and those for mortality include deaths overseas during the First and Second World Wars. (*From P. H. Jacobson, Differentials in divorce by duration of marriage and size of family. Amer. sociol. Rev., 1950, 15:235–244. Used by permission.*)

child and 4.6 divorces in 1,000 marriages where there are four or more children (Jacobson, 1950).

Legal separations and desertion are likewise indications of poor marital adjustment. A legal separation is a trial divorce in that it leaves the door open for a possible reconciliation as time goes on. Desertion of the wife, on the other hand, has no legal implications. A man who has found his marriage intolerable simply leaves his wife and children high and dry to get along as best they can. This is often referred to as a "poor man's divorce" because it gives the man the freedom he wishes from a marriage that has not proved to be satisfactory to him without, at the same time, the cost and legal complications of a divorce. Regardless of the cause or causes given by one or both marriage partners for the breakup of the marriage, the fundamental cause is poor adjustment (Anderson, 1949).

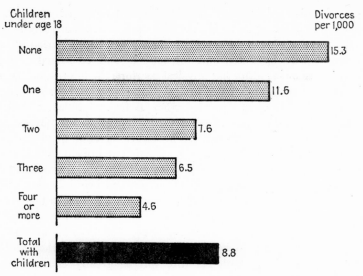

Fɪɢ. 54. Divorces per 1,000 married couples, according to size of family, in the United States, 1948. (*From P. H. Jacobson, Differentials in divorce by duration of marriage and size of family. Amer. sociol. Rev., 1950, 15:235–244. Used by permission.*)

ADJUSTMENT TO PARENTHOOD

The first step in the adjustment to parenthood comes with the recognition of pregnancy. At first, if the child has been desired, both parents rejoice. But, as they settle down to consider what parenthood really means, the realization has a sobering effect on them. For the woman, it means a period of restrictions in activities, physical discomforts, a temporary period of embarrassment about her changed figure and of wonder if her distorted body will cool her husband's love for her, the necessity for giving up any career she may have established for herself and changing her occupation to that of housewife, and the necessity of giving up many plans for the future to provide for the new arrival.

Adjustments of Woman. When the child has been seriously and sincerely wanted, these adjustments will be made willingly and gladly by the woman. When, however, motherhood was not sincerely wanted, the adjustments will be poor and she may turn against her husband for his role in the position she now finds herself. This will put a serious strain on the husband-wife relationship and may even threaten the marriage. As pregnancy progresses, she may make satisfactory adjustments and welcome the prospects of motherhood. And yet she may not. How the woman will react will depend largely not upon the physical or glandular changes that accompany pregnancy but rather upon her own attitude toward pregnancy and motherhood.

For the average woman, however, pregnancy is a happy period of anticipation, marked only by occasional forebodings and emotional upsets. The solicitude of her husband for her physical comfort, the interest her family and her in-laws take in the anticipated arrival of the baby, and the realization that her childhood dream of motherhood is about to be fulfilled, all add to her happiness and thus help her to adjust satisfactorily to the physical discomforts and deprivations of pregnancy. The higher secretion of progestin during pregnancy adds to her emotional calm and self-contentment (Benedek, 1946).

Adjustments of Man. The man's adjustment to the pregnancy period is not always so satisfactory, even though a son and heir has been one of his lifelong ambitions. Now he realizes that parenthood will mean many sacrifices in finances as well as in comforts and pleasures, that his life will have to be readjusted once again as it was at marriage, that he will have to assume greater responsibilities than he did when he married, and that the chances are that his relationship with his wife will be greatly changed when she assumes the burdens of caring for a child.

The examples he has seen in the marriages of his friends or of his own family after the arrival of a baby do not always serve to calm his forebodings. Added to this is the necessity of adjusting his sexual relationships with his wife during the pregnancy period and the changed attitude on his wife's part toward the sexual relationships that existed before pregnancy began. And, finally, his wife's preoccupation with her own health, her tendency to be irritable and complaining, and her inability or lack of desire to do many of the things they formerly did together do not help to ease his adjustment to this new change in his life.

Parenthood. Early parenthood, provided all goes well at delivery and the mother and child get along well, is a period of emotional excitement for the young parents. The father as well as the mother have a period of ego-inflation when they are the center of attention of relatives and of friends. This, however, does not last long. It is followed by a period of difficult adjustments to the cares and responsibilities of a helpless infant, combined with many deprivations and harder work, more sacrifices, and less opportunity for living their own individual lives than they have ever before experienced. There has been a general shake-up in their lives, and adjustment to the changes is not always easy for them to make (Cohen, 1943). For the man, the adjustment is often more difficult than for the woman because he has little of the pleasure that comes from constant care and personal contact with the baby and, because of the preoccupation of his wife with the baby's needs, he feels as if he is literally being "shoved aside," a fact which proves to be a great blow to his ego.

So long as the baby is helpless and appealing, parents make the sacrifices necessary for his care with willingness and cheerfulness. They adjust happily to their parental role and to each other. But, as time goes on and the baby develops into a troublesome child and an even more troublesome adolescent, parental attitudes toward the child very often change. The parent-child relationship worsens as time goes on (see discussion of this in chapters on Childhood and Adolescence). The larger the family, the more work and economic strain this entails, and the less harmony there is between the children, the more difficult the adjustment of the parents to their role as parents.

As adolescence draws to a close and the children begin to plan their own lives, parents frequently rebel at relinquishing their roles. The mother especially, for whom the role of motherhood has been her chief occupation for many years, is more reluctant than the father to see her life occupation come to an end. As a result, far too many mothers cling to their children and oppose their marriages or their desires to have a career that will take them away from the parental roof. Instead of welcoming the easing of the burden they have carried for so many years, they cling to it in the hope that their lives will not seem empty and futile now that their main work has been completed.

Factors Influencing Adjustment. The *age* of the adult and his previous occupation play roles of importance in determining how well he will adjust to parenthood. Both men and women, in their twenties, can adjust better to the responsibilities and restrictions of their freedom that parenthood brings than can older men and women. As is true of adjustments to one another, they make these adjustments with greater difficulty with each passing year. The mental rigidity and the formation of well-established habits, both of which are normal accompaniments of middle and old age, militate against successful adjustment to the role of parenthood. This does not mean that older parents do not make good parents. As a matter of fact, they often make parents who are too good because they are overprotective and oversolicitous in their attitudes toward their children both of which, as was pointed out earlier, are damaging to the healthy personality development of the child.

The individual's *occupation*, likewise, plays a role of importance in determining how successfully he will adjust to parenthood. In the case of a man, this factor is less important than in the case of the woman. While it is true that an occupation that gives rise to nervous tension, as one frequently finds in executive business and professional occupations, makes adjustment to parenthood harder than adjustments would be if the occupation were less emotion-provoking, the man can adjust with fair success if he has the desire to do so. For the woman, on the other hand, adjustments to the all-absorbing and time-consuming role of motherhood are handicapped by training for and experience in a given line of work, when that work has been interesting to the woman. In a study of the effects of a premarital career on the woman's adjustments to marriage and parenthood, Seward (1945) found that poor maternal adjustments came when the woman's career was interrupted by marriage and parenthood. Seward concluded: "These results would seem to indicate that a premarital profession is a poor risk for adjusting to the traditional wife and mother role."

Managing a Home. With the modern laborsaving devices and the ease with which all the necessities for running a home can be obtained in our present culture, adjustment to managing a home would appear to be the simplest adjustment the adult must make. If money were unlimited and if domestic help were readily available at a price the average young couple could afford to pay, this would be true. But, during the early years of marriage, when rearing a family takes the major part of the mother's time and when labor-saving devices and domestic help would be of the maximum help, that is the time when the family income can usually not provide such help. The tendency is for most families to leave the burden of responsibility for the management of the home in the hands of the wife. Some women are quick and efficient with the result that they run their homes with minimum effort and need little help from the other members of the family. Other women, by contrast, are slow and inefficient or they begrudge the time they must spend on housework. As a result, their homes are not well kept, the meals are poorly prepared, and the children are either neglected or they are subjected to the constant grumblings of a mother who is poorly adjusted to the management of her home.

The second important aspect of running a home consists of budgeting the family income. Traditionally, in our culture, the money is earned by the husband and control of all financial matters lies in his hands. Today, as a result of their premarital training and experience in the business world, wives are as capable of managing the family finances as the husband and they often resent not being given this part of the home management. Furthermore, it is often extremely difficult for a woman who, before her marriage, earned and managed her own money to find herself in a position where she has only what money her husband will give her or who has no control whatsoever over the family finances. As time passes and as the husband's income increases, managing a home becomes easier for the woman. And, when money is more plentiful, the wife finds herself in possession of more money for her needs and for the needs of the family. Unless illness, death, or divorce take the breadwinner in middle age, the family-management problems generally are well solved by then. Only as the man approaches the retirement age or when failing health causes him to stop work are the years of middle age likely to present as many financial problems as the years of early marriage did. Then, too, at this time the demands made by growing children are over and most middle-aged couples find themselves in a position where their income can be spent for some of the things they have wanted through the early years of their marriage.

ADJUSTMENT TO SINGLENESS

For both men and women, marriage is the sought-after goal of maturity. When conditions prevent marriage, whether they come from within the individual or from environmental pressures, the individual is likely to be unhappy, lonely, and thwarted in his normal desires for sex expression, for parenthood, for affection from an admired member of the opposite sex, and for the prestige that marriage and family living give the individual. In many communities there is no place for the bachelor or spinster, except as an extra man at a dinner party or a baby sitter for married relatives.

The unmarried man frequently finds satisfactory sexual outlets either in autoerotic practices, in extramarital intercourse with women of his acquaintance, or in intercourse with prostitutes. Whatever outlet he uses, he generally makes fairly satisfactory adjustments to the normal sex drive (Kinsey *et al.,* 1948). In a study of the sex lives of a large and unselected group of men, it was found that, in the twenty- to twenty-eight-year group, only 20 per cent were virgins. Virginity was higher among the more educated than among those of lower educational and economic status. Ninety per cent of the nonvirgins and 87 per cent of the virgins admitted that they masturbated at some time (Hohman and Schaffner, 1947).

Women have less chance than men to make satisfactory adjustments to singleness. While women, as is true of men, engage in autoerotic practices, opportunities for extramarital intercourse, strongly tabooed for women, are limited and always surrounded by the danger of loss of social status for the woman. In a group of 1,000 unmarried women, the highest percentage of happiness was found in the group which denied all sex feelings and experiences, the next highest in the group with sex feelings but no observations of periodicity in their sex feelings, and the lowest percentage of happiness was found in the group that recognized periodicity of sex feelings (Davis, 1929).

Because, in our culture, the man is thought of as superior to the woman, an unmarried woman has even more difficult adjustment problems than has the unmarried man. As a result, many women try to reject the typically feminine role and replace it with a more masculine role. In this way, they compensate for feelings of inadequacy which are likely to arise because of their unmarried status. This desire is often accentuated by the unmarried woman's realization that she is regarded as "queer" by society because she has not followed the conventional pattern for women by marrying and settling down to the job of rearing children.

While there are many reasons why men and women do not marry, such as family responsibilities, disillusionment, and self-sufficiency, the unmarried man or woman is usually less well adjusted than is the married person, and this poor adjustment has militated against his marriage. Absence of one parent from the home, because of death or divorce, has little influence on the young woman's interest in and desire for marriage. But, in the case of young men, the situation is very different. When the father is absent from the home, the young man shows a lower level of courtship behavior than young men of his age do whose fathers are at home (Winch, 1949). In many instances, young men with the responsibility of caring for a widowed mother remain unmarried throughout their mother's lives.

SEX-ROLE ADJUSTMENT

In every culture, whether primitive or civilized, there are certain patterns of behavior approved for women and others for men. When a man's behavior does not conform to the appropriate masculine pattern, he is labeled "effeminate," and this is a form of derision. When a woman's behavior does not conform to the socially approved pattern for her sex, she is called "masculine" and, in our society, a masculine woman is as much a misfit as an effeminate man. The patriarchal or antifeminist attitude on the part of men and the extreme feminist attitude on the part of women is usually associated with marital maladjustments (Kirkpatrick, 1939).

The socially approved masculine role for members of our culture consists of wage earner, head of the family, and citizen. The man is given a wide leeway to select the role he wishes to play in life, whether it be in one line of work or in another, and how he will behave in the home or in the community. The pattern in every area is flexible so that the man may select what he wants to do. This is very important because it offers opportunities for expression of individual interests and preferences. The woman in our culture finds herself confronted with a more rigidly prescribed role and one that offers little opportunity for her to deviate in order to satisfy her own interests, ambitions, and abilities. While the unmarried woman is free to select her own role in much the same way as the man is, the social attitude toward the unmarried woman is unfavorable, except in the large cosmopolitan centers.

For the married woman, there are three separate roles she may play (Kirkpatrick, 1936), (1) the *traditional wife and mother role,* carrying privileges of security, respect, domestic authority, economic support, loyalty of the husband and obligations of rearing the children, making a home, and rendering domestic service; (2) the *companion role,* which enables the wife to share pleasures with her husband and to enjoy leisure time for social and educational contacts; (3) the *partner* with economic independence, equal authority in family finance, and social acceptance on an equal footing.

When Seward (1945) asked a group of young women to record their attitudes toward their roles in a 40-item test which included such statements as,

"I shall want to discontinue paid work outside the home if I have a child," and "I shall expect the same working conditions, pay, and hours as men in the same jobs," she found the women put emphasis on equality between men and women in education, vocational opportunities, working conditions, community activities, and social contacts. Inconsistently, there was a reactionary belief in the traditional subordinate feminine role of wife and mother. This shows the cultural conflict concerning the "feminine role," with emphasis on equality between the sexes in certain spheres but not in others. This is bound to cause personal conflict for both men and women, a conflict that is social, not biological.

Measures of Masculinity-Femininity. Because there are fairly definite cultural standards of what a man should be in our culture and of what a typically feminine woman should be, it is interesting to see how the average man or woman conforms to the cultural standards. To measure the degree of conformity, Terman and Miles (1936) have constructed an attitude-interest test based on activities which have been found to be different between large groups of men and women. When this test was applied to a large group of men and women of different cultural, educational, and intellectual backgrounds, some of the important findings were:

1. There is a correlation between masculinity and height, femininity and length of trunk in relation to height. Exceptionally early puberty is associated with excessive masculinity in the late teens and excessive femininity at this age.

2. Masculinity is definitely correlated with extroversion and femininity with introversion.

3. High-scholarship men are more feminine, while low-scholarship men are more masculine. The interests of high-scholarship men are more cultural while those of the low-scholarship men are more mechanical and athletic.

4. Athletes tend to be strongly masculine, especially among the women.

5. Divorced women are more masculine than either happy or unhappy wives. By contrast, the unhappily and happily married men are more masculine than the divorced.

6. For both sexes, there is a tendency throughout maturity toward femininity. The peak of masculinity for men is reached during the high-school period, while the most feminine scores are made in old age. The peak of femininity for girls comes in the eighth grade, while the greatest extreme of masculinity comes in the college period (see Fig. 55). Feminizing of men during maturity is due to increasing age and to the greater length of married life today.

7. High-school and college education exert a more masculinizing influence than grade-school education on men. For women, college training has a more masculinizing influence than has high-school or grade-school education.

8. The more intellectual and better educated women are more masculine than feminine. If married, they score higher in femininity, regardless of their occupation.

9. Masculinity in men is associated with active and mechanical pursuits and with indifference to artistic and cultural pursuits. Femininity in men is associated

with cultural interests. In women, masculinity is associated with activity and intellectuality; feminism with the arts of home and social life. The masculine man has typically masculine interests; the feminine man has cultural interests. The feminine woman has typically feminine interests, while the masculine woman has intellectual interests.

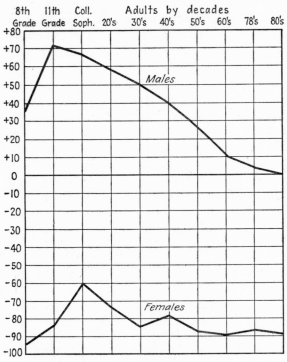

FIG. 55. Changing masculinity-femininity scores of males and females by age groups. Among males the most masculine interests and attitudes are found in the eleventh grade and the most feminine at old age. Among females the most feminine scores are found in the eighth grade and the most masculine among college sophomores. (*Based on L. M. Terman, and Catherine Cox Miles, Sex and Personality. New York: McGraw-Hill, 1936. From F. K. Shuttleworth, The adolescent period: a graphic atlas, Monogr. Soc. Res. Child Develpm., 1949, 14, No. 1. Used by permission.*)

10. The effects of home environment are shown in such situations as part orphans who are contrastingly masculine or feminine, according to whether they are brought up by the mother or by the father. Whole orphans are more feminine than the average. With increasing size of the family, the father and mother become more feminine except in the case of fathers of boys only, when they become more masculine as the number of boys increases. Mothers tend to be less feminine when the children are all boys.

As explanations of the sex differences they found, Terman and Miles (1936, p. 449) stated:

In so many ways too familiar to realize, each sex gives and receives such different treatment as largely to explain the divergences in expression or in fact revealed by the material we have studied. Singularly powerful in shaping our development are other people's expectations of us, past and present, as shown by their practice and their precept. Whether the boy is innately more aggressive and fearless, more handy with the electric lighting than with the cooking stove, more interested and informed about public affairs and about science, more active and enterprising physically; and whether the girl is more sympathetic, gentle, timid, fastidious, more attracted to pots and pans than to rods and guns, more punctilious in dress, personal appearance, manners, and language; at any rate society in the shape of parents, teachers, and one's own fellows of whichever sex expects these differences between the sexes, and literature reflects them. Irresistibly each sex plays the role assigned, even in spite of its own protests.

ADJUSTMENT AND HAPPINESS

The degree of success the individual has in making satisfactory adjustments to the important problems he faces in adult life will determine the degree of his happiness. For, in the adult years as is true of all ages of life, good adjustment and happiness go hand in hand just as poor adjustment and unhappiness are closely associated. As Watson (1930) has pointed out, a person is called happy if he *believes* himself happier than most other people of a similar age and sex, and if he believes his prevailing moods are cheerful. The well-adjusted person is pleasantly satisfied with life in its various aspects. He may not achieve great success or fame but he manages to get along with reasonable success and to adapt himself to the problems that arise in his life activities. Happy and unhappy people are very much alike in their problems and interests. The people who are unhappy do not have peculiar interests or problems but they make less satisfactory adjustments to them than do those who achieve happiness. Happy people are more concerned with affairs outside themselves while unhappy people are concerned with themselves and their relationships to others.

Other ways in which happy and unhappy people differ consist of such situations as follows: The happy people are most concerned with facing reality and adjusting to it; the unhappy are most concerned with their own unhappiness, their intimate relationships with other people, and their frustrations. Unhappy people are less concerned with personal attractiveness than are happy people, they find a philosophy of life more of a problem than an interest, and they are much concerned about goals, ideals, and ambitions (Symonds, 1937a).

When Watson had a group of adults rate their happiness and then correlated the degree of happiness they reported with different factors, he found the following correlates with happiness in adult years: Intelligence has no relationship to happiness; failure in love is a major cause of unhappiness; enjoyment of and success in love is a major factor in happiness; good health in childhood is the foundation for happiness; popularity contributes to happiness as does success in dealing with people; music and poetry tend to be refuges for the unhappy; youth is not the golden age for happiness nor is old age; fears, sensitiveness, and shyness are rightly regarded as major factors in unhappiness. In conclusion, Watson (1930) pointed out: Happiness is associated with serious, deliberate, responsible, earnest, hard-working living, rather than with light, amusing dilettantism."

In early adulthood, the individual has more adjustment problems than he will have as time goes on. While he is solving these problems, he frequently goes through a period of emotional tension that is far from happy (Havinghurst, 1950). By early or mid-forties, he has generally resolved his problems with enough satisfaction to be able to feel contented and happy. When psychological problems do arise in middle age, they usually consist of frustrations within personalities who have reached maturity with certain character deficiencies. The cultural milieu in which the adult finds himself may also contribute to his adjustments and, hence, to the state of his happiness. In fact, even the best adjusted adult cannot find happiness in a milieu which is totally unsuited to him but into which he has been forced by conditions beyond his control.

CHAPTER 13

Old Age
(Sixty Years to Death)

Old age is a new social problem. True, we have always had the aged with us, but they were far less numerous than they are today and they did not present the social problems they now do. In the past, the few individuals who lived to a ripe old age were accepted by families, the community, and society in general with little or no disruption of the pattern of living. Because of the new problems old age has created, there has recently been more scientific interest in this period of life than ever before. The two new areas of scientific research which have developed recently to study the aged are *gerontology* and *geriatrics*. Gerontology is the science of aging. It is derived from the Greek *geron*, meaning "old man" and *ology*, meaning the "study of." As a science, gerontology is concerned with all facets of aging, with all forms of life, not human alone, and even with inanimate objects. Geriatrics, on the other hand, is that area of medical practice concerned with the physiologic and disease problems of those in later maturity and of the elderly. It deals with the health of the aged, just as pediatrics deals with the health of infants and of children.

Period of Decline. While marked individual differences exist in the ages at which physical and mental decline set in, sixty years is taken as the arbitrary dividing line between late maturity and old age. With age comes a decline, a regression, or a return to an earlier pattern of behavior and a simpler level of function. Only in very old age is there *deterioration,* or spoilage and disorganization. The period when the decline is of an earlier pattern of behavior is known as "senescence." The individual may become senescent in the fifties or not until the early or late sixties, depending upon the rate of physical and mental decline that occurs. "Senility," in contrast to senescence, means the period of old age when a more or less complete physical breakdown takes place and when there is mental disorganization. This may come in the early sixties or even late fifties, or it may never occur because the individual dies before deterioration sets in. Many more people become senescent than senile.

Because old age is a period of decline, whether slow and gradual or rapid and disorganizing, it gives rise to a defensive strategy of holding on to life, rather than to seizing more of it, as is true of the earlier years. This defensive strategy is especially marked in the physical, mental, and economic spheres. The individual must work hard to hold on to what he has and, even then, he finds life slipping through his fingers (Havinghurst, 1950). As a result, he frequently becomes unhappy, thwarted, and poorly adjusted to his role in life. As a general rule, the senescent individual finds adjustments more difficult than does the senile person because the former is aware of the slipping, over which he can exercise little or no control, while the latter is so mentally disorganized that he is incapable of recognizing how rapidly he is slipping.

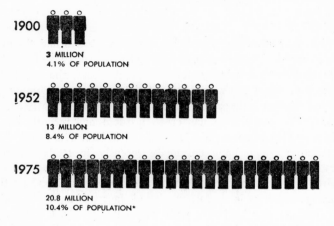

1900
3 MILLION
4.1% OF POPULATION

1952
13 MILLION
8.4% OF POPULATION

1975
20.8 MILLION
10.4% OF POPULATION*

*ESTIMATED

Fig. 56. The percentage of the population sixty-five years and over has more than doubled since 1900 and is still growing. (*From M. Gumpert, Our "Inca" ideas about retirement. The New York Times, July 27, 1952. Used by permission.*)

Social Problems of Old Age. The aged have created many social problems that have never before existed to such a marked degree or had such a strong influence on the lives of such large segments of the entire population. The important social problems created by the aged are as follows:

INCREASE IN THE AGED. How marked the increase in life span has been in recent years can best be appreciated by comparing the average life expectancy of men and women today with that of men and women of the past. In Rome, the mean length of life was 23 years, and in Greece, it was 29.4 years. The first American life tables, "Wiggleworth's Table" constructed from data gathered in several towns in Massachusetts and New Hampshire, appeared in 1789 and showed the mean life expectancy at that time to be 35.5 years. By 1850, the life expectancy had risen to 40 years, by 1900, to 47 years, by 1930, to 60 years, and by 1940, to 63 years.

Owing to a decline in the birth rate and an increase in the length of life, the proportions of old people are becoming steadily greater (see Fig. 56). In

1850, for example, 15.1 per cent of the population was four years of age or younger as compared with 8 per cent in that age group in 1940. On the other hand, the increase in percentages of the population of sixty-five years of age and older has risen from 2.6 in 1850 to 6.8 in 1940. By 1980, it is predicted that there will be 26 million men and women over sixty-five years of age in America, as compared with 9 million today (U.S. Bureau of the Census data). This means that at that time, 27 per cent of our population will be sixty years or older (Havinghurst, 1950).

There have been a number of causes of the increase in life span and the shifts in population proportions. Of these causes, the most important are reduction of infant mortality and the practical elimination of certain diseases in childhood and youth, such as typhoid fever and smallpox; the elimination of epidemic diseases, such as those that wiped out large segments of the adult population many years ago; improved prenatal and postnatal care which enable the individual to live longer; and modern medical methods of prolonging life, as well as of curing diseases which formerly shortened life (Valaoras, 1950).

Shifts in population structure are not new. In the past, however, they were due to destructive forces, such as wars, famines, floods, and pestilences. Today, by contrast, the shifts come from constructive forces, such as medical science, improved sanitation, and the diminished rigors of modern civilization. This has enabled the unfit to survive, a situation which has never before existed to such a marked degree. Even wars have not cut down the percentage of young as happened in the past because war is more mechanized today than formerly. As Goodenough (1945) has pointed out: "The average span of life has increased not so much because the old live to be older but because a greater number of the young live to be old."

Some of the important effects of the gradually increasing proportions of old people in the population have already begun to be felt. Of the effects, the most important noted to date are as follows: fall in standards of living due to the burden of old people on those of productive age to take care of their own old age, those who did not provide for their old age when they were younger, and the aged who are unable to work; greater conservatism because of the larger number of old people in society and their resistance to departures from the accustomed ways; concerted action against daily risks of life because of the conservatism of age; accumulated wisdom due to age resulting in the utilization of natural resources, the curtailment of waste, and the guidance of the channels of production and distribution; and, finally, a disturbance in the sex ratio, in favor of women, which may upset the social and economic balance of life in old age (Cowdry, 1939).

ECONOMIC STATUS. When a population is primarily rural, care of the aged does not present a problem of any real significance for the younger generation. But when a population becomes primarily urban, as is true in

America today, and when the trend is toward smaller homes, smaller families, and simplified living, the aged become a real burden for the younger generation to fit into their lives. An extra room for an elderly parent means a dislocation of the entire family living arrangements in many cases and an added burden on the family budget to provide the necessary food for an extra family member. The role and function in society of elderly people have been greatly disturbed and lowered by the transition from rural to urban economy (Burgess, 1949). Many of the problems associated with old age are thus not the result of old age per se but rather of the socioeconomic problems old age presents.

How great the economic burden of old age is may be appreciated better when one realizes that only about one-third of all Americans over sixty-five years of age are self-supporting. The remaining two-thirds must depend in part or in whole on outside help. Of this group, about 50 per cent are supported by relatives and friends and the other 50 per cent by public assistance or private charities. There is, however, at the present time, a decreasing tendency for the dependent aged to be supported by families and friends, not because of a decrease in family affections or a sense of loyalty on the part of members of the family but rather because of such factors as the high cost of living, higher taxes, smaller homes, and reduced social pressure for members of the family to take care of an aged relative.

✓SOCIAL ATTITUDES TOWARD OLD AGE. Society's attitude toward old age and toward the role the aged can play is of utmost importance in determining how successful the adjustments of the aged will be. The individual, as he grows older, is aware of society's attitude toward him. This, he knows, is generally far from favorable. He realizes that his family considers him a nuisance, a burden, and a source of financial drain. He knows, too, that his position in the business world is one of little importance and that, no matter how efficient he is or how successful he has been in the past, his days are numbered so far as his work is concerned. And, he is aware of the fact that society regards him as an "old fogy," who is "out of step" with modern times.

A very interesting study of how children feel about old people has revealed some interesting facts. Reminiscent answers to the question of how, as children, they felt toward old people, revealed that 80 per cent expressed negative or pessimistic views, as a dislike for old people because they would not allow them to run and play, they were sometimes cross, or they interfered with their pleasures. Their aversion to old people came sometimes from the appearance of the old people rather than from their behavior, such as aversion to wrinkles, their slowness, unsteady gait, untidiness of dress or eating, loss of teeth, etc. Only 20 per cent gave favorable answers. They regarded the old people as wise, free to do as they wanted, they liked their power as storytellers, they were kind, and they interceded with their parents (Scott, 1896).

A recent study regarding adults' attitudes toward old people has revealed attitudes as unfavorable as those of children. According to this study, our culture places emphasis on speed and youth, and it expects old people to give up gainful employment, to withdraw from participation in civic and social activities, and to be content to end their lives without recognition of their capacities, abilities, needs, and drives. This cultural expectation has led to erroneous ideas and equally erroneous stereotypes about old age. In order to determine how closely people of different ages and backgrounds accept these attitudes and stereotypes, a questionnaire with 137 statements dealing with physical changes, personality characteristics, adjustment, conservatism, family relationships, activities, interests, insecurity, and attitude toward the future was given to graduate students, college sophomores, and a group of old people ranging from sixty to eighty-eight years of age.

The reactions of these groups showed a considerable agreement with the stereotypes and misconceptions relating to old age. The attitudes of old people toward retirement are a reflection of our cultural attitudes toward old age. To most of the subjects questioned, there was a negative attitude toward retirement. This led them to the conclusion that "Old people and older workers are living in a social climate which is not conducive to feelings of adequacy, usefulness, security, and good adjustment to their later years" (Essert et al., 1951, p. 73).

ROLE OF THE AGED IN SOCIETY

What role old people play in society depends not upon the degree of civilization but rather upon the customs and patterns of life that have been built up over a period of time. A social group made up almost exclusively of warriors, for example, will have less use for old people than a social group where the major pursuits are those of peacetime activities. This is true of civilized as well as of primitive peoples. The economic condition of the social group is also a factor of great importance in determining the attitude of the group toward the aged and the status accorded the aged. When conditions are favorable and when the group as a whole is prosperous, each member can afford to share what he has with a nonproductive member.

Among Primitive Peoples. The effect of the environment and of the economic status of the social group is especially marked among primitive peoples. When living conditions are good, the prestige of the aged is high. When, on the other hand, living conditions are poor, when food is scarce, and when epidemics strike, the aged are poorly treated. Among some tribes, the aged are killed or they are deserted and allowed to die. Among the less highly organized forms of tribal life, where there is a common store of food, all share equally, regardless of age. Thus, even the aged are not discriminated against when provisions are short or when conditions are unfavorable. In still other tribes, the position of the aged is high and they are revered by the younger members. They hold sway not only as rulers but as teachers of the young.

It is interesting to note that sex differences in the status of the aged are pronounced among primitive peoples. Aged women have more nearly equal rights with men in very primitive societies than when the social structure of the group becomes more complex. Men have greater prestige in tribes where patriarchal family organization exists, while women have greater prestige in the matriarchal forms of family organization. The latter is more often found in the simpler societies. In political, civic, and judicial activities, men who in the prime of life have already attained positions of prominence and responsibility have a greater chance of becoming the leaders of the different secret societies and initiatory rites than have men who, as younger men, were not outstanding. In many primitive groups, aged men were regarded as repositories of knowledge and imparters of valuable information. They were looked upon as experts in solving the problems of life, such as predicting the future and controlling the weather, and they were expected to treat disease and officiate at childbirth and at all similar important events in the life of the tribal members. Rarely did the elderly women attain positions of respect and responsibility equal to those of the men.

Among Civilized Peoples. The position of the aged among civilized peoples has varied markedly. In ancient times, because of wars, famines, and diseases, there was a high mortality rate among younger people. As a result, few lived to be old. Among the ancient Greeks, for example, data from 2,022 sepulchral inscriptions showed that the highest mortality rate fell between the ages of childhood and mid- to late forties. Among the distinguished Greeks, there was remarkable vitality. Philosophers, historians, and poets lived to be 60 years of age or older. Statesmen were found to be the oldest of all, with an average age of 78.6 years (Richardson, 1933). In Sparta, the Council of Twenty-eight Men was composed of those who were 60 years of age or older, and they held great power. In the Homeric Age, by contrast, even the king, when his bodily vigor waned, could be pushed aside for younger and stronger men.

In Rome, old people had a higher position than in Greece. The Roman Senate, with its great power, was composed of old men. In all areas of life, even in the home, the old were revered. Much the same was true among the Jewish peoples of ancient times. The father was the head of the family with complete power over all members. The grandparents were provided for and respected, but their authority and influence diminished as age crept on. A kindly, tolerant attitude prevailed at all times, even when authority and influence diminished.

The position of the aged in Eastern countries has been higher and more powerful than in any of the Western civilizations. While this has proved to be an advantage for the aged themselves, it has proved to be a stagnating influence on the country. Little is known about the position of the aged throughout the Middle Ages. With the Christian influence and emphasis on the care of the weak, it is logical to assume that the aged were well taken care of in all Christian countries during this time. Women, throughout the Christian era, have fared less well than men. In many European countries, as well as in Puritan America, old women were often accused of being witches and sorceresses, positions which held them in disrepute if not in actual danger. As a result, many women as they approached middle age feared the thought of old age and did everything within their power to ward it off as long as possible.

The most outspoken revolt against the aged in this era came in Germany at the time Hitler was in supreme power. Because he thought old people stood in the way of progress by their "dangerous thoughts," the lives of the aged were in constant danger during his regime. Unquestionably, society's attitude toward old age is far from favorable today. Instead of revering and using the wisdom accumulated over the years, there is a strong tendency to relegate the old people to positions of minor importance in every area of American life. This has had a marked influence on the attitudes and behavior of the aged. As Lawton (1939) has pointed out: "The tribulations of old age are as much sociological as they are biological, perhaps even more. Many of the disagreeable traits of old people and of the tragic aspects of aging are the results of the kind of civilization we have built up in this country." According to Lindeman (1950), our old people lack honor and status for three reasons: our frontier heritage and our present factory society have fostered a crass, utilitarian philosophy; an extraordinary premium has been placed on youth because of the emphasis on aggressiveness and acquisitiveness; and our society lacks deep-rooted traditions regarding the aged.

Literary Comments on Old Age. Throughout the literature of the world, there have been frequent references to old age. These literary references have, for the most part, stressed the miseries, both physical and psychological, of old age. This type of writing has helped to strengthen the popular belief that old age is a time when the good things of life gradually slip away and when the individual is left with little to comfort him except the thought of death. A few of the better known literary references to old age are worthy of mention because of their emphasis on the miseries of old age. One of the oldest writers to describe the miseries of old age was Maximiamus, a Latin poet of the sixth century A.D. who devoted six elegies to the infirmities and miseries of old age. Among these he emphasized the progressive diminution of the acuity of the higher senses, especially hearing, taste, and vision; the impairment of memory for recent events; physical changes of the skin, hair, teeth, and body form; growing conservatism and intellectual rigidity; loss of sexual pleasure; and early waking accompanied by vexations from interruptions of sleep (Neuberger, 1947).

According to Talleyrand, the French statesman, "Everyone wants to live long, but no one wants to be old." This stresses the prevailing attitude of people toward old age and suggests that centuries ago, as today, old age was a period of life when the best is believed to be over. Shakespeare twice vividly described the misfortunes of old age, when he wrote.

> And so from hour to hour we ripe and ripe,
> And then from hour to hour we rot and rot;
> And thereby hangs a tale.

And again,

> Last scene of all,
> That ends this strange eventful history,
> Is second childishness, and mere oblivion,
> Sans teeth, sans eyes, sans taste, sans everything.

The most cheerful reference to old age in literature is the picture painted by Browning when he wrote:

> Grow old along with me!
> The best is yet to be,
> The last of life, for which the first was made.

INDIVIDUAL DIFFERENCES IN OLD AGE

There is no such thing as a pattern of physical or mental development that will fit all. So it is with physical and mental decline. Chronological age is not a true index of the degree of decline. Old people, therefore, cannot all be treated alike because they are not all alike any more than children are. There are no characteristics as such that may be found in the aged alone nor are there any that may be described as typically those of old age. Traits of the aged vary according to sex, socioeconomic status, and educational backgrounds (Morgan, 1937). Studies of large groups of old people have revealed that aging progresses at different rates for different physical and mental characteristics. Aging generally progresses at a diminishing rate as the individual grows older. As a general rule, physical aging precedes mental aging, though this is not always the case. Sometimes the reverse occurs, especially when the individual believes he is growing old and, as a result, lets go mentally when the first signs of physical aging appear.

Causes of Differences. While many attempts have been made to explain individual differences in aging, most of these emphasize the importance of heredity and the slightly less important role played by environmental forces. At the present, there is a dearth of information relating to the role played by heredity due not so much to lack of interest as to the fact that vital statistics have been available only recently. All studies that have been made to date, however, show a positive correlation between the life spans of parents and children. Furthermore, they show that females live longer, on the average, than males, even within the same family. The ratio of females over males among people over sixty-five years of age has been found to be 570 females for every 478 males (Kallman and Sander, 1948).

A recent report of studies of the causes of aging stresses the fact that the basic, primary causes of aging are not yet known nor is it known how they can be found. The reason for this is that there is a wide range of obscuring secondary causes of aging, which include glandular deficiencies; hardening of the arteries; and degeneration of the heart, liver, kidneys, and other organs. Until science learns more about these secondary causes, it will be impossible to determine the primary causes. Hormone deficiency, especially deficiency of the sex hormones, has been looked upon as a primary cause of aging. A number of years ago, attempts at rejuvenation by treating the sex glands of old men were made but these have since proved to be far less successful than was originally believed. The two famous experimental approaches were the sex-gland-operation technique used by Steinach, and Voronoff's method of transplanting the gonads of anthropoid apes to aging men.

Recent experiments have shown that it is impossible to rejuvenate or to make aging men young again. The administration of hormones can, however, build up the health and vigor of the individual, thus preventing senility and premature death. Deficiencies of hormones late in life may accelerate and intensify the process of aging, but they must be considered secondary causes of aging. When hormones are given to hormone-deficient elderly men, they have ended depression and improved the individual's muscular activity. Thyroid extracts, given to elderly men who need them, have often staved off heart ailments and brain hemorrhages. Male hormones have been found to have an antiaging effect on the thyroids, kidneys, the heart, skeletal muscles, and the metabolic rate (Korenchevsky, 1952).

At the present, evidence points to the fact that all one can do is to stave off the process of aging by dealing with its secondary causes and by improving the general health condition of the individual as well as his manner of living. A life pattern that is too active for an individual who is beginning to age will, unquestionably, hasten the process of decline. In short, "Within the genetically controlled limits of variability, human life can be lengthened or shortened by outside factors and the degree of efficiency in utilizing constitutional potentialities, but in terms of present knowledge it cannot be prolonged beyond the present boundaries of man's vital capacity" (Kallman and Sander, 1948).

PHYSICAL CONDITION AT SENESCENCE

It is assumed that with the passage of time, the individual will deteriorate physically to such a point that his bodily mechanism will be of little use to him. The different ailments that are traditionally associated with old age are believed to be inevitable. In the case of teeth, for example, it is taken for granted that after a certain age, the individual will have to part with his own and make use of artificial teeth. While it is unquestionably true that physical changes do occur with aging and that these changes are, for the most part, in the direction of deterioration, individual differences are so marked that, at a given age, no two individuals are at the same state of deterioration. Some people at sixty may be as aged as others at seventy or even eighty.

Causes of Physical Deterioration. The earliest explanations of aging on record trace back to the Greek philosophers and physicians who explained aging as a result of a decline of an "innate heat" within the body. Arabic medical writers attributed aging to a progressive loss of moisture in the body, thus causing shrinking and hardening of the tissues. This is the fundamental theory back of the saying that is used so widely today, "A man is as old as his arteries." More recently, biologists have suggested that when differentiated germ plasm is no longer produced, senescence ensues. Others maintain that old age is a generalized kind of disease, not one specific thing. Their justification for this is the recognition that the old are often chronically ill.

Today it is widely recognized that the physical condition of old age depends partly upon the individual's inherited constitution, partly upon his manner of living, and partly upon environmental factors. Overwork, lack of repose, dietary errors, infectious diseases, and endocrine disorders are just a few of the more specific causes of aging (Oliver, 1950). With age, it is known that the vitality or quality of life of millions of individual cells of the body tissues are affected in such a manner that their capacity to perform their normal functions is reduced. Because the various structures of the body are interdependent, the effects of old age are very complex. A minor change in one group of cells performing a specialized function may, for example, affect the balance of the rest of the organism. As old age advances, atrophy of the tissues becomes more and more apparent. The endocrine glands, it has been established, play a role of great significance in bringing about the different physical changes that come with aging. No one gland is solely responsible for the physical ravages characteristic of old age, though they themselves are the victims of decreased blood supply because of generalized vascular sclerosis. Their consequent decreased efficiency plays a contributory part in the atrophic and degenerative changes which follow (Hall, 1948).

Bodily Changes with Aging. There are certain changes, both external and internal, which are so characteristic of old age that no one can fail to recognize them. Other changes, which are just as characteristic of old age, may not be recognized as such and may be regarded as belonging only to the individual who possesses them. On the exterior of the body, the usual changes are so marked that even the best beauty aids are incapable of hiding them. The face tells the individual's age more forcibly than any other part of the body. There are changes in the soft areas of the face, such as the nose, mouth, and ears that come from the actual addition of substance and from the lack of firmness that formerly existed.

Changes in the facial *skin,* as well as in the skin covering the entire body, are very marked. The epidermis, or outer covering of the skin, gradually thins and becomes more flexible and flaccid with age. Under the epidermis, the tissues are less elastic than they formerly were because of atrophy of many of the elastic fibers that make up a considerable share of the intercellular matrix. Because of loss of elasticity, the skin springs back less readily, it sags here and there, and creases or folds because the habitual expressions of the individual are fixed as wrinkles. Atrophy of the oil and sweat glands makes the skin rather dry and coarse. Perspiration is less profuse even in areas of the body where formerly it was abundant. In true senility, dark spots or white scaly plaques often appear in exposed areas of the skin. These are the beginnings of skin cancers, though many will never develop. Moles, warts, and other skin blemishes often appear as age advances.

The *hair* on the head becomes thin and gray. Gradually it becomes so thin that the head is bald or nearly bald, especially in the case of men. The gray color turns into white, often with a yellowish cast. Tough, bristly hairs come around the opening of the external ear and the nose. The hairs of the eyebrows usually become coarse and more bristly, though they may not change in color as the hair on the head does. The *nails* of the hands and feet become thick and tough, with a slight increase in brittleness. The *eyes* seem dull and lusterless and there is often a watery look to the eyes, due to the poor functioning of the tear glands. By old age, most people have lost some of or all their *teeth* and even with the best dentures, this is likely to change the shape of the mouth as well as their facial expression. Any teeth that remain are likely to be yellowed and discolored with age.

The individual's *stature* decreases, there is a stooping of the *shoulders,* often a decline in *weight,* a gradual shrinking of the *secondary sex characteristics* so that the body does not seem to be either masculine or feminine. The *hands* show the ravages of age not only by the toughened, rough skin that characteristically develops at this time but also by the veins that show clearly on the backs of the hands. The *arms* and *legs* are likely to be flabby and unattractive with veins showing through in the legs. The *feet* frequently grow larger because of sagging muscles and they develop corns, bunions, and other disfigurations which necessitate the wearing of larger and less attractive shoes than the individual formerly wore.

Changes in the *skeleton* come through hardening of the bones, deposits of mineral salts, and modifications of the internal structures of the bones. As a result of these changes, the *bones* become brittle and are subject to fractures and breaks which are increasingly slow in healing as age progresses. Changes in the *nervous system* are especially marked in the case of the brain. In old age there is a loss in brain weight, the lateral ventricles tend to be dilated, and the ribbon of cortical tissue is narrowed. The *viscera* go through a marked transformation with advancing age, as has been determined from autopsies of senile bodies. Atrophy is particularly marked in the spleen, liver, testes, heart, lungs, pancreas, and kidneys. There is increased density of the solid organs. The color of the different organs changes to gray or a brownish tone, there is a change in translucency, atrophy of adipose tissue, and increased dryness and toughness of the muscles. In men, there is no evidence of spermatogenesis.

Perhaps the most marked change of all is to be found in the heart. In the early years of life, the position of the heart is more nearly in the center of the chest than it is in advanced age. Also, its position is more erect in the young individual while later, in middle and old age, it assumes a horizontal position. It increases in bulk with age and continues to grow even after the body has ceased to do so. Therefore, the ratio of heart weight to body weight decreases gradually with age. The softness and pliability of the valves gradually change because of an increase in fibrous tissue from deposits of fat and calcium, and from changes in the quality of the elastic tissue. It is uncommon not to find some deformity in the heart in old age. The gastrointestinal tract, the urinary tract, and the smooth muscle organs generally are the least and last affected by aging. Central nervous system changes come early, as is shown first in a decrease in the speed and later in the power of intelligence (Atkin, 1940).

SENSE ORGANS. There is a general but unmistakable downward trend in *sensitivity* as age progresses. All the *sense organs* function less efficiently in old age than they did when the individual was younger. However, because the decline in efficiency of use is slow and gradual in most cases, it gives the individual an opportunity to make adequate adjustments to these changes. Furthermore, modern aids in the form of glasses for impaired vision and hearing aids for impaired hearing compensate for the decline to such an extent that the adjustments can be almost perfect. Of all the sense organs, the most useful, the *eyes* and *ears,* are most seriously affected by old age. The marked decrease in the efficiency of the eyes may be due partly to poor care during the years of maturity and to generally lowered physical condition with old age rather than to any marked changes in the eyes themselves. Most old people suffer from presbyopia, or farsightedness, because of diminishing elasticity of the lens which makes it impossible for the lens to change its shape adequately to accommodate for near vision. This necessitates reading glasses for all near-vision work.

There is no evidence of deterioration in color efficiency up to the age of sixty years. After that, an abnormally high color-blind rate has been found. In a relatively small sample of old people, the percentage of cases of color blindness was 20, higher than the normal expectancy. This, however, may have been due to the smallness of the sample used (Boice *et al.*, 1948). A significant reduction in pupil size with age has also been found (Birren *et al.*, 1950). Visual perception in terms of reading also shows the effect of age, especially with a decline in both speed and accuracy. It is probable, though not yet tested, that visual perception in all areas is affected unfavorably by old age.

Deterioration in hearing is greatest for high-pitched sounds, from the high *C* in the musical scale upward. Sensitivity is entirely lost for extremely high tones because of atrophy of the nerve and end organ in the basal turn of the cochlea. For tones below high *C*, most old people have hearing as good as younger people do. Old people as a rule regard hearing difficulties as caused by stimulus rather than by response. In other words, they blame others for "mumbling" and do not in any way feel that the trouble lies within themselves. In personal conversations with just one person, the elderly individual has little difficulty in hearing because he can face the speaker directly and can read lips. In groups, on the other hand, the old person must be close to the speaker and must face him directly if he is to hear what is being said. Both seeing and hearing among old people are complicated by emotional receptivity. There is a tendency for the person to see and to hear what he wants to, regardless of its importance or its clarity. This is a form of imaginary invalidism and, like the child, the old person finds it a convenient way to get attention or to avoid doing things he does not want to do on the grounds that he "did not see" or "did not hear" what he was asked to do. To a certain extent also, lack of attention, or wandering of attention, is responsible for poor hearing and poor vision in the elderly.

Changes in the sense of *taste* are marked in old age. A study of human cadavers of persons twenty to seventy years of age, and also from birth to eighty-five years of age, revealed that from birth to twenty years, the average number of taste buds per papilla was surprisingly constant, at about 245. From maturity to early old age, the average dropped to 208 and from seventy-four to eighty-five years, the drop went to an average of 88. The same type of drop was noted in the taste buds in the trench wall surrounding the papillae (Arey *et al.*, 1935). The taste buds at the end of the tongue atrophy first. As age advances, the atrophy extends gradually further and further back on the tongue. Taste buds likewise become fewer on the inner surface of the cheeks. The sense of smell also becomes less acute with age, and this tends to make food seem tasteless.

With the drying and hardening of the skin, the sense of *touch* becomes less and less acute. *Pain* is dulled in the aged with the result that it is less valuable as a danger signal than it is in younger people. Among old people, for example, the pain of appendicitis is less intense than in youth and, as a result, they are likely to ignore this danger signal for too long thus accounting for the high mortality rate from appendicitis among the aged. Upsets of the *labyrinthine* and *kinesthetic* sensations result in liabilities to falls, trippings, and imbalance among old people. In general, the decline in sensory efficiency that is so characteristic of old age has a marked influence on the individual's life. Diminution of sensory experiences removes for him one of the chief sources of enjoyment from life. No longer, for example, is eating as pleasurable as it formerly was nor can the individual enjoy to the same extent what he sees and hears because of poor vision or poor hearing. Declining sensitivity is likely to result in social isolation, especially when the sense organs that are most seriously affected are the eyes and ears. And, finally, personality maladjustments are frequent among old people, the use of whose senses declines to the point where they are cut off from social contacts and must live within themselves.

MUSCLES AND JOINTS. Loss of *muscular tone* and *stiffness of the joints* cause difficulties in locomotion. The gait of the aged shows a shortened step, lack of elasticity, a widened base, and forward leaning in a slightly flexed attitude. *Tremors* of the hands, forearms, head, and lower jaw are common among old people though not necessarily continuously present. The tremor does not occur in sleep or if the area is supported. It is, however, usually increased by fatigue, emotions, or activity in the area involved. Restless movements, such as tapping, twitching, patting, or rocking the body are common in old age.

CLIMACTERIC. The male climacteric has only recently been identified as such. The reason for this is that there is no specific demarcation of involution, such as in the female menopause. The climacteric is known now to come later in men than the menopause comes in women (see the discussion of menopause in the chapter on Adulthood) and to require more time than the menopause does. There is a greater variation in ages at which the male climacteric comes than is true of the menopause, though the average age is between fifty-five and sixty-five years.

While the climacteric may result in loss of power of fertilization, owing to absence of sperm cells from the semen, the man may not be aware of this fact because there is little or no relationship between it and sexual desire or even potency. There is usually, however, a gradual diminution of both desire and potency as the climacteric progresses. The common symptoms, in addition to decrease in sexual desire and potency, are increasing fatigability and mental and physical lassitude, associated with insomnia. When emotional turmoil does occur at this time, it is generally caused not by the glandular condition of the man but by his awareness of advancing age.

Because there are no "old wives' tales" to exaggerate the significance of or the discomforts associated with the male climacteric, as is true of the female menopause, most men are affected little either physically or psychologically by this change that deprives them of their powers of procreation. There are, however, some evidences of the changes that have occurred with the climacteric in the form of waning of the secondary sex characteristics. The voice becomes higher in pitch, the hair on the face and body becomes less luxuriant, and the heavy musculature of the body gives way to a general flabbiness and sinking of the skin in different areas. In general, the old man is less "masculine" than he was in the prime of his life.

BODY FUNCTIONS. The automatic regulation of the body's functions comes about more slowly with each advancing year. Regulation of body temperature is impaired by impairment of the regulatory devices. Reduced metabolic rate and lessened muscular vigor make regulation of body temperature difficult in cold environments. It is also difficult in hot environments because of the degeneration of the capillaries and sweat glands in the skin. On the whole, old people feel the cold more than the heat. When an old person becomes short of breath as a result of unusual exertion, it takes longer to restore breathing and heart action to normal than it did when he was younger.

In old age, there is a decline in the amount of *sleep* needed and in the quality of sleep. By middle age, the individual has been sleeping about one hour less than he did when he was in the twenties and thirties. By the age of sixty or seventy years, the daily amount is reduced an hour or two more and brief periods of rest and sleep, "cat naps," generally replace the longer periods of sleep of the younger person. Most old people suffer from insomnia with the result that nights are difficult times for them and they like to get up and wander around the house when they find that they cannot sleep.

Digestive changes are perhaps the most marked of the regulatory functions. Difficulties in eating come partly from loss of teeth which is fairly universal in old age. This loss comes not from old age per se but rather from dietary deficiencies in prenatal and postnatal life and from neglect in dental hygiene. Even with well-fitted dentures, the old person has difficulties in chewing his food and, as a result, often shuns certain food even though he may like it. In addition, as was pointed out in the section related to sensation, there is a decline in smell and taste sensitivity with old age and this causes even the best food to be somewhat tasteless. As a general rule, old people eat less than they did when they were younger primarily because they do not feel the need or the desire for food as they formerly did. When they do eat, it is usually in smaller quantities and at more frequent times.

Gradual atrophy of the glands lining the walls of the stomach and bowels means a decrease in the ferments and juices that carry out *digestion*. As a result, the old person needs more fluids to lubricate and to dissolve food elements and he should discard foods that are hard to digest. To avoid over-taxing the weakened digestive system, meals should be smaller and, if neces-sary, at more frequent intervals. The lower bowel, or colon, is more sensitive to irritation by roughage because it is less well lubricated with mucus. This is especially serious for old people whose loss of teeth makes it difficult for them to chew well.

Sodium, water, chloride, and calcium show definite increases with age. Potassium, magnesium, phosphorus, nitrogen, and ash, on the other hand, show a decrease. Basal-metabolism values tend to decrease, though wide variations are noted. There is a reduction in oxygen consumption and a diminution in carbohydrate tolerance. Strength and work capacity decrease as the ability to use the muscles as they were formerly used declines as a result of muscular flabbiness and general weakness. The ability for brief and violent effort diminishes with age while the ability to withstand a long, steady grind increases. Physical fatigue requires longer time for recuperation with advancing age. This is true also of fatigue from continued mental work or from nervous strain. As a result, most old people learn to cut down on any work that requires either strength or speed.

Health. Old age is a period of increasingly *poor health*. Even if there is no illness, there is a tendency to feel less well than usual. Illness, however, is even more common than in babyhood, the least healthy of all ages prior to senescence. There are few diseases limited to this period, but some occur more commonly in old age than at any other time. This is particularly true of cancer and heart diseases of all kinds. There is also a greater tendency to constipation, hemorrhoids, and digestive disturbances of all kinds than at other ages. The diseases that are peculiar to senescence are circulatory dis-orders, metabolic disorders, involutional mental disturbances, disorders of the joints, and tumors, both benign and malignant. The older organism repairs itself much more slowly after mechanical and chemical injury than the younger one does. For example, during the First World War Alexis Carrel found that the rate of healing of uninfected wounds varied with the age of the patient so precisely that the relation could be expressed in a mathe-matical formula. Knowing only the surface area of a wound and its rate of healing, the age of the soldier could be calculated with surprising accuracy. Broken bones knit more slowly and more poorly in older people than in younger.

When the characteristics of the common diseases are compared among the aged and youth, some marked differences are apparent. In youth, most diseases arise from without (infectious); among the aged, they come from within (noninfectious). In youth, they are due to specific, identifiable agents; in old age, to multiple, obscure causes. In youth, diseases begin abruptly and follow a stormy course; in old age, they begin slowly and follow a gradual and insidious course. In youth, the disease leaves the patient immunized; in old age, it makes him more vulnerable. And, finally, in youth the disease is painful, while in old age it is not, thus making its diagnosis difficult. Among men and women in the sixties, poor general health is less common than it is when individuals live to be over seventy years of age. After seventy, fully half of all men and women can anticipate several years of invalidism before they die (Havinghurst, 1950). Poor vision, poor hearing, lameness, weak or ailing heart, lung trouble, and a general physical weakness are also very common (Miles, 1935). Many old people suffer from imaginary illness and concentrate on any ache or pain they may have. Talking about aches,

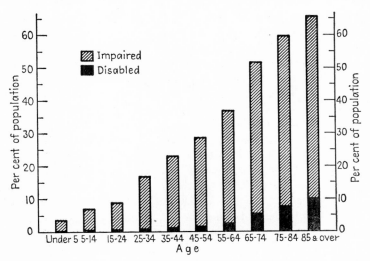

Fig. 57. Per cent of population impaired and disabled according to age. (*Based on data from L. I. Dublin, A. J. Lotka, and M. Spiegelman, Length of Life, rev. ed. New York: Ronald, 1949. From N. W. Shock, Trends in gerontology, Stanford, Calif.: Stanford Univ. Press, 1951. Used by permission.*)

pains, medicine, and doctors is a favorite pastime of many old people (Gardiner, 1949). The marked increase in physical disability with advancing age is shown in Fig. 57.

There are a number of *physical hazards* of old age which require serious consideration. The old person needs suitable living quarters the maintenance of which will not overtax his strength and which are as free as possible from hazards of falls. He must have proper food for his age and general health, proper heating because of the inability of his body to adjust as well to changes in temperature as when he was younger, and a minimum of noise to interfere with his sleep. Because everyone recognizes, sooner or later, that he is growing old, there must be an acceptance of this fact. Some old people try to prove to themselves and others that they are as young as ever and, as a result, engage in activities far too strenuous for their age. Others go to the opposite extreme and take too little exercise to maintain good health. Accidents from driving a car or from being confused by heavy traffic to the point where he is a victim of an accident are common experiences of the aged (Selling, 1944).

In general, the old person's health and safety need guarding in much the same way as do those of the child. With each advancing year, the individual becomes less and less able to assume this responsibility for himself. And yet, without reasonably good health, the downward descent will be faster than it would otherwise be. So long as old people can remain in fairly good health with a minimum of physical defects, their motor and mental efficiency can be maintained at a relatively high level. Decline in physical health, on the other hand, brings about a more rapid decline in motor and mental activities than would otherwise occur.

MOTOR ABILITIES

It is a widely recognized fact that old people are slower and less sure of their movements than are the younger. They seem less well coordinated than they did when they were younger and, as very old age sets in, they become clumsy and awkward in their movements.

Awkwardness. The awkwardness of old people is so common that it has become customary to expect old people to spill and drop things, to trip and fall, just as one expects such behavior during the "awkward age" of early adolescence. This tendency to be awkward, together with the greater amount of energy needed to do things than was formerly necessary, very often causes old people to shun motor activities whenever possible. They will ride rather than walk whenever they can, they will go up and down stairs in an elevator in preference to walking, they will welcome an opportunity to be waited on by others, and they will give up many of the sports and hobbies they formerly enjoyed. As a result of this voluntary giving up of activities, often before it is necessary, many old people are more in danger of wearing out from disuse than from sensible activity (Stieglitz, 1950).

Strength. Decline in physical strength begins in the late twenties and advances throughout the years of adulthood. Whatever type of strength test is used, the results are the same. They indicate that the individual becomes progressively less strong as he gets older. When measures of hand strength, by means of the dynamometer were made on men, it was found that by the age of sixty years, there was a decline in average strength of $16\frac{1}{2}$ per cent from the maximum (Fisher and Birren, 1947). Decline in strength with age varies, however, with different groups of muscles. The decline is most pronounced in the flexor muscles of the forearm and in the muscles which raise the body. Declining strength is shown also in the speed with which the elderly person becomes fatigued. It takes only a short time and a minimum of use for him to complain of fatigue in this or that set of muscles.

Skills. Motor coordinations become increasingly difficult for the elderly person. As a result, he frequently does things in a careless, untidy manner, cutting corners whenever possible. The breakdown of motor skills proceeds in inverse order to that in which skills were formed. The earliest formed skills are retained longest and the most recently formed ones are lost first. With advancing age, however, even the most firmly established coordinations begin to break up and the individual reverts to the state of semihelplessness characteristic of the early months of his life.

Learning new skills in old age is a rare experience. Not only is learning extremely difficult but lack of motivation on the individual's part further militates against the learning. This is well illustrated in such tasks as learning a maze where a drop from 100 per cent for the eighteen- to twenty-nine-year-old group to 55 per cent for the seventy- to eighty-nine-year group was noted (Miles, 1933). In such a task, the older subject has little motivation to learn and, hence, his learning is unfavorably affected. Learning skills where there will be some benefit to him personally, however, may have the necessary motivating force but, even then, the learning progresses slowly and the end results are inferior to those of younger learners.

Inability to learn new skills or to make modifications in previously learned skills is a handicap to the elderly person in our modern business and industrial life. New machinery and new techniques of work require new learning or modification of skills previously learned. This is where the old person is at a distinct disadvantage. The tendency to become emotionally disturbed and confused when working under pressure or when there are crowds present makes new learning even more difficult than it would otherwise be for the old person and militates against his ability to use the skills he already has to their maximum efficiency. This is especially apparent in the way old people become confused while driving a car or walking in traffic, and it explains why there are so many traffic accidents among old people.

MENTAL ABILITIES

The decline in mental abilities, begun in middle age, continues as old age sets in. The mental deterioration of old age is one of its most characteristic qualities. As in all other areas of human behavior, deterioration in the mental area varies from individual to individual. There is no one age at which the decline begins and no specific pattern of decline that is characteristic of all old people. In general, among the highest intellectual levels, there is relatively less decrease in mental efficiency than among those of the lower intellectual levels. The rate of mental decline, as is true of decline of motor abilities, is dependent to a marked extent upon the physical condition of the individual.

The healthier the old person, other factors being equal, the slower will be the decline in his mental functions. Lack of environmental stimulation will likewise leave its mark on the rate of mental decline (Anderson, 1949).

Mental activities that are dependent in part or in whole on physical activities decline faster than do those that are purely psychological. In the case of perceptual activities, for example, the individual is dependent upon the use of the different sense organs. As the efficiency of functioning of the sense organs, especially the eyes and ears, declines in old age to a point where the individual must rely upon artificial aids if he is to obtain any sensory experiences of real value, it is obvious that the visual and auditory perceptions of the aged would decline fast as the efficiency of the sense organs upon which they depend declines. To determine just how great the mental decline of the individual is as he reaches senescence, it is not adequate to compare his mental capacity at that time with the mental capacities of his contemporaries. A true measure of the amount of decline consists of having an accurate measure of the individual's intellectual abilities at their peak and then determine from this standard the percentage of decline that sets in at different ages.

This, unfortunately, is rarely possible because the individuals who are old today grew up at a time when intelligence tests were in limited use. One way of meeting this difficulty has been to use the Babcock Test of Vocabulary on the assumption that vocabulary does not increase materially after maturity, that it is highly correlated with mental ability, and that it shows a marked resistance to the ravages of age. In this way, it is possible to determine with a fair degree of accuracy the original intellectual level of the subjects studied in old age. The degree of mental deterioration suffered can be measured by determining the discrepancy between the vocabulary-test score and the scores on speed-and-learning tests, since speed and learning have been proved to be mental abilities subject to deterioration with age (Gilbert, 1944).

Areas of Decline. Tests of general intelligence show that from the age of sixty years on, there is a pronounced decline in mental efficiency as measured by these tests. While the decline starts in the forties and progresses at a slow rate until sixty, after sixty, the decline is much more marked (Miles, 1935). Individuals in the earlier part of the sixty-year-old group show a greater mental efficiency than do those in the latter part of this group. This shows a progressive deterioration in mental efficiency within that one decade of the individual's life. This deterioration progresses at a rapid rate with each successive decade of the individual's life (Gilbert, 1944). While there is a definite decrease in mental efficiency at senescence for individuals of all levels of intelligence, there is a marked tendency for those of the highest level of intelligence to show relatively less decrease in mental efficiency than those of lower intellectual levels.

This would suggest that the brighter individuals retain their original equipment longer than do those who are not so bright (Gilbert, 1941). There is no question about the fact that the brighter individuals make more use of their intellectual powers during the years of adulthood than do those who are not so bright and this is thus partly responsible for the maintenance of a higher level of mental efficiency for a longer time. An analysis of the different mental abilities as measured by the different parts of the intelligence test has revealed that although there is general and marked deterioration on all types of efficiency tests, the deterioration is greatest in the tests involving learning and formation of new associations, facility of perceptual relations, and motor ability. Least deterioration has been found in tests of giving opposites, general information, and simple repetitions. The average loss for all tests has been found to be 29 per cent, with the greatest, 57 per cent, in learning paired associates, and the least, 12 per cent, in general information (Gilbert, 1944). There has also been noted a marked deterioration in auditory memory for digits and words, in immediate visual memory, and in arithmetical reasoning (Beeson, 1920).

Causes of Deterioration. To date, no one has been able to determine just what is primarily responsible for the deterioration of general mental efficiency in old age. There is no question about the fact that there is a marked relationship between the gradual physical deterioration that takes place at this time and mental deterioration. For example, declines in physical strength and vigor, decrease in sensory acuity, and brain changes and diseases common in old age all affect not only the general physical well-being of the individual but also his emotionality, his outlook on life, and his desire to do good work. Furthermore, old people are not, as a rule, as alert or interested in what goes on in the environment as younger people are. This attitude affects their adjustment to a test situation and, as a result, they do less well than the younger person whose motivation may be stronger.

As was pointed out earlier, the mental deterioration that is associated with old age may not be as great as is popularly supposed. There is a possibility that what is assumed to be a deterioration of general mental ability may be caused by discrepancies in the choice of groups of different age levels for comparisons and by the differences in education that exist today and at the time the elderly groups were school children. Only when genetic studies of large and well-selected groups are made will it be possible to determine the amount of mental deterioration that actually takes place and in what areas this deterioration is most marked.

In addition, because it is a known fact that speed of action is less with advancing age, the tests which are used to measure mental deterioration must not put as much emphasis on speed as intelligence tests in use today do (Lorge, 1936). And, finally, the maintenance of mental practice and intellectual interests throughout the years of adulthood may go a long way toward warding off the mental deterioration that generally accompanies aging. The "inference of mental decline is an unfortunate libel upon adults," Lorge (1936) maintains as there may be no actual mental decline but decline in other abilities and interests which are responsible for the older person's doing less well than he otherwise would on a test of intelligence. Also, since many of the old people who are used as subjects for these studies are unemployed, they may lack proper work habits and practice in intelligence tests.

Tradition holds that as the individual grows older, he is "too old a dog to learn new tricks." Most elderly people accept this point of view and make little effort to learn new things. In addition, society calls upon them little for new adjustments (Hollingworth, 1928). Feelings of insecurity and inadequacy on the part of the elderly person add to his already present difficulties in learning and this tends to slow down the rate of learning. The type of work he has done throughout the years of adulthood and the amount of time he has devoted to intellectual activities are likewise factors of importance in determining how easily he will learn new material. The more out of practice he is, due to interests and activities pursued during the adult years, the more slowly and laboriously will he learn (Gilbert, 1941). Almost anything is learnable up to fifty or later (Thorndike, 1928). After that, old people show less aptitude in dealing with novel material than do younger.

However, they often compensate for their loss in learning ability by added incentives or better selection of material to be learned (Thorndike, 1928). When a decrease in learning ability does occur, and this is more often the case than not, the trouble can be traced to lack of motivation or disuse, or to both. Because of decreased flexibility and adaptability, the formation of new associations is especially difficult if they interfere in any way with those previously formed. Old people can and do learn new material but the learning is slower, more laborious, and less efficient than that of younger people (Gilbert, 1944). Because relatively few of the individuals sixty years of age or older studied by Gilbert were capable of attacking with normal efficiency tasks involving new learning, he maintained that this supported the contentions of those who insist on the necessity of a retirement age fixed in the sixties and of those who refuse new employment to persons in the sixties.

Forgetfulness. Forgetfulness is one of the popular criteria of approaching senility. When a person whose hairs are beginning to turn gray forgets a name or a date, his hearers immediately put two and two together and come to the conclusion that he is getting old. As a matter of fact, this same individual may never have had a good memory for names and dates but, during the earlier years of his life, no one paid any attention to his forgetfulness. Now, however, attention is focused on it because of the belief that forgetfulness is a certain accompaniment of old age.

Old people have poor recent memories but good remote memories. According to Hollingworth (1928), "The most recent impressions and experiences are the first to be lost; later those of adult life; then those of youth; and finally those of early childhood." Because motivation is important in memory, youthful experiences which are emotionally toned are more likely to be remembered than are those of old age. Furthermore, the old person is less attentive to what he may later want to remember than is the younger person and his brain is no longer so soft and plastic. Feelings of inadequacy may cause withdrawal of attention from the details of external reality with the result that many old people are more forgetful than they need to be (Cowdry, 1939).

The following suggestions for compensating for the normal memory declines that come with age have been made (Gilbert, 1941):

1. Get greater practice on things to be remembered.
2. Form methodical habits of jotting down things one wishes to remember.
3. Make memoranda of new material to be learned and remembered and then study it at leisure.
4. Avoid forming the habit of depending on younger people to remember things for the older individual.
5. Keep active and alert mentally.
6. Maintain the intellectual quality of reading throughout the years of adulthood.

Reasoning. Reasoning ability reaches its peak among the last of all the mental abilities and it is among the last to go at old age. How rational or irrational the old person will be depends not so much upon his age as upon his experience and knowledge. Some people in the sixties have logic-tight minds but, if one had a case history of their past, one would discover that logic-tight thinking characterized the major part of their lives. It did not develop suddenly as they became old though, like all other traits, it became more pronounced with age. Driving accidents among old people are frequently the result of confused and slow reasoning. The ability to form comparisons and to reason by analogy declines rapidly after the age of sixty years. At eighty, the average person can reason about as well as an eight-year-old child.

Vocabulary. Because vocabulary is in constant use and because the words used have, for the most part, been learned when the individual was a child, the deterioration in vocabulary at old age is very slight as compared with other mental abilities. This is true of all previously learned and constantly used material, not of vocabulary alone. After the age of sixty years, there is some decline in size of vocabulary (Foulds and Raven, 1948), though, on the whole, the decline is not great. A comparison of a group of seventy- to seventy-nine-year-olds with a control group made up of forty- to forty-nine-year-olds showed no significant difference in vocabulary ability in the two groups as measured by a vocabulary test (Fox, 1947). In sixty- to sixty-nine-year-old subjects, decline in vocabulary and comprehension tests is less than that in all tests (Fox and Birren, 1950).

Mental Rigidity. The mental rigidity that sets in during middle life becomes increasingly pronounced as age advances. Most old people become so mentally rigid or "set in their ways" that adjustments to new situations are difficult for them to make. They are fixed in their opinions, attitudes, and reactions to such an extent that any deviation from the customary pattern is extremely difficult if not impossible for them to make. This lack of mental elasticity turns the youthful radical into an elderly conservative.

While individuals differ in the degree of mental rigidity they experience, it is unusual for a person over sixty years of age not to be prejudiced in his opinions, unwilling to adapt his points of view to meet new conditions, and set in ways of doing things. Part of this mental rigidity comes, unquestionably, from the fact that learning is slow and laborious as age advances. As a result, the old person takes the easiest way out by doing things in the old and tried way (Cavan *et al.,* 1949). Men, as a group, are more flexible than women not because of greater masculine intelligence but rather because the mode of life of men gives them opportunities to adjust to new situations more often than is offered to women throughout the course of their adult lives. Experience thus acts as an aid in warding off mental rigidity.

EMOTIONAL REACTIONS

According to traditional beliefs, with old age comes the dying down of the "fires" of the emotional life. The result is that the old person is devoid of emotions as experienced by the younger person and is even incapable of experiencing many of the feelings of the younger person. The explanation for the waning of the emotional life at senescence is that decreased vigor, decreased physical strength, and decreased sexual drives all rob the old person of the sources of emotional reactions that he had during the early years of life.

Studies of the aged have shown that the affective life "tends toward a level of apathy" (Hollingworth, 1928). The rigidity that is characteristic of motor performances and thought is apparent in the affective life of the elderly person. He is less responsive emotionally than he was when he was younger, and he shows less enthusiasm. Typically, the emotional responses are more specific, less varied, and less appropriate to the occasion than are the emotional responses of younger people. They are, thus, inadequate because they are not comprehensive and varied enough to deal with new situations. It is not unusual for the elderly person to show signs of regression in his emotional behavior, such as negativism, temper tantrums, and excitability characteristic of a child (Banham, 1950).

The *emotional rigidity* of the elderly, which shows itself in repetitiveness in behavior and lack of affective adaptability, is due, Banham explained, to the fact that emotional organization undergoes a certain amount of consolidation, constriction, and disintegration in later life. When stimulated by an exciting or terrifying event, the individual acts in a specific, repetitive fashion as contrasted with the child whose behavior may be inappropriate because it is violent or random. In the elderly, it is inappropriate because of the limited nature of the response and its unchangeability.

Recovery from emotional experiences also differs as the individual grows older. The young child may spend his energy, mobilized for emotional responses, in play or constructive activity of some sort. The elderly person, by contrast, may be exhausted, less able to turn to other things, and may remain anxious and depressed for a long time. According to Banham (1951, p. 178), "The emotions of old people are characterized by paucity rather than overabundance of affective energy. The form of their behavior tends to narrow, like a stream in a drought, into one channel rather than to brim over into general hyperactivity and tension."

Characteristics. While the affective life of the old person does, on the whole, show less intensity than is characteristic of the younger years, the resistant emotions show an unaccustomed intensity. The old person is likely to be irritable, quarrelsome, crotchety, and contrary. Fears and worries, disappointments, disillusionments, and beliefs of persecution are far more common than the pleasanter emotional states. Old age is far from passive and peaceful and the elderly person is more likely to be belligerent than peace-loving. Like the child, the elderly person's belligerent attitudes come from feelings of being rejected and from thwartings. The appearance of the old person, his manners, and his attitudes are often unpleasant, if not actually repulsive to others. Neglect of personal hygiene, disagreeable odors, physical distortions, and annoying mannerisms, combined with poor health and the accompanying fussiness and egocentricity that are usual in such cases, all add to social neglect of the elderly.

Furthermore, old people are thwarted by not being able to do many of the things they did when they were younger. Physical activities are reduced to a minimum and they are deprived of many of the pleasures that rely upon the use of the senses, especially the eyes and ears. The old person senses society's attitude toward him and he resents this attitude. All in all, there are few things in our culture to make an old person happy and many things to make him cross, irritable, and generally disagreeable to live with. Financial dependency, which is becoming more frequent every year, often makes the old person feel ashamed and unhappy, another common cause for the predominance of unpleasant emotions in old age (Gilbert, 1944).

Neuroticism. Old people are often accused of being neurotic. The explanation for their neuroticism is that they are mentally rigid and, hence, cannot adjust successfully to changed conditions in everyday life. But rigidity is unquestionably a normal characteristic of old age, not necessarily a sign of neuroticism. The traits indicative of maladjustment and neuroticism which old people are thought to show include feelings of inadequacy, of rejection, of depression and self-pity, hypochondria, anxiety, emotional sensitivity, irritability, quarrelsomeness, tearfulness, boredom, apathy, negativism, social withdrawal, guilt feelings, rigidity, narrowing of interests, conservatism, and regressive tendencies, especially in the sex area (Banham, 1951).

These Pollak (1943) attributes partly to environmental frustrations and the limited opportunities old people have for the satisfaction of thwarted needs and partly to changes in mental and physical capacities and functions. Even with changed environmental conditions, it is questionable whether the tendency toward unpleasant emotional reactions could be completely eliminated. The waning health and lowered physical resistance characteristic of old age would of itself be responsible for this emotionality. When a group of old people ranging in age from sixty to one hundred and two years was questioned, more than two-thirds felt their worst fault was their irritability and quick temper (Gardiner, 1949).

CHANGES IN INTERESTS WITH ADVANCING AGE

After the age of fifty years, most people develop a pronounced dislike for any change and, as a result, their interests remain static. But, as their health fails and their energy decreases with advancing age, their interests reflect this change in that there is an increase in sedentary pursuits and a decrease in activities that require strength and energy. After the mid-sixties, there is little, if any, change in the type of interests the individual has though there is a shift of emphasis on interests because of the changes in general health conditions.

Types of Interest. No matter how strong the interest in sports was earlier in life, few old people retain enough interest in them to bother to read sports events or to attend athletic contests. Even over television and radio, where they may watch or hear about the sports event with no effort whatsoever on their part, few old people are sports enthusiasts to the point where they follow athletic teams and take a real interest in the outcome of sports events. Even talking about sports, a favorite topic of conversation among adult men, sinks into oblivion as age advances. Why interest in sports declines so rapidly and so markedly as old age advances may be explained partly by the declining health and physical vigor of the old person.

Interest in *appearance* continues to wane as old age advances. While it is true that some old people are as appearance-conscious as they were when they were younger, they are definitely the exception to the rule. Declining interest in appearance and *clothes* may be a form of compensation. Instead of being reminded of deterioration in looks with age, which would be inevitable if the old person spent as much time in front of the mirror as the younger person does, the old person avoids the mirror and develops an "I don't care" attitude toward clothes. As a result, he is frequently careless and slovenly instead of well-groomed. The mental rigidity that shows itself in other areas of behavior is very apparent in the old person's attitude toward new styles in clothing. Not only is the old person conservative in the clothes he selects but, whenever possible, he selects clothes of the style that approximates the style that prevailed when he was younger.

Increase in body odors, caused partly by changes in the sweat glands and partly by poor personal hygiene, adds to the unattractiveness of the old person. The more senile he becomes, the more unattractive and the less interested he is in either clothes or appearance. Old men, as a rule, are more interested in their appearance than are old women (Anderson, 1949). This is in direct contrast to the prevailing interests of younger people and may be explained by the fact that women use this as a compensation for the distress that failing looks bring them.

Interest in *money,* which started to wane during middle age, generally becomes more intense as old age sets in. With retirement or unemployment, the elderly person usually finds himself with a greatly reduced income or with no income at all. This focuses his attention on money and stimulates an interest in the problem of how he can get more. This interest is not for the purpose of having more possessions but rather to maintain independence and an opportunity to live where he wishes, free from dependency on relatives or charity.

As a general rule, the *recreational interests* of elderly people are similar to those of the middle-aged, with a gradual narrowing down of interests as health fails. It is rather unusual when an old person cultivates a new recreational interest during the closing years of his life. He may, however, devote his time to an activity which interested him greatly when he was younger but which he had to put aside during the years when he was busy making money or rearing a family. Men and women who, in the sixties or seventies, take up painting as an avocation are usually those whose interest in painting did not begin then but who, because of lessened responsibilities, are able to resume activities related to a dormant interest. Likewise, an old person is very unlikely to develop an interest as readily in old age if there was no interest along that line during the earlier years of the individual's life.

Reading is one of the common pastimes of old people. How much they read, however, depends partly upon reading habits established during the earlier years of their lives and partly upon the quality of their eyesight (Conkey, 1933). On the whole, what they read in old age changes little from what they read when they were younger. Listening to the *radio* and watching *television* increase in popularity for many old people as their eyesight fails and as they find it increasingly difficult to go out of doors. While the tastes of older people are more conservative than those of the younger, they generally listen to much the same type of program as younger people do. There is a marked tendency, for example, for older people to dislike *jazz music* (Conkey. 1933). Attending *movies* becomes a rare diversion for old people. This may be explained partly by the fact that the old people alive today never really formed the movie-going habit when they were younger but mostly because going out in crowds becomes increasingly difficult and confusing for older people.

To be a source of real satisfaction, a *hobby* must be selected earlier in life and must be a well-established part of the individual's life pattern. When a group of old people was questioned about their hobbies, 35.1 per cent said that they had some sort of hobby; the rest said that they had none. Of those who claimed to be happy, 47 per cent had hobbies and only 17.2 per cent of the unhappy group did. The common hobbies reported by men included gardening, cards, baseball, reading and participation in music; hobbies popular with women included sewing, embroidery, gardening, reading, cards, housekeeping, church work, and listening to music. When those who once had hobbies were asked why they gave them up, the reasons were poor health, too expensive, old age, no opportunity, lost interest, and no time (Morgan, 1937). The number of hobbies and the amount of time devoted to hobbies decrease after sixty-five years of age (Briggs, 1938).

Interest in *religion* and in a *philosophy of life* becomes increasingly important as life draws to a close. The poorer the individual's physical condition, the more likely he is to become deeply interested in some sort of religious or philosophical thought. While old people as a rule attend church less than they did when they were younger, this does not necessarily mean a waning of interest in religion. Failing health and a tendency to become confused and emotionally disturbed when in a crowd make many older people stay at home when they would really enjoy a church service.

When a group of people of different ages was asked why they attended church, marked differences in reasons were given by the younger and older members of the group. The reasons given by the younger members of the group for going to church were to gain new friends and acquaintances, to aid in formulating a philosophy of life, and to get light on civic, moral, and social issues. While some of the older members of the group claimed that they went to church for the same reasons, the numbers were much less. For example, only 18 per cent of the older group went to gain new friends and acquaintances while 63 per cent of the younger group did so. Likewise, 36 per cent of the older group said they attended church to help formulate a philosophy of life as compared with 71 per cent of the younger group. Among the older people questioned, the desire to "join with others in keeping alive the spirit of Christ" and to encourage church attendance on the part of families and others were reasons that grew increasingly strong with age (Kingsbury, 1937).

SOCIAL BEHAVIOR

As an old person's interest in self increases, interest in other people decreases. Each year, as the person becomes older, his interest in other people becomes weaker. At first, he loses interest in acquaintances or in those whom he knows least of all. Then, gradually, with advancing age, his interest in friends wanes and he finally narrows himself down to a few intimate friends or "cronies" with whom he spends what time he can. His social interests and behavior regress to a stage characteristic in many respects to that of childhood.

Companions. To an elderly person, the family circle constitutes the nucleus of his social life. While the members of his family may not be as congenial as his contemporaries would be, there is the advantage of having them ready and available for companionship. The older he is, the more he must rely upon his family for companionship because his contemporaries have died or are in a physical or mental condition that makes it impossible for them to do things with him.

The person of sixty or more finds it difficult, if not impossible, to keep up to the pace set by his former friends who are now only middle-aged. Furthermore, he discovers that he is no longer a welcome member of a younger group because his age makes it impossible for him to do what the group does. As a result, after 30 or 40 years of associating with individuals of different ages, he now finds it necessary to limit his friends to individuals of his own age. This adjustment is often very difficult for an elderly person to make (Havinghurst, 1950).

From the point of view of the older person, social contacts with his contemporaries have advantages that far outweigh any disadvantages there might be. His contemporaries have interests in common with his and, because the older person finds it difficult to adjust to new situations easily, this is important to him. He can feel at home with people with whom it is unnecessary to make radical adjustments and whose interests are similar to his because they are contemporaries. Then, too, his contemporaries move physically and mentally at a tempo similar to his. This puts far less strain on him than when he tries to keep up to the pace set by younger people. And, finally, social contacts with his contemporaries offer him an opportunity for prestige that he would not have in a group where there are younger people. His past achievements and successes are remembered and give him a status in the group which he would not likely have in a group where there are younger people whose successes are in the present rather than in the past.

Social Activities. As age advances, interest in social activities not only declines but its scope narrows. Many of the things the individual formerly enjoyed doing with members of the family and friends he now finds too tiring or too boring. As a result, he gives them up. This is especially true of parties, dancing, and going to places of amusement. Even card playing, which requires a minimum of physical exertion, comes to be too much of a mental strain as people become older. As a result, it is less popular as a form of social activity than it was during earlier years. Most old people find their social activities narrowing down to visiting with friends and talking (Gardiner, 1949).

Until senility sets in, the typical older person derives keen enjoyment from being with people who will listen to him. For the most part, he finds that younger people, even the members of his own family, seem disinterested in what he has to say. They either do not listen or they pay so little attention that they do not know what has been said. Furthermore, they are likely to show impatience at the endless talking of the older person. His contemporaries, on the other hand, will usually listen to him if he, in turn, will listen to them. Consequently, talking becomes one of the most popular social activities of the aged.

While it is true that memories of the present fade out first, that alone is not what makes old people talk about the past rather than about the present. They talk about the past because they realize that it held more for them than the present and future do and thus was a period in their lives when more of interest happened to talk about. When the individual becomes senile to the point where his motor coordinations are poor, his speech likewise becomes poor. Frequently it is difficult if not actually impossible to understand what the senile person is saying because his speech becomes a series of sounds with little or no meaning or relationship. When this happens, the individual who is already somewhat helpless becomes even more so. Like the baby, he is unable to make his needs and wants known through speech but, unlike the baby, he generally does not use crying as a means of language communication. Consequently, he remains thwarted with unsatisfied desires, a fact which helps to contribute to the unhappiness of old age.

CHAPTER 14

Old Age
(Continued)

With each passing year, the productivity of the individual declines. He is not only capable of producing less than he was when he was younger but his failing strength and energy sap his motivation, and society gives him relatively little chance to do even what he is capable of doing. As a result, the output of the older person, when measured either in terms of achievements or in terms of income, falls far short of that of the individual in middle age or earlier, when he is at the peak of his chosen line of work. This has been well illustrated by Lehman's curves for productivity in many lines, all of which show a drop after forty-five, to a low in the sixties and seventies (Lehman, 1943).

The psychological effects of decreased output are far greater than is commonly recognized. To the younger person whose days are crowded often to the breaking point with duties and responsibilities, retirement or semiretirement seems like a golden period in life. But, when the time comes and the days of retirement are here, the situation seems far less rosy than it did when viewed through the eyes of a younger person.

Types of Work. The type of work an old person engages in determines to some extent the duration of his usefulness. In executive positions, his days of employment in large or even in small organizations are limited by retirement rules which generally stipulate that he must retire at the age of sixty-five years. Several years prior to that, he is aware of the fact that a younger man is being groomed to succeed him and that his influence in the organization is waning. Clerical workers are generally retired at the age of sixty-five years, if they have been able to retain their jobs that long. When conditions in the business world are poor, the elderly worker is generally the first to be laid off. The skilled, semiskilled, or unskilled worker finds that, as his speed and strength decrease with age, his usefulness to his organization likewise decreases and, as a result, he is often laid off at slack times, only to be replaced by a younger worker when conditions improve.

Only when a person is in business for himself can he continue to work without an arbitrarily set retirement age. If his health and vigor are still good, he may do as much work and work of a caliber as high as he did when he was at the peak of his career. Or, if he wishes, he may do part-time work, at his own speed and in his own way. In this way, he is able to retain some interest in the activities that formerly engrossed his time and attention and he may earn enough to supply his diminishing needs and wants. Few individuals today, however, are in this fortunate position. With the growth of corporations and with the tendency for people to work for an employer instead of for themselves, the old person of today is governed by rules set by his employer.

Not only does the type of work the individual engages in determine how long he will be able to retain his job but it also determines the ease or difficulty he encounters in changing jobs or in getting a job if he is unemployed. As a general rule, individuals at the two extremes of the business and industrial ladders are in the least favorable positions in this respect. The higher the position, the more difficult it is to attain when one reaches middle age. After fifty, stepping into an important executive position is almost impossible. The less skilled the older worker, the less chance he has of getting a new job. It is feared that he is "too old a dog to learn new tricks" and that he is not quick enough to keep up to the pace that modern business and industry demand.

Women are generally in a far less favorable position than are men both in holding their jobs and in getting new jobs as they grow older. The traditional belief that women, after the menopause, are no longer capable of doing what they did when they were younger affects their vocational lives just as it affects their sex lives. The first sign of graying hair or the first wrinkle is likely to be interpreted as meaning that the woman is "getting too old" to work. Studies of elderly people have shown that marked individual differences exist in their abilities to hold jobs and to do the work that these jobs require. Many old people retain their vigor and faculties to an advanced age and can, as a result, successfully hold down their jobs far beyond the time of compulsory retirement. There are other old people who, through accident, disability, debility, or simple decline in powers, have less ability than they had when they were younger and yet who are not unemployable. Still others are incapable of earning a living because of some permanent illness or disability (Clague, 1949).

Advantages of Older Workers. Most people emphasize the disadvantages to business and industry brought about by the employment of old people. There is a strong popular idea that older workers are unable to work under younger supervisors, that they resist changes in work methods or the introduction of new machinery, and that they are difficult to work with (Esser *et al.,* 1951; Tuckman and Lorge, 1952). Employees under thirty years of age have been found to be neutral toward the employment of older workers; those thirty or older become increasingly more favorable as they grow older (Kirchner *et al.*, 1952). Looking at the other side of the situation, it becomes apparent that there are advantages as well as disadvantages to the employment of the elderly. Whether the advantages will outweigh the disadvantages, or vice versa, can be determined only when a reasonable number of elderly people are kept on the job beyond the compulsory retirement age and an opportunity is thus given to measure the degree of deterioration in their work from its peak.

The older worker, through his greater experience, tends to do things with less waste motion than does the younger, less experienced worker. He is less inclined to distractions from home and other outside sources than is the worker whose interests are centered around his romances or his family life. There is a greater conscientiousness among older workers because of their more mature attitudes and their realization of the importance of doing their

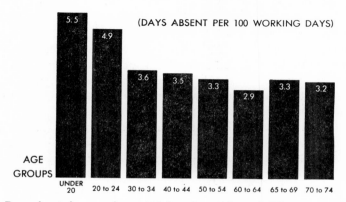

Fig. 58. Days absent from work per 100 days for workers of different ages. (*From M. Gumpert, Our "Inca" ideas about retirement. The New York Times, July 27, 1952. Used by permission.*)

best to hold onto a job. In industry, it has been found that older workers spoil less material and cause less turnover than do younger workers. These advantages compensate, in part at least, for less speed and decreased adaptability, both of which are characteristic of old age.

Absenteeism, due to illness or disinclination to work, is a problem that plagues most employers. In our modern business and industrial life, where most workers work for someone else, absenteeism is a major problem. Studies of the Bureau of Labor Statistics have revealed that absenteeism is highest among the workers under twenty years of age and less frequent among the older workers (see Fig. 58). Furthermore, the record for older workers in regard to disabling injuries and illnesses is better than for the younger age groups. Even among workers from sixty-five to seventy-four years, almost half are not found to be affected by any chronic disability (Gumpert, 1952),

No age group over fifty years has been found to have a rate for disabling injuries as high as the thirty-five- to forty-four-year group (Shock, 1951).

An interesting side light on this matter is shown in the reaction of employers to older employees. A survey of 1,000 employers by the New York State Joint Legislative Committee on the Problems of the Aging has revealed that employers rate older workers as more loyal and steadfast than and as productive as their juniors. Three out of every four employers interviewed believed the older workers produced as much as the younger (Desmond, 1949). A similar study in California showed similar results. Although some employers said they believed some jobs were more appropriate for older workers, many said they preferred the older workers for jobs requiring judgment and experience and for jobs where quality is more important than speed (California Department of Industrial Relations, 1930). And yet, in spite of the prevailing opinion among employers that older workers are better for certain types of jobs, the practice of personnel officers is usually to discriminate against them (Shock, 1951).

Vocational Opportunities. After middle age, the vocational opportunities for both men and women decrease rapidly. In a recent study of the positions the older workers hold in the American labor market today, it was found that these positions were far below the standards the individuals would find satisfying. It is therefore not surprising that the workers would find little satisfaction in their jobs. When the capacities and opportunities for the aged were explored, it was found that the age group over sixty-five was disproportionally in agriculture, forestry, animal husbandry, and public service. In industry, the older workers are found in dead-end jobs, in monotonous, repetitive jobs, and in highly skilled and responsible jobs. Almost 50 per cent of all men in age group sixty-five to seventy-four years are employers or self-employed. Under such conditions, they can remain in the type of work they have been accustomed to doing until their health fails or until they have a real desire to retire (Pollak, 1950).

Unemployment. Unemployment strikes hard at any age but, as the individual approaches old age, being unemployed is a very serious problem. Not only is it increasingly difficult for him to get another job as he grows older, but the effects on his personality are far more serious and far-reaching than is true of the younger worker. The younger worker knows that his chances of obtaining future employment are good, even if he must take a temporary setback in wages. With the older worker, however, there is a far less hopeful outlook (Harsh and Schrickel, 1950). He knows that most business and industrial organizations are not favorably disposed toward the older worker. He knows, further, that if he is lucky enough to get a job, it will be far below his capacities. Furthermore, the older worker has, in most instances, restricted his vocational training and activity to a rather limited area of work in which, as the years passed, he became proficient. In addition, the time-

and energy-consuming tasks of earning a living and raising a family have given him little opportunity to prepare himself for another line of work. Then, too, old people, believing that they are "too old dogs to learn new tricks," make no effort to prepare themselves for another type of work in which their age would not be so great a handicap (Harsh and Schrickel, 1950).

Studies of the *mental effects of unemployment* on older workers have revealed how serious they are. Measures of the mental efficiency and attitudes of unemployed and employed men in their sixties have shown that those who engage in regular, gainful occupation are, on the average, superior intellectually to those who are unemployed. Lack of practice and unfavorable mental attitudes are important contributing factors to this deterioration. This is shown also in the differences between those who are unemployed for shorter periods as compared with those who are unemployed for longer times (Gilbert, 1936). While it is difficult or almost impossible in our present cultural setup completely to eliminate unemployment among the older workers, some of the unemployment could be eliminated by constructive measures. Suggestions for this consist of educational efforts directed at correcting prejudices that lead to the discrimination against older workers; research concerning the determination of what jobs the older workers can do; and attempts to prevent workers from becoming technologically and physiologically obsolete as they grow older (Willard, 1949).

Retirement. Since the First World War, there has been a growing tendency in America to enforce retirement on workers at an arbitrarily set age, regardless of the capacities of the individual when he reaches that age. This tendency has increased and has become more widespread since the depression years of the thirties and the Second World War. When attempts have been made to find out how workers feel about retirement, the results have shown that most of them would rather work than be inactive. In interviews with women and men, ages fifty to eighty years, the majority said they desired to become active again. This desire for work came from a need for self-respect and to escape self-preoccupation, depression, and restlessness. This need was especially strong among those who had been unexpectedly dismissed (Fried, 1949).

If the economic side of the picture could be eliminated, retirement might not prove to be the psychological problem for the elderly that it is. But retirement brings with it economic problems that have serious effects on the individual's concept of self and, as such, lead to many emotional conflicts with their damaging effects. In a *Fortune Magazine* (1946) survey of the incomes of the aged, based on 1945 data, it was reported that 39 per cent of the aged were dependent upon public and private assistance, such as government, churches, institutions, friends, and relatives. Thirty-four per cent derived their income from earnings through employment, 19 per cent depended upon incomes from pensions, and 9 per cent on incomes from investments. Percentages of families, with heads sixty-five years of age and older, are shown in Fig. 59.

An analysis of the records of retired industrial workers showed the main source of dissatisfaction was economic need. This also affects the wife's attitude toward her husband's retirement. Activity is important to good adjustment on the part of the retired worker, whether this be paid or unpaid work. Changes in living conditions help also, as do hobbies (Moore, 1948). When given a choice, most retired workers on pensions elect to continue to work at their jobs if given an opportunity. Because most pensions are so small, retirement under present conditions does not permit a happy and abundant life for most workers (Hochman, 1950). When a group of retired workers

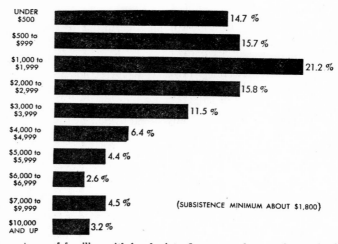

FIG. 59. Percentages of families, with heads sixty-five years of age and over, in the various income groups. (*From M. Gumpert, Our "Inca" ideas about retirement. The New York Times, July 27, 1952. Used by permission.*)

was graded on the basis of degree of satisfaction with their retirement, it was found that the excellently adjusted had retired voluntarily, they had looked forward to retirement, they were better off financially, and had wives who were better satisfied than the dissatisfied group (Moore, 1948). According to Alexis Carrel (1939), "The aging man should neither stop working nor retire. Inaction further impoverishes the content of time. Leisure is even more dangerous for the old than for the young. To those whose forces are declining appropriate work should be given. But not rest."

Psychological Effects. Unquestionably some of the most serious emotional problems of old age stem from enforced retirement. At the present time, the old people who are being forced into retirement in the early or mid-sixties grew up in a period in our culture when retirement was voluntary and when old people could continue to work as long as they wished or were physically able to do so. As a result, they did not make adequate psychological provisions for retirement. True, they may have saved money or they took out all forms of insurance and pensions to guarantee financial security in old age but preparation for a life of idleness was not made.

The unfavorable effects of obligatory cessation of work are many. If the individual is still at his peak or near the peak of productivity, there will be marked feelings of frustration if he is suddenly thrown into an inactive state and is replaced by someone else who may be less able than he. Because of reduced income, he may be forced to forgo the social contacts he formerly had and, because he no longer goes to work, he loses contact with the people he was accustomed to seeing daily. Loss of status in the home is likewise a source of emotional conflict for the retired worker. He must frequently move from the home he has occupied for a major part of his adult life; he may even have to go to live as a dependent in the home of a grown child or in a public institution; and he will unquestionably find that the members of the family feel that his authority as head of the home is no longer what it was before, when he was a wage earner.

Constructive Suggestions. There have been many suggestions offered to ease the emotional shock to the elderly person of compulsory retirement. For the most part, these suggestions all stress the need for psychological preparation for retirement. If retirement is to produce the least psychological damage, it must be gradual, not sudden. As Gitelson (1948) has pointed out: "If retirement is necessary, it should be gradual and seldom complete. The old one's own impulse will remain stronger and more regular if he can continue to keep a finger on the pulse of his affairs. To the fullest extent possible, collateral interests should be mobilized or revived, or created. In other words, retirement should be to something, not from something."

Cushing (1952) has suggested four essentials of successfully meeting the problems of retirement. These include financial security, a time-consuming interest, a gradual tapering off of work, and companionship of one's own compeers. Planning for retirement, he further maintains, is a responsibility the individual cannot take alone. It must be done with his family, the company for which he works, and with community help.

One of the most important constructive suggestions for successful retirement deals with the economic problem that arises with retirement for most old people. It is difficult, if not impossible, to maintain a healthy attitude when one feels that he or she is an unwanted dependent upon a son or daughter who already has a heavy financial burden to carry. And yet, many of our old people today are being robbed of their lifetime savings by inflation. According to the United States Bureau of the Census, over 30 per cent of American citizens sixty-five years of age and older have no money income. Of the remainder, 60 per cent have an income of less than $1,000 a year, while the rest have $3,000 or more. This means that only approximately 10 per cent of all old people are financially independent (Gumpert, 1952).

Even those who during the years of earning saved to pay premiums on annuities, old-age-benefit plans, or insurance now find their annual incomes from these savings inadequate to meet the high cost of living. In December, 1950, the average size of monthly social-security benefits for a retired worker was $42, or for a retired worker and his wife, $72. At that time, according to the Bureau of Labor Statistics, a minimum annual income of $1,800, or $150 monthly, was necessary for a man and wife to live on. To make matters worse, a rule in force stipulated that these benefits be withheld from a person under seventy-five years of age who earned more than $50 a month. In June, 1952, a bill was passed which increased the monthly payments by $5 and extended the limits of outside earnings to $70 monthly. Even this revision is hopelessly inadequate to meet the present high cost of living (Gumpert, 1952).

In addition, some change should be made in the policy of the recently developed pension plans. At the present time, a single premium for a worker hired at the age of forty years may cost the employer as high as $6,823. Each year, as the worker grows older, the cost to the employer for such a premium grows larger. By the age of sixty years, the cost is approximately $13,860. It is natural, under such conditions, that the employer shies away from employing anyone over forty years of age if he can fill his ranks with younger workers. At the present time, it is estimated that there are 53 million Americans forty years of age and older, and as time goes on, there will be many more millions as the number of old people increases (Gumpert, 1952).

Employers alone cannot meet the problem of employment of older workers. The worker himself must be willing to accept types of work different from those that he has been accustomed to performing, he must accede willingly to changes in pay for such work, and he must undertake any training or retraining necessary to retain his employability. Most older workers at the present time are in a position where they will have to depend upon self-employment if they want to work after sixty-five. This means that they will have to depend upon their own initiative and inner resources (Shock, 1951).

FAMILY RELATIONSHIPS

The pattern of family life, established during the early years of adulthood, starts to change with the onset of middle age. Interest in sex, as a rule, declines and the duties and responsibilities connected with rearing a family gradually come to an end as the children grow up, marry, and go to homes of their own. With the diminishing family size and curtailment of income frequently come changes in living conditions. These changes are often made more pronounced by retirement with its reduced income or by the death of the spouse. At a time in life when adjustments to new conditions are difficult to make, the aging individual is frequently called upon to make radical changes in the pattern of his life. This is especially difficult for women, not because women adjust less well than men but rather because the woman's life is centered around the home much more than is that of the man.

Of the many adjustments in family relationships the elderly person must make, the following are the most important:

Sexual Behavior. It is popularly believed that with old age come sexual impotence and loss of interest in sex. Furthermore, social taboos make many aged men and women feel that showing an interest of any sort in sexual matters is "not nice" and that such interest should be limited to younger people. When the individual passes middle age, any behavior of a sexual sort is regarded as a form of perversion. Women, according to tradition, become sexually impotent with the menopause, and at that time their sexual lives are expected to have come to an end. An interesting side light on the social reactions to sexual behavior in older people has been reported by Hamilton (1942), who asked a group of young adults what was their first reaction to the realization that their parents engaged in sexual intercourse. While many did not give their reactions, 20 per cent of the men and 29 per cent of the women said they were distressed. To them, the realization that older people might have any sexual desires or engage in any sexual activity was repulsive. Even when it was not considered repulsive, they thought it undignified and nonaesthetic. This attitude was found to carry on frequently to old age. Many individuals feel that people should be done with sex as a personal issue when they reach middle or old age.

In recent years, it has become apparent from scientific research that most of the "old wives' tales" are faulty. Sexual interest and sexual desire do not decline as early as is popularly believed and the sexual needs of the aged are too widespread to be considered pathological. It has become apparent that sexual impotence comes much later than was formerly believed and that interest in sex after fifty is normal, not pathological. Direct questionings of elderly people have revealed interesting facts regarding their sex lives. When a group of fifty- to sixty-four-year-old men and women was asked about their sexual behavior, 70.6 per cent said they still had sexual relations but that intercourse was spaced further apart and the man's preliminary orgastic phase was longer. In most cases, marital relations improved marital harmony. When this was not the case, marital friction had existed before the libidinal decline in the wives. Of those who had terminated sex relationships, it was mostly because of physical illness. Among the group of sixty-five and over, only one reported continued sexual intercourse (Fried and Stern, 1948).

Kinsey reported that, in a group of 126 men, sixty years of age and older, questioned by him, there was no sudden cessation of sexual activity with age but rather a gradual diminishing of this activity. For the sixty-five-year-old group Kinsey questioned, the mean frequency of sexual outlet was 1.0 per week; for the seventy-five-year-old group, 0.3 per week; and for the eighty-year-olds, 0.1 per week. At the age of sixty, 5 per cent of the men he questioned were totally inactive sexually as compared with 30 per cent at seventy. Heterosexual intercourse was found to be the most frequent sexual outlet. There was little masturbation reported and few nocturnal emissions. Erective impotence is common among old men. Ejaculatory impotence, or the inability to ejaculate when in erection, on the other hand, is very rare. By the age of seventy years, 27 per cent of the men reporting were found to be impotent; at seventy-five years, 55 per cent; and at eighty years, 75 per cent (see Fig. 60). This, Kinsey believes, is more often due to psychological than to

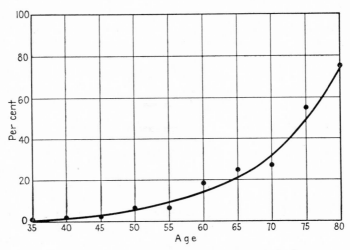

FIG. 60. Age of onset of impotence. (*From H. C. Kinsey, W. B. Pomeroy, and C. E. Martin, Sexual behavior in the human male. Philadelphia: Saunders, 1948. Used by permission.*)

physical causes. They *expect* to be impotent and this expectation frequently leads to impotence (Kinsey *et al.*, 1948).

Because of the strong social taboos that interfere with the satisfaction of the sexual needs of old people, and because of the increasing tendency to be preoccupied with bodily sensations in general, such as eating, eliminating, and sleeping, there is need for some sexual outlets, either through contacts with members of the opposite sex or through forms of sexual expression used in early adolescence, especially *masturbation*. There is evidence that it is widely practiced among those for whom there are few if any other sexual outlets. It is more common in the sixties than in the forties and fifties, and it generally is more often practiced among those who are becoming senile than among those who are senescent (Hamilton, 1929). Masturbation is more frequent among women than among men. This may be due to the social taboos against direct sexual expression through intercourse which affects women in middle and old age more than it affects men. It is a type of compensation for lack of sexual activities, especially among the widowed and unmarried women, though it is by no means limited to these groups. Married women in old age indulge in it also (Hamilton, 1929).

The psychological effects of unfavorable social attitudes toward sexual behavior in the elderly are far more serious than is generally recognized. Feelings of guilt, emotional storm and stress from thwarted sex desires, and feelings of inadequacy may and do lead to sexual impotence or to sexual outlets more characteristic of adolescence than of adulthood. As a result, there is a decrease in the frequency of coitus and an increase in other sexual outlets. As general physical decline sets in, in the sixties or seventies, there are glandular and physical changes in the sex organs and in the body as a whole which lead to a decline in sexual interest and potency. This, however, generally comes later than declines in interest and potency due to psychological causes. In men, impotence for physical reasons alone is rare under the age of sixty years (Kinsey *et al.*, 1948).

One indication of senility is sexual recrudescence, or foolish infatuations on the part of elderly people for young people of the opposite sex. This may be diffuse or localized in one love object. Among men, it usually takes the form of wanting to make love to all pretty young girls, or it may result in seduction or rape of children or adults. It is not uncommon for a man who is becoming senile to want to marry a girl who is young enough to be his granddaughter. Aged women may play with dolls, may mother children, or take a strong interest in young men. It is not uncommon for women who show this form of sexual regression to be infatuated with a man young enough to be a grandson.

Death of Spouse. Widowhood is a common problem in old age. Both men and women find, as they reach the sixties, that loneliness is a problem they must face, should they lose a spouse through death. Because it is more customary for women to marry men older than they than for men to marry women who are their seniors, and because men, on the average, die sooner than women (see Fig. 61), widowhood is a far more common problem for women than for men. According to the 1940 census, women in America outlive men by 8 years. At that time, there were nearly 6 million widows as compared with slightly more than 2 million widowers. Fifty per cent of the women over sixty years of age were widows. By the age of eighty-five years, however, 85 per cent of the women are widows (Havinghurst, 1950). While statistics of widowers of that age are not available, there is evidence to show that the percentage would be far less.

Adjustments to the death of a spouse are difficult for both men and women in old age because, at this age, all adjustments are increasingly difficult to make and because it is a time when their interests are contracting. This is especially true, as was pointed out in the preceding chapter, of social interests. As a result, loneliness becomes a major problem for an elderly person who is left alone. Furthermore, there is usually a decreased income when the husband dies and this frequently necessitates giving up interests that the widow might otherwise retain. It may even necessitate moving to smaller

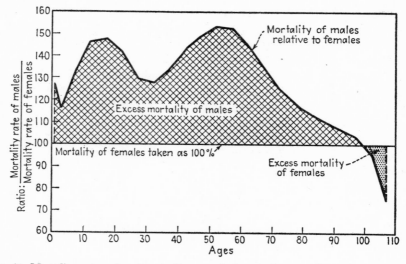

FIG. 61. Mortality rates of males at all ages relative to the mortality rates of females. On the average for the entire life span the mortality rate for males is higher than that for females by 36.8 per cent. Only at ages one hundred and over are the rates for males lower than for females. (*Based on data of United States Life Tables, 1939–1941. Vital Statistics—Special Reports, 1944, 19 (4). From F. K. Shuttleworth, The adolescent period: a graphic atlas, Monogr. Soc. Res. Child Develpm., 1949, 14, No. 1. Used by permission.*)

and less desirable living quarters which, likewise, means serious adjustments (Pollak and Heathers, 1948).

When a group of 75 men and women of different socioeconomic groups was questioned, 16 of the 31 who discussed the death of a spouse said that they had made plans for it. The possibility of the spouse's death was contemplated without emotional disturbance, though the majority contemplated loneliness. This, however, did not disquiet them (Fried and Stern, 1948). It is questionable, however, when the death occurred with the many problems it presented, whether the individual who had contemplated it with the emotional calm reported would not have markedly different attitudes.

Death of a spouse at middle age, in the late forties and fifties, by contrast, means marked loneliness for the remaining spouse, and this is intensified by the frustrations of the normal sex desires which are still strong. If, however, the individual remains widowed for 10 or more years, he generally makes fairly satisfactory adjustments to his single state. There is, however, a tendency to be lonely and to find the single state unsatisfactory. Those whose marriages had been happy usually react to the death of a spouse by idealizing the deceased, combined with a form of spiritual reunion, or they escape loneliness through social distractions, especially social-service activities. Those who are satisfied with widowhood are glad to be liberated from a resented mate (Fried and Stern, 1948).

Divorce. Young adults frequently solve the problem of an unsatisfactory marriage by divorce. As was pointed out in Chapter 12, divorce is more frequent in the first few years of marriage than it is later, especially when there are children. The number of divorces decreases as age progresses, though there are cases of divorce in the sixties and seventies. Even after celebrating a golden anniversary, couples occasionally obtain a divorce (Jacobson, 1950). No matter how dissatisfied elderly people are with their marriage, most of them do not contemplate ending it in a divorce court. When they do think of the possibility of ending their marriages in old age or when they decide to do so, it is generally not a new decision but rather something they had contemplated since the early days of marriage but which they never did because of the children or because of economic circumstances (Fried and Stern, 1948).

Remarriage. The older women whose marriage has been ended by death or divorce has poorer remarriage prospects than has the man. This is true not only because there are proportionally more elderly women than there are men but also because women may hesitate to give up their pension rights or inheritance should they remarry (Glick and Landau, 1950). An analysis of marriages in New York State, exclusive of New York City, for the years 1945 to 1948, showed that 5.2 per cent of the men and 3 per cent of the women married at fifty or over. For the men, 16.6 per cent of these marriages were first marriages as compared with 13.7 per cent for the women (Bossard, 1951a). It is popularly believed that old men marry women much younger than they. In an analysis of census data for the year 1949, it was found that men sixty-five to seventy-four years of age married women 4 years younger than they, on the average, when it was their first marriage. For their second wives, by contrast, they selected women whose average age was 10 years below theirs (Glick and Landau, 1950).

A statistical analysis of age differences of men and women who remarried during the latter years of life showed that for men fifty years of age and older, only 3.5 per cent married women who were 30 or more years younger than they. This would indicate that the December–May marriage is not as common as it is believed to be. The majority of older men do, however, marry women younger than they. In Bossard's analysis of marriages among elderly people in New York State, 76.2 per cent of the men were found to have married women younger than they as compared with the 16.5 per cent who married in the same five-year-age group and with 7.3 per cent who married women older than they. Beginning at the age of fifty, the tendency for elderly men to marry younger women increases appreciably. After fifty-five, this tendency is marked and it reaches its maximum after seventy.

Up to middle age, women usually marry men older than they or of approximately the same age. After that, the reverse trend appears. In the group of women fifty years of age and older studied by Bossard (1951a), 23.3 per cent had married men younger than they. Like the men, the tendency to marry younger men increased with age, as is shown by the fact that 47.6 per cent of the women over seventy-five years of age married men younger than they as compared with 19 per cent of the fifty- to fifty-four-year-old group. Often the men selected for a second or later marriage are 15 to 20 years younger than the women. While both men and women in the later years of their lives do marry individuals of approximately their own age, the number who marry individuals younger than they is "surprisingly large." In an attempt to explain why it is that both men and women in old age select as mates individuals who are younger than they, Bossard has suggested: "Apparently, after middle age, both men and women seem to reach out to regain in their mates the youth that they themselves have lost."

An interesting discussion of the advantages of remarriage in older people by Harsh and Schrickel (1950) has brought out points often overlooked in regard to this matter. According to them, "While there are psychologically sound reasons for frowning upon a wedding of spring with fall or winter, the marriage of two older persons has been shown in many instances to yield very satisfactory results for both individuals, as well as for society, in which they continue to be more useful and effective as a result." The arguments they give in favor of such marriages are that older people are likely to make more of a success of their marriage than are younger because they take into consideration more of the lasting features of marriage in making their decisions. They are less likely than younger people to make a match based almost solely upon physical sexual desire, though love and affection in the broadest sense are not restricted to the tensional releases of sexual intercourse.

Singleness. The popular belief that an old person, who has never married and who, as a result, is "alone in the world," will face an unhappy, lonely old age is not borne out by real experiences. Not having had the companionship of a family of his own, he has learned through the years to develop interests and activities to compensate for this companionship. As a result, he is less likely to face a lonely old age than is the individual who married, whose interests were tied up in home and in family, and who now, in old age, finds himself widowed and with his children in homes of their own. Furthermore, the person who marries is far less likely to have made the necessary adjustments to meet old age alone than is the person who has been alone for the major part of his adult life. Consequently, old age is more likely to be lonely for the widow or widower than for the bachelor or spinster, unless the former remarry.

Those who reach old age without having married do this from choice, not from necessity in most cases. In the group of elderly men and women interviewed by Fried and Stern (1948), only 21 per cent of those who had never married said they remained unmarried against their will. The rest had personal attitudes that did not favor marriage. Of the unmarried, few were found to live alone. Most of them lived with relatives or friends of their own age. They accepted their childless state as calmly as they accepted their single state. For the elderly person who has remained unmarried, there are two forms of compensation which generally prove to be satisfying. One consists of caring for the children of relatives and friends, thus compensating for lack of parenthood. The second form of compensation is an affectional attitude toward persons of the same age. Unlike the married person who detaches himself from the companionship of his contemporaries for the sake of his family, the unmarried person reaches old age with friends of the same age whose interests are in common with his.

It is commonly believed that the unmarried person faces a dull and lonely old age and because of this should be pitied. It is questionable whether such is always the case. True, the unmarried woman who makes her home with a married brother or sister and "does her part" by yielding to the demands of the family will, unquestionably, find old age a lonely and dreary period of life. But such women are few and far between today. The modern woman has built up a life of her own. As a result, she has much to keep her happy and occupied in old age. Even though she is retired from her life career, she doubtless has been able to save enough money to do many of the things she always wanted to do. And, because her leisure time was never at the beck and call of a family, she has had an opportunity to establish many avocational interests which will be of great help to her when she reaches the retirement age. Much the same is true of the unmarried man. In both cases, old age is less likely to be lonely than it is for those who have devoted the adult years of their lives to family and home, only to find both slipping away from them when it is too late to build new lives for themselves.

Relationship with Offspring. The relationship of elderly people with their children may be a very pleasant one and it may not. Much depends upon the type of relationship that was established earlier in life. When parents are willing to shift their attitudes toward their children to suit the age and developmental level of the children, the chances are that the parent-child relationship will be a wholesome one as the years go on. As a result, it is probable that the elderly person will find much satisfaction in the companionship of sons and daughters. When, on the other hand, the parent has been unwilling, through the years, to adjust his attitude to meet the changing needs of growing children, he is likely to face a lonely old age. The strain in parent-child relationship which began in adolescence will likely grow worse rather than better as time goes on.

For the most part, elderly women are more absorbed in the relationship with their children and grandchildren than are elderly men. This is a continuation of the parent-child relationship that started at the time of the child's birth. When the relationship between themselves and their children was rated as satisfactory or unsatisfactory by a group of elderly people, mothers reported more friction than did fathers. In the case of the mothers, 48.9 per cent reported a satisfactory relationship as compared with 51.1 per cent who said the relationship was unsatisfactory. Among fathers, on the other hand, 73.1 per cent said their relationship with their children was satisfactory as compared with 26.9 per cent who said it was unsatisfactory. The explanation given was that the mother's relationship with her children is more intense than is that of the father and, as a result, there is likely to be more friction (Fried and Stern, 1948). If the parent-child relationship has been satisfactory up to the age of fifty or fifty-five years of one or of both parents, it is unlikely that new alienations will develop after that.

EMOTIONAL DEPENDENCY. It is popularly believed that elderly parents become emotionally dependent upon their children and that, for old people, the companionship of their children is essential to happiness. While it is true that a happy parent-child relationship contributes much to the happiness of old age, especially as health fails and opportunities for social contacts with outsiders diminish, it is less important than is popularly believed. Fried and Stern (1948), from questioning a group of old people of different socio-economic backgrounds, found that older parents are not as emotionally dependent upon their children as is often assumed. As their children grow up and make homes of their own, parents gradually achieve a certain degree of independence, though this is generally less than the independence achieved by their children. Even when the parent-child relationship is good, children often drift apart because they live in different communities, because they are preoccupied with work and child rearing, or because they have made friends of their own ages. As a result, the parents gradually develop new interests of their own to fill the gaps left by their children's absence from the home.

The emotional independence of elderly parents is shown by the number of times they see their grown children. Of the 90 per cent of elderly people questioned by Fried and Stern (1948) who lived in the same town as their children and who could, as a result, see them frequently, 26.8 per cent said that they saw their children at least once a week; 65.8 per cent, at least once a month; and 7.4 per cent, less than once a month. Only two of the group complained that they did not see their children often enough. Only a minority of the parents showed a high degree of emotional dependence on their children when the children had reached maturity. These, it was found, were not happily married or were isolated from their mates by death. This was true more often of the women in the group than of the men.

FINANCIAL DEPENDENCY. It is difficult for the individual to adjust to financial dependency at any age after childhood. Adolescent boys and girls generally begin to rebel against being dependent upon their parents for spending money long before their high-school days are over. It is difficult enough to be dependent upon others at any time, but when the dependency falls upon their children, who they know are struggling to establish homes of their own, it is a bitter pill for most old people to swallow. How strongly old people feel about such dependency is shown by the reactions of the group of elderly people questioned by Fried and Stern (1948). Of the 65 per cent of the group who faced the possibility of having to become dependent upon their children at some time or other during their old age, an overwhelming majority of them rejected with intense feeling the possibility of any form of economic support from their children. They maintained that they preferred government pensions or other subsidies to dependence upon their children. The reasons they gave for this attitude were that their children should have economic responsibilities toward their own families, not toward them, that it was humiliating to them to have to be supported by their children, that by doing so it signified the relinquishment of parental authority, and that it was a challenge they wanted to meet alone. Those who did accept the idea of financial help usually came from countries where the cultural background differed from that which prevails in America today.

Relationship with Grandchildren. The role of the grandparent in the home life of modern America is less important than it was in the past. Then families lived closer together than they do today, the social unit of family life was made up of members of the family, and the authority of the grandparents over their children and grandchildren was supreme. A tradition has grown up that the grandparent is a stabilizing influence in family life, that the grandparent understands and is more tolerant of children than parents are, and that children just "naturally" love old people. With changes in living conditions, grandparents play a less important role in family life now than they did in the past. Not only do families live farther apart today than formerly but respect for parental authority is less. Furthermore, because there have been marked changes in child-rearing practices in recent years, there has been a growing tendency to question the tradition that grandparents understand children better than parents do.

While many parents of today call upon grandparents to help them to meet family emergencies, there is a growing tendency to put grandparents on the shelf and to keep them from interfering with parental methods of rearing the children. This has built up a certain barrier between children and their grandparents which has been intensified by the lack of close contact the child of past generations had with his grandparents. Furthermore, evidence has shown that children more often dislike than like old people because of their behavior or their looks or both. There is less chance for a child to grow to love his grandparents today than there was in the past when close contacts made favorable conditioning possible. As a result, the normal childish antipathy for old people frequently spreads to grandparents and conditions the child's attitude.

From the point of view of the grandparents, the attitude toward grandchildren is more favorable. When a group of elderly people was questioned regarding this matter, they remarked that they enjoyed their contacts with youth. But, of the group, more than two-thirds said that their children meant more to them than their grandchildren did. Few of the grandmothers said that their husbands did more for their grandchildren than they had done for their own children (Fried and Stern, 1948). Of the two, the grandmother is more likely to be absorbed in the grandchildren than is the grandfather. Furthermore, it is the grandmother rather than the grandfather who is called upon to help parents meet family emergencies. As a result, the grandmother is put in a better position to come in contact with her grandchildren than the grandfather is.

While the virtues of grandmothers have been extolled for generations, there is reason to believe that the grandmother's influence on the grandchild is not as favorable as it is supposed to be. This point of view has been expressed by Vollmer (1937), who maintains, "Grandmothers exert an extraordinarily pernicious influence on their grandchildren. . . ." The grandmother is not a suitable custodian of the care and rearing of her grandchild. She is a disturbing factor against which we are obligated to protect the child to the best of our ability. The disturbing influence produced by the grandmother is not the result of her age but rather of her attitude toward the child. Also, the hardening of the older person's personality causes unbending and didactic opinions about child care. The grandfather is a less disturbing influence than is the grandmother because he is more remote from the child.

Marital Happiness. It is often said that old people stay together through habit rather than because of love. Having spent the major part of their adult life together, it would be a great adjustment on the part of both husband and wife if they should dissolve their marriage and each go his or her separate way. This belief implies that old people find little happiness in marriage and that what happiness existed when they were younger gradually wanes as age progresses. This point of view is unquestionably based on the belief that there can be no marital happiness unless there is a sexual basis for it.

Recent investigations of marriage have shown that marriages which are happy during the early years generally continue to be so as time goes on. Unhappy marriages, on the other hand, are generally those which were unhappy almost from the start and which were never dissolved because of moral or religious beliefs, or because of feelings of obligation to remain together for the sake of the children. The fate of a marriage is generally decided during its early years. It is more usual than unusual for it to follow much the same pattern that was established during its early months or years. Marital disharmony, it has been found, is frequent among elderly male identical twins because of the jealousy of the wives over the close relationship of the brothers (Kallman and Sander, 1948). This is not a new pattern in old age but one of long duration.

Questioning a group of old people regarding their happiness in marriage revealed that 48.7 per cent felt that their marriages had been satisfactory as compared with 51.3 per cent who felt they had been unhappily married. Nearly all the marriages that were reported as satisfactory had always been good and nearly half of them had become even more satisfactory as the marriage partners aged. Most of those who felt that their marriages were unsatisfactory had been more or less dissatisfied from the beginning and nearly half felt that their marriages had deteriorated further with advancing age. The causes found for decline in marital satisfaction were emotional immaturity of one or both partners, increased incompatability with age as shown in nagging, domineering, and faultfinding, few interests in common, especially after the children left home, and differences in sexual demands, especially when the marriage was based mainly on sexual attraction.

When increase in marital satisfaction was reported, it was found to be due to emotional maturity of one or both partners as shown in their being less irritable, egotistical, demanding, and temperamental; to almost identical habits and interests; to the children's growing up and going away from home, thus drawing the partners closer together as in the early days of marriage; to enforced retirement or serious illness which made one partner enjoy being important to the other; to the death of demanding and dominating parents-in-law; and to increased economic security, often brought about by the earnings of the wife (Fried and Stern, 1948).

LIVING QUARTERS

One of the most difficult adjustments old people are frequently forced to make is that of changed living quarters. Having spent many years of their adult lives in saving and planning for homes of their own, it is a source of great concern to them if economic necessity forces them out of these homes. Not only are there many happy memories associated with their homes but they have become accustomed to every inch of the home and feel safe and secure there. In the past, old people, far more often than is possible today, remained in their homes until death. When poor health made it impossible for them to live alone, it was considered the duty of a daughter to move back to the parental home to take charge of things for her parents. When reduced income threatened the parental home, the children either contributed to the support of it or one of the married children moved back to the home and shared the expenses of running it. In that way, the old person was guaranteed the security of the home he had lived in for the major part of his adult life.

Conditions have changed so radically, not only financially but also in feelings of responsibility toward aging parents, that many old people of today are forced to move out of their homes when health or financial conditions become poor. This is presenting a serious adjustment problem for the older members of our culture. Compulsory retirement, with its accompaniment of reduced income from pensions or savings, frequently makes it financially impossible to maintain the home any longer. And, because of high taxes and high cost of living, grown children have difficulties in making two ends meet in their own homes without the added burden of contributing to the support of the parental home. Furthermore, social pressures against those who do not contribute to the family home are far less severe than they formerly were, with the result that many children no longer feel they must make the personal sacrifices necessary to help their parents maintain the home.

In addition, there is a widespread feeling that it is unwise for "three generations to live under one roof." This has cut down on the former practice of married children's returning to the parental home with their families. The belief that children are better off in their own homes than in the home of someone else has further strengthened the tendency. Modern living conditions militate against married children's opening their doors to their aging parents. Modern homes are small and space is at a premium. As a result, the family must usually be dislocated when parents come to make their home with their married children. Then, too, the presence of an elderly person in the home adds to the already heavy burdens of the modern housewife.

Some interesting statistics compiled by Havinghurst (1950), based on census reports for 1940, show where and how most old people live. Most old people cling to the living quarters of their middle age. Of the men, 78 per cent lived in private households as heads of the family. In the case of the women, 38 per cent lived in private households as the wives of the heads of the household and 30 per cent as the heads. Of the women who were not living in their homes, 18 per cent lived with their children and 3.3 per cent in hotels, lodging homes, and homes for the aged. Of the men not living in their own homes, 8 per cent lived with their children, 5 per cent as lodgers in private homes, and 4.5 per cent in hotels, lodging homes, and homes for the aged (see Fig. 62). While old people tend to live in low-rent and low-value structures in the older neighborhoods of a community, in houses that are dilapidated and deficient in plumbing facilities, they are less crowded than younger families who live in more modern types of homes (Silk, 1952).

When it is impossible for an old person to maintain his home, it is frequently necessary for him to move into the home of a married son or daughter. Most old people accept this as a last resort. Only parents who grew up in other countries where this is a common practice accept without resistance the idea of living in the homes of their grown children. When a group of old people were asked how they felt about living with their children, two-thirds of the group said they felt that they were unwanted and in the way. They also reported that two-thirds of the family criticism centered around

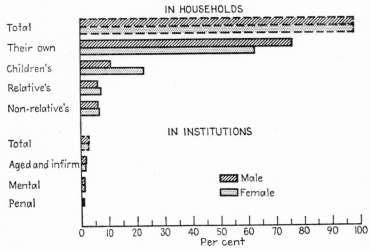

FIG. 62. Per cent of male and female population, sixty-five years of age and older, in households and institutions. "Nonrelatives" include quasi households. (*Based on data from Sixteenth Census, 1940. Population, Vol. IV, Part 1, and Special report on institutional population. Washington, D.C.: Government Printing Office, 1948. From N. W. Shock, Trends in gerontology. Stanford, Calif.: Stanford Univ. Press, 1951. Used by permission.*)

their interference in family affairs and their personal habits (Gardiner, 1949).

Less than one-fourth of a group of old people, ages sixty to sixty-five and of different socioeconomic backgrounds, and less than one-tenth of those over sixty-five years of age, said that they wanted to live with their children. The reasons given by these elderly parents for not wanting to live with their children was that they feared the resentment of their in-laws, they feared the restrictions on their individual freedom, and they did not want to give up their own homes, which were symbols of their independence (Fried and Stern, 1948). In spite of the strong feeling many old people have toward living with their children, it is often a necessity and unquestionably contributes to the unhappiness and poor adjustments of old age.

There are certain pitfalls that must be avoided if the aging parent who, through necessity, must make his home with a married son or daughter is to be happy. These include such problems as failure to recognize the fact that some parents cannot live happily with their children and prefer to board with a friend, relative, or stranger; being too proud to allow the parent to live in a publicly or privately supported home for the aged; failure of all the children of the family to share the responsibility for the care or support of the parent, thus putting all the burden on the shoulders of one child, who is certain to feel abused and thus develop an unfavorable attitude toward the parent.

Other important pitfalls are refusing to accept board money from parents, which takes away from the parents the last prop to their feeling of independence; forgetting to provide spending money for an aged parent who has no money of his own; discarding personal possessions which are especially precious to the aged parent because of their happy associations; letting the aged parent lose his old friends and limiting his social contacts to the family circle; expecting the grandparents to be every-ready baby-sitters; failing to make the parent feel that he is a real member of the family; and forgetting that old people often need outside activities (Stern and Ross, 1952).

Suitable living quarters for old people must take into consideration the matter of physical health and declining motor abilities. Many homes that are suitable for young children, adolescents, or adults are unsuitable for old people because of their hazards to the health and safety of the old person. As was pointed out in the preceding chapter, declining motor coordinations make the old person subject to awkwardness. This, when combined with a poor sense of equilibrium in old age, may readily result in falls which cause broken bones or other serious injuries. Since bones heal slowly in old age— if they heal at all—the individual may spend the last years of his life as a helpless invalid. Then there is the matter of heating. Old people cannot stand the cold as well as younger people can. As a result, their homes must be well heated and evenly heated if they are to avoid colds which may, and frequently do, lead to pneumonia. The size of the home and its location, whether in the city, country, or suburbs, will determine how much housework there is to be done.

Since the physical hazards of a home are serious for old people, some attention must be given to the "provision of physical safeguards such as suitable staircase railings and the elimination from rooms much used by the aged members of the family of small rugs and similar objects likely to cause stumbling. Hazardous places such as the tops of staircases should be kept well lighted. Young persons in a household where there are elderly people should give some thought to these matters, not only on account of the old persons themselves but for the sake of the entire household" (Goodenough, 1945, p. 490). When old people are living alone or with older people, the provision for protection against household hazards is even more important than when they are with younger people.

Because of serious hazards of heavy traffic in our modern cities and because of the constant noise and confusion on the streets, the question of the location of a home for elderly people becomes an important one. Ideally, old people should live in a warm climate with few changes in temperature from season to season, they should be located in the less heavily populated sections of a city or in a suburban community where they can go to church or to other community meeting places without running into the dangers of heavy traffic, and they should be living in a one-story house with no stairs to climb or in an apartment house that is supplied by elevator service. To meet this ideal, the average old person would have to move into a new environment since such a home is not usually practical for younger people.

Studies of the geographic distribution of old people have shown that more old people live in nonfarm rural areas or villages than in cities. This may be due to a back-migration of the elderly or to the conditions of the two types of area that affect longevity or to both. Whatever the cause, conditions in villages are more favorable to the aged than in cities (Pollak and Heathers, 1948). In recent years, there has been a migration of elderly people to more favorable climates in this country. Florida and the West Coast have, as a result, had a proportionally greater increase in old people than have other areas of the country. Between 1940 and 1948, the population over sixty-five in California increased 41.4 per cent as compared with 20 per cent in the entire country (Shock, 1951). Unquestionably better climatic conditions and absence of the emotional tensions of large cities favor the old person.

The personal and social adjustments of the old person are greatly influenced by his mode of living. With retirement and decreased strength, the individual spends more hours in the home than he did during his more vigorous years. Restrictive living arrangements breed discontent and restlessness while living conditions similar to what he has been used to during the major part of his adult life lead to contentment. Furthermore, life falls into a pattern as the individual grows older. Any change in this pattern means breaking habits of many years' duration with the necessity for making new adjustments. Not only is this difficult, but if satisfactory adjustments are not made the individual is unhappy. Men who remain in their own homes throughout their old age have the most advantageous position from the point of view of health, activity, and attitudes. Poorest adjustment comes when they live in rooming houses or hotels. Old women, like old men, are best adjusted if they remain in their own homes or in homes of relatives. In institutions, where the individual is deprived of the independence he enjoyed for the major part of his life, the old person makes the poorest adjustments and is the least happy (Cavan, 1949).

PERSONALITY CHANGES

Personality is never static. It constantly changes, not markedly but to a slight degree. With the marked changes in physique, in bodily functions, in interests, activities, and mental abilities which come with old age, it would be surprising if there were not changes in personality also. It is popularly believed that these changes are invariably for the worse. There is a traditional personality pattern associated with old age that is far from attractive. According to popular belief, the old person is selfish, self-centered, egotistical, mean, stingy, quarrelsome, demanding, and generally impossible to live with. Regardless of what sort of personality pattern he had when he was younger, it is believed that he will develop into an ogrelike creature as he grows older. Furthermore, it is popularly believed that all individuals deteriorate into childlike personalities in the closing years of their lives and that they must be treated as children.

While scientific studies of personality changes in the aged have been few, except in the case of mental disorders, there is enough evidence today to contradict the popular concepts of senescent personality. Observations of individuals over a period of time and reports regarding their behavior from family and friends seems to point to the belief that the personality pattern of the old person is fundamentally the same as that which was established early in his life. As Lawton (1951) has pointed out, "Aging is like applying a magnifying glass to the personality." In other words, personality changes are quantitative rather than qualitative. The fundamental pattern of personality hardens and becomes more set with advancing age (Harsh and Schrickel, 1950).

Concept of Self. The fundamental core of the personality pattern of the individual is his concept of self. What he thinks of himself, his abilities, and his disabilities will determine the characteristic form of his behavior. This concept of self is established in the early years of life, taking its fundamental form in the years of babyhood and childhood. While it unquestionably does change to a certain extent, the changes are, for the most part, slight. What the individual thinks of himself is a reflection of what those with whom he comes in contact think of him.

Throughout the years of life, the concept of self is constantly influenced by people's reactions to him. When, during adult years, he achieves success and the accompanying social and economic status that success brings, there is likely to be an inflation of the ego. The concept of self, established earlier, is now revised to meet his new status in the social group. When the reverse happens, the concept of self deteriorates. That frequently happens during middle age, when parents begin to see that their children find them "old-fashioned" and when they become aware of the fact that they are no longer so necessary to their children as they were when the children were younger. The approach of old age brings about changes in society's attitude toward the individual. In the business world, his position is gradually threatened by younger workers and in community affairs, he finds younger people taking over.

Awareness of Aging. G. S. Hall (1923) made an attack upon the problem of the individual's awareness of approaching old age by asking old people such questions as, "How and at what age did you first realize the approach of old age?" Subjective awareness of aging has received some attention lately. Giese (1928) asked a group of subjects how they noticed for the first time that they were growing old and discovered that physical symptoms of aging were noticed twice as often as mental ones. Of the physical symptoms most often reported, the order of frequency in which they were given is as follows: breakdown in the locomotor apparatus, nervous difficulties, sense-organ impairment, deterioration of the skin and hair, increased tendency to fatigue, and greater need for sleep. Among men, there were frequent mentions of decline in sexual potency. Most people suddenly realize that they are no longer young.

At what age the individual becomes subjectively old varies markedly. For the average person, this is just before they reach the half-century mark, at the age of forty-nine years (Jones, 1935). Subjective appraisal of failing physiological and psychological functions is markedly influenced by both levels of aspiration and cultural pressures. Failing strength and motor-skill decline may be due more to lack of practice and motivation than to old age. And yet, if these are used as criteria for estimating age, the individual will begin to think of himself as "old." Likewise, the cumulative effects of experience, frustrations, and awareness of limitations may have more influence in the area of psychological aging than any physiological deficit (Malamud, 1942).

In short, then, what the individual thinks he is he is likely to become. If he thinks of himself as old, he is very likely to think and behave as an old person is supposed to. This concept of himself, unquestionably, is markedly influenced by popular beliefs and cultural pressures. As was pointed out earlier in this chapter, the belief that a man loses his sexual desires and potency when he reaches mid-fifties or early sixties more often causes impotency than any physiological deterioration of his sex organs or decline in their functioning. So it is with his personality. He thinks as society expects him to think and consequently develops a personality pattern that conforms to social expectancy.

Causes of Personality Change. While few individuals retain the same personality pattern in old age that they had when they were younger, the degree of change that takes place varies markedly from one individual to another. In few is the change so marked that it is impossible to recognize the characteristic pattern that has prevailed throughout the major part of their lives. Qualities which were apparent when the individual was younger are apparent as he grows older, only to a more marked degree. Many attempts have been made to explain the personality changes that accompany aging. Of the causes most often given, the following are the most important.

PHYSICAL CAUSES. With decline in physical strength, with the tendency to experience poor health, and with gradual decline in the usefulness of the different sense organs, it would be surprising if there were not some accompanying changes in personality. To the elderly person, physical decline is meaningful. He is aware of the fact that this means the beginning of the end and that any hope of regaining his former health or abilities is vain. As a result, he experiences frustrations and emotional tensions which leave their stamp on his personality. By far the most universal physical cause of personality change experienced by the elderly person is that of the climacteric. While women reach the end of their sex lives during middle age, the effects on their personalities may not be felt for several years when they recognize the fact that society in general but men in particular regard them as "old." For men, in whom the climacteric comes more slowly and later, the effects may be even more pronounced because of the ego involvement. To a man, loss of his sexual powers is an even more bitter pill to swallow than it is for women.

The changes in attitudes, interests, and personality that accompany the climacteric in both men and women have been studied and reported by Hamilton (1942, pp. 471–472). According to him,

Many women find that, with the subsidence of the menopause, there comes a withdrawal of interest from environmental concerns, a dreary sense of unsatisfaction, preoccupation with gastrointestinal and other bodily functions which may pass over into a more or less serious morbid melancholy and anxiety, sexual frigidity, a generally egotistic outlook upon life and a resultant unsympathetic, selfish, querulous attitude toward persons with whom they formerly sustained a more wholesome relationship. They are easily offended, feel slighted when there is no adequate objective ground for this reaction, develop a host of petty grievances, expend a good deal of emotion on self-pity and look for scapegoats onto whom they can project their inner self-dissatisfactions. A comparable phase is encountered in men in the sixth, seventh, or even as late as the eighth decade.

PAST EXPERIENCES. In general, those who have made good adjustments to life during their earlier years will make better adjustments in old age than will those whose earlier years were characterized by poor adjustments. The individual himself is not entirely responsible for the adjustments he makes. Sometimes environmental forces beyond his control make good adjustment difficult, if not impossible, for him. Other individuals, more fortunate than he, had less severe problems to cope with when they were younger and, as a result, can make better adjustments with less effort. While the first individual enjoys the declining years of his life, secure and well provided for, the second individual becomes an unwelcome dependent upon a grown child or finds himself in a charitable institution.

The importance of individual differences in past experiences has been emphasized by Jones and Kaplan (1945, p. 92) as follows:

It is frequently emphasized that the pressures incidental to age do not fall uniformly upon all. Some enjoy physical health to the very end; others suffer varying degrees of physical handicap and discomfort. Some are financially secure, no matter how long they may live; others face the future with no certainty except that of privation. Some enjoy the declining years of life in the company of loved ones; others are doomed to years that become increasingly more friendless. Some are honored and favored; others are surrounded by a social atmosphere that might well be expected to nourish malignant attitudes.

Jones and Kaplan further point out that the influence of the individual's previous experiences depend upon the personality traits that he developed earlier in his life. This is well illustrated in the case of personality maladjustments in later life. For, as they emphasize, while the relationship between earlier and later personality is not necessarily primary, it is true that the problems of old age may prove to be too much for a person with a long history of instability and, as a result, may precipitate mental disease. Abnormal traits have been found to be the rule in the case histories of senile dements, especially those having delusions of persecution. Such persons were often suspicious, quarrelsome, and loveless personalities in their earlier years (Lange, 1934).

IDLENESS AND USELESSNESS. Idleness at any age tends to make a person restless and irritable. Not knowing what to do to occupy his time, the individual becomes fretful and is annoyed by things which, if he were busy, he would overlook. In the case of the elderly person, idleness is especially difficult because many of the activities he engaged in during his free time when he was younger he now no longer has the strength or energy to enjoy. Furthermore, he feels that he is too old to develop new interests. As a result, his time is spent in idleness with its accompanying boredom. With idleness come loss of ambition and a spiritless, apathetic attitude. Typically, the elderly person seems to have lost the joy of living, to derive little satisfaction from anything that other people enjoy, and to feel that he is a useless, unwanted member of society. Many old people who must become dependent upon others for support develop a persecution complex which is expressed through constant grumblings and faultfinding or by feeling sorry for themselves.

SOCIETY'S ATTITUDE TOWARD OLD AGE. The attitude of the social group to which the elderly person belongs will influence his attitude toward his age. As Harsh and Schrickel (1950, p. 281) have pointed out,

The meaning of middle and old age for a member of our society can be understood only in terms of the social attitudes and values which have developed in our tradition regarding these matters. Every society makes some provision for the aged, whether it be exposure to the elements in some barren place or, at the other extreme, elevation to the highest positions of honor and responsibility. The individual introjects many of the attitudes and values of his society regarding middle and old age so that when he reaches these stages in his own development he interprets them in the light of these acquired meanings. Thus aging is not a process the meaning of which comes to the person exclusively from psychophysiological changes; he interprets these changes through the meanings and values his society has provided.

THE INDIVIDUAL'S ATTITUDE TOWARD HIS WANING ABILITY. Some old people meet recognitions of change constructively while most meet them in a destructive, negative manner. Because aging takes place in an uneven manner, with decline in physical abilities usually preceding decline in mental abilities, some old people compensate for their aging by drawing attention away from areas of decline to areas where decline has not yet started to be apparent. Covering up wrinkles by make-up, dyeing hair that is turning gray, or developing a youthful figure by exercise and diet help to create a youthful appearance to draw attention away from inability to engage in activities of a strenuous sort.

Most old people do not, however, learn to compensate for their awareness of waning abilities. Instead, they constantly compare themselves now with what they were when they were younger and, when the comparisons become too painful, the individual refuses to face the present or the future, but rather lives mentally in the past. The constant thinking and talking about the past, with emphasis on the important role the individual played when he was younger, is a common characteristic of many old people. It is a form of compensation for an unhappy present. Other old people, realizing that their abilities are waning and that their social usefulness is fading, compensate by bidding for attention and sympathy through complaining about poor health, by bemoaning their hard lot in life, or reporting imaginary slights from their families and friends.

Common Personality Patterns. Because no two people age in exactly the same way, and because no two are influenced in the same manner by environmental forces, there is no such thing as a "typical" personality pattern of old age. There are, however, certain personality traits which are so characteristically found among old people that they might be considered "typical." For the most part, these traits are not due to physical or mental decline but rather to the individual's awareness of society's attitude toward old age and the way he is treated by the social group. The following are the most common of the personality traits that are typically found in old age.

INTEREST IN SELF. The old person is interested in himself, his aches and pains, his bodily functions, and his personal comforts. He is egocentric to the point where his interests must come first or he will feel abused and unhappy. Much of the selfishness and thoughtlessness of the old person stems from his focusing of attention upon himself. Failing health, deterioration of the sense organs, and enforced retirement gradually narrow his outside interests. The fewer his interests and the fewer his opportunities to develop new interests, the more self-centered he will become.

CONSERVATISM. Most old pople are conservative and reactionary to the point where they are unwilling to try anything new or different. They are intolerant of any change or of anyone who thinks or acts in a manner that differs from their standards. There are reasons for the conservatism of old age and these, for the most part, stem from society's treatment of the aged. Long-established practices and beliefs, which served him well when he was younger, are clung to now because they give him the feeling of security that he lacks. The old person is frequently socially isolated which makes it difficult for him to keep up to date with the changes that are taking place.

SELF-DEPRECIATION. There are few old people who are able to retain any feeling of adequacy they may at one time have possessed. Men, as a whole, have a greater subjective sense of inferiority than is typical for women of the same age. Not only are they more self-conscious of their increasing physical and mental handicaps than women are, but they are aware that their role in life is less useful than is that of elderly women (Miles, 1933a). For the woman, there is always work to do in the home and there are usually children to take care of for grown sons, daughters, or neighbors.

INTROVERSION. Cut off from social contacts formerly experienced, and aware of his less important place in the social group than he formerly held, the elderly person turns inward and is preoccupied with his own thoughts, feelings, and emotions. Having few social contacts, he learns to become self-sufficient. As a result, when he is with people, he has little to say and he shows little feeling for anything or anyone but himself. Almost all old people develop their introvertive side as age advances (Gray, 1947).

APATHY. Only a few old people retain their youthful expectations of the future. With the disappearance of the consciousness of the future comes a feeling of the emptiness of the present accompanied by an unrest, a craving for distractions, and a state of depression. When the life of the aging person is dominated by experiences of the present or when the past is relived, retrospection in many aging persons produces a feeling of vain regret and even of despair (Vischer, 1947). Few older people retain the joy of living they had when they were younger. Their emotional reactions to the present, to all people, and to all things become, as a result, weak as compared with their emotional reactions to similar experiences when they were younger.

LONELINESS. As he sees his relatives, family, and friends die off, move to other areas, or become incapacitated so that they can no longer maintain their earlier friendships, the older person not only feels that he is alone in the world but he feels that without social ties, he is unprotected and insecure (Jones and Kaplan, 1945). Some old people react to this by becoming increasingly introverted, thus deriving a feeling of security from memories of the past. Others complain and try to bid for the attention of younger people by complaining of being afraid of being alone or by stressing their poor health. Relatively few adjust by cultivating new friendships and new social interests.

ANXIETY. Worries at this age are often based on general tension which comes partly from poor health, partly from feelings of insecurity, and partly from loneliness. Like the younger person, the older person frequently worries about things which will never happen but the effects on his health and mental state are equally as bad as if they did happen. In a study of a group of old people, Morgan (1937) found that the most common sources of worry related to financial dependency, concern for spouse or family, and poor health with its accompanying physical dependency. The least common sources of worry were death, family estrangements, and inability to work.

FEELINGS OF MARTYRDOM. When feelings of persecution become strong in old age, they may lead to delusional ideas. These are frequently the result of the individual's realization that he is not wanted or that he is an unwelcome dependent upon a member of the family or friend. The delusional productions of the elderly frequently caricature the basic worries of normal individuals of their own age. Fear of poisoning, of being robbed, or of bodily harm are the most common forms. These occur more frequently among old people of the lower intellectual levels (Jones and Kaplan, 1945).

REGRESSION. Contrast between the present and the past is often so painful to the old person that he turns away from the present and lives within the daydream world of the past. This is accompanied by an unwillingness to face the present. Through reliving the past, either in a daydream world or by constant talking about the past, the old person is able to compensate for the feelings of inferiority and inadequacy that the present brings.

Goodenough (1945, p. 592) aptly expressed this point of view when she said:

Senescence, which Hall so aptly calls the "youth of old age," is a time when a new kind of psychological weaning must take place if the years that follow are to be satisfying. The adolescent must free himself from emotional dependence upon his parents; the senescent in like manner must free himself from emotional dependence upon his own youth. Each age has its own satisfactions for the person who will take them. Growing old is as normal a part of life as growing up. In age, as well as in youth, the well-integrated personality lives in the present and plans for the future.

OVERDEPENDENCY. In many cases, the younger people in our culture over-protect the old people with the resulting damage to their personalities. The damaging effects of this are stressed by Overholser (1942), who maintains, "The same errors of management which often retard the progress by which a child matures into mature independence may at the other end of the age scale accelerate the entrance into a condition of dependent helplessness." Instead of overprotection of individuals in old age, there should be encouragement given to them to be as independent as their physical and mental states will permit. Much of the frustration, with its accompanying feelings of inadequacy, could thus be eliminated. With the first sign of aging, most old people start to give up. They expect others to do things for them which they could do for themselves, even though at a slower rate and with less proficiency.

Personality Breakdown. With advancing age and its pressures comes an increase in the number of personality breakdowns and in the proportional number of individuals committed to mental institutions. In the milder forms, these breakdowns consist of such disorders as disturbances of memory; forgetting and falsifications of memory; faulty attention; disturbances of orientation as to time, place, and person; egoism; suspiciousness; irritability; disturbances in the ethical domain; hallucinations, and delusions, especially of persecution.

Mental disease shows a marked increase in old age. In the sixties, psychoses with cerebral arteriosclerosis and senile psychoses begin to predominate and these groups increase steadily to the end of life. After the age of seventy, senile psychoses mostly prevail. Since 1920, the increase in the number of cases in mental institutions has been greater for those over sixty years of age than for those under the 60-year-old group (Malzberg, 1948). Dementia precox and manic-depressive psychoses are less frequent, as is true also of general paralysis and alcoholic psychoses. Involutional melancholia shows a slight increase after the age of sixty (Malzberg, 1935).

Many of the mental breakdowns in later life trace their origin to the experiences of childhood and adolescence. It is believed that early experiences play a prominent role in schizophrenia and manic-depressive psychosis as well as in senile dementia and involutional melancholia (Jones and Kaplan, 1945). Abnormal traits are frequently found in the past histories of senile dements, especially those having delusions of persecution (Lange, 1934). Many persons are not clinically diagnosed as schizophrenics until well in the senile period (Kaplan, 1940). The proportion of mental cases in old age without any formal education exceeds its quota by 90 per cent (Malzberg, 1948).

ADJUSTMENTS IN OLD AGE

How well the individual adjusts to life at any age depends largely upon his earlier experiences. In middle and old age, difficulties in adjustment are at their peak not only because these ages present more and more difficult problems but also because the ability to make adjustments becomes increasingly difficult with advancing age. The difficulties experienced in adjustments in old age are, for the most part, the product of earlier learning of certain forms of adjustment that are not adequate to present circumstances. When the individual discovers this, he must make new adjustments. This means a flexibility which is difficult for those who are old. "The conflicts and frustrations to be found in aging personalities provide one of the best examples of the fundamental truth that the most adequate adjustments are those which are made in profit from the past, with full regard for the present, and in anticipation of the future" (Harsh and Schrickel, 1950).

Many old people react with emotional tension to their own aging, to loss of health, to loss of occupation, to loss of persons dear to them, and to financial or physical dependency. In spite of the emotional disturbances these problems present, most old people manage to keep their equilibrium within fair balance. The severity of the problems of old age, the individual's reactions to them, and their solutions are dependent on the previous life experiences of the individual. They are, as a result, predominantly individual and to a large extent different in each person (Frohlich, 1949). Old women are, for the most part, better adjusted than old men because men do not have enough to do when they retire (Landis, 1942).

Good adjustment in old age depends largely upon the individual's attitude. When the individual has a resistant attitude toward growing old, it will be an obstacle to successful adjustment. How resistant the attitude is will depend not only upon society's attitude toward old people which, in our culture, is far from favorable, but also upon the individual's own status. The individual who is financially secure, whose family status is favorable, and whose health enables him to continue activities that are enjoyable to him will adjust better to old age than will the individual whose status is less secure and less satisfactory.

Poor Adjustments. Idleness and the accompanying feeling of uselessness, of "being through," which comes when the individual has been retired from his life work, predisposes the old individual to poor adjustment. An extensive study of the adjustments of old people living in high, low, and middle socioeconomic areas of the same communities has recently been made to see what factors are responsible for poor adjustments as measured by the Cavan-Burgess-Havinghurst-Goldhamer questionnaire "Your Activities and Attitudes." For both men and women in all three of the socioeconomic groups, 20 factors were found to be related to poor adjustment. Among these were poor present position in life; past position in life is same as or worse than the present; feeling of lack of permanent security; unmarried or not living with spouse; less visits with friends now; no close friends that are seen often; poor or merely fair present health; health worse now than formerly; serious health problem.

In addition, the following factors were found to play an important role in the poor adjustments made by these individuals: physical complaint; not living in own household; no, or infrequent, church attendance; less frequent church attendance now than in the past; no, or less than three, plans for the immediate future; recognition of having a happiest period of life; recognition of having a least happy period of life; not an officer in any club ten years ago; officer in no organizations at present; low social morale (feelings of being discriminated against in life); and low activity score (low degree of social participation) (Schmidt, 1951).

Interesting sex differences were found to exist. For old women, the factors most often associated with poor adjustment in old age were less activity in organizations now than ten years ago and poor economic position of the family when in the teens; for old men, stationary or downward social mobility, poor economic position of family in childhood, and no church membership were found to be the most common factors. For women alone in old age, the factors associated with poor adjustment were poor or fair health when in the teens; regular reader of no, or less than three, magazines; high physical mobility; low degree of family intimacy; and same or greater church attendance now than ten years ago. For elderly men who are alone, not believing in an afterlife or not sure of it, less frequent church attendance now than ten years ago, and not an officer in any clubs ten years ago were associated with poor old-age adjustments (Schmidt, 1951).

Poor adjustment is also indicated by the marked increase in mental breakdowns in old age (see section Personality Changes above) and in the number of suicides or attempts at suicide in old age. Up to sixty years, there is a steady increase in the rate of suicide for white people, after which the rate remains more or less constant. Men at all ages and of all races have a higher suicide rate than do women. The gap between the two sexes widens appreciably as age advances. In the case of forty-five- to fifty-four-year-old whites, for example, the suicide rate in males is 44.1 and in females, 14.0. By the age of seventy-five and over, however, the rate for males has jumped to 65.2 and for females, it has fallen to 8.7. Among Negroes, the rate of suicides decreases after middle age (Jones and Kaplan, 1945; Stokes, 1948).

Suicide at all ages fluctuates with economic conditions. During periods of economic depression, suicide is more frequent than during periods of prosperity. While many suicides in old age are traceable to poverty or to economic insecurity with its accompaniment of dependency, not all suicides in old age are due to economic factors alone. Of the many other causes of suicide, the following are the most important: loss of a loved one; physical ailments, especially those of hopeless prognosis; and mental disease. In the latter cause, suicidal tendencies are especially prominent in involutional melancholia, though they sometimes occur among senile dements and psychotics with arteriosclerosis (Jones and Kaplan, 1945).

Good Adjustments. As a general rule, there are indications that those who made good adjustments when they were younger will make good adjustments when they are old. The cultural milieu in which the individual lived during the formative years of his life will also affect the type of adjustment he makes to old age. For example, more neuroticism has been found among adults who had almost all their maturity since the depression of the thirties than among those who were brought up in the twenties. Those who were established before the depression had fewer cases of neuroticism than those who were children at the time of the depression. All old people worry some, especially about health, dependency, and finances. To be well adjusted, there must be a minimum of worry. Idleness at any age predisposes the individual to worry and, because old age is a period of relatively greater idleness than any other life period, there are plenty of opportunities for the elderly person to worry. Feelings of having enough to do are very important to good adjustment in old age.

This point of view has been emphasized by Landis (1942, p. 470) who maintains:

If old people are to be happy and well adjusted they must be busy. . . . It seems that our culture requires individuals to feel that they are doing something creative and worthwhile or they are not contented. When aged people get to the place where they can no longer prove their worth or when they are deprived of their work they become discontented and unhappy. Thus it would seem that if a society is to deprive its aged citizenry of work at a certain time it must go further than just offering financial assistance. It must provide a program which will keep the aged contented by enabling them to feel that they still have a useful place in society.

In addition to the feeling of uselessness that comes with idleness in old age is the tendency to reminisce. Those who live in the past, recalling with strong emotional reactions their previous successes and happinesses, find it difficult to adjust to the present. This tendency to reminisce, which is so common in old people, is exaggerated and made even more harmful to good adjustment by two factors, failing memory and the keeping of cherished relics of bygone days. With age, memory begins to fail and there is a tendency to fill in the gaps of recalled facts by products of the imagination. The old person, in his reminiscences, frequently embroiders them to the point where they bear little resemblance to the real experiences. Furthermore, keeping reminders of these past events and bringing them out from time to time help to recall the events they symbolize (Conkey, 1933).

Being busy alone is not all that is required for good adjustment in old age. Studies of well-adjusted and poorly adjusted old people have revealed that there are a number of other factors associated with good adjustment, the most important of which are strong and varied interests; economic independence with its accompaniment of feelings of security; good health and freedom from physical handicaps; many social contacts including old friendships with one's contemporaries as well as new friendships, especially with younger people; pleasant social and emotional relations with members of the family; the quiet, privacy, and independence which come from homes or living quarters of their own; some form of work which is pleasurable while not overtaxing of waning strength and energy; participation in or contribution to community organizations, especially the church; invigorating experiences; hobbies and forms of recreation suited to their health and interests; delegation of authority and responsibility to younger associates thus enabling them to pursue interests of their own; a high degree of education which helps to foster interests; a marriage contracted not too early or too late in life; living with the spouse; and belief in afterlife (Conkey, 1933; Folsom and Morgan, 1937; Morgan, 1937; Landis, 1942; Johnson, 1948; Cavan *et al.*, 1949; Lawton, 1943; J. H. Britton, 1951; J. O. Britton, 1951; Pressey, 1951; Shanas, 1951).

Criminality. An interesting indication of the relatively good adjustment old people make is to be found in the information now available regarding criminality among the aged. In general, statistics indicate that, in America, in spite of the rapid increase in proportions of individuals who are criminals, the crime rate becomes progressively lower after middle age. In the year 1940, only 171 persons seventy years of age and older were sent to prisons or reformatories, and of this number, 169 were males. This contrasted markedly to 12,073 persons between the ages of twenty-one and twenty-four years imprisoned in the same year. At that time, there were in different penal institutions in this country 4,624 males over sixty-five years of age and 244 females as compared with 92,279 males and 5,363 females between the ages of twenty-five and thirty-four years. Some of the older people had been committed at earlier ages and were serving long terms (U.S. Bureau of the Census, 1943, 1943*a*).

The most common causes of arrest among old people are drunkenness, assault, disorderly conduct, vagrancy, driving while intoxicated, theft, and sex crimes (FBI Report, 1944). There have been many explanations given for the decline in the criminality rate among old people, most important of which are the leniency of many judges and juries, the greater unwillingness of older people to expose themselves to physical dangers, physical incapacity to undertake certain types of crime, learning from past experience that crime does not pay, and increasing conformity to the law with advancing age as an outgrowth of their greater conservatism. Some of the crimes of old age come from the individual's attempts to adjust to conditions influenced by or imposed by old age (Jones and Kaplan, 1945).

MENTAL HYGIENE OF OLD AGE

Because the individual's attitudes and patterns of adjustment are established while he is still young, preparation for old age should be started while the individual is at his peak of achievement or even before. Healthy attitudes toward old age as a normal part of the life span, toward the abilities and disabilities of old age, and toward the activities and interests old age can enjoy should all be established while the individual is able to make adjustments easily. Waiting until he is old is often too late. Without proper preparation, psychologically as well as physically, the individual is almost doomed to an unhappy and fruitless period at the end of his life. According to the old saying, "Unhappy in old age is he who failed to learn to play solitaire in his youth" (Anderson, 1949).

However, since a large part of our old-age population today grew up at a time when such preparation was not given or never anticipated the changes that old age would bring into their lives because, in their youth, retirement and its accompanying problems had not become a part of our cultural pattern, or because they had not anticipated living as long as people of today live, there are many who are urgently in need of mental-hygiene help to enable them to make satisfactory adjustments to old age so that the closing years of their lives will be at least reasonably happy. The following mental-hygiene rules have been suggested for helping old people of today to make more satisfactory adjustments (Lewis, 1943):

1. Use the old person in an economic way, or in a fashion to assure him that he is still a part of the world of affairs.

2. Changes of work and frequent rest periods will help to retard mental senility.

3. Relieve him as much as possible from worry, mental strain, anxieties, and feelings of financial insecurity.

4. Avoid physical discomforts and overeating.

5. Protect him from injuries to avoid a post-traumatic constitution, with its characteristic changes in disposition.

6. Avoid any heavy burden on the sense organs.

7. Younger and more able associates should recognize and make allowances for his occasional loss of acuity in dealing with situations.

8. Use tolerance and understanding.

9. Give the older person some understanding of his personality in terms of the psychology of old age.

In addition, several other suggestions are worthy of consideration. Because the senses grow duller with age, many old people are partially or totally cut off from social contacts. It is, therefore, important to use every possible artificial aid to compensate for increasing sensory weakness. Not only should old people be taken care of financially but every effort should be made to enable them to retain their independence as far as possible even when they have the status of a dependent. And, finally, the encouragement necessary to develop new skills and interests should be given so that the individual's old age will not be empty and meaningless. This can be done by making use of the difference in rate of decline of different abilities. Most abilities decline slowly enough to enable the individual to participate in many activities if he wishes to do so (Goodenough, 1945).

Preparation for Old Age. Because the problems of old-age adjustments are becoming a social problem of great importance today, it is not enough to deal with those who are already old. It is even more important to prepare those who are still young or who are approaching middle age for the problems they will have to meet when they become old. The mental hygiene of old age is thus deeply concerned with how this is to be done effectively. Several suggestions for preparing young people for old age have been offered. They include (Lawton, 1939; Essert *et al.,* 1951):

1. Intensive study, over a long period of time and preferably using the genetic approach on the same groups of individuals, of the mental abilities, interests, recreational activities, emotional problems, and personalities of old people.

2. Instruction for changing previously learned attitudes of younger people toward aging. This should emphasize the positive aspects in terms of abilities rather than disabilities, and should point out the variabilities of old age instead of its uniformity.

3. Old-age guidance clinics similar to the child guidance clinics, to help the individual not only at retirement but also at earlier periods of his life to enable him to be prepared for old age and retirement.

4. Educational programs in schools and colleges to help young people to prepare for the problems they will face when they are old and to help them to understand old people better.

5. Consultant services in business and industry to help the older worker not only while he is on the job but also to prepare himself for retirement.

6. Social planning for the aged, especially housing and recreational facilities.

HAPPINESS IN OLD AGE

How happy the individual is at any age depends largely upon the degree of adjustment attained. This, in turn, depends not so much upon present environmental conditions or upon the attitudes of the individual as it does upon the success or failure of past adjustments. At no time in life do unsuccessful past adjustments make present adjustment as difficult as in old age, and at no other life period is the adjustment to existing conditions as hard as it is in old age. As a result, the old person's chances for happiness are far less than they are at earlier periods in his life. Because old age is a period of life associated with disintegration and loss, the characteristic feeling tone which prevails at that time is likely to be one of unpleasantness as compared with the happiness that more frequently prevails during earlier periods (Marcus, 1927). The more upset the pattern of the older person's life is, the more predisposed he will be to unhappiness.

According to Lawton (1943), "Happiness" shifts its meaning as people grow older. In old age, the elements of happiness are health, religion, contentment, economic security, acceptance by society, etc. In youth, by contrast, happiness means freedom from care and responsibility, gaiety and going out with members of the opposite sex, setting goals and achieving them, and, most of all, activity. Old age cannot know the same kind of happiness as can youth. It is a period when existence is much more passive and contemplative than the active period of youth.

When Lawton (1943) asked a group of old people whether they would exchange an older life period for a younger one, the answers he received showed both satisfactions and discontents with old age. The assets of old age, as pointed out by this group, consisted of good health, trust in God, a cheerful state of mind, money, friends, gainful occupation (or the equivalent in interesting and useful activity), pleasant relationships with members of one's family, contemplation of one's children and grandchildren, the satisfaction of doing things for others, and kindly treatment from others. The sources of discontent and unhappiness given by this group included ill health, lack of religious belief, lack of emotional discipline (poor childhood training in the way of meeting hardships and disappointments), lack of money, lonesomeness, absence of occupation or interests, self-centeredness, and unkind treatment from others.

There are many sources of worry in old age and, when these are strong, they accentuate the already existing unhappiness or predispose the individual who might otherwise be contented to be unhappy. Of these, the most important are financial worries and dependence, concern for spouse or family, poor health and physical dependence, inability to work, family estrangements, and death (Morgan, 1937). For most old people, death is not the source of worry that is popularly believed. Most old people's attitude toward their own death is calm as is contemplation of death of a spouse (Fried and Stern, 1948).

Factors Related to Happiness. Happiness has been found to bear a strong positive relationship to economic independence (Gardiner, 1949). But economic security is not enough to produce happiness in old age. The factors that have been found to be most strongly associated with happiness at that time are good health and freedom from physical disabilities, especially in men;

pleasant social and emotional relationships with friends and members of one's family, for women especially; possession of hobbies and outside interests; the quiet, privacy, and independence of action provided by living in their own homes, especially for those brought up in our American culture as opposed to those whose childhood was spent in some foreign country where different customs prevail; and some form of work or worklike, useful activity, as compared with the more recreational activity of a hobby. American people, on the whole, are workers. Without work, they do not know how to spend their time. This is especially true of the older generation who grew up during the time when the work day was longer than it is today (Morgan, 1937).

According to Morgan (1937), one of the most acute problems of old age is what to do with the time formerly taken up by work. She feels that a large part of the happiness and social adjustment of old people depend upon an adequate solution to the problem of leisure time. Of the group questioned by Morgan, nearly one-third found time hanging heavily upon their hands. For the group as a whole, the happiest periods of their lives were the busiest. Women find it easier to occupy themselves than men do because the woman can always keep herself occupied with household tasks. For the old man, retirement means 8 to 12 extra hours a day to fill in. When Morgan asked a group of old people listed in *Who's Who* whether they believed the sources of unhappiness in old age were inherent in old age, few answered in the affirmative. Most of them stressed the fact that old age is a period with its own peculiar needs, not financial alone.

Missing things one has been accustomed to is a source of great unhappiness to most people. For old people, adjustment to losses of accustomed things is especially difficult. When asked what were the things most missed from younger years, a group of old people reported that in order of frequency, they consisted of deceased members of the family; health and physical activity; work; miscellaneous, such as hobbies, travel, and church; social activities; money; deceased friends; or their own homes. Of the group, 14.2 per cent said they missed nothing while 4.9 per cent reported that it was "hard to say" (Morgan, 1937).

Periods of Happiness. Retrospective studies, in which the old person looks back over his life and tries to decide which was the happiest period, have revealed some interesting facts which throw additional light on the problem of happiness in old age. A group of 450 people, sixty-five to ninety-eight years of age, questioned by Landis (1942) maintained that, for half of them, young adulthood was the happiest period. One-fifth said that youth, or the teens and early part of young adulthood, was the happiest, while the third happiest period was childhood. Only 5 per cent said that middle age and old age were the happiest. Those who stressed the happiness of young adulthood referred to marriage and family as the chief source of their happiness, in spite of the work and responsibilities these brought. Others mentioned good health and hopes for success. Among the unmarried, youth and childhood were looked upon as the happiest periods and emphasis was placed on their associations with young people and parties. To them, later life seemed empty.

Almost identical findings were reported by Morgan (1937). In her study, only 5.1 per cent said old age, from sixty on, was the happiest period. Once again, in both the late teens and early adulthood, happiness traced its origin to social responsibility, to the feeling of being part of the working world, and to being a necessary unit of the family group. It is thus apparent that old people can be happy but only if society gives them the chance. If they are permitted to be as active as their health and strength allow, and if their activity produces results that are of some value to the social group, they too will be happy in the knowledge that their lives are useful until the grave claims them.

Lawton (1951) has suggested a "bill of rights" for old people which, if fulfilled in every aspect, would bring both happiness and contentment to old age. The ten "rights" an old person is entitled to are the following:

1. The right to be treated as a person.
2. The right to be treated as an adult.
3. The right to a fair chance on our merits.
4. The right to a say about our own life.
5. The right to a future.
6. The right to have fun and companions.
7. The right to be romantic.
8. The right to your help in becoming interesting to you.
9. The right to professional help whenever necessary.
10. The right to be old.

Bibliography

ABERNETHY, E. M.: 1925. Correlations in physical and mental growth. *J. educ. Psychol.,* 16:458–466, 539–540.

ABRAHAM, W.: 1952. The reading choices of college students. *J. educ. Res.,* 45:459–465.

ABT, L. E., MENDENHALL, P., and PARTRIDGE, E. D.: 1940. The interests of scouts and nonscouts. *J. educ. Sociol.,* 14:178–182.

ACHESON, E. M.: 1933. A study of graduate women's reactions and opinions on some modern social attitudes and practices. *J. abnorm. soc. Psychol.,* 28:42–63.

ACKERSON, L.: 1931. *Children's behavior problems.* Chicago: Univ. Chicago Press.

ADDITON, H.: 1930. And what of leisure? *J. soc. Hyg.,* 16:321–334.

ADLER, A.: 1930. *Problems of neurosis.* New York: Cosmopolitan Book Corp.

ALDRICH, C. A.: 1947. The pediatrician looks at personality. *Amer. J. Orthopsychiat.,* 17: 571–574.

ALDRICH, C. A., NORVAL, M. A., KNOP, C., and VENEGAS, F.: 1946. The crying of newly born babies. IV. A follow-up study after additional nursing care had been provided. *J. Pediat.,* 28:665–670.

ALDRICH, C. A., SUNG, C., and KNOP, C.: 1945. The crying of newly born babies. *J. Pediat.,* 26:313–326; 27:89–96, 428–435.

ALLEN, I.: 1948. Facial growth in children of five to eight years of age. *Hum. Biol.,* 20:109–145.

ALLEN, L., BROWN, L., DICKINSON, L., and PRATT, K. C.: 1941. The relation of first name preferences to their frequency in the culture. *J. soc. Psychol.,* 14:279–293.

ALLPORT, G. W.: 1937. *Personality: a psychological interpretation.* New York: Holt.

ALLPORT, G. W., GILLESPIE, J. M., and YOUNG, J.: 1948. The religion of the freshman college student. *J. Psychol.,* 25:3–33.

ALPERT, A.: 1941. The latency period. *Amer. J. Orthopsychiat.,* 11:126–132.

ALTMANN, M., KNOWLES, I., and BULL, H. D.: 1941. A psychosomatic study of the sex cycle in women. *Psychosom. Med.,* 3:199–225.

AMEN, E. W.: 1941. Individual differences in apperceptive reaction: a study of the responses of preschool children to pictures. *Genet. Psychol. Monogr.,* 23:319–385.

AMES, L. B.: 1937. The sequential patterning of prone progression in the human infant. *Genet. Psychol. Monogr.,* 19:409–460.

AMES, L. B.: 1940. The constancy of psycho-motor tempo in individual infants. *J. genet. Psychol.,* 57:445–450.

AMES, L. B.: 1941. Motor correlates of infant crying. *J. genet. Psychol.,* 57:445–450.

AMES, L. B.: 1948. Postural and placement orientation in writing and block behavior: developmental trends from infancy to age ten. *J. genet. Psychol.,* 73:45–52.

AMES, L. B.: 1949. Development of interpersonal smiling responses in the preschool years. *J. genet. Psychol.,* 74:273–291.

AMES, L. B., and LEARNED, J.: 1946. Imaginary companions and related phenomena. *J. genet. Psychol.,* 69:147–167.

AMMONS, R. B., and AMMONS, H. S.: Parent preferences in young children's doll-play interviews. *J. abnorm. soc. Psychol.,* 44:490–505.

ANASTASIA, A.: 1948. A methodological note on the "controlled diary" technique. *J. genet. Psychol.*, 73:237–241.

ANASTASIA, A., COHEN, N., and SPATZ, D.: 1948. A study of fear and anger in college students through the controlled diary method. *J. genet. Psychol.*, 73:243–249.

ANASTASIA, A., and MILLER, S.: 1949. Adolescent "prestige factors" in relation to scholastic and socio-economic variables. *J. soc. Psychol.*, 29:43–50.

ANDERSON, A., and DVORAK, B.: 1928. Differences between college students and their elders in standards of conduct. *J. abnorm. soc. Psychol.*, 23:286–289.

ANDERSON, H. H.: 1937. Domination and integration in the social behavior of young children in an experimental play situation. *Genet. Psychol. Monogr.*, 19:343–408.

ANDERSON, J. E.: 1949. *The psychology of development and personal adjustment.* New York: Holt.

ANDERSON, J. P.: 1940. A study of the relationship between certain aspects of parental behavior and attitudes and the behavior of junior high school pupils. *Teach. Coll. Contr. Educ.*, No. 809.

ANDERSON, W. A.: 1932. Some vocational factors associated with the vocational choices of college men. *Amer. J. Sociol.*, 6:100–113.

ANDREWS, R. O., and CHRISTENSEN, H. T.: 1951. Relationship of absence of a parent to courtship status: a repeat study. *Amer. sociol. Rev.*, 16:541–549.

ANONYMOUS: 1949. Ambivalence in first reactions to a sibling. *J. abnorm. soc. Psychol.*, 44:541–548.

ANTONOV, A. N.: 1947. Children born during the siege of Leningrad in 1942. *J. Pediat.*, 30:250–259.

APPEL, M. H.: 1942. Aggressive behavior in nursery school children and adult procedures in dealing with such behavior. *J. exp. Educ.*, 11:185–199.

AREY, L. B., TREMAINE, M. J., and MONZINGO, F. L.: 1935. The numerical and topographical relations of taste buds in human circumvallate papillae throughout the life span. *Anat. Rec.*, 64:9–25.

ARLITT, A. H.: 1942. *Family relationships.* New York: McGraw-Hill.

ARRINGTON, R. E.: 1939. Time-sampling studies of child behavior. *Psychol. Monogr.*, 51, No. 2.

ASHLEY-MONTAGU, M. F.: 1946. *Adolescent sterility.* Springfield, Ill.: Charles C Thomas.

ASHLEY-MONTAGU, M. F.: 1950. The existence of a sterile phase in female adolescence. *Complex,* 1:27–39.

ATKIN, S.: 1940. Old age and aging: the psychoanalytic point of view. *Amer. J. Orthopsychiat.,* 10:79–84.

AUSTIN, F. M.: 1931. An analysis of the motives of adolescents for the choice of the teaching profession. *Brit. J. educ. Psychol.,* 1:87–103.

AUSTIN, M. C., and THOMPSON, G. G.: 1948. Children's friendships: a study of the bases on which children select and reject their best friends. *J. educ. Psychol.,* 39:101–116.

AUSUBEL, D. P.: 1950. Negativism as a phase of ego development. *Amer. J. Orthopsychiat.,* 20:796–805.

AYER, M. E., and BERNREUTER, R. G.: 1937. A study of the relationship between discipline and personality traits in young children. *J. genet. Psychol.,* 50:165–170.

BABER, R. E.: 1936. Some mate selection standards of college students and their parents. *J. soc. Hyg.,* 22:115–125.

BAIR, G. M.: 1950. What teachers should know about the psychology of adolescence. *J. educ. Psychol.,* 41:356–361.

BAKWIN, H.: 1947. The emotional status at birth. *Amer. J. Dis. Child.,* 74:373–376.

BAKWIN, H.: 1948. Pure maternal overprotection. *J. Pediat.,* 33:788–794.

BAKWIN, H.: 1949. Emotional deprivation in infants. *J. Pediat.*, 35:512–521.

BAKWIN, H.: 1950. Lateral dominance. *J. Pediat.*, 36:385–391.

BALDWIN, A. L.: 1945. Differences in parent behavior toward three- and nine-year-old children. *J. Person.*, 15:143–165.

BALDWIN, A. L.: 1947. Changes in parent behavior during childhood. *Amer. Psychol.*, 2:425–426.

BALDWIN, A. L.: 1948. Socialization and the parent-child relationship. *Child Develpm.*, 19:127–136.

BALDWIN, A. L.: 1949. The effect of home environment on nursery school behavior. *Child Develpm.*, 20:49–62.

BALDWIN, B. T.: 1921. The physical growth of children from birth to maturity. *Univ. Ia. Stud. Child Welf.*, 1, No. 1.

BALDWIN, B. T.: 1928. The determination of sex maturation in boys by a laboratory method. *J. comp. Psychol.*, 8:39–43.

BANHAM, K. M.: 1950. The development of affectional behavior in infancy. *J. genet. Psychol.*, 76:283–289.

BANHAM, K. M.: 1951. Senescence and the emotions: a genetic theory. *J. genet. Psychol.*, 78:175–183.

BANHAM, K. M.: 1952. Obstinate children are adaptable. *Ment. Hyg., N.Y.*, 36:84–89.

BARR, E. D.: 1934. A psychological analysis of fashion motivation. *Arch. Psychol., N.Y.*, No. 171.

BARSCHAK, E.: 1951. A study of happiness and unhappiness in the childhood and adolescence of girls in different cultures. *J. Psychol.*, 32:173–215.

BARTLETT, E. R., and HARRIS, D. B.: 1936. Personality factors in delinquency. *Sch. & Soc.*, 43:653–656.

BAYLEY, N.: 1932. Study of the crying of infants during mental and physical tests. *J. genet. Psychol.*, 40:306–329.

BAYLEY, N.: 1940. *Studies in the development of young children.* Berkeley: Univ. California Press.

BAYLEY, N.: 1940a. Skeletal X-rays as indicators of maturity. *J. consult. Psychol.*, 4:69–73.

BAYLEY, N.: 1943. Size and body build of adolescents in relation to rate of skeletal maturing. *Child Develpm.*, 14:51–89.

BAYLEY, N.: 1946. Tables for predicting adult height from skeletal age and present height. *J. Pediat.*, 28:49–64.

BAYLEY, N., and DAVIS, F. C.: 1935. Growth changes in bodily size and proportions during the first three years. *Biometrika*, 27:26–87.

BEAN, C. H.: 1932. An unusual opportunity to investigate the psychology of language. *J. genet. Psychol.*, 40:181–202.

BEAN, C. H.: 1933. The psychology of adherence to the old and of acceptance of the new. *J. soc. Psychol.*, 4:340–352.

BEESON, M. F.: 1920. Intelligence at senescence. *J. appl. Psychol.*, 4:219–234.

BEESON, M. F., and TOPE, R. E.: 1928. A study of vocational preferences of high school students. *Voc. Guid. Mag.*, 7:115–119.

BELL, H. M.: 1934. *The adjustment inventory.* Stanford University, Calif.: Stanford Univ. Press.

BELL, H. M.: 1938. *Youth tell their story.* Washington, D.C.: American Council on Education.

BELLER, E. E.: 1949. Two attitude components in younger children. *J. soc. Psychol.*, 29:137–151.

BELLINGRATH, G. C.: 1930. Qualities associated with leadership in the extra-curricular activities of the high school. *Teach. Coll. Contr. Educ.*, No. 399.

BENDER, L.: 1950. Anxiety in disturbed children. *In* Hoch, P. H., and Zubin, J., *Anxiety.* New York: Grune & Stratton.

BENDER, L., and LOURIE, R. S.: 1941. The effect of comic books on the ideology of children. *Amer. J. Orthopsychiat.,* 11:540–550.

BENDER, L., and VOGEL, B. F.: 1941. Imaginary companions of children. *Amer. J. Orthopsychiat.,* 11:56–65.

BENEDEK, T.: 1946. Psychosexual functions in women. *In* Harriman, P. L., *Encyclopedia of psychology.* New York: Philosophical Library, pp. 667–678.

BENEDICT, R.: 1938. Continuities and discontinuities in cultural conditioning. *Psychiatry,* 1:161–167.

BENJAMIN, H.: 1932. Age and sex differences in the toy preferences of young children. *J. genet. Psychol.,* 41:417–429.

BENTON, A. L.: 1940. Mental development of prematurely born children. *Amer. J. Orthopsychiat.,* 10:719–746.

BERGER, I. L.: 1948. Psychopathologic attitudes of frustrated previously employed mothers toward their offspring. *J. nerv. ment. Dis.,* 108:241–249.

BERNARD, J., and SONTAG, L. W.: 1947. Fetal reactivity to tonal stimulation: a preliminary report. *J. genet. Psychol.,* 70:205–210.

BERNARD, W. S.: 1938. Student attitudes on marriage and the family. *Amer. sociol. Rev.,* 3:354–361.

BERNARDA, M.: 1949. Wat den Kenjonge mensen over den dood? *Vlaam. Opvoedk. Fijdschr.,* 30:32–40.

BERNREUTER, R. G.: 1933. The measurement of self-sufficiency. *J. abnorm. soc. Psychol.,* 28:291–300.

BERNSTEIN, M. E.: 1952. Studies in the human sex ratio. 2. The proportion of unisexual siblings. *Hum. Biol.,* 24:35–43.

BESKOW, B.: 1949. Mental disturbances in premature children at school age. *Acta paediatr. Stockh.,* 37:125–149.

BIRREN, J. E., and FOX, C.: 1950. Accuracy of age statements by the elderly. *J. abnorm. soc. Psychol.,* 45:384–387.

BISHOP, B. M.: 1951. Mother-child interaction and the school behavior of children. *Psychol. Monogr.,* 65: No. 11.

BLANTON, S.: 1929. Speech disorders. *Ment. Hyg., N.Y.,* 13:740–753.

BLATZ, W. E.: 1938. *The five sisters.* New York: Morrow.

BLATZ, W. E., and BOTT, E. A.: 1927. Studies in mental hygiene of children. 1. Behavior of public school children—a description of method. *J. genet. Psychol.,* 34:552–582.

BLATZ, W. E., BOTT, E. A., and MILLICHAMP, D. A.: 1935. *The development of emotions in the infant.* Child Develpm. Ser., Univ. Toronto Press, No. 4.

BLOCK, V. L.: 1937. Conflicts of adolescents with their mothers. *J. abnorm. soc. Psychol.,* 32:193–206.

BLONSKY, P. P.: 1929. Früh-und Spätjahrkinder. *Jb. Kinderheilk.,* 124:115–125.

BLUM, L. H.: 1952. Pediatric practices and the science of child development. *Nerv. Child,* 9:233–241.

BLUMER, H.: 1933. *Movies and conduct.* New York: Macmillan.

BOAS, F.: 1932. Studies in growth. *Hum. Biol.,* 4:307–350.

BODMAN, F., MACKINLEY, M., and SYKES, K.: 1950. Adaptation of institution children. *Lancet,* 258:173–176.

BOGARDUS, R., and OTTO, P.: 1936. Social psychology of chums. *Sch. & Soc.,* 20:260–270.

BOICE, M. L., TINKER, M. A., and PETERSON, D. G.: 1948. Color vision and age. *Amer. J. Psychol.,* 61:520–526.

BONNER, A.: 1936. Adolescent anxieties. *Child Study,* 13:206–208.

BONNEY, M. E.: 1942. A study of the relation of intelligence, family-size, and sex differences with mutual friendships in the primary grades. *Child Develpm.*, 13:79–100.

BONNEY, M. E.: 1943. Personality traits of socially successful and socially unsuccessful children. *J. educ. Psychol.*, 34:449–472.

BONNEY, M. E.: 1944. Sex differences in social success and personality traits. *Child Develpm.*, 15:63–79.

BONNEY, M. E.: 1949. A study of friendship choices in college in relation to church affiliation, in-church preference, family size, and length of enrollment in college. *J. soc. Psychol.*, 29:153–166.

BONNEY, M. E.: 1951. A sociometric study of the peer acceptance of rural students in three consolidated high schools. *Educ. Adm. Supervis.*, 11:234–240.

BOSE, R. G.: 1929. Religious concepts of children. *J. relig. Educ.*, 24:831–837.

BOSSARD, J. H. S.: 1932. Residential propinquity as a factor in marriage selection. *Amer. J. Sociol.*, 38:219–224.

BOSSARD, J. H. S.: 1951. Process in social weaning: a study of childhood visiting. *Child Develpm.*, 22:211–220.

BOSSARD, J. H. S.: 1951a. Marrying late in life. *Social Forces*, 29:405–408.

BOSSARD, J. H. S., and BOLL, E. S.: 1948. Rite of passage—a contemporary study. *Social Forces*, 26:247–255.

BOSSARD, J. H. S., and BOLL, E. S.: 1950. *Ritual in family living*. Philadelphia: Univ. Pennsylvania Press.

BOSSARD, J. H. S., and SANGER, W. P.: 1952. The large family system—a research report. *Amer. sociol. Rev.*, 17:3–9.

BOTT, E. A., BLATZ, W. E., and BOTT, H.: 1928. Observation and training of fundamental habits in young children. *Genet. Psychol. Monogr.*, 4:5–161.

BOTT, H.: 1928. Observation of play activities in a nursery school. *Genet. Psychol. Monogr.*, 4:44–88.

BOUSSION-LEROY, A.: 1950. Dessins en transparence et niveau de développement. *Enfance*, 3:276–287.

BOWDEN, A. O.: 1926. A study of the personality of student leaders in colleges in the United States. *J. abnorm. soc. Psychol.*, 21:149–160.

BOYD, E.: 1935. The growth of the surface area of the human body. *Univ. Minn. Inst. Child Welf. Monogr.*, No. 10.

BOYNTON, B.: 1936. The physical growth of girls. *Univ. Ia. Stud. Child Welf.*, 12, No. 4.

BOYNTON, M. A., and GOODENOUGH, F. L.: 1930. The posture of nursery school children during sleep. *Amer. J. Psychol.*, 42:270–278.

BOYNTON, P. L.: 1936. The vocational preferences of school children. *J. genet. Psychol.*, 49:411–425.

BOYNTON, P. L.: 1942. An analysis of the responses of women teachers on a personality inventory. *Peabody J. Educ.*, 20:13–18.

BOYNTON, P. L., and BOYNTON, J. C.: 1938. *Psychology of child development*. Minneapolis: Educational Publishers.

BRACKETT, C. W.: 1933. Laughing and crying in preschool children. *J. exp. Educ.*, 2:119–126.

BRACKETT, C. W.: 1934. Laughing and crying in preschool children. *Child Develpm. Monogr.*, No. 14.

BRADLEY, C.: 1947. Early evidence of psychoses in children. *J. Pediat.*, 30:529–540.

BRECKENRIDGE, M. E., and VINCENT, E. L.: 1943. *Child development*. Philadelphia: Saunders.

BRIDGES, J. W.: 1927. Emotional instability of college students. *J. abnorm. soc. Psychol.*, 22:227–234.

BRIDGES, K. M. B.: 1931. *Social and emotional development of the pre-school child.* London: Kegan Paul.

BRIDGES, K. M. B.: 1932. Emotional development in early infancy. *Child Develpm.,* 3:324–341.

BRIGGS, E. S.: 1938. How adults in Missouri use their leisure time. *Sch. & Soc.,* 47:805–808.

BRILL, A. A.: 1921. *Fundamental conceptions of psychoanalysis.* New York: Harcourt, Brace.

BRITTON, J. H.: 1951. A study of the adjustment of retired school teachers. (Unpublished data, summarized by Schmidt, 1951.)

BRITTON, J. O.: 1951. A study of the adjustment of retired Y.M.C.A. secretaries. (Summarized by Schmidt, 1951.)

BROWN, A. W., MORRISON, J., and COUCH, G. B.: 1947. Influence of affectional family relationships on character development. *J. abnorm. soc. Psychol.,* 42:422–428.

BROWN, F. J.: 1939. *The sociology of childhood.* New York: Prentice-Hall.

BROWN, R. R.: 1938. Effect of age on the speed-power relationship with reference to tests of intelligence. *J. educ. Psychol.,* 29:413–418.

BRUCH, H.: 1940. Obesity in childhood. *Amer. J. Dis. Child.,* 60:1082–1109.

BRUCH, H.: 1941. Obesity in childhood and personality development. *Amer. J. Orthopsychiat.,* 11:467–474.

BRUCH, H.: 1943. Food and emotional security. *Nerv. Child,* 3:165–173.

BRUEN, C.: 1933. Variations of basal metabolic rate per unit surface area with age. II. The pubertal acceleration. *J. Nutrit.,* 6:383–395.

BRUSH, A. L.: 1938. Attitudes, emotional and physical symptoms commonly associated with menstruation in 100 women. *Amer. J. Orthopsychiat.,* 8:286–301.

BRYAN, E. S.: 1930. Variations in the responses of infants during first 10 days of postnatal life. *Child Develpm.,* 1:56–77.

BÜHLER, C.: 1927. *Das Seelenleben der Jugendlichen.* Vienna: Gustav Fischer.

BÜHLER, C.: 1930. *The first year of life.* New York: John Day.

BÜHLER, C.: 1933. The social behavior of children. *In* Murchison, C., *A handbook of child psychology,* 2d ed. rev. Worcester: Clark Univ. Press, Chap. 15.

BÜHLER, C.: 1935. The curve of life as studied in biographies. *J. appl. Psychol.,* 19:405–409.

BÜHLER, C.: 1935a. *From birth to maturity.* London: Routledge and Kegan Paul.

BÜHLER, C., and HETZER, H.: 1928. Das erste Verständnis von Ausdruck im ersten Lebens-Jahr. *Z. Psychol.,* 107:50–61.

BÜHLER, K.: 1930. *The mental development of the child.* New York: Harcourt, Brace.

BURGESS, E. W.: 1934. *The adolescent in the family.* New York: Appleton-Century-Crofts.

BURGESS, E. W.: 1949. The growing problem of aging. *In* Tibbitts, C., *Living through the older years.* Ann Arbor: Univ. Michigan Press.

BURGESS, E. W., and COTTRELL, L. S.: 1939. *Predicting success or failure in marriage.* New York: Prentice-Hall.

BURGESS, E. W., and LOCKE, H. J.: 1940. *The family.* New York: American Book.

BURGESS, E. W., and WALLIN, P.: 1943. Homogamy in social characteristics. *Amer. J. Sociol.,* 49:109–124.

BURKE, B. S., BEAL, V. A., KIRKWOOD, S. B., and STUART, H. C.: 1943. Nutrition studies during pregnancy. *Amer. J. Obstet. Gynaec.,* 41:38–52.

BURKE, B. S., HARDING, V. V., and STUART, H. C.: 1943. Relation of protein content of mother's diet during pregnancy to birth length, birth weight, and condition of infant at birth. *J. Pediat.,* 23:506–515.

BURLAGE, S. R.: 1923. The blood pressure and heart rate in girls during adolescence. *Amer. J. Physiol.,* 64:252–284.

BUTTERFIELD, O. M.: 1939. Love problems of adolescent girls. *Teach. Coll. Contr. Educ.*, No. 768.

BUTTERWORTH, R. F., and THOMPSON, G. C.: 1951. Factors related to age-grade trends and sex differences in children's preferences for comic books. *J. genet. Psychol.*, 78:71–96.

CABOT, P. S. DEO.: 1938. The relationship between characteristics of personality and physique in adolescence. *Genet. Psychol. Monogr.*, 20:3–120.

CAILLE, R. K.: 1933. Resistant behavior of preschool children. *Child Develpm. Monogr.*, No. 11.

CALDWELL, O. W., and LUNDEEN, G. E.: 1934. Further study of unfounded beliefs among junior-high-school pupils. *Teach. Coll. Rec.*, 36:35–52.

CALDWELL, O. W., and WELLMAN, B.: 1926. Characteristics of school leaders. *J. educ. Res.*, 14:1–13.

CALIFORNIA DEPARTMENT OF INDUSTRIAL RELATIONS: 1930. *Middle-aged and older workers.* Special Bull., No. 1.

CAMERON, W. J.: 1938. A study of early adolescent personality. *Prog. Educ.*, 15:553–563.

CAMPBELL, E. H.: 1939. The social-sex development of children. *Genet. Psychol. Monogr.*, 21:461–552.

CAMPBELL, H. M.: 1940. *Sex differences obtained by the "guess who" technique in reputation assessments given and received by adolescent boys and girls.* Ph.D. dissertation, Univ. of Chicago.

CANNING, L., TAYLOR, K. VON F., and CARTER, H. D.: 1941. Permanence of vocational interests of high-school boys. *J. educ. Psychol.*, 32:481–494.

CAPPE, J.: 1947. Les manifestations artistiques chez l'enfant. *Nouv. Rev. Pedag.*, 3:89–93.

CARLSON, A. J., and GINSBURG, H.: 1915. The tonus and hinder contractions of the stomach of the newborn. *Amer. J. Physiol.*, 38:352–360.

CARLSON, J. S., COOK, S. N., and STROMBERG, E. L.: 1936. Sex differences in conversation. *J. appl. Psychol.*, 20:727–735.

CARREL, A.: 1939. *Man the unknown.* New York: Harper.

CARROLL, J. B.: 1939. Determining and numerating adjectives in children's speech. *Child Develpm.*, 10:215–229.

CASE, A.: 1921. Children's ideas of God. *Relig. Educ.*, 16:143–146.

CASON, H.: 1930. Common annoyances. *Psychol. Monogr.*, 40: No. 2.

CASON, H., and CHALK, A.: 1933. Annoyance and behavior. *J. soc. Psychol.*, 4:143–155.

CATTELL, P.: 1928. *Dentition as a measure of maturity.* Cambridge, Mass.: Harvard Univ. Press, Monog. in Educ., No. 9.

CATTELL, R. B.: 1934. Friends and enemies: a psychological study of character and temperament. *Character & Pers.*, 3:55–63.

CAVAN, R. S.: 1949. Family life and family substitutes in old age. *Amer. sociol. Rev.*, 14:71–83.

CAVAN, R. S., BURGESS, W. E., HAVINGHURST, R. J., and GOLDHAMER, H.: 1949. *Personal adjustments in old age.* Sci. Res. Assoc.

CAVANAUGH, J. R.: 1949. The comics war. *J. crim. Law Criminol.*, 40:28–35.

CENTER, S. S., and PERSONS, G. L.: 1936. The leisure reading of New York City high school students. *Eng. J.*, 25:717–726.

CHAFFEY, J.: 1941. *"Reputation records" development in adolescence.* Berkeley, Calif.: Institute of Child Welfare, Vol. 1.

CHOWDHRY, K., and NEWCOMB, T. M.: 1952. The relative abilities of leaders and non-leaders to estimate opinions of their groups. *J. abnorm. soc. Psychol.*, 47:51–57.

CLAGUE, R.: 1949. Aging and employability. *In* Tibbetts, C., *Living through the older years.* Ann Arbor: Univ. Michigan Press, pp. 141–153.

CLARK, H. F., and WITHERS, W.: 1931. The findings of a world study of the best distribution of people in occupations. *The New York Times,* Dec. 27.

CLARK, K. B., and CLARK, M. P.: 1939. The development of consciousness of self and the emergence of racial identification in Negro preschool children. *J. soc. Psychol.,* 10:591–599.

CLARK, K. B., and CLARK, M. P.: 1950. Emotional factors in racial identification and preference in Negro children. *J. Negro Educ.,* 19:341–350.

CLARK, L. M.: 1949. Sex life in the middle aged. *Marriage Fam. Living,* 11:58–60.

CLARK, W. R.: 1940. Radio listening habits of children. *J. soc. Psychol.,* 11:131–149.

CLARKE, A. C.: 1952. An examination of the operation of residential propinquity as a factor in mate selection. *Amer. sociol. Rev.,* 17:17–22.

CLARKE, T. W.: 1952. Allergy and the "problem child." *Nerv. Child,* 9:278–281.

CLOSE, K.: 1948. Grandpa wants to work. *Survey-Graphic,* 37:288–292.

COBB, K.: 1952. Measuring leadership in college women by free association. *J. abnorm. soc. Psychol.,* 47:126–128.

COFFIN, T. E.: 1948. Television's effects on leisure-time activities. *J. appl. Psychol.,* 32:550–558.

COHEN, L. H.: 1943. Psychiatric aspects of child-bearing. *Yale J. Biol. and Med.,* 16:77–92.

COLE, L.: 1944. *Attaining maturity.* New York: Rinehart.

COLEMAN, J. H.: 1931. Written composition interests of junior- and senior-high-school pupils. *Teach. Coll. Contr. Educ.,* No. 494.

COLM, H.: 1951. Help and guidance as discipline for pre-adolescents. *Nerv. Child,* 9:131–138.

CONKEY, F.: 1933. The adaption of fifty men and women to old age. *J. Home Econ.,* 25:387–389.

CONKLIN, E. S.: 1933. *Principles of adolescent psychology.* New York: Holt.

CONKLIN, E. S.: 1936. Childhood and adolescence. *In* Skinner, C. E., *Educational psychology.* New York: Prentice-Hall, Chap. 11.

CONKLIN, E. S., BRYON, M. E., and KNIPS, A.: 1927. Some mental effects of menstruation. *J. genet. Psychol.,* 34:357–367.

CONN, J. H.: 1939. Factors influencing development of sexual attitudes and awareness in children. *Amer. J. Dis. Child.,* 58:738–745.

CONN, J. H.: 1940. Sexual curiosity of children. *Amer. J. Dis. Child.,* 60:1110–1119.

CONN, J. H.: 1948. Children's awareness of the origin of babies. *J. child Psychiat.,* 1:140–176.

CONN, J. H.: 1951. Children's awareness of sex differences. II. Play attitudes and game preferences. *J. child Psychiat.,* 2:82–99.

CONN, J. H., and KANNER, L.: 1940. Spontaneous erections in early childhood. *J. Pediat.,* 16:337–340.

CONN, J. H., and KANNER, L.: 1947. Children's awareness of sex differences. *J. child Psychiat.,* 1:3–57.

COOK, W. M.: 1931. Ability of children in color discrimination. *Child Develpm.,* 2:303–320.

COURTENAY, M. E.: 1938. The persistence of leadership. *School Rev.,* 46:97–107.

COWDRY, E. V.: 1939. *Problems of aging.* Baltimore: Williams & Wilkins.

COWLEY, W. H.: 1931. The traits of face-to-face leaders. *J. abnorm. soc. Psychol.,* 26:304–313.

CRAMPTON, C. W.: 1908. Anatomical or physiological age versus chronological age. *Ped. Sem.,* 15:230–237.

CROWLEY, J. J.: 1940. High-school backgrounds of successful men and women graduates. *Sch. Rev.,* 48:205–209.

CRUDDEN, C. H.: 1937. Reactions of newborn infants to thermal stimuli under constant tactual conditions. *J. exp. Psychol.*, 20:350–370.

CUMMINGS, J. D.: 1944. The incidence of emotional symptoms in school children. *Brit. J. educ. Psychol.*, 14:151–161.

CUNLIFFE, R. B.: 1927. Whither away and why: trends in choice of vocation in Detroit. *Person. J.*, 6:25–28.

CUNLIFFE, R. B.: 1929. Why this career? *Person. J.*, 7:376–384.

CUSHING, J. G. N.: 1952. Problems of retirement. *Ment. Hyg., N.Y.*, 36:449–455.

DAHLBERG, G.: 1948. Do parents want boys or girls? *Acta Genetica et Statistica Medica*, 1:163–167.

DALE, E.: 1935. *Children's attendance at motion pictures.* New York: Macmillan.

DAMRIN, D. E.: 1949. Family size and sibling age, sex, and position as related to certain aspects of adjustment. *J. soc. Psychol.*, 29:98–102.

DASHIELL, J. F.: 1917. Children's sense of harmonies in colors and tones. *J. exp. Psychol.*, 2:466–475.

DAVENPORT, F. I.: 1923. Adolescent interests. *Arch. Psychol., N.Y.*, No. 66.

DAVIS, A.: 1944. Socialization and adolescent personality. *43d Yearb. nat. Soc. Stud. Educ.*, p. 209.

DAVIS, D. M.: 1939. The relation of repetition in the speech of young children to certain measures of language maturity and situational factors. Part I. *J. Speech Disorders*, 4:303–318.

DAVIS, E. A.: 1932. The form and function of children's questions. *Child Develpm.*, 3:57–74.

DAVIS, E. A.: 1937. Mean sentence length compared with long and short sentences as a reliable measure of language development. *Child Develpm.*, 8:69–79.

DAVIS, H. V., SEARS, R. R., MILLER, H. C., and BRODBECK, A. J.: 1948. Effects of cup, bottle, and breast feeding on oral activities of newborn infants. *Pediat.*, 3:549–558.

DAVIS, K. B.: 1926. Periodicity of sex desire. *Amer. J. Obstet. Gynaec.*, 12:824–838.

DAVIS, K. B.: 1929. *Factors in the sex life of twenty-two hundred women.* New York: Harper.

DAWE, H. C.: 1934. An analysis of two hundred quarrels of preschool children. *Child Develpm.*, 5:139–157.

DAWSON, G. E.: 1900. Children's interest in the Bible. *Ped. Sem.*, 7:151–178.

DAWSON, M. A.: 1937. Children's preferences for conversational topics. *Elem. Sch. J.*, 37:429–437.

DEARBORN, G. V. N.: 1919. The psychology of clothing. *Psychol. Rev. Monogr.*, 26:1–72.

DENNIS, W.: 1935. The effect of restricted practice upon the reaching, sitting, and standing of two infants. *J. genet. Psychol.*, 47:17–32.

DENNIS, W.: 1938. Historical notes on child animism. *Psychol. Rev.*, 45:257–266.

DENNIS, W.: 1939. Is infant behavior appreciably affected by cultural influences? *Psychol. Bull.*, 36:398–399.

DENNIS, W.: 1940. Does culture appreciably affect patterns of infant behavior? *J. soc. Psychol.*, 12:305–317.

DENNIS, W.: 1941. Infant development under conditions of restricted practice and minimum social stimulation. *Genet. Psychol. Monogr.*, 23:143–189.

DENNIS, W., and DENNIS, M. G.: 1937. Behavioral development in the first year as shown by forty biographies. *Psychol. Rec.*, 1:349–361.

DENNIS, W., and DENNIS, M. G.: 1938. Infant development under conditions of restricted practice and a minimum of social stimulation; a preliminary report. *J. genet. Psychol.*, 53:149–157.

DESMOND, T. C.: 1949. *Never too old*. New York State Joint Legislative Committee on Problems of the Aging, Legislative Document, No. 32.

DESPERT, J. L.: 1946. Psychosomatic study of fifty stuttering children. *Amer. J. Orthopsychiat.*, 16:100–113.

DESPERT, J. L.: 1949. Sleep in preschool children: a preliminary study. *Nerv. Child*, 8:8–27.

DILLON, M. S.: 1934. Attitudes in children toward their own bodies and those of other children. *Child Develpm.*, 5:165–176.

DIMOCK, H. S.: 1935. A research in adolescence. 1. Pubescence and physical growth. *Child Develpm.*, 6:285–302.

DIMOCK, H. S.: 1935a. A research in adolescence: the social world of the adolescent. *Child Develpm.*, 6:285–302.

DIMOCK, H. S.: 1936. Some new light on adolescent religion. *Relig. Educ.*, 31:273–279.

DIMOCK, H. S.: 1937. *Rediscovering the adolescent*. New York: Association Press.

DINGWALL, M.: 1949. Maintenance of mental health. 3. Going to school—the second five years. *Ment. Hyg., Lond.*, 9:31–33.

DOCKERAY, F. C.: 1934. Differential feeding reactions of newborn infants. *Psychol. Bull.*, 31:747.

DOLGER, L., and GINANDES, J.: 1946. Children's attitudes toward discipline as related to socioeconomic status. *J. exp. Educ.*, 15:161–165.

DOLL, E. A.: 1935. A genetic scale of social maturity. *Amer. J. Orthopsychiat.*, 5:180–186.

DOLL, E. A.: 1938. Social maturation. *Proc. 5th Inst. except. Child, Child Res. Clin. Ser.*, 5:31–36.

DOUGLASS, H. R.: 1925. The development of number concepts in children of preschool and kindergarten age. *J. exp. Psychol.*, 8:443–470.

DOW, P., and TORPIN, R.: 1939. Placentation studies: correlations between size of sac, area of placenta, weight of placenta, and weight of baby. *Hum. Biol.*, 11:248–258.

DREIKURS, R.: 1935. The choice of a mate. *Int. J. ind. Psychol.*, 1, No. 4:99–112.

DUBLIN, L. I., KARSNER, H. T., PEPPER, O. H. P., and BROOKS, B.: 1941. *Medical problems of old age*. Philadelphia: Univ. Pennsylvania Press.

DUDYCHA, G. J.: 1933. The religious beliefs of college students. *J. appl. Psychol.*, 17:585–603.

DUDYCHA, G. J.: 1933a. The superstitious beliefs of college students. *J. abnorm. soc. Psychol.*, 27:457–464.

DUDYCHA, G. J.: 1934. The beliefs of college students concerning evolution. *J. appl. Psychol.*, 18:85–96.

DUNBAR, F.: 1944. Effect of the mother's emotional attitudes on the infant. *Psychosom. Med.*, 6:156–159.

DUNKERLEY, M. D.: 1940. A statistical study of leadership among college women. *Stud. Psychol. Psychiat. Cathol. Univ. Amer.*, 4, No. 7.

DUREA, M. A.: 1935. Mental and social maturity in relation to certain indicators of the degree of juvenile delinquency. *Child Develpm.*, 6:154–160.

DUROST, W. N.: 1932. Children's collecting activity related to social factors. *Teach. Coll. Contr. Educ.*, No. 537.

DYKMAN, R. A., HEIMAN, E. K., and KERR, W. A.: 1952. Lifetime worry problems of three diverse adult cultural groups. *J. soc. Psychol.*, 35:91–100.

EAGLESON, O. W.: 1946. Students' reactions to their given names. *J. soc. Psychol.*, 23:187–195.

EAST, W. N.: 1942. *The adolescent criminal*. London: Churchill.

EBLIS, J. H., TISDALL, F. F., and STOTT, W. A.: 1941. The influence of prenatal diet on the mother and child. *J. Nutrit.*, 22:515–526.

ECKSTRAND, R.: 1931. The variation of behavior problems with size of family. *Smith Coll. Stud. soc. Work,* 1:291–300.

EDMAN, M.: 1940. Attendance of school pupils and adults at moving pictures. *Sch. Rev.,* 48:753–763.

EDWARDS, A. S.: 1950. The myth of chronological age. *J. appl. Psychol.,* 34:316–318.

EISENBERG, A. L.: 1936. *Children and radio programs.* New York: Columbia Univ. Press.

EKHOLM, E., and NIEMINEVA, K.: 1950. On prenatal changes in the relative weights of the human adrenals, the thymus, and the thyroid gland. *Acta paediatr. Stockh.,* 39:67–86.

ELLINGSON, R. J., and LINDSLEY, D. B.: 1949. Brain waves and cortical development in newborn and young infants. *Amer. Psychologist,* 4:248–249.

ELLIS, A.: 1949. A study of human love relationships. *J. genet. Psychol.,* 75:61–71.

ELLIS, A.: 1949a. Some significant correlates of love and family attitudes and behavior. *J. soc. Psychol.,* 30:3–16.

ELLIS, R. W. B.: 1947. Growth in relation to maturity. *Edinb. med. J.,* 54:269–283.

ELLIS, R. W. B.: 1950. Age of puberty in the tropics. *Brit. med. J.,* 1:85–89.

ENGLAND, A. O.: 1946. Non-structural approach to the study of children's fears. *J. clin. Psychol.,* 2:364–368.

ENGLE, E., and SHELESNYAK, M.: 1934. First menstruation and subsequent menstrual cycles of pubertal girls. *Hum. Biol.,* 6:431–453.

ENGLE, T. L.: 1945. Personality adjustments of children belonging to two minority groups. *J. educ. Psychol.,* 36:543–560.

ENGLISH, O. S.: 1947. Adolescence. *Philad. Med.,* 42:1025–1026.

ESPENSCHADE, A.: 1940. Motor performance in adolescence. *Monogr. Soc. Res. Child Develpm.,* 5, No. 1.

ESPENSCHADE, A.: 1947. Development of motor coordination in boys and girls. *Res. Quart. Amer. phys. Educ. Ass.,* 181:30–43.

ESSERT, P. L., LORGE, I., and TUCKMAN, J.: 1951. Preparation for a constructive approach to later maturity. *Teach. Coll. Rec.,* 53:70–76.

FAHS, S. L.: 1932. Should Peggy and Peter pray? *Relig. Educ.,* 27:596–605.

FAHS, S. L.: 1950. The beginnings of mysticism in children's growth. *Relig. Educ.,* 45:139–147.

FASTEN, N.: 1950. The myth of prenatal influence. *Today's Health,* 27 (October):42–43.

FEDERAL BUREAU OF INVESTIGATION REPORT: 1943. *Uniform crime reports for the United States and its possessions.* Washington, D.C.: Federal Bureau of Investigation, Vol. 14.

FEIFEL, H., and LORGE, I.: 1950. Cumulative differences in the vocabulary responses of children. *J. educ. Psychol.,* 41:1–18.

FELDER, J. C.: 1932. Some factors determining the nature and frequency of anger and fear outbreaks in preschool children. *J. juv. Res.,* 16:278–290.

FELDMAN, S.: 1941. Origins of behavior and man's life-career. *Amer. J. Psychol.,* 54:53–63.

FENTON, J. C.: 1925. *A practical psychology of babyhood.* Boston: Houghton Mifflin.

FENTON, N.: 1943. *Mental hygiene and school practices.* Stanford University, Calif.: Stanford Univ. Press.

FERGUSON, L. W.: 1941. The cultural genesis of masculinity and femininity. *Psychol. Bull.,* 38:584–585.

FESSLER, L.: 1950. The psychopathology of climacteric depression. *Psychoanal. Quart.,* 19:28–42.

FINGER, F. W.: 1947. Sex beliefs and practices among male college students. *J. abnorm. soc. Psychol.,* 42:57–67.

FISHER, M. B., and BIRREN, J. E.: 1941. Age and strength. *J. appl. Psychol.,* 31:490–497.

FISHER, M. S.: 1934. *Language patterns of preschool children.* New York: Teachers College, Columbia Univ.

FLEEGE, U. H.: 1945. *Sex-revelation of the adolescent boy.* Milwaukee: Bruce Pub.

FLEMING, E. G.: 1932. Best friends. *J. soc. Psychol.,* 3:385–390.

FLEMING, E. G.: 1932a. Pleasing personality. *J. soc. Psychol.,* 3:100–107.

FLEMING, E. G.: 1935. A factor analysis of the personality of high-school leaders. *J. appl. Psychol.,* 19:596–605.

FLORY, C. D.: 1936. Osseous development in the hand as an index of skeletal development. *Monogr. Soc. Res. Child Develpm.,* 1, No. 3.

FLUHMANN, C.: 1934. The length of the human menstrual cycle. *Amer. J. Obstet. Gynaec.,* 27:73–78.

FOLSOM, J. K., and MORGAN, C. M.: 1937. The social adjustment of 381 recipients of old age assistance. *Amer. sociol. Rev.,* 11:223–229.

FOLSOM, J. K., et al.: 1938. *Plan for marriage.* New York: Harper.

FORMAN, H. J.: 1935. *Our movie made children.* New York: Macmillan.

Fortune Magazine: 1946. Our aging population. 34, No. 6:250–254.

FOSTER, S.: 1927. A study of the personality make-up and social setting of fifty jealous children. *Ment. Hyg., N.Y.,* 11:53–73.

FOULDS, G. A.: 1949. Variations in the intellectual activities of adults. *Amer. J. Psychol.,* 62:238–246.

FOULDS, G. A., and RAVEN, J. C.: 1948. Normal changes in the mental abilities of adults as age advances. *J. ment. Sci.,* 94:133–142.

FOX, C.: 1947. Vocabulary ability in later maturity. *J. educ. Psychol.,* 38:482–492.

FOX, C., and BIRREN, J. E.: 1950. The differential decline of subtest scores of the Wechsler-Bellevue Intelligence Scale in 60–69-year-old individuals. *J. genet. Psychol.,* 77:313–317.

FRANCIS, K. V.: 1933. A study of the means of influence of socio-economic factors upon the personality of children. *J. juv. Res.,* 17:70–77.

FRANK, L. K.: 1944. Adolescence as a period of transition. *43d Yearb. nat. Soc. Stud. Educ.,* Chap. 1.

FRANK, L. K.: 1950. The concept of maturity. *Child Develpm.,* 21:21–24.

FRANKEL-BRUNSWIK, E.: 1948. A study of prejudice in children. *Hum. Relat.,* 1:295–306.

FRAZIER, A., and LISONBEE, L. K.: 1950. Adolescent concerns with physique. *Sch. Rev.,* 58:397–405.

FREEMAN, H. A.: 1931. First graders' religious ideas. *Sch. & Soc.,* 34:733–735.

FREEMAN, L.: 1952. Youth delinquency growing rapidly over the country. *The New York Times,* Apr. 20.

FREUD, S.: 1920. *A general introduction to psychoanalysis.* New York: Boni.

FRIED, E. G.: 1949. Attitudes of the older population groups toward activity and inactivity. *J. Geront.,* 4:141–151.

FRIED, E. G., and STERN, K.: 1948. The situation of the aged within the family. *Amer. J. Orthopsychiat.,* 18:31–54.

FRIES, M. E.: 1937. Factors in character development, neuroses, psychoses, and delinquency. *Amer. J. Orthopsychiat.,* 17:142–181.

FRIES, M. E.: 1941. Mental hygiene in pregnancy, delivery, and the puerperium. *Ment. Hyg., N.Y.,* 25:221–236.

FRIES, M. E., and LEWI, B.: 1938. Interrelated factors in development. *Amer. J. Orthopsychiat.,* 17:726–752.

FROHLICH, M. M.: 1949. Mental hygiene in old age. *In* Tibbitts, C., *Living through the older years.* Ann Arbor: Univ. Michigan Press, pp. 85–97.

FURFEY, P. H.: 1926. *The gang age: a study of the preadolescent boy and his recreational needs.* New York: Macmillan.

FURFEY, P. H.: 1927. Some factors influencing the selection of boys' chums. *J. appl. Psychol.,* 11:47–53.

FURFEY, P. H.: 1929. Pubescence and play behavior. *Amer. J. Psychol.,* 41:109–111.

GARDINER, L. P.: 1949. Attitudes and activities of the middle-aged and aged. *Geriatrics,* 4:33–50.

GARDNER, G. E.: 1929. The adolescent "nervous breakdown." *Ment. Hyg., N.Y.,* 13:769–779.

GARDNER, L. P.: 1943. A survey of attitudes and activities of fathers. *J. genet. Psychol.,* 63:15–53.

GARDNER, L. P.: 1947. An analysis of children's attitudes toward fathers. *J. genet. Psychol.,* 70:3–28.

GARRISON, K. C., and CUNNINGHAM, J.: 1952. Personal problems of ninth-grade pupils. *Sch. Rev.,* 60:30–33.

GARTH, T. R., and PORTER, E. P.: 1934. The color preferences of 1,032 young children. *Amer. J. Psychol.,* 46:448–451.

GATES, A. I., and TAYLOR, G. A.: 1926. An experimental study of the nature of improvement resulting from practice in motor functions. *J. educ. Psychol.,* 27:226–236.

GATES, G. S.: 1926. An observational study of anger. *J. exp. Psychol.,* 9:325–336.

GEISEL, J. B.: 1951. Discipline viewed as a developmental need of the child. *Nerv. Child,* 9:115–121.

GERBERICH, J. R., and THALHEIMER, J. A.: 1936. Reader interests in various types of newspaper content. *J. appl. Psychol.,* 20:471–480.

GESELL, A.: 1928. *Infancy and human growth.* New York: Macmillan.

GESELL, A.: 1930. *The guidance and mental growth of infant and child.* New York: Macmillan.

GESELL, A.: 1933. The mental growth of prematurely born infants. *J. Pediat.,* 2:676–680.

GESELL, A.: 1940. *The first five years of life.* New York: Harper.

GESELL, A.: 1941. Genesis of behavior form in fetus and infant: the growth of the mind from the standpoint of developmental morphology. *Proc. Amer. phil. Soc.,* 84:471–488.

GESELL, A.: 1946. Behavior aspects of the care of the premature infant. *J. Pediat.,* 29:210–212.

GESELL, A.: 1949. The developmental aspect of child vision. *J. Pediat.,* 35:310–317.

GESELL, A.: 1949a. Growth potentials of the human infant. *Sci. Mon., N.Y.,* 68:252–256.

GESELL, A.: 1952. Developmental pediatrics. *Nerv. Child,* 9:225–227.

GESELL, A., and AMATRUDA, C. S.: 1945. *The embryology of behavior.* New York: Harper.

GESELL, A., AMATRUDA, C. S., CASTNER, B. M., and THOMPSON, H.: 1939. *Biographies of child development.* New York: Hoeber.

GESELL, A., and AMES, L. B.: 1947. The development of handedness. *J. genet. Psychol.,* 70:155–175.

GESELL, A., and AMES, L. B.: 1947a. The infant's reaction to his mirror image. *J. genet. Psychol.,* 70:141–154.

GESELL, A., and HALVERSON, H. M.: 1936. The development of thumb opposition in the human infant. *J. genet. Psychol.,* 48:339–361.

GESELL, A., and THOMPSON, H.: 1934. *Infant behavior, its genesis, and growth.* New York: McGraw-Hill.

GESELL, A., and THOMPSON, H.: 1938. *The psychology of early growth.* New York: Macmillan.

GIESE, F.: 1928. Erlebnis formen des Alters, Umfrageergebnisse über merkmale person-lichen. *Verfalls: Deutsch. Psychol.*, Halle, Marhold, 5, No. 2.

GIESECKE, M.: 1936. The genesis of hand preference. *Monogr. Soc. Res. Child Develpm.*, 1, No. 2.

GILBERT, J. G.: 1935. Mental efficiency in senescence. *Arch. Psychol.*, N.Y., No. 188.

GILBERT, J. G.: 1936. Senescent efficiency and employability. *J. appl. Psychol.*, 20:266–272.

GILBERT, J. G.: 1941. Memory loss in senescence. *J. abnorm. soc. Psychol.*, 36:73–86.

GILBERT, J. G.: 1944. Measuring mental efficiency in senescence. *Amer. J. Orthopsychiat.*, 14:267–272.

GILLILAND, A. R.: 1940. The attitude of college students toward God and the church. *J. soc. Psychol.*, 11:11–18.

GITELSON, M.: 1948. The emotional problems of elderly people. *Geriatrics*, 3:135–150.

GLADSTONE, R.: 1948. Do maladjusted teachers cause maladjustment? *J. except. Child*, 15:65–70.

GLASER, K., PARMELEE, A. H., and PLATTNER, E. B.: 1950. Growth patterns of pre-maturely born infants. *Pediatrics, Springfield*, 5:130–144.

GLICK, P. C., and LANDAU, E.: 1950. Age as a factor in marriage. *Amer. sociol. Rev.*, 15:517–529.

GLUECK, S., and GLUECK, E. T.: 1934. *One thousand juvenile delinquents*. Cambridge: Harvard Univ. Press.

GLUECK, S., and GLUECK, E. T.: 1950. *Unravelling juvenile delinquency*. New York: Commonwealth Fund.

GOLDSTEIN, M. S.: 1939. Development of the head in the same individuals. *Hum. Biol.*, 11:197–219.

GOODE, M. J.: 1951. Economic factors and marital stability. *Amer. sociol. Rev.*, 16:802–812.

GOODENOUGH, F. L.: 1926. *Measurement of intelligence by drawings*. Yonkers, N.Y.: World.

GOODENOUGH, F. L.: 1931. *Anger in young children*. Minneapolis: Univ. Minnesota Press.

GOODENOUGH, F. L.: 1945. *Developmental psychology*, 2d ed. New York: Appleton-Century-Crofts.

GOODENOUGH, F. L., and HARRIS, D. B.: 1950. Studies in the psychology of children's drawings. II. 1928–1949. *Psychol. Bull.*, 47:369–433.

GOODMAN, M. E.: 1951. The education of children and youth to live in a multiracial society. *J. Negro Educ.*, 19:397–407.

GOTTEMOLLER, R.: 1943. The sibling relationship of a group of young children. *Nerv. Child*, 2:268–277.

GOUGH, H. G., HARRIS, D. B., MARTIN, W. E., and EDWARDS, M.: 1950. Children's ethnic attitudes. II. Relationship to certain personality factors. *Child. Develpm.*, 21:83–91.

GOUGH, H. G., McCLOSKY, H., and MEEHL, P. E.: 1952. A personality scale for social responsibility. *J. abnorm. soc. Psychol.*, 47:73–80.

GRACE, A. G.: 1929. The reading interests of adults. *J. educ. Res.*, 19:265–275.

GRANT, E. I.: 1939. The effect of certain factors in the home environment upon child behavior. *Univ. Ia. Stud. Child Welf.*, 17:63–94.

GRAVES, C. E.: 1948. Factors in the development and growth of children's personalities. *J. Iowa State Med. Soc.*, 38:437–539.

GRAY, H.: 1947. Psychological types and changes with age. *J. clin. Psychol.*, 3:273–277.

GRAY, H.: 1949. Psychological types in married people. *J. soc. Psychol.*, 29:189–200.

GRAY, S.: 1944. The vocational preferences of Negro school children. *J. genet. Psychol.*, 64:239–247.

GRAY, W. S., and MONROE, R.: 1929. *The reading interests and habits of adults.* New York: Macmillan.

GREEN, E. H.: 1933. Group play and quarreling among preschool children. *Child Develpm.,* 4:302–307.

GREGG, A.: 1928. *An observational study of laughter in three-year-old children.* New York: Columbia Univ. Library. (Unpublished master's thesis.)

GREULICH, W. W.: 1950. The rationale of assessing the developmental status of children from roentgenograms of the hand and wrist. *Child Develpm.,* 21:33–44.

GREULICH, W. W., et al.: 1942. Somatic and endocrine studies of puberal and adolescent boys. *Monogr. Soc. Res. Child Develpm.,* 7, No. 3.

GRIFFEN, H. C.: 1929. Changes in the religious attitudes of college students. *Relig. Educ.,* 24:159–164.

GUILFORD, R. B., and WORCESTER, D. A.: 1930. A comparative study of the only and non-only children. *J. genet. Psychol.,* 38:411–426.

GUMPERT, M.: 1952. Our "Inca" ideas about retirement. *The New York Times,* July 27.

GUTTERIDGE, M. V.: 1939. A study of motor achievements of young children. *Arch. Psychol., N.Y.,* No. 244.

GUYON, R.: 1948. The child and sexual activity. *Int. J. Sexol.,* 2:26–32.

HABBE, S.: 1937. Nicknames of adolescent boys. *Amer. J. Orthopsychiat.,* 7:371–377.

HAGMAN, E. P.: 1933. The companionships of preschool children. *Univ. Ia. Stud. Child Welf.,* 7, No. 4.

HAGMAN, S. R.: 1932. A study of fears of children of preschool age. *J. exp. Psychol.,* 1:110–130.

HALL, C. E.: 1948. Age and the endocrine glands. *Tex. Rep. Biol. Med.,* 6:321–336.

HALL, G. S.: 1904. *Adolescence.* New York: Appleton-Century-Crofts.

HALL, G. S.: 1907. *Aspects of child life and education.* Boston: Ginn.

HALL, G. S.: 1923. *Senescence.* New York: Appleton-Century-Crofts.

HALL, O. M.: 1934. Attitudes and unemployment. *Arch. Psychol., N.Y.,* No. 165.

HALL, W. E., and ROBINSON, F. P.: 1942. The role of reading as a life activity in a rural community. *J. appl. Psychol.,* 26:530–542.

HALVERSON, H. M.: 1931. An experimental study of prehension in infants by various systematic cinema records. *Genet. Psychol. Monogr.,* 10:107–286.

HALVERSON, H. M.: 1940. Genital and sphincter behavior of the male infant. *J. genet. Psychol.,* 56:85–136.

HAMILTON, G. V.: 1929. *A research in marriage.* New York: Boni.

HAMILTON, G. V.: 1942. Changes in personality and psychosexual phenomena. *In* Cowdry, E. V., *Problems of aging,* 2d ed. Baltimore: Williams & Wilkins, Chap. 30.

HAMILTON, G. V., and MACGOWAN, K.: 1929. *What is wrong with marriage?* New York: Boni.

HANLON, C. R., BUTCHART, J. B., and KEMPF, P. R.: 1949. Injuries in childhood. *J. Pediat.,* 34:688–698.

HARDY, J. D., GOODELL, H., and WOLFF, H. G.: 1941. Sex differences in temperature regulation. *J. Nutrit.,* 21:383.

HARDY, M. C.: 1937. Social recognition of the elementary school age. *J. soc. Psychol.,* 8:365–384.

HARDY, M. C.: 1937a. Adjustment scores of adolescents having a history of frequent illness in childhood. *Amer. J. Orthopsychiat.,* 7:204–209.

HARDY, M. C., BOYLE, H. H., and NEWCOMB, A. L.: 1941. Physical fitness of children from different economic levels in Chicago. *J. Amer. med. Ass.,* 117:2154–2161.

HARMS, E.: 1943. The development of humor. *J. abnorm. soc. Psychol.,* 38:351–369.

HARMS, E.: 1944. The development of religious experience in children. *Amer. J. Sociol.,* 50:112–122.

HARRIS, D.: 1935. Age and occupational factors in the residential propinquity of marriage partners. *J. soc. Psychol.*, 6:257–261.

HARRIS, D. B.: 1950. Behavior ratings of post-polio cases. *J. consult. Psychol.*, 14:381–385.

HARRIS, D. B.: 1950a. How children learn interests, motives, and attitudes. *49th Yearb. nat. Soc. Stud. Educ.*, Chap. 5.

HARRIS, D. B., GOUGH, H. G., and MARTIN, W. E.: 1950. Children's ethnic attitudes. II. Relationship to parental beliefs concerning child training. *Child Develpm.*, 21:169–181.

HARRIS, D. B., and MARTIN, W. E.: 1950. Mothers' child training preferences and children's ethnic attitudes. *Amer. Psychologist*, 5:467.

HARRIS, J. A., JACKSON, C. M., PATTERSON, D. G., and SCAMMON, R. I.: 1930. *The measurement of man*. Minneapolis: Univ. Minnesota Press.

HARSCH, C. M., and SCHRICKEL, H. G.: 1950. *Personality*. New York: Ronald.

HART, F. W.: 1934. *Teachers and teaching*. New York: Macmillan.

HATTENDORF, K. W.: 1932. A study of the questions of young children concerning sex: a phase of an experimental approach to parent education. *J. soc. Psychol.*, 3:37–64.

HATTWICK, L. A.: 1940. Group life of the young child. *J. educ. Psychol.*, 14:205–216.

HATTWICK, L. A., and SANDERS, M. K.: 1938. Age differences in behavior at the nursery school level. *Child Develpm.*, 9:27–47.

HAVINGHURST, R. J.: 1949. Old age—an American problem. *J. Geront.*, 4:298–304.

HAVINGHURST, R. J.: 1950. *Developmental tasks and education*. New York: Longmans.

HAVINGHURST, R. J., ROBINSON, M. Z., and DORR, M.: 1946. The development of the ideal self in childhood and adolescence. *J. educ. Res.*, 40:241–257.

HAY-SHAW, C.: 1949. Maintenance of mental health. *Ment. Hlth., Lond.*, 9:3–6.

HEALY, W.: 1915. *The individual delinquent*. Boston: Little, Brown.

HEALY, W., and BRONNER, A. F.: 1935. *New light on delinquency and its treatment*. New Haven: Yale Univ. Press.

HEATH, C. W., and GREGORY, L. W.: 1946. Problems of normal college students and their families. *Sch. & Soc.*, 63:355–358.

HEIDLER, J. B., and LEHMAN, H. C.: 1937. Chronological age and productivity in various types of literature. *Eng. J.*, 26:284–304.

HEISLER, F.: 1948. A comparison between those elementary school children who attend moving pictures, read comic books, and listen to serial radio programs with those who indulge in these activities seldom or not at all. *J. educ. Res.*, 42:182–190.

HENRIQUES, B. L. G.: 1949. The adolescent delinquent boy. *Practitioner*, 162:299–304.

HERRING, J.: 1947. Aetiology and incidence of foetal malformation. *Med. Pr.*, 218:814–817.

HERTZLER, A. E.: 1940. Problems of the normal adolescent girl. *Calif. J. second. Educ.*, 15:114–119.

HESS, J. H., MOHR, G. J., and BARTELME, P. F.: 1934. *The physical and mental growth of prematurely born children*. Chicago: Univ. Chicago Press.

HETZER, H.: 1926. Der Einfluss der negativen Phase auf soziales Verhalten und Literarischeproduktion pubertierender Mädchen. *Quellen und Studien*, 5:1–143.

HETZER, H.: 1927. Systematische Dauerbeobachtungen an Jugendlichen über dem Verlauf der negativen Phase. *Zeitsch. f. Pädogog. Psychol. u. Experim. Pädagog.*, 28:80–96.

HETZER, H., and TUDOR-HART, B. H.: 1927. Die frühesten Reactionem auf die menschliche Stimme. *Quellen und Studien*, 5:103–124.

HEWITT, L. E., and JENKINS, R. L.: 1946. *Fundamental patterns of maladjustment: the dynamics of their origin*. Springfield: State of Illinois.

HICKS, J. A., and HAYES, M.: 1938. Study of the characteristics of 250 junior high school children. *Child Develpm.*, 9:219–242.

HILDRETH, G.: 1933. Adolescent interests and abilities. *J. genet. Psychol.*, 43:65–93.

HILDRETH, G.: 1936. Developmental sequence in name writing. *Child Develpm.*, 7:291–303.

HILDRETH, G.: 1941. *The child's mind in evolution.* New York: King's Crown Press.

HILDRETH, G.: 1949. The development and training of hand dominance. *J. genet. Psychol.,* 75:197–220.

HILDRETH, G.: 1950. The development and training of hand dominance. *J. genet. Psychol.,* 76:39–144.

HILGARD, J. R.: 1932. Learning and maturation in preschool children. *J. genet. Psychol.,* 41:36–56.

HILL, D. S.: 1930. Personification of ideals by urban children. *J. soc. Psychol.,* 1:379–393.

HOCH, P. H., and ZUBIN, J.: 1949. *Psycho-sexual development.* New York: Grune & Stratton.

HOCHMAN, J.: 1950. The retirement myth. *In* New York Academy of Medicine, *The social and biological challenge of our aging population.* New York: Columbia Univ. Press, pp. 130–145.

HOFFEDITZ, E. L.: 1934. Family resemblances in personality traits. *J. soc. Psychol.,* 5:214–227.

HOGBEN, H., WATERHOUSE, J. A. L., and HOGBEN, L.: 1948. Studies on puberty. Part 1. *Brit. J. soc. Med.,* 2:29–42.

HOHMAN, L. B., and SCHAFFNER, B.: 1947. The sex lives of unmarried men. *Amer. J. Sociol.,* 52:501–507.

HOLLINGSHEAD, A. B.: 1950. Cultural factors in the selection of marriage mates. *Amer. J. Sociol.,* 15:619–627.

HOLLINGWORTH, H. L.: 1928. *Mental growth and decline.* New York: Appleton-Century-Crofts.

HOLLINGWORTH, L. S.: 1926. *Gifted children, their nature, and nurture.* New York: Macmillan.

HOLLINGWORTH, L. S.: 1928. *The psychology of the adolescent.* New York: Appleton-Century-Crofts.

HOLLINGWORTH, L. S.: 1933. The adolescent child. *In* Murchison, C. A., *A handbook of child psychology,* 2d ed. rev. Worcester: Clark Univ. Press, pp. 882–908.

HOLLINGWORTH, L. S.: 1940. Personality and adjustment as determiners and correlates of intelligence. *Yearb. nat. Soc. Stud. Educ.,* 39:271–275.

HOLMES, M. H.: 1951. The child's need for identification. *Ment. Hlth., Lond.,* 10:64–65.

HOPKINS, J. W.: 1947. Height and weight of Ottawa elementary school children of two socio-economic strata. *Hum. Biol.,* 19:68–82.

HOROWITZ, R. E.: 1939. Racial aspects of self-identification in nursery school children. *J. Psychol.,* 7:91–99.

HORROCKS, J. E., and BULSER, M. E.: 1951. A study of the friendship fluctuations of preadolescents. *J. genet. Psychol.,* 78:131–144.

HOUGH, E.: 1932. Some factors in the etiology of maternal over-protection. *Smith Coll. Stud. soc. Work,* 2:188–208.

HOWARD, P. J., and MORRELL, C. H.: 1952. Premature infants in later life. *Pediatrics,* 9:577–584.

HOWARD, R. W.: 1946. Intelligence and personality traits of a group of triplets. *J. Psychol.,* 21:25–36.

HOWARD, R. W.: 1946a. The language development of a group of triplets. *J. genet. Psychol.,* 69:181–188.

HOWARD, R. W.: 1947. The developmental history of a group of triplets. *J. genet. Psychol.,* 70:191–204.

HOWELLS, T. H.: 1928. A comparative study of those who accept and those who reject religious authority. *Univ. Ia. Stud. Charact.,* 2, No. 2.

HUANG, I.: 1943. Children's conception of physical causality: a critical summary. *J. genet. Psychol.,* 63:71–121.

HUGHES, W. L.: 1926. Sex experiences of boyhood. *J. soc. Hyg.*, 12:262–273.

HUNTER, E. C., and JORDAN, A. M.: 1939. An analysis of qualities associated with leadership among college students. *J. educ. Psychol.*, 30:497–509.

HURLOCK, E. B.: 1929. *The psychology of dress.* New York: Ronald.

HURLOCK, E. B.: 1929a. Motivation in fashion. *Arch. Psychol.*, *N.Y.*, No. 111.

HURLOCK, E. B.: 1943. *Modern ways with children.* New York: McGraw-Hill.

HURLOCK, E. B.: 1943a. The spontaneous drawings of adolescents. *J. genet. Psychol.*, 63:141–156.

HURLOCK, E. B., and JANSING, C.: 1934. The vocational attitudes of boys and girls of high school age. *J. genet. Psychol.*, 44:175–191.

HURLOCK, E. B., and KLEIN, E. R.: 1934. Adolescent "crushes." *Child Develpm.*, 5:63–80.

HURLOCK, E. B., and McDONALD, L. C.: 1934. Undesirable behavior traits in junior high school students. *Child Develpm.*, 5:278–290.

HURLOCK, E. B., and SENDER, S.: 1939. The "negative phase" in relation to the behavior of pubescent girls. *Child Develpm.*, 1:325–340.

HURLOCK, E. B., and THOMPSON, J. L.: 1934. Children's drawings: an experimental study of perception. *Child Develpm.*, 5:127–138.

ILG, F. L., and AMES, L. B.: 1950. Developmental traits in reading behavior. *J. genet. Psychol.*, 76:291–312.

ILG, F. L., LEARNED, J., LOCKWOOD, A., and AMES, L. B.: 1949. The three-and-a-half-year-old. *J. genet. Psychol.*, 75:21–31.

ILLINGWORTH, R. S., HARVEY, C. C., and GIN, S. Y.: 1949. Relation of birth weight to physical development in childhood. *Lancet,* 257:598–602.

IRWIN, O. C.: 1930. The amount and nature of activities of newborn infants under constant external stimulating conditions during the first ten days of life. *Genet. Psychol. Monogr.,* 8, No. 1.

IRWIN, O. C.: 1932. The distribution of the amount of motility in young infants between two nursing periods. *J. comp. Psychol.*, 14:429–445.

IRWIN, O. C.: 1948. Infant speech: the effect of family occupational status and of age on sound frequency. *J. Speech and Hearing Disorders,* 13:320–323.

IRWIN, O. C.: 1948a. Infant speech: speech-sound development of sibling and only infants. *J. exp. Psychol.*, 38:600–602.

IRWIN, O. C.: 1951. Infant speech: consonant position. *J. Speech and Hearing Disorders,* 16:159–161.

IRWIN, O. C., and CHEN, H. P.: 1941. A reliability study of speech sounds observed in the crying of newborn infants. *Child Develpm.*, 12:351–368.

IRWIN, O. C., and WEISS, L. L.: 1934. The effect of clothing on the general and vocal activity of the newborn infant. *Univ. Ia. Stud. Child Welf.,* 9, No. 4.

ISAACS, S.: 1940. Temper tantrums in early childhood in their relation to internal objects. *Int. J. Psycho-Anal.*, 21:280–293.

JACK, L. M.: 1934. An experimental study of ascendant behavior in preschool children. *Univ. Ia. Stud. Child Welf.,* 9, No. 3.

JACOBSON, P. H.: 1950. Differentials in divorce by duration of marriage and size of family. *Amer. sociol. Rev.,* 15:235–244.

JAHODA, G.: 1949. Adolescent attitudes toward starting work. *Occup. Psychol., Lond.,* 23:184–188.

JALAVISTO, E.: 1950. Mother's youth held key to longer life. *The New York Times,* July 12.

JAMES, S. Q.: 1943. An investigation of the relationship between children's language and their play. *J. genet. Psychol.*, 62:3–61.

JAMES, W.: 1890. *The principles of psychology.* New York: Holt.

JAMESON, S. G.: 1940. Adjustment problems of university girls because of parental patterns. *Soc. sociol. Res.,* 24:262–271.

JANNEY, J. E.: 1938. A quantitative study of fad and fashion leadership among undergraduate women. *Psychol. Bull.,* 35:696.

JENKINS, L. M.: 1930. *A comparative study of motor achievements of children, five, six, and seven years of age.* New York: Bureau of Publications, Teachers College, Columbia Univ.

JENNINGS, H. C.: 1930. *The biological basis of human nature.* New York: Norton.

JENSEN, K.: 1932. Differential reactions in newborn infants. *Genet. Psychol. Monogr.,* 12:361–479.

JERSILD, A. T.: 1939. Radio and motion pictures. *38th Yearb. nat. Soc. Stud. Educ.,* pp. 153–173.

JERSILD, A. T.: 1947. *Child psychology.* 3d ed. New York: Prentice-Hall.

JERSILD, A. T., and FITE, M. D.: 1939. The influence of nursery school experience on children's social adjustments. *Child Develpm. Monogr.,* No. 25.

JERSILD, A. T., GOLDMAN, B., and LOFTUS, J. J.: 1941. A comparative study of the worries of children in two school situations. *J. exp. Educ.,* 9:323–326.

JERSILD, A. T., and HOLMES, F. B.: 1935. Children's fears. *Child Develpm. Monogr.,* No. 20.

JERSILD, A. T., MARKEY, F. V., and JERSILD, C. L.: 1933. Children's fears, dreams, wishes, daydreams, likes, dislikes, pleasant and unpleasant memories. *Child Develpm. Monogr.,* No. 21.

JERSILD, A. T., and TASCH, R. J.: 1949. *Children's interests.* New York: Bureau of Publications, Teach. Coll., Columbia Univ.

JOHNSON, B. L.: 1932. Reading interests as related to sex and marital status. *Sch. Rev.,* 40:33–43.

JOHNSON, B. L.: 1932a. Children's reading interests as related to sex and grade in school. *Sch. Rev.,* 40:257–272.

JOHNSON, H. M.: 1933. *The art of block building.* New York: John Day.

JOHNSON, K. B.: 1941. The training needs of the delinquent girl. *Train. Sch. Bull.,* 38:6–14.

JOHNSON, W. B., and TERMAN, L. M.: 1940. Some highlights in the literature of psychological sex differences published since 1920. *J. Psychol.,* 9:327–336.

JOHNSON, W. M.: 1946. Adjustment to age. *Med. Ann. Dist. Columbia,* 17:661–701.

JONES, H.: 1951. Maintenance of mental health. *Mental Hlth., Lond.,* 10:40–42.

JONES, H. E.: 1943. *Development in adolescence.* New York: Appleton-Century-Crofts.

JONES, H. E.: 1944. The development of physical abilities. *43d Yearb. nat. Soc. Stud. Educ.,* Chap. 6.

JONES, H. E.: 1946. Skeletal maturing as related to strength. *Child Develpm.,* 17:173–185.

JONES, H. E.: 1946a. Physical ability as a factor in social adjustment in adolescence. *J. educ. Res.,* 40:287–301.

JONES, H. E., and CONRAD, H. S.: 1933. The growth and decline of intelligence: a study of a homogeneous group between the ages of ten and sixty years. *Genet. Psychol. Monogr.,* 13:223–298.

JONES, H. E., and JONES, M. C.: 1928. A study of fear. *Childhood Educ.,* 5:136–143.

JONES, H. E., and KAPLAN, C. J.: 1945. *Psychological aspects of mental disorders in later life.* Stanford, Calif.: Stanford Univ. Press.

JONES, L. W.: 1935. Personality and age. *Nature, Lond.,* 136:779–782.

JONES, M. C.: 1924. The elimination of children's fears. *J. exp. Psychol.,* 7:382–390.

JONES, M. C.: 1926. The development of early behavior patterns in young children. *J. genet. Psychol.,* 33:537–585.

JONES, M. C.: 1938. Guiding the adolescent. *Prog. Educ.,* 15:605–609.

JONES, M. C., and BAYLEY, N.: 1950. Physical maturing among boys as related to behavior. *J. educ. Psychol.,* 41:129–148.

JONES, V.: 1936. Attitudes of college students toward war, race, and religion and the change in such attitudes during four years in college. *Psychol. Bull.,* 33:731–732.

JONES, V.: 1946. A comparison of certain measures of honesty at early adolescence with honesty in adulthood—a follow-up study. *Amer. Psychologist,* 1:261.

JORDON, A. M.: 1942. *Educational psychology,* 3d ed. New York: Holt.

JORDON, H. M.: 1930. What five thousand children said they liked in magazines. *North Carolina Teacher,* 7:136–137.

KAHN, E., and SIMMONS, L. W.: 1940. Problems of middle age. *Yale Rev.,* 29:349–363.

KALLMAN, F. J., and SANDER, G.: 1948. Twin studies on aging and longevity. *J. Hered.,* 39:349–357.

KAMBOUROPOULON, P.: 1926. Individual differences in the sense of humor. *Amer. J. Psychol.,* 37:208–278.

KAMBOUROPOULON, P.: 1930. Individual differences in the sense of humor and their relation to temperamental differences. *Arch. Psychol., N.Y.,* No. 121.

KAPLAN, C. J.: 1940. *Studies in the psychopathology of later life.* Berkeley: Univ. California Press.

KARN, M. N.: 1947. Length of human gestation with special reference to prematurity. *Ann. Eugen., Camb.,* 14:44–59.

KASSER, E.: 1945. The growth and decline of children's slang vocabulary at Mooseheart, a self-contained community. *J. genet. Psychol.,* 66:129–137.

KATES, S. L.: 1951. Suggestibility, submission to parents and peers, and extrapunitiveness, intrapunitiveness, and impunitiveness in children. *J. Psychol.,* 31:233–241.

KATZ, D., and ALLPORT, F. H.: 1931. *Students' attitudes.* Syracuse, N. Y.: The Craftsman's Press.

KATZ, D., and BRALY, K. W.: 1935. Racial prejudice and racial stereotypes. *J. abnorm. soc. Psychol.,* 30:175–193.

KATZ, E.: 1940. The relationship of I.Q. to height and weight from three to five years. *J. genet. Psychol.,* 57:65–82.

KAUFMAN, M. R.: 1940. Old age and aging: the psychoanalytic point of view. *Amer. J. Orthopsychiat.,* 10:73–79.

KEISTER, M. E.: 1950. Relation of mid-morning feeding to behavior of nursery school children. *J. Amer. diet Assoc.,* 26:25–29.

KELCHNER, M.: 1941. Motive jugendlichen Rechtsbrecher. *Psychol. Abstr.,* 15, No. 4763.

KELLY, E. L.: 1936. Concerning the validity of Terman's weights for predicting marital happiness. *Psychol. Bull.,* 36:202–209.

KELTING, L. S.: 1934. An investigation of the feeding, sleeping, crying, and social behavior of infants. *J. exp. Educ.,* 3:97–106.

KENDERDINE, M.: 1931. Laughter in the preschool child. *Child Develpm.,* 2:228–230.

KENT, E.: 1949. A study of maladjusted twins. *Smith Coll. Stud. soc. Work,* 19:63–77.

KEY, C. B., WHITE, M. R., HONZIG, W. P., HEIMEY, A. B., and ERWIN, D.: 1936. The process of learning to dress among nursery school children. *Genet. Psychol. Monogr.,* 18:67–163.

KIMMINS, C. W.: 1928. *The springs of laughter.* London: Methuen.

KINGSBURY, F. A.: 1937. Why do people go to church? *Relig. Educ.,* 32:50–54.

KINSEY, H. C., POMEROY, W. B., and MARTIN, C. E.: 1948. *Sexual behavior in the human male.* Philadelphia: Saunders.

KIRCHNER, W., LINDBOM, T., and PATERSON, D. G.: 1952. Attitudes toward the employment of older workers. *J. appl. Psychol.,* 36:154–156.

KIRKENDALL, L. A.: 1948. Sex problems of adolescents. *Marriage Hyg.,* 1:205–208.

KIRKPATRICK, C.: 1936. An experimental study of the modifications of social attitudes. *Amer. J. Sociol.,* 41:649–656.

KIRKPATRICK, C.: 1939. A methodological analysis of feminism in relation to marital adjustment. *Amer. sociol. Rev.,* 4:325–334.

KIRKPATRICK, C., and COTTON, J.: 1951. Physical attractiveness, age, and marital adjustment. *Amer. sociol. Rev.,* 16:81–86.

KLOPFER, B.: 1939. Personality differences between boys and girls in early childhood. *Psychol. Bull.,* 36:538.

KNEHR, C. A., and SOBOL, A.: 1949. Mental ability of prematurely born children at early school age. *J. Psychol.,* 27:255–261.

KOCH, H. L.: 1933. Popularity in preschool children: some related factors and a technique for its measurement. *Child Develpm.,* 4:164–175.

KOCH, H. L.: 1935. An analysis of certain forms of so-called "nervous habits" in young children. *J. genet. Psychol.,* 46:139–170.

KOCH, H. L.: 1944. A study of some factors conditioning the social distance between the sexes. *J. soc. Psychol.,* 20:79–107.

KOCH, H. L., DENTLER, M., DYSART, B., and STREIT, H.: 1934. A scale for measuring attitude toward the question of children's freedom. *Child Develpm.,* 5:253–266.

KOFFKA, K.: 1925. *The growth of the mind.* New York: Harcourt, Brace.

KORENCHEVSKY, V.: 1952. Primary causes of aging unknown. *The New York Times,* Sept. 14.

KROGER, R., and LOUTTIT, C. M.: 1936. The influence of father's occupation on the vocational choices of high-school boys. *J. appl. Psychol.,* 19:203–212.

KROGMAN, W. M.: 1948. A handbook of the measurement and interrelation of height and weight in the growing child. *Monogr. Soc. Res. Child Develpm.,* 13, No. 3.

KUHLEN, R. G.: 1940. Social change: a neglected factor in psychological studies of the life span. *Sch. & Soc.,* 52:14–16.

KUHLEN, R. G.: 1941. Effect of war developments on attitude toward countries. *J. abnorm. soc. Psychol.,* 36:423–427.

KUHLEN, R. G.: 1948. Trends and problems in later maturity. *In* Pennington, L. A., and Berg, I. A., *An introduction to clinical psychology.* New York: Ronald, Chap. 11.

KUHLEN, R. G., and ARNOLD, M.: 1944. Age differences in religious beliefs and problems during adolescence. *J. genet. Psychol.,* 65:291–300.

KUHLEN, R. G., and LEE, B. J.: 1943. Personality characteristics and social acceptability in adolescence. *J. educ. Psychol.,* 34:321–340.

KUNST, M. S.: 1948. A study of thumb- and finger-sucking in infants. *Psychol. Monogr.,* 62, No. 3.

KUPKY, O.: 1927. Jugendlichen Psychologie. Ihre Hauptprobleme. *Verlag der Dürrschen Buchhandlung,* p. 122.

LANDAU, R. L.: 1951. The concept of the male climacteric. *Med. Clin. N. Amer.,* 35:279–288.

LANDIS, C.: 1927. National differences in conversations. *J. abnorm. soc. Psychol.,* 21:254–257.

LANDIS, C., and FARWELL, J. E.: 1944. A trend analysis of age at first admission, age at death, and years of residence for state mental hospitals: 1913–1941. *J. abnorm. soc. Psychol.,* 39:3–25.

LANDIS, C., LANDIS, A. T., and BOLLES, M. M.: 1940. *Sex in development.* New York: Hoeber.

LANDIS, J. T.: 1942. What is the happiest period of life? *Sch. & Soc.,* 55:643–645.

LANDIS, J. T.: 1943. Social-psychological factors of aging. *Social Forces,* 20:468–470.

LANDIS, J. T., POFFENBERGER, T., and POFFENBERGER, S.: 1950. The effects of first pregnancy upon the sexual adjustment of 212 couples. *Amer. sociol. Rev.,* 15:766–772.

LANDIS, M. H., and BURTT, H. E.: 1924. A study of conversations. *J. comp. Psychol.,* 4:81–89.

LANDRETH, C.: 1941. Factors associated with crying in young children in the nursery school and the home. *Child Develpm.*, 12:81–97.

LANGE, J.: 1939. Seelische Störungen im Greisenhalter. *Münch. med. Wschr.*, 81:1959–1964.

LATHAM, A. J.: 1951. The relationship between pubertal status and leadership in junior high school boys. *J. genet. Psychol.*, 78:185–194.

LAUE, H. G.: 1950. Recreational needs and problems of older people. *In* Donahue, W., and Tibbitts, C., *Planning the older years.* Ann Arbor: Univ. Michigan Press.

LAWTON, G.: 1938. Fears: their cause and prevention. *Child Develpm.*, 9:151–159.

LAWTON, G.: 1938a. Mental abilities at senescence: a survey of present-day research. *J. appl. Psychol.*, 22:607–619.

LAWTON, G.: 1939. Mental hygiene at senescence. *Ment. Hyg., N.Y.*, 23:257–267.

LAWTON, G.: 1940. A long-range research program of old age and aging. *J. soc. Psychol.*, 12:101–114.

LAWTON, G.: 1943. *New goals for old age.* New York: Columbia Univ. Press.

LAWTON, G.: 1943a. Happiness in old age. *Ment. Hyg., N.Y.*, 27:231–237.

LAWTON, G.: 1951. *Aging successfully.* New York: Columbia Univ. Press.

LAZAR, M.: 1937. *Reading interests, activities, and opportunities of bright, average, and dull children.* New York: Bureau of Publications, Teachers College, Columbia Univ.

LAZARSFELD, P. F.: 1940. *Radio and the printed page.* New York: Duell, Sloan & Pearce.

LAZARSFELD, P. F.: 1941. *Radio research.* New York: Duell, Sloan & Pearce.

LAZARSFELD, P. F., and KENDALL, P. L.: 1948. *Radio listening in America.* New York: Prentice-Hall.

LEAL, M. A.: 1929. *Physiological maturity in relation to certain characteristics of boys and girls.* Philadelphia: Univ. Pennsylvania Press.

LEAL, M. A.: 1931. Personality traits and maturing in children of normal I.Q. *J. educ. Res.*, 23:198–209.

LEAL, M. A.: 1932. The relationship between height and physiological maturing. *J. educ. Res.*, 25:168–177.

LEDERER, R. K.: 1939. An exploratory investigation of handed status in the first two years of life. *Univ. Ia. Stud. Child Welf.*, 16, No. 2.

LEHMAN, H. C.: 1936. The creative years in science and literature. *Sci. Mon., N.Y.*, 43:151–162.

LEHMAN, H. C.: 1937. The creative years: "best books." *Sci. Mon., N.Y.*, 45:65–75.

LEHMAN, H. C.: 1938. Most proficient years at sports and games. *Res. Quart. Amer. Assoc. Health and phys. Educ.*, 9:3–19.

LEHMAN, H. C.: 1941. The creative years: medicine, surgery, and certain related fields. *Sci. Mon., N.Y.*, 52:450–461.

LEHMAN, H. C.: 1942. The creative years: oil paintings, etchings, and architectural works. *Psychol. Rev.*, 49:19–42.

LEHMAN, H. C.: 1943. Man's most creative years: then and now. *Science*, 98:393–399.

LEHMAN, H. C.: 1949. Some examples of creative achievement during later maturity and old age. *J. soc. Psychol.*, 30:49–79.

LEHMAN, H. C., and WITTY, P. A.: 1926. Playing school—a compensatory mechanism. *Psychol. Rev.*, 33:480–485.

LEHMAN, H. C., and WITTY, P. A.: 1927. *The psychology of play activities.* New York: A. S. Barnes.

LEHMAN, H. C., and WITTY, P. A.: 1927a. The compensatory function of the movies. *J. appl. Psychol.*, 11:33–41.

LEHMAN, H. C., and WITTY, P. A.: 1930. A study of play in relation to pubescence. *J. soc. Psychol.*, 1:510–523.

LEHMAN, H. C., and WITTY, P. A.: 1936. Sex differences in vocational attitudes. *J. appl. Psychol.*, 20:576–585.

LEONARD, E. A.: 1932. Problems of freshmen college girls. *Child Develpm. Monogr.*, No. 9.

LERNER, E., and MURPHY, L. B.: 1941. Methods for the study of personality in young children. *Monogr. Soc. Res. Child Develpm.*, 6, No. 4.

LEUBA, C.: 1933. An experimental study of rivalry in young children. *J. comp. Psychol.*, 16:367–378.

LEUBA, C.: 1941. Tickling and laughing: two genetic studies. *J. genet. Psychol.*, 58:201–209.

LEVINSON, E. D.: 1949. Fetal defects following rubella in pregnant mothers. *McGill med. J.*, 18:183–198.

LEVY, D. M.: 1928. Finger-sucking and accessory movements in early infancy. *Amer. J. Psychiat.*, 7:881–918.

LEVY, D. M., and TULCHIN, S. H.: 1925. The resistant behavior of infants and children. *J. exp. Psychol.*, 8:209–224.

LEWIN, K.: 1935. *Dynamic theory of personality.* New York: McGraw-Hill.

LEWIS, N. D. C.: 1943. Mental hygiene rules for dealing with age. *In* Lawton, G., *New goals for old age.* New York: Columbia Univ. Press.

LINDEMAN, E. C.: 1950. The sociological challenge of the aging population. *In* New York Academy of Medicine, *The social and biological challenge of our aging population.* New York: Columbia Univ. Press, pp. 171–183.

LIPPITT, R.: 1941. Popularity among preschool children. *Child Develpm.*, 12:305–332.

LIPPMAN, H. S.: 1927. Certain behavior responses in early infancy. *J. genet. Psychol.*, 34:424–440.

LOCKE, H. J., and KARLSSON, G.: 1952. Marital adjustment and prediction in Sweden and the United States. *Amer. sociol. Rev.*, 17:10–17.

LOCKHART, E. G.: 1930. The attitude of children toward law. *Univ. Ia. Stud. Charact.*, 3, No. 1.

LOEB, N.: 1941. *The educational and psychological significance of social acceptability and its approach in an elementary school setting.* Unpublished Ph.D. dissertation, Univ. of Toronto.

LONG, A.: 1941. Parents' reports of undesirable behavior in children. *Child Develpm.*, 12:43–62.

LONG, L.: 1940. Conceptual relationships in children: the concept of roundness. *J. genet. Psychol.*, 57:289–315.

LORGE, I.: 1936. The influence of the test upon the nature of mental decline as a function of age. *J. educ. Psychol.*, 27:100–110.

LORGE, I.: 1936a. Attitude stability in older adults. *Psychol. Bull.*, 33:759.

LORGE, I.: 1940. Psychometry: the evaluation of the mental status as a function of the mental test. *Amer. J. Orthopsychiat.*, 10:56–59.

LOWRIE, S. H.: 1951. Dating theories and study responses. *Amer. sociol. Rev.*, 16:334–340.

LUCINA, M.: 1940. Sex differences in adolescent attitudes toward best friends. *Sch. Rev.*, 48:512–516.

LUNDBERG, G. A., and DICKSON, L.: 1952. Selection association among ethnic groups in a high school population. *Amer. sociol. Rev.*, 17:23–35.

LUNDEEN, G. E., and CALDWELL, C. W.: 1930. A study of unfounded beliefs among high-school seniors. *J. educ. Res.*, 22:257–273.

LUNGER, R., and PAGE, J. D.: 1939. Worries of college freshmen. *J. genet. Psychol.*, 54:457–460.

LURIE, O. R.: 1941. Psychological factors associated with eating difficulties in children. *Amer. J. Orthopsychiat.*, 11:452–466.

LYND, R. S., and LYND, H. M.: 1929. *Middletown.* New York: Harcourt, Brace.

MCANDREW, SISTER M. B.: 1943. An experimental investigation of young children's ideas of causality. *Stud. Psychol. Psychiat. Cath. Univ. Amer.*, 6, No. 2.

MACAULAY, E.: 1929. Some notes on the attitude of children to dress. *Brit. J. med. Psychol.*, 9:150–158.

MACAULAY, E., and WATKINS, S. H.: 1926. An investigation into the development of the moral conceptions of children. *Forum Educ.*, 4:13–32, 92–108.

McCANN, W. H.: 1941. Nostalgia: a review of the literature. *Psychol. Bull.*, 38:165–182.

McCANN, W. H.: 1943. Nostalgia: a descriptive and comparative study. *J. genet. Psychol.*, 62:97–104.

McCARTHY, D. A.: 1930. *The language development of the preschool child.* Minneapolis: Univ. Minnesota Press.

McCARTY, S. A.: 1924. *Children's drawings: a study of interests and activities.* Baltimore: Williams & Wilkins.

McCASKILL, C. L., and WELLMAN, B.: 1938. A study of common motor achievements at the preschool ages. *Child Develpm.*, 9:141–150.

McCUEN, T. L.: 1929. Leadership and intelligence. *Education*, 50:89–95.

MACDONALD, M., McGUIRE, C., and HAVINGHURST, R. J.: 1949. Leisure activities and the socioeconomic status of children. *Amer. J. Sociol.*, 54:505–519.

McFARLAND, M. B.: 1938. Relationships between young sisters as revealed in their overt responses. *Child Develpm. Monogr.*, No. 24.

McGINNIS, J. M.: 1930. Eye-movements and optic nystagmus in early infancy. *Genet. Psychol. Monogr.*, 8:321–430.

McGRAW, M. B.: 1931. A comparative study of a group of Southern white and Negro infants. *Genet. Psychol. Monogr.*, 10:1–105.

McGRAW, M. B.: 1932. From reflex to muscular control in the assumption of an erect posture and ambulation in the human infant. *Child Develpm.*, 3:291–297.

McGRAW, M. B.: 1935. *Growth: a study of Johnny and Jimmy.* New York: Appleton-Century-Crofts.

McGRAW, M. B.: 1939. Swimming behavior of the human infant. *J. Pediat.*, 15:485–490.

McGRAW, M. B.: 1940. Suspension grasp behavior of the human infant. *Amer. J. Dis. Child.*, 60:799–811.

McGRAW, M. B.: 1941. Development of the plantar response in healthy infants. *Amer. J. Dis. Child.*, 61:1215–1221.

McGRAW, M. B.: 1941a. Neural maturation as exemplified in the changing reactions of the infant to pin pricks. *Child Develpm.*, 12:31–42.

McKINNEY, F.: 1939. Personality adjustment of college students as related to factors in personal history. *J. appl. Psychol.*, 23:660–668.

MACKINTOSH, J. M.: 1947. Child guidance in old age. *Lancet*, 252:659–660.

McLAUGHLIN, SISTER M. A.: 1930. The genesis and constancy of ascendance and submission as personality traits. *Univ. Ia. Stud. Child Welf.*, 6, No. 5.

MACLEAN, A. H.: 1930. The idea of God in Protestant religious education. *Teach. Coll. Contr. Educ.*, No. 410.

MADDOCK, E.: 1947. A collection and analysis of conversational patterns of children. *Speech Monogr.*, 14:214–215.

MALAMUD, W.: 1942. Mental disorders of the aged: arteriosclerosis and senile psychoses. *Mental health in later maturity*, Suppl. No. 166, U.S. Publ. Hlth. Rep., pp. 104–110.

MALLER, J. B.: 1937. Juvenile delinquency in New York City: a summary of a comprehensive report. *J. Psychol.*, 3:1–25.

MALLINSON, G. G., and CRUMRINE, W. M.: 1952. An investigation of the stability of interests of high school students. *J. educ. Res.*, 45:369–384.

MALONEY, J. C.: 1948. Authoritarianism and intolerance. *Int. J. Psycho-anal.*, 29:236–239.

MALZBERG, B.: 1935. A statistical study of age in relation to mental disease. *Ment. Hyg., N.Y.,* 19:449–476.

MALZBERG, B.: 1948. Mental diseases among the aged in New York State. *Ment. Hyg., N.Y.,* 33:599–614.

MANGUS, A. R.: 1948. Personality adjustment of rural and urban children. *Amer. sociol. Rev.,* 13:566–575.

MARCUS, H.: 1927. Die Paradoxien Gefühls. *Z. angew. Psychol.,* 29:197–228.

MARKEY, F. V.: 1935. Imaginative behavior in preschool children. *Child Develpm. Monogr.,* No. 18.

MARSH, C. J.: 1942. The worries of the college woman. *J. soc. Psychol.,* 15:335–339.

MARTIN, A. R.: 1943. A study of parental attitudes and their influence upon personality development. *Education,* 63:596–608.

MARVIN, D.: 1938. Occupational propinquity in marriage selection. *In* Partridge, E. D., *Social psychology of adolescence.* New York: Prentice-Hall, pp. 187–188.

MASSLER, M., and SAVARA, B. S.: 1950. Natal and neonatal teeth. *J. Pediat.,* 36:349–359.

MATHER, W. G.: 1934. The courtship ideals of high-school youth. *Sociol. soc. Res.,* 19: 166–172.

MATTHEWS, S. M.: 1934. The effect of mothers' out-of-home employment upon children's ideas and attitudes. *J. appl. Psychol.,* 18:116–136.

MAUDRY, M., and NEKULA, M.: 1939. Social relations between children of the same age during the first ten years of life. *J. genet. Psychol.,* 54:193–215.

MAXWELL, C. H., and BROWN, W. P.: 1948. The age-incidence of defects in school children: their changing health status. *J. sch. Health,* 18:65–80.

MAYO, S. C.: 1951. Social participation among the older population in rural areas of Wake County, North Carolina. *Social Forces,* 30:53–59.

MEAD, M.: 1928. *Coming of age in Samoa.* New York: Morrow.

MEAD, M.: 1949. *Male and female.* New York: Morrow.

MEANS, M. H.: 1936. Fears of one thousand college women. *J. abnorm. soc. Psychol.,* 31:291–311.

MEEK, L. H.: 1940. *The personal-social development of boys and girls with implications for secondary education.* New York: Progressive Education Association, Committee on Workshops.

MEIER, N. C.: 1939. The graphic and allied arts. *Yearb. nat. Soc. Stud. Educ.,* 38:175–184.

MELCHER, R. T.: 1937. Development within the first two years of infants prematurely born. *Child Develpm.,* 8:1–14.

MELTZER, H.: 1933. Students' adjustments to anger. *J. soc. Psychol.,* 4:285–308.

MELVILLE, A. H.: 1912. An investigation of the function and use of slang. *Ped. Sem.,* 19:94–100.

MEREDITH, H. V.: 1935. The rhythm of physical growth. *Univ. Ia. Stud. Child Welf.,* 11, No. 3.

MEREDITH, H. V., and BROWN, A. W.: 1939. Growth in body weight during the first ten days of postnatal life. *Hum. Biol.,* 11:24–77.

MEYER, C. T.: 1947. The assertive behavior of children as related to parent behavior. *J. home Econ.,* 39:77–80.

MEYERS, C. E.: 1944. The effect of conflicting authority on the child. *Univ. Ia. Stud. Child Welf.,* 20:31–98.

MEYERS, C. E.: 1946. Emancipation of adolescents from parental control. *Nerv. Child,* 5:251–262.

MILES, C. C.: 1933. Age and certain personality traits of adults. *Psychol. Bull.,* 30:570.

MILES, C. C.: 1935. Sex in social psychology. *In* Murchison, C., *A handbook of social psychology,* Worcester: Clark Univ. Press, Chap. 16.

MILES, C. C., and MILES, W. R.: 1932. The correlation of intelligence scores and chronological age from early to late maturity. *Amer. J. Psychol.,* 44:44–78.

MILES, W. R.: 1931. Measures of certain abilities throughout the life span. *Proc. nat. Acad. Sci., Wash.,* 17:627–633.

MILES, W. R.: 1931a. Correlation of reaction and coordination speed with age in adults. *Amer. J. Psychol.,* 43:377–391.

MILES, W. R.: 1933. Age and human ability. *Psychol. Rev.,* 40:99–103.

MILES, W. R.: 1934. Age and kinephantom. *J. educ. Psychol.,* 10:204–207.

MILES, W. R.: 1935. Age and human society. *In* Murchison, C., *A handbook of social psychology.* Worcester: Clark Univ. Press, pp. 596–682.

MILLER, R. A.: 1936. The relation of reading characteristics and social indexes. *Amer. J. Sociol.,* 41:738–756.

MILLS, C. A.: 1950. Temperature influence over human growth and development. *Hum. Biol.,* 22:71–74.

MILLS, C. A., and OGLE, C.: 1936. The sterility of adolescence. *Hum. Biol.,* 8:607–615.

MINARD, R. D.: 1931. Race attitudes of Iowa children. *Univ. Ia. Stud. Charact.,* 4, No. 2.

MISSILDINE, W. H., and GLASNER, P. J.: 1947. Stuttering: a reorientation. *J. Pediat.,* 31: 300–305.

MOHR, G. J.: 1948. Psychosomatic problems in childhood. *Child Develpm.,* 19:137–142.

MOLILCH, M., and COUSINS, R. F.: 1934. Variations of basal metabolic rate per unit surface area with age. *J. Nutrit.,* 8:247–251.

MOORE, E. H.: 1948. Industrial workers in retirement. *Sociol. soc. Res.,* 32:691–696.

MOORE, H. T.: 1922. Further data concerning sex differences. *J. abnorm. soc. Psychol.,* 17:210–214.

MOORE, J. K.: 1948. Speech content of selected groups of orphanage and non-orphanage preschool children. *J. exp. Educ.,* 16:122–133.

MOORE, L. H.: 1935. Leadership traits of college women. *Sociol. soc. Res.,* 20:136–139.

MORGAN, C. M.: 1937. The attitudes and adjustments of recipients of old age assistance in upstate and metropolitan New York. *Arch. Psychol., N.Y.,* No. 214.

MORGAN, H. G.: 1946. Social relationships of children in a war-boom community. *J. educ. Res.,* 40:271–286.

MOTT, S. M.: 1937. Mother-father preference. *Character & Pers.,* 5:302–304.

MUHSAM, H. V.: 1947. Correlation in growth. *Hum. Biol.,* 19:260–269.

MULL, H. K.: 1947. A comparison of religious thinking of freshmen and seniors in a liberal arts college. *J. soc. Psychol.,* 26:121–123.

MULLEN, F. A.: 1950. Truancy and classroom disorders as symptoms of personality problems. *J. educ. Psychol.,* 41:97–109.

MUMMERY, D. V.: 1947. An analytical study of ascendant behavior in preschool children. *Child Develpm.,* 18:40–81.

MURPHY, D. P., SHIRLOCK, M. E., and DOLL, E. A.: 1942. Microcephaly following maternal pelvic irradiation for the interruption of pregnancy. *Amer. J. Roentgenology and Radium Therapy,* 48:356–359.

MURPHY, G., and MURPHY, L. B.: 1947. *Experimental social psychology.* New York: Harper.

MURPHY, L. B.: 1937. *Social behavior and child personality.* New York: Columbia Univ. Press.

MURRAY, H. A.: 1938. *Explorations in personality.* New York: Oxford.

MUSTE, M. J., and SHARPE, D. F.: 1947. Some influential factors in the determination of aggressive behavior in preschool children. *Child Develpm.,* 18:11–18.

MYERS, R. J.: 1949. War and postwar experience in regard to the sex ratios at birth in various countries. *Hum. Biol.,* 21:257–259.

MYERS, R. J.: 1949a. Same-sexed families. *J. Hered.,* 40:268–270.

NATIONAL CONFERENCE ON AGING: 1951. *Man and his years.* Raleigh, N.C.: Health Publications Institute, Inc.

NATIONAL RECREATION ASSOCIATION REPORT: 1935. *The leisure hours of 5,000 people.* New York: National Recreation Association.

NEILON, P.: 1948. Shirley's babies after fifteen years: a personality study. *J. genet. Psychol.,* 73:175–186.

NEUBERGER, M.: 1947. The Latin poet Maximianus on the miseries of old age. *Bull. hist. Med.,* 21:113–119.

NEWBERRY, H.: 1941. The measurement of three types of fetal activity. *J. comp. Psychol.,* 32:521–530.

NEWMAN, H. H., FREEMAN, F. N., and HOLZINGER, J. K.: 1937. *Twins: a study of heredity and environment.* Chicago: Univ. Chicago Press.

NICE, M. M.: 1925. Length of sentence as a criterion of a child's progress in speech. *J. educ. Psychol.,* 16:370–379.

NICE, M. M.: 1933. A child's attainment of the sentence. *J. genet. Psychol.,* 42:216–224.

NIMKOFF, M. F.: 1942. The child's preference for father or mother. *Amer. sociol. Rev.,* 7:517–524.

NOBLE, G. V., and LUND, S. B. T.: 1951. High school pupils report their fears. *J. educ. Psychol.,* 25:97–101.

NORVAL, M. A.: 1946. Sucking responses of newly born babies at breast. *Amer. J. Dis. Child.,* 71:41–44.

OAKLEY, C. A.: 1940. Drawings of a man by adolescents. *Brit. J. Psychol.,* 31:37–60.

OESTING, R. B., and WEBSTER, F.: 1938. The sex hormone excretion of children. *Endocrinology,* 22:307–314.

OJ'EMANN, R. H.: 1934. The measurement of attitude toward self-reliance. Researches in parent education. III. *Univ. Ia. Stud. Child Welf.,* 10:103–111, 345–356.

OLIVER, J.: 1950. Structural aspects of the process of aging. *In* New York Academy of Medicine, *The social and biological challenge of our aging population.* New York: Columbia Univ. Press, pp. 25–43.

OLNEY, E. E., and CUSHING, H. M.: 1935. A brief report of the responses of preschool children to commercially available pictorial material. *Child Develpm.,* 65:52–55.

ORGEL, S. Z., and TUCKMAN, J.: 1935. Nicknames of institutional children. *Amer. J. Orthopsychiat.,* 5:276–285.

ORR, A. E., and BROWN, F. J.: 1932. A study of out-of-school activities of high-school girls. *J. educ. Sociol.,* 5:266–273.

OVERHOLSER, W.: 1942. *"Orientation"—mental health in later maturity,* Suppl. No. 168, U.S. Publ. Hlth. Rep., pp. 3–5.

PAGE, M. L.: 1936. The modification of ascendant behavior in preschool children. *Univ. Ia. Stud. Child Welf.,* 12, No. 3.

PARKER, V. H.: 1938. What young people want to know about sex. *Child Study,* 16:88–98.

PARTEN, M. B.: 1933. Social play among preschool children. *J. abnorm. soc. Psychol.,* 28:136–147.

PARTRIDGE, E. D.: 1934. Leadership among adolescent boys. *Teach. Coll. Contr. Educ.,* No. 608.

PARTRIDGE, E. D.: 1938. *Social psychology of adolescence.* New York: Prentice-Hall.

PASAMANICK, B.: 1946. A comparative study of the behavioral development of Negro infants. *J. genet. Psychol.,* 69:3–44.

PEARL, R.: 1930. Alcohol: biological aspects. In *Encyclopedia of the social sciences.* New York: Macmillan, pp. 620–622.

PEATMAN, J. G., and HIGGONS, R. A.: 1940. Development of sitting, standing, and walking of children reared with optimal pediatric care. *Amer. J. Orthopsychiat.,* 10:88–110.

PECHSTEIN, L. A., and MUNN, M. D.: 1939. The measurement of social maturity in children. *Elem. Sch. J.,* 40:113–123.

PEOPLE'S LEAGUE OF HEALTH, INTERIM REPORT: 1942. Nutrition of expectant and nursing mothers. *Lancet,* 2:10–12.

PETERSON, F., and RAINEY, L. H.: 1910. *Beginnings of mind in the newborn.* New York: Bulletin of the Lying-in Hospital of the City of New York.

PHILLIPS, W. S., and GREENE, J. E.: 1939. A preliminary study of the relationship of age, hobbies, and civil status to neuroticism among women teachers. *J. educ. Psychol.,* 30:440–444.

PHIPPS, M. J.: 1949. Some factors influencing what children know about human growth. *Amer. Psychologist,* 4:391–392.

PIAGET, J.: 1929. *The child's conception of the world.* New York: Harcourt, Brace.

PINTNER, R., and FORLANO, G.: 1933. The influence of month of birth on intelligence quotients. *J. educ. Psychol.,* 24:561–584.

PINTNER, R., and FORLANO, G.: 1934. The birth month of eminent men. *J. appl. Psychol.,* 18:178–188.

PINTNER, R., and FORLANO, G.: 1939. Season of birth and intelligence. *J. genet. Psychol.,* 54:353–358.

PINTNER, R., and FORLANO, G.: 1943. Season of birth and mental differences. *Psychol. Bull.,* 40:25–35.

PINTNER, R., FORLANO, G., and FREEDMAN, H.: 1937. Personality and attitudinal similarity among classroom friends. *J. appl. Psychol.,* 21:48–65.

PINTNER, R., and LEV, G.: 1940. Worries of school children. *J. genet. Psychol.,* 56:67–76.

PIXLEY, E., and BECKMAN, E.: 1949. The faith of youth as shown by a survey in public schools of Los Angeles. *Relig. Educ.,* 44:336–342.

PLANT, J. S.: 1941. Negativism: its treatment and its implications. *Amer. J. Dis. Child.,* 61:358–368.

POLLAK, O.: 1943. Conservatism in later maturity and old age. *Amer. sociol. Rev.,* 8:175–179.

POLLAK, O.: 1950. The older worker in the labor market. *In* Derber, M., *The aged and society.* Champaign, Ill.: Individual Relations Research Assoc., pp. 56–64.

POLLAK, O., and HEATHERS, G.: 1948. *Social adjustment in old age.* New York: Social Science Research Council, Bull. 59.

POPE, C.: 1943. Personal problems of high school pupils. *Sch. & Soc.,* 57:443–448.

POPENOE, P.: 1932. How can young people get acquainted? *J. soc. Hyg.,* 18:218–224.

PRATT, K. C.: 1934. The effects of repeated auditory stimulation upon the general activity of newborn infants. *J. genet. Psychol.,* 44:96–116.

PRATT, K. C.: 1945. A study of the "fears" of rural children. *J. genet. Psychol.,* 67:179–194.

PRATT, K. C., NELSON, A. K., and SUN, K. H.: 1930. *The behavior of the newborn.* Columbus: Ohio State Univ. Press.

PRESSEY, L. C.: 1929. *Some college students and their problems.* Columbus: Ohio State Univ. Press.

PRESSEY, S. L.: 1951. Differentia of success in old age. *Amer. Psychologist,* 5:369.

PRESSEY, S. L., and ROBINSON, F. P.: 1944. *Psychology and the new education.* New York: Harper.

PRESTON, M. I.: 1940. Physical complaints without organic basis. *J. Pediat.,* 17:279–304.

PREYER, W.: 1888. *The mind of the child.* New York: Appleton-Century-Crofts.

PRONKO, N. H., BOWLES, W. J., SNYDER, F. W., and SYNOLDS, D. L.: 1949. An experiment in pursuit of "color blindness." *J. genet. Psychol.,* 74:125–142.

PRYOR, H. B.: 1936. Certain physical and physiological aspects of adolescent development in girls. *J. Pediat.,* 8:52–62.

PUNKE, H. H.: 1936. Leisure-time attitudes and activities of high-school students. *Sch. & Soc.,* 43:884–888.

PUNKE, H. H.: 1944. Dating practices of high-school youth. *Bull. nat. Ass. Second. Sch. Princ.*, 28, No. 119.

PUNKE, H. H.: 1950. Neglected social values of prolonged human infancy. *Sch. & Soc.*, 71:369–372.

RABBAN, M.: 1950. Sex-role identification in young children in two diverse social groups. *Genet. Psychol. Monogr.*, 42:81–158.

RADKE, M. J.: 1946. *The relation of parental authority to children's behavior and attitudes.* Minneapolis: Univ. Minnesota Press.

RADKE, M. J., and SUTHERLAND, J.: 1949. Children's concepts and attitudes about minority and majority American groups. *J. educ. Psychol.*, 40:449–468.

RADKE, M. J., TRAGER, H. G., and DAVIS, H.: 1949. Social perceptions and attitudes of children. *Genet. Psychol. Monogr.*, 40:327–447.

RAINEY, H. P., BRANDON, A. L., and CHAMBERS, M. M.: *How fare American youth?* New York: Appleton-Century-Crofts.

RAMSEY, G. V.: 1943. The sex information of younger boys. *Amer. J. Orthopsychiat.*, 13:347–352.

RAMSEY, G. V.: 1943a. The sexual development of boys. *Amer. J. Psychol.*, 56:217–233.

RAMSEY, G. V.: 1950. Sexual growth of Negro and white boys. *Hum. Biol.*, 22:146–149.

RAND, W., SWEENY, M. E., and VINCENT, E. L.: 1942. *Growth and development of the young child.* Philadelphia: Saunders.

RAPP, G. W., and RICHARDSON, J. C.: 1952. A salivary test for prenatal sex determination. *Science,* 115:265.

RARICK, G. L., and McKEE, R.: 1949. A study of twenty third-grade children exhibiting extreme levels of achievement on tests of motor proficiency. *Res. Quart. Amer. Ass. Health,* 20:142–152.

RATCLIFF, J. D.: 1950. Miscarriage. *Woman's Home Companion,* December, pp. 42, 75.

RAUTH, J. E., and FURFEY, P. H.: 1932. Developmental age and adolescence. *J. soc. Psychol.,* 3:469–472.

RAVEN, J. C.: 1948. The comparative assessment of intellectual ability. *Brit. J. Psychol.,* 39:12–19.

REANY, M. J.: 1916. The psychology of the organized group game. *Brit. J. Psychol., Monogr. Suppl.,* No. 4.

REID, J. W.: 1951. Stability of measured Kuder interests in young adults. *J. educ. Res.,* 45:307–312.

REMMERS, H. H., MYERS, M. S., and BENNETT, E. M.: 1951. Some personality aspects and religious values of high school youth. *Purdue Opin. Panel,* 10, No. 3.

REMMERS, H. H., and WELTMAN, N.: 1947. Attitude, inter-relationships of youth, their parents, and their teachers. *J. soc. Psychol.,* 26:61–68.

REMMERS, H. H., WHISLER, L., and DUVALD, V. F.: 1938. "Neurotic" indicators at the adolescent level. *J. soc. Psychol.,* 9:17–24.

REMMLEIN, M. K.: 1938. Analysis of leaders among high school seniors. *J. exp. Educ.,* 6:413–422.

REYNOLD, E. E.: 1949. The fat/bone index as a sex determinating character in man. *Hum. Biol.,* 21:199–204.

REYNOLDS, E.: 1946. Sexual maturation and the growth of fat, muscle, and bone in girls. *Child Develpm.,* 17:121–144.

REYNOLDS, F. J.: 1944. Factors of leadership among seniors of Central High School, Tulsa, Oklahoma. *J. educ. Res.,* 37:356–361.

REYNOLDS, M. M., and MALLAY, H.: 1933. The sleep of young children. *J. genet. Psychol.,* 43:322–351.

RIBBLE, M. A.: 1943. *The rights of infants.* New York: Columbia Univ. Press.

RICCIUTI, P. A.: 1951. Children and radio: a study of listeners and non-listeners to various types of radio programs in terms of selective ability, attitude, and behavior measures. *Genet. Psychol. Monogr.*, 44:69–143.

RICHARDS, T. W.: 1936. The importance of hunger in the bodily activity of the neonate. *Psychol. Bull.*, 33:817–835.

RICHARDS, T. W., and NEWBERRY, H.: 1938. Can performance on test items at six months be predicted on the basis of fetal activity? *Child Develpm.*, 9:79–86.

RICHARDS, T. W., NEWBERRY, H., and FALLGATLER, R.: 1938. Studies in fetal behavior. II. Activity of the human fetus in utero and the relation to other prenatal conditions, particularly the mother's basal metabolic rate. *Child Develpm.*, 9:69–72, 79–86.

RICHARDSON, B. E.: 1933. *Old age among the ancient Greeks*. Baltimore: Johns Hopkins Press.

RICHARDSON, H. M.: 1939. Studies of mental resemblance between husbands and wives and between friends. *Psychol. Bull.*, 36:194–220.

RICHEY, R. G.: 1937. The relation of accelerated, normal, and retarded puberty to the height and weight of school children. *Monogr. Soc. Res. Child Developm.*, 2, No. 1.

RICKETTS, A. F.: 1934. A study of the behavior of young children in anger. *Univ. Ia. Stud. Child Welf.*, 9, No. 3:161–171.

RIEMER, M. D.: 1949. The effect on character development of prolonged or frequent absence of parents. *Ment. Hyg., N.Y.*, 33:293–297.

RIESS, B. F., and DECILLIS, O.: 1940. Personality differences in allergic and nonallergic children. *J. abnorm. soc. Psychol.*, 35:104–113.

ROCKWOOD, L. D., and FORD, M. E. N.: 1945. *Youth, marriage, and parenthood*. New York: Wiley.

ROETHLISBERGER, F. J., and DICKSON, W. J.: 1943. *Management and the worker*. Cambridge: Harvard Univ. Press.

ROGERS, R. H., and AUSTIN, O. L.: 1934. Intelligence quotients of juvenile delinquents. *J. juv. Res.*, 18:103–106.

ROSANDER, A. C.: 1939. Age and sex patterns of social attitudes. *J. educ. Psychol.*, 30: 481–496.

ROSE, A. A.: 1947. A study of homesickness in college freshmen. *J. soc. Psychol.*, 26:185–203.

ROSS, B. M.: 1930. Some traits associated with sibling jealousy in problem children. *Smith Coll. Stud. soc. Work*, 1:364–376.

ROSS, C. L.: 1928. Interests of adults and high school pupils in newspaper reading. *Sch. & Soc.*, 27:212–214.

ROSS, E. A.: 1917. *Social psychology*. New York: Macmillan.

ROTH, J., and PECK, R. F.: 1951. Social class and social mobility factors related to marital adjustment. *Amer. sociol. Rev.*, 16:478–487.

ROTHNEY, J. W. M.: 1937. Interests of public secondary-school boys. *J. educ. Psychol.*, 28:561–594.

ROUSSEAU, J. J.: 1911. *Émile, or education*. New York: Dutton.

ROWAN-LEGG, C. E.: 1949. Self-demand feeding of infants. *Canad. med. Ass. J.*, 60:388–391.

RUBIN-RABSON, G.: 1940. The influence of age, intelligence, and training on reactions to classic and modern music. *J. genet. Psychol.*, 22:413–429.

RUBINOV, O.: 1933. The course of man's life—a psychological problem. *J. abnorm. soc. Psychol.*, 28:206–215.

RUCH, F. L.: 1933. Adult learning. *Psychol. Bull.*, 30:387–411.

RUCH, F. L.: 1934. The differentiative effects of age upon human learning. *J. genet. Psychol.*, 11:261–286.

RUGG, H., KRUEGER, L., and SONDERGAARD, K.: 1929. A study of the language of kindergarten children. *J. educ. Psychol.,* 20:1–18.

RUJA, H.: 1948. The relation between neonate crying and length of labor. *J. genet. Psychol.,* 73:53–55.

RUNNER, J. R.: 1937. Social distance in adolescent relationships. *Amer. J. Sociol.,* 43: 428–439.

RUST, M. M.: 1931. The effect of resistance on intelligence test scores of young children. *Child Develpm. Monogr.,* No. 6.

SCAMMON, R. E., and CALKINS, L. A.: 1929. *The development and growth of the external dimensions of the human body in the foetal period.* Minneapolis: Univ. Minnesota Press.

SCHALTENBRAND, C.: 1928. The development of human motility and motor disturbances. *Arch. Neurol. Psychiat., Chicago,* 20:720–730.

SCHMEIDLER, G. R.: 1941. The relation of fetal activity to the activity of the mother. *Child Develpm.,* 12:63–68.

SCHMIDT, J. F.: 1951. Pattern of poor adjustment in old age. *Amer. J. Sociol.,* 57:33–42.

SCHONFELD, W. A.: 1943. Primary and secondary sexual characteristics. *Amer. J. Dis. Child.,* 65:535–549.

SCHONFELD, W. A.: 1950. Inadequate masculine physique as a factor in personality development of adolescent boys. *Psychosom. Med.,* 12:49–54.

SCOTT, C.: 1896. Old age and death. *Amer. J. Psychol.,* 8:67–122.

SCOTT, R. B., et al.: 1950. Growth and development of Negro infants. III. Growth during the first year of life as observed in private pediatric practice. *J. Pediat.,* 37:885–893.

SEAGOE, M. V.: 1931. The child's reactions to the movies. *J. juv. Res.,* 15:169–180.

SEAGOE, M. V.: 1933. Factors influencing the selection of associates. *J. educ. Res.,* 27:32–40.

SEARS, P.: 1951. Doll-play aggression in normal young children: influence of sex, age, sibling status, father's absence. *Psychol. Monogr.,* 65, No. 4.

SEARS, R.: 1950. Ordinal position in the family as a psychological variable. *Amer. J. Sociol.,* 15:397–401.

SEDER, M.: 1940. Vocational interests of professional women. *J. appl. Psychol.,* 24:130–143, 265–272.

SEIDENFELD, M. A.: 1944. Measuring mental competency in the aging. *Amer. J. Orthopsychiat.,* 14:273–276.

SELLING, L. S.: 1944. Old age from the standpoint of the traffic situation. *Amer. J. Orthopsychiat.,* 14:276–279.

SEWALL, M.: 1930. Two studies in sibling rivalry. 1. Some causes of jealousy in young children. *Smith Coll. Stud. soc. Work,* 31:1, 6–22.

SEWARD, G. H.: 1944. Psychological effects of the menstrual cycle on women workers. *Psychol. Bull.,* 41:90–102.

SEWARD, G. H.: 1945. Cultural conflict and the feminine role: an experimental study. *J. soc. Psychol.,* 22:177–194.

SEWARD, G. H.: 1946. *Sex and the social order.* New York: McGraw-Hill.

SEWARD, J. P., and SEWARD, G. H.: 1934. The effect of repetition on reactions to electric shock with special reference to the menstrual cycle. *Arch. Psychol., N.Y.,* No. 168.

SEWARD, J. P., and SEWARD, G. H.: 1937. Psychological effects of estrogenic hormone therapy in the menopause. *J. comp. Psychol.,* 24:377–392.

SHANAS, E.: 1951. The personal adjustment of recipients of old age assistance with special consideration of the methodology of questionnaire studies of older people. (Summarized by Schmidt, 1951.)

SHANNON, J. R.: 1929. The post-school careers of high-school leaders and high-school scholars. *Sch. Rev.,* 37:656–665.

SHERIF, M., and CANTRIL, H.: 1947. *The psychology of ego-involvements.* New York: Wiley.

SHERMAN, A. W.: 1948. Personality factors in the psychological weaning of college women. *Educ. and psychol. Measurement,* 8:249–256.

SHERMAN, M., and SHERMAN, I. C.: 1925. Sensori-motor responses in infants. *J. comp. Psychol.,* 5:53–68.

SHERMAN, M., and SHERMAN, I. C.: 1929. *The process of human development.* New York: Norton.

SHIRLEY, M. M.: 1931. *The first two years of life.* Minneapolis: Univ. Minnesota Press, Vol. 1.

SHIRLEY, M. M.: 1933. *The first two years: personality manifestations.* Minneapolis: Univ. Minnesota Press, Vol. 3.

SHIRLEY, M. M.: 1938. Development of immature babies during their first two years. *Child Develpm.,* 9:347–360.

SHIRLEY, M. M.: 1939. A behavior syndrome characterizing prematurely born children. *Child Develpm.,* 10:115–128.

SHIRLEY, M. M.: 1941. The impact of the mother's personality on the young child. *Smith Coll. Stud. soc. Work,* 12:15–64.

SHOCK, N. W.: 1944. Physiological changes in adolescence. *43d Yearb. nat. Soc. Stud. Educ.,* 56–79.

SHOCK, N. W.: 1945. Creatine excretion in adolescents. *Child Develpm.,* 16:167–180.

SHOCK, N. W.: 1947. Physiological factors in development. *Rev. educ. Res.,* 17:362–370.

SHOCK, N. W.: 1948. Metabolism in old age. *Bull. N.Y. Acad. Med.,* 24:166–178.

SHOCK, N. W.: 1951. *Trends in gerontology.* Stanford, Calif.: Stanford Univ. Press.

SHULMAN, H. M.: 1949. The family and the juvenile delinquent. *Ann. Amer. Acad. polit. Sci.,* 261:21–31.

SHUTTLEWORTH, F. K.: 1937. Sexual maturation and the physical growth age six to nineteen. *Monogr. Soc. Res. Child Develpm.,* 2, No. 5.

SHUTTLEWORTH, F. K.: 1938. Sexual maturation and skeletal growth of girls age six to nineteen. *Monogr. Soc. Res. Child Develpm.,* 3, No. 5.

SHUTTLEWORTH, F. K.: 1939. The physical and mental growth of girls and boys age six to nineteen in relation to age at maximum growth. *Monogr. Soc. Res. Child Develpm.,* 4, No. 3.

SHUTTLEWORTH, F. K.: 1949. The adolescent period: a graphic atlas. *Monogr. Soc. Res. Child Develpm.,* 14, No. 1.

SILK, L.: 1952. The housing circumstances of the aged in the United States. *J. Geront.,* 7:87–91.

SILVERMAN, S. S.: 1945. Clothing and appearance: their psychological significance for teen-age girls. *Teach. Coll. Contr. Educ.,* No. 912.

SIMMONS, K.: 1944. The Brush Foundation study of child growth and development. *Monogr. Soc. Res. Child Develpm.,* 9, No. 1.

SIMMONS, L. W.: 1945. *The role of the aged in primitive society.* New Haven: Yale Univ. Press.

SIMPSON, M.: 1935. *Parent preferences of young children.* New York: Teachers College, Columbia Univ.

SLOANE, A. E., and GALLAGHER, J. R.: 1950. Changes in vision during adolescence. *J. Ophthalmol.,* 33:1538–1542.

SMITH, C. A.: 1947. Effects of maternal undernutrition upon the newborn infant in Holland, 1944–1945. *J. Pediat.,* 30:229–243.

SMITH, G. F.: 1924. Certain aspects of the sex life of the adolescent girl. *J. appl. Psychol.*, 8:347–349.

SMITH, H.: 1931. Families with ambitions unsuitable for their children. *Smith Coll. Stud. soc. Work,* 1:406.

SMITH, J. M.: 1936. The relative brightness values of three lines for newborn infants. *Univ. Ia. Stud. Child Welf.,* 12:93–140.

SMITH, M., and NYSTROM, W. O.: 1937. A study of social participation and of leisure time of leaders and non-leaders. *J. appl. Psychol.,* 8:347–349.

SMITH, M. E.: 1926. An investigation of the development of the sentence and the extent of vocabulary in young children. *Univ. Ia. Stud. Child Welf.,* 3, No. 5.

SMITH, M. E.: 1932. The preschool child's use of criticism. *Child Develpm.,* 3:137–141.

SMITH, M. E.: 1933. The influence of age, sex, and situation on the frequency, form, and function of questions asked by preschool children. *Child Develpm.,* 4:201–213.

SMITH, M. E.: 1935. A study of the speech of eight bilingual children of the same family. *Child Develpm.,* 6:19–25.

SMITH, M. E.: 1949. Measurement of vocabularies of young bilingual children in both the languages used. *J. genet. Psychol.,* 74:305–310.

SOLOMON, P.: 1948. Emotional maturity. *Ann. West. Med. Surg.,* 2:12–15.

SONTAG, L. W.: 1940. Effect of fetal activity on the nutritional state of the infant at birth. *Amer. J. Dis. Child.,* 60:621–630.

SONTAG, L. W.: 1941. The significance of fetal environment. *Amer. J. Obstet. Gynaec.,* 42: 996–1003.

SONTAG, L. W.: 1946. Some psychosomatic aspects of childhood. *Nerv. Child,* 5:296–304.

SONTAG, L. W., and RICHARDS, T. W.: 1938. Studies in fetal behavior. 1. Fetal heart rate as a behavioral indicator. *Monogr. Soc. Res. Child Develpm.,* 3, No. 4.

SONTAG, L. W., and WALLACE, R. F.: 1934. Preliminary report of the Fels Foundation: study of fetal activity. *Amer. J. Dis. Child.,* 48:1050–1057.

SONTAG, L. W., and WALLACE, R. F.: 1936. Changes in the rate of the human fetal heart in response to vibratory stimuli. *Amer. J. Dis. Child.,* 51:583–589.

SOWERS, A.: 1937. Parent-child relationships from the child's point of view. *J. exp. Educ.,* 6:205–231.

SPAULDING, C. B.: 1933. Types of junior-college leaders. *Sociol. soc. Res.,* 18:164–168.

SPIEGEL, L. A.: 1950. The child's concept of beauty: a study in concept formation. *J. genet. Psychol.,* 77:11–23.

SPITZ, R. A.: 1946. The smiling response: a contribution to the ontogenesis of social relations. *Genet. Psychol. Monogr.,* 34:57–125.

SPITZ, R. A.: 1949. The role of ecological factors in emotional development in infancy. *Child Develpm.,* 20:145–155.

SPRAGUE, E. M.: 1929. *Conversational contacts of nineteen nursery school children.* New York: Columbia Univ. (Unpublished master's essay.)

SPRINGER, D. V.: 1950. Awareness of racial differences by preschool children in Hawaii. *Genet. Psychol. Monogr.,* 41:215–270.

SPRINGER, D. V.: 1951. Development of concepts related to the clock as shown in young children's drawings. *J. genet. Psychol.,* 79:47–54.

SPRINGER, N. N.: 1938. The influence of general social status on the emotional stability of children. *J. genet. Psychol.,* 53:321–327.

STAGNER, R.: 1935. Economic status and personality. *Sch. & Soc.,* 42:551–552.

STAGNER, R.: 1948. *Psychology of personality,* 2d ed. New York: McGraw-Hill.

STAGNER, R., and KATZOFF, E.: 1936. Personality as related to birth order and family size. *J. appl. Psychol.,* 20:340–346.

STAPLES, R.: 1932. The response of infants to color. *J. exp. Psychol.,* 15:119–142.

STECKEL, M. A.: 1929. Intelligence and birth order in family. *J. educ. Psychol.,* 20:641–642.

STENDLER, C. B.: 1949. A study of some socio-moral judgments of junior high school students. *Child Develpm.*, 20:15–28.

STENDLER, C. B.: 1952. Critical periods in socialization and overdependency. *Child Develpm.*, 23:3–12.

STERN, E. M., and ROSS, M.: 1952. *You and your aging parents.* New York: Wyn.

STIEGLITZ, E. J.: 1950. Orientation in gerontology. *In* N.Y. Acad. Med., *Biological foundations of health education.* New York: Columbia Univ. Press, pp. 96–116.

STOCKARD, C. R.: 1931. *The physiological basis of personality.* New York: Norton.

STOGDILL, R. M.: 1937. Survey of experiments of children's attitudes toward parental control and the social adjustments of children. *J. appl. Psychol.*, 51:293–303.

STOKE, S. M., and CLINE, W. F.: 1929. The avocations of one hundred college freshmen. *J. appl. Psychol.*, 13:257–265.

STOKE, S. M., and WEST, E. D.: 1930. The conversational interests of college students. *Sch. & Soc.*, 32:567–570.

STOKE, S. M., and WEST, E. D.: 1931. Sex differences in conversational interests. *J. soc. Psychol.*, 2:120–126.

STOKES, A. B.: 1948. Old age from the psychiatric viewpoint. *Canad. med. Assoc. J.*, 59:518–521.

STOLZ, H. R., JONES, M. C., and CHAFFEY, J.: 1937. The junior-high-school age. *Univ. high Sch. J., Calif.*, 15:63–72.

STOLZ, H. R., and STOLZ, L. M.: 1944. Adolescent problems related to somatic variations. *43d Yearb. nat. Soc. Stud. Educ.*, 80–99.

STOLZ, H. R., and STOLZ, L. M.: 1951. *Somatic development of adolescent boys.* New York: Macmillan.

STONE, C. P., and BARKER, R. G.: 1934. On the relationship between menarcheal age and certain aspects of personality, intelligence, and physique in college women. *J. genet. Psychol.*, 45:121–135.

STONE, C. P., and BARKER, R. G.: 1937. Aspects of personality and intelligence in postmenarcheal and premenarcheal girls of the same chronological age. *J. comp. Psychol.*, 23:439–455.

STONE, C. P., and BARKER, R. G.: 1939. The attitudes and interests of premenarcheal and postmenarcheal girls. *J. genet. Psychol.*, 54:27–71.

STOTT, L. H.: 1938. An analytical study of self-reliance. *J. Psychol.*, 5:107–118.

STOTT, L. H.: 1939. Personality development in farm, small-town, and city children. *Univ. Neb. Agr. Exper. Sta. Res. Bull.*, No. 114.

STOTT, L. H.: 1940. General home setting as a factor in the study of the only versus the non-only child. *Character & Pers.*, 8:156–162.

STOTT, L. H.: 1940a. Parental attitudes of farm, town, and city parents in relation to certain personality adjustments in their children. *J. soc. Psychol.*, 11:325–339.

STOTT, L. H.: 1940b. Home punishments of adolescents. *J. genet. Psychol.*, 57:415–428.

STOUFFER, G. A. W.: 1952. Behavior problems of children as viewed by teachers and mental hygienists. *Ment. Hyg., N.Y.*, 36:271–285.

STOUGHTON, M. L., and RAY, A. M.: 1946. A study of children's heroes and ideals. *J. exp. Educ.*, 15:156–160.

STOUT, I. W., and LANGDON, G.: 1951. A study of the home life of well-adjusted children in three areas of the United States. *J. educ. Sociol.*, 25:67–85.

STRANG, R.: 1931. Knowledge of social usage in junior- and senior-high schools. *Sch. & Soc.*, 34:709–712.

STRANG, R.: 1938. *An introduction to child study*, rev. ed. New York: Macmillan.

STRANG, R.: 1943. Why children read the comics. *Elem. Sch. J.*, 43:336–342.

STRANG, R.: 1951. What discipline means to adolescents. *Nerv. Child*, 9:139–146.

STRATTON, G. M.: 1927. Anger and fear: their probable relation to each other, to intellectual work, and to primogeniture. *Amer. J. Psychol.,* 39:125–140.

STRAY, H. F.: 1933. Leadership traits of girls in girls' camps. *Sociol. soc. Res.,* 18:241–250.

STRONG, E. K.: 1931. *Changes in interest with age.* Stanford University, Calif.: Stanford Univ. Press.

STRONG, E. K.: 1936. Interests of men and women. *J. soc. Psychol.,* 7:49–67.

STRONG, E. K.: 1951. Permanence of interest scores over 22 years. *J. appl. Psychol.,* 35: 89–91.

STUART, J. C.: 1926. Data on the alleged psychopathology of the only child. *J. abnorm. soc. Psychol.,* 20:441–445.

STUTSMAN, R.: 1935. Constancy in personality trends. *Psychol. Bull.,* 32:701–702.

SULLENGER, T. E.: 1930. Modern youth and the movies. *Sch. & Soc.,* 32:459–461.

SULLENGER, T. E.: 1934. Economic status as a factor in juvenile delinquency. *J. juv. Res.,* 18:233–245.

SULLENGER, T. E.: 1938. Extracurricular leisure time activities. *Recreation,* 32:509–510.

SULLIVAN, SISTER C.: 1934. A scale for measuring developmental age in girls. *Stud. Psychol. Psychiat. Cathol. Univ. Amer.,* 3, No. 4.

SUPER, D. E.: 1939. Occupational level and job satisfaction. *J. appl. Psychol.,* 23:547–564.

SUPER, D. E.: 1941. Avocational and vocational adjustment. *Character & Pers.,* 10:51–61.

SUTLIFF, W. D., and HOLT, E.: 1925. The age curve of pulse rate under basal conditions. *Arch. intern. Med.,* 35:224.

SWARD, K.: 1931. Temperament and religious experience. *J. soc. Psychol.,* 2:374–396.

SWARD, K.: 1933. Temperament and direction of achievement. *J. abnorm. soc. Psychol.,* 4:406–429.

SWEET, C.: 1946. Enuresis: a psychologic problem of childhood. *J. Amer. med. Ass.,* 32:279–281.

SYMONDS, P. M.: 1935. Seriousness of personal problems of adolescents and degree of interest in these problems. *Psychol. Bull.,* 32:707–708.

SYMONDS, P. M.: 1936. Comparison of the problems and interests of young adolescents living in city and country. *J. educ. Sociol.,* 10:231–236.

SYMONDS, P. M.: 1936a. Changes in problems and interests with increasing age. *Psychol. Bull.,* 33:789.

SYMONDS, P. M.: 1936b. Life problems and interests of adults. *Teach. Coll. Rec.,* 38:144–151.

SYMONDS, P. M.: 1937. Changes in sex differences in problems and interests of adolescents with increasing age. *J. genet. Psychol.,* 50:83–89.

SYMONDS, P. M.: 1937a. Happiness as related to problems and interests. *J. educ. Psychol.,* 28:290–294.

SYMONDS, P. M.: 1938. A study of parental acceptance and rejection. *Amer. J. Orthopsychiat.,* 8:679–688.

SYMONDS, P. M.: 1945. Inventory of themes in adolescent fantasy. *Amer. J. Orthopsychiat.,* 15:318–328.

SYMONDS, P. M.: 1949. *Adolescent fantasy: an investigation of the picture-story method of personality study.* New York: Columbia Univ. Press.

SYNOLDS, D. L., and PRONKO, N. H.: 1949. An exploratory study of color discrimination of children. *J. genet. Psychol.,* 74:17–21.

TAYLOR, K. VON F., and CARTER, H. D.: 1942. Retest consistency of vocational interest patterns of high school girls. *J. consult. Psychol.,* 6:95–101.

TELFORD, C. W.: 1950. A study of religious attitudes. *J. soc. Psychol.,* 31:217–230.

TER KEURST, A. J.: 1939. The acceptance of superstitious beliefs among secondary school pupils. *J. educ. Res.,* 32:673–685.

TERMAN, L. M.: 1922. *The measurement of intelligence.* Boston: Houghton Mifflin.

TERMAN, L. M.: 1926. *Genetic studies of genius.* Stanford University, Calif.: Stanford Univ. Press, Vol. 2.

TERMAN, L. M., and BUTTENWIESER, P.: 1935. Personality factors in marital compatability. *J. soc. Psychol.,* 6:143–176.

TERMAN, L. M., BUTTENWIESER, P., FERGUSON, L. W., and JOHNSON, W. B.: 1938. *Psychological factors in marital happiness.* New York: McGraw-Hill.

TERMAN, L. M., and LIMA, M.: 1927. *Children's reading.* New York: Appleton-Century-Crofts.

TERMAN, L. M., and MERRILL, M. A.: 1937. *Measuring intelligence.* Boston: Houghton Mifflin.

TERMAN, L. M., and MILES, C. C.: 1936. *Sex and personality.* New York: McGraw-Hill.

TERMAN, L. M., and ODEN, M. H.: 1947. *The gifted child grows up.* Stanford University, Calif.: Stanford Univ. Press.

THOMPSON, G. G., and WITRYOL, S. L.: 1948. Adult recall of unpleasant experiences during three periods of childhood. *J. genet. Psychol.,* 72:111–123.

THOMPSON, H.: 1936. Sleep requirements during infancy. *Psychol. Monogr.,* 47:212.

THORNDIKE, E. L.: 1921. The correlation between interests and abilities in college courses. *Psychol. Rev.,* 28:374–376.

THORNDIKE, E. L.: 1928. *Adult learning.* New York: Macmillan.

THORNDIKE, E. L.: 1935. The interests of adults. *J. educ. Psychol.,* 26:401–410, 497–507.

THORNDIKE, E. L.: 1949. Note on the shifts of interest with age. *J. appl. Psychol.,* 33:55.

THORNDIKE, R. L., and HENRY, F.: 1940. Difference in reading interests related to differences in sex and intelligence level. *Elem. Sch. J.,* 40:751–763.

THRUM, M. E.: 1935. The development of concepts of magnitude. *Child Develpm.,* 6:120–140.

THURSTONE, L. L.: 1931. Influence of motion pictures on children's attitudes. *J. soc. Psychol.,* 2:291–305.

TINKLEPAUGH, O. L.: 1933. The nature of periods of sex desire in women and their relation to ovulation. *Amer. J. Obstet. Gynaec.,* 26:335–345.

TODD, T. W.: 1937. *Atlas of skeletal maturation.* Vol. 1, *The hand.* St. Louis: Mosby.

TORRANCE, P.: 1945. The influence of the broken home on adolescent adjustment. *J. educ. Sociol.,* 18:359–364.

TROUP, E., and LESTER, O. P.: 1942. The social competence of identical twins. *J. genet. Psychol.,* 60:167–175.

TRYON, C. M.: 1939. Evaluation of adolescent personality by adolescents. *Monogr. Soc. Res. Child Develpm.,* 4, No. 4.

TUCKMAN, J., and LORGE, I.: 1952. Attitudes toward older workers. *J. educ. Psychol.,* 36:149–153.

TUDOR-HART, B. E.: 1926. Are there cases in which lies are necessary? *J. genet. Psychol.,* 33:586–641.

UNITED STATES BUREAU OF THE CENSUS: 1943. *Sixteenth census of the United States: 1940: Population: Special report on institutional population fourteen years and older.* Washington, D.C.: Government Printing Office.

UNITED STATES BUREAU OF THE CENSUS: 1943a. *Prisoners in state and federal prisons and reformatories:* 1940. Washington, D.C.: Government Printing Office.

UPDEGRAFF, R.: 1930. The visual perception of distance in young children and adults: a comparative study. *Univ. Ia. Stud. Child Welf.,* 4, No. 4.

UPDEGRAFF, R., and KEISTER, M. E.: 1937. A study of children's reactions to failure and an experimental attempt to modify them. *Univ. Ia. Stud. Child Welf.,* 13, No. 4.

VALAORAS, V. G.: 1950. Pattern of aging of human populations. *In* N.Y. Acad. Med., *The social and biological challenge of our aging population.* New York: Columbia Univ. Press, pp. 67–85.

VALENTINE, W. L.: 1936. Common misconceptions of college students. *J. appl. Psychol.,* 20:633–658.

VANCE, T. F., and McCALL, L. T.: 1934. Children's preferences among play materials as determined by the method of paired comparisons of pictures. *Child Develpm.,* 5:267–277.

VAN DALEN, D. B.: 1949. A differential analysis of the play of junior high school girls. *J. educ. Res.,* 43:22–31.

VAN DUSEN, C. R.: 1939. An anthropometric study of the upper extremities of children. *Hum. Biol.,* 11:277–284.

VAN DYKE, G. E.: 1930. The effect of the advent of puberty on the growth in height and weight of girls. *Sch. Rev.,* 38:211–221.

VAN DYNE, E. V.: 1940. Personality traits and friendship formation in adolescent girls. *J. soc. Psychol.,* 12:291–303.

VECERKA, L.: 1926. Das soziale Verhalten von Mädchen während der Reifezeit. *Quellen und Studten,* 4:49–121.

VISCHER, A. L.: 1947. Psychological problems of the aging personality. *Akad. Med. Wiss.,* 2:280–286.

VOLBERDING, E.: 1948. Out-of-school behavior of eleven-year-olds. *Elem. Sch. J.,* 48:432–441.

VOLLMER, H.: 1937. The grandmother: a problem in child-rearing. *Amer. J. Orthopsychiat.,* 7:378–382.

VOLLMER, J.: 1946. Jealousy in children. *Amer. J. Orthopsychiat.,* 16:660–671.

VREELAND, F. M., and CORY, S. M.: 1935. A study of college friendships. *J. abnorm. soc. Psychol.,* 30:229–236.

WAGNER, I. F.: 1938. A note on the hiccough of the neonate. *J. genet. Psychol.,* 52:233–234.

WAGONER, L. C., and ARMSTRONG, E. M.: 1928. The motor control of children as involved in the dressing process. *J. genet. Psychol.,* 35:884–897.

WALL, W. D.: 1948. Happiness and unhappiness in the childhood and adolescence of a group of women students. *Brit. J. Psychol.,* 38:191–208.

WALL, W. D.: 1948a. The newspaper reading of adolescents and adults. *Brit. J. educ. Psychol.,* 18:26–40.

WALLACE, W. J.: 1947. The girl's puberty rite of the Mahave. *Proc. Ind. Acad. Sci.,* 57:37–40.

WALLIN, W.: 1937. The rating and dating complex. *Amer. sociol. Rev.,* 2:727–734.

WARD, A.: 1939. The only child. *Smith Coll. Stud. soc. Work,* 1:41–55.

WARKANY, J.: 1944. Congenital malformations induced by maternal nutritional deficiency. *J. Pediat.,* 25:476–480.

WARREN, W.: 1949. Abnormal behavior and mental breakdown in adolescence. *J. ment. Sci.,* 95:589–624.

WASHBURNE, J. N.: 1941. Factors related to the school adjustment of college girls. *J. soc. Psychol.,* 13:281–289.

WATERS, J.: 1949. *Achieving maturity.* New York: McGraw-Hill.

WATSON, G.: 1930. Happiness among adult students of education. *J. educ. Psychol.,* 21:79–109.

WATSON, G.: 1934. A comparison of the effects of lax versus strict home training. *J. soc. Psychol.,* 5:102–105.

WATSON, J., BREED, W., and POSMAN, H.: 1948. A study of urban conversations: sample of 1,001 remarks overheard in Manhattan. *J. soc. Psychol.,* 28:121–133.

WATSON, J. B.: 1925. *Behaviorism.* New York: Norton.

WATSON, J. B.: 1925a. What the nursery has to say about instincts. *J. genet. Psychol.,* 32:293–327.

WATSON, J. B., and WATSON, R. R.: 1921. Studies in infant psychology. *Sci. Mon., N.Y.,* 19:493–515.

WATTENBERG, W. W.: 1949. Delinquency and only children: study of a "category." *J. abnorm. soc. Psychol.,* 44:356–366.

WATTENBERG, W. W.: 1950. Family recreation and delinquency. *Focus,* 29:6–9.

WEAVER, P.: 1944. Youth and religion. *Ann. Amer. Acad. pol. soc. Sci.,* 236:152–160.

WEISS, L. A.: 1934. Differential variations in the amount of activity of newborn infants under continuous light and sound stimulation. *Univ. Ia. Stud. Child Welf.,* 9, No. 4.

WELLMAN, B.: 1937. Motor achievement of preschool children. *Childhood Educ.,* 13:311–316.

WHEELER, O. A.: 1931. Variations in the emotional development of normal adolescents. *Brit. J. educ. Psychol.,* 1:1–12.

WHITE, M. W.: 1931. Some factors affecting the night sleep of children. *Child Develpm.,* 2:234–235.

WHITLEY, M. T.: 1929. Children's interest in collecting. *J. educ. Psychol.,* 20:249–261.

WICKMAN, E. K.: 1929. *Children's behavior and teachers' attitudes.* New York: Commonwealth Fund.

WILE, I. S., and DAVIS, R.: 1941. The relation of birth to behavior. *Amer. J. Orthopsychiat.,* 11:320–334.

WILLARD, J. W.: 1949. Employment problems of older workers. In *Proc. nat. Conf. soc. Work.* New York: Columbia Univ. Press, pp. 395–402.

WILLIAMS, R. M., and MATTSON, M. L.: 1942. The effect of social groupings upon the language of preschool children. *Child Develpm.,* 13:233–245.

WILLOUGHBY, R. R.: 1927. Family similarities in mental-test abilities. *Genet. Psychol. Monogr.,* 2:235–277.

WILLOUGHBY, R. R.: 1929. Incidental learning. *J. educ. Psychol.,* 20:671–682.

WILLOUGHBY, R. R.: 1935. Emotionality as a function of age, sex, and conjugal condition. *Psychol. Bull.,* 32:728.

WILLOUGHBY, R. R.: 1936. Neuroticism in marriage. *J. soc. Psychol.,* 7:19–48.

WILLOUGHBY, R. R.: 1937. The emotionality of spinsters. *Character & Pers.,* 5:215–223.

WILSON, C. O.: 1931. *A study of laughter situations among young children.* Lincoln, Nebr.

WILSON, F. T.: 1939. Expressed wishes of elderly persons, college men, and birthday wishes of first grade children. *J. genet. Psychol.,* 55:81–101.

WILSON, F. T.: 1941. Reading interests of young children. *J. genet. Psychol.,* 38:363–389.

WILSON, F. T.: 1943. Stories that are liked by young children. *J. genet. Psychol.,* 63:55–69.

WILSON, F. T.: 1943a. Young children's favorite stories and characters, and their reasons for liking them. *J. genet. Psychol.,* 63:157–164.

WINCH, R. F.: 1949. The relation between the loss of a parent and progress in courtship. *J. soc. Psychol.,* 29:51–56.

WINKER, J. B.: 1949. Age trends and sex differences in the wishes, identifications, activities, and fears of children. *Child Develpm.,* 20:101–200.

WINSLOW, C. N.: 1937. A study of the extent of agreement between friends' opinions and their ability to estimate the opinions of each other. *J. soc. Psychol.,* 8:433–442.

WITTY, P. A.: 1931. A study of deviates in versatility and sociability of play interests. *Teach. Coll. Contr. Educ.,* No. 470.

WITTY, P. A.: 1932. The reading interests and habits of five hundred adults. *Education,* 52:554–562.

WITTY, P. A.: 1941. Children's interest in reading the comics. *J. exp. Educ.*, 10:100–104.

WITTY, P. A.: 1941a. Reading the comics—a comparative study. *J. exp. Educ.*, 10:105–109.

WITTY, P. A., and COOMER, A.: 1942. Reading the comics in Grades IX–XII. *Educ. Adm. Supervis.*, 28:344–353.

WITTY, P. A., COOMER, A., and McBEAN, D.: 1946. Children's choices of favorite books: a study conducted in ten elementary schools. *J. educ. Psychol.*, 37:266–278.

WITTY, P. A., GARFIELD, S., and BRINK, W. G.: 1941. Interests of high-school students in motion pictures and the radio. *J. educ. Psychol.*, 32:176–184.

WOLFLE, H. M.: 1949. The import of the caress in modern child psychology. *Amer. Psychologist*, 4:249.

WOMEN'S BUREAU, U.S. DEPARTMENT OF LABOR: 1941. *Lifting heavy weights in defense industries.* Washington, D.C.: Government Printing Office.

WOOD, M. W.: 1946. *Living together in the family.* Washington, D.C.: American Home Economics Association.

WOODS, A. H., and CHASE, G.: 1937. Forms of personality obstructive to progress in college. *J. soc. Psychol.*, 8:411–431.

WOOFTER, A. C.: 1940. Preliminary survey of relation of physical defects to scholastic standing. *Child Develpm. Abstr.*, 14, No. 150.

WRIGHT, B. A.: 1942. Altruism in children and the perceived conduct of others. *J. abnorm. soc. Psychol.*, 37:219–233.

YARNELLE, E. C.: 1932. The relation of children's preferences to the preferences and attitudes of their parents. *Smith Coll. Stud. soc. Work*, 2:376–377.

YEDINACK, J. G.: 1949. A study of the linguistic functioning of children with articulation and reading disabilities. *J. genet. Psychol.*, 74:23–59.

YELLOWLEES, H.: 1940. The problem of adolescence. *Lancet*, 238:233–235.

YOUNG, F. M.: 1941. An analysis of certain variables in a developmental study of language. *Genet. Psychol. Monogr.*, 23:3–141.

YOUNG, K.: 1940. *Personality and problems of adjustment.* New York: Appleton-Century-Crofts.

ZACHRY, C. B.: 1940. The child's social and emotional adjustment. *Proc. 6th Conf. on Educ. and the except. Child,* Child Research Clinic of the Woods School, pp. 8–15.

ZELIGS, R.: 1941. Environmental factors annoying to children. *Sociol. soc. Res.*, 25:549–556.

ZELIGS, R.: 1945. Social factors annoying to children. *J. appl. Psychol.*, 29:75–82.

ZELIGS, R.: 1950. Children's concepts and stereotypes of Polish, Irish, Finn, Hungarian, Bulgarian, Dane, Czecho-Slovakian, Hindu, and Filipino. *J. genet. Psychol.*, 76:73–83.

ZELIGS, R.: 1950a. Reasons given by children for their intergroup attitudes. *J. genet. Psychol.*, 76:145–161.

ZELIGS, R.: 1950b. Intergroup attitudes of Gentile, Jewish, and Apache Indian children. *J. educ. Psychol.*, 41:243–248.

ZUCKER, H. J.: 1943. Affectional identification and delinquency. *Arch. Psychol., N.Y.,* No. 286.

ZYVE, C. I.: 1927. Conversations among children. *Teach. Coll. Rec.*, 29:46–61.

LIST OF VISUAL AIDS

The visual aids listed below can be used to supplement the material in this book. For the convenience of film users, the films have been grouped by chapter subjects, although in some instances a film may be used in connection with several different chapters. It is recommended that each film be reviewed before using in order to determine its suitability for a particular group.

Both motion pictures and filmstrips are included in this list of visual materials, and the character of each one is indicated by the self-explanatory abbreviations "MP" and "FS." Immediately following this identification is the name of the producer; if the distributor is different from the producer, the name of the distributor follows. The addresses of the distributors are listed at the end of the bibliography. In most instances, the films can be borrowed or rented from local or state 16-mm film libraries. (A nationwide list of these local sources is given in *A Directory of 2002 16mm Film Libraries,* available for 35 cents from the Superintendent of Documents, Washington 25, D.C.) Unless otherwise indicated, the motion pictures are 16-mm sound black-and-white films, and the filmstrips are 35-mm black-and-white and silent.

This bibliography is suggestive only, and film users should examine the catalogue of the National Institute of Mental Health, *Mental Health Motion Pictures,* and the latest annual edition and quarterly supplements of *Educational Film Guide,* a catalogue of some 10,000 films published by the H. W. Wilson Co., New York. The *Guide,* a standard reference book, is available in most college and public libraries.

CHAPTER 1

He Acts His Age (MP, CNFB/McGraw, 14 min, color or b&w). An over-all picture of a child's emotional, physical, and psychological growth from one to fifteen years of age. Followed by specific "ages and stages" films, two of which are currently available: *The Terrible Twos and Trusting Threes* and *The Frustrating Fours and Fascinating Fives.*

Human Growth (MP, Brown, 19 min, color). Traces the changes in human growth, male and female, from birth to adulthood. Setting of film is in a seventh-grade class and its study of the problem of human growth and development.

CHAPTER 2

Birth and the First Fifteen Minutes of Life (MP, NYU, 10 min, silent). Shows the birth of a baby and its reactions to stimuli presented 15 minutes after birth and to the first feeding 24 hours later. Also shows a second newborn baby and its contrasting reactions to the same stimuli. Distribution restricted to advanced classes in psychology and to medical students.

Human Reproduction (MP, McGraw, 20 min). Portrays by means of animated drawings the process of human reproduction, including the menstrual cycle, male and female reproductive organs, fertilization of the ovum, development of the embryo, and the process of birth. (Correlated filmstrip, same title, 30 frames, also available.)

CHAPTERS 3 TO 4

Baby Meets His Parents (MP, EBF, 11 min). Explains, with life situations, how the personality of infants is influenced by the extent to which a baby finds fulfillment of his basic needs—food, elimination, sleep, and loving care.

Child Development (MP series, EBF). Series of 11 motion pictures, each one 10 minutes in length, based upon the research of Dr. Arnold Gesell at the Yale Clinic of Child Development. Titles of the individual films are:

Baby's Day at Twelve Weeks
Behavior Day at 48 Weeks
Behavior Patterns at One Year
Early Social Behavior
From Creeping to Walking
Growth of Infant Behavior: Early Stages
Growth of Infant Behavior: Later Stages
Learning and Growth
Life Begins
Posture and Locomotion
Thirty-six Weeks Behavior Day

How a Baby Grows (MP series, EBF). Ten films, each one 15 minutes and silent, produced at the Yale Clinic of Child Development with the collaboration of Dr. Arnold Gesell. Different stages in the physical and psychological development of infants are shown. Titles of the individual films are:

The Baby's Bath
Bottle and Cup Feeding
The Conquest of the Spoon
Early Play
Growth of Adaptive Behavior
Growth of Motor Behavior
How Behavior Grows
Infants Are Individuals
Self-discovery in a Mirror
Twins Are Individuals

Know Your Baby (MP, CNFB, 10 min). Presents happy family relationships, particularly the acceptance of a new baby by the other children, and illustrates the fundamental principles for safeguarding the psychological and emotional health of children.

Life with Baby (MP, MOT/McGraw, 18 min). Pictorial summary of the Gesell studies at Yale and of the physical and mental growth of children from age one to age six.

Your Children and You (MP, BIS, 31 min). Realistic portrayal of a home with average imperfect parents and average imperfect children. Emphasizes the psychological handling of children through affection and security.

CHAPTERS 5 TO 6

Answering the Child's Why (MP, EBF, 13 min). Dramatizes situations in which children meet with positive or negative attitudes toward their questions and suggests the resulting effect upon their personalities.

Child Development (MP series, McGraw). Series of five motion pictures and correlated filmstrips dealing with various phases of child development. Titles of the individual films and their running times are:

Child Care and Development (17 min)
Children's Emotions (22 min)
Heredity and Pre-natal Development (21 min)
Principles of Development (17 min)
Social Development (16 min)

Fears of Children (MP, MHFB/IFB, 32 min). Dramatizes some of the emotional problems of a five-year-old boy, his fears of the dark, of being alone, of new situations. Explains that these fears are common to children of his age and are accentuated when parents become either unduly protective or overly severe.

Children Growing Up with Others (MP, BIS/UWF, 30 min). Illustrates stages in the growth of children showing by example their constant adaptation to the world around them.

Children Learning by Experience (MP, BIS/UWF, 40 min). Develops the themes that all children want to learn, they enjoy practicing skills, they strive to understand the world around them, they learn some things at second hand and a great many things by play and imagination.

The Frustrating Fours and Fascinating Fives (MP, CNFB/McGraw, 22 min, color or b&w). Explains the psychological characteristics of ages four and five—from childish helplessness and inconsistent destructiveness to imaginative play and independence.

Preface to a Life (MP, USPHS/UWF, 29 min). Parental influences on a child's developing personality illustrated by a series of episodes showing the effects of an overly solicitous mother and an overly demanding father; and, in contrast, the healthy childhood resulting when both parents accept their child as an individual.

The Terrible Twos and Trusting Threes (MP, CNFB/McGraw, 20 min, color or b&w). Presents a close examination of the growing years between two and four, and particularly the contrast between the seemingly aimless activity of two-year-olds and the organizational play activities of three-year-olds.

CHAPTERS 7 TO 9

Adolescent Development (MP series, McGraw). Series of five films and correlated filmstrips portraying the interests, problems, and activities of teen-age boys and girls. The titles and running times of the individual films are:

Age of Turmoil (20 min).
The Meaning of Adolescence (16 min)

Meeting the Needs of Adolescents (19 min)

Physical Aspects of Puberty (19 min)

Social-Sex Attitudes in Adolescence (22 min)

Farewell to Childhood (MP, MHFB/IFB, 20 min). Dramatized story of a teen-age girl, full of the swift emotions typical of adolescence, longing for and fearing the privileges of adulthood. Portrays the adolescent moods of rebellion and trust, anger and irresolution, self-pity and idealism, and her parents' bewilderment and confusion.

CHAPTERS 10 TO 12

Breakdown (MP, CNFB/McGraw, 40 min). Story of a young woman's schizophrenic breakdown, treatment, and recovery in a modern mental hospital.

The Feeling of Hostility (MP, CNFB/McGraw, 27 min). Case study of Clare, an outwardly successful but inwardly incomplete personality; and through dramatized flash backs into her early life at home and at school, an understanding of the reasons for her hostility toward herself and others.

The Feeling of Rejection (MP, CNFB/McGraw, 23 min). A case history of a neurotic young woman suffering from headaches and physical fatigue and an explanation, through scenes of her early life, of the psychosomatic reasons for her physical ills.

Feelings of Depression (MP, CNFB/McGraw, 30 min). Case history of a man in his early thirties who suffers periods of great despondency and an explanation, through scenes of his early life, of the psychological reasons for his condition.

Marriage for Moderns (MP series, McGraw). Five films and follow-up film-strips, correlated with Bowman's *Marriage for Moderns,* portraying through dramatized situations various problems before and after the marriage and the psychological reasons behind such problems. The titles and running times of the individual films are:

Choosing for Happiness (14 min)

It Takes All Kinds (20 min)

Marriage Today (22 min)

This Charming Couple (19 min)

Who's Boss? (16 min)

Over-dependency (MP, CNFB/McGraw, 32 min). Case study of a young man who has been crippled mentally and emotionally by overdependency upon his mother, sister, and wife.

Shades of Gray (MP, USA/UWF, 67 min). Portrays through dramatized situations and case histories various mental disorders experienced by soldiers during training and combat ranging from mild anxiety states to severe depressive reactions and paranoid psychoses; traces the life patterns of each affected soldier and relates his early familial and environmental experiences to the circumstances which precipitate his mental breakdown; demonstrates methods of psychotherapy, including emotional catharsis, narcoanalysis, hypnotic suggestions, and group therapy; and makes the point that in terms of mental health, no one is either "black" or "white"; everyone is a "shade of gray."

CHAPTERS 13 TO 14

Grandma Moses (MP, AFF, 22 min, color). Scenes of the life and accomplishments of Grandma Moses, American primitive painter, who reached the age of 90 in 1950. Of interest as an illustration of a "success story" in meeting the problems of old age.

The Steps of Age (MP, MHFB/IFB, 25 min). Dramatizes the emotional problems and interpersonal relationships within a family which are faced by a woman of 62 who must retire from her job. Emphasizes that one must begin early in life to adjust to the problems of old age.

DIRECTORY OF SOURCES

AFF—A. F. Films, 1600 Broadway, New York 19.

BIS—British Information Services, 30 Rockefeller Plaza, New York 20.

Brown—E. C. Brown Trust, 220 S.W. Alder St., Portland 4, Oreg.

CNFB—National Film Board of Canada, 1270 Avenue of the Americas, New York 20.

EBF—Encyclopaedia Britannica Films, Inc., 1150 Wilmette Ave., Wilmette, Ill.

IFB—International Film Bureau, 57 E. Jackson Blvd., Chicago 4, Ill.

McGraw—McGraw-Hill Book Co., Text-Film Dept., 330 W. 42d St., New York 36.

MHFB—Mental Health Film Board, 166 E. 38th St., New York 16.

MOT—March of Time Forum Films, 369 Lexington Ave., New York 17.

NYU—New York University Film Library, 26 Washington Pl., New York 3.

USA—U.S. Dept. of the Army, Washington 25, D.C.

USPHS—U.S. Public Health Service, Washington 25, D.C.

UWF—United World Films, Inc., 1445 Park Ave., New York 29.

INDEX